With Liberty for Some

Northeastern University 1898–1998

Advisor in Criminal Justice to
Northeastern University Press

GIL GEIS

WITH

500 Years of Imprisonment in America

LIBERTY

Scott Christianson

FOR

Northeastern University Press

SOME

Boston

NORTHEASTERN UNIVERSITY PRESS

Library of Congress Cataloging-in-Publication Data

Christianson, Scott.
    With liberty for some : 500 years of imprisonment in America / Scott Christianson.
      p. cm.
    Includes bibliographical references and index.
    ISBN 1-55553-364-7 (cloth : alk. paper)
      1. Prisoners—United States—History.   2. Imprisonment—United States—History.
   3. Prisons—United States—History.   I. Title.
    HV9466.C47   1998
    365′.973—dc21   98-23541

Composed in Bulmer by Graphic Composition, Inc., in Athens, Georgia.
Printed and bound by The Maple Press Company, York, Pennsylvania.
The paper is Sebago Antique Cream, an acid-free sheet.

Manufactured in the United States of America

02 01 00 99 98   5 4 3 2 1

For Tamar Gordon

CONTENTS

PREFACE

The train rolls past the scarred and weathered walls of Sing Sing Prison. The engineer toots his horn. The tower guard nods. But none of the other passengers around me seems to stir.

Prisons are all around us but we choose not to notice, and more than we admit, perhaps more than we realize, so-called corrections is a central feature of American society. It has become one of the leading growth industries and ways of life in the post-industrial United States, a multi-billion-dollar enterprise that directly affects tens of millions of Americans and, indirectly, all of us.

More than one million inmates are confined in American prisons and jails, and the trend, which has been surging upward each year since 1974, shows no signs of abating, even though most criminologists contend that incarceration does not reduce crime. Certainly it hasn't made us feel any safer. Never mind that the institution's mission is unclear. Never mind that most people believe the correctional system doesn't work. The only outcry is for more of the same. Politicians get elected by demanding tougher punishment, scurrying to outdo each other in penal severity. Three strikes and you're out. Life without parole. Lock 'em up and throw away the key. Ours is the biggest penal complex in the world. We resort to incarceration more than other nations. But we still can't get enough of it.

- What explains the paradox of a country that prides itself as being the citadel of individual liberty, yet imprisons more persons per capita than any other nation in the world with the possible exception of Russia?
- Why does a country founded on equality imprison mostly people of color, showing a rate of incarceration of blacks that is more than eight times that of whites?

- How is it that the United States, which epitomizes and sancti-
  fies democracy, continues to build and maintain such a huge
  and growing complex of totalitarian institutions in its midst?
- What's gone on inside the secret world of prisons?
- What role has imprisonment played in American history?

It was nearly thirty years ago that I first entered a prison. As a young
newspaper reporter in Albany, New York, I drove up to Dannemora, near
the Canadian border, to interview a convict who had started serving a
fourteen-year maximum term for heroin possession. He was black. A three-
time loser. I'd never met him face-to-face, but I'd written stories about him,
after which he'd been convicted and sent away for a long time. I felt guilty.

New York's embattled prison system was reeling from the bloody Attica
uprising that had occurred a few months earlier, and getting into the 116-
year-old Clinton State Correctional Facility for an interview had required
me to obtain the inmate's formal consent, the warden's verbal okay, and the
commissioner's written permission, as well as my editor's approval.

Upon arriving, I was asked to sign my name on a register and produce
my personal identification. Then I was fingerprinted for the first time in
my life, one set to go into Albany's criminal identification bank, another to
be sent off to Washington for J. Edgar Hoover's FBI. Then, I was x-rayed,
hand-searched, and sharply questioned—treated, it seemed, like a criminal
myself. Doors clanged behind me. Beefy guards watched. As one steel gate
after another clamped shut in my wake, I felt strangely afraid, powerless,
and imprisoned, wondering if I'd ever get out.

I met my prisoner in the lawyers' interview room, which in those days
provided little privacy. Accompanied by a stern-faced corrections lieutenant, Jimmy Parker was wearing greens and sneakers. He looked older than
I expected. His eyes were bloodshot. He took every cigarette I offered.
Throughout our brief meeting, I tried to get him to tell me what he knew
about police corruption back home. But he wouldn't squeal on anyone,
admitting nothing, except that he missed his son.

I left that day without the story I had sought. But I was spurred to find
out more about the justice system that had singled out a black hustler for
long-term cold storage while passing over so many others who seemed to
have committed worse crimes.

As an adventurous young investigative reporter, I believed prison to be
the ultimate stonewall, the cover-up of cover-ups, the darkest scoop. Precisely because the inner workings of the penal system appeared so physically inaccessible and secret, I was challenged to see if I could get inside,
and intensely curious to discover what prisons were really about.

To try to find out, I enrolled in a graduate school and began studying all about criminal justice. One day I joined in a class field trip to another fabled maximum-security institution, Great Meadow Correctional Facility in rural Washington County. After a long ride we crossed a frozen barge canal, along which stood the warden's stone mansion, and beyond it, ugly as sin, the prison itself.

As an academic, I was allowed to explore some parts of the institution that journalists never got to see. Suddenly I was peering into horrific "mental observation units" where naked madmen raved, strolling past tiny open-faced cells that displayed one infamous criminal after another, many of them sitting on bunks in their underwear, doing pushups on the stone floor, writing letters, or sleeping. Great Meadow was crammed with 1,350 inmates, most of them blacks or Puerto Ricans from New York City, 200 miles away, yet all 600 or so staff members (and indeed virtually all of the entire county's free residents) were white, rural antipodes.[1]

Here was the warden, a relic from another century, who gruffly said he'd already served forty-one years inside prisons, and then proceeded to instruct his visitors on some of the finer points of prison administration, such as "how to handle the coloreds." Our escorts, a succession of stone-faced guards, seemed uncomfortable with university types and responded to our questions with only a word or two, particularly when inmates were around.

Then we talked with some convicts. At first, only two or three. Quickly, there were more. Some were the same impassioned black militants who'd been on television during the Attica rebellion the previous September. Here they were complaining to anyone who'd listen about how badly they'd been treated. One of them, Champ, held forth as smoothly as a skilled trial lawyer arguing his case. Several students were mesmerized. Somebody whispered they couldn't believe he was the prisoner and the other fellow was the warden.

The sight that left the deepest impression was set off in a corner of the prison grounds, where a lonely chimney belched putrid smoke into the frigid air. It came from one of the decrepit industrial shops, the Soap Factory. Entering it that bitter-cold day, I went from far below zero to eighty above in one step. The first gasp seemed to glaze my throat and guts with slime, like shampoo, and when I breathed bubbles seemed to appear. White officers stood around, bellies hanging over their belts, looking disgusted; the prisoners' muscular black bodies glistened with sweat as they stirred the huge, bubbling cauldrons of boiling lard. And as they stirred, the prisoners sang. The lyrics that day in 1972 sounded like old Negro spirituals. Somebody later remarked that the songs had probably been

brought north via prison camps and other institutions from their origin on
Southern slave plantations.[2] This scene and its connections would not
leave my mind.

I became fascinated and began to study prisons seriously, putting aside
my journalistic career to pursue a doctoral degree, plunging into libraries
and field work, reading everything I could find. Having decided that I
needed some "inside" experience, I took a position as a research analyst.
Over the next twenty years I held several high-ranking posts in state government that gave me unusual access to prison operations and criminal
justice policy making; all the while, I continued to study and reflect upon
the history of American imprisonment. Some of those who were lively inmates or correction officers when I started, all those many years ago, remained confined where I had first encountered them, but their hair had
turned white and they shuffled stooped and stiff.

What began as a journalistic foray into prisons and the criminal justice
system gradually evolved into a more than twenty-year study of the origins
of the modern prison. This eventually grew into a book that examines the
role of imprisonment in American history from Columbus to the present.
Unlike other, more narrowly focused histories, this one considers five hundred years of imprisonment, involving not just the model state prisons that
arose here in the nineteenth century, but other forms as well: the system
of convict transportation to America (and later Australia); the thriving international trade in captive indentured servants, slaves, and military conscripts; life under slavery; the transition from colonial to revolutionary and
post-revolutionary prisons; the experience of domestic prisoners of war
and political prisoners; the invention of the penitentiary; and the evolution
of contemporary corrections. In doing so, it looks at the history of imprisonment in a light different from that of previous works. For instance, it
unites the literatures of two related institutions—prison and slavery—that
are usually considered as separate.[3] As David Brion Davis has pointed out:
"We seldom think of black slavery as a penal institution. Yet throughout
history enslavement has been used as a form of punishment, while some
penal systems have acquired many of the characteristics of chattel slavery."[4]
And, as we shall see, there are many other connections and interrelation-
ships between these two distinct types of imprisonment throughout American history.

I have tried to explore imprisonment in the specific context of time and
place. The narrative generally employs historical details above theoretical
postulates in order to render the story more unobtrusively. Many of the
issues covered remain as problematic and vexing today as they were when

first confronted, centuries ago. However, this work is not intended as a blueprint for reform or as a call for alternatives to incarceration, either of which would have properly become a treatise in its own right. Rather, it is a history of how we got to where we are.

This book differs from many conventional prison histories in the extent to which it focuses on prisoners instead of just prison reformers or specific prisons. Furthermore, many of its observations were obtained through the lens of my own experience within and around the prison scene. Consequently, it is more of an insider's account of imprisonment than is usually the case in scholarly works. I have long considered it odd that prisoners have been glaringly left out of many standard prison histories. Instead of ignoring them, I have tried to listen to what they had to say. Although I have sought to not glorify captives, I have also struggled against the convention to demonize them. And what a convention it has been.

Who were these prisoners? What do we know about them and the circumstances of their imprisonment? Yes, many were or are anonymous low-lifes, losers, riffraff, rogues, scoundrels, thugs, hoodlums, killers, rapists, robbers, psychopaths, or fiends—call them what you wish. But consider some of the more familiar figures who have been locked up, albeit briefly in some cases, at one time or another:

Jack Abbott, Nelson Algren, Ethan Allen, Jim Bakker, Roger Baldwin, Alexander Berkman, Daniel Berrigan, Philip Berrigan, Billy the Kid, Black Hawk, Robert Blake, Daniel Boone, William Bradford, H. Rap Brown, Henry Box Brown, James Brown, John Brown, Lenny Bruce, Louis Lepke Buchalter, Sitting Bull, Aaron Burr, William Burroughs, Al Capone, Rubin "Hurricane" Carter, Chief Wild Cat, Caryl Chessman, Cinque, Christopher Columbus, Eldridge Cleaver, Chief Mangas Colorado, Charles Colson, Gregory Corso, Crazy Horse, J. Hector St. John de Crèvecoeur, David Crosby, Leon Czolgosz, Angela Davis, Jefferson Davis, Dorothy Day, John Dean, Eugene Debs, David Dellinger, Legs Diamond, John Dillinger, Frederick Douglass, Robert Downey, Jr., Thomas Eddy, John Ehrlichman, Paul E. Erdman, Leslie Fiedler, Lawrence Ferlinghetti, Philip Freneau, William Franklin, Joey Gallo, William Lloyd Garrison, Marcus Garvey, Geronimo, Gary Gilmore, Ralph Ginzburg, Emma Goldman, John Gotti, Alexander Graydon, Dick Gregory, Merle Haggard, H. R. Haldeman, Nathan Hale, Gus Hall, Julian Hawthorne, Bob Hayes, Big Bill Haywood, Leona Helmsley, Joe Hill, Chester Himes, Jimmy Hoffa, Abbie Hoffman, Billie Holiday, Samuel

Gridley Howe, O Henry, E. Howard Hunt, John Irwin, Andrew
Jackson, George Jackson, Mother Jones, Meir Kahane, Alvin
Karpis, Ken Kesey, Stacey Keach, Machinegun Kelly, Don King,
Rev. Martin Luther King, Jr., Lyndon LaRouche, Henry Laurens,
Dr. Timothy Leary, Ann Lee, Charles Lee, G. Gordon Liddy,
Leadbelly, Light Horse Harry Lee, Jack London, Robert Lowell,
Charles "Lucky" Luciano, Malcolm X, Charles Manson, Russell
Means, Herman Melville, Michael Milken, Robert Mitchum, Tom
Mooney, Robert Morris, Thomas Morton, Elijah Muhammad,
Huey Newton, Solomon Northrup, Kate O'Hare, James Edward
Oglethorpe, Osceola, Tom Paine, Leonard Peltier, William Penn,
Miguel Piñero, John Pintard, Pocahontas, Roman Polanski,
Gabriel Prosser, James Earl Ray, Wilhelm Reich, Moses Roper,
Pete Rose, Julius and Ethel Rosenberg, Mary Rowlandson, Jerry
Rubin, Jack Ruby, Bayard Rustin, Satanta, Dred Scott, the Scotts-
boro Boys, Bobby Seale, Rev. Al Sharpton, Daniel Shays, O. J.
Simpson, Sirhan Sirhan, Iceberg Slim, Agnes Smedley, Captain
John Smith, Joseph Smith, Jr., Morton Sobel, Son of Sam, Martin
Sostre, Richard Speck, Benjamin Spock, Robert Stroud, Willie
Sutton, Frank Tannenbaum, Piri Thomas, Henry David Thoreau,
John Trumbull, Sojourner Truth, Harriet Tubman, Nat Turner,
Mike Tyson, Gustavus Vassa, Sol Wachtler, Mae West, Henry
Wirz, Cole Younger . . .[5]

They are a mixed bag, to be sure. If we try, many of us could probably
add other names from our own circle of friends and acquaintances, even
from our own families. By and large, though, we may tend to believe that
prisoners represent "them," the "other" side, the lumpenproletariat—just
the kind of people we would most hope to avoid being with or thinking
about. Just the type of branches to be snipped from our genealogical tree.
But this does not diminish prisoners' importance in society or negate their
suitability as objects for historical study. Can we honestly think there are
no longer any political prisoners in America?

And what about the multitudes who served as keepers: the slave traders
and spirits and crimps and transporters and outfitters and masters and
drivers and overseers and locksmiths and jailers and wardens and judges
and bail bondsmen and bailiffs and guards and chaplains and prison
reformers and inspectors and jurors and executioners and sheriffs and marshals and cops and probation officers and parole officers and correction
officers and their families? Many of them were also imprisoned, in shifts.
It is their history too. Having worked alongside many such men and

women over the years, I've tried to be sensitive to their concerns and fair to them as well.

Much of this nation's prison heritage has been officially and culturally suppressed. Avoidance and amnesia have kept us from facing this dirty, hidden history. Prisons are repositories of failure that remind us of problems which would prove unsettling if put in open view. So we hide them in remote places and keep them guarded and inaccessible to outsiders. Few of us want to face what seems so messy, so troubling, so well concealed. We don't want to know. Yet prison has been an important piece of the American experience. The flip side. Another part of the paradox.

This book traces the development of imprisonment in the context of the larger society, showing how the two sides have played out together. In that sense, it is different from most standard penology and most American history.

ACKNOWLEDGMENTS

Over the more than twenty years I have spent on this project, hundreds of prisoners, wardens, correction officers, relatives of incarcerated men and women, prison inspectors, civil rights attorneys, ex-cons, historians, penologists, and other helpful persons shared some of their thoughts about prison. During that time my role took various forms, among them that of journalist, graduate student, researcher, teacher, investigator, probation and parole official, gubernatorial aide, advocate, and ordinary citizen. I was not imprisoned, nor did I work full-time in a prison every day, but I enjoyed rare access to the physical world and historical records of dozens of jails and maximum-security prisons for many of those years. Thus, I got to see and learn things that often remain off-limits even to some insiders.

Many personal debts must remain confidential. However, some persons who helped me over the years that I can acknowledge include Dr. Michael Baden; Karomoko Baye; Herb Blyden; John Boston; Alvin J. Bronstein of the American Civil Liberties Union, National Prison Project; W. Haywood Burns; Warden J. Leland Casscles; Agenor Castro; Donald B. Chamberlin of the New York City Department of Corrections; Commissioner William Ciuros, Jr.; Allison Coleman; Jim Corsaro of the New York State Library; Chuck Culhane; Governor Mario M. Cuomo; Jomo Davis; Frank W. Dunbaugh; Tom Engelhardt; Assemblyman Dan Feldman; Robert G. Fichenberg; Jim Fox; H. Bruce Franklin; Alice G. Fraser; Bob Gangi of the Correctional Association of New York; Liz Gaynes of the Osborne Association; Dr. Charles T. Gehring of the New Netherland Project; Prof. Gilbert Geis of the University of California at Irvine; Prof. Daniel Georges-Abeyie; Diana R. Gordon; Jonathan Gradess of the New York State Defenders Association; John Gresham; Dr. Alice Green; Dr. Larry Hackman of the New York State Archives; Petrita Hernandez-Rojas of the New York State Department of Correctional Services; Andy Hall; Russ Immarigeon; Kenny

Jackson; Prof. James B. Jacobs; Prof. Robert Johnson; Charles 37X Kenyatta; Paul W. Keve; Fay Honey Knopp of the American Friends Service Committee; Ed Koren of the National Prison Project; Prof. Dick Korn; Lawrence T. Kurlander; Barb Leonard; David C. Leven of Prisoners' Legal Services; Tom Lewis; June License; Linda Loffredo of the New York State Division for Women; Prof. Lucien X. Lombardo; Jose Lopez; Superintendent Elaine Lord of Bedford Hills Correctional Facility; Janet Lugo of the Society of Friends; Prof. Patrick D. McAnany of the University of Illinois at Chicago Circle; Sam McDowell; Carey McWilliams; Jess Maghan; Bea Milwe; Jim Murphy; Tom Murton; John Nelson; Prof. Lloyd Ohlin of Harvard; Dr. Tom Obrig of Albany Medical College; JoAnn Page of the Fortune Society; Hal Pepinsky; Lenny Perlmutter; Joan Petersilia of the Rand Corporation; Dan Pochoda; John J. Poklemba; John Rakis; Lanier Ramer; Dr. Jon L. Regier of the New York State Council of Churches; Bill Rowley; Barry C. Sample of the New York State Division of Criminal Justice Services; Tony Schulte; Prof. Herman Schwartz; Henry Schwarzschild of the American Civil Liberties Union; Prof. Beverly A. Smith; Hal Smith of the New York State Office of Mental Health; Sharon Smolick; Margaret Stinson; Rabbi Bill Strongin; Dennis Sullivan; Prof. Paul Takagi; Phil Tarbell; Jeanne Thelwell; Piri Thomas; Prof. Hans Toch; Commissioner Anthony K. Umina of the New York State Board of Parole; Mrs. Helen Vanderbilt; Lynn Walker; Lanny E. Walter; Ed Weldon of the National Archives; Malcolm Willison; S. Brian Willson of the National Moratorium on Prison Construction; Norma Sue Wolfe; Yevgeny Yevtushenko; Father Peter G. Young; and Chris Zimmerman. Some influential teachers include Fred Cohen, Evan Hill, Michael J. Hindelang, Donald J. Newman, Graeme R. Newman, Vincent O'Leary, David J. Rothman, Hans Toch, and Leslie T. Wilkins. Among the graduate students who assisted at some stage of my work are Nicky Hahn, William Oliver, Dave Parry, Barb Rockell, Rich Dehais, and Ed Reed.

Many thousands of published and unpublished works were consulted for this book. In their pursuit, I was fortunate to spend most of a year immersed in the rare-book collections of the New York Public Library, the New-York Historical Society, and the New York State Library. Other assisting institutions were the Albany Institute of History and Art, Albany Law School Library, Albany Medical College Library, Auburn Public Library, Bethlehem Public Library, Buffalo and Erie County Public Library, George Arents Research Library of Syracuse University, Hamilton College Library, Harmanus Bleecker Public Library, G. W. Blunt Library of Mystic Seaport, British Museum, British Admiralty, Chicago Public Library, Chicago Historical Society, Connecticut State Library, University of Chicago

Library, Correctional Association of New York, Friends Historical Library at Swarthmore College, John Jay College of Criminal Justice Library, Mariner's Museum of Newport News, Virginia, Middlebury College Library, National Archives, National Association of Blacks in Criminal Justice, National Council on Crime and Delinquency, New Jersey Historical Society, New Jersey State Library, New London County Historical Association, New York County Clerk's Office, New York Historical Association, New York State Archives, New York State Commission of Correction, New York State Department of Correctional Services, New York State Library, New York State Museum, Old Newgate Historical Commission, Princeton Theological Seminary, Princeton University Library, Queens College Library, Rensselaer County Historical Society, Rensselaer Polytechnic Institute Library, Schomburg Collection of Black Literature, History and Art, State University of New York at Albany, Troy Public Library, Union Theological Seminary, University of California at Irvine Library, University of Connecticut, University of Hawaii, U.S. Library of Congress, Virginia Historical Society, and the Virginia State Archives.

Pals from the old Marketplace gang, especially Bill Kennedy, Tom Smith, Bill Herrick, Vinny Reda, Larry Reiss, Jim Hart, Barbara Fischkin, Bill Rowley, and Lee Berry, provided song and good cheer in low times. The New York State Writers Institute supplied many great talks and chances to socialize with other writers. I was also fortunate to receive helpful feedback from several discerning readers, among them Gil Geis, Alan Nadel, Nikki Smith, Tony Schulte, and Hans Toch. I am grateful for the thoughtful encouragement of William Frohlich of Northeastern University Press. Frank Austin proved himself a magnificent copyeditor. Emily McKeigue, Tara Mantel, and others were enormously helpful.

To my family, who gave succor and support throughout all these years—particularly my daughter Kelly, who commented on an earlier version of the manuscript—and my other children, Emily and Jonah, thank you for going without me for so long in order that I might finish this work. Without the magnificent insight, understanding, and nurturance of my wife, Tamar Gordon, this book might not have emerged from the dust bin. She read and critiqued several drafts at various stages and helped to rethink and discover many central ideas.

With Liberty for Some

CHAPTER ONE

The Rise of the Prisoner Trade

EXPLORERS

A MONG the ninety or so assorted crewmen whom Cristóbal Colón—
alias Christopher Columbus—assembled for his voyage of discovery
were a black youth taken from the Canaries and at least four convicts,
maybe more. How many others had previously been prisoners at some
time will never be known, nor did it matter. Once they set sail, any ordinary
seaman aboard the three ships became an inmate, subject to flogging or
worse if he stepped out of line; upon the mighty ocean that separated the
crews from the real world, the cramped vessels in which they were held
were as isolating and potentially fatal as the darkest stone dungeon or the
cruelest iron cage. Nobody was free to leave if he wished; none could be
sure of surviving the indeterminate term that lay ahead.

But, as luck would have it, thirty-three days after leaving from Gomera,
at two o'clock in the morning on October 12, 1492, Rodrigo de Triana,
a watchman on the *Pinta,* spied something on the moonlit horizon and
shouted "Tierra! Tierra!" His shipmates then alerted their counterparts
on the nearby flagship, *Santa María,* and their sister caravel, the *Niña.*
When told the news, Columbus wisely decided to hold back their approach until daylight to avoid running aground on coral reefs.

At dawn an armed search party stepped from a boat onto terra firma
and waded onto a little island, lush and green, which turned out to be
simply one link in a chain. Columbus, mistakenly believing he had found
the fabled Passage to India, christened this archipelago the "Indies," so
that when a band of mostly naked, tawny-skinned natives appeared, they
became "Indians."[1] As the two groups struggled to communicate by sign

language and sounds, he discovered they called the island "Guanahani."
Because they kept saying "taino, taino" (which in their language apparently meant "good"), Columbus named them the Taino Indians.[2]

The Tainos were extraordinarily friendly and gentle, especially the well-
proportioned, receptive women who tarried with his bearded men.[3] He
reported the natives "invite you to share anything that they possess, and
show as much love as if their hearts went into it."[4] He was quick to add,
"They should be good servants and intelligent, for I observed that they
quickly took in what was said to them."[5] He took six of them as prisoners
and resumed his journey.[6]

Columbus made it back to Spain with relative ease, and even though
nobody yet understood exactly what new world he had discovered, clearly
he had found a path of wind that could carry trade ships across the Atlantic
and back.[7] He proudly displayed an assortment of booty that included
aloe, rhubarb, cinnamon, spices, cotton, brightly colored birds, and the
exotic-looking Tainos, whom the Spaniards now referred to as "slaves."[8]
The strutting explorers did not know it yet, but some of the Indian women
with whom they had coupled apparently had transmitted *Treponema pal-
lidum*, the spirochete of syphilis, which eventually would take its toll in
horrible suffering and deaths throughout Spanish ports, just as the natives
left behind had contracted measles and smallpox from the whites that
would spread among their villages with fatal effect.[9]

A few months later, Columbus left Spain on a second voyage, commanding a fleet of seventeen ships with fifteen hundred men, including five
of the Indians he had seized.[10] When he finally returned home, two years
and nine months later, he had failed to bring back most of his ships and
company, much less any treasure. The most he could report was that he
had encountered "a wild people fit for any work, well proportioned, and
very intelligent, and who, when they have got rid of their cruel habits to
which they have been accustomed, will be better than any other kind of
slaves."[11] At first, the Spanish Crown rejected his appeal to open a major
slave trade, but the government did order the enlistment of three hundred
convicts, thirty of them women,[12] and authorized the realm's justices to
ship away any condemned criminals (except for heretics, traitors, counter-
feiters, and sodomites) who might be convinced to go.[13]

Columbus's third expedition arrived to find Hispaniola's new colonial
capital, Santo Domingo, embroiled in a settlers' revolt, which he quickly
crushed in an effort to head off an even more dangerous Indian rebellion.
In only a few years, he had conscripted Spanish convicts and other unfor-
tunates on his voyages, many of whom he later had abandoned abroad. On
one trip alone he had sent back six hundred Indian captives.[14] But what

goes around comes around, for in 1500 the Spanish sovereigns dispatched a new commissioner, who arrested Columbus on political charges and hauled him back to Spain to face inquisition. He entered Cádiz still in chains and was taken to Las Cuevas monastery in Seville, where he was kept for several months until finally being stripped of his powers and released.[15] Like his idol, Marco Polo, who had written his epic journal in prison, Columbus had paid a price for discovery.[16] One humorist later quipped that he had "discovered America and they put him in jail for it."[17]

But Columbus was undeterred. Shortly after being freed from prison, he made a fourth voyage to the New World just prior to his death. Oddly, the lands he had discovered came to be known to Europeans, not as "Columbus," but as "America," in honor of another Italian explorer, Amerigo Vespucci of Florence, who claimed to have reached the New World a year before him, but who really had not done so till a year after.[18] (Some historians later suggested that Amerigo had a criminal past, prompting Ralph Waldo Emerson to comment, "Strange . . . that broad America must wear the name of a thief.")[19]

Spain's discovery of precious-ore deposits led to further exploitation of the natives. War, disease, overwork, and suicide caused the population of the Antilles to sink like a rock in deep water. Historians have estimated the decline as proceeding from 300,000 in 1492 to 60,000 in 1508, 46,000 in 1510, 20,000 in 1512, and 14,000 in 1514; a Catholic priest who lived through it figured that fully three million Indians had died between 1494 and 1508, comprising one of the worst genocides in recorded history.[20]

One Spaniard who was horrified by what was happening to the natives was a former explorer, Bartolomé de Las Casas, who vowed to devote the rest of his life to securing "the justice of those Indian peoples, and to condemn the robbery, evil and injustice committed against them."[21] To save them from extinction, he beseeched his king to introduce Negroes from Guinea as a substitute, arguing that "the labour of one Negro was more valuable than that of four Indians." The king agreed, and in 1517 the first *asiento* was arranged, enabling four thousand Negroes to be imported to the West Indies over the next eight years.[22] African slaves started arriving a few months later, and by 1540 an estimated thirty thousand men, women, and children had been taken to Hispaniola alone.[23]

At first the Spanish considered these Africans to be ideally suited for slavery in the mines and fields. But in his old age, Las Casas came to realize he had made another terrible mistake.[24] Black slavery did not save the Indians but merely added another oppressed race—and the colony became even more dependent on slavery for its survival. From their base in Hispaniola, Spanish conquistadors under Hernando Cortés plunged into Mexico and liquidated the golden Aztec empire. More conquerors sailed up to Florida and fanned out into the Texas panhandle, Santa Fe, the Mississippi, the Grand Canyon, and California. Among their earliest constructs in North America, Spanish soldiers in 1570 erected the first substantial prison, at St. Augustine, Florida.

By then a few brave Spaniards had begun to criticize the slave trade publicly. Bartolomé de Albornoz attacked it as morally and legally wrong, but his views were officially suppressed. Tomas Mercado condemned the trade as being based upon deceit, robbery, and force.[25] Alonso de Sandoval declared, "God created man free. . . . Slavery is not exile, but also subjection, hunger, sorrow, nakedness, insult, prison, perpetual persecution, and, in short, is a Pandora's box of all the evils."[26]

Nevertheless, more explorers of the New World brought more convicts and Africans whom they held as prisoners; the latter were to be useful in case they encountered other blacks. Vasco Núñez de Balboa had thirty Africans with him when he discovered the Pacific Ocean in 1513, and Francisco Pizarro brought some on his conquest of Peru. Blacks went with Francisco Vásquez de Coronado to New Mexico and with Pánfilo de Narváez and Álvar Núñez Cabeza de Vaca as they crossed Florida, New Mexico, and Arizona a few years later. Hernando de Soto's expedition included African slaves and Indians; in his travels he discovered some Cherokees who had taken other Indians as prisoners of war and made them slaves— a practice that was common to other tribes as well. Many early Spanish and French accounts used the terms "prisoner" and "slave" interchangeably when referring to the Indians' captives. However, the distinctions could actually be sharp, even fatal, since some women or children prisoners of the Indians were subsequently adopted, whereas adult male captives were usually tortured to death.

Before long, other European nations began competing with Spain and Portugal in overseas exploration, and they too utilized convicts to fill out their crews. Jacques Cartier of France combed the jails for fifty convicts, men and women, whom he employed on his expedition to Newfoundland in 1542.[27] Pierre du Guast, sieur de Monts, and Samuel De Champlain used convicts as sailors on their northern voyages.[28] Blacks accompanied French explorers into Canada and the Mississippi River Valley.

During the 1560s, John Hawkins and Francis Drake started trafficking slaves between England, Africa, and Spanish America, and Richard Hakluyt later called for a large-scale conscription of criminals as a better way to settle the New World. But England's colonization efforts waned until 1606, when policies abruptly changed. Sir John Popham's venture at

Kennebec, or Maine, was stocked "out of all the gaols [jails] of England," prompting one critic to complain, "It is a shameful and unblessed thing to take the scum of people, and wicked and condemned ones, to be the people with whom you plant."[29] That same year, the Virginia Company sent an expedition to America, which landed several hundred miles to the south.[30] One of its voyagers, Captain John Smith, then twenty-six, was a soldier of fortune who claimed to have escaped from slavery under the Turks. Arrested en route to Virginia for conspiring to mutiny, he remained imprisoned in the hold until the end of the voyage, whereupon he was unshackled to help defend the colony.[31] (He turned out to be one of only 38 of Jamestown's original 105 colonists to survive the first year.)[32] But one day, as he foraged for food, Smith was captured by Indians. As he later told the tale, just as he was about to be executed, the Indian emperor's favorite daughter "got his head in her arms, and laid her own upon his to save him from death."[33] Smith eventually made it home to England to tell his story in various printed versions, thus marking the beginning of one of the first American literary genres—the captivity narrative.

The Virginia Company authorized its colonists to seize native children wherever they could "for conversion . . . to the knowledge and worship of the true God and their redeemer, Christ Jesus." One of those abducted— Smith's rescuer, young Pocahontas—was ransomed, taken as a wife by one of the Englishmen, and brought as a trophy to London, where she soon died.[34]

Company officials ignored the colonists' urgent pleas for better living conditions, insisting instead that greater discipline was needed. In 1610 a tough new governor, Lord Delaware, arrived and imposed a dictatorship.[35] His successor, Thomas Dale, was even more severe. Under his regime, Virginia's colonists were literally held as prisoners, and punishments became more and more harsh.[36] For uttering "base and detracting words" against the governor, Richard Barnes was ordered to be "disarmed and have his arms broken and his tongue bored through with an awl and [he] shall pass through a guard of 40 men and shall be butted by every one of them and at the head of the troop kicked down and footed out of the fort; and he shall be banished out of James City and the Island, and he shall not be capable of any privilege of freedom in the country."[37] Men caught trying to escape were tortured to death. Seamstresses who sewed their lady's skirts too short were whipped.[38] Governor Dale pronounced his methods justified and the company backed him up. Back in London, an official said that the Virginians were "dangerous, incurable members, for no use so fit as to make examples to others."[39]

KIDNAPPED

O N his first voyage, Columbus had encountered Tainos toting rolls of dried leaves, called "tobacco," which they lit and inhaled in curls of smoke through their nostrils.[40] By the early seventeenth century tobacco smoking had become so popular in England that one observer remarked, "Many a young nobleman's estate is altogether spent and scattered to nothing in smoke [and] a man's estate runs out through his nose, and he wastes whole days, even years, in drinking of tobacco; men smoke even in bed."[41] Soon the leaf's value equalled that of silver.[42]

The weed grew wild in Virginia, and English entrepreneurs sought to cultivate it there for shipment home. Investors liked its high yield per acre, excellent keeping properties, and light shipping weight. Once colonists succeeded in growing a nonbitter strain from seeds acquired in the Caribbean, Virginia was perched to take the first step toward becoming a lucrative plantation.[43] The colony finally had an attractive product to export.[44]

But establishing a successful tobacco trade posed a tremendous challenge. Land in Virginia was fertile and free, yet cultivating any crop, especially tobacco, required a large and constantly replenished supply of labor—large because of the innumerable manual tasks that had to be performed, constantly replenished because of the workers' short life expectancy. The cargoes also had to be transported across the ocean. After only three or four crops the soil would become exhausted and no longer able to produce tobacco; sometimes it would not even yield corn, which meant that more and more land would have to be cleared and planted. All this demanded laborers to chop trees, pull stumps, lay fences, and manage the crops. Fortifications had to be built, roads constructed, firewood split, fuel carted, water fetched, game hunted, fish caught, corn and wheat planted. There was a need for carpenters, boatwrights, blacksmiths, brickmakers, joiners, coopers, sawyers, fowlers, bakers, tanners. In 1618, the prospect of this happening seemed remote, since after eleven years of struggle and considerable investment by the stockholders only about six hundred of eighteen hundred colonists had survived.[45]

That year, however, the Virginia Company underwent a shakeup that put Sir Edwin Sandys in control. Under his direction the company launched an intensive promotional campaign to attract more investors, settlers, and servants.[46] Publicists wrote enticing broadsides, promising everything from daily sustenance to eternal bliss to anyone who would go to Virginia. Drummers marched from village to village, beating up interest. Hucksters combed the fairs and groghouses, enlisting recruits. Minstrels sang seductive ballads. From Parliament to pulpit, Virginia's colonization was depicted as a noble effort of Christian reformation, for, as one pious supporter asked, "What can be more excellent, more precious, more glorious, than to convert a heathen nation from worshipping the devil to the saving knowledge and true worship of God in Jesus Christ?"[47] Sandys offered a promise of something that was generally not available in England: an opportunity for upward mobility. Piece by piece, he and his image makers created the American Dream.

Tracts of land were apportioned for persons who performed a service for the company. This "headright" system was expanded for every person, or head, who was transported to Virginia.[48] Private ownership of land was authorized in the belief that it would encourage people of means to emigrate with their families and servants.[49] A modified version of apprenticeship, known as "indenture," was devised to attract servants who otherwise could not afford the costs of passage. Named from the Latin *indentare* or *indentura* (to cut into teeth, to give a jagged edge), an indenture was a kind of contract between two or more parties. Legally, the term signified a covenant, drawn on parchment and cut into pieces; the peculiar fit between its parts marked the meeting of the minds between the party of the first part (the master) and the party below (the servant). Typically its terms bound a person as servant for a determinate period—usually from four to seven years, or (if a minor) until he or she reached twenty-one years of age.[50]

The authorities also examined the feasibility of sending large numbers of persons abroad against their will. Such an approach could supply workers for the plantations and help to rid the home front of undesirables. A legal way of doing this had not yet been worked out, but one option was to utilize the vagrancy laws to round up society's outcasts. Vagrancy statutes had been in use since the fourteenth century, with the usual penalties being execution, branding, whipping, or penal slavery.[51] Under Elizabeth I the measures had begun to provide for exile beyond the seas as an alternative to capital punishment, and the definition of "rogues" and "vagabonds" had been widened to an exceptional degree. But large-scale unloading to the colonies was not yet feasible. Some legal scholars objected that the Magna Carta prohibited exile "but by lawful judgment of [an individual's] peers and by the law of this province."[52] Others reasoned that exporting known troublemakers to the fledgling colonies might fatally contaminate any effort to build a successful plantation. Thus one company official initially opposed plans to send criminals abroad on the grounds that "the weeds of their native country . . . would act as a poison with the body of a tender, feeble, and yet unreformed colony."[53] Even if some were sent, the basic question remained whether evildoers should be segregated or spread around. If concentrated, could they be governed? If dispersed, would they corrupt the good?

Back in Virginia, Governor Dale confided that "[e]very man laments himself of being here" and wondered how the plantation might ever succeed with "such disordered persons, so profane, so riotous . . . besides of such diseased and crazed bodies." In desperation he urged the king to "banish hither all offenders condemned to die out of common gaols," arguing that it "would be a ready way to furnish us with men and not always with the worst of men, either for birth, for spirit, or body," and adding that many "would be glad to escape a just sentence and make this their new country . . . with all diligence, cheerfulness and comfort."[54]

Although Dale's request was denied, his ideas gained support as a means of ridding the gaols (jails) and countryside of the growing hordes of rabble who were thought to be threatening the kingdom's physical, moral, and political health. England's overcrowded gaols often made criminals more dangerous to society. The prisons were breeding grounds for typhus ("gaol fever") and other diseases, which often spread beyond the walls, endangering the whole population. Sir Francis Bacon described gaol fever as the "most pernicious infection, next to the plague."[55] One such epidemic at Oxford in 1577 claimed more than five hundred lives and helped give rise to the notion that *all* prisoners were dangerous and that their disease, perhaps even their criminality, might contaminate anyone around them. This reinforced images of prisons as "schools of crime" in which younger pupils became corrupted by older, more hardened offenders.

From this perspective even quarantine seemed insufficient; banishment out of the country appeared more sensible. Surely such rabble were of no use to society in society. In America, on the other hand, criminals could at least be put to use earning a profit for company and crown, and they could serve the interests of Christendom at the same time. Having already established the "reformative" value of colonization for heathen savages, it required no great leap to apply this standard to others.

Thus it was that a royal commission concluded that any felon, except those convicted of murder, witchcraft, burglary, or rape, could legally be transported to Virginia or the West Indies to become servants on the plantations. Those prisoners who were physically able to work, or whose "other abilities shall be thought fit to be employed in foreign discoveries or other services," were henceforth authorized for banishment beyond the seas.[56] The plan to transport "notorious and wicked offenders that will not be reformed but by severity of punishment, in order that they may no more infect the places where they abide within our realm," was the subject of a royal proclamation dated December 23, 1617.[57] Almost immediately prisoners were selected from county jails "to yield a profitable service to the Commonwealth in parts abroad." The economic purpose of this policy was clear from the start. In one case, a man convicted of manslaughter and condemned to death was reprieved "because he was a carpenter and the plantation needed carpenters."[58]

Soon afterward Sandys proposed sending over maids as breeders, "that wives, children and family might make them less movable and settle them, together with their posterity in that soil."[59] The costs of passage could be paid by the planters who took them as "wives."[60] Twelve women were accordingly obtained by the Virginia Company and shipped to Jamestown as wives to colonists. A month later, fifty more were sent. Sandys went on record as hoping that their marriage would be "free according to the law of nature," asking Virginia's governor and council to be "fathers to them in this business, not enforcing them to marry against their wills." He cautioned against making them servants "but in case of extremity," since the company needed their condition to be viewed favorably in order that "multitudes may be allured thereby to come unto you."[61]

A scandal arose from allegations that some maids had been taken by force or bought from their parents for a few pieces of silver; some even whispered that King James himself had received a kickback ("royalty") from the scheme.[62]

The king had begun sending children away as servants as well.[63] The president of the company begged London's mayor for permission to hold such children in the city's Bridewell jail and put them to work until a ship was ready to transport them; the Common Council ordered "100 children out of the swarms that swarm in the place to be sent to Virginia . . . as apprentices for certain years."[64] Sandys reported to the Crown that the council had "appointed 100 children from the superfluous multitude to be transported to Virginia, there to be bound apprentices for certain years, and afterward with very beneficial conditions for the children." But he was careful to request legal authorization that would enable him to coerce the youngsters.[65]

As it granted Sandys's request, the Privy Council commended the city fathers for "redeeming so many poor souls from misery and ruin and putting them in a condition of use and service to the State."[66] If any children were found "obstinate to resist or otherwise to disobey such directions as shall be given in this behalf," company officials were henceforth empowered to "imprison, punish and dispose of any of those children, upon any disorder by them or any of them committed, as cause shall require, and so to ship them to Virginia with as much expedition as may stand for conveniency."[67]

Once the procedure had been worked out, roundups became routine. Soon the Virginia Company's request for another 100 children was quickly approved and another batch was swept up and sent away. It is unclear how many boys and girls were taken, but company records indicate that additional cargoes were authorized, at least in 1620 and 1622, and a letter of 1627 mentions 1,400 to 1,500 children as being shipped to Virginia.[68] The policy of allowing, even encouraging, private companies to forcibly apprehend, detain, transport, and sell into service lower-class children was legitimized by every branch and level of government and praised by the highest church officials. Shipping such persons abroad, John Donne said, "is not only a spleen to drain the ill humors of the body, but a liver to breed good blood."[69] This seizure (or "napping") of children ("kids") for shipment to America as servants became so well-known that the practice acquired a new name: "kidnapping."[70] Its original practitioners and defenders included government officials, corporate executives, clergymen, and parents.

Important developments often coincide, and the year 1619 was marked by another event, barely noticed at the time, that would prove of great significance for many generations to come. That was when John Rolfe reported to Sandys that at the end of August there had come to Virginia a Dutch man-of-war that "sold us twenty and odd Negers."[71]

The precise circumstances surrounding the arrival of these first Africans in Virginia are not clear. But historians have concluded that twenty or more black prisoners were taken to Point Comfort by Captain Jope in a Dutch ship of 160 tons that was guided by an English pilot named Master Marmaduke Rayner. Virginia's governor, George Yeardley, and his cape merchant, Abraham Piersey, appear to have purchased them with provisions. Their Dutch supplier seems to have taken them from a Spanish slaver, which the warship had captured as booty, Spain and Holland then being at war.[72]

Although Elizabeth's policy of noninvolvement in the African slave trade was still in effect, only a few months before—simultaneous with the roundup of maids and children—King James had created the Company of Adventurers of London Trading into Parts of Africa.[73] England was just beginning to make another attempt to colonize the Dark Continent.

THE GROWTH OF THE PRISONER TRADE

THE infusion into Virginia of kidnapped children, maids, convicts, and Africans, all to work as servants on the plantations, marked the beginning of a pattern that would continue for nearly two centuries. By 1650, most British emigrants to colonial America went as prisoners of one sort or another. Some were forcibly "kidnapped" or "arrested" (a legal distinction that can prove hard to make out, particularly for those seized) and shipped here against their will. Some were tricked or enticed into giving up their liberty. Others bound themselves as servants in order to avert execution, starvation, imprisonment, or boredom. There were some significant distinctions between indentured servants, transported convicts, slaves, and seamen or soldiers compelled into military service (impressed), but all of them qualified as prisoners, since they were deprived of their liberty to leave.

British America was not the first prison colony. Many earlier empires had used transplanted prisoners to cultivate foreign plantations, dig mines, and perform other hard labor.[74] Starting in the early seventeenth century and continuing for 150 years, however, an organized, international prisoner trade, of which the African slave trade was just one important part, provided the foundation for England's colonial wealth and America's identity. To the extent that American history is the story of immigration,[75] then American colonial history is largely the story of the immigration of prisoners.

Following sea routes discovered by their explorers, European merchants transported iron, alcohol, and other goods to Africa, exchanging them for human cargoes. These people were brought by force to the West Indies and the Americas and traded for tobacco, sugar, gold, silver, and other items that were taken back to English and European ports. Prisoners manned the ships, prisoners were carried to the colonies to work in the mines and fields, prisoners were brought in chains from Africa and Europe to the Caribbean and the Americas as slaves.

An organized system soon developed to get servants and send them overseas. Some enterprising souls functioned as agents working on commission. Offices sprang up that offered laborers on order "at a day's warning." Investors ventured into the systematic speculation in servants. Shipbuilders, outfitters, and insurers got involved, and colonial planters discovered a new means of exchange for greater volumes of goods. A successful trading company stood to realize profits of as much as 800 percent.[76]

One Londoner observed that the "usual way of getting servants hath been by a sort of men nick-named spirits, who take up all the idle, lazy, stupid people they can entice, such as have professed idleness, and would rather beg than work."[77] Around 1638 the lord mayor and aldermen of London complained to the Privy Council that "usually for the supply of soldiers into divers parts, and sending of men to the several plantations beyond the seas, without lawful press, certain persons called spirits, do inveigle and by lewd subtleties entice away youth, against the consent either of their parents, friends, or masters; whereby of times great tumults and uproars are raised within the city, to the breach of the peace, and the hazard of men's lives."[78]

Once persons disappeared, their relatives or friends had little chance of finding them again. Even if a victim managed to tell somebody in authority that she had been taken against her will, she was not likely to be freed. Officers of the law were expected to *apprehend* persons, not release them. Moreover, England lacked a professional system of police, so that the powers of law enforcement, especially arrest, belonged to those with the right political connections—in short, to those who were behind the manstealing.[79] The number and variety of officials and semiofficials authorized to take prisoners into custody made it difficult to determine who was a "kidnapper" and who was not.[80] Some thugs were licensed to apprehend persons and bind them as servants to foreign plantations; others stole without a license to steal. The line between kidnapping and arrest was literally paper thin. Not everyone was entitled to take people, but there was tremendous potential for abuse. Instead of rounding up 100 "vagrants," as legally authorized, a gang might grab 150 and sell the excess for their own aggrandizement. The gangs might resort to force when force was forbidden or unnecessary, or seize someone who did not fit the approved description. Many victims were not in a position to resist.

During his conquest of Ireland, Oliver Cromwell ordered mass roundups of Irish for the plantations.[81] He also favored impressment, and seized Jamaica with an army that was composed primarily of "common cheats, thieves, cutpurses and such like persons."[82] The ship *Unity* was used to transport some captive Scots to Boston and Charlestown.[83] Two London merchants, John Jeffries and Robert Lewellin, negotiated through their Irish agent to transport two hundred "passengers" from Dublin to Virginia in the vessel. The contract called for them to be taken from Irish prisons, but when only thirteen or fourteen could be obtained there the *Unity*'s master "laid out a considerable sum of money" to meet his quota. The spirit he hired organized a press-gang to comb the city.[84] Later the ship was used in the African slave trade, carrying captive blacks between Antigua, Angola, Nevis, Barbados, Sierra Leone, and Sherbro Island.[85] John Jeffries, meanwhile, engaged in the trafficking of not only political prisoners but indentured servants and black slaves as well.[86]

It was during the Restoration (which began in the summer of 1660) that the prisoner trade really became a moving force of English colonial policy. The return of Charles II to the throne inaugurated an age of great monopoly in which the prevailing powers ruled by using kidnapping, violence, and imprisonment on a massive scale. Plans were made for expanded trafficking in felons and Africans, and the Company of Royal Adventurers Trading to Africa dispatched its first forty ships in search of gold and slaves. It was a system that would thrive for more than a century. (General James Edward Oglethorpe, the "prison reformer" who founded Georgia in 1732–33 with colonists obtained from English prisons, was a director of the Royal African Company.[87] Micajah Perry was both a leading colonial agent for servants and convicts and a secretary to the company.[88])

England's trafficking of prisoners would continue for generations, outlasting most of the kings and businessmen who temporarily controlled it. Without the seizure, imprisonment, shipment, and sale of human beings to America, immense fortunes would not have been made from tobacco, sugar, and rum.

Although the wide scope and high level of organization of spiriting were self-evident, the real powers behind it were rarely revealed. A notable exception occurred in 1670 when a convicted spirit named William Haverland testified against sixteen cohorts.[89] Among his allegations was that John Steward of St. Katherine's Parish had taken away five hundred persons a year for the last twelve years.[90] For this Steward was paid forty shillings per head, the same amount usually imposed as a fine for forcible kidnapping at that time. But even Haverland's sensational disclosures failed to produce stiff penalties for kidnapping, and the higher-ups—the merchants and planters who employed the spirits and bought the servants from them—were rarely implicated. Very few disappearances ever resulted in prosecution; even when they did, the convicted kidnapper was seldom punished more severely than with a small fine—a remarkable fact considering that various forms of petty theft, such as filching a lady's petticoat or a gentleman's spoon, drew sentences of whipping, branding, penal servitude, and even death.[91] By 1680, the Reverend Morgan Godwyn estimated that ten thousand souls were being spirited to the colonies every year.[92]

Although the English had been relatively late starters in the African slave trade, by the last quarter of the seventeenth century they had begun to dominate it. Once they had established a colony capable of turning out a lucrative product, such as tobacco or sugar, and could staff their plantations with a white labor force capable of overseeing black slaves, all that remained was to develop the legal and moral justification for racial slavery.[93]

Africans qualified for slavery because they were black, "primitive" strangers, infidels. It seemed to follow that the African was eligible for less humane treatment than other (white, Christian) servants. Once black prisoners began to receive worse treatment, they assumed less humanity in the eyes of their captors. And once they had been made to seem subhuman, their capture, custody, and living conditions became much more harsh.

The captive Africans, some of them loaded down with heavy stones to prevent escape, were tied to each other to form long columns and prodded through the jungle until they reached a place where other prisoners were being held. At the Niger Delta they were herded into an immense outdoor cage (a barracoon); at Wydah, monsters shoved them into a stinking storehouse called the "trunk."[94] Brought down to Fida from the inland country, one Guinea slaver wrote, the captives were "put into a booth, or prison, built for that purpose, near the beach, all of them together; and when the Europeans are to receive them, they are brought out into a large plain, where the surgeons examine every part of everyone of them, to the smallest member, men and women being all stark naked."[95]

Africans who were too old or deformed or maimed or missing too many teeth or lame or too seriously wounded or sick—particularly if it was with obvious venereal disease that might infect a white man—were pulled out and "rejected." The rest were often branded, then put back into their cages, where they might stay for a day, a week, or a month, if they survived, until their time came to be moved. Like the Portuguese, the Royal African Company hoarded its slaves and other goods in huge stone castles along the shore.[96] Accommodations for the officers at Cape Coast Castle were so luxurious that Captain Thomas Phillips wrote in his journal: "I believe there are not better barracks anywhere than here." Slaves in silk livery served him punch and fanned away the heat. But beneath the brick-lined apartment with its feather bed and arcaded balcony, below the "handsome staircase" leading to the "stately hall," deep underground a thousand slaves groaned in a vaulted dungeon carved in the sweating rock, bats flapping about them in the darkness of their tomb.[97]

THE ROLE OF PRISONS

PRISONS were an essential part of the prisoner trade, whether the captives were Africans, servants, convicts, or pressed men. In the British Isles as well, after a person had been taken into custody he or she was brought to a holding place near the shore to await shipment abroad. If the apprehension was lawful, the captive might be kept in a local gaol, prison, or house of correction until being moved aboard a vessel. Some prisons from the twelfth century were still in use in England. One of the oldest was the Fleet, an immense stone fort surrounded by a sewer, which had nearly been destroyed by London's Great Fire of 1666. The most famous was Newgate, which dated back to the reign of King John and perhaps even to Roman times.[98] This prison took its name from a gate in the wall that surrounded the ancient City. Like many fortifications it had contained dungeons, some of which (such as Cripplegate, Ludgate, and this one) remained the foundation upon which subsequent prisons had been built over centuries.

By the mid-seventeenth century, Newgate was a dark, damp warren of stone yards, winding staircases, and narrow passageways. Some of the latter led to well-furnished apartments, others to black dungeons like the condemned hold—a stone pit with an open sewer running through its middle, hooks and chains fastened to its moist walls, and floors covered with lice that cracked under one's feet like shells strewn on a garden walk. Newcomers were placed into the prison's "common side" with rogues and rabble who could not afford to pay for better accommodations; moreover, new prisoners oftentimes started out in shackles, iron collar, or fetters until they paid a special fee to ease their irons. Those wanting to receive visitors had to pay. A captive could send for his servant, his wife, or an occasional prostitute; he could enjoy as much liquor or other items as he could buy. Candles, firewood, and food were available for a price; they were not available to those without means. Besides these lawful fees, there were unofficial charges. A new arrival (or "rat," as he was often called) quickly found himself beset by a gang of brutish-looking ruffians who, one visitor explained, "eyed me as if they would look me through, and examined every part of me from head to toe, not as tailors to take measure of me, but as footpads that survey the goodness of the clothes first, before they grow intimate with the linings." Anyone wanting protection or other privileges had better pay for that as well.[99]

The usual English prison was an old house, medieval dungeon, or some other privately owned structure. The prison in Halifax was owned by the Duke of Leeds, Maccesfield's by Lord Derby, Dunham's by the local bishop, Exeter's belonged to Mr. J. R. Walter, Chesterfield's to the Duke of Portland.[100] Some trading companies maintained dozens of their own lockups, complete with oak doors, manacles, and guards. Even Bristol, the second biggest city in England and one of the greatest places of embarkation for the colonies, lacked its own public prison, except for a small cage

erected in 1647, until the eighteenth century.[101] Norwich had only one de-
caying fourteenth-century structure as its all-purpose prison, bridewell,
and gaol.[102]

A London observer of 1649 reported that most persons bound for the
colonies were "put up in cook's houses about St. Katherine's," where they
were "kept as prisoners until a master fetches them off; and they lie at
charges in these places a month or more, before they are taken away. When
the ship is ready, the spirits' charges and the cook for dieting paid, they
are shipped, and this charge is commonly 3 [pounds]."[103] Press-gangs
brought their unwilling recruits to similar houses of detention, called
"press-rooms," until the navy could take custody.[104]

Operating such private prisons became a lucrative clandestine trade in
many ports. Guards were hired to prevent escapes, lookouts watched for
worried relatives searching for missing kin, informers reported bits of intelligence in exchange for rewards, and the manufacturers of leg irons and
other hardware of restraint enjoyed a thriving business.

A newspaper writer calling himself the English Rogue described being
taken by a spirit to a narrow room so filled with tobacco smoke that he
could barely make out the occupants' faces. He wrote that there was

> little discourse amongst them, but of the pleasantness of the soil
> of that continent we were designed for, (out of a design to make
> us swallow their gilded pills of ruin) and the temperature of the
> air, the plenty of fowl and fish of all sorts; the little labor that is
> performed or expected having so little trouble in it, that it rather
> may be accounted a pastime than anything of punishment; and
> then to sweeten us the farther, they insisted on the pliant loving
> natures of the women there; all which they used as baits to catch
> us silly gudgeons.[105]

Thirty years later, Ned Ward reported peeping into a London gateway,
"where we saw three or four blades well dressed, with hawks' countenances, attended with half a dozen raggamuffinly fellows, showing poverty
in their wages, and despair in their faces, mixt with a parcel of young wild
striplings like run-away prentices." A friend told him that the place was
"an office where servants for the plantations bind themselves."[106]

By the early eighteenth century, spiriting and other forms of organized
crime were still in full swing. After learning the tricks of his trade while
himself imprisoned, Jonathan Wild went on to become a legendary receiver
in stolen goods and thief-taker.[107] As one of London's leading spirits, Wild
fenced people as well as inanimate property, and his mask of respectability

extended to calling his warehouses "offices for the recovery of stolen property." Daniel Defoe, the pioneering London journalist and novelist who had been imprisoned himself for blasphemy and debt, got to know Wild and other underworld characters and wrote about them in several popular accounts. He also devoted part of his highly factual novel, *Colonel Jack,* to the kidnapping trade.[108]

QUAKERS

S HORTLY after the English Civil War, there had arisen in northern England a radical religious movement comprised of persons who called themselves Friends and whom others called Quakers because they quaked and shook with zeal. Its founder, George Fox, spent much of his time locked up for his beliefs, and it was in prison that he convinced many others to join his sect.[109]

In 1652 a group of Fox's converts, the Valiant Sixty, began to spread his message aggressively, hoping eventually to convince the whole world.[110] Quakerism spread among the middle class with astonishing speed. The convinced met in remote homes or open fields, attracting anywhere from a few dozen to two hundred people. "Their speaker . . . standing, with his hat on," one Puritan eyewitness wrote, "his countenance severe, his face downward, his eyes mostly fixed towards the earth, his hands and fingers expanded, continually [struck] gently on his breast."[111]

By the winter of 1655–56, Friends were meeting in almost every county, despite severe repression. The more they were imprisoned, the stronger their resolve; the stronger their resolve, the more converts they gained; the more members they attracted, the more threatening they were considered and the more of them that were imprisoned; and the more that were imprisoned, the more converts they made. Thus it was that the prisons became their primary meeting places and suppliers of new members. Fox himself was frequently shifted from one prison to another and often released because he was more of a threat inside than out. But the more that he and his supporters were mistreated, the more they seemed to thrive.[112] Thrust into a dank cell among toadstools and rats, young Ann Audland wrote glowingly to another Friend, "This is indeed a place of joy, and my soul doth rejoice in the Lord."[113] Shortly before he died from his own ordeal, William Dewsbury exulted that he had "joyfully entered prisons as palaces, telling mine enemies to hold me there as long as they could; and in the prison house I sung praises to my God and esteemed the bolts and locks put upon me as jewels."[114]

Many Friends found ready converts in prison. They also attracted streams of visitors, some of whom asked for permission to trade places with their captive sisters and brothers.[115] As their deaths in prison mounted, word of their martyrdom spread. Some captives composed reams of writs and testimonies about their sufferings. These tracts were taken out by visitors and passed on, hand to hand, to waiting printers. Fox himself saw published several books that he had dictated in prison.[116]

CONVICT TRANSPORTATION

ENGLISH prisons continued to be generally used to detain offenders, not to punish them. "Real" punishments were intentionally painful, and the criminal law of the period often required the death penalty for minor property offenses. Beginning in the late seventeenth century and continuing into the eighteenth, more and more crimes were made punishable, at least in statute, by hanging. The system of penalties became known as the Bloody Code, and the threat of execution was held over a large portion of the criminal population.[117] With the passage of the Black Act in 1723, an already voluminous list of capital offenses was expanded to no less than fifty, to include such crimes as poaching fish, damaging trees, stealing a silver spoon, and appearing disguised in a game preserve. (As before, kidnapping was not among them.)[118]

Outcries against such policies were surprisingly rare, except on the part of Quakers, and support for the death penalty may actually have been just as strong or stronger among the lower classes than it was among the rich. Public executions remained immensely popular with the masses—too much so, according to some officials.

In London a hanging day began with the somber toll of buffeted churchbells.[119] Visitors streamed in for the occasion, drawing pickpockets from miles around, and hawkers sold the day's "last dying confessions" to throngs who lined the winding route to the gallows. Newgate's doomed convicts were brought out of the condemned hold to the prison chapel, where the prison ordinary prepared them as best he could. Then they were taken to the press-yard, where a procession was formed. Then the carts went out the gate, surrounded by soldiers and ministers and undertakers, the latter usually eliciting scattered hoots and jeers from the crowd. The cavalcade clattered along the city's busiest street at Smithfield and crossed the Fleet River Bridge, then moved slowly up Holborn Hill, where patrons often rushed from taverns to get a look and sometimes give a final swig of wine to a condemned wretch.

Bernard de Mandeville's description was typical of a gentleman's distaste, not so much for the event itself, as for the mob that invariably turned out to watch. "All the way, from Newgate to Tyburn, is one continual fair, for whores and rogues of the meaner sort," he wrote.[120]

The arriving carts were backed up beneath Albion's fatal tree. Spectators stretched to get a view of the prisoners, gaping wide-eyed and bewildered, as the executioner, moving like a cat, got into position. Some executioners were themselves convicted criminals, and in time a few of them would be put to death by means of the very apparatus they had used against others.[121]

Capital punishment might have been viewed differently if the government strictly enforced the capital laws. But it did not. Seventeenth-century courts continued to recognize benefit of clergy, so that a convicted felon was entitled to "call the book"—if he was able to read a passage from the Bible, he might escape death and have his thumb branded instead.[122] Some illiterates abused the privilege by simply dropping to their knees and reciting the "neck verse," usually the first verse of the Fifty-first Psalm. Accordingly, in 1705 Parliament removed the literacy requirement and substituted a list of twenty-five felonies not subject to clerical intervention, including murder, piracy, treason, arson, burglary, highway robbery, and theft of goods valued at more than one shilling. In addition, royal pardons replaced benefit of clergy as the preferred instrument of mercy.[123]

Both devices were an ingenious legal legerdemain, since without them banishment might have been illegal. The Magna Carta and the Habeas Corpus Act may have forbidden the government from imposing exile or transportation.[124] But it was not illegal for an offender to be exiled "voluntarily." The courts could not be faulted for allowing a condemned felon to be pardoned by the Crown on the condition that he or she leave the country for a specified term. Criminals were not likely to want to go to America on their own, but facing death they might agree to anything to save their lives. This arrangement also allowed the Crown to show mercy, thereby boosting its image and eliciting compliance.

Thus, while Parliament kept adding to the list of capital crimes the number of persons executed actually decreased over time.[125] (Between 1607 and 1616 the average annual volume of hangings in London and Middlesex was 140, but between 1749 and 1799 it had dropped to 33.)[126] In fact, most of those condemned to death during the eighteenth century did not go to the gallows; they were pardoned. As a result, the prerogative of mercy was made to appear as much a feature of the administration of justice as blind severity seemed the keystone of law.

The workings of this process of "mercy" could be extremely complex and mysterious, occurring behind closed doors. Above all it was a system of discretion. Loyalty, patronage, and influence were integral, as a man without them discovered with his demise. For without a person of consequence to speak in his behalf, a condemned felon's doom could be quickly and irrevocably sealed. With such backing, he or she might look forward to fourteen years' servitude on a foreign plantation.

The code established mandatory death sentences for a wide array of offenses and was seemingly blind to class distinctions. The spectacle of public trials riveted attention on individual transgression and appeared to treat every defendant impartially. Pomp and solemnity filled the air. Everyone in the hushed courtroom sprang up as the judges, bedecked in wigs and robes, paraded in, and everyone sat after the judges had ascended to their perch. Great pains were taken to make the law seem magisterial and the courts incorruptible, impartial, and venerable. Knowing that judges held the power of life or death in their hands, defendants strained to appear cooperative, penitent, and even thankful during the proceedings. They clung to etiquette even as they were being sentenced to death, in the hope that their good behavior would ultimately help to spare their lives, which it usually—but not always—did. Thus, the system maintained the loyalty and obedience of its subjects.

Judges welcomed this process as a means of ameliorating the harsh sentences that law required them to dispense, and they were grateful that it also protected them from cries of excessive leniency. Technically judges were not empowered to grant pardons; they simply recommended clemency. A pardon had to be sealed with the Great Seal and issued by authority of the king or the Privy Council. If a judge was not disposed to recommend a pardon, his conscience could always be eased by the knowledge that a convict might still petition to higher authority up to the moment of execution. In this way neither the lawmakers, the judges, the king or Privy Council, nor any other authority was forced to accept personal accountability for an execution. Judges also had discretion to stay an execution by granting a reprieve. If a female convict pleaded her belly and a jury of matrons concluded that she was quick with child, the court might order her held in prison until she delivered, whereupon the woman would be called down to her former judgment and her child turned over to the house of orphans. Occasionally a judge was dissuaded by the prison ordinary, but not even he could always be counted on to plead for mercy, since an ordinary's reputation and livelihood might depend upon his ability to extract penitent dying confessions.[127]

But tenderheartedness was not the only factor accounting for the frequent use of pardons, any more than simple cruelty explained why there were so many capital crime laws. Above all, the system supplied workers to the colonies, providing labor that the government could get very cheaply and sell at a fat profit to private contractors; labor that otherwise would not have been forthcoming; labor that was worth more abroad than at home; labor that the mother country was glad to be rid of and the colonial merchants were eager to traffic; labor that could be easily regulated in volume, since the government could always decrease or increase the number of pardons; captive labor that nevertheless pleaded for the chance to go to America rather than to the gallows; white labor to lighten the rising tide of black slaves and thus reduce the difficulties of control on the plantations; labor that could be enormously profitable to transfer as well as to use.[128]

In 1717 Parliament passed an act empowering courts to sentence offenders directly to transportation.[129] Persons convicted of clergyable felonies or petty larceny could now be sent to American plantations for seven years instead of being whipped or burnt on the hand. This meant that a large portion of England's offenders were eligible to be shipped abroad and sold as servants for seven-year terms. Felons convicted of capital crimes could, with royal consent, be commuted to a term of fourteen years' transportation or, in some cases, life. Anyone who returned before her or his term expired or who helped a convict to escape was liable to be hanged.

Jonathan Forward, a young London merchant with extensive contacts in Maryland, obtained a lucrative subsidy of three pounds for every Newgate felon and five pounds for every convict taken from the provinces. In exchange, he agreed to ship any and all criminals sentenced to transportation, and to pay all costs, including gaol fees, for their conveyance.[130] Forward was experienced in the African slave trade and had recently shipped two vessels with 171 convicts to Maryland. Operating out of his Cheapside house on Fenchurch Street, London, he collaborated with Jonathan Wild, who helped to provide "felons" for shipment abroad.

On April 26, 1718, 29 malefactors at the Old Bailey were ordered to be transported.[131] Four months later the *Historical Register* reported that 106 convicts "that were ordered for transportation, were taken out of Newgate and put on board a lighter at Blackwall Stairs, from whence they were carried through the Bridge to Long Reach, and there shipped on board the *Eagle* galley, Captain Staples commander, bound for Virginia and Maryland."[132] (The *Eagle* was a well-known slave ship that had sailed for the Royal African Company for more than a decade, so the transport of prisoners to America was nothing new for her.)[133]

Forward retained his monopoly for over twenty years until April 1739, when Andrew Reid was added to the payroll. Although Forward continued to transport felons from provincial gaols until the late 1740s, Reid assumed

main control of the convict trade. He had several partners, including
Andrew Armour of London and James Stewart of Scotland. Reid held the
Treasury contract until March 1757, when Stewart succeeded him. Stewart
described his predecessor as a "person against whom almost every species
of complaint was made" and observed that the transporting of felons was
carried on by the "most corruptible class" of traders. Stewart himself
remained in the trade until his death in February 1772; he was followed by
his partner, Duncan Campbell, also of Scotland.[134] From 1771 to 1775 the
Scottish commission for the contract trade to Maryland and Virginia was
held by Patrick Colquhoun, a young Glasgow trader and future police
reformer.[135]

France pursued a similar policy. John Law, a Scottish entrepreneur and
gambler who had sought refuge on the Continent for killing a man in London, had won access to the inner circle of the French court through the
gaming table. Law used his contacts to gain permission to try out some of
his banking schemes, and in August 1717 he was granted approval to
attempt the development of the vast Louisiana territory in America. Using
a gang called the Mississippi Bandits, he scoured French jails and hospitals, picking up inmates to serve as his first colonists. One observer said
these recruits included "beyond such small-fry as a few drunkards, confirmed blasphemers, dangerous intriguers and procuresses—chiefly mur-
deresses, prostitutes, thieves, knife experts, and female criminals branded
on the shoulder with the *fleur-de-lys,* associates of coiners or of the bands
of brigands infesting the forest of St. Germain." A few of the women apparently "scratched the faces of the children in charge of them" and vanished
into nearby fields, but most prisoners were not so lucky.[136]

By the April 1718 session of the Old Bailey, more than half of the convicted felons—twenty-seven of fifty-one—were ordered transported. From
then until 1769, more than two-thirds (69.5 percent) were banished to
America, making transportation the leading punishment for serious crime
in Great Britain. The list of "serious crimes" also kept growing; from 1720
to 1765, Parliament passed sixteen acts establishing transportation as a
penalty for additional crimes ranging from perjury to poaching.[137] In addition to these "seven-year passengers" and capital convicts sentenced to
fourteen years abroad, during the 1730s an estimated ten thousand debtors
were released from British prisons to settle the new colony of Georgia. The
man who organized the project was General James Edward Oglethorpe,
deputy governor of the Royal African Company.[138]

Based upon his analysis of many official records regarding convict transportation, the historian Abbot Emerson Smith figured that the total number of convicts reaching Virginia and Maryland during the eighteenth

century was slightly more than twenty thousand from England and about half that from Ireland, making a total of roughly thirty thousand convicts transported to America.[139] His estimate is generally lower than those of other historians.

A more recent study by A. Roger Ekirch concluded that well over 30,000 convicts were transported from England to America between 1718 and 1775; he set the total number sent here from England at 36,000. Adding more than 13,000 shipped from Ireland and another 700 sent from Scotland during the same period, Ekirch put the number transported from Britain at 50,000 and concluded: "Convicts represented as much as a quarter of all British emigrants to colonial America during the 18th century."[140] But even these numbers appear low, since they may underestimate the numbers sent from Britain before 1718, ignore debtors, and do not include criminals transported by the French, Spanish, and Dutch.[141]

In any event, the convict trade to America was big business. Some of the larger convict traders also dealt in indentured servants, sometimes carrying them and dry goods in the same ships. On their return voyages, convict vessels often brought colonial exports like tobacco, wheat, and pig iron back to Britain. Some ships were also engaged in the African slave trade. Jonathan Forward's *Anne* and *Eagle* carried slaves, servants, and convicts during the same period. So did some of Samuel Sedgley's ships out of Bristol and James Gildart's from Liverpool. Profits sometimes exceeded 30 percent. One leading convict trader wrote to his partner that their business "if properly managed will in a few years make Us very genteel fortunes."[142]

PENAL SLAVERY MADE FASHIONABLE

PENAL slavery became fashionable due in part to one of the most influential essays ever written, the brief but elegant *On Crimes and Punishments*, attributed to a young Milanese aristocrat and economist, Cesare Bonesana, Marchese di Beccaria.[143] Hailed by Voltaire as *le code de l'humanité*, and embraced by many of Europe's royal courts, Beccaria's work gained fame as the definitive plea for "humane" treatment of criminals. To this day it remains a classic work in criminology and penology.[144]

Beccaria thought punishments should deal only with lawbreakers, and carry "only that degree of severity which is sufficient to deter others." Urging an end to torture and secret trials, he wanted every accused person to enjoy both humane treatment and the legal rights to defend himself. He considered swift and certain punishments as more effective deterrents than severe penalties. He also thought they should be carefully measured out to be the least possible given the circumstances and proportionate to the offense.

Just as important, he favored imprisonment, not only for detaining the accused until his case was decided but also as a punishment for crime. In fact, Beccaria recommended penal slavery as the appropriate punishment for robbery, and he advocated corporal punishment on top of it if violence had accompanied the stealing. In place of capital punishment, he preferred "perpetual slavery," saying it offered "all that is necessary to deter the most hardened and determined, as much as the punishment of death." His arguments constituted a "humanitarian" justification for penal slavery—one that helped ensure its adoption by Enlightenment thinkers.

CONVICT VESSELS

AFTER a convict had been pardoned and the transportation order signed, he might languish in prison for as long as three or four months until a ship was ready to carry him away. When that time finally came, the inmate was brought out into the prison yard, in irons, and chained to a line of fellow transports. Soldiers with fixed bayonets ensured there were no shenanigans. Coffles of as many as a hundred men and women were prodded out through the gate, clanking over the cobblestones in a wretched-looking train, heading toward a waiting ship at Gravesend.[145] All along the narrow route, curious crowds formed to watch them pass, dogs barked, and boys tossed mud and stones.

Among one such group were Anthony Carnes, convicted of stealing goods valued at forty shillings; Timothy Featherstonehaugh Scutt, convicted of taking two letters from the post office; Henry Porte, imprisoned for taking ten pence worth of goods; and Edward Coleman, who had ripped a lead pipe from a house belonging to the East India Company.[146] Shabbily dressed, often looking haggard and sick, with sullen or contemptuous expressions, most transports were young men, although as many as a fifth were women; nearly all of them had been convicted of small-time theft. Very few were professional criminals from London's underworld or persons of consequence.

Most vessels used in the prisoner trade weighed less than two hundred tons. Though not Britain's largest commercial carriers, they could haul substantial loads, typically holding ninety or more passengers, who sometimes included a mix of convicts and indentured servants.

Common convicts were marched aboard and transferred to the custody of the shipmaster, who recorded their names in a log and put them under the hatches in the hold. A visitor touring one of John Stewart's convict vessels wrote, "I went on board, and . . . saw this poor man . . . chained to a board in a hole not above 16 feet long, more than 50 with him; a collar and padlock about his neck, and chained to five of the most dreadful creatures I ever looked upon."[147]

THE MIDDLE PASSAGE

THE next shock in the ordeal of the kidnapped Africans began when the prison door was opened and they were pulled out, naked and afraid, into the bright light. Men, women, and children were herded into separate groups. It all happened so quickly that the men barely had time to recover before guards bound their necks and ankles with heavy iron chains and started pushing them toward the beach. Many inlanders had never seen the sea and they were filled with wonder. Astonishment turned to terror as the white guards shoved them into boats and pushed off from the shore, heading toward a huge vessel with tall masts waiting in the harbor. In a few minutes they were being hoisted aboard.

Thirty years later, the former slave Equiano remembered thinking at the time that he was entering a "world of bad spirits, and that they were going to kill me." Many feared being eaten. When he saw water boiling in a large copper kettle and a "multitude of black people of every description chained together, every one of their countenances expressing dejection and sorrow," he was so horror stricken that he fainted on the deck.[148]

Slavers considered boarding particularly dangerous; their prisoners were not only terrified but close to shore, and some were not yet aware of the extraordinary precautions that had been taken to prevent their escape. Those trying to get away were beaten back or shot. Some jumped overboard only to become tangled like flies in a spider's web, the slavers having hung nets around the ship. Others who made it into the water sank under the weight of their fetters.[149]

The men were prodded down the ladder to the upper hold, where the guards pushed them onto a long shelf and fastened each in place by wrist and ankle. Equiano recalled that when he was thrust between the decks he received "such a salutation in my nostrils as I had never experienced in my life; so that, with the loathesomeness of the stench, and crying together, I became sick and low that I was not able to eat, nor had the least desire to taste anything."[150] Some captives passed out, or gagged and vomited in the suffocating heat. As many as 300 to 400 persons might be crowded into the ship's belly, each occupying a space only 5 or 6 feet long by as little as

16 inches wide by 3 or 4 feet high.[151] The only air and light inside seeped through the iron gratings over the hatches. The only way to dispose of body waste was for it to leak through the cracks between the unplaned boards on which the captives lay, dripping upon those below.

Sometimes they stayed in the hold for as long as the ship was in port (which could be as long as three to ten months), the master of a slave ship usually considering it too risky to let his prisoners on deck except for feeding. Once the men were secured below, the women and children were brought aboard. From the moment of their arrival, a former slaver wrote, the women and girls were "often exposed to the wanton rudeness of white savages. . . . In imagination the prey is divided on the spot, and only reserved till opportunity offers."[152] From the hold Equiano could hear their shrieks, but like all of the men he was powerless to help. Only the shipmaster could decide how the women would be treated, and as one master explained it, "Perhaps some hard-hearted pleader may suggest that such treatment would indeed be cruel in Europe; but the African women are negroes, savages, who have no idea of the nicer sensations which obtain among civilized people."[153]

The hold contained prisoners of many tribes and backgrounds, which complicated communication.[154] It was also a perfect incubator for all sorts of diseases.[155] Many contracted measles, smallpox, gonorrhea, or syphilis from their European captors, and some transmitted in return various tropical ills. Yellow fever, malaria, and amoebic dysentery were common disorders on the slave ships. Perhaps the worst, however, was the flux, which began with intermittent fevers, chills, and dizziness, and then racked the bowels with a bloody, grayish mucous discharge that left such a stink that even barrels of vinegar poured over the decks could not remove it.

A slave ship's crew suffered from some of the same perils and privations as its prisoners.[156] Some seamen had themselves been coaxed or kidnapped into the voyage; regardless of how they had entered, once aboard ship they were prisoners too, relinquishing all liberty to the shipmaster and officers. Wayward crewmen faced severe floggings, keelhauling, and even summary execution, virtually without legal rights.[157]

Outranked by the master and officers, vastly outnumbered by the blacks, the common seamen worked in a state of constant tension, mortally vulnerable to attack from above and from below. To survive, the guards tried to use conflict to their own advantage. Unlike the master, whose profit depended on delivering the maximum number of slaves to market, the crew were simply engaged in a job and interested only in their own survival. Generally it made no difference to them whether the slaves were kept healthy or alive; all that mattered was that they—the guards—lasted long enough to get paid or jump ship. Besides having to operate the vessel, their duties included the custody and care of the prisoners, and they were not inclined to want to take needless risks, though they did have to obey the master's commands or face the consequences.

Some slaves saw no difference between the master or his officers and the crew, viewing them all as white oppressors. The crew, on the other hand, often considered themselves in the middle. In order to be protected from the master, they had to make him realize that they were all that stood between him and the prisoners. Thus the guards were quick to remind those in authority of the dangerousness of the blacks and of their own importance in maintaining order and control on the vessel. Mutinies by the crew were rare, but the guards often tried to use other, more subtle methods to increase their power. If some guards had their way, the prisoners never would have been allowed to leave the hold. But they were not in command, so they had to go along as ordered. This usually entailed allowing the male slaves to be brought onto the main deck or forecastle to be fed. Ordinarily this was done twice a day, in the morning and late afternoon. Very tight security was maintained during these feedings, with the crew either distributing victuals or standing by with loaded firearms, "some with lighted matches at their great guns that yawn upon them, loaded with partridge, till they have done and gone to their kennels between decks."[158]

Prisoners who refused to eat were whipped. If they still refused, the guards held them down and inserted metal bars between their teeth. The device was screwed until their jaws were pried open, sometimes crunching teeth in the process, and food was jammed down their throats.[159]

Few slaving captains described their experiences in public print, but those who did invariably depicted themselves as compassionate fellows. As proof, one second-generation slaver with more than twenty years' experience in the Guinea trade cited his practices of allowing the blacks' irons to be removed soon after the ship was at sea, providing two tasty meals a day, permitting the slaves to remain on deck all day if they wished, and providing them with pipes of tobacco one day per week. Another captain described himself as a liberal among slave traders because he did not resort to cutting off the legs and arms of the "most wilful" captives in order to "terrify the rest."[160] A third said: "We often at sea in the evenings would let the slaves come up into the sun to air themselves, and make them jump and dance for an hour or two to our bag-pipes, harp, and fiddle, by which exercise to preserve them in health; but not withstanding all our endeavour, 'twas my hard fortune to have great sickness and mortality among them."[161]

Slavers used informers and other surreptitious means to defuse possible conspiracies. Captain Phillips appointed thirty or forty Gold Coast blacks to oversee his Wydah captives.[162] Ottobah Cugono, a kidnapped Fantee who later escaped to tell his story, reported a plot among the women and boy slaves to destroy their ship in a mass suicide, but said they were betrayed by one of their countrywomen.[163] Even if the prisoners managed to overcome their captors, they faced the problem of having to operate the ship. As a result, slave mutinies seldom succeeded.[164]

The human cost of the slave trade was incalculable. Besides those killed during capture, or who succumbed en route to the holding pens, or who died in prison, the Middle Passage alone probably claimed from 10 to 55 percent of those who were shipped.[165] Records of the Royal African Company's purchases and deliveries for the period 1680–88 indicate an average loss in transit of about 23.4 percent.[166] Captain Phillips, whose vessel the *Hannibal* left the Guinea coast in 1693 with 700 slaves, delivered only 372 alive to Barbados.[167] The identities of those who perished will forever remain a mystery.

The end of the voyage was marked by sudden attention to the slaves' condition. Whenever possible, rations were increased and exercise was extended. Each slave was physically examined, hair was cut, bodies were washed. Wounds were disguised by cosmetics, and skin chafed raw was rubbed with oil until it glistened. After permission was received for the ship to dock, the final count was taken and the cargo was appraised. Spectators watched, heard, and smelled the chained Africans step hesitantly onto the wharf.

SERVANT CROSSINGS

CONVICTS and indentured servants experienced a comparable ordeal. Once a ship had set sail, a passenger's overriding concern was to survive the voyage. This was no easy task. Some ships leaving Ireland or England suffered higher mortality rates than warring armies sustained in whole campaigns.[168] During the seventeenth century, losses of over 50 percent were not unusual, and occasional records indicate that as many as 100 or 130 of 150 were lost. The 300-ton vessel, *Welcome* (which often served as a slave ship), that took Quaker William Penn to America in 1682 lost 30 of 100 passengers to smallpox.

Shipboard losses among convicts probably averaged 15 to 30 percent during the seventeenth century, dropping to as low as 3 percent by the last quarter of the eighteenth. All told, 5,000 or so convicts may have perished en route to America, many of them from smallpox and typhus.[169] A ship sailing from Ireland to Philadelphia in 1729 lost 100 of its 190 passengers and crew to starvation. The sloop *Sea-Flower* left Belfast in 1741 with 106 passengers; 46 of them starved to death. On the *Owners Goodwill* out of London in 1721, 19 of 50 convicts died before reaching America. In 1726, as many as 48 of the 108 felons aboard the *Rappahanock* never made it to Virginia.

"As I am grieved so many healthy young People die in the voyage," Andrew Reid, the convict contractor, wrote in 1742, "I would do all in my power to prevent it." After twenty years in the convict trade, Duncan Campbell said more than a seventh of the transports died on the voyage. He figured that a death rate of 10 percent during the crossing was considered a "moderate Loss," and he counted a total of more than 14 percent of transports as dying somewhere between British prisons and American soil.[170]

Not all convict traders evinced such concern. In 1743 the commander of the *Justitia,* Barnet Bond, left London for Maryland with 170 felons aboard. Despite having ample water reserves, Bond allotted each transport only one pint a day, enforcing his will by keelhauling and flogging. By voyage's end, nearly 50 convicts had expired.[171]

There were other dangers as well. The threat of piracy was real—anyone who went to sea faced the threat of being taken prisoner and held indefinitely. Fierce Atlantic tempests sent many ships to the bottom with all hands aboard, or marooned like some woebegone survivor on a Caribbean deserted island. Passengers who had spent their whole lives on solid ground quickly learned that the relentless waves that made men sick could also suddenly rise like mountains and smash a hapless craft into match sticks. The racing wind that threw a weight of five hundred tons across the water for more than one hundred miles a day might suddenly stop, leaving a vessel motionless and adrift for days or even weeks while supplies ran out.

Given the slim chances of surviving an escape attempt at sea, insurrections were relatively rare. Servant mutinies were so unusual that few shipmasters were very concerned with security unless they had felons aboard. Convict insurrections were much more frequent, even in the face of the extra precautions. In 1735 forty Irish convicts ran their vessel aground off Nova Scotia, killed the crew, and escaped onto land. Off the North Carolina coast in 1751, convicts from Liverpool seized control, shot the captain, imprisoned the crew, and escaped onto land. The same year, another shipmaster was killed by convicts before the crew could regain control. Consequently, many captains followed the same security procedures adopted for slave ships. But if the vessel was attacked at sea, even convicts might be turned loose to join the fight.[172]

A petition to Parliament in 1659 described how 72 servants were locked belowdecks during an entire voyage of over five weeks "amongst horses, [so] that their souls, through heat and steam under the tropic, fainted in them."[173] Crowding was often at its worst at night, when the servants in the hold were often so numerous that they had to sleep in shifts and in pairs, sometimes one on top of another. On Gottlieb Mittelberger's journey to Philadelphia in 1750, passengers were packed so tightly that one "person receives a place of scarcely 2 feet width and 6 feet length in a bedstead, while many a ship carries 4 to 600 souls; not to mention the innumerable implements, tools, provisions, water-barrels, and other things which likewise occupy much space."[174]

Philadelphia eventually passed an ordinance requiring a legal limit of at least six feet square for every four whole "freights" (persons)—children being considered only a fraction of a freight, based on their age—but even that minimum was regularly exceeded. Overcrowding produced an environment that was extremely noisy, smelly, and unhygienic. Besides having to endure a lack of privacy and constant scrutiny by their keepers, passengers experienced enforced intimacy with strangers. Most distasteful for some was that they had to live in close quarters with persons not of their own choosing. Friction among passengers was commonplace. Travel accounts by "persons of quality" bristle with indignation over the insolent behavior of commoners. Writing of his crossing in 1686, Durand the Huguenot complained about the lewd conduct of the twelve prostitutes aboard his vessel, saying he "saw those wenches behave so shockingly with the sailors and others, in addition to the distress caused by their songs and dances, that it awakened within me so intense a hatred of such persons that I shall never overcome it."[175] Some adults, especially crewmen, resented having children aboard, claiming the little ones got in their way and disrupted the normal operations of the ship.

For most passengers, though, the problem was not so much distraction as helplessness, idleness, and monotony—the common fate of prisoners. A passenger was powerless to affect either the course or the outcome of the voyage. Some whimpered, sighed, and cried piteously for their homes. Those who perished were cast into the sea, leaving their relatives and others who had persuaded them to undertake the journey in such despair that it was almost impossible to pacify and console them. "In a word, the sighing and crying and lamenting on board the ship continues night and day, so as to cause the hearts even of the most hardened to bleed when they hear it."[176]

When land was finally sighted and the ship approached shore, the servants' bodies were washed and their hair was trimmed. Clothes were mended, and some convicts were given wigs to make them appear more respectable to prospective buyers. The survivors were gathered on deck and their names and other information about them was logged. James Revel, one of the few transported convicts to leave a written account of his experience, wrote:

> *We were wash'd and cleaned,*
> *That to our buyers we might better seem;*
> *Our things were gave to each they did belong,*
> *And they that had clean linnen put it on.*

> *Our faces shav'd, com'd out our wigs and hair,*
> *That we in decent order might appear,*
> *Against the planters did come down to view,*
> *How well they lik'd this fresh transported crew.*[177]

HUMAN CARGOES

BY the early eighteenth century, a ship's arrival was announced by a local newspaper, which advertised the kind and quality of incoming cargoes, the scheduled date and place of landing, and other particulars about the merchandise for sale. The *American Weekly Mercury* of February 18, 1729, declared: "Lately arrived from London, a parcel of very likely English servants, men and women, several of the men tradesmen; to be sold reasonable and time allowed for payment. By Charles Read of Philadelphia, or Captain John Ball, on board his ship, at Anthony Milkinson's Wharf."[178] A notice in the *Maryland Gazette* of June 29, 1758, reported: "Last week arrived here from Bristol, the *Snow Eugene,* Capt. Jonathan Tallimay, with 69 of His Majesty's Seven Years' Passengers, 51 men and 18 women."[179] Noteworthy ads were picked up by editors in other colonies.

Most convict ships arrived in late spring and summer, and the Chesapeake convict trade was more regularized than the trade in slaves or indentured servants.[180] Slave ship arrivals were announced in the same way, and the tearsheets were tacked up beside the servants' notices on the walls of merchants' coffeehouses in Boston, New York, Philadelphia, Charleston,

Annapolis, Newport, New London, and other towns. When the *Martha* put into Philadelphia from South Carolina in 1737, the *Gazette* informed its readers of "A PARCEL of likely young Negro boys and girls, to be sold by Robert Ellis in Water-Street."[181]

Residents of Charleston were notified of the sale of wine, slaves, and indentured servants:

> TO BE SOLD on board the ship *Bance Island,* on Tuesday the 6th
> of May next, at Ashley-Ferry; a choice cargo of about 250 fine
> healthy NEGROES just arrived from the Windward & Rice Coast.
> The utmost care has already been taken, and shall be continued,
> to keep them free from the least danger of being infected with
> the SMALL-POX, no boat having been on board, and all other com-
> munication with people from Charleston prevented. Austin,
> Laurens & Appleby. N.B. Full one half of the above Negroes
> have had the SMALL-POX in their own country.[182]

Henry Laurens (of Austin, Laurens & Appleby) had pursued the slave trade to become the richest man and leading citizen in South Carolina.[183] As a partner in Charleston's largest and most successful slave-trading firms, he was the biggest slave trafficker in America.

Laurens personally involved himself in every aspect of the business, complaining on one occasion to his Rhode Island associates: "God knows what we shall do with what remain, they are a most scabby flock, all of them full of crockeraws—several have extreme sore eyes, three very puny children and add to this the worst infirmity of all others with which 6 or 8 are attended (vizt) Old Age."[184]

Some of the concern about incoming passengers stemmed from fears that they would transmit disease, and there was good reason to worry. In 1741 a ship carrying servants and convicts from Dublin was blamed as the source of a fatal fever epidemic in Philadelphia. In Virginia, a wealthy Northern Neck planter reported that his household was "much alarmed . . . about a Jail disorder brought into the Neighbourhood by Col. Frank Lee's servant bought of Somervill."[185] In 1767 the deaths of a widow and more than twenty of her slaves on Maryland's Eastern Shore were attributed to jail fever, throwing residents into a panic and prompting Governor Horatio Sharpe to write back to London: "That scores of People have been destroyed here by the Jail Fever first communicated by Servants from on board crowded infectious Ships is notorious."[186]

Slave imports were especially suspect. Dr. James Killpatrick reported that in 1738 "Charleston, the unfortunate capital of this province, was visited . . . with a bilious fever, which was probably imported from Africa, or the Caribee-Islands."[187] Although Africans appeared less susceptible than American Indians to smallpox, and suffered a lower mortality rate from malaria and yellow fever than European slavers, they were by no means immune to the viruses they encountered during their passage and entry into America. Smallpox, pestilential fever, flux, pleurisies, influenza, pneumonia, and tuberculosis claimed thousands of lives.[188] Thus the colonists' tendency to blame newcomers, especially slaves and convicts, for outbreaks of disease was especially ironic.

Nor were prisoners ever credited for their part in bringing cures. During the spring of 1721, for instance, Boston was struck by a smallpox epidemic that infected half the city's ten thousand residents and claimed more than eight hundred lives. Some attributed the malady to a Negro slave who had recently arrived from the Caribbean, but there was really no way to determine its cause. What was worse, there was no known effective treatment. Then Cotton Mather, the Puritan preacher and scientist, recounted an old tale he had heard from African slaves. Some Negroes had said that in their homeland the disease was prevented by cutting open a healthy person's skin and administering some of the pox's secretion into the wound. Mather's story horrified many of his fellow Puritans. But on June 26, 1721, Dr. Zabdiel Boylston took the risk and inoculated two of his slaves and his own young son with smallpox. The treatment worked. But the incident created a furor in Boston, since many elders argued that it was sinful to employ "pagan" methods, even if they seemed successful. Better to just accept the epidemic as a judgment from God.

About the same time, the disease hit London, resulting in many deaths. Lady Mary Wortley Montagu convinced the Princess of Wales to support inoculation experiments, and she in turn convinced the king to pardon several convicts on the condition that they submit to infection. Six condemned Newgate felons were accordingly inoculated on August 9 by Dr. Charles Maitland. Again, the treatment apparently worked. And again, prisoners received no credit for originating a cure or for serving as human guinea pigs.[189]

By the 1760s, several colonies had enacted quarantine laws that threatened to penalize any captain who brought in diseased convicts. As a result, convict contractors were encouraged to improve the design of their vessels to make them more hygienic, and their ships began to feature gratings, portals, and ventilators.[190]

PRISONERS FOR SALE

BEING sold was a common experience of white convicts, indentured
servants, redemptioners, and black slaves. Most prisoners had become articles of trade before their arrival in America, and some would
change hands several times before they ended up working on American
soil. Those who indentured themselves might have been bound to a merchant in England, who in turn had sold them to a shipmaster or agent for
conveyance to the colonies. Convicts had moved from the sheriff to the
gaoler to the hands of contractors like Jonathan Forward and on to agents
abroad. Africans, too, had often passed through the clutches of so many
manstealers, cages, and ships that many had lost count.

A good number of persons were sold on the ship that had transported
them. Once they had been cleaned up, convicts or other servants were
brought up on deck and displayed. Males were separated from females and
other groupings were formed—rows of pale gaunt faces, pocked cheeks,
intent expressions, lean bodies, worn shoes, filthy stockings, torn petti-
coats, stained shirts, coughs, wheezes, clinks, and mutters. Prospective
customers passed among them to inspect the goods. Look them over, ask
questions. James Revel, the convict, later wrote:

> *Examining like Horses, if we're sound,*
> *What trade are you, my Lad, says one to me,*
> *A Tin-man, Sir, that will not do, says he.*
>
> *Some felt our hands and view'd our legs and feet,*
> *And made us walk, to see we were compleat;*
> *Some view'd our teeth, to see if they were good,*
> *Or fit to chew our hard and homely Food.*
>
> *If any like our look, our limbs, our trade,*
> *The Captain then a good advantage made.*[191]

On land, servant and convict sales often resembled slave auctions. A
London weaver who was new to Williamsburg noted in 1758:

> They all was sett in a row, near a hundred man & women & the
> planter come down the cuntry to buy. . . . I never see such pasels
> of pore raches [wretches] in my life some all most naked and
> what had cloths was as black as chimney swipers, and all most
> starved by the ill usidge in ther pasedge by the capn, for they are

used no bater than so many negro slaves that are brought in hare and sold in the same manner as horss or cows in our market or fair.[192]

Another colonist that year reported: "[They] are Brought in hare and sold in the same maner as horses or Cows in our market or fair."[193] From Philadelphia in 1773, a British officer wrote home to his father in Dublin: "They sell the servants here as they do their horses, and advertise them as they do their beef and oatmeal."[194]

William Green, a convict, noted: "They search us there as the dealers in horses do those animals in this country, by looking at our teeth, viewing our limbs, to see if they are sound and fit for their labour." Another reported: "He asked My Trade, My Name, and whence I came, And, what vile Fact had brought Me to this Shore."[195]

Servants were exchanged for all kinds of goods. Most favored were bills payable on demand from reputable British firms, but agents also accepted gold or other precious metals, tobacco, sugar, livestock, turpentine, wine, or rum. In Pennsylvania in 1683, indentured servants were bought for six pounds sterling and sixhundredweight of beef, "with the hide and tallow."[196]

Many masters naturally preferred indentured servants over convicts. However, labor was often in such short supply that landowners could not be choosy. An anxious Maryland planter, Turbutt Wright, wrote to James Cheston on April 11, 1773: "[I] would chuse an indented servant in preference to a convict, but rather than not have one some [time] this summer or next autumn, would consent to take a convict."[197]

Convicts usually were cheaper than slaves. In the late colonial period, an adult male slave in the Chesapeake sold for about £35–44 sterling, whereas convicts fetched less than £13.[198] Slaves served for life, compared to seven or fourteen years for convicts. And slave progeny also belonged to the master. But slaves had to be supported for life, regardless of age or condition, whereas convicts and other servants served limited terms. Like slaves, and unlike regular indentured servants, convict servants generally were not entitled to receive freedom dues (severance pay).

Yet, distinctions could be blurred. Many convict transporters and sellers simply referred to "servants" for sale, without specifying whether they were felons. A surveyor of customs at Annapolis observed that Marylanders "too generally conceive an opinion that the difference is merely nominal between the indented servant and the convicted felon; nor will they readily believe that people, who had the least experience in life, and whose characters were unexceptionable, would abandon their friends and families, and their ancient connexions, for a servile situation in a remote appendage to the British empire." In fact, he added that he thought the colonists "rather consider the convict as the more profitable servant, his term being for seven, the [indentured servant's] only for five years."[199]

Through it all the buyers complained that they were getting the short end of the deal. "You have no idea of the plague we have with servants on this side of the water," a colonist wrote from Philadelphia in 1769. "If you bring over a good one he is spoilt in a month. Those born in the country are insolent and extravagant. The imported Dutch are to the last degree ignorant and awkward. The Irish . . . are generally thieves, and particularly drunkards; and the Negroes stupid and sulky, and stink damnably."[200]

CHAPTER TWO

A Land of Prisoners and Keepers

PURITAN CRIMES AND PUNISHMENTS

THE Puritans who had founded Massachusetts in 1630 viewed their war on crime as a moral necessity, for they considered every crime a sin and every sin a crime.

The most common crime in their colony was drunkenness, and repeated offenders were treated harshly by today's standards.[1] Ralph Golthorpe was whipped for his second offense, and Robert Coles was disenfranchised and ordered to wear a large red "D" on his clothes upon his third conviction. Believing that public humiliation would help deter others, the Puritans constructed stocks in every public square.[2] It was not enough for lawbreakers to be found guilty; they had to be made to look guilty and feel guilty.

As believers in visible signs of sainthood or sinfulness, Puritans often attached appropriate physical stigmata to convicted lawbreakers. A woman who skipped worship might have to stand at the church door with a sign around her neck, or, if the offense was more serious, the town fathers might force her (like Hester Prynne) to wear a scarlet letter on her clothes for life. Some markings were made permanent by the removal of an ear or two, or the branding of a shoulder, hand, forehead, or cheek. The punitive alphabet included "A" (adulterer), "B" (blasphemer), "D" (drunk), "F" (fighter), "M" (manslaughterer), "R" (rogue), and "T" (thief).[3]

Although upper-class persons were practically never flogged, unless their crime was extraordinarily shameful, whipping was a standard punishment for servants, seamen, or Indians who could not meet fines or restitution requirements.[4]

The Massachusetts Bay Company charter required a "House of Correction [to] be erected and set up, both for the punishment of such offenders, and to deter others by their example."[5] In the fall of 1632, when Boston still consisted of less than forty houses, the General Court decided that "there shall be a House of Correction and a house for the beadle [keeper] built at Boston" as quickly as possible.[6] More than two centuries later, Nathaniel Hawthorne, a descendant of one of the original Puritan settlers, began *The Scarlet Letter* by observing, "The founders of a new colony, whatever Utopia of human virtue they might originally project, have invariably recognized it among their earliest practical necessities to allot a portion of the virgin soil as a cemetery, and another portion as the site of a prison." He continued, "In accordance with this rule . . . the forefathers of Boston . . . built the first prison house, somewhere in the vicinity of Cornhill, almost as seasonably as they marked out the first burial-ground, on Isaac Johnson's lot."[7] Boston's prison, graveyard, and church were congregated together, directly across the street from the marketplace. One account described the small but secure wooden structure as a "house of meagre looks and ill smells."[8] John Winthrop, the colony's first governor, himself visited a condemned murderer who was "shut up in an inner room within the prison."[9]

Besides establishing prisons, other criminal punishments, and a system of servitude for members of their community, the Puritans soon began using even more extreme measures against the local Indians. In 1636 the Massachusetts Standing Council waged war against the Pequots, ostensibly to avenge the killing of a white trader who had died trying to ransom some Indians he had kidnapped. The Puritans held a Pequot ally, Chausop, in Boston's prison, then moved him to Castle Island "to be a slave for life to work, unless we see further cause."[10] They also carried out one of the bloodiest attacks on Indians in history, teaming up with Narragansett and Mohegan warriors to murder as many as seven hundred Pequot women and children at Mystick (Connecticut), after which they sold some of the survivors to the Narragansetts and loaded seventeen others onto a Marblehead-built ship, the *Desire*. Captain William Pierce of Salem guided the vessel to the Caribbean, where he exchanged them for "cotton, tobacco, salt and negroes," which he took back to Boston.[11]

A few months later, the Massachusetts Court of Assistants began sentencing white offenders to be "slaves" as punishment for various crimes.[12] Gyles Player, convicted of housebreaking and theft, was sentenced to be severely whipped and "delivered up for a slave to whom the Court shall appoint." Thomas Dickerson, Thomas Savory, and Jonathan Hatch were also sentenced to be "slaves," though it appears that they may have eventually been released. However, in 1641 the Massachusetts General Court adopted a new penal code, which carefully distinguished between the liberties of freemen, women, children, foreigners, and servants, each according to "his [or her] place."[13] The Body of Liberties prohibited the arrest, restraint, banishment, dismemberment, or other punishment of any person, except by virtue of some specific law. Manstealing was deemed a capital offense, and bond slavery, villenage, or captivity were forbidden, "unless it be lawful captives taken in just wars, and such strangers as willingly sell themselves, or are sold to us."[14] Yet within a few months after the code's adoption the number of Indian and black slaves had increased significantly, and the court had sentenced half a dozen whites to "slavery" for various crimes.[15]

Based upon his reading of the law, Emmanuel Downing privately acknowledged that it would be wrong to seize the Narragansetts without justification. But, he added:

> If upon a just war, the Lord should deliver them into our hands, we might easily have men, women and children enough to exchange for Moors, which will be more gainful pillage for us than we can conceive, for I do not see how we can thrive until we get a stock of slaves sufficient to do all our business, for our children's children will hardly see this great Continent filled with people, so that our servants will still desire freedom to plant for themselves, and not stay but for very great wages.[16]

PERSECUTING QUAKERS

AMONG those the Puritans considered to be the most threatening and dangerous were "witches" and Quakers. Margaret Jones of Charlestown was hanged in Boston in 1648 after it was shown she "had a malignant touch . . ., produced deafness, practiced physic, and that her harmless medicines produced violent effects."[17] And beginning in 1656, when the first Quaker proselytizers arrived in Boston, Massachusetts enacted more and more severe laws against the heretics.[18]

Even though threats of fines and other punishments discouraged many shippers from conveying more of them into New England, the Quakers themselves were not deterred. One built his own vessel and sailed it to New England with eleven other Friends. Boston's government thereafter proclaimed that any Quaker male who returned there after being banished "shall for the first offense have one of his ears cut off, and be kept at work in the House of Correction till he can be sent away at his own charge, and for the second offense shall have his other ear cut off . . . and be kept in the House of Correction." Third-time offenders would have their tongues bored through with a hot iron. To show it meant business, the court ordered every town to maintain at least one cage for potential law-breakers.[19]

Even these drastic measures failed, however, and by June 1658 the Quakers had actually begun to win some supporters. The authorities responded by arresting any sympathizers. Even after three Quakers were thrown into prison to await their execution, they continued to attract so many supporters that the General Court quickly ordered a fence erected around the building—not to prevent a breakout, but to keep others from conversing with or aiding the prisoners.[20]

Scarcely more than two decades later, the Quakers' fortunes had so improved that one of them obtained a royal charter to begin a new colony called Pennsylvania, one that would offer complete religious freedom and a criminal code that eschewed sanguinary punishments in favor of imprisonment.[21] The founder, William Penn, had himself been imprisoned three times for political reasons before starting his "Holy Experiment" at Philadelphia. As governor, many years later, he would end up being imprisoned again in London, this time for debt. His health ruined, he died shortly after being released.[22]

SERVANTS AND MASTERS

BY the end of the seventeenth century, three main classes (besides the Indians) had emerged in the North American colonies. Black slaves occupied the lowest rung. Convicts and other white servants, though often held under hard conditions, were somewhat better off, primarily in their chances for eventual upward mobility. And free white persons constituted the most privileged group in colonial society. Regardless of class, women generally enjoyed fewer rights and privileges than their male counterparts.

White servants were usually the most numerous part of the population, and they fell into several categories.[23] These included persons who had arrived under some sort of temporary servitude. "Redemptioners," for example, had voluntarily bound themselves in exchange for the cost of passage. Convicts, on the other hand, had been bound as punishment for their crimes; like other indentured servants, their terms of service were limited to a determinate period of years.

Another group of white servants consisted of persons, mostly young apprentices, who were already residing in the colonies as freemen but who later had become indentured for a fixed term.[24] Some apprentices had been bound in accordance with laws regulating the poor, but most apprenticed themselves to a master more or less of their own free will in order to learn a trade. Boys were customarily apprenticed for seven years, until they turned twenty-one; girls usually were bound until they reached the age of eighteen or were married. Terms could be longer or shorter, depending upon the servant's age.[25]

Colonial records indicate that apprentices were trained in such skilled trades as those of the cooper, sailmaker, and wheelwright, to name a few. In 1718 Josiah Franklin, a tallow chandler and soap boiler of Boston, looked about for a trade for his twelve-year-old son, Benjamin. In order to gauge his interests and abilities, he took the boy to observe joiners, bricklayers, braziers, and other craftsmen at work. After considering the cutler's trade, the father finally decided on printing, and Benjamin was apprenticed to his elder brother, James, till he was twenty-one years of age, a pattern Franklin males had followed for generations.[26]

Servitude was a legal and social institution in which an individual was required by contract to serve a particular master for a specified period. So long as the servant remained under contract, he or she was considered movable property and could be transferred from one master to another, and from one place to another, subject to basic legal requirements. This meant that a servant might have to undergo a major, unanticipated change in living and working conditions. Theoretically, an individual rented his labor and not his person. In fact, servants were often treated more as things than as human beings. They had to perform whatever tasks the master required and obey all commands of that master and his duly appointed agents. Violations were punishable as crimes.

Servants had to remain in their master's custody and within the boundaries he established, whether the area was as large as a plantation or as small as a ship's hold or a cage. Servants were forced to live with others not of their own choosing. Sometimes this meant having to maintain intimacy with persons they detested. Their living quarters, tools, clothing, and other property belonged to the master, not to them. Any servant who left that custody or crossed the boundary without proper permission committed an offense. Any wayward servant could be tracked down, recaptured, and punished according to the master's discretion, provided the penalty did not violate local laws.

Family, marital, sexual, and other personal associations by servants were the master's prerogative. In order to marry, a servant ordinarily had to get the master's permission; if the prospective spouse was bound to another master, he also had to approve the marriage.[27] Servants who engaged in unauthorized sexual relations could be punished and the illegitimate off-spring confiscated, even if the "bastard" or "base-born child" had been sired by the master himself. Even when laws were adopted to prevent "dissolute masters" from impregnating their maids in order to acquire another servant and to increase the maid's term of service, they did not provide for any punishment for the master. Where the maidservant had a criminal record, the law often continued to entitle a master to service from her illegitimate child.[28]

Proponents said servitude helped to reform the labor force, improve an individual's moral fiber, inculcate good habits, and cleanse a sinner through retribution. Many believed that bondage ensured a more well ordered and productive society, figuring that close supervision generally deterred persons who otherwise might engage in antisocial behavior or fail to pay their debts. But the primary functions and objectives of servitude were economic: it existed to make profits for masters, agents, and suppliers.

Not much is known today about servant overseers of servants, except that they enjoyed greater freedom of movement and more privileges than those they supervised. Servants and overseers both probably exhibited many of the behaviors and attitudes characteristic of other prisoners and keepers throughout history. For although historians have seldom considered them as such, colonial American servants were, after all, prisoners. Held in captivity, under forcible restraint if necessary, indentured servants were treated as inferiors and faced severe punishment if they resisted authority.

Yet even though many contemporary accounts depicted servants and slaves as being more "sinful" and more "criminal" than free white persons, it is difficult to determine if that was really so. First of all, many servant crimes were punished privately, outside the courts, so they were not recorded. Frequently, judicial records do not indicate who was a servant and who was not. The historian Lawrence Towner, who studied servant protest in Puritan society from 1629 through 1750, found only about a dozen criminal cases involving servants per year, which led him to conclude that there was "neither a mass movement aimed at servile rebellion nor a total rejection of the system."[29] The perception that servants were "more criminal" is also attributable, at least in part, to the fact that they were under more legal strictures than free persons. In many instances, criminality or criminal severity was determined, not by an act's inherent harm, but by the status of the person who had committed it. (Thus, the most frequent servant crime was "theft," and the most common theft was stealing oneself—running away.) Servants and slaves were also held under tighter supervision than free persons, making it more likely that their crimes would be detected, and they were punished more severely if they stepped out of line.

Both the Scriptures and the penal codes treated murder as a capital offense, and certainly any servant who murdered (or sometimes only threatened to kill) his master was liable to be executed. But masters who killed their servants were not punished for murder, and in some instances they were not punished at all. Consider some cases from early Maryland: Ann Nevill was acquitted of beating to death her maidservant, Margaret Redgearne, despite convincing evidence to the contrary; Mr. and Mrs. Thomas Ward were fined three hundred pounds of tobacco for fatally whipping their maidservant Alse Lutt with a peach-tree rod; Captain Thomas Bradnox and his wife escaped indictment for murdering their servant, Thomas Watson, whom they had starved nearly to death before finally killing him by blows to the face; John Grammar whipped young Thomas Simmons more than one hundred stripes with a corded rope after he had lapsed into unconsciousness, continuing even until Simmons died, yet despite extensive eyewitness testimony the grand jurors refused to indict; and the cooper Pope Alvey beat his servant, Alice Sandford, till her body turned to "jelly," then forced cold hominy down her throat, and yet got off with a brand on his hand.[30]

A servant who had completed his term of service might expect to receive "freedom dues"—usually amounting to no more than a few coins, a suit of clothes, a bag of seeds, or some tools—to ease the formidable transition into the free world.[31] In Maryland in 1640 this reward consisted of "one good cloth suit of kiersy or broad cloth, a shift of white linen, one pair of stockings, and shoes, two hoes, one axe, 3 barrells of corn and 50 acres of land"; the Massachusetts code of 1641 simply provided that discharged servants must "not be sent away empty."

Despite such ameliorative efforts, the treatment of servants in Virginia during the late seventeenth century could be extremely harsh, with masters resorting to whippings, reduced rations, and cruel abuses.[32] Most of the major servant protests in that colony took place between 1661 and 1682. This was the period when lifetime racial slavery was being imposed or expanded and Negroes were beginning to replace indentured servants as the primary source of plantation labor.

In 1661 servants in York County organized such a revolt. Led by Isaac Friend, forty of them planned to seize arms and "go through the country and kill those who made any opposition," vowing to either "be free or die for it." But the plot was exposed by an informer and the rebellion was defused.[33] Two years later another incident occurred to the north in grow-ing Gloucester County, where nine servants allegedly conspired to seize their master's arms and attack the governor's mansion to demand their free-dom. Again, an informer alerted the authorities before the plan could be carried out. Several participants were executed and the informer was pub-licly rewarded with his freedom and five thousand pounds of tobacco. The arrest day, September 13, was made an annual holiday.[34]

During the late 1660s and early 1670s Virginia authorities repeatedly expressed concern about the dangerous "giddy multitude" of servants, convicts, and recently liberated workers. In 1668 the Virginia House of Burgesses called for every county to erect a Bridewell, or workhouse, and empowered the county courts to "take poor children from indigent parents to place them to work in these houses."[35] Two years later the General Court voiced alarm over the "danger to the colony caused by the great number of felons and other desperate villains sent over from the prisons of England," adding that convict imports had given Virginia an undeserved reputation as "a place only fit to receive such base and lewd persons." The Court issued an "order about jail birds," forbidding any person to bring into the colony any capitally convicted offender from England.

As more servants completed their terms, the swelling ranks of impover-ished freedmen presented Virginia officials with a dilemma. The lack of opportunity was breeding discontent, not only among the free poor but also among the servants, who saw little incentive to be cooperative.[36]

Led by Nathaniel Bacon, Virginia's former servants erupted in 1676 in the largest rebellion to date in any English colony. Freedmen rose up again in 1682 in the plant-cutting rebellion in Gloucester County.[37]

According to the historian Edmund S. Morgan, "The substitution of slaves for servants gradually eased and eventually ended the threat that the freedmen posed: as the annual number of imported servants dropped, so did the number of men turning free."[38] Morgan has argued that unfreedom and freedom advanced together, along with the gap between them.

It is difficult to determine how many servants managed to move on to assume better positions in colonial society, but indications are that the number was relatively low. Abbot Emerson Smith calculated that probably only one of ten indentured servants ultimately became a farmer in comfort-able circumstances, and that only one other attained artisan status. The remaining eight, he figured, either died, left the country, or succumbed to a life of propertyless vagrancy, maritime service, chronic dependency, or trouble with the law.[39]

"A RACE OF CONVICTS"

AS for the British and Irish prisoners who had been transported into servitude, a leading American historian of the subject figured that "their ultimate fate is shrouded in mystery, where it is perhaps as well that it should remain," since most of them were, in his judgment, "certainly . . . worthless and dangerous."[40] Many historians have simply dismissed the transports as unsavory types who did not play any significant role in American development. Likewise, generations of genealogists have regarded them with a mixture of embarrassment and scorn, snipping them from family trees as if they were diseased branches. Wrote a visitor to Maryland in 1708: "You'd blush (if one could blush) for shame," if you knew "who from Bridewell or Newgate came."[41]

Firsthand accounts by transported convicts are extremely rare. One of them—*The Poor Unhappy Transported Felon's Sorrowful Account of His Fourteen Years Transportation, at Virginia, in America,* by James Revel— did not appear until the mid-1700s, and some historians have suggested that it may have been written as early as the late seventeenth century.[42] All that is known about the author is what is contained in his rhymed chapbook account, leaving doubts about its authenticity. Yet many details seem accurate, indicating that Revel may have arrived sometime between 1656 and 1671. He claimed to have been born near London's Temple Bar and apprenticed at age thirteen to a tin-man at Moorfields. There he fell into "wicked company" and ran away from his master. After some time prowling the streets with a gang of rogues he was apprehended. Three of his companions were hanged; he drew fourteen years' transportation.

Five of the threescore convicts aboard his vessel died during the seven-week crossing. After the ship entered port, young Revel was cleaned up and then inspected by a stream of planters who examined his teeth and questioned him about his background. Eventually he was bought by a "grim old man" and taken in chains to a waiting sloop. He later learned that his new master had himself been transported before settling in Wicoccmoco, in Rappahannock County. Arriving at the plantation, the boy was issued a canvas shirt and trousers and put to work hoeing among the tobacco plants. He worked there from dawn to dusk, six days a week, for his master's good; on the seventh day he worked to produce his own food. With him in the fields were five other convicts and eighteen black slaves, all of whom fared the same in work and food. In the master's house, four convict servants waited upon the owner's daughter and spouse. Any who tried to run away were made to serve a day for every hour gone, and for every day a week, for every month a year.

Twelve years passed. Revel's master died and the young man was put up for sale. A rich lawyer from Jamestown bought the black slaves but refused to have anything to do with a transported felon. So Revel and his fellow jailbirds were auctioned off to the highest bidder. He was fortunate to be sold to a kind master, and upon the completion of his fourteen-year sentence he was freed and returned home to England.

Many historians have portrayed transported felons as losers in their own day who generally failed to rise very much in economic or social status, a class that over generations formed the basis for what came to be known as Southern "poor white trash." But there is reason to question these assumptions. Even though some respectable colonists viewed convicts with distaste, if not revulsion, it is also true that many others—including Captain Augustine Washington and his son, George—purchased transported felons as trusted personal servants. Some "king's passengers" performed important gentlemanly tasks as well as essential hard labor. Young George Washington was tutored by a convict. As an adult, he purchased convicts for all sorts of jobs, among them John Winter of Charles County, Maryland, who was known as a "very compleat House Painter" who could "imitate Marble or Mahogany very exactly" and "paint Floor Cloths as neat as any imported from Britain." In 1759 Winter went to work painting Mount Vernon.[43]

Some convicts managed to avoid being sold after their arrival. Dr. David Benfield, an Oxford physician who had been transported for poaching and allowed to buy his way out of servitude, wrote home to his former Oxford gaoler in 1772: "I have had very Great Success in My undertakings. I have folloed nothing but physick and Surgorey since I have been heare." Benfield estimated that he would clear a hundred pounds that year, adding, "I Lives Like a Ientleman."[44] Another transport, John Jones Van de Huville, practiced medicine in Prince Georges County, Maryland, with his master's permission.[45]

Daniel Defoe, the English journalist and novelist whose reporting career brought him into close contact with the London underworld and who had been imprisoned and pilloried in England for his political views, popularized stories about transported convicts who achieved happiness and fortune in America.[46] None better personified this than his fictional heroine in *The Fortunes and Misfortunes of the Famous Moll Flanders,* published in London in 1722.[47] In the novel, Moll's aging mother-in-law confided that "many a Newgate-bird becomes a great man, and we have . . . several justices of the peace, officers of the trained bands, and magistrates of the towns they live in, that have been burnt in the hand." With that the old lady removed her glove to expose a scar, saying: "'You need not think such a thing strange, daughter, for as I told you, some of the best men in this country are burnt in the hand, and they are not ashamed to own it. There's Major————,' says she, 'he was an eminent pickpocket; there's Justice Ba———r, [he] was a shoplifter, and both of them were burnt in the hand, and I could name you several such as they are.'"[48]

Three decades after *Moll Flanders* was published, an Englishman returned from a tour reported that "the convicts . . . sometimes prove very worthy creatures and entirely forsake their former follies."[49] Eleven years after that, Malachy Postlethwayt observed, "Even your transported felons, sent to Virginia instead of Tyburn, thousands of them, if we are not misinformed, have, by turning their hands to industry and improvement, and (which is best of all) to honesty, become rich, substantial planters and merchants, settled large families, and been famous in the country; nay, we have seen many of them made magistrates, officers of militia, captains of good ships, and masters of good estates."[50]

Anthony Lamb served out his sentence in Virginia and moved north to become America's "most celebrated and skilful optician, and maker of mathematical instruments." His son, John, was a general in the Continental army.[51] Patrick Colquhoun, a Scotsman who got his start working in the convict trade, went on to achieve fame as a pioneer police official and banking expert in London. Years later he said many former convicts had risen to positions of prominence. "Possessed in general (as every adroit thief must be) of good natural abilities," he wrote, "they availed themselves of the habits of industry they acquired in the years of their servitude— became farmers and planters on their own account; and many of them, succeeding in these pursuits, not only acquired that degree of respectability which is attended to property and industry; but also in their turn became masters, and purchased the servitude of future Transports sent out for sale."[52]

Nevertheless, many colonists strongly resented and opposed convict transportation, and their legislatures passed ordinances restricting shipments of prisoners. In 1683 Pennsylvania proposed that "no felons be brought into this country."[53] In 1721 an act was finally passed that fixed a duty of five pounds on every convict brought into the commonwealth; it also required the importer to put up security in the amount of fifty pounds for the transport's good behavior during the first year. Any person bringing convicts into Pennsylvania was also required to present a certified inventory of those transported, listing their names, offenses, and other information. Justices of the peace were also empowered to inquire into every importation. The stated reason for this act and others like it was economic. Upon being sold as servants, many convicts allegedly ran away or commit-

ted further crimes, resulting in great loss to their owners.[54] Like impressment, the Crown's policy of convict transportation was alleged to be
injuring American colonial interests.

An act barring convict imports into Maryland was passed in 1676, but
not enforced.[55] Afterward the province became the favorite dumping
ground for transported felons. Fear of convict rebellions became acute in
early 1721, when a band of felons was arrested for conspiring to seize the
town's arms and ammunition depot at Annapolis. But the plot was uncov-
ered before it could be carried out. Some Marylanders charged that the
influx of known criminals had resulted in an inordinate number of prosecu-
tions and felony trials, "as well as common trespasses, breaches of the
peace, and other misdemeanors since the late importation of convicts from
Great Britain into this province."[56]

Lawsuits were brought against Jonathan Forward, the importer, and in
1723 an act was passed to restrict convict shipments.[57] In 1728 another act
was passed, requiring all captains to furnish a certificate for every convict
brought into Maryland. Any captain who refused to declare under oath
whether any of his passengers were convicts was subject to a stiff fine.[58]
South Carolina took similar steps about the same time, and in 1741 another
bill was proposed there to "prevent convicts being brought into this province."[59] But despite colonists' repeated protests against convict transportation, and local laws enacted to discourage the practice, Britain continued
to send greater numbers of felons to America.

Public opinion in Maryland was aroused once again in March 1751. Jer-
emiah Swift, a convict field hand for John Hatherly, in Anne Arundel
County, had been hoeing soil in a tobacco field with two of his master's
young sons. He went berserk and beat both boys to death, then entered
the house and slaughtered their fourteen-year-old sister with an axe. He
also stabbed another child, but the youth survived. Swift was tried and
executed, but his ferocious attack sent waves of panic throughout Maryland and beyond.[60]

Benjamin Franklin, who had himself been the victim of a burglary, was
among those who reacted strongly. Writing as Americanus in the *Pennsylvania Gazette*, he called England's unloading of felons "an insult and
contempt, the cruellest, that ever one people offered to another."[61] In
exchange, Franklin proposed that the colonies ship some of their indige-
nous rattlesnakes to Britain. There, they could be carefully distributed in
St. James's Park and other haunts of the nobility and gentry, "but particularly in the gardens of the prime ministers, the lords of trade, and members
of Parliament, for to them we are most particularly obliged." Franklin
acknowledged there might be obstacles to such a scheme, but added

sarcastically, "What is a little house-breaking, shop-lifting, or highway-robbing; what is a son now and then corrupted and hanged, a daughter debauched, and pox'd, a wife stabbed, a husband's throat cut, or a child's brains beat out with an axe, compared with this 'Improvement and well peopling of the colonies.'"

But transportation continued. One distinguished British magistrate proclaimed that transporting felons "out of the way" was the wisest, most humane punishment available, saying it "immediately removes the evil, separates the individual from his abandoned connections, and gives him a fresh opportunity of being a useful member of society."[62] When the British ministry appeared to be bowing to American pressures against convict transportation, London's Dr. Samuel Johnson roared in disgust to James Boswell, "Why they are a race of convicts, and ought to be thankful for anything we allow them short of hanging!"[63]

PERPETUAL SLAVES

INDENTURED servants generally served six-year terms, and convicts seven or fourteen, but slaves were bound for life. Although convicts and other white servants were often held under harsh conditions, slaves were even more oppressed. Servants enjoyed a chance to become free someday, but slaves remained as such perpetually, so that their status was transmitted from one generation to the next, from the living to the as yet unborn.[64]

In time, blacks took the place of the Irish as the colonies' most degraded class, and some former servants became overseers of the slaves. The development of racial slavery helped to ease some of the tensions building among the rising servant class, and it provided present and former white servants with a sense of higher status, if only because there was now a more degraded group of servants who could never compete with them.

One of the first legal references to inheritance of the slave status occurred in 1662, when the Virginia House of Burgesses declared: "Children got by an Englishman upon a Negro woman shall be bond or free according to the condition of the mother, and if any Christian shall commit fornication with a Negro man or woman, he shall pay double the fines of a former act."[65] This statute—which reversed English common-law tradition holding that a child's status should depend upon the status of the father—proved instrumental in perpetuating black slavery. From that point, every female slave assumed additional value, because she could be used to produce more slaves; every product of her unions, including those with the master himself, was born into slavery, and their children, and their children's children. This was true not only of native Africans and their black progeny, but of any racially mixed infant who had at least one black ancestor.

Maryland enacted similar laws in 1663 and 1664, stipulating that blacks were to serve *Durante Vita.*[66] Slavery in Carolina was authorized from the early days of the proprietorship, when the Puritan-educated John Locke helped to write into the Fundamental Constitution a provision that "every Freeman of Carolina shall have absolute power and authority over Negro slaves."[67] (Although he was later credited with inventing the concept of man's "inalienable rights" and esteemed as champion of the social contract, Locke was also a staunch advocate of slavery who had made a fortune from his slave-trade investments.)[68]

In 1670, even Puritan Massachusetts stopped exempting children who had been born there under slave parents, thus paving the way for perpetual slavery of blacks.[69] Neighboring Connecticut, although it never established slavery by law, nevertheless allowed it in practice through various statutes and court decisions.[70] Rhode Island acted early to limit bondage to ten years, but that restriction was openly violated and the colony became one of the leading slavery centers in the Northeast.[71] Slavery in New Hampshire was officially acknowledged in 1645.[72] After the British took over control of New Netherlands from the Dutch, in 1684 New York officially adopted hereditary slavery.[73] New Jersey had slavery from the beginning of the proprietary period and the institution continued after royal-province status was granted.[74] Delaware (formerly New Sweden), which had originally prohibited the buying or keeping of slaves, also resorted to slavery after it passed into English hands.[75] Pennsylvania employed slavery at its inception.[76] Georgia lifted its ban against slavery in 1750 to become a major slave colony.[77]

Colonial governments tried to prohibit imports of political prisoners or professional criminals into their jurisdictions, on the grounds that they would cause trouble. Colonies also discouraged imports of "seasoned" slaves, who had been sent to America by way of the West Indies or other transitional points. Such persons already had been exposed to slavery, and many had learned at least some English. However, it also meant that they had learned how to beat or sabotage the system, possibly even how to escape or attack. Seasoned slaves were often suspected of having been sent as punishment for crimes they had committed in the West Indies. Consequently, many colonists preferred to import slaves directly from Africa.

Douglas Greenberg conducted a computer analysis of the fifty-three hundred criminal cases contained in New York's court records for the period 1691 to 1776; he concluded that blacks were actually prosecuted at a disproportionately lower rate than whites, even though whites generally regarded blacks as "more criminal." Although blacks made up about 11.5 percent of the colony's population, they accounted for only 7.4 percent of the criminal cases appearing in the court minutes. Among the alternative explanations that Greenberg explored was the possibility that most slaves were kept in relative isolation from each other and held under constant surveillance, which may have deterred them from offending. Blacks also faced harsher punishments than whites, including discipline that their masters dispensed without ever going to court.[78]

Every colony developed its own slave code and control apparatus.[79] Police powers and punishments were bolstered, and communications networks among the colonies were improved. The foundation for slavery already had been laid with indentured servitude. Systems of control already were established; housing arrangements and supervisory staff were in place. People had become conditioned to accept the notion of human beings as property to be bought, sold, taxed, and transferred. What remained was to tighten the shackles that bound servants to masters and masters to the slavery system. In fact, much of America's early government was devised and strengthened to protect slavery.

The transformation from servitude to racial slavery entailed an escalation of imprisonment from temporary restraints to total control. Blacks were increasingly segregated from whites, housed in separate (and inferior) quarters. On Southern plantations, these usually took the form of detached huts or shanties; in the North, slaves were assigned to a remote section of the master's house in which whole families crowded into a tiny, spartan space. Slaves were fed apart from other servants, and even buried apart. Most colonies adopted statutes prohibiting them from leaving their owner's plantation without a pass, and then only under necessary circumstances. Nighttime curfews were imposed. The level of supervision increased and greater use was made of chains, fetters, cages, and locks. Blacks were made more regimented, more conspicuous and identifiable. Hair was closely cropped and skin was branded. Greater attention was paid to clothing, on the grounds that a slave should always look like a slave, both to prevent escapes and to deny any sense of prestige or individuality. South Carolina law, for example, specified what garb was permitted: "negro cloth, duffelds, coarse kearsies, osnabrigs, blue linen, checked linen, or coarse garlix or calicoes, checked cottons, or scotch plaids, not exceeding ten shillings per yard."[80]

The possibility of a black person becoming free amidst all of this was sealed off. A South Carolina code of 1722 required masters who wished to manumit or set free one of their slaves to provide "for his departure out of this Province; and such slave who shall not depart this Province by the space of 12 months next after such manumission (being at liberty to do so), shall lose the benefit of such manumission, and continue to be a slave."[81] Later laws limited a master's right to free his slaves to cases in which the slave had performed some valuable public service, such as revealing a plotted slave revolt, and mere conversion to Christianity was eliminated as a possible escape route to freedom. Slaves were also forbidden to trade or own property without their master's consent, and any unauthorized property was supposed to be confiscated and the slave punished for receiving stolen merchandise. Horses, boats, guns, or other articles that might be used for escape or revolt were strictly forbidden. Blacks were barred from serving in the militia. Slaves were denied legal rights that other servants enjoyed, such as the right to bring a case to court or the right to testify in court, unless it was against another slave. They were treated as an inferior species, to be degraded, shunned, ridiculed, mastered, detested, disciplined, and sold and acquired through the last wills and testaments of their deceased white superiors.

PLANTATIONS

ISOLATED from its neighbors by wide stretches of open fields, dense woods, and running water, the rural Southern plantation was a prison without walls: self-contained, stratified, paternalistic, coercive; a society unto itself with its own laws, rules, customs, and language. Plantations varied in size from a couple of dozen acres to vast tracts of thirty thousand acres or more, containing anywhere from a few to a thousand slaves, who ranged in age from newborns to wizened old folks.

A mid-eighteenth-century visitor who approached from the long and dusty road leading to one Savannah estate described coming to an opening "occupied by a miniature palace, elegant in its exterior and embellished by the most refined taste, in the midst of a noble plantation, and surrounded by a little village of Negro huts."[82]

Most slave quarters were about 8 by 10 feet, or 10 by 12, with dirt floors and only a hole in the roof or a wooden chimney to let the smoke out, and no furniture inside. Commissary Alexander Garden observed about Negroes in South Carolina: "They are as 'twere a Nation within a Nation, in all Country Settlements," and added, "they live in Contiguous houses, and often 2, 3, and 4 Families of them in one house Slightly partitioned into so many Apartments, they labour together and converse almost wholly among themselves."[83]

George Washington was a third-generation slaveholder who grew up accepting slavery as natural, necessary, and moral. One of his inventories listed 216 slaves. He both inherited and acquired some by marriage, and he bought and sold slaves throughout his life. When his slaves gave him trouble he could not handle, he shipped them to the West Indies. Like his father before him, he also imported convicts to work on his plantation. On one occasion, he purchased four felons for £110.[84] (Washington was not the only prominent colonist to own convicts, servants, and slaves; some others included Alexander Spotswood and Landon Carter in Virginia, and William Fitzhugh and Charles Carroll in Maryland.)[85]

By the eighteenth century, the system had evolved to the point that Washington could employ a white overseer in 1762. The contract specified that the man should "take all necessary and proper care of the Negroes . . . using them with proper humanity and discretion." He expected his overseers' wives to work as house servants and to make clothes for Negroes.[86]

In Virginia and South Carolina, Negroes gradually replaced whites as the preferred domestic servants, and no self-respecting plantation lady could do without at least one Negro to perform household chores. "I shall keep young Ebba to do the drudgery part, fetch wood, and water, and water and scour, and learn as much as she is capable of Cooking and Washing," Eliza Pinckney of Charleston wrote. "Mary-Ann Cooks, makes my bed, and makes my punch. Daphne works and makes the bread, old Ebba boils the cow's victuals, raises and fattens the poultry, Moses is imployed from breakfast until 12 o'clock without doors, and after that in the house. Pegg washes and milks."[87] Sharp distinctions arose between slaves who worked in the fields and those assigned to the master's house.

A slave's choices were essentially those of any prisoner. He or she could try to escape by running away or committing suicide. In either instance, such actions could also have painful effects for loved ones left behind, since besides losing forever all contact with their fugitive kin such relatives might suffer whippings or sale. A slave could try to subvert the institution through malingering, sabotage, arson, pilfering, slowdowns, poisonings, and secret reprisals. He or she could seek to overthrow the captors by force, or submit as much as necessary and simply try to do his or her time in the least painful manner.

Slavery elicited all of these responses, and all of the attending physical and psychological consequences. It also produced powerful fear and paranoia in slaveholders. Whites always had to remain alert, vigilant. They

could not relax. Many worried that one day they might suddenly be overcome and butchered, or even enslaved as they had done to others. Some
whites were tormented with guilt.

Rebellion was not confined to the North or the South. Among colonial
American slave revolts, the bloodiest occurred in New York City in 1712
and 1741, and in South Carolina in 1739.[88] South Carolina had a black
majority, whereas New York's slave population probably constituted less
than 10 percent of the city's total population. All three conspiracies
occurred during a period of general economic and social unrest. Each was
preceded by the passage of a strict new slave code and took place amidst a
climate of fear or anxiety aroused by a recent precipitating incident. In
each instance, the slaves' apparent plan was thwarted before it could be
fully carried out, and the number of black fatalities exceeded those of
whites. After each revolt there was a public inquiry, quickly followed by
mass public executions of slaves. Anyone suspected of playing even an
indirect role was severely punished, placed under tight security, or sold far
away. Reports about the conspiracy were widely circulated throughout the
slaveholding world, alerting masters everywhere about potential dangers
and contagions.

Master-dominated legislatures enacted protective measures that immu-
nized the slaveholders, as well as overseers, patrollers, and any other white
person having "sufficient cause or lawful authority," so they could not be
held liable for their actions.[89] Limitations on the killing or maiming of
slaves were few and far between, usually being reserved for the most sadistic kinds of punishment.[90]

Lawmakers also expanded the number of capital crimes for slaves. In
Georgia execution became mandatory for any slave who had killed a white
person, except when it could be proved that the slave had done so by
accident "or in defense of his master or other person under whose care
and government such slave shall be." Additional capital offenses peculiar
to slaves included the grievous wounding, maiming, or bruising of a white
person; the raising or attempting to raise of an insurrection; the enticement
of any slave to run away from the province; the assistance of anyone who
had run away; the willful and malicious destruction of any stack of rice,
corn, or other grain produced in the province; the destruction of tar-kiln
barrels of tar, turpentine, or resin; and poisoning. Slaves could also be
executed for teaching or instructing another slave in "the knowledge of
any poisonous root, plant, herb, or other sort of poison" and for giving
false information.[91]

Formal court trials were seldom held; slaves were summarily killed. And the manner of killing could be extremely brutal in order to terrify others.[92] Colonial records are filled with accounts of slaves being disemboweled, roasted, decapitated.

As early as 1669 the Virginia Assembly formally declared what had already become plantation practice—no master who killed one of his slaves should be judged guilty of a felony, "since it cannot be presumed that pre-pensed malice . . . should induce any man to destroy his own estate."[93] The protection of masters did not end when the offending slave was dead. Laws were also passed that recognized the value of a slave's life in terms of the loss it posed to the master. Thus, for every slave killed or put to death by law, the master was entitled to be reimbursed from the public treasury.[94]

RUNAWAYS

SOME servants and slaves tried to escape. Convicts were the most apt to run away, but even so only a small minority of felons—maybe 5 to 10 percent—bolted. After all, most slaves and servants knew precious little about what lay beyond the plantation where they were kept. In some places, the whole region consisted of plantations, and escape was difficult. The masters, on the other hand, were intimately familiar with every corner of their district, and most of them knew each other by name. Planters kept in touch by word of mouth and correspondence, and their control system was aided by information exchanged in books, broadsides, and newspapers. Each newspaper edition contained notices about the latest servants and slaves who had deserted, the first lost-and-found columns.

Thus William and Thomas Bradford of Philadelphia advertised on July 19, 1775, for a runaway servant lad of nineteen, John Cass, who they said "may pass for a Printer or Book-binder, as he understands a little of both."[95] Another master announced:

> Ran away from the subscriber, living in Annapolis, on May 23, a Convict Servant Woman named Hannah Boyer, about 23 years of age. Pitted much with Small Pox, has a Scar in one of her Eye Brows, not very tall, but strong, fresh colour'd, robust, masculine Wench. She had on and took with her a blue Jacket, an old whitish Cloak, a brown Petticoat, a double Mobb [cheap hood], an Osnabrigs Shift, no Shoes nor Stockings; but without doubt will change her cloathing. She had a Horse Lock and chain on one of her Legs.[96]

Ads for fugitive whites often appeared next to descriptions of runaway blacks. Where whites and blacks had run away together, the advertisers usually described the white suspect as a transported convict, a known criminal, or an Irishman, who had become romantically involved with a slave. For example, the *South Carolina Gazette* reported that a young sandy-haired convict had stolen a horse and "enticed with him a short lusty well-set Negro wench" who spoke plain English and was last seen wearing men's clothes.[97] Ironically, a white and a black fugitive traveling together were better able to pass themselves off as master and slave.

The runaway ads often appeared in several cities simultaneously, especially if the fugitive was suspected to be heading in a particular direction. "The wicked and bad of them that come into this Province, mostly run away to the Northward," one Marylander said. Convicts commonly were pictured as wearing iron collars, or a darby on each leg with a chain to one of them, all double riveted. Many columns noted a missing finger, a broken wrist, or a face badly pitted by smallpox. Fugitives were known to walk with a limp and to have backs scarred from whippings—or backs freshly wounded. And they bore other telltale marks of hard life, such as a swelled testicle said to have been caused from a kick on the convict ship, an unhealed rupture, or a saber cut or gunshot wound gained in struggle. Notices often testified to the runaway's defiant character and "bold" or "insolent" manner. Such was the case of William Hatton, who was described as having a scar running from the corner of his mouth to his chin, and a "very remarkable way of staring any body in the face" who spoke to him.[98]

A white prisoner's chances of escaping were vastly greater than a black's because whites were less conspicuous. Some white runaways improved their chances by dressing like free persons, often after stealing some of their master's clothes. Thus one newspaper notice pointed out that Anne Barret had left home fully attired in a striped Holland gown, a quilted callimanco petticoat, ruffles, aprons, and new pumps with red heels. Mary Holland, whom her master angrily described as "much conceited in her beauty," had fled with an elegant wardrobe complete with a fine lawn apron and a flowered handkerchief.[99]

A modern study of newspaper notices in eighteenth-century South Carolina concluded that only 1 of 221 missing whites was reported caught, whereas 862 of 2,001 fugitive slaves were captured alive.[100] Still, the slaves kept trying. The more they tried, the more their masters took steps to prevent escape. Heads were shaved, skin was branded, legs were clamped in heavy irons. Chains, padlocks, handcuffs, and neck yokes were standard equipment.[101] When such restraints failed, fugitives risked being set upon by yelping hounds or shot down as they ran.[102]

Indentured servants who were caught could expect to serve more time—in some places, a week for every day gone, or a year for every week.[103] A runaway could also be whipped up to thirty-nine lashes for the first offense, be branded or lose an ear for the second, have his nose split for the third, and be executed for the fourth.[104] Anyone who helped or harbored a fugitive servant or apprentice was subject to a stiff fine or worse.[105] If the fugitive was a slave, punishments were more severe, and in some cases the offended master was actually legally required to take certain measures, for the good of the system.[106] Masters commonly offered a reward for the capture of a runaway. Sometimes a bounty was promised if the slave was brought back dead or alive, as did the owner who offered ten pounds to "any man who will bring him Toney's head."[107]

Owners formed networks of volunteers to patrol their areas. The first were conducted sporadically, on a rotating basis; patrols eventually became the duty of the local militia, whose primary function in some places grew to be "police supervision of the slaves."[108] Officers were appointed and given lists of all the slaves residing in their district, and the units travelled the countryside gathering intelligence and making arrests.

A South Carolina statute of 1734 organized the task into districts and set requirements for the makeup and operation of the patrols. Five-man units were instructed to make the rounds at least once a month, with authority to question any travelling Negro, search Negro homes, and confiscate firearms and other contraband. Their license included the right to kill or torture any Negro who resisted arrest.[109]

Similar systems were developed in the other plantation colonies. Georgia's code of 1735 empowered commissioned militia officers to "disperse, suppress, kill, destroy, apprehend, take or subdue . . . any company of slaves, who shall be met together or who shall be lurking in any suspected places, where they may do mischief or who shall have absented themselves from the service of their owners."[110]

Thus was born the first organized system of police in plantation country.

JAILS

JAILS were among the first public structures built in colonial America.[111] Besides being an essential part of the prisoner trade and a useful receptacle and staging place for arriving reluctant emigrants, they were an integral part of the system of servitude and slavery. A plantation was organized for labor, but a jail was meant as a holding pen for persons who somehow had managed to escape from bondage: fugitives, unruly servants, debtors, vagrants, and common criminals awaiting trial or execution. Flaws in the imprisoning ability of the plantation had led to the rural South's first police system and jails. Elsewhere, in the coastal cities of Charleston, Philadelphia, Boston, Newport, and New York, the apprehending was performed by an expanding corps of nightwatchmen, constables, and marshals. In North and South alike, many of the fugitives and other lawbreakers caught by slave patrols and city police were first taken to jail to await their fate. Jails helped to enforce the laws of bondage and to uphold the authority of masters. For men who owned men and women, a world without prisons was inconceivable.

As reliance on servitude grew, colonial governments required every local jurisdiction to establish and maintain its own jail at public expense. Keepers were appointed and salaries set. Eventually a locked room in the sheriff's house was replaced by a wooden structure erected for the specific purpose of detaining offenders. Reinforced walls were introduced and boards gave way to stone and brick. Jails became more pervasive, more secure, more permanent. By the 1720s every city and virtually every county had at least one detention house, and most had several. Colonial America had more jails than public schools or hospitals.

In Virginia, the economic losses that masters incurred as a result of slaves and servants escaping resulted in several laws being passed. In 1657 the General Assembly made the counties liable for damages for any inmate who escaped for want of a sufficient prison.[112] Four years later it announced that any county that did not construct a "good strong prison" within eight months of the passage of the act would be fined five thousand pounds of tobacco.[113] In 1669 the General Assembly authorized the construction of a new capitol and other buildings, including a "substantial Brick Prison, thirty foot long in the clear and twenty foot wide in the clear [with] three rooms on the lower floor, one with Chambers above for the gaolers or prison keepers owne use and for confinement of small offenders, and the other two smaller on the lower floor . . . for the criminals of both sexes."[114]

In Maryland, the preference for public prisons arose in the spring of 1662, when the assembly stated the need to create a prison "for the securing of malefactors and other exorbitant persons."[115] In 1663 funds were appropriated for building a log house at St. Mary's, because "divers inconveniences have happened within this province through want of places for securing offenders."[116] In 1666 another institution was authorized to be "well and sufficiently built" near a spring on the east side of St. Mary's and furnished with irons and other restraints.[117] In 1674 a substantial sum was

appropriated to construct a brick statehouse and prison at St. Mary's, and
every county was ordered to erect its own courthouse and jail.[118] Two years
later an act was passed by which each sheriff who "voluntarily or negli-
gently" allowed a prisoner to escape was to be fined twenty thousand
pounds of tobacco, indicating that some sheriffs had been incompetent, if
not corrupt.[119]

In April 1640 the Connecticut Court of Election ordered a jail to be
built at Hartford, citing the "many stubborn and refractory persons [who]
are often taken in these liberties, and no meet place is yet prepared for the
detaining and keeping of such to their due and deserved punishment."[120]

Within a few years jails could be found in the smallest towns. By the
middle of the eighteenth century, an observer wrote, the tiny village of
Bristol, Pennsylvania, had only one road "marked by anything like a conti-
nuity of building," but that cluster included an Episcopal church with its
lonely graveyard, a Quaker meeting-house, and a brick jail.[121]

The colonial American jail was as minuscule as a plantation was large—
often merely a cage, no bigger than the closets that later were introduced
into American homes, and rarely more than twenty square feet—and neither its face nor its interior bore any trace of elegance. The structure built
at Henrico County, Virginia, in 1683 was designed to be "15 feet square,
the floor laid out with stout plank, the ceiling lined with cedar, and the
roof covered with shingles [with] a single chimney . . . placed on the outside of the house."[122] The one put up in Salem, Massachusetts, that year
was twenty feet square, with a "convenient yard, fenced and closed," a
brick chimney, "a lock on the door . . . , iron bars for the lights," and a
dungeon.[123]

In some institutions the jailkeeper, and occasionally his family as well,
resided in a separate wing. But neither his quarters, nor his status, resembled that of a plantation master. He was more like an overseer, except that
his prisoners generally did not have to work.[124] A prisoner's lot could
depend on his ability to pay the keeper for food, blankets, fuel, and other
necessities. He usually was forced to sleep on straw that often had been
used before. The room in which he was kept was likely to be smelly, poorly
ventilated, and dark. Oftentimes it was crowded.

A minister who visited the Charleston jail in 1767 reported: "A person
would be in better situation in the French King's galleys, or in the prisons
of Turkey or Barbary, than in this dismal place—which is a small house
hir'd by the Provost Marshal containing 5 or 6 rooms, about 12 feet square
each and in one of these rooms have 16 debtors been crowded." He added
that the occupants "often have not room to lie at length, but succeed each
other to lie down—one was suffocated by the heat of the weather of this

summer—and when a coffin was sent for the corpse, there was no room to admit it, till some wretches lay down, and made their wretched carcasses a table to lay the coffin on. Men and women are crowded promiscuously—no necessary houses to retire."[125]

Benjamin Franklin's brother, James, printed an early newspaper. One edition carried an article that was deemed seditious, and when he would not reveal its author he was committed to Boston's stone jail. He remained there for a month until a physician certified that his health had suffered from confinement.[126] Writing from the same stone prison thirty years later, another incarcerated journalist complained, "If there is any such thing as a hell upon earth, I think this place is the nearest resemblance of any I can conceive of."[127] That winter in New York the debtors issued a public appeal that they had not "one stick to burn" and were freezing to death.[128]

The jail's importance as a receptacle for bondsmen was not limited to the South. Boston's almshouse, constructed in 1685 as a supposed refuge for the poor, was used mostly as a prison for troublesome servants and slaves.[129] In 1721 a new bridewell was established for the detention of "unruly servants and minor offenders."[130] Newport's prison was utilized for keeping runaway or recalcitrant slaves.[131] New York's almshouse was designed to hold "beggars, servants running away or otherwise misbehaving themselves, trespassers, rogues, vagabonds, [and] poor people refusing to work."[132] As such, the various kinds of jails were a key component of the system for disciplining unfree laborers.

But even shackles or jails could not restrain people who were determined to be free. The most frequent public complaint about prisons was that they permitted too many escapes. Governor Culpeper of Virginia said there was none in his colony that could not be "easily broken." After three pirates busted out of Charleston's prison, an editor snapped that "few criminals stay till the times appointed to make their trials."[133] The Philadelphia Common Council called their jail "a public nuisance . . . it being too notorious that criminals frequently escape."[134] In Newport in 1737 the escapees added insult to embarrassment by leaving a chalked message on the prison floor. "Fare you well Davis," it said, "your prisoners are fled; your prison's broke open while you are in bed."[135]

In response to such embarrassments, jail breaking was made a felony, law enforcement was bolstered, more and stronger prisons were called for, and authorities paid closer attention to separating different types of offenders—both by creating a greater variety of institutions and by segregating inmates within the same prison.

One of the most advanced institutions in its day was the sturdy stone jail at Third and High Streets in Philadelphia, which had been designed in 1722 by Quakers under the influence of John Bellers, an English prison reformer. Consisting of two connected buildings with a yard and high wall, it featured cellular housing and separate wings for debtors and common criminals, with the latter being housed in locked cells. There was also improved ventilation and exercise facilities. But not even those features could eliminate escapes: from 1729 to 1732 at least fifteen inmates broke out.[136] By the depression of the 1760s, the old place had become severely overcrowded, and conditions had deteriorated so much that concerned residents solicited donations to keep the distressed inmates alive. In 1772 at least three prisoners starved to death.[137]

Government's unwillingness to provide for inmates' most basic needs was typical during the seventeenth and eighteenth centuries. To some extent it reflected a desire to ensure that jails were unpleasant places. By withholding food and other necessities, authorities increased the pressure on inmates to confess or otherwise cooperate. Starving prisoners were more vulnerable to "voluntary" servitude, military "enlistment," and other forfeitures of liberty. Their misery served warning to others. The wretchedness of some inmates—most often, the debtors—also provided an outlet for "humanitarian" impulses. Sometimes the debtors' pleas for assistance were answered by gifts of food from kind-hearted residents, and occasionally someone even stepped forward to pay off the problem debt.[138]

In New York, a legislature hardly known for soft-heartedness responded to the debtors' plight in 1732 by enacting a law stating that "many poor persons may be imprisoned a long time for very small sums of money . . . to the ruin of their families, great damage to the public who are in Christian charity obliged to provide for them and their families . . . and without any real benefit to their creditors." The statute provided that debtors owing less than two pounds could be assigned to service for five months if they were male and seven months if they were female.[139] Prisoners may not have been forced to work inside the institution, but they were now compelled to bind themselves to work outside.

PROTESTS AND REBELLIONS

CRITICISM of the prisoner trade increased during the eighteenth century. Although officials and merchants in England denied complicity in anything illegal, scandals occasionally surfaced that implicated prominent, seemingly respectable people in kidnapping and other sordid schemes.

In 1739, on the Isle of Skye and neighboring islands, over a hundred men, women, and children who had been forcibly seized from their beds at night and loaded onto ships for transportation to America managed to escape and get help. A judicial inquiry later ordered them freed.[140] In 1753 in Philadelphia the Quarter Sessions freed young Ann Dempsey from her indenture after she proved she had been kidnapped in Ireland.[141] Joshua Brown, a Quaker, later wrote about his mother being kidnapped in Scotland and sold off to America when she was just thirteen.[142] George Eskridge, who was kidnapped and sold in Virginia, went on to become a member of the colony's House of Burgesses and the legal guardian of George Washington's mother.[143]

One famous case involved a boy named Peter Williamson, who claimed to have been stolen out of his aunt's home in Aberdeen and sent to Philadelphia.[144] In another, James Annesley, son and heir to Lord Altham, alleged that his uncle had conspired to have him kidnapped and sent to America in order to gain his inheritance.[145]

Yet many masters apparently felt little remorse over the fact that persons they had bought and sold as servants or slaves had been illegally kidnapped into bondage. After all, their reasoning went, they had not performed the manstealing; they had merely purchased servants who were already bound, so that everything they had done was perfectly legal and respectable. As far as polite society was concerned, complications arose only in that rare instance when a victim turned out to be some "reputable" person, like themselves.

At the same time, some critics on both sides of the Atlantic assailed impressment, or military conscription, as "repugnant to the liberties of an Englishman, and irreconcilable to the established rules of law, viz. that a man without offense by him committed, or any law to authorize it, shall be hurried away like a criminal from his friends and family, and carried by force to a remote and dangerous service."[146] Still, the practice continued. Many of the protests against it followed a common theme: freeborn white English subjects did not deserve to be treated like common criminals or sooty slaves. Or, put another way, criminals and Negroes did.

Impressment was extremely unpopular in America, and especially provoked violent reactions in Boston, where victims and bystanders often physically resisted depredations by press-gangs. Many local merchants there opposed impressment because it was their servants, apprentices, and employees who were being taken, at considerable loss to themselves. Seizures of the pool of available seamen and laborers worsened the labor shortage and boosted the costs of doing business.[147]

In 1746 a Boston town meeting petitioned the House of Representatives to put an end to the roundups, saying that the city had lost three thousand men to the "lawless rabble" of press-gangs.[148] A year later, after several violent incidents involving press-gangs, Governor William Shirley ordered the militia to put down a major riot that had erupted after a gang had seized some men without warrants. Public sentiment against press-gangs was so strong that no militiamen, except officers, would obey the order.[149] Continued resistance prompted officials to enact a statute in 1751 for suppressing unlawful assemblies and riots.[150]

Popular resistance to press-gangs intensified during the 1760s. Mobs freed some victims, assaulted procurers, and burned naval vessels.[151] Following one incident, and in defense of some whalers who had killed an officer while resisting an attempted impressment, attorney John Adams contended that it was not the townspeople who were the rioters, but the kidnappers who went about apprehending citizens without lawful authority.[152] Impressment sparked further protests in Boston, New York, and other cities in 1770, one of which resulted in the Boston Massacre.

The New England colonies were also the scene of frequent brawls, tumults, tax protests, rent strikes, tenant uprisings, attacks on inoculation centers, jailbreaks, mob attacks, and riots. Historians have disagreed over whether the general occurrence of these disturbances was purposive and ideologically motivated or represented spontaneous and anarchic expressions of underlying discontent and rage, and some writers have questioned the role of local political leaders in fomenting revolt. But few have disagreed that collective unrest was widespread, intense, and growing prior to the outbreak of armed rebellion.[153]

Slavery as well came under increasing attack. Some tracts contended that the slave trade was encouraging wars and grave crimes in Africa, that enslavement was not the necessary and humane result of sparing a captive's life in war, that it was wrong to punish when no criminal act had been committed, that compulsory labor without recompense was illegal, that manstealing was a mortal sin and a serious crime, that enslavement compelled men to act cruelly in order to force compliance, and that slavery led to the separation of families and the breaking of God's commandments.[154]

"Man is born free, and yet we see him everywhere in chains," Jean-Jacques Rousseau wrote in *The Social Contract* (1762). "Those who believe themselves the masters of others cease not to be even greater slaves than the people they govern." Rousseau rejected the notion that some men were slaves by nature. He argued that slavery was not a natural right or condition, but a forcibly imposed and maintained status. "Force made the first slaves," he wrote, "and slavery, by degrading and corrupting its victims, perpetuated their bondage."[155]

Others challenged slavery on economic grounds. David Hume observed that a disproportionately large ratio of slaves to freemen necessarily resulted in insecurity and harsh discipline and that it retarded population growth to such an extent that the slave system would eventually begin to consume more than it produced.[156] Benjamin Franklin also used economic arguments to condemn slavery, asserting that, if the colonies continued their dependence on slave labor, they would be at a fatal disadvantage in trade.[157] Such views about slavery received their fullest development in Adam Smith's *Wealth of Nations* (1776), which contended that slavery was flawed because it was less productive than the work done by free men.

Fiery rhetoric about slavery also found its way into the political discourse of many prominent colonists, although a good number of them were slaveholders. Richard Henry Lee and other leading Virginians urged an end to further slave imports, in part because they wanted to protect their investments, fearing that a further influx would depreciate the value of slaves they already owned, property for which they were already taxed.[158]

John Dickinson, formerly Philadelphia's leading slaveholder, complained, "Those who are taxed without their consent . . . are slaves."[159] John Adams described his fellow colonists as "the most abject sort of slaves."[160] Washington and other leaders of the independence movement openly asserted that the British government was attempting to implement a deliberate plan to enslave the colonies and bring them under arbitrary control. The "MONSTER of a standing army," one orator claimed, was part of "a PLAN . . . systematically laid, and pursued by the British ministry, near 12 years, for enslaving America." The Stamp Act, insisted another, had been calculated to "enslave the colonies."[161]

Virginia's Patrick Henry, patriot and slaveowner, rose to advise his fellow legislators. Standing with his head bowed and his wrists crossed, as if to imitate a manacled slave, he asked: "Is life so dear, or peace so sweet, as to be purchased at the price of chains and slavery?" After a pause, he shouted: "Forbid it, Almighty God! I know not what course others may take. But as for me—give me liberty, or give me death!"[162]

No wonder that Dr. Samuel Johnson asked, "How is it that we hear the loudest yelps for liberty among the drivers of Negroes?"[163]

A clause of Thomas Jefferson's original draft of the Declaration of Independence included a passage that attacked the Crown for waging "cruel war against human nature itself, violating its most sacred rights of life & liberty in the persons of a distant people who never offended him, captivating & carrying them into slavery in another hemisphere, or to incur miserable death in their transportation thither." But this section was deleted at the request of South Carolina and Georgia.[164] The final version cited a "long train of abuses and usurpations," some of which plainly involved the prisoner trade. They included complaints the Crown had obstructed the administration of justice, sent swarms of officers to harass the people, deprived many of the benefits of trial by jury, transported persons beyond the seas for pretended offenses, and committed other injustices. Having failed by peaceful means to gain an end to these oppressions, the "Representatives of the United States of America" solemnly declared their colonies as "Free and Independent States."

CHAPTER THREE

Prisoners of the Revolution

A CITY OF PRISONERS

ARMED conflict began. By November of 1776, as many as 5,000 captured rebels were being held by British forces in New York City.[1] After the debacle at nearby Fort Washington, 230 rebel officers and 2,607 soldiers had been taken prisoner.[2]

One of them, Jonathan Gillett, described his experience in a letter sent home to Connecticut. "[T]hey first disarmed me, then plundered me of all I had, watch, buckles, money and sum clothing, after which they abused me by bruising my flesh with the butts of there [guns]," he wrote. "They knocked me down; I got up and they [kept on] beating me almost all the way to there. . . . The next thing I was allmost starved to death."[3] Another prisoner from Connecticut, William Slade, wrote in his diary that the Americans had been "verry much frowned upon by all we saw" and "called Yankey Rebbels a going to the gallows."[4] He and his companions were lined up near the Jews' Burying Ground, counted, and marched off to confinement at Manhattan's North Church.

Alexander Graydon, a young officer and gentleman from Pennsylvania, who now found himself among the glum and defeated captives, took offense at being called a "rebel," a label he found "too much interwoven with the idea of state criminality."[5] Actually, the term's use reflected the official British policy of recognizing captured American soldiers and merchant marines, not as prisoners of war, but as criminals engaged in insurrection against the Crown. Therefore, members of the American armed forces were not considered subject to the rules and privileges of warfare, and they could not be sure what to expect if taken prisoner.[6] British troops at Bunker Hill had spared the lives of only eleven of thirty-one rebel captives, and the fates of prisoners on both sides were increasingly linked together and connected to the vagaries and outcome of the war.[7]

Washington put his counterpart, General Henry Gage, on notice that he would regulate his conduct "towards those gentlemen who are or may be in our possession, exactly by the rule you shall observe towards those of ours now in your custody." He also warned, "If severity and hardship mark the line of your conduct, painful as it may be to me, your prisoners will feel its effects."[8]

Gage replied that "Britons, ever pre-eminent in mercy, have outgone common examples, and overlooked the criminal in the captive. Upon these principles, your prisoners, whose lives by the law of the land are destined to the cord, have hitherto been treated with care and kindness, and more comfortably lodged than the King's troops."[9]

The British army had occupied New York only two months earlier, and confusion reigned.[10] Many residents had fled with everything they could carry. One-third of Manhattan's structures lay in charred ruins, and all remaining houses owned by rebels were declared forfeited. With winter approaching and food and fuel in limited supply, the city's military garrison suddenly had to provide for the care of five thousand ill-clothed and hungry prisoners.

One of the conqueror's first steps was to rip out the pews from confiscated rebel churches in order to make needed jail space. The stripped wood was hauled away as fuel to warm bivouacked British and Hessian troops. Many of the makeshift prisons lacked fireplaces or other living facilities, and their inhabitants were not provided any blankets or beds, not even straw. The Middle Dutch Church on Nassau Street and the North Dutch Church on William Street became prisons, holding nearly two thousand persons.[11] The Brick Church on Beekman Street functioned as a jail.[12] The Friends' Meeting-house on Pearl Street, the Presbyterian Church on Wall Street, and the French Church on Pine Street were converted into military hospitals.[13] Columbia College and City Hall became prisons.[14]

The British also employed several empty sugarhouses, which formerly had been storehouses for sugar, rum, and molasses.[15] The largest and most infamous, which adjoined the Middle Dutch Church on Liberty (Crown) Street, held as many as five hundred men in damp, unheated, poorly ventilated, and unsanitary conditions.[16] An inmate of the Sugar-House observed there was "not a pane of glass, not even a board to a single window in the house, and no fire but once in three days to cook our small allowance of provision." He also told of old shoes that were "bought and eaten with as much relish as a pig or a turkey" and said that "a beef bone of four or five ounces, after it was picked clean [by the captors], was sold by the British guard for as many coppers."[17]

Many rebel prisoners were confined aboard ships in New York harbor, partly because it was feared they would spread disease throughout the city if allowed on land. On one of these early makeshift prison ships, a Yankee diarist wrote: "Friday [December], 27th. Three men of our battalion died last night. The most melancholyest night I ever saw. Small pox increases fast. This day I was blooded. Drawd bisd and butter. Stomach all gone. At noon, burgo. Basset is verry sick. Not like to live I think."[18]

Before the occupation, New York had but two regular places of confinement for criminals. Now the new and still unfinished Bridewell on the north side of the Commons had become crammed with as many as eight hundred prisoners, mostly militiamen and Continental privates.[19] The Provost gaol, a rough-stone structure three stories high with a large cupola, had been built in 1757 as a debtor's prison. It now held "problem" inmates who were thought to pose special security risks: political prisoners of superior rank, as well as ordinary felons awaiting execution.[20]

Rebels called the Provost "New City Hall" because it was the headquarters of the British provost marshal, Captain William Cunningham. He had been involved in the prisoner trade, trafficking indentured servants. (So had John Paul Jones.)[21] After the British takeover, Cunningham and his assistant, a young mulatto named Richmond, who had been the slave of a rebel officer, reportedly carried out numerous executions of rebel prisoners, one of them a young schoolteacher and spy, Nathan Hale.[22]

After being informed of the deplorable prison conditions in New York, General Washington said he hoped the prisoners' "scanty allowance" was due to the "state of Genl. Howe's Stores and not to any desire to add Famine to the misfortunes of Captivity."[23] But winter greatly increased the captives' sufferings. Later accounts described men freezing to death in unheated buildings with smashed windows, their bodies covered with drifting snow; stiff corpses were stacked like logs onto carts and buried in latrines, where they were eaten by pigs or wild animals.[24] A former captive reported: "The distress of the prisoners cannot be communicated by words. Twenty or thirty die every day. They lie unburied. What numbers of my countrymen have died by cold and hunger, perished for want of the common necessities of life! . . . Nothing can stop such treatment but retaliation."[25]

Seemingly overnight, New York had become a city of prisoners. It would remain such for the rest of the War for Independence.

PRISONERS OF CLASS

WHILE captured rebel soldiers were living under terrible conditions, their officers were allowed to be at liberty on parole. General Charles Lee, one of America's highest-ranking military commanders, was confined in one of the city's finest rooms, provided with ample food and liquor, and allowed to entertain as many as six dinner guests each evening, all at Congress's expense.[26] His valet was permitted to come up from Virginia with choice selections from the general's wardrobe and library.[27]

Captain Alexander Graydon also enjoyed special privileges. After purchasing civilian clothes, he rented a room in a confiscated house on Queen's Street, which was now being managed by the mistress of the British commandant, General James Robertson. Graydon later acknowledged that while he and other privileged gentlemen were enjoying the "benefit of free air and the use of our limbs, our poor devoted soldiers were enclosed within walls, scantily supplied with provisions of bad quality, wretchedly clothed, and destitute of sufficient fuel, if indeed they had any." Out of a sense of obligation, he ventured into the prisons where some of his former comrades had been taken. But after concluding that he could offer them neither comfort nor assistance, he never returned. Like many rebels at the time, Graydon blamed the British for cruel treatment of those interned, but he also faulted Congress for not doing more to arrange a prisoner exchange.[28]

One of the captain's fellow parolees, Lieutenant Jabez Fitch of Connecticut, likewise reported that he had "[m]ade the poor Prisoners a Visit, found them in a very Pityfull Cituation," and then returned to his rented quarters to dine on "Beef Stakes and Rost Pig," though as he ate he could only lament the fate of the captive enlisted men.[29] Fitch kept a detailed diary on heavy brown paper, wherein he described making visits to prisons whose entrances were often littered with corpses.

After a few months in Manhattan, Captain Graydon and some of his fellow officers were removed to bucolic Long Island, where their parole was restricted to New Lots, Flatbush, Gravesend, and Flatlands. Although their situation remained reasonably comfortable, Graydon griped that "no longer thought of by friends or foes, we were destined to waste the best of our days in a state of hopeless captivity." Besides roaming the countryside, they read, swam, played ball, ate and drank in taverns, and took employment from the local residents. Some of them even married local girls.[30]

Meanwhile, in a communiqué of September 1777, the Provost prisoners notified Washington that they were being

[c]lose confined in jail . . . amongst felons (a number of whom
are under a sentence of death), without their friends being
suffered to speak for them, even through the gates. On the
scanty allowance of 2 lbs. hard biscuit and 2 lbs. raw pork per
man per week, without fuel to dress it. Frequently supplied with
water from a pump where all kinds of filth is thrown . . . when
good water is easily obtained. Denied the benefit of a hospital;
not allowed to send for medicine, nor even a doctor permitted to
visit them when in the greatest distress; married men and others
who lay at the point of death, refused to have their wives or relations admitted to see them, who, for attempting it, were often
beat from prison. Commissioned officers and other persons of
character, without a cause, thrown into a loathesome dungeon,
insulted in a gross manner, and vilely abused by a provost marshal, who is allowed to be one of the basest characters in the British army.[31]

One of the prisoners was Colonel Ethan Allen of Vermont, the colorful
hero of Ticonderoga, who had been moved to the Provost for violating his
parole after learning that back home his eleven-year-old son had died of
smallpox.[32] (Allen later wrote a rousing captivity narrative.)[33]

Washington ordered his commissary of prisoners, Elias Boudinot, to
investigate.[34] Boudinot, a courtly New Jersey aristocrat, went over to New
York in his own sloop and was politely received at tea by his counterpart.[35]
He quickly obtained evidence about the rebel officers' cruel treatment.
Armed with this information, he confronted the provost marshal, William
Cunningham, and asked him point-blank if the complaints were true.
According to Boudinot, Cunningham sneered that "every word was
true."[36] Boudinot promptly reported this confession to the British com-
mandant, and, apparently as a result, Cunningham was removed to Phila-
delphia and the American officers were paroled to Long Island.[37]

Lewis Pintard, the agent for American prisoners in New York, also took
Boudinot to two hospitals, which held 211 prisoners "in tolerably good
order," and to the Sugar-House, where they found 190 more. The old
warehouse now had stoves in each room, the windows had shutters, and a
blanket had been provided to each prisoner. Inmates reported that their
situation had lately improved and that Pintard had raised their rations
above the British allowance.[38]

Elsewhere in the city, however, they discovered appalling prison conditions. Boudinot went to the old French Church on Pine Street, where his
father had been baptized, and was shocked to find so many prisoners

inside—three or four hundred—that they could not all lie down at once. Some claimed that from October 15 to January 1 "they never recd a single stick of wood, and . . . for the most part . . . eat their Pork raw when the Pews & Door & Window facings failed them for fuel."[39]

Shortly after receiving these reports, Washington agreed to a general exchange of prisoners and appointed a commission to negotiate one. But the process became mired in politics, dragging out as more deadly epidemics swept the city's holding pens.[40] By May 1777, the *New York Gazette* reported that "of 3,000 prisoners taken at Fort Washington, only 800 are living."[41]

TORIES AND QUAKERS

AMERICAN rebels were not the only prisoners to complain about their treatment. Colonel Campbell, a British officer, wrote to General William Howe from the Concord Jail on February 14, 1777: "With respect to your treatment of General Lee, I can scarcely believe it similar to mine. I am lodged in a dungeon of 12 by 13 feet square, the sides black with grease and litter of successive criminals."[42]

Ensign Thomas Hughes of the Fifty-third Regiment, who had guarded rebel prisoners before being captured at Ticonderoga, was moved from one makeshift jail to another, including a prison ship at Boston that was jammed with two hundred famished inmates. His chief complaint was boredom, but he also resented that the officers' servants were treated the same as themselves.[43]

The most notorious American prison was an old copper mine in Simsbury, Connecticut.[44] "Newgate," as it was called, was designed to be escape proof, and Washington himself personally committed the first military prisoner there for safekeeping.[45] Although the place continued to hold as many as thirty or forty prisoners at a time—including prisoners of war, Tories, deserters, court-martialed American soldiers, and common criminals, most of whom were kept chained underground and forced to work twelve-hour stretches in the damp, dark mines—a number managed to escape.[46]

In December 1776 Philadelphia's Quakers had circulated an epistle signed by John Pemberton that tried to counteract the rising hostility they were encountering due to their alleged Tory sympathies.[47] The pamphlet restated the Friends' traditional opposition to war, military service, special taxes, and oaths of allegiance, and it stressed their neutrality in the present conflict. A few days later, patriot soldiers seized and imprisoned two Quakers who had refused to bear arms or work at the entrenchments that were being built around the city.[48] Pressure quickly grew for the Friends to take sides, but they refused.[49]

Charles Willson Peale, the portrait painter and president of the Committee of Correspondence of the Whig Society of Pennsylvania, urged that all Tories should be prosecuted.[50] With a military confrontation at Philadelphia drawing near, Congress ordered the apprehension of all persons "notoriously disaffected." Houses of those who had not "manifested their attachment to the American cause" were ordered searched.[51] The Supreme Executive Council of Pennsylvania authorized the arrest of forty-one Quakers as "dangerous" to the state.[52]

Musketeers rounded them up. Those refusing to submit to an oath (parole) that they would not communicate with the British were taken to the Free Masons' Lodge and held under guard.[53] On September 11, twenty-two Quakers in flatbrims and drab clothes were forced into wagons and driven out of Philadelphia, banished to western Virginia without a hearing.[54] Hundreds of spectators stood silently along the route, some of them dejected poor blacks who shook John Pemberton's hand as he rode by.[55]

The exiles arrived at Reading four days later and were greeted by a mob, whose members pulled some of them from their wagons and began pummeling them. Officers finally intervened and stopped the violence, and some friendly townspeople appeared bearing pies and other gifts.[56] Among those who observed the exiles at an inn there was Captain Alexander Graydon, recently released from captivity as a rebel prisoner of war at New York. One of the banished Quakers, who knew him, commented that he did not look as if he had been starved by the British. Graydon in turn observed that the Quakers did not look like victims of persecution.[57]

After the British evacuated Philadelphia, the rebels held court at City Hall to hear indictments against scores of suspects.[58] Forty-eight persons were later executed.[59] Many other Tory prisoners were treated roughly, such as a fellow who was stripped naked and painted in different colors.[60]

Although deserted by the lawful government, still troubled by the banishment of some of their members to Virginia, and with many more of their number facing possible confiscation of property and other persecution, Philadelphia's Quakers were nonetheless stunned when two Friends were arrested and charged with treason.[61]

A three-judge panel ordered them to be executed and their property attainted and seized.[62] More than four thousand persons attended their funeral.[63]

JOHN HOWARD, PRISON REFORMER

MEANWHILE, one disastrous effect of the American Revolution-ary War upon the mother country was that it disrupted the prisoner trade.[64] Slave trafficking to America, which had been operating at full tilt on the eve of the Revolution, virtually ceased during the hostilities, along with the supply of indentured servants. The once-flowing stream of trans-ported felons to Maryland and other ports also stopped, resulting in longer court backlogs and terrible prison overcrowding throughout the realm. England's ancient prison system was experiencing its worst crisis in memory.

A plan was suggested for sending some offenders to an island in the Gambia, but it was rejected in favor of an act that established convict gal-leys—another inadequate response. To make matters worse, an additional two thousand or so American prisoners, many of them captured privateers and fishermen, were taken all the way to prisons in Plymouth and other locations in England, adding even more to the overcrowding problem at home.[65] England's outmoded penal machinery needed a thorough exami-nation.

It appeared in print on April 5, 1777: the most comprehensive study of English prisons ever undertaken—a 489-page indexed volume, printed at the author's expense—*The State of the Prisons in England and Wales, with Preliminary Observations and an Account of Some Foreign Prisons* (America was not included).[66] It had been written by a distinguished gen-tleman of property, John Howard.

Born to wealthy parents, Howard had been orphaned as a teenager and had inherited a sizable fortune.[67] While he was leading the genteel life of a country squire, a ship on which he was traveling was seized by French marauders and he was taken prisoner. Howard was held for several months and almost died. From that time onward he became concerned about bar-barous prison conditions. In 1773, seventeen years after his own brief imprisonment, he was appointed high sheriff of Bedfordshire. He took the job seriously. Ascending into his elegant post chaise, he set off into the countryside to inspect all of the gaols within his jurisdiction. Howard soon discovered that his fine garments stank so badly from the gaols that he could no longer endure being inside an enclosed carriage, so he switched to riding horseback, sprinkled himself with vinegar to counteract the stench and disease, and continued on. In 1775 and 1776, he visited over one hundred prisons throughout Great Britain.[68]

Howard visited local houses of correction, which had been instituted in the sixteenth century as receptacles for the poor. But instead of finding

Bridewells that provided useful employment or taught a trade, as was their stated purpose, he discovered dark dens of idleness and misery, packed with beggars, paupers, vagrants, and petty thieves. The structures themselves had fallen into deeper disrepair during the period of reliance upon transportation to the American colonies, but now that Maryland and other ports were no longer open to the convict trade, the level of crowding had pushed the buildings beyond their breaking point.

In 1776 a law was passed that provided that any male who was lawfully convicted of a crime punishable by transportation to America shall be "kept to hard labour in the raising of sand, soil and gravel, and cleansing the river Thames, or any other service for the benefit of the navigation of the said river."[69] In October of that year, Howard made his first visit to the newly employed prison hulks on the Thames, craft that had been enlisted as a stopgap measure to hold the convict overflow.[70] After going aboard one ship he inspected all the convicts upon the deck, including a man who appeared extremely ill and was said to be suffering from venereal disease. Learning that the vessel had no surgeon or apothecary, Howard scanned their sickly looks and noted that many had no shirts, some no waistcoats, stockings, or shoes. Fearing reprisals, the nervous convicts would only whisper their complaints.

He methodically set about writing down his prison impressions. Although reserved in conversation, Howard asked good questions as an interviewer and sharpened his powers of observation to a keen point. A steady, deliberate worker, he kept precise notes and maintained fastidious records, prompting one modern writer to observe, "It was Howard who first applied to the field of social distress the empirical method of collecting and comparing personal experience."[71]

Howard pointed out that during the period 1773 to 1775 more persons had died in gaols than were executed for crime, although such destruction was neither just nor prudent. Certainly some of them could "be useful at home or abroad; if proper care were taken of them in prison, to keep them healthy and fit for labour."[72] He criticized the existing institutions for being "seminaries" of idleness and vice.[73]

To set matters right, he urged better prison conditions: sufficient wholesome food, sanitary improvements, and ventilated rooms.[74] He recommended that free clothing be provided for indigent convicts and that prison surgeons and apothecaries be appointed. He advocated strict separation of males and females, and of youths from hardened offenders, adding that each group should have its own common room but that every offender should sleep in a separate cell. "If it be difficult to prevent their being together in the daytime, they should by all means be separated at night. Solitude and silence are favorable to reflection, and may possibly lead them to repentance."[75]

Howard specified that a jailer must be "honest, active and humane" as well as sober. Jailers should be paid an adequate salary and forbidden to accept fees or favors from the prisoners. If possible, "The gaoler should not only reside on the spot, but be constantly at home."[76]

Like Adam Smith, he believed that slavery was not as productive as free labor, and he doubted that prison labor would ever prove profitable. He did think, however, it might enable the institutions to at least become self-sufficient.[77] Howard's works proved to be the most detailed and humane call for prison reform published to that point, setting a standard against which all subsequent reform efforts would be judged.

THE INFAMOUS PRISON SHIPS

SIMULTANEOUS with the introduction of the hulks on the Thames, the British had begun using a British warship, the *Whitby*, as a prison ship in New York harbor.[78] Over the next several months, the list of vessels grew into a small squadron of hospital ships and prison ships that included the *Kitty, Scorpion, Good Hope, Falmouth, Prince of Wales, Hunter, Providence, Bristol, Clyde, Woodlands, Scheldt, Glasgow, Grosvenor,* and *Strombolo*.[79]

The most infamous, HMS *Jersey*, was anchored in a small channel in the East River called the Wallabout, roughly 100 yards from the Brooklyn shore and across from the lower tip of Manhattan (near the future site of the New York Naval Shipyard).[80] Built in 1736, she had seen extensive action as a warship, first as a store ship and later as a hospital ship with the *Solebay* and the *Strombolo*. Then, in 1779, stripped of her masts, sails, and 60 guns, her ports boarded shut, with even her lion figurehead and rudder ripped away, her barnacled hulk was put to use as a receiving ship for captured privateers and other rebel prisoners. A vessel of 1,065 tons, measuring 144 feet in length, with a beam of 41.5 feet and a depth in her hold of 16.11 feet, the *Jersey* was designed for a crew of 400, but now held as many as 1,200 prisoners, under shocking conditions.[81]

In the daylight the ship could be seen from shore. Hundreds of forms, looking like stunned insects, some of them waving their gaunt arms, covered her upper deck and bowsprit. Shortly before sunset only her sentinels became visible, and any approaching visitors could make out only occasional moving shapes inside the hold through tiny airholes that ringed the ship.[82] Those coming closer were suddenly struck by a hideous stench, and many had to cup their hands over their faces to keep from retching. Voices inside the hulk cried for water or for news as the latest arrivals were brought up a ladder and through a heavily guarded barricado door, then lined up on deck and searched.

Each prisoner was ordered to give his name and rank to a scribe, who registered the information in a huge log. This done, the captives were directed through another barricade on the starboard side and down a ladder leading to the main hatchway. Marines prodded or shoved them below, into the smelly hold.

"And now a scene of horror, which baffled all description, presented itself," a former prisoner recalled. "On every side, wretched, desponding shapes of men could be seen."[83] As another remembered, "Here were men who had once enjoyed life while riding over the mountain wave or roaming through pleasant fields, full of health and vigor, now shrivelled by a scanty and unwholesome diet, ghastly with inhaling an impure atmosphere, exposed to contagion . . . and surrounded by the horrors of sickness and death."[84]

Those who had not brought their own hammocks or other bedding with them were left to sleep without covers on the slimy planks. Heads and bodies soon crawled with lice, and the hold was reputed to be home to smallpox, against which some of the terrified uninitiated sought to inoculate themselves by using infected fellow inmates and whatever instruments they could find, usually common pins or rusty nails.[85] Diseased and healthy mingled together.[86] They remained in the hold for sixteen hours, until 9 A.M.

The *Jersey*'s crew were relieved each week, to reduce their contamination.[87] Some survivors later reported having never seen the captain.[88]

The prisoners were organized into six-man mess groups.[89] Each unit sent a representative to receive its rations. When the cook decided the food had been heated long enough he rang a bell, and the mess leader would be expected to lift the portion from a huge copper pot, the inside of which was coated with verdigris and partitioned into several compartments. One side might contain peas and oatmeal, boiled in fresh water; another might have meat boiled in salt water that had been drawn from the side of the ship, near places where the garbage and excrement of a thousand men had been dumped.[90]

Rations were officially set at two-thirds of a British seaman's allowance; in fact, they amounted to much less and were of very inferior quality.[91] Accounts describe the biscuits as so bad that prisoners rapped them on the deck to dislodge the worms, or so moldy that "a slight pressure of the hand reduced them to dust, which rose up in little clouds of unsubstantial aliment, as if in mockery of the half-famished expectants."[92] Flour and oatmeal tended to be sour, the suet pungent, and the meat rotten. One survivor remembered the time a joker almost caused a riot by throwing a bag of apples among hundreds of famished inmates.[93]

To survive, some tars had sewn money in pieces of canvas hidden in their clothes, which they later used to buy food or bribe clerks to facilitate escapes and record the absences as deaths. According to William Dunlap, "A boat would be brought to the ship at night and by a system of collusion, the person who had bought his liberty would be removed by some specious pretense."[94]

The more privileged captives congregated in the former gun room, located in the extreme afterpart of the ship. The two decks below were occupied by common seamen. Frenchmen and other foreigners tended to be held in the bottom part, where conditions were worst and the chances of being exchanged were slimmest.[95] "The inhabitants of this lower region were the most miserable and disgusting looking objects that can be conceived," one surviving inmate recalled.[96] "Daily washing in salt water, together with their extreme emaciation, caused the skin to appear like dried parchment. Many of them remained unwashed for weeks; their hair long and matted, and filled with vermin; their beards never cut except occasionally with a pair of shears, which did not improve their comeliness, though it might add to their comfort. Their clothes were mere rags, secured to their bodies in every way that ingenuity could devise."[97]

British officers often came aboard ship and ordered the prisoners to line up on deck for inspection. These counts helped to determine if anyone was missing; they also offered opportunities for the British to find deserters or recruit men into the Royal Navy.[98] Bounties were offered for those willing to enlist, but few men accepted, though Ebenezer Fox of Massachusetts later claimed he had signed up in order to escape, which he later did in Jamaica.[99] Defectors were often jeered by their former shipmates until they were out of sight.[100]

Escape attempts were usually detected by the guards or betrayed by other prisoners.[101] Those trying to swim to shore often found the river too cold, as in the case of six escapees who had managed to slip away undetected until one of them gasped too loudly. Five were shot dead and the sixth survived by clinging to the anchor with only his nose above the surface.[102] But in warmer weather a few swimmers succeeded: Thomas Andros eventually made it onto Long Island, two and a half miles away, and from there took a whaleboat to Connecticut.[103] Lieutenant Eliakim

Palmer swam off with his clothes bundled over his head, but lost his trousers and had to cross the whole length of the island half-naked, subsisting on berries and cow's milk, until he finally reached some friends at Oyster Point Pond who smuggled him to safety.[104]

The prisoners formed their own government, complete with written bylaws, to which, one rebel wrote, "a willing submission was paid, so far as circumstances would permit."[105] The rules required that personal cleanliness should be preserved as much as possible, profane language avoided, and drunkenness, theft, and smoking belowdecks prohibited; every man was encouraged to come to the Sabbath observance cleanshaven; and the senior officer was designated to act as judge over alleged infractions. Remarkable discipline, considering their situation. An accused violator was entitled to be read the rule in question before his trial, and if convicted his punishment had to be approved by the whole company.[106]

They also established a work party to perform the daily chores. Commanded by an officer of the day, twenty or so of the most able-bodied men scrubbed the deck and gangways, spread the awning, hoisted supplies from the delivery boats, removed body waste, aided the sick to bunks on the center deck, and gathered the dead. In exchange, they received an extra one-third ration and a half-pint of rum, often using their privileges to gather intelligence and steal precious supplies like food, grease, pins, and wood.[107] Thomas Philbrook was among those who served on a work party, and he later described struggling up the ladder from the hold one morning with a corpse on his back. "What, you alive yet?" the guard exclaimed. "Well, you are a tough one."[108]

The dead, as many as six to twelve per day, were piled upon gratings on the upper deck and sewn inside old blankets.[109] A work party attached each parcel to a tackle and lowered the remains to a waiting launch from the hospital ship. Some prisoners actually volunteered for the burial party in order to get ashore. Under armed guard, the gravediggers rowed to a low wharf near Remsen's Mill and trudged to a hut to pick up their wheelbarrows and shovels. The bodies were then loaded on and wheeled to the bank of the Wallabout, from which the members of the detail could gaze back at the *Jersey*. Andros recalled watching from the ship each morning as the party rowed ashore and dumped their cargo, noting that the bodies were so lightly covered with sand that they must eventually have been washed away by the tides.[110] Sometimes a digger brought back a handful of moist dirt to share with his comrades; it was passed "by them from hand to hand, and its smell inhaled, as if it had been a fragrant rose."[111]

At least three prison vessels caught fire and sank during the Revolution. Two were hospital ships that were destroyed, in October 1777 and February 1778, and the *Good Hope* went down on March 5, 1780, reportedly during an escape attempt.[112]

The most famous firsthand account of the prison ships was written during the Revolution by the poet Philip Freneau. Born in 1752 to a prominent Huguenot family, he had grown up on a thousand-acre plantation in New Jersey. Later, he attended Princeton with such luminaries as James Madison, Aaron Burr, and Hugh Henry Breckenridge (with whom he had collaborated to write America's first known work of fiction, *Father Bombo's Pilgrimage to Mecca in Arabia*).

After spending some time on a privateer in the West Indies, young Freneau had served in the New Jersey militia, rising to the rank of sergeant.[113] In the bitter winter of 1780, he let his enlistment expire and signed up as third mate aboard the *Aurora*, a twenty-gun Letter of Marque that was bound for St. Eustacia with tobacco. Shortly after leaving Delaware Bay they were spotted by a British frigate, the *Iris*, which forced their surrender. Because the ship's records mistakenly listed him as a "gunner," Freneau was treated as a common prisoner. Taken to New York, he sought in vain to purchase his parole.[114]

On the *Scorpion* prison ship, he suffered many hardships and became delirious with fever. Three weeks later, he ended up on a filthy and overcrowded hospital ship moored in the East River.[115] Finally, numb and exhausted, Freneau was released after six weeks of captivity. While convalescing at home, he penned an epic poem, *The British Prison-Ship*. Published first as a broadside in the fall of 1780, it was reissued countless times thereafter. As the finest expression of the horrors of the prison ships, it established him as the "Poet of the Revolution."[116]

LEGACIES

JOHN Trumbull, the Connecticut patriot and painter, was another prominent American prisoner of war. He had been studying art in England under Benjamin West when he was arrested and jailed in retaliation for the hanging of Major John André, Benedict Arnold's contact. He was held on suspicion of treason; later, he became the leading American painter of the Revolutionary period.

The highest-ranking American prisoner taken during the war was Henry Laurens, the former Charleston slavetrader and signer of the Declaration of Independence, who had gone on to become president of the Continental Congress. He ended up in the Tower of London, where he was held on suspicion of high treason. He remained confined under close

guard and was denied the right to receive visitors or conduct correspondence. After the British defeat at Yorktown, he was paroled and exchanged
for Lord Charles Cornwallis.[117]

In the spring of 1781, British dragoons and Tories waged a fierce campaign against American rebels in South Carolina. Loyalties were so divided
that the fighting more closely resembled a civil war than a revolution.
Among those conducting raids for the Americans were a thirteen-year-old
boy, Andrew Jackson, and his brother, Robert. As the two hid out in their
cousin's home, an informer alerted the enemy and British troops surrounded the house, burst in, and began smashing the furniture.

The story goes that a lieutenant of the Light Dragoons ordered young
Andrew to clean his muddy jackboots, to which the youth replied: "Sir, I
am a prisoner of war, and claim to be treated as such." With that the officer
smashed his saber at Jackson's head, but the young man ducked and raised
his left hand to deflect the blow. He received a deep gash in his hand and
a bad cut on his head. As Andrew lay stunned and bleeding on the floor,
the officer ordered Jackson's brother to clean his boots; he, too, refused
and was sent sprawling and cut. Later the wounded brothers and 20 other
prisoners were taken on horseback for forty miles, without water, food, or
medical care, to Camden, where the British had established their regional
headquarters. The Jacksons were thrown into a horrific prison enclosure
with 250 other captives, held without medicine or beds, and nearly starved
to death. Robbed of their shoes and jackets, they fell ill and their hunger-
tautened skin turned yellow. Smallpox swept the camp and a tenth of the
prisoners died. Both brothers contracted the disease and became covered
with sores. Their mother appeared at the camp with two horses just as a
prisoner exchange was being worked out and managed to bring them away.
Both youths were deathly ill, dressed in tattered rags, and looked like skeletons. Within a few days of reaching home, Robert died and Andrew was
"a raving maniac." Elizabeth Jackson spent several months nursing him
back to health. As soon as he was well enough to be left alone, she rode
off to Charleston to nurse some of her other kin who were being held in
the prison ships there. As a result she contracted "ship fever" and died.
She was buried in an unmarked grave. Her son, Andrew Jackson, the
future president of the United States, was deeply marked by these wartime
experiences.[118]

Thomas Jefferson narrowly avoided being taken prisoner. Another leg-
islator who was not so lucky was a young representative from Fayette
County in the Kentucky district, Daniel Boone, who was briefly imprisoned before being paroled.[119]

By war's end, more Americans had perished as prisoners than had been killed in combat.[120] As many as 11,500 men had died on the *Jersey* alone—far more than were lost in all of the battles of the Revolution.[121] Abandoned where she lay when her last prisoners were liberated, the worm-eaten *Jersey* eventually collapsed and sank, taking with her the names and other graffiti that her captives had scratched on her planks.[122] Dozens of accounts by some of her former inmates were later published, and many thousands of stories were passed on by word of mouth to younger generations, making the prisoners' horrible sufferings one of the best-known episodes in American revolutionary history.[123] Many American families had lost a loved one to the prison ships and other prisons that had operated during the war, and the consciousness of many survivors about issues of punishment and freedom had been raised to new levels.

ENDING THE REBELLION

THE Treaty of Paris, ending the war, was signed in September 1783. Two months later, on November 26, Washington's army triumphantly entered Manhattan. By then the surviving military prisoners had gradually been freed, but a general who was at the Provost jail that morning recalled that a "few British criminals were yet in custody, and O'Keefe [the jailer] threw his ponderous bunch [of keys] on the floor and retired, when an American guard relieved the British guard, which joined a detachment of British troops, then on parade in Broadway, and marched down to the Battery, where they embarked for England."[124] All jail keys were now in American hands.

Over thirty thousand people, including military personnel and ten thousand Loyalists, servants, and slaves, had recently fled the city or been taken away. Many of the slaves, having learned from British proclamations that military authorities would free them from their rebel masters, were anxious to escape before the Americans returned. Three of these slaves had belonged to Washington himself.[125] (Quakers such as Thomas Eddy had slipped south to New Jersey and then on to Philadelphia and Virginia; his elder brother Charles had headed to Ireland, and his brother-in-law Lawrence Hartshorne to Halifax.)[126] William Cunningham, David Sproat (the commissary of naval prisoners), and other detested keepers were also gone.[127] Behind them the British had left gutted buildings, a drained economy, and a surrounding countryside that had been stripped of forest and game. With them they had taken an established government and way of life, leaving the city and the colonies, for better or for worse, independent.[128]

The city's recovery started immediately. Within a few months, a new government was installed, New York harbor was clustered with merchant ships, the population was increasing, and new construction was under way. Exiles returned to reclaim their property, and the victors began extensive forfeiture proceedings to seize their spoils.

The war was over, but the Revolution was not. Some patriots still pursued principles for which the struggle had been waged, expecting those ideals would become law. Yet soon it became apparent that some rights that had been apotheosized in revolutionary rhetoric remained dangerous notions to those in power. Now that they were fully in charge, many of the men who had organized and led the rebellion against the Crown suddenly worried that *they* might become the object of revolt and their developing new order the target for continued insurrection. Revolutionaries became counterrevolutionaries almost overnight. Human rights were subsumed under property rights. A flood of civil actions ensued. The number of new lawyers soared (among them were Alexander Hamilton, John Jay, Aaron Burr, and Gouverneur Morris, to name a few). So did the public's antipathy toward attorneys, courts, and prisons, particularly on the part of debtors, who now found themselves tangled in sticky webs of claims and complaints, judgments and seizures.[129]

In Massachusetts, the birthplace of the Revolution, a rabble-rouser named Samuel Ely was convicted for trying to prevent the sitting of a court of common pleas at Northampton, but a mob forced his release from jail. When the ringleaders were caught and imprisoned, another crowd tried to spring them, too. A militia of fifteen hundred men was marched over to protect the prison, but the protests continued. Elsewhere, more mobs marched on courthouses, shutting them down, and insurrection spread. At Great Barrington, a thousand-man militia, called out to protect the General Court, became divided among itself and dispersed, leaving a mob to break open the jail and free the debtors.[130]

Stephen Burroughs, a young New Englander who was locked up in the Northampton jail for counterfeiting, left a lively account of his experiences. Conditions there resembled those suffered in New York a decade earlier; there was scarce food or warmth during the bitter-cold winter. Burroughs tried desperately to escape, but was caught, beaten, and subjected to even worse deprivation. After trying to burn down the jail, he was stomped, bludgeoned, and shoved into a dungeon, where he probably would have died but for the intervention of an uncle who helped him to purchase food and arrange for a transfer.[131]

The biggest postwar revolt was centered in economically distressed central and western Massachusetts, which was struggling under a heavy tax burden imposed to meet state debts. There the rebellion was led by Captain Daniel Shays, a wounded Revolutionary War veteran and debtor, who, like so many former combatants, still had not been paid his promised wages. Shays's armed insurgents, numbering several hundred, tried to close the courts to prevent further actions against the debtors, but Shays's Rebellion was finally smashed by federal troops. Several rebels were hanged, but Shays himself was pardoned and allowed to leave.[132]

ANTISLAVERY, WITHIN LIMITS

IMPORTS of slaves, convicts, and servants had virtually ceased during the war, and some transported convicts and other servants had managed to slip away to freedom during the confusion.[133] The war had closed with all of the new states ending the international slave trade.[134] Slave trafficking was also banned within Massachusetts, Connecticut, Rhode Island, Pennsylvania, Virginia, North Carolina, and Georgia.[135]

Yet most slaves remained slaves, and the system continued to be the law of the land. Only two Northern states had gone so far as to outlaw the institution: the Republic of Vermont had prohibited slavery by its constitution of 1777, and three years later Pennsylvania had become the first state to begin the gradual emancipation of all slaves within her borders.[136] Emancipation was being discussed in Delaware and Virginia, and slavery's legitimacy was coming under widespread assault; however, the institution still endured in most of the United States.[137]

Some Americans expressed concern that the Revolution's ideals were being forsaken. Referring to the Declaration of Independence, David Cooper, a Quaker from Burlington, New Jersey, wrote: "If these solemn truths . . . are self-evident . . . the very people who make these pompous declarations are slave-holders, and, by their legislative conduct, tell us, that these blessings were . . . only meant to be the rights of white-men not of all men."[138]

At war's end, English antislavery activities became better organized. Thomas Clarkson published his *Essay on the Slavery and Commerce of the Human Species, Particularly the African* in London in 1785, and it created an immediate sensation throughout the British empire and North America.[139] Although he was not a Quaker, Clarkson identified strongly with the sect's ideas, and his treatise claimed that the work of emancipated Negroes was superior in quantity and quality to that of slaves. As a result, fewer were needed to do the same work, which meant that plantation owners could increase their profits.[140]

Clarkson distinguished between "voluntary" and "involuntary" slavery.

The first, such as with military volunteers, indentured servants, and "half-free" laborers, entailed a consensual contract. The latter, involving prisoners of war, conscripted soldiers, and slaves, rested on sheer coercion. In his view, slaves, whether "publicly seized by virtue of an authority of the prince" or "privately kidnapped by individuals," had been "collected by means of violence and oppression; by means, repugnant to nature, the principles of government, and the common notions of equity, as established among men." As he saw it, the African slave trade could not be morally justified, either as a spoil of war or as a punishment for crime.[141]

Clarkson exposed the prevailing, shocking conditions in the international slave trade, primarily as they affected British seamen. He noted how British subjects were often lured into serving on slave ships to avoid being sent to gaol, and he disclosed appalling mortality rates—more than a fifth of each crew—aboard the slave ships. This, he said, meant that instead of being the "great nursery of British seamen," the African slave trade was better described as their grave.[142]

He advocated an end to international slave trafficking, claiming it would improve slavery's material conditions and make the institution more efficient and profitable. In short, Clarkson sought to reform African slavery, not immediately eliminate it. This perspective was further evident when he considered penal slavery. For whose benefit, he asked, must the convict (slave) labor? If it was for the benefit of the state, then slavery was justified in his estimation. But if the prisoner was enslaved to benefit an individual, it was not just, because "[t]he State alone is considered to have been injured, and as injuries cannot possibly be transferred, the State alone can justly receive the advantages of his labour."[143]

Spurred on by British reformers such as Clarkson, and capitalizing on American revolutionary rhetoric, Anglo-American antislavery forces focused upon winning some significant legislative victories, and they seemed on their way to eradicating slavery once and for all. Even Washington, who still personally owned 216 slaves, confided to his friend Robert Morris, the financier: "I can only say, that there is not a man living, who wishes more sincerely than I do, to see a plan adopted for the abolition of it [slavery]; but there is only one proper and effectual mode by which it can be accomplished, and that is by legislative authority; and this as far as my suffrage will go, shall never be wanting."[144]

Pennsylvania's emancipation law was considered a model. It provided that all persons who were slaves on the date the statute was passed would remain in bondage, while slaves who were born in the future would be freed later, after serving for a set period (twenty-eight years), under a sort of extended indentured servitude. Masters could still sell their free-born slaves, subject to certain restrictions. This complicated approach aimed to free a future generation of potential slaves without liberating those presently held in slavery; the loophole allowing masters to sell their free-born slaves to other jurisdictions indicated that lawmakers were seeking to phase out the existence of slavery locally without necessarily causing owners any serious loss.[145]

At the time, Negroes constituted only about 12 to 15 percent of New York State's population. As many as three of every five slaves lived upstate, but New York City's upper class depended on slaves to do much of its domestic work.[146] In January 1785 a group of seventeen leading New Yorkers, mostly major slaveholders or Quakers, formed the New-York Manumission Society.[147] One of their first acts was to order two hundred copies of Clarkson's essay. They also petitioned the state legislature to enact gradual emancipation. The lawmakers prohibited slave imports into New York, but they rejected gradual emancipation on the grounds that the plan did not adequately protect paramount property rights.[148]

Antislavery efforts were firmly blocked in the lower South. Blacks there continued to be denied any rights and privileges, and they were increasingly viewed as threatening to whites. Their condition became even more restricted and their race vilified by thinkers like Jefferson, whose *Notes on the State of Virginia* articulated deep-seated beliefs in black inferiority.[149]

In 1784 Congress had appointed Jefferson to chair a committee to plan the government of the territory north of the thirty-first parallel (an area that now includes the states of Kentucky, Tennessee, Mississippi, and Alabama). This committee had recommended that, after 1800, neither slavery nor involuntary servitude should be permitted there. But that policy fell one vote short of passage. Three years later, Jefferson wrote another provision that "forever" prohibited slavery in the territory known as the National Domain (later the states of Ohio, Indiana, Illinois, Michigan, and Wisconsin). Under the plan, the land south of the Ohio River would retain slavery, while the area to its north would be free. But not entirely. That is, the Northwest Ordinance of July 13, 1787, forbade slavery and involuntary servitude in the Northwest Territory *except as a punishment for crime,* specifying: "There shall be neither slavery nor involuntary servitude in the said territory, otherwise than in the punishment of crimes whereof the party shall have been duly convicted: Provided always, that any person escaping into the same, from whom labor or service is lawfully claimed in any one of the original States, such fugitive may be lawfully reclaimed and conveyed to the person claiming his or her labor aforesaid."[150]

Such actions reflected a growing trend among lawmakers in the North to try to link slavery with criminal punishment. Outside the South, private slavery was being drastically curtailed, whereas state-sponsored penal slavery was being encouraged. Thus, Pennsylvania's Quakers failed to gain the complete abolition of capital punishment, but it was removed for all but four felonies (murder, treason, rape, and arson) in favor of "continued hard labor, publicly and disgracefully imposed."[151]

One of their top supporters, Dr. Benjamin Rush, the Philadelphia physician and signer of the Declaration of Independence, called capital punishment "the natural offspring of monarchial governments" and said he favored imprisonment instead, on the grounds that "a prison sometimes supplies the place of a church and out-preaches the preacher in conveying useful instruction to the heart."[152] Still, Rush opposed forcing convicts to undergo hard labor disgracefully imposed because it might render labor itself "ignominious." Like other utilitarians of the time, he favored making criminal punishments proportionate, not only to the crimes involved but also "according to the temper of criminals and the progress of their reformation." He also wanted the duration of the punishment to be concealed from the offender. Rush said he considered this to be "of the utmost importance in reforming criminals and preventing crimes," for "[t]he imagination, when agitated with uncertainty, will seldom fail of connecting the longest duration of punishment, with the smallest crime."[153]

One of Rush's frequent Quaker correspondents—Dr. John Coakley Lettsom, a popular London physician—favored condemning convicts to public labor out-of-doors, partly to deter other criminals. But even as he advocated establishing penal slavery for convicts, he also cheered progress in the Anglo-American campaign to abolish the African slave trade, never seeing that there might be any inconsistency between his two positions.[154] Support for such stances was growing by the day, and within a few months England began transporting convicts, not to America, but to a new penal colony: Australia.[155]

By March 1787, convicts with shaved heads and dark blue-and-brown uniforms with parti-colored woolen caps were being used to clean Philadelphia's streets, prompting one resident, Mrs. Ann Warder, to note in her diary: "They have an iron collar around their neck and waist to which a long chain is fastened and at the end a heavy ball. As they proceed with their work this is taken up and thrown before them. . . . A guard accompanies each gang." At first some prisoners were so embarrassed that they professed to prefer execution. But they got used to it, for as Warder later concluded: "Two things I think need regulating, suffering [allowing] people to talk to them, and to prevent their receiving money."[156]

The Pennsylvania Abolition Society, which had been founded before the Revolution, resumed its activities in 1784. Three years later, none other than Benjamin Franklin became its president and changed the name to the "Pennsylvania Society for promoting the abolition of slavery, the relief of free Negroes unlawfully held in bondage, and for improving the condition of the African race." Old Franklin corresponded with antislavery leaders and labored with James Pemberton and other Quakers to abolish the international slave trade, extirpate slavery, and address the needs of emancipated Negroes.[157]

Parallel developments occurred in New York. On the one hand, the Manumission Society organized a boycott of slave auctioneers, lobbied for gradual emancipation, and focused on improving the Negro condition through education. At the same time, the legislature enacted the new state's first slave code—New York's first since 1730—as well as a harsh new penal code, which provided the death penalty for treason, murder, forgery, counterfeiting, rape, forcible detaining of women, robbing a church, housebreaking by day or night involving an occupied dwelling, robbery, willful burning of any house or barn, and malicious maiming.[158] And the Massachusetts General Court banned citizens from engaging in the slave trade, and the next day passed an act "for suppressing and punishing of Rogues, Vagabonds, common Beggars, and other idle, disorderly, and lewd Persons," with provisions that barred foreign Negroes from tarrying within the commonwealth for longer than two months, under penalty of being jailed, whipped, or banished.[159]

ESTABLISHING CONTROL

THE proper organization and structure of American government was still very much under debate when there began to appear in New York's newspapers a series of public letters arguing for a strong federal government. The stream of essays continued for several months. The collection was later reissued as *The Federalist* and attributed to Alexander Hamilton, John Jay, and James Madison, who were among the authors of the proposed new Constitution of the United States, which was then up for ratification.[160] The Federalist Papers contended that the administration of criminal and civil justice was government's paramount purpose. The writers viewed punishment as an important and necessary function of government, saying that "every government ought to contain in itself the means of its own preservation" and warning that a government without punishment was "a strong incitement to sedition—and the dread of punishment—a proportionately strong discouragement to it."[161]

On September 13, 1788, the state's adoption of the Constitution was

announced in New York City, which was then the seat of the federal and
state governments. Washington's election as the first president of the
United States was unanimous and unopposed, and he was inaugurated in
Manhattan on April 30, 1789. Hamilton assumed office as secretary of the
treasury and reported that the United States already had a national debt of
$54,124,465.56, plus interest.[162]

Despite the removal of British prison ships and the release of thousands
of prisoners of war from rebel churches and other makeshift jails, the capital of the new nation still retained a panoply of busy penal machinery. The
long, gray-stoned Bridewell, which had served as a British prison throughout the Revolution, kept in full swing after the British left. Its keeper and
his assistants occupied the first floor; the second floor was divided into an
Upper Hall for less desperate criminals and a Chain Room for common
prisoners, including slaves.[163] Constables received a bounty for every
vagrant they brought there.[164] In 1785 the legislature had authorized the
common council to compel offenders at the institution to perform hard
labor inside the prison, and by 1787 vagrants were engaged in a variety of
tasks, including fishing, nail making, and manual labor along the water-
front, just as they might be under English rule.[165]

East of the Bridewell, near the present site of City Hall, stood the aging
two-story stone Almshouse. Although only 56 feet long by 24 feet deep, in
November 1785 it had held 301 inmates; by May 1787, the number had
swelled to 426.[166] Beyond the Almshouse loomed the infamous Provost,
now called the Jail and used as a debtors' prison. In December 1788 the
Society for the Relief of Distressed Debtors reported that 1,162 debtors
had been committed to the Jail in less than two years—an astronomical
number in a city of only 25,000 persons—and that many of those being
held owed less than 20 shillings.[167]

Soon after the British evacuation, a new gallows had been constructed
in a brightly painted pagoda that was located, appropriately, between the
Jail and the Almshouse. Nearby stood the whipping post and stocks.[168]
Larceny was punishable by up to thirty-nine lashes, and indigent strangers
who returned after being banished were subject to whippings of up to
thirty-nine lashes for males and twenty-five for females.[169]

During the postwar depression, however, even these controls were
strained beyond their limits, for it seemed that many residents did not have
a lot to lose. In April 1788 rumors circulated that human corpses had been
secretly dug up from New York's potter's field and Negroes' Burial Ground
for use by medical students at New York Hospital. A riot broke out, which
pitted Alexander Hamilton, John Jay, and other prominent citizens against

the outraged masses, some of whom stormed the hated Jail. Jay was struck by a rock and knocked unconscious. When the soldiers' gunsmoke had cleared, five persons lay dead and eight were seriously wounded.[170]

FEARS OF CONTAGION

A MERICAN newspapers of the day also devoted close attention to growing unrest in Europe. On July 14, 1789, a Paris mob had stormed the notorious Bastille prison, killed the guards, freed the inmates, and destroyed the fortress. In that instance a prison riot gradually escalated into a revolution. In September 1792 a massacre started at one prison and spread to another, as the revolutionaries cut off their enemies' heads and stuck them on pikes.[171] The French Revolution attracted tremendous interest in the United States and contributed to the Bill of Rights being hurriedly added to the Constitution. Such violence abroad horrified most of America's Founding Fathers, who worried that the terror might spread.

Thomas Paine was an exception. He had gone to France to support the cause of liberty, only to be arrested by the Committee of General Safety and taken to Luxembourg Prison on the pretense of being a British agent. The American minister to France, Gouverneur Morris, shunned him as a provocateur, and some of his other former comrades, including Washington and Jefferson, provided no help. As he languished in prison, 300 of his fellow inmates went to the guillotine. In the first 13 months, France carried out at least 1,220 executions, and then the Revolution spun even more out of control, taking 1,376 heads in just seven weeks. Paine's own cell door was scratched with chalk, marking him for death, but the cross had been inscribed when the door was open, not closed, thereby removing it from view of the authorities, so that he was accidentally spared. At last, after eleven harrowing months in captivity, James Monroe finally arranged his release.[172]

Public opinion about the French Revolution was particularly divided in Philadelphia, a haven for French émigrés. Tensions were heightened in 1793 by a major outbreak of yellow fever, which turned out to be the worst plague not involving Indians in American history to that point.[173] Over a four-month period, the disease claimed more than one-tenth of the city's population, or more than the number killed in France by the guillotine. Its cause was not yet known, but the menace was considered so contagious that Charles Willson Peale, the former patriot and persecutor of the Quakers, hurried throughout his house sprinkling vinegar on everything in sight and firing smoky musket charges in an effort to ward off the danger.[174] Dr. Benjamin Rush suspected Negroes as the carriers and recommended quarantine.[175]

Such anxiety increased as the potent ideas of liberty, equality, and fraternity collided with slavery. France too had maintained a colonial slave empire, and when the Bastille fell, the French West Indian island of St. Dominique (Haiti) had a population of over half a million persons, 80 percent of them black. In 1791 these slaves erupted in the first truly large-scale African slave rebellion.[176] As a result, many whites in the United States, which had seven hundred thousand potentially rebellious slaves of its own, followed these events with alarm. A few stubborn radicals actually applauded Toussaint L'Ouverture's success. One of them, Boston's J. P. Martin, compared blacks' right to revolt with that of Americans who had rebelled against the Crown.[177]

But such views were not widely shared by white Americans. John Adams suggested that white workers' resentment toward blacks, not their concern for them, had contributed to the end of slavery in New England. "If the gentleman had been permitted by law to hold slaves," he wrote, "the common white people would have put the negroes to death, and their masters too, perhaps."[178] Racist attitudes had become deeply engrained. Blacks were increasingly being depicted by whites of all classes as irresponsible, lazy, treacherous, and crime prone.

Jefferson was one of the leading commentators who fostered this image. Now that he had become afraid that he and his former liberty-loving revolutionaries might have created a monster, he looked up from the news of the bloodbaths sweeping France and St. Dominique and warned that "if something is not done, and done soon, we shall be the murderers of our own children [and] the revolutionary storm, now sweeping the globe, will be upon us."[179]

White paranoia increased, and not without reason. Reported American slave revolts during the 1790s grew by 150 percent over the previous decade.[180] In 1793 alone, slaves in New York raised a liberty pole honoring the West Indies revolt and attached a sign, FREEDOM TO AFRICANS; gangs of Negroes roamed through Philadelphia's streets, knocking into white men and saying they would "show them San Domingo"; and attempts to set Albany, New York, afire were attributed to rebellious Negroes.[181]

Indeed, some whites worried that freedom itself might be contagious, for, as Jefferson observed, "The course of things in the neighboring islands of the West Indies appears to have given considerable impulse to the minds of the slaves in different parts of the U.S. . . . A great disposition to insurgency has manifested itself among them."[182] Governor Charles Pinckney of

South Carolina sent his condolences and support to the Colonial Assembly of St. Dominique, noting that their two white-minority societies had much in common.[183]

At the same time, slavery's legal status was becoming more complicated and controversial. In 1791 the Pennsylvania Society for the Abolition of Slavery petitioned the governor of Virginia to extradite three men who had kidnapped a free Negro in Pennsylvania and carried him to Virginia against his will. When the governor demurred, saying he lacked sufficient legal basis, a congressional committee was appointed to draft legislation permitting the seizure of anyone "charged in any State with treason, felony or other crime."[184] The resulting Fugitive Slave Law of 1793 provided the "mode by which a person held to service or labor in one State under the laws thereof, escaping into another, shall be delivered up on the claim of the party to whom such labor may be due." Instead of helping to curtail slavery, it set a hefty fine of $500 for anyone who aided a fugitive slave anywhere in the United States.[185]

THOMAS EDDY

FUGITIVE Tories fared better than fugitive slaves. Since fleeing New York to evade possible persecution, Thomas Eddy, the former Philadelphia Quaker, had headed south to Virginia, where he and his brother carried on the tobacco trade.[186] Using slave-harvested leaves as barter, their fledgling company had financed the terms of the British surrender at Yorktown, though years later Eddy confessed that the Virginia business had turned out badly and said his "being much exposed to extravagant and dissipated company was a great injury to me in every respect."[187]

In 1790 he returned to New York, apparently without worry that he might be prosecuted for his wartime activities. (He had been briefly imprisoned in New Jersey as a suspected spy.) With $250 borrowed from his father-in-law and assistance from a prominent Quaker merchant, Eddy began work as an insurance broker, later becoming an underwriter.[188] Within three years he had grown rich through successful speculation and was elected a director of the Western Inland Lock Navigation Company, a New York–based corporation fostering westward development. Its chief director was General Philip J. Schuyler, the upstate aristocrat and father-in-law of Hamilton.[189] Legislation had been enacted in Pennsylvania to convert a wing of the Walnut Street jail into a "penitentiary-house," providing for solitary confinement, imprisonment at hard labor, and other reforms. Jay's Federalist friend, General Schuyler, was sent to Philadelphia to gather information about the new penal system, and he brought with him his business associate, Eddy, the former Philadelphian. While they were there, Eddy consulted his old Quaker acquaintance Caleb Lownes, who had become an inspector at the redesigned Walnut Street prison.[190]

Upon returning to New York, Eddy enlisted Cadwallader D. Colden to help him draft a comprehensive new penal code, modeled after Pennsylvania's. Their finished product abolished the death penalty in all cases except treason against the state, murder, aiding or abetting murder, and stealing from a church; it also eliminated whipping as a punishment for crime. The act gave broad discretion to judges to regulate the length of prison terms at hard labor and called for the erection of two state prisons. Convicts were to be provided "coarse clothing" and "inferior food." No outside visitors were allowed. Corporal punishment of convicts was forbidden.[191] Eddy's legislation was passed with only one dissenting vote in the New York senate and nine in the state assembly, and it became law on March 26, 1796.[192]

Chief Justice Ambrose Spencer appointed a committee to build the state prison at New York. Besides Eddy, the New York Committee included Matthew Clarkson, who had served in the Revolution, chartered the Bank of New York in 1791, and been a key figure in the New-York Manumission Society; John Watts, Jr., a prominent Federalist and former speaker of the assembly and congressman; Colden; Eddy's boyhood friend and business associate, John Murray, Jr.; and Isaac Stoutenburgh, another prosperous Quaker.[193] The committee designated Eddy to supervise the task. He selected as architect Joseph-François Mangin, a Frenchman who had fled the Reign of Terror, and also hired the workmen and directly supervised the construction.[194] In July, Caleb Lownes himself came up from Philadelphia to New York to assist in drawing plans.[195]

Like the new Walnut Street jail, Eddy's plan provided for two housing wings that extended backward from a central structure holding administrative offices. But Eddy's institution was designed exclusively for felons, and debtors were excluded. He also incorporated a large chapel for inmate worship. The new prison followed many of John Howard's suggestions: it was built near a river, on an airy spot, and provided for separation of male and female, as well as younger and older, offenders. However, Eddy's design favored congregate housing rather than solitary confinement, except for a few special-punishment cells. He also opted for more-lenient punishments, rejecting flogging, marks of disgrace, and torture.[196]

Eddy admired John Howard and resembled him in several ways. (Howard had continued his prison visits until the end, dying of gaol fever in a Russian army typhus ward at Kherson, in Ukraine, in 1791.)[197] Like Howard, he had grown up with a strong commitment to order, work, moderation, sacrifice, temperance, and obedience to God. Both were punctual, precise, methodical, neat, courteous, pious, prudent. Both were members of persecuted religious groups. Both had experienced imprisonment at first hand, and then, after a lapse of seventeen years, had suddenly devoted themselves to prison reform. Both had travelled extensively, lobbied indefatigably, written prolifically. Both were wealthy and well-connected. No wonder that Eddy already was on his way to being called "the Howard of America."[198] Indeed, the life of the "Father of New York State Prison" is worth remembering in some detail. He had lived through the turmoil of the Revolution, experienced persecution, and been forced to flee from home to avoid prosecution. He also had witnessed Southern plantation slavery and had followed Quaker antislavery efforts in England and America. He had been both bankrupt and rich, blacklisted and elected to elite societies, all within the space of a few years. As an enterprising young businessman and a pioneer in New York's burgeoning insurance business, immersed in actuarial tables and geometric progressions, he had become skilled at calculating personal risks and at projecting profits—notions that now became integrated into determinate, time-based prison sentences. Exposed to the idea of contagions, he had also been personally affected by infectious disease, which had claimed his son's ability to hear and speak—events that may have later influenced him to favor solitary instead of congregate prisoner housing and bars against verbal communication among convicts.

STATE PRISON

THE first New York state prison was located on the east bank of the Hudson River, in upper Greenwich Village (formerly the Algonkian village of Sappokanican), which was one of the oldest habitations of white persons on Manhattan Island.[199] The spot was about a block from the Christopher Street ferry slip and a mile and a half from City Hall. At the site, one could smell the fresh salt air, hear the gulls, and scan the surrounding rolling green countryside, and Eddy claimed that a "more pleasant, airy, and salubrious spot could not have been selected in the vicinity of New-York."[200]

Construction was started on an outside wall, 23 feet high along the river and 14 feet high in front, 500 feet long on one side and 297 feet in breadth, with matching watchtowers. (It would not be completed until 1799.) The front of the main building was 204 feet long and two stories high, designed in the Doric style. At its center was a pediment with a handsome cupola containing a bell to sound the alarm. Another pediment adorned the west front. The roof was slate, the walls were freestone. Its numerous windows were grated with iron inlaid with steel and hardened. The center of the main structure contained apartments for use by the inspectors and agent, the keeper, his family, and assistants. From each end of the main body there projected a wing, extending towards the river, and from them two smaller wings. The regular inmate housing consisted of 54 rooms, each of which measured 12 by 18 feet and was designed to accommodate up to eight prisoners. A chapel capable of holding up to 500 persons was located in the first north wing, and the dining hall was in the southern compartment. Adjoining the end of each wing was a separate building containing seven solitary cells measuring 8 feet long, 6 feet wide, and 14 feet high with windows 8 feet above the floor. Outside the west wall was a river wharf for loading and unloading prison goods. Watchtowers at each end overlooked the yards and a brick workshop. The latter measured 200 feet long and 20 feet wide and was sectioned into individual work compartments.[201]

The cost to New York State for the land, buildings, and wharf was $208,846—a very substantial sum at that time, particularly given the lack of public revenues. In fact, the prison was the state's first significant capital construction project and its leading expenditure—more than roads or schools or canals or the military or any other activity. Operating funds were another matter. The legislature expected the prison to pay as many of its expenses as possible with the proceeds from convict labor, yet the institution might not have been considered fiscally viable without Eddy's business acumen.

A committee governed the prison until January 1799, when a board of seven inspectors was appointed. Four members, including Eddy, were prominent Quakers. Eddy also served as principal keeper, at a salary of $875. In addition, the prison employed a deputy keeper and nine assistants, at salaries of $400 and $250 respectively, plus room, board, and washing.

After a few years of on-the-job experience, Eddy observed that "[t]he success of the whole system depends on a principal keeper being proposed of suitable qualifications," saying it was "therefore essentially necessary, that he should have a handsom salary, and he should be a sober, religious, exemplary Man, of a humane good disposition, of a decent good understanding, and a strong firm & resolute mind." He added that a prison keeper "should be a person of sound understanding, quick discernment, and ready apprehension; of a temper cool, equable and dispassionate; with a heart warmed by the feelings of benevolence, but firm and resolute; of manners dignified and commanding, yet mild and conciliating; a lover of temperance, decency and order; neither resentful, talkative, or familiar; but patient, persevering, and discreet to all in his conduct."[202]

The first convict sentenced to the New York state prison was Richard (alias Robert) Dawson, a twenty-eight-year-old white carpenter with a fair complexion and gray hair, who on April 22, 1796, received a life sentence in Albany for burglary. In May three more offenders were sentenced in Manhattan. David Green (alias Alexander Howard), twenty-six, an Englishman with a pockmarked face and a large mole on his right cheek, resided in Albany and listed his occupation as "clerk." Green was sentenced to life in prison for forgery, as was Amanda Coe, a silversmith from Litchfield, Connecticut, who was listed as being thirty years old, with dark complexion and black hair. Thomas Donnelly, a twenty-three-year-old seaman from Scotland who resided in Philadelphia, drew two years for grand larceny.

The first convicts were not received at New York until November 28, 1797. According to the state prison's original record book for 1797, of 123 persons committed to the prison, 92 were white men, 21 black men, 6 white women, and 4 black women. About 40 percent were listed as foreign born. Most of the 21 black men were slaves or former slaves, some of whom were identified only by their first name and owner; 3 were apparently originally from Africa, and most of the rest had been in New York for some time. Their listed occupations included farmer, laborer, tailor, cook, butcher, barber, hairdresser, blacksmith, mason, stevedore, and seaman. Two of the Negro females were girls who apparently had been domestic servants. The convicts' sentences ranged from one month to life, for offenses that included forgery, grand larceny, petty larceny, burglary, passing counterfeit money, stealing from a church, and manslaughter.[203]

Eddy favored reformation and felt that it was best achieved through "that system of regular labour and exact temperance by which habits of industry and sobriety are formed." Although he acknowledged that some offenders would not be easily or quickly reformed, he still thought that the chief aim of criminal punishment should be to eradicate the "evil passions and corrupt habits which are the sources of guilt." Like John Howard, he also insisted: "Cleanliness is the *very first* consequence, as order, and of course reformation, could not be supported without the *strictest* attention to it. It cannot be carried too far."[204] Accordingly, as soon as a new inmate was admitted, he or she was bathed, provisioned, interrogated, and told the rules. Prison regulations strictly prohibited uncleanliness, swearing, indecent language or vulgar stories, and quarrelling, and called for any infraction to receive immediate punishment by confinement in a solitary cell on bread and water.[205] Yet, that was the only mode of punishment allowed; Eddy even eschewed the use of irons and other common restraints. On the second day, the convict was assigned to the prison workshop.

Eddy's efforts to develop prison industry were also significant. Young Samuel Slater, the "creator of the American factory system," had recently started to develop industrial capacity in textile production at his Pawtucket cotton mill. Eddy tried to take some of Slater's ideas to a new level. The first industry he introduced was the manufacture of shoes and boots, inaugurated when a convict who had been a cobbler was used to instruct his fellow inmates. Soon there were about sixty shoemakers working at a long table, instructed by other inmates who had been trained in prison. Efforts were also made to utilize inmates' existing work skills at tailoring, weaving, gardening, cooking, and record keeping.[206] Prisoners were expected to labor alone or in small groups, without leaving their assigned area or communicating with each other. Assistant keepers supervised them closely. As soon as the convicts left work they were locked in their rooms with their fellow occupants. Watchmen moved throughout the prison during the night, lighting and extinguishing candles, checking locks, and performing other duties.

Eddy reportedly approved of the maxim that, to get labor from an animal, he should be fed good wholesome food, however coarse. "We find Rye coffee, sweetened with Mollasses, a very cheap & good Breakfast," he wrote. "Ox head soup or Dry cod fish & potatoes for Dinner and for Supper mush & mollasses. Cost of the whole 5 to 6 cents." Still, the kitchen was "conducted with as good management as in any public establishment in Europe."[207]

Developing successful prison industry took time, but progress was already evident by April 28, 1798, when William Dunlap visited with a small group of New Yorkers. Dunlap wrote in his diary that Eddy had escorted them through the partially built institution, where the workshops were still not finished and many "melancholy" prisoners were loitering without employment. But he added that "in the Hall & apartments devoted to those who make shoes, all looked if not well at least tolerable. All was clean, decent & orderly & the appearance of the victims approaching to cheerfulness."[208] Based upon his visit that October, Chancellor James Kent pronounced the operation "the most finished and best conducted institution of the kind upon earth." He added, "Thomas Eddy, the principal promoter and superintendent of the thing, deserves great credit, and will probably acquire lasting fame by the success of the scheme.

The Quakers are certainly the most spirited and active class of citizens in the community in promoting humane and benevolent undertakings."[209]

Eddy established religious worship in the prison chapel and encouraged local ministers to come and preach. The convicts sang psalms, read Scriptures, and prayed, in a solemn atmosphere. He also started a night school, with classes restricted to well-behaved convicts, who were charged four shillings' worth of extra labor to learn reading, writing, and arithmetic. He devised a system of incentives to improve inmate conduct and productivity. A well-behaved convict might get to see his wife and children every three months in the presence of a keeper. Inmates were also charged a set amount for their prison clothes, the expenses of their transport to prison, and fifteen cents a day for their maintenance. A convict clerk kept a daily account of each man's labor; he provided a weekly return to the prison administration, which entered the amount to the convict's credit. If an inmate had, according to the inspectors, maintained a record of good behavior, upon his discharge he could receive a share of the profits he had helped to generate.[210]

After only a year or two of operation, Eddy said he wished he had avoided congregate housing in favor of Howard's suggestion of separate cells. Although recognizing individual differences, he considered convicts "wicked and depraved, capable of every atrocity, and ever plotting some means of violence and escape."[211]

Prison escapes and disturbances had been almost routine before Eddy took office. His institution, too, had its share of problems. By the end of 1797 four "escapes" were listed. There were also four deaths, all involving inmates serving sentences for grand larceny.[212] In June 1799 fifty or sixty convicts revolted and seized several keepers as hostages. The takeover was put down by musket fire.[213] The following June saw another riot, which required military assistance to break up. The press reported that three or four ringleaders had been injured and a keeper knifed in the face.[214] On March 11, 1801, the common council noted that Eddy had appeared before it and reported that "several of the Prisoners had lately broken out & escaped & suggested the necessity of a small Guard to walk round the Wall of the Prison Yard during the night." As a result the board directed that eight additional watchmen equipped with firearms be employed and stationed at the state prison at the inspectors' expense.[215]

Eddy expressed frustration over the prison's apparent failure to reform many convicts. In 1798 a pair of former inmates was returned to the prison on a second conviction. The following year, another 2 were sent back. In 1800 the number grew to 9; in 1801 it reached 17. Of the 155 prisoners received in 1803, 25 were serving time for second offenses—15 for petit larceny and 10 for grand larceny. (Twelve of the 25 were black.)[216] One of the worst recidivists was Charlotte Thomas, a white woman who had originally been sentenced in New York on January 28, 1797, to four years for grand larceny, when she was twenty-eight years old. She was pardoned on July 14, 1800. Nine months later, she was recommitted for petit larceny and sentenced to two years. Shortly after her discharge she was arrested again and sentenced to three more years. Let out in 1805, she was recommitted again on August 12, 1806. After her release she was sentenced again for grand larceny, marking her fifth prison term over a period of sixteen years.[217]

Although such outcomes today might not seem so bad, at the time they appeared to signal failure. The inspectors were embarrassed to find that some inmates who had shown good behavior, and received freedom dues as a reward, had later committed further crimes and been sent back to prison. The inspectors felt hoodwinked. As a result, they adopted a new rule whereby even a prisoner who appeared meritorious was given only a trifling sum upon release. If, after three months of freedom, he could produce a certificate signed by creditable citizens to the effect that he had remained orderly, sober, and industrious, he might get more money.[218]

Eddy grandly predicted that the New-York state prison

> will furnish a model for others, which the increase of population
> and growth of luxury may render necessary in the distant parts
> of this extensive country. And, whatever may be the future condi-
> tion of mankind, this institution will reflect lasting honour on
> the State; become a durable monument of the wisdom, justice,
> and humanity of its legislators, more glorious than the most
> splendid achievements of conquerors or kings; and be remem-
> bered when the magnificent structures of folly and pride, with
> their founders, are alike exterminated and forgotten.[219]

In 1800, however, the Democrats swept the Federalists out of office, and the influence of the Quakers was diminished. By 1803, the prison's average daily population had soared to about 400, 109 were released when their sentence expired, 27 were pardoned, and 26 died.[220] That April, when Eddy was away on business, 20 inmates tried to escape by scaling the walls. The guard ordered them to stop. When they did not, the soldiers fired, killing four convicts, one of them an innocent bystander.[221]

Amidst the furor, Eddy's relations with some of the newly appointed inspectors became so unpleasant that he decided to resign from the board.[222] Shortly after Captain White Matlack replaced him as agent, a fire destroyed the roof of the prison's north wing; the institution remained plagued by problems for the rest of its existence.[223]

Whatever their shortcomings, the Walnut Street and New-York prisons had started a trend. By 1800, within the space of just a few years, new state prisons had been built in Pennsylvania, New York, New Jersey, Massachusetts, Kentucky, Vermont, Maryland, New Hampshire, Ohio, Georgia, and Virginia.[224]

The latter might have been called "Jefferson's Penitentiary," for during the Revolution he had suggested that the death penalty should be abolished for all offenses but treason and murder, to be replaced by penal slavery.[225] He had personally drafted some prison designs after plans by P. G. Bugniet of France, researching his project down to the finest detail. ("It has been suggested to me that fine gravel mixed in the mortar prevents the prisoners from cutting themselves out," he noted, "as that will destroy their tool.")[226] But his proposed penal code was considered too lenient, and it was not decided on until December 1786, when it still fell one vote short. Ten years later, Virginia finally authorized the construction of a new state penitentiary house capable of holding as many as two hundred convicts at hard labor. Benjamin Latrobe served as architect, using Eddy's advice and Jefferson's sketches.[227]

IMPRISONMENT FOR DEBT

BUT even though common criminals were being hanged or whipped or imprisoned at hard labor, higher-class offenders often managed to escape punishment, even when they had committed huge frauds. Many leading public officials, including President Washington, Secretary of the Treasury Hamilton, Governor George Clinton, Walter Livingston, Robert Morris, James Duane, Chancellor Kent, and John Jay, were implicated in shady land deals, and some of them also reeled from heavy debts that could have landed them in jail.[228] Yet most managed to avoid prosecution.

Alexander Macomb, the front man in the land scandal, went bankrupt and was imprisoned for debt. William Duer was said to have lost $2.5 million through speculation, setting off a financial panic, and his irate creditors forced him to seek refuge in jail.[229] John Pintard, secretary of New York's first insurance company, who had served during the Revolution as assistant commissary of prisoners in New York, also ended up being imprisoned, in Newark, from July 15, 1797, to August 6, 1798. General Light Horse Harry Lee went to prison for debt as well.[230]

The biggest fish to get caught was Robert Morris, "Financier of the American Revolution," and the richest man in the country. (As one historian put it, "The Revolution financed Robert Morris, not the other way around.")[231] Scarcely a decade after the war, Morris was unable to pay his personal debts.[232] Some of his creditors included Eddy's brothers, who would not forgive the debt. At their insistence, Morris was arrested on February 14, 1798, and taken the next day to Prune Street, the debtors' apartment at the Walnut Street jail. His sons offered to pay a high rent for a private room, but none was available, so he was housed in an apartment with other prisoners until he finally obtained his own cell. The family delivered a writing desk, books, a copying press, maps, a bed, furniture, looking glasses, and other items for his use. Prune Street prisoners sometimes were allowed to walk abroad, receive visitors, host dinner guests, and enjoy other privileges. Morris's wife and daughter often visited. Late in 1798, when he was in Philadelphia recruiting an army for a possible war against France, George Washington dropped by to see his old friend and they dined together in Morris's prison cell. Morris remained confined until 1801, when he was freed by a new law regulating bankruptcy. By then he had served three years, six months, and ten days in prison.[233]

In his diary covering this period, Thomas Eddy preserved an extraordinary letter bearing on some of these topics. It had apparently been sent to him by Thayendanegea (Two-Sticks-of-Wood-Bound-Together), the Mohawk leader also known as Joseph Brant, whom Eddy had gotten to know through his philanthropic activities.[234] Brant had been schooled in Connecticut and later educated at Dartmouth College, where he had translated the Bible into Mohawk. During the American Revolution he had fought for the British and was reported to have massacred American civilians. In one instance he was said to have been trying to interrogate a prisoner, became enraged because the man would not answer, and killed him with a single blow. Afterward, he learned the man had not been able to respond due to a speech impediment, and he always thereafter regretted what he had done. In his letter, however, Brant defended Indian people from charges that they were less "civilized" than whites.[235]

"In the government you call civilized, the happiness of the people is constantly sacrificed to the splendour of empire," he wrote.

> [A]mong us we have *no* prisons. We have no pompous parade of
> courts; we have no written laws, and yet judges are as highly
> revered among us as they are among you, and their decisions as
> much regarded. Property, to say the least, is as well guarded, and
> crimes are as impartially punished. We have among us, no splen-

did villains above the control of our laws. Daring wickedness is here never suffered to triumph over helpless innocence; the estates of widows and orphans are never devoured by enterprising sharpers. In a word, we have no robbery under the colour of law.

His letter continued:

The palaces and prisons among you form a most dreadful contrast. . . . Go to one of your prisons;—here description utterly fails. Kill them, if you please—kill them, too, by torture; but let the torture last no longer than a day. Those you call savages, relent; the most furious of our tormentors exhausts his rage in a few hours, and dispatches the unhappy victim with a sudden stroke. Perhaps it is eligible that incorrigible offenders should sometimes be cut off—Let it be done in a way that is not degrading to human nature; let such unhappy men have an opportunity, by the fortitude of their death, of making an atonement, in some measure, for the crimes they have committed during their lives.

. . . And will you ever again call the Indian nation cruel? Liberty, to a rational creature, as much exceeds property, as the light of the sun does that of the most twinkling star. . . . I had rather die by the most severe tortures ever inflicted on this continent, than languish in one of your prisons for a single year.

FROM CHATTEL SLAVERY TO PENAL SLAVERY

AT least one form of imprisonment seemed to have reached a crisis stage. Slavery appeared doomed. For many American slaveowners had become so threatened by slave insurrection, so haunted by their own guilty consciences, or, spurred by their disdain for racial mixture, so worried about what would happen when Negroes were emancipated, that they increasingly gave serious thought to deporting blacks back to Africa.[236] Jefferson had proposed removing slaves "beyond the reach of mixture" of free Negroes. But another Virginian, St. George Tucker, contended there were only three sensible options: "either to incorporate them with us, to grant them freedom without any participation of civil rights, or to retain them in slavery." Tucker himself favored some "middle course, between the tyrannical and iniquitous policy" of slavery and one that would "turn loose a numerous, starving, and enraged banditti, upon the innocent descendants of their former oppressors." He devised an intricate plan for gradual emancipation which held that female slaves who were born after the plan was adopted would not be free but would transmit the potential to be free to their offspring. Those children, in turn, would serve their mothers' masters until they were 28 years old, when they would receive freedom dues amounting to $20 and some clothing and then begin to enjoy the same rights as white indentured servants. Tucker figured that his plan would not end slavery for 105 years. Even then, Negroes should never be treated equally with whites: they would never be allowed to serve as jurors, lawyers, witnesses against whites, executors, trustees, public officeholders, or landholders (with a few limited exceptions). Nor could they ever marry whites.

Tucker's writings, especially a book published in Philadelphia in 1796, were widely circulated.[237] That same year, the New-York Manumission Society pushed legislation for gradual abolition, but the assembly defeated it on the grounds that it did not provide adequate compensation of masters.[238] (Compensating slaves for their losses was not considered.) In 1798 antislavery legislation passed the assembly by twenty-six votes but failed in the senate.

Finally, on March 29, 1799, Governor Jay signed a bill providing for the gradual emancipation of slaves in New York State.[239] (The vote had strictly followed party lines; the bill passed by 68 to 23 in the assembly and cleared the senate by 10 votes.) The measure provided that persons born after July 4, 1799, whose mothers were slaves were to be bound for service to their mother's master under the same conditions as children bound to service by the overseers of the poor, until they turned twenty-five if women or twenty-eight if men. A master entitled to the services of a young black slave under the law was allowed to release him before he reached the age of one year, and thereafter the child was to be supported as a pauper by the overseers of the poor. The new law had the effect of limiting slavery but not eliminating it, not immediately. Some New York Negroes would remain slaves for a generation. What was more, Negroes or anyone else could now be imprisoned and enslaved by the state as a punishment for crime.

State prisons in New York, Pennsylvania, and elsewhere were not created exclusively for blacks, but they were designed to arrest and counteract slavery's traits without ending slavery itself. Some of the barriers to slavery's abolition were also among the forces pushing the growth of imprisonment as a punishment for crime—sentiments such as the fear of large numbers of free blacks, a perceived inability to accommodate large numbers of newly liberated slaves in a free society, racial prejudice, fear of radicalism and revolution, the need for a cheap and servile labor force for the state, and the fear of crime. As a convenient means of forcing compliance, obedience, and performance, imprisonment remained crucial to the control and conditioning of free Negroes and other members of the labor force. Prison was intended to improve on slavery by eliminating slacking and economic inefficiency. It offered a setting that in some ways resembled slavery, but minus certain distasteful features, such as sexual licentiousness, irreligiousness, idleness, and unjustified captivity. Prison silence would replace plantation singing. Masters would now erect walls to keep the captives in, the opponents out, and the do-gooders in check, leaving it to the great masses of the general public to only imagine what horrors lurked inside. Instead of being bred on plantations, these prisoners would be kept celibate and prevented from multiplying. Rather than being enslaved, not for any fault of one's own, but for being a member of the Negro race, convicts now would be committed pursuant to conviction of a specific crime. Who could quarrel with that? Except in cases of particularly serious offenses, individuals would not be held for life, only for a set term of years. Persons would no longer be born into bondage; they would have to achieve it by their own illegal deeds. Individual masters would no longer own slaves, perhaps inherited with the livestock. Now, all citizens would relinquish such ownership to the state, and the state alone would serve as master and keeper. Such was the modus operandi of the new state prison.

Before the state prison was invented, imprisonment had entailed all sorts of pains for captives, but sexual abstinence was not necessarily among them. In the past, many prisons routinely had allowed inmates to be joined or at least visited by their wives or by prostitutes; indeed, many "holding" rooms had not been segregated by sex or policed to prevent sexual activity. Blacks and whites, young and old, healthy and ill, married and chaste, all were thrust together in the dark and in the light, sometimes beyond earshot of any prudish keeper.[240] As a result, early jails and prisons often were the scene of raucous and often promiscuous intercourse between prisoners and their spouses, prisoners and other prisoners, prisoners and keepers, or various combinations thereof.

This changed in the late eighteenth and early nineteenth centuries, when enforced sexual deprivation became a standard feature of penal policy. Convicts were cut off from their families, including spouses, barred from having any physical contact with another person. Now they were segregated by sex, often to such an extent that a male prisoner might spend entire years without ever seeing a woman or hearing her voice. Mates were torn from each other. Inside the prisons the sexes were kept separated. Closer surveillance was introduced to prevent any sexual liaison. And so, sexual deprivation became another cardinal feature of American imprisonment, joining other disentitlements like the denial of liberty, the loss of goods and services, and the loss of security and autonomy.

But prison sexual policy went further. Taking a cue from the gradual emancipationists, and sanitizing the sordid sexual arrangements of slavery, creators of the state prison demanded sexual abstinence from predominantly youthful males who were at the height of their sexual needs and at an age when they would normally be most likely to procreate. Sexual incapacitation of such young men and women was more than a denial of pleasure, it was a method of birth control in an age that lacked contraceptive options, a way of restricting and controlling the population growth of an otherwise fecund and troublesome class who in future generations threatened to become still more dangerous and costly to maintain. Above all, the state prison promised to sever sexual relations, once and for all, between the keepers and the kept, ending generations of sexual licentiousness and rape by slave traders, masters, and overseers—the kind of conduct that had given slavery a bad name.

These values were enhanced by the most fashionable contemporary economic theories. Influenced by Benjamin Franklin and other birth-rate pioneers, a celibate young English clergyman named Thomas Robert Malthus published his *Essay on the Principle of Population,* in which he postulated a universal tendency for populations to grow in geometric progression, doubling every generation or so unless they were checked, until they exceeded the earth's finite resources.[241] Malthusian theory predicted that millions of the earth's people would be driven to starvation or crime. Such grim forecasts led some policy makers to favor an "iron law of wages" that would help to hold workers at a bare subsistence level and serve to retard further population upsurges. More attention became focused on efforts to control marriage and procreation, especially where classes of "dependent" or "degraded" poor were involved. Malthus considered poverty as the best and most necessary stimulus to industry, and favored a system of laws and politics that would foster habits of sobriety, independence, and prudence. Malthusian influence immediately took hold at the end of the eighteenth century, just as American states were being formed, and reached its zenith in the 1830s and 1840s.[242] Malthus's theory buttressed the need for prisons.

Meanwhile, in all of the states, "free blacks" remained less free than free whites.[243] Generally, they could not vote. They could rarely obtain licenses for the trades, except the most menial. In the majority of states they were not allowed to testify in court against a white person or serve on a jury. In

Maryland, free blacks accused of attending noisy or suspicious meetings were eligible to be committed to jail unless they could prove their good behavior and furnish an acceptable guarantee that they would reappear to face charges. In the nation's capital, free blacks as well as slaves and "mulattoes" were subject to whippings for "nightly and other disorderly meetings."

Everywhere the burden was upon blacks to prove they were free, not on others to establish that they were not. Without a certificate of freedom or other evidence, any Negro was liable to arrest and imprisonment; those who lacked proof might be judged to be fugitives and sold into bondage. Ohio required free blacks to "procure and record a certificate of freedom and to give bond and security for the sum of $500 for their good conduct, and that they will not become a charge upon the township." New Jersey prohibited free Negroes from entering the state.[244]

One of the first prisoners to enter Virginia's still-unfinished state penitentiary was Gabriel Prosser, a twenty-eight-year-old slave. He had been arrested for trying to lead a major slave insurrection, planned for Henrico County on the night of August 30, 1800. A burly blacksmith who stood six feet, two inches tall and wielded a powerful intellect as well as a fiery temper, Gabriel claimed to have been inspired by the example of Moses leading his people to rise up against the pharaoh. According to the charges against him, Gabriel and his mostly urban followers had plotted to overthrow their masters, burn Richmond to the ground, take hostages, and carry out a chain-reaction liberation of rural slave plantations. The plan called for identified white oppressors to be secretly marked for retribution; Quakers, Methodists, and Frenchmen—those considered most sympathetic to the antislavery cause—would be spared and enlisted in the cause of freedom.[245]

But Gabriel's conspiracy had been betrayed by two of his fellow slaves, and his rebellion was delayed by a violent thunderstorm just long enough for Governor James Monroe to defuse it. Gabriel was captured in flight and taken to Richmond's new penal institution, where the keeper was ordered to place him in solitary confinement under constant watch and prevent him from having any communications whatsoever unless authorized by the governor. There, despite every means of persuasion that was used to get them to confess, he and his disciples stayed silent to the end. "The accused have exhibited a spirit, which, if it becomes general, must deluge the Southern country in blood," one alarmed Virginian who visited them in prison warned. "They manifested a sense of their rights, and contempt of danger, and a thirst for revenge which portend the most unhappy consequences."[246] Soon afterward, Gabriel was tried and executed with no less than thirty-four other slaves.[247]

Gabriel's failed rebellion prompted many prominent Virginians to reconsider various colonization schemes, including the development of a suitable receptacle for troublesome Negroes. Now that he had become president, Jefferson actively sought to find a means of unloading a wide array of problem blacks. On July 13, 1802, he wrote, "It is material to observe that they are not felons, or common malefactors, but persons guilty of what the safety of society, under actual circumstances, obliges us to treat as a crime." A few months later, Jefferson and Monroe arranged the Louisiana Purchase. Meanwhile, the Virginia House of Delegates favored creating a penal colony for rebellious slaves and free-black criminals. About the same time, a Philadelphia Quaker named John Parrish asked Congress to set aside wilderness lands as homesteads for Negroes, and another Quaker devised a complex scheme to maximize profits from such philanthropy.[248]

Gabriel Prosser's treatment stood in sharp contrast to what white criminals could expect at that time. In 1807 Aaron Burr, the former vice president of the United States under Jefferson and the acknowledged killer of Alexander Hamilton in a pistol duel three years earlier, was brought to the same Virginia State Penitentiary on treason charges. According to Burr's own account, the jailer there did not treat him badly. In fact, Burr wrote to his daughter, Theodosia, that his door would have remained unlocked but for his own concern for his safety, and he was allowed candles to keep reading late into the night. He was also showered with gifts of messages, oranges, lemons, pineapples, raspberries, apricots, cream butter, and ice, as well as some ordinary articles.[249] After receiving a fair trial, free of torture, Burr was ultimately acquitted of treason, and he returned to New York to practice law—quite a different fate from Gabriel Prosser's.

But slavery still demanded to be changed. In March 1807 Congress outlawed the international slave trade, effective January 1, 1808. Yet although the external slave trade was now illegal, the act did not apply to domestic slave trading, and it ignored those who already had been enslaved.[250]

Enactment of the new law, and Britain's prohibition of the international slave trade a few weeks later, temporarily relieved growing sectional tensions concerning slavery. But over the next few years, tensions between the United States and Great Britain escalated again. During the presidency of James Madison, Southern "war hawks" protested against what they claimed was Britain's continued impressment of American seamen, violation of U.S. territorial waters, and other abuses. War was declared. Once again, the British forces outnumbered the Americans, but this time they were too preoccupied with Napoleon to devote more than passing attention to North America.[251]

During the War of 1812, more than twenty thousand American prisoners of war, mostly captured sailors, were confined in British prisons; others were held at occupied sites within the United States.[252] On September 13, 1814, after British troops had attacked and burned the capital of Washington, an American lawyer named Francis Scott Key boarded a British ship near Baltimore to try to arrange for the release of one of the captives. As he watched the British bombardment of Fort McHenry, Key gained the inspiration to write the "Star-Spangled Banner."

During the war, ordinary convicts at the New York state prison and other recently founded penal institutions were pushed to new levels of productivity as the nation was spurred to meet the increased demands for domestic manufactures that had been brought on by the British embargo. This apparent industrial success may have encouraged some politicians to think that prison labor might somehow be made profitable in peacetime as well.[253] When peace was declared, in 1815, the surprising victory by the United States launched the nation into a period of profound change. Nationalist feelings increased. Americans gained a greater sense of mission. Victory also marked the beginning of American economic independence, much as the Revolution had signified American political independence.

With the end of the Napoleonic Wars, European emigration to the United States also resumed, introducing hordes of workers to fill the growing number of industrial jobs in New York and other cities. For the first time in several years, the supply of white skilled labor exceeded the demand. Newly arrived whites took over trades that might otherwise have become open to native-born free blacks. At the same time the cotton economy also expanded, with plantation slavery spreading south into Alabama and Mississippi as well as westward. A rationale for American expansionism was taking root. This would be the era in which modern capitalism and the modern state would come into being. The years after the War of 1812 would also bring increased repression, suppression of individual liberties, contempt for idlers and slackers, and heightened concern about inebriety, illiteracy, and pauperism.[254]

CHAPTER FOUR

Little Man in the Big House

AUBURN

ONE of the early white settlers of New York's rolling western frontier was Captain Daniel Shays, the leader of the unsuccessful rebellion. Another Revolutionary War veteran, Captain John L. Hardenburgh, arrived about the same time at nearby Aurelius, bringing with him his young daughter and two Negro slaves, Harry and Kate Freeman, who cleared the land and built a cabin on a site that came to be known as Auburn. Situated at the head of Owasco Lake, on the rutted wagon road used by westward-moving migrants, Auburn had become a county town in 1805, and it was incorporated as a village ten years later.[1]

In 1816, after the second triumph over Great Britain, the reins of New York's state government passed into Democratic hands, due in some measure to the party's victory in Auburn's own Cayuga County. At the time, sympathy toward criminals was so low that the state prison inspectors supported establishing a federal penal colony in the Pacific Northwest; if that was not feasible, they wanted to create a new prison in western New York. Auburn's local politicians capitalized on their newfound clout in the state legislature, where their own John H. Beach headed the assembly's prison committee, and a prison plan was adopted. Coincidentally, Beach was among the three local citizens authorized to build the new state prison at Auburn; the site they selected, of which Beach and his son, Ebenezer, were part owners, was located on the swift-running Owasco's outlet, at a point where a dam could generate valuable water power.[2] (As it would turn out, the soon-to-be-started Erie Canal would pass seven miles from the site.)[3] Besides getting approval for the prison, Beach and others secured from the legislature a coveted charter for a new Auburn bank.[4] A prison literally meant money in the bank; it would hold the convicts, and the bank would hold the fruits of convict labor. The bank would help to create the power structure and the prison would help to protect it.

Architectural plans, imitating the New-York state prison at Greenwich Village, were hastily drafted and approved.[5] Beach hired his longtime business associate, William Brittin, as general contractor, and he put as many local builders and workmen on the prison payroll as he could. A carpenter who knew nothing of masonry, Brittin was aided by Isaac Little, an experienced stonemason from New York City who already had erected several major public buildings; Little brought Ralph DeCamp with him as foreman.[6]

On June 16, 1816, a crowd huddled for the laying of the southeast cornerstone of the structure that was to be the Auburn prison wall. Unbeknownst to the proud politicians and clergymen who had come to break ground for the project, DeCamp had slipped in a bottle of whiskey and was murmuring a prayer for the prison's future occupants as thunder boomed from the heavens.[7] Subsequent excavations unearthed a Cayuga graveyard, and workers turned up piles of Indian bones, bits of ancient pottery, and utensils.[8]

By year's end, the foundations of the main building and the south wing were finished and the south wall had reached a height of four feet. Auburn prison faced north toward the village and stood only eighty feet from the main road.[9] In early 1817, the south wing was ready to receive its first convicts. Wagons arrived with manacled prisoners who had been brought from nearby county jails, and they too were put to work building the prison and the Prison Hotel across the street.[10]

Thomas Eddy had been instrumental in getting the legislature to appropriate funds for this new state prison, as well as for an asylum for the insane. During the next legislative session, in 1817, he helped to gain passage of legislation for the gradual emancipation of New York's slaves.[11] It provided that "every negro, mulatto, or mustee within this state, born before the 4th day of July, 1799, shall, from and after the 4th day of July, 1827, be free."[12] Once again, the waning of racial slavery and the waxing of the prison system were inextricably linked.

Captain Elam Lynds, a former military man, was hired as principal keeper at Auburn. Standing ramrod straight at six feet, one inch tall, with a slender waist and powerful shoulders, Lynds was an imposing figure who kept his wavy hair swept back from a large forehead and often wore a high beaver hat and a dark coat with knee-length tails that made him look even taller. He kept his face clean shaven, showing off a bulldog jaw and a jagged red scar that ran from his left eye to the corner of his mouth. His small dark eyes seemed to penetrate any gaze.[13] Born in Connecticut in 1784, Lynds had seen action at Lundy's Lane, been promoted to major and permanent captain in the Eighth New York, and finished the war as a battalion commander in the Eighth Division, regular army.[14] Upon leaving the military, he had returned to Troy to look for work and through his political connections there had landed a job at the emerging Auburn prison. He also practiced the hatting trade with Nathaniel Garrow, a prominent local politician.[15]

Lynds's arrival signalled harsher new methods at the prison, and Auburn's inmates did not accept their worsening fate without a struggle. In June 1818 many of them revolted and threatened to destroy the institution. Military force was summoned to quell the disturbance. Once order was restored, one hundred ringleaders were placed in solitary confinement on restricted status, but the uproar later resumed to such an extent that sentinels patrolling the walls were ordered to fire their muskets among the transgressors. This finally crushed the rebellion.[16]

In April 1819 stricter legislation was enacted that marked a drastic departure from Thomas Eddy's humane penal code. It empowered prison officials to put offenders on bread and water in solitary confinement, use irons or stocks, and whip up to thirty-nine lashes any male convict who violated prison rules. They could also employ convicts on public roads throughout the county.[17] As the new agent and keeper, the inspectors chose the contractor William Brittin, who had served as de facto warden since the project's inception.[18] John D. Cray, a young local architect who had recently lost all his possessions and was desperate for employment, was hired to oversee the prison's discipline and police; Lynds was put in charge of the prison's finances, setting him into immediate conflict with Cray.[19] Rumors arose that Cray had deserted his post during the war, and factions developed within the guard force.

One Saturday afternoon in October 1820, the roof of the unfinished north wing suddenly caught fire and flames threatened to engulf the main building. An inmate escaped during the confusion and others were caught apparently planning their flight. As nightfall approached, and a bucket brigade of local women continued to pass water to the embattled fire fighters, Brittin ordered the convicts back to their cells; they refused to go, so Brittin had them herded into their cages at bayonet point. After the blaze was extinguished, twenty-two prisoners were indicted for arson or attempted escape.[20] The incident prompted the formation of a New York State Prison Guard, armed and equipped to put down riots and other disturbances.[21] Soon afterward, Brittin fell ill, leaving Cray and Lynds to vie for control of

Auburn. Cray ended up resigning "with feelings of unkindness and morti-fication," and early in 1821 Elam Lynds was named agent and keeper at the handsome annual salary of $1,800.[22]

At the same time, the legislature authorized an experiment to determine how the prison regime should be organized. Auburn's inmates were di-vided into three classes: the most hardened offenders would be placed in constant solitary confinement as soon as the north wing could accommo-date them; a less dangerous group would be kept in solitary except when permitted to work in groups; and the "least guilty and depraved" would be allowed to work together in the daytime and be separated at night. Work was started on a small south wing, containing tiny cells that measured only 7 feet long by 3½ feet wide by 7 feet high. Each was designed to hold a single prisoner.[23]

Lynds tightened discipline, insisting on total obedience from convicts and staff alike. He issued each assistant keeper a "cat," the handles of which were made of common cowhide, about eighteen inches long, wound with leather, with six or nine strands about twelve or fifteen inches long, knotted at the end to keep them from unravelling. Lynds himself carried a long bullwhip that he kept looped and ready for use.[24]

His tough methods were quickly challenged. In one incident that spring, Lynds ordered three convicts to be whipped, but three keepers in succession refused to obey his command. Each keeper was summarily fired on the spot; finally, Jonathan Thompson, a blacksmith who was work-ing nearby, entered the fray and flogged the prisoners. That evening when Thompson left the prison he was greeted by a crowd of townspeople who'd heard about what had happened inside. The vigilantes ripped off Thompson's clothes, covered him with hot tar from head to toe, and car-ried him around the prison on a rail. The ringleader, Lewis Warren, skipped alongside Thompson with a shrieking hen under his arm, pluck-ing feathers and sticking them onto the hot tar. When the convicts caught wind of this commotion, some of them revolted and began setting fire to the workshops, but they were quickly restrained. Warren and three others were subsequently arrested, tried, and convicted of riot. Warren went free after paying a fine of $80; the others were held in jail for two months. As a result of the episode, Lynds's authority was bolstered.[25]

When a sufficient number of solitary cells were complete, on Christmas Day, 1821, eighty "hardened" convicts were put inside. Held in complete isolation, monitored day and night to keep them from communicating with anyone except the chaplain, they remained idle and alone in their dark cells and were even prevented from lying down in daytime, presumably to prevent muscular atrophy. The legislature also authorized Auburn's agent to furnish them with Bibles.[26] By January 1, 1823, at least five had died from "consumption" and forty-one were seriously ill. According to the prison physician, their "sedentary life in the prison, as it calls into aid the debilitating passions of melancholy, grief, etc., rapidly hastens the progress of pulmonary disease." Several had apparently gone insane. When one convict's door was opened, he sprang out and leaped from the fourth-floor gallery onto the stone pavement. Another was discovered to have bashed his head against the cell wall until he had destroyed one of his eyes. Another had slashed his veins with a piece of tin and bled to death.[27] Governor Joseph C. Yates personally visited the prison and was so horrified by what he saw that he pardoned some survivors on the spot.

Nevertheless, a number of government officials continued to believe in the need for strict security. News had recently arrived about the burning of a prison in Virginia, and authorities in New York City had narrowly quashed an insurrection attempt there. Some prison keepers argued that Eddy's old congregate housing arrangement had made them more vulnerable to the deadly contagions of riot and disease, and they called again for solitary cells.[28]

So, New York State instituted a radical new program. All convicts would remain housed in solitary cells at night, be prevented from communicating with each other, and subjected to strict military discipline. During the day they would have to labor at various industries within the prison, which was reorganized as an industrial center. A whole routine was developed to impose the regularity, discipline, and frugality of factory work. Although it was already commonplace in some British mills to lock the factory gates and impose absolute discipline over everybody inside, the fortress factory of Auburn prison would take such features to radical new extremes. "Industry, obedience, silence" were the guiding principles of the system.

Each arriving convict was admitted according to a carefully developed ritual. First his irons were taken off and he was stripped naked by other convicts (usually Negro men) under the watchful eyes of a keeper. Then he was subjected to a thorough cleansing process known as the "ceremony of ablution." Dunked into a huge wooden tub of hot soapy water, he was scrubbed and scoured of the filth and vermin he had brought from the county jail. His face was shaved and his hair was cropped. After being clad in a coarse, clean prison uniform, he was brought to the clerk's office, where a detailed description of him was taken and entered in the prison register. Each admission was assigned a number, his new identity. Then convict number such-and-such was brought to the agent's ornate office for a face-to-face meeting with his new master. Lynds surveyed him closely, then proceeded to interrogate him sternly about his actions, habits, and character. All the while, the agent made sharp remarks that were calculated to impress upon the new arrival his guilt and degraded status, the justness of his punishment, and the importance of his using his seclusion as a means of improving himself and showing deep repentance. Lynds instructed his subject in the prison rules and told him some of what would happen if he failed to obey. Convict dismissed!

An assistant keeper then assigned the convict to a trade and a cell. Each prisoner was packed into his own tiny room, which separated him from others like a cavity in a honeycomb. Convicts were forbidden to receive or send any letters or other intelligence. No relatives or friends were allowed to speak to a convict except in some extraordinary case, and then only in the company of the agent or a deputy keeper.

Auburn carried asceticism and frugality—other hallmarks of factory organization in the outside world—as far as possible, short of death. Its institutional regimen was made totally formal and impersonal, symbolic of the new industrial relationship. Persons were identified by numbers, uniformed, and treated to the extent possible as the gray, faceless cogs of a machine. Daily schedules and workplans became highly refined and were regarded as almost sacrosanct. Clocks, bells, whistles, and horns marked the time relentlessly. The common factory ban against talking during working hours was extended to all hours, and fiercely enforced. Keepers and foremen who did not abide by and uphold the rules faced immediate dismissal. Written regulations admonished keepers to "refrain from singing, whistling, scuffling, loud immoderate laughter, provoking witticisms or severe sarcasms" and forbade turnkeys to curse at each other when convicts were present.[29] Any inmate who failed to submit to the prison's rigid rules or who committed any other violation faced severe punishment. Auburn's discipline, one official explained, "takes measures for convincing the felon that he is no longer his own master; no longer in a condition to practise deceptions in idleness; that he must learn and practise diligently some useful trade, whereby, when he is let out of the prison to obtain an honest living."[30]

In January of 1825, a prestigious three-member inspection committee reported that, compared to free workmen, convicts

> have no cares, incumbrances, or extra labor, or burdens of any
> kind . . . no families to provide for . . ., no interruptions of any
> kind; and all possible means are provided to enable them to
> work to the best advantage: such as excellent shops and imple-
> ments, and the utmost personal accommodation, with the exact

and regular supply of every article wanted. If, then, the prisoner
who is master of a trade, does not accomplish as much work as
an out-door workman, it is merely because he will not. The question then, between such a prisoner and the public, is simply,
whether he shall be compelled to do it, or be supported by the
community in comparative idleness.[31]

Prison officials took extraordinary measures to try to ensure noninter-
course and industry among the convicts. At night this involved holding
them in separate cells under close guard. The challenge was greater during
the day, when the prisoners were congregated at work. But the need was
all the more practical, since unsupervised convicts were known to try to
commit sabotage by spoiling their work. Tight supervision was economically unfeasible, since it would require almost as many keepers as convicts.
One way such control was attempted at Auburn was by constructing secret
"inspection avenues," which, according to one account, consisted of "narrow passages along the back part of the shops, and separated from them
by only a thin board partition, through which are cut, at short distances,
along the whole length of the shops, numerous small apertures, for the
purpose of looking through from the avenues upon the convicts in the
shops." These avenues were built to admit only a little light and had stationed within them several officers, wearing moccasins, who constantly
crept from one end of the prison to the other, spying on the shops, without
being seen or heard by any of the convicts or keepers. Noting that the
secret corridors had proven "a most effectual guard against forbidden
intercourse among the convicts," the legislative committee added: "[N]o
convict knows, at any time, but that the invisible eye of a keeper is fastened
directly on him. Thus the apertures of the partition between the avenue
and the shop, are like so many eyes constantly fixed on the convicts; and
the effect is, to make them feel, at all times, that any violation of the rules
of the institution, whether under the eye of their shopkeeper or not, must
be at the risk of incurring a severe penalty."[32]

Public visitors were also allowed to tour approved sectors of the prison,
provided they paid a twenty-five-cent visiting fee. This charge was imposed, not only to generate revenue, but to keep away a "certain class"
who "overthronged the prison"—the class from which most of the convicts
and their families had come; in France the class that had stormed the Bastille.[33] The practice also extended surveillance to include the citizens at
large, many of whom now delighted in peeking at the hapless convicts
through secret watchposts.

Every convict movement, from work to cell and back again, or from work to dining hall and back, had to be performed in a regimented manner. Prison authorities invented a method of marching known as the lockstep, which called upon the convicts to become interlocked into a human chain that kept them in strict formation to prevent any communication between them. One prison official said the lockstep was designed "to give the spectator somewhat similar feelings to those excited by a military funeral; and to the convicts, impressions not entirely dissimilar to those of culprits when marching to the gallows."[34] In time the word "lockstep" became a household expression for a method or procedure that was mindlessly adhered to or that minimized individuality.

Many visitors were astonished by what they saw. A British tourist who observed Auburn's dining hall later wrote that he would have supposed it "morally impossible" for so many people—635 at the time of his visit, 22 of them women—to be congregated in one spot with so little noise and confusion.[35] And a Boston clergyman who visited Auburn in 1826 found it a shining example of what could be accomplished by proper discipline and design. "The whole establishment, from the gate to the sewer, is a specimen of neatness," he wrote. "The unremitted industry, the entire subordination and subdued feelings of the convicts, have probably no parallel among an equal number of criminals." Reverend Louis Dwight and his associates in prison reform said that after "wading through the fraud, and material, and moral filth" of other prisons, they felt pleasure in contemplating such a "noble institution" and added: "We regard it as a model worthy of the world's imitation."[36]

A HINT OF SCANDAL

BUT Auburn was not perfect. This became plain shortly after Lynds had left town to supervise the building of a new state prison (Mount Pleasant, or Sing Sing) in Westchester County. The scandal involved a female convict, Rachel Welch, who had died in the prison on January 12, 1826, only a few days after giving birth to a child who had apparently been conceived while she was being held in solitary confinement. Upon autopsy Welch's body showed signs that she had been whipped, even though state law specifically forbade the flogging of women convicts.

Newspaper reports prompted investigations by the local district attorney and the state senate. They established that Welch, an Irish immigrant, had been sentenced at Rochester shortly after arriving in the country, and she had entered Auburn prison on January 5, 1825. Because her sentence also included a requirement of three months' solitary confinement, she had to be isolated even from the other female convicts, who, unlike the men, were generally congregated in an upstairs attic and not subjected to strict rules of silence, separation, and industry. As it turned out, the only suitable single room for her was a second-floor storeroom—Number 15—located above the keeper's hall and heated by pipes leading from the keeper's stove below.[37]

The senate inquiry found that Welch had been impregnated in early March, about two months after she had entered No. 15. Any sexual access to her, by anyone, during that period was an abuse and a violation of her sentence of solitary imprisonment. So, one question was, who was the father?

Some prison employees testified that John White, a convict cook, usually was assigned to bring Rachel her meals. The normal procedure called for a keeper to stand at the foot of the stairs and watch White as he ascended with her food and exchanged the dishes and tubs. However, the committee added, "There is some testimony leading to a suspicion that this duty was not always observed with perfect vigilance."[38] At least one guard claimed that Welch and White were later discovered to have carried on a personal relationship, with romantic overtones. Yet, years later, a local minister alleged in print what others had only whispered: that Lynds himself was the father.[39] The senate committee did not go that far, but it did not exonerate him, either. "We are perfectly aware, and justice requires us to mention," they wrote, "that Mr. Lynds was to our knowledge absent a considerable part of the session, in the spring, on public business; and towards the latter part of the session, in the spring, and during the examinations regarding the new state prison, and the preparations for the work, we ourselves engaged a good deal of his attention, and kept him from his charge." They added, "Still, neither he nor ourselves could understand that he was the less obligated to have the prison kept with all due vigilance; and we are bound therefore to say, that the exposed condition of Rachel Welch's room, or at the least the exposure from the keeper's hall, amounted to an abuse, for which Mr. Lynds stands responsible."[40]

But pregnancy was only part of the scandal. Rachel Welch had also been beaten, in violation of the law of 1819 that expressly forbade the whipping of any female convict.[41] In her case the treatment was more outrageous because she had been whipped when pregnant.

Upon completing her term of solitary, Welch had been moved to the south wing, second story, No. 7, with the other women convicts. The whole department was under the control of Ebenezer Cobb, an assistant keeper who had lost an arm defending his country at the Battle of Lake Champlain. Cobb acknowledged that Welch had complained she was pregnant. Therefore, he had referred her to the prison physician, Dr. Erastus D. Tuttle. Cobb said Dr. Tuttle had responded that she was a "troublesome, outrageous hussey" and had prescribed a whipping as treatment. Welch had also used lewd, profane, and abusive language toward her keepers and thrown bowls of mush and other objects from her cell, according to Cobb. Finally, he said, on July 27, he went to her cell with a cowskin whip. He swore he had struck her only a few strokes on her bare shoulders and a few more over her knees as she sat on her bed. Cobb claimed he had brought with him two Negro convicts, to help defend himself, but under questioning he acknowledged that, as convicts, they could not legally be considered as competent witnesses.

Dr. Tuttle testified that Welch had later told him she had been held down by the two Negroes while Cobb whipped her very severely. He also described having found injuries that were much worse than those Cobb had admitted inflicting. During this examination conducted after her flogging, Dr. Tuttle said he had discovered that she was five months' pregnant and that she was suffering from high fever, uterine hemorrhage, labor pains, inflammation and swelling of the back, shoulder, thighs, and loins, and other problems. Dr. Tuttle said he and another local physician, Dr. Leander B. Bigelow, had commenced treatment immediately and bled her several times.

In September, Welch had become sicker and threatened to miscarry, but she ultimately went to term and delivered a baby in prison on December 5. A month later, after showing signs of being angry and despondent and walking bare-footed on the cold stone floor, she had contracted pneumonia. She died on January 12, 1826.[42]

Within a few days, Cobb was convicted of assault and battery and fined $25, but allowed to stay on the job.[43] More investigations followed, but they were hampered because convicts could not present evidence. Testimony conflicted over whether the whipping or other abuses had contributed to Welch's death. Nothing was said on the record about the fate of her baby.

A grand jury found that Auburn's keepers had been permitted to flog inmates without a higher official being present, a violation of state law. Yet neither Lynds nor any other prison authority was prosecuted; as a result, the use and intensity of flogging drastically increased.[44]

Reforms of New York's imprisonment of women were slow in coming. Proposals for a separate penitentiary for women were rejected by the legislature on the grounds that Auburn prison relied on female inmates to do its washing, ironing, and mending.[45] Auburn did not hire a matron for the women convicts until eight years after Welch's death.[46] Meanwhile, state inspectors continued to describe the women's quarters as "a specimen of the most disgusting and appalling features of the old system of prison management at the worst period of its history."[47] (New York's first separate prison building for women would not open until 1839, and the first separate women's prison was not erected until 1893.)[48]

In the wake of the Welch scandal, a writer in Auburn's *Cayuga Patriot* commented: "It is impossible that the people of this country should feel wholly indifferent to an institution officered by our own citizens and located amongst us. If abuses exist, shall we not sound the tocsin of alarms?"[49]

ILLUSTRIOUS VISITORS TO SING SING

M ANY Americans of the day took pride in what apparently had been accomplished in their model new prison systems, which were merely one of innumerable "internal improvements" then occupying the country. For its part, New York led the way in developing vast plans for turnpikes, canals, railroads, bridges, schools, houses of refuge, and other institutions. The fact that some convicts did not always appreciate their new abodes did not tarnish the allure they held for many of their free countrymen. On the contrary, whatever prisoners appeared to loathe the most often held the greatest popular appeal.

Inspection of American prisons by the public had become, like zoo visiting, a popular form of recreation, and many convicts resented being put on display.[50] But being subjected to stares was not the only public humiliation that convicts in Massachusetts endured. In 1815 the directors of the Charlestown prison had declared that discipline "should be as severe as the laws of humanity by any means tolerate." One of the things they came up with was to dress inmates in parti-colored uniforms—one arm was red, the other blue, one leg was green, the other gray—that were designed to increase mortification and the chances of recapture if its wearer ever escaped. Convicts were also permanently tattooed with the words "Mass. State Prison."[51] Other states followed suit.

Maine went to extremes to keep its convicts out of sight and out of mind. Its state prison, at Thomaston, had been founded by Dr. Daniel Rose, a physician who insisted that prisons should be as dark and comfortless as possible. He designed underground cells that could be entered when a rope ladder was lowered through a two-foot-square hole. Convicts were planted inside like so many potatoes.[52]

Most early-nineteenth-century penal institutions were anything but "model" places. Boston's Reverend Louis Dwight, who had been so impressed with Auburn's "perfect order," visited the District of Columbia jail as a roving agent for the American Bible Society and was particularly aroused by a sight he came upon in a small room containing three women and four children. Two white females were wrapped only in blankets, "like Indian women," and when he looked in they tried to hide. The children— three mulatto brothers and their sister, ranging from four to twelve years old—had been imprisoned without a parent to keep them from falling into the hands of slavetraders. Their father, a white man, was dead, and his slave—their mother—was unable to protect them. Although their father's last will had given them their freedom, his executor had sought to sell them to clear his debts, and the local marshal had committed the children to prison to save them from bondage. There they languished in darkness and filth, unable to wash themselves. Dwight reported that the little girl was ill and sprawled on the floor without any bedding, surrounded by her brothers. The minister said he regretted he could do nothing to help them. "I have seen so many in similar circumstances," he wrote, "that I am constrained to go on my way with an assurance, that when I shall bring before the church of Christ a statement of what my eyes have seen, there will be a united and powerful effort in the United States to alleviate the miseries of prisons."[53] True to his word, he founded the influential Boston Prison Discipline Society in 1826.[54] Published reports by Dwight's group and other organizations were widely distributed, drawing more important visitors from abroad.

On May 11, 1831, two French magistrates arrived in Manhattan to begin a tour of American prison systems on behalf of the French government. Alexis de Tocqueville, twenty-six, was generally interested in observing America's political system during this period of profound economic and political change. Even though he would eventually use the observations made on this trip as the basis for his two-volume work, *Democracy in America* (1835, 1840), at the time of the journey he privately confided: "Intellectually, I have an inclination for democratic institutions, but I am an aristocrat by instinct—that is to say, I despise and fear the mass. . . . I have a passionate love for liberty, law, and respect for rights—but not for democracy."[55] Tocqueville's maternal grandfather and an aunt had been imprisoned and guillotined during the French Revolution. Both his parents had also been imprisoned.

His friend and travelling companion, Gustave de Beaumont (three years his elder), was also a writer; like Tocqueville, he had prosecuted some criminal cases and visited some French prisons before coming to America.

Prison was not his primary concern, either, for Beaumont was most interested in slavery, which he would later explore in a novel, *Marie, ou l'esclavage aux États-Unis: Tableau des moeurs Américaines* (1835).[56]

While they were in New York City, Beaumont and Tocqueville visited the House of Refuge, the Bridewell, and Blackwell's Island penitentiary. (Thomas Eddy's state prison was no more, having been transferred to the custody of the city in 1828 and later closed.) Wherever the two Frenchmen went, they dined and socialized with members of the local elite, gathering anecdotes, books, and other materials.

On May 29, they set off on a tour of New York State, starting up the Hudson River to Sing Sing, where the biggest prison in the United States—Mount Pleasant prison—had been erected by convicts under Elam Lynds's direction. Sing Sing was becoming famous for its strict discipline and sound management, and lately its appeal seemed to be entering another dimension—the prison actually appeared to be making a profit for the state.[57]

Mount Pleasant was nestled in idyllic surroundings along the east bank of the Hudson, thirty-three miles north of New York City and ten feet above the high-water mark, at one of the most picturesque spots that Tocqueville and Beaumont would ever encounter in America. The prison's nearness to the water, however, also allowed the institution to drain its foul discharges directly into the river, prompting one sarcastic ex-convict to remark, "Hence, it appears that that place is well selected for the purposes for which it is intended."[58] The area was the site of extensive marble beds and former silver- and copper-ore deposits. Local legends figured in many Washington Irving stories. The prison could be approached by vessels drawing twelve feet of water, which made it ideally situated for stonecutting. In fact, extensive excavation was going on there. Explosives were used to break open the ground, and convicts lugging heavy sledgehammers pounded and pounded and pounded the rocks, leaving large marble chunks to be transported from the quarries to the prison yards. To accomplish this, four to six convicts were yoked to a cart, and a heavy block of stone was fastened to it; they were forced to haul the load away by brute strength—a practice that many visitors found repulsive.[59] When the marble had been finished in the yard for market, convicts loaded it onto ships for transport to New York, Albany, and other ports. In time, Sing Sing marble would adorn many churches, city halls, banks, and other respectable buildings.

Mount Pleasant prison covered 130 hilly acres. At its southeast corner, the keeper's large house—a three-story marble mansion—commanded a good view of the river, the prison, and its quarries. Running north and south along the river was the famous cellblock, five stories high, 480 feet long, and only 44 feet wide, containing 1,000 separate cells.[60]

As they spied the colossus and its workshops, Tocqueville and Beaumont were shocked not to see any outside walls. (They had not yet been added.) Although convicts were laboring in an open courtyard and nearby quarries without balls or chains, and were under a remarkably light guard, the Frenchmen were immediately struck by the prisoners' absolute silence and extraordinary discipline.[61] Likewise, an Englishman who had toured the site a few years earlier had been amazed to find only two armed sentinels pacing along a hilltop that overlooked two hundred "hardened ruffians" at work in complete order and subordination. "There was something extremely imposing in the profound silence with which every part of the work of these people was performed," he had written. "During several hours that we continued amongst them, we did not hear even a whisper, nor could we detect in a single instance an exchange of looks amongst the convicts, or what was still more curious, a sidelong glance at the strangers."[62]

Beaumont later wrote to his mother that "the guardians well appreciate their numerical weakness, and as they are 30 against 900, they must at each instant fear to see a revolt break out." But he added, "It's that which generally makes them just in the punishments they inflict; they understand that every oppression of theirs might bring on a rebellion." Beaumont went on to ask: "But if they are materially the stronger, have they the same moral force as the small number of individuals charged with watching them? No, because they are isolated, one from the other. All strength is born of association; and 30 individuals united through perpetual communication, by ideas, by plans in common, by concerted schemes, have more real power than 900 whose isolation makes them weak."[63]

The main prison was as long and slender as a ship, its numbered stone cells stacked in rows. Five hundred faced east and five hundred faced west, with a hall in between. The cells were even smaller than Auburn's, measuring only 6' 7" high, 7' long, and 3' 3" wide—hardly big enough to allow an occupant to pace two or three steps, provided he shuffled sideways to avoid the elevated plank that served as a bunk. The tiny rooms were dirty and damp. Their heavy iron doors were made to swing outward, allowing scant light and air to come in through the small openings on top. Newcomers complained about the smells. Other than blankets, and the convict with the clothes on his back, the only other contents were a Bible, a gill cup, a pint cup, a spoon, and sometimes a comb. It was in that cell that all sleeping, eating, and other bodily functions took their course. The convicts were normally marched one-by-one to the kitchen to get their little tub of food (a keeper with a cudgel stood by to rap anyone who tried to snitch extra rations) from a conveyer belt that was cranked by hand from the kitchen. Eventually one convict invented a new lever-lock system with elaborate bolts and pulleys connected to an iron bar. Stretching 250 feet long, it enabled a single keeper to lock or unlock fifty cell doors in the time it previously took to operate one, thus reducing the load on staff resources and reducing convict movement time.[64]

Almost since its inception, Sing Sing had received the services of a full-time chaplain, whose salary was paid by private donations. The chapel could accommodate nine hundred persons. After holding divine service there, the Reverend Gerrish Barrett spent several hours speaking to the men in their cells. "I have found no one yet, who showed any disrespect, or unwillingness to hear what was said," he reported. "It is surprising to see, sometimes, how a few minutes' conversation, concerning the soul, will make the muscles of a hardy-looking face relax, and his eyes fill with tears." Every evening at 7 P.M., Barrett stood near the center of the ground floor of the hushed cellblock and shouted the Scriptures in a booming voice that echoed through the hall. This was usually followed by a brief sermon.

Sing Sing's chaplain also taught selected convicts to "read" the Bible by having them do rote memorization of selected verses. He calculated that his pupils, during one 18-month period, had recited 770 chapters containing 19,328 verses. One convict had successfully committed 1,296 verses to memory; another, 1,605. At the time of Tocqueville's visit, only 60 to 80 of the 900 convicts were admitted to the prison Sunday school. But, Tocqueville noted, "A poor Negro, who had learned to read in the prison, recited by heart in front of us two pages of the Bible, which he had studied in his leisure hours of the week, and he did not make the slightest mistake in memory."[65]

Tocqueville jotted in his diary that the current chaplain, Mr. Prince, "likened the warden [Robert Wiltse] of the establishment to a man who has tamed a tiger that may one day devour him."[66] Although the Frenchmen spent nine fascinating days at Sing Sing, trying to understand it, Wiltse did not allow them to interview any convicts and they did not record any abuses.[67]

Had they spoken with convicts or ex-convicts, they might have gained a different impression. Colonel Levi S. Burr had served three years in Mount Pleasant for perjury and had later written a book about his experience, claiming he was innocent and detailing all kinds of brutal and inhumane treatment. Burr argued that Americans had a general sense of what justice was being administered in the courts, because trials were open to public view, but citizens could never know what really went on inside Sing Sing, because it was closed to scrutiny. Unlike Auburn, there were no inspection avenues. Burr claimed that not even the prison inspectors fully knew what happened in the prison; they only knew what the agent told them. Consequently, people could only learn from the "pen of some unfortunate sufferer who has tenanted that horrid place." As far as he was concerned, if the public learned what went on there, Sing Sing would fall like the Bastille.

Burr called Sing Sing's government a "Cat-ocracy and Cudgel-ocracy." The frequency and intensity of the floggings varied according to the will and temper of the keeper at that moment. Burr estimated the usual dose at from 20 to 50, 70, 80, 90, or more lashes. He wrote: "On one occasion I counted 133; and while the afflicted subject was begging upon his knees, and crying and writhing under the laceration, that tore his skin in pieces from his back, the deputy keeper approached and gave him a blow across the mouth with his cane, that caused the blood to flow profusely; and then, as if conscious of my feelings at beholding so barbarous a spectacle, turned and faced me with an agitated stare."

Burr also described the lockstep from the convict's vantage point: "The keeper, with his cane or cudgel in his hand, raises this proud ensign of authority, and orders, Step! Go on! If the novice happen to step off left foot first, with the rest of the company, and do not break his step (imitating, or rather mocking, a military drill), he passes very well. But if the *novice* either by ignorance, or want of use, once mistakes his step, the company is then halted, and he is reprimanded in the harshest terms."[68]

The publication of Burr's exposé in 1833 unleashed a torrent of horror stories about Sing Sing's alleged abuses. Some convicts were said to have received over four hundred lashes with the cat-o'-nine-tails. Keepers admitted sticking hot pokers into prisoners' cells; beating convicts for making slight noises in their cells or for talking or smiling or refusing to work; and slopping salt and vinegar or beef brine onto wounds. An insane prisoner ate his own excrement until he died. A convict was flogged for asking for clean trousers. Public reports described the flogging post as consisting of two iron rings fastened into a prison wall, next to piles of cats and rawhide gags. Some keepers fashioned their own cats using strands of wire so as to better lacerate convict skin, but most preferred cudgels.[69]

Next to beating, hunger was the worst suffering endured by Sing Sing prisoners, particularly since they worked so hard at manual labor. Meat rations were seldom larger than a hen's egg. Survivors told of eating roots, weeds, grass, or clay.[70] Such complaints continued for years. One former convict, James R. Brice, depicted the year 1837 as "a general time of starvation throughout the whole prison" and recounted how convicts who asked for more food were flogged.[71]

Horace Lane had spent five years as a convict in Sing Sing and was there when Tocqueville and Beaumont visited. He later recalled being repeatedly awakened at night by the sound of a hammer nailing up coffins: "it was a dismal sound in their cells, and to hear them rapping on their iron doors, (you know how they rap with their spoons on the door, when they want a keeper), and groaning when they were taken, how awful a sound!"[72]

Official statistics confirmed a high rate of mortality at Sing Sing compared to most other American prisons. Some attributed the high incidence of deaths to cruelty by particular keepers. But most observers simply suggested that the prison's spartan living conditions, severe discipline, and slave-labor practices, which contributed to the death rate, were the result of an unchecked desire to make a profit. Many more convicts left the prison alive, but broken in health and spirit.

Under the labor arrangement then in effect at Sing Sing, the state owned only the bare walls of the prison workshop, with the prison contractors functioning as "the owners of the slaves and stock" and "owners of the prisoners." The contractors purchased from the state the labor of a certain number of prisoners per month, pledging their property in the shops as security in the event that they defaulted on their monthly payments. Besides operating a marble shop, contractors employed convicts at shoemaking, hatmaking, and carpentry, and they maintained a blacksmith shop, a brass foundry or saddler's stirrup shop, and other industries, depending upon what businessmen contracted with the state. James Brice went so far as to say that Sing Sing was not really a state prison, but "a monstrous individual speculating, money-making prison, where these very contractors are pocketing the hard earnings of the convicts, except the trifling monthly payment they make to [Warden] Robert Wiltse." Levi Burr likened the prisoners' treatment to that of slaves at Tripoli, except that Sing Sing's slaves were treated more cruelly.

Bit by bit, through these accounts the prison took on the appearance of a slave plantation. The prison "overseers" were paid about the same amount as their Southern counterparts. Some resorted just as much to the whip, and they were expected to record their floggings in punishment logs like those that were kept down South. Keepers and clerks dutifully recorded data about each and every convict as he or she was acquired, substituting in their neat ledgers "sentence" columns for "price." Prison authorities increasingly began using slavekeepers' devices, such as iron masks and other restraints, that could be ordered through the agricultural journals.

Militant labor leaders in the Northeast already were complaining that

New England mill hands and other workingmen were in worse economic condition than European laborers or Southern slaves. Groups of mechanics throughout New York State alleged that convict labor was being used to undercut law-abiding workers. Some demanded that convicts should not be permitted to learn any new trades while in prison, since that would give them an unfair advantage over honest journeymen and apprentices. Many assailed the philosophy of reformation of prisoners, saying that it provided rewards and incentives for lawbreaking. These critics also charged that there was rampant corruption and fraud in the awarding of prison contracts.[73]

In June 1835 the stonecutters of New York City banded together to protest the use of Sing Sing convicts to build a university and several private houses there. Tempers flared and troops were finally called out at Five Points to disperse the malcontents. The soldiers remained encamped at Washington Square for four days and four nights.[74] In such an atmosphere, an English visitor predicted that Sing Sing might remain profitable for many years to come, provided that New York's developing labor organizations did not overturn it as unfair competition. Certainly, lawbreaking in New York City would continue to supply Sing Sing with inmates, he said, so that "crime and luxury will thus feed each other, and the marble that now lies peaceably under Mount Pleasant, will be torn from its bosom by the outcasts of that city it is destined to enrich and embellish."[75]

AN INTERVIEW WITH ELAM LYNDS

B EAUMONT and Tocqueville had heard many colorful stories about Elam Lynds. According to one tale, a convict was overheard to swear he would kill him at the first opportunity. When Lynds learned of the threat, he sent for the prisoner, ordered him to come into his bedroom, gave him a straight razor, exposed his own throat, and demanded to be shaved. The convict obeyed. When he had finished the job, Lynds looked him in the eye and said: "I know you intended to kill me, but I despise you too much to believe that you would ever be bold enough to execute your design. Single and unarmed, I am always stronger than you are."[76]

The two Frenchmen were so intrigued that they wanted to meet him. At the time, he was politically out of power and not affiliated with any prison. However, his harsh prison methods still attracted intense public interest at home and abroad, and Beaumont and Tocqueville considered him a major figure in American prisons. Lynds was an archetypal autocrat, who in many ways resembled and modeled himself after the two "great men" of his age, Napoleon Bonaparte and Andrew Jackson. Like them, he was a military man, rigid and erect; he was extremely disciplined and he required discipline from everyone below him. He also demanded absolute authority to do what he deemed correct and fiercely resisted sharing any power whatsoever. He prided himself on being a self-made man, a man of determination and iron will, strength, and courage, and he was totally convinced of the moral rightness of his cause.

When they finally met him, they were disappointed. "He was dressed like a salesman and performed the duties of one," Tocqueville noted.[77] At first Lynds could not be interviewed because he had no one to watch his hardware store. But he later joined them at the inn where they were staying, and they had a fascinating conversation that Tocqueville recorded as close to verbatim as possible.[78]

Lynds said he had spent the last ten years of his life involved in prison administration. "I have been for a long time a witness of the abuses which predominated in the old system," he told them; "they were very great." He explained that "[p]risons then caused great expenses, and the prisoners lost all the morality which they yet had left."

Based upon his experience, he said the director of a prison must be invested with an "absolute and certain power"—a state of affairs that, he conceded, was often at odds with the spirit of a democratic republic. "My principle has always been, that in order to reform a prison, it is well to concentrate within the same individual, all power and all responsibility. When the inspectors wished to oblige me to act according to their views, I told them: you are at liberty to send me away; I am dependent upon you; but as long as you retain me, I shall follow my plan; it is for you to choose."

One of his guests asked, "What is then the secret of this discipline so powerful, which you have established in Sing Sing, and of which we have admired the effects?"

"It would be pretty difficult to explain it entirely," he responded. "The point is, to maintain uninterrupted silence and uninterrupted labour; to obtain this, it is equally necessary to watch incessantly the keepers, as well as the prisoners; to be at once inflexible and just."

"Do you believe that bodily chastisement might be dispensed with?"

Lynds shook his head. "I am convinced of the contrary. I consider the chastisement by the whip, the most efficient, and, at the same time, the most humane which exists; it never injures health, and obliges the prisoners to lead a life essentially healthy. Solitary confinement, on the contrary, is often insufficient, and always dangerous. . . . I consider it impossible to govern a large prison without a whip. Those who know human nature from books only, may say the contrary."

"Don't you believe it imprudent at Sing Sing, for the prisoners to work in an open field?"

"For my part, I should always prefer to direct a prison in which such a state of things existed. . . . [I]f you have once completely curbed the prisoner under the yoke of discipline, you may, without danger, employ him in the labour which you think best."

"Do you really believe in the reform of a great number of prisoners?"

Lynds chose his words with care. "We must understand each other; I do not believe in a complete reform, except with young delinquents. Nothing, in my opinion, is rarer to see [than] a convict of mature age become a religious and virtuous man. I do not put great faith in the sanctity of those who leave the prison. . . . But my opinion is, that a great number of old convicts do not commit new crimes, and that they even become useful citizens, having learned in prison a useful art, and contracted habits of constant labour. This is the only reform which I have ever expected to produce, and I believe it is the only one which society has a right to expect."

"What do you believe proves the conduct of the prisoner in the prison, as to his future reformation?"

"Nothing. If it were necessary to mention a prognostic, I would even say that the prisoner who conducts himself well, will probably return to his former habits, when set free. I have always observed, that the worst subjects make excellent prisoners. They have generally more skill and intelligence than the others; they perceive much more quickly, and much more thoroughly, that the only way to render their situation less oppressive, is to avoid painful and repeated punishments, which would be the infallible consequence of insubordination; they therefore behave well, without being the better for it. . . . [Prisons] are filled with coarse beings, who have had no education, and who perceive with difficulty ideas, and often even sensations. . . ."

"Which is, in your opinion, the quality most desirable in a person destined to be the director of prisons?"

"The practical art of conducting men," Lynds replied. "Above all, he must be thoroughly convinced, as I have always been, that a dishonest man is ever a coward. This conviction, which the prisoners will soon perceive, gives him an irresistible ascendency, and will make a number of things very easy, which, at first glance, may appear hazardous."

Beaumont and Tocqueville later expounded Lynds's views in their book about American prison systems, *On the Penitentiary System in the United States and Its Application in France* (Philadelphia, 1833), writing that "[w]hile society in the United States gives the example of the most extended liberty, the prisons of the same country offer the spectacle of the most complete despotism."[79] Their report included statistics indicating that Negroes were disproportionately overrepresented in American prisons. In states where whites outnumbered blacks by thirty to one, the prisons nevertheless contained one Negro for every four white persons. These statistics led them to several conclusions. First, they assumed a connection between race and crime, claiming that the "states which have many Negroes must therefore produce more crimes." (Yet, that reason alone could not validly explain the phenomenon at work in America. After all, a majority of Negroes were being held in the South in slavery, where most of their offenses were privately punished by masters rather than by government.) Beaumont and Tocqueville also contended that "we should deceive ourselves greatly were we to believe that the crimes of the Negroes are avoided by giving them liberty; experience proves, on the contrary, that in the South the number of criminals increases with that of manumitted persons; thus, for the very reason that slavery seems to draw nearer to its ruin, the number of freed persons will increase for a long time in the South, and with it the number of criminals." In other words, rather than finding slavery to be a criminogenic factor, capable of producing rather than restraining crime, Beaumont and Tocqueville actually cited manumission as a special cause of crime; moreover, they thought that *emancipation* increased the number of persons subject to imprisonment. "The slaves, as we have seen before, are not subject to the Penal Code of the whites; they are hardly ever sent to prison," they explained. "To manumit a slave, therefore, actually amounts to introducing into society a new element of crime."[80]

When it came to examining the background and lot of New York's convicts, Beaumont and Tocqueville's accounts were woefully incomplete. Institutional logs containing information about the convicts who were imprisoned in Auburn at the time of their visit actually are more revealing. Some typical entries read:

No. 421—D.B.—(Mulatto girl.) True name is D.J. Age 21; born in Schoharie County; her mother was a slave; knows nothing of a father; ran away from her master when she was 14, and has been in trouble ever since; in Ballston jail 30 days for petit larceny; has had a child which died in three months; became a common prostitute; no education. Convicted of petit larceny, 2d offence, in Rensselaer county, June 1, 1827, and sentenced 3 years. Discharged by expiration of sentence.

No. 467, a black man from Greene County who was a slave until Emancipation Day, jailed for stealing an umbrella. . . .

No. 471, a Mulatto who refused to reveal his real name. . . .

No. 488, a 35-year-old Negro male, has been a slave; brought up in perfect ignorance, and disregard of everything serious. . . .

Prison records such as these offer some telling insights into prevailing American values. A bigamist, for example, was released after serving a sentence of four years. This was more than the time served by a father of seven who had raped a ten-year-old girl, but not nearly as much as the forty-two-year sentence handed out to a Jewish forger. The convicts' personal histories cataloged a different side of the American experience than was ever presented in newspaper accounts or history books.

Many already had been imprisoned numerous times in their lives. By 1831, No. 409—a fifty-eight-year-old convict from Massachusetts—had been in New York prison five times for an aggregate of twenty-six years' confinement. No. 431, whose father was in the Ohio State Prison, had been discharged as an eighteen-year-old after serving three years for petit larceny, second offense, but within a few weeks he was back in prison again. Likewise,

> No. 404—E.J.—Aged 40; born in New-Jersey; lost his parents when an infant; brought up by his grandfather, at blacksmithing; no early education; has learnt to read a little late years, and can write his name after a fashion; has had a great deal of trouble in his day; in 1818 was convicted of jail breaking and assaulting the jailer, in Genesee county, and sentenced 8 years; pardoned in about 5; was 2 years in solitary; soon after his discharge, was in this county jail 30 days, for stealing blacksmiths' tools; in 1825 was convicted, in this county, of stealing three or four young cattle, which he "was driving along without intending any thing wrong," and sentenced 5 years. Says he was never addicted to any very bad habits. Discharged by expiration of sentence, March 11, 1830. This man has lately been overtaken "driving along" some cows, and is on his way back to prison for the third time.

By the end of their sentence, some prisoners showed signs of derangement, either real or feigned, though it was unclear how many may have gotten that way because of their imprisonment. Some appeared to have improved during their confinement, such as those who were listed as having learnt to read, write, and cipher in the prison's Sabbath school. Others were discharged as bad or worse than when they entered, such as an inmate who claimed to have been unjustly convicted and was described by the prison authorities as "a bad convict" who "goes out full of revenge," or another prisoner about whom it was simply said: "He has been a hard convict." Convict No. 411 had been attacked by another inmate, but he had taken away the assailant's knife and stabbed him with it several times, for which he was sentenced to spend three years of his term in solitary.

Sing Sing's principal keeper told a legislative committee that his convicts "must be made to know, that *here* they must submit to every regulation and obey every command of their keepers." This often prompted testing by the prisoners. Keepers had to respond immediately and with as much force as they could muster. Any attack on a keeper by an armed convict, in the presence of other inmates, was considered an assault against the discipline of the prison, for it jeopardized not only the life of the individual keeper but the government of the entire institution. That was why it could never be allowed to succeed. In all such cases, it was necessary both to subdue the offender and to make an example of him. Otherwise, there could be no discipline and no order.[81]

PENITENTIARY

UNLIKE Auburn and Sing Sing, Pennsylvania's Eastern Penitentiary was intended to keep convicts apart even as they worked. It was meant to be the culmination of John Howard's ideas for a pure penal institution that would totally separate offenders from all forms of earthly corruption, contamination, or infection and enable them to repent and be reformed. Thus the term "penitentiary."

Eastern's planners had wanted its exterior to "exhibit as much as possible great strength and convey to the mind a cheerless blank indicative of the misery which awaits the unhappy being who enters within its walls."[82] The whole design and construction sought to impart a severe and awful character to its face, producing an effect on the imagination of every approaching spectator that was "peculiarly impressive, solemn, and instructive," and conveying a picture like that of some magnificent medieval castle. The architect John Haviland won the contract over his rival, William Strickland, in 1821, and his creation was finally "opened" for its first convicts in October 1829.[83] So successful was the design that a distinguished architectural critic, writing in the *Metropolitan Museum of Art Bulletin* in

1955, declared that "this prison comes nearer to being a work of art than any other building of its kind."[84]

Eastern Penitentiary was perched on the site of a former orchard called Cherry Hill, on the outskirts of Philadelphia.[85] Surrounded by a gigantic wall, thirty feet high, twelve feet thick at its base and two and one-half feet wide at its top, with crenellated towers, a façade composed of large blocks of hewn, squared granite, and a massive iron gate, Haviland's entrance was said to be "the most imposing in the United States." The wall alone had cost over $200,000—an extraordinary sum for any American public structure at that time, much less for a prison exterior.

The challenge of its interior was to devise individual cell arrangements wherein prisoners could be kept in absolute solitary confinement without being driven insane or physically broken and debilitated beyond repair, such as had happened at Auburn. It was the largest, most expensive structure in America, full of many remarkable innovations.[86] Every cell contained taps delivering running water, plus a new invention: the flush toilet. (One champion delicately hailed it as a "novel and ingenious contrivance [that] prevents the possibility of conversation, preserves the purity of the atmosphere of the cells, and dispenses with the otherwise unavoidable necessity of leaving the apartment, except when the regulations permit.")[87] Flues conducted heated air from large underground cockle stoves to each living area, though in winter the temperature inside the cells rarely rose above sixty degrees.[88] Individual yards enabled the convicts to exercise one hour per day, and some were allowed to use their yards to grow vegetables or flowers.[89]

A black hood was drawn over the head of every arriving prisoner, blotting out any glimpse of the exterior world or the winding interior route leading to the lonely tomb where he would pass his entire sentence. (The hood would remain in use until 1904.)[90] Even an awareness of the prison's size or configuration was shrouded, and the newcomer could not tell where he was in it. His world changed. From that point, all identity was left behind and he became a number. His name and other personal information were recorded in a book accessible only to the warden and the prison chaplain. Every convict wore a coarse cotton uniform. Hair was cut short. All contact with family or friends, whether in person or by letter, was eliminated. Any communication with persons other than prison staff was prevented, though some convicts devised tapping codes for transmitting messages via the plumbing or heating pipes or tossed crumpled messages to each other over the exercise area walls. All contact with the outside world effectively ceased. The only official visitors allowed in the penitentiary included the governor, members of the senate and house of representatives, the secretary of the commonwealth, the judges of the supreme court, the attorney general and his deputies, the president and associate judges of all the state courts, the mayor and selected city officials, and board members of the prison society. Penitentiary officials said the separation was so complete that a convict might remain unaware that a cholera epidemic was spreading panic outside the walls, or never know that his best friend had been incarcerated in the adjoining cell for the last two years.[91]

A convict knew only his own cell. Measuring 11' 9" long, 7' 6" wide, and 16' high—about twice the size of Sing Sing's—each room consisted of plastered whitewashed walls and a small, solid door of sturdy oak and grated iron with a specially constructed feeding drawer and peephole. When opened, the drawer allowed food to be passed in and out of the cell; when closed, it folded into a small table. The device was designed in such a way as to prevent the convict from catching even a glimpse of anyone outside, while the tiny aperture enabled a keeper to observe him at will. There, in a silent and isolated tomb, the penitent prisoner ate, slept, defecated, worked, and thought, day and night, week after week, month after month, year after year. According to the prison inspectors, the convict should regard this solitary cell as "the beautiful gate of the Temple leading to a happy life and by a peaceful end, to Heaven." The only source of natural light in that cell was a tiny hole, eight inches in diameter, in the ceiling. If punishment was required, that too could be sealed off.[92] An occupant was allowed to have a Bible, a slate and pencil (and under certain conditions other books, and pen and ink and paper), as well as a razor, a plate and can, and a basin. During the day his bed was turned up against the wall to allow more room for using a loom, bench, wheel, or other work equipment.

Auburn's inmates were kept separate at night but forced to work together at hard labor during the day. At Eastern, convicts were not prescribed work as punishment; labor was seen as a reward, a privilege, which an inmate fervently requested to relieve himself from complete, maddening inactivity. A prisoner worked by himself, if he was lucky. If he was not lucky, he did not get to work at all. In fact, many convicts complained that Sundays seemed even longer than workdays because they were not allowed to labor on the Sabbath.[93]

Both the Auburn and Philadelphia systems were predicated upon a belief in the changeability of inmates, and as such both embodied a new flowering of the reformative ideal in American prisons.[94] The two systems relied on silence, separation, discipline, regimentation, and industry to achieve positive human change. Perhaps because they were so much alike, their proponents became engaged in a fierce rivalry, as if they were competing for nothing less than the approbation of the civilized world.

Beaumont and Tocqueville visited Eastern Penitentiary eight times over twelve days in October 1831, two years after it opened. They said it was "incontestable that this perfect isolation secures the prisoner from all fatal contamination."[95] Eastern's officials were stunned when Tocqueville asked for permission to interview each convict alone in his cell without a keeper present, but they were so convinced of their system's merits that they granted his wish. Not only was he allowed to tour the institution but to his credit he privately conversed with forty-six inmates in their solitary cells, pencilling meticulous notes about what he found.[96]

When Tocqueville asked one veteran convict whether he thought the new penitentiary was superior to the old prison, the man replied, "It is as if you asked me if the sun were more beautiful than the moon."[97]

Venturing deeper into the interior, Tocqueville came upon a light-skinned Negro in excellent health. He had become the penitentiary's first convict nearly two years earlier. Of No. 1, he wrote:

> This man works with ardor; he makes ten pair of shoes a week.
> His mind seems very tranquil; his disposition excellent. He con-
> siders his being brought to the Penitentiary as a signal benefit of
> Providence. His thoughts are in general religious. He read to us
> in the Gospel the parable of the good shepherd, the meaning
> of which touched him deeply; one who was born of a degraded
> and depressed race, and had never experienced any thing but
> indifference and harshness.[98]

No. 28, a convicted murderer who denied his guilt, said his only companion was a cricket that had entered his cell a few months ago. "If a butterfly, or any other animals, enters my cell," he said, "I never do it any harm."[99]

Deeper inside still, No. 41, a young man who could not stop crying, blurted that he was happy nobody could see him there and sobbed that he could only hope of one day returning to society without being rejected. No. 35, more than eighty years old, kept reading the Bible as the Frenchman entered his cell.[100]

A couple of years later, after having operated the penitentiary for about four years, Eastern's inspectors offered some observations about a convict's desired adjustment process.

We mark, generally, that at first the prisoner indulges in morose
or vindictive feelings, and is guilty of turbulent and malicious
conduct; but after a few weeks he adopts a more subdued tone,
becomes reasonable, and his countenance indicates a more ami-
able state of mind; is disposed to talk of his past life as one of
misery and folly; begins to think that the barrier between him
and a good reputation is not impossible; and that there are those
in the community, whose prejudices against the condemned are
not so strong as to induce the withholding a friendly countenance to his attempts at restoration. In many, the retrospect of
life becomes a horrible and loathsome subject of reflection—
the sense of shame and feelings of remorse drives them to some
source of consolation, and the ordinary means of stifling an
actively reproving conscience being denied by reason of their
solitariness, the comforts of the Bible and the peace of religion
are eagerly sought for.[101]

Nevertheless, some convicts still engaged in forbidden behavior. One of
the most common evils was the "secret vice" (masturbation), which Dr.
William Darrach, the prison physician, cited as a leading cause of insanity,
suicide, chronic pleurisy, and pulmonary tuberculosis.[102] To deter it and
other misconduct, Eastern's staff utilized all sorts of punishments, ranging
from starvation diets and denial of work, to the use of straitjackets, "iron
gags," and ducking in the shower bath, to immurement in the dark cell or
the "mad chair."[103]

After the suspicious death of convict No. 102 (Matthew Maccumsey) in
1833, an investigating committee described the iron gag as "a rough iron
instrument resembling the stiff bit of a blind bridle, having an iron palet in
the center, about an inch square, and chains at each end to pass around
the neck and fasten behind." They explained:

This instrument was placed in the prisoner's mouth, the iron
palet over the tongue, the bit forced back as far as possible, the
chains brought round the jaws to the back of the neck; the end
of one chain was passed through the ring in the end of the other
chain drawn tight to the "fourth link" and fastened with a lock;
his hands were then forced into leather gloves in which were
iron staples and crossed behind his back; leather straps were
passed through the staples, and from thence round the chains of
the gag between his neck and the chains; the straps were drawn

tight, the hands forced up toward the head, and the pressure consequently acting on the chains which press on the jaws and jugular vein, producing excruciating pain, and a hazardous suffusion of blood to the head.[104]

In Maccumsey's case the device was "so forcibly fastened that his blood collected and suffused up into his brain and he suddenly died under the treatment."[105]

The "shower bath" was not much better. It consisted of the repeated dumping of cold water from a considerable height onto an exposed convict who was under restraint. According to an official investigation into the case of Seneca Plumley, "In the depth of winter, he was tied up against the wall attached to his cell by the wrists, while buckets of extremely cold water were thrown upon him from a height which partly froze on his head and his person, and he was shortly after discharged as incurably insane."[106] (Eastern was by no means alone; prisons throughout the United States used the shower bath for decades to come.)

The "mad chair" had been invented by the "father of American psychiatry," Dr. Benjamin Rush.[107] It was so called because the contraption resembled a large boxlike chair, into which a (usually mentally disturbed) prisoner was strapped and bound in a manner that prevented his body from resting, which caused extreme pain.

Eastern's most astute observer was a thirty-year-old English novelist, Charles Dickens, who visited the institution on March 8, 1842.[108] Like Beaumont and Tocqueville, he toured the penitentiary's dreary passages under official escort, sometimes pausing to hear the profound silence that was broken only by the faint, almost imperceptible sound of a lone weaver's shuttle or the taps of a shoemaker's hammer. He spent a whole day passing from cell to cell, talking with inmates.[109]

The first man he saw was working at a loom. Convict No. 1066 wore spectacles and a paper hat. When addressed, the man paused for a long time and spoke very deliberately. He said he had been there for six years and was due to remain three more. Convicted of receiving stolen goods, second offense. Insisted he wasn't guilty. Dickens noticed the fellow had painted some figures on the wall, including a female form over the door whom he called "The Lady of the Lake." Dickens noticed his lip trembled when the subject of his wife was raised, after which the man shook his head, turned aside, and covered his face with his hands. "Time is very long, gentlemen, within these four walls!" he said.

Far into the block, pungent smells drifted from the vicinity of an inmate

who apparently was allowed to keep rabbits in his cell. When he was called
into the sunlight, the prisoner appeared haggard and unearthly pale, and
he was clutching and stroking a white rabbit at his breast. Dickens thought
his manner resembled a rabbit's.

He found others. A tall, strong black man, who had been born a slave
and imprisoned for burglary. A just-arrived English villain, who, Dickens
felt, gladly would have stabbed him if given the chance. A swarthy mariner
who wrote poetry. A "fat old Negro" whose leg had been amputated in the
penitentiary, and who was being attended by a fellow inmate who was "an
accomplished surgeon." A thirteen-year-old colored boy. Three beautiful
young light-skinned black women, all convicted of conspiracy to rob the
same man. A mulatto sailor—No. 58—looking helpless and crushed, who
had been imprisoned there upward of eleven years; now near the end of
his term, he was addicted to peeling the skin from his fingers.

Dickens later wrote that he was impressed by the prison's "perfect
order" and accepted as admirable the motives of those who governed. But
he believed Pennsylvania's system of rigid, strict, and hopeless solitary confinement was, in its effects, "cruel and wrong." He held

> this slow and daily tampering with the mysteries of the brain,
> to be immeasurably worse than any torture of the body, and
> because its ghastly signs and tokens are not so palpable to the
> eye and sense of touch as scars upon the flesh; because its
> wounds are not upon the surface, and it exhorts few cries that
> human ears can hear; therefore I the more denounce it, as a
> secret punishment which slumbering humanity is not roused
> up to stay.[110]

INDIAN REMOVAL

DEALING with white transgressors and blacks was one thing, but
how to cope with a huge population of American Indians was
another matter. When Jefferson had purchased Louisiana, he had been
exploring plans to remove free blacks to remote sections of the country
west of the Mississippi River. But the scheme was deemed unfeasible, and
besides, some advocates of colonization preferred Africa instead.[111]
Numerous proposals were made for sending convicts abroad, but they
never bore fruit. Large-scale Indian removal to remote sections of the west,

on the other hand, seemed much more appealing—the Indians occupied land that whites wanted.

The usual process called for the government to make a treaty with a particular tribe and purchase specified parts of its lands. The Indians would then receive some new territory in which they could settle, and occasionally get some assistance in moving. That, at least, was how it was supposed to work.

In 1828, after gold was discovered on Cherokee territory, the State of Georgia quickly nullified all existing treaties and imposed a series of humiliating and restrictive laws on the tribe, who, since Oglethorpe's day, had been considered the friendliest and "most civilized" of the Southern Indians. Like the Georgia slave codes, the new laws barred Indians from testifying against whites and held that no Indian legal claim would be considered valid.[112]

A few months later, Andrew Jackson, the tough old Indian fighter whom Seminoles knew as "Sharp Knife," was elected president of the United States, due in large part to Southern support. Jackson concentrated on the five Southern nations—the Seminoles, who inhabited lands that contained mineral deposits and other valuable resources, and the Creek, Choctaw, Chickasaw, and Cherokee. The principal states involved were Georgia, Alabama (created as a state in 1819, mainly from Cherokee and Creek land), and Mississippi (created in 1817, mainly from Choctaw and Chickasaw country).

In his annual message to Congress in 1829, Jackson squarely addressed the Indian question, claiming that former policies had simply caused the Indians to recede westward while retaining their "savage habits." Unless something was done, he warned, the Choctaw, Cherokee, and Creek would quickly succumb to the same fate as the Mohegan, the Narragansett, and the Delaware. Thus, for the sake of humanity and justice, he proposed to remove Southern Indians to ample districts west of the Mississippi, "and without the limit of any State or Territory now formed, to be guaranteed to the Indian tribes as long as they shall occupy it, each tribe having distinct control over the portion designated for its use."[113]

Jackson sought and obtained congressional approval to uproot the Indians. Congress passed the Indian Removal Act of 1830, which authorized the president to negotiate with the tribes for their relocation.[114] The law took effect that spring.

Under the new federal policy, the Creeks were quickly defrauded. Six months after signing their treaty, the nation's council told the U.S. secretary of war: "Instead of our situation being relieved as was anticipated . . ., we are surrounded by the whites with their fields and fences, our lives are in jeopardy, we are daily threatened. . . . We have for the last six months lived in fear, yet we have borne it with patience, believing our father, the President, would comply on his part with what he had pledged himself to do."[115]

Driven to starvation, the Creeks finally revolted; in 1836 their resistance brought down military action. As a result, nearly two thousand of them were taken prisoner. Their eighty-four-year-old leader, Eneah Emathla, was manacled and forced to march away with them, but he never uttered a complaint.[116]

Some Cherokees refused to leave their reservation in Georgia and took their claims to court. Chief Justice John Marshall ruled that the governments of Georgia and the United States were duty-bound to honor Cherokee land claims, and he affirmed the tribe's legal right to its reservation. But Georgia ignored the ruling and Jackson refused to enforce it, thus encouraging more white traders to enter the area with federal blessing. The Indians had won their case in the U.S. Supreme Court, but the white governments had refused to comply with their own law. Although the Cherokees had violated no federal or state laws, it was they who were treated like criminals.[117]

Black Hawk, an elderly chief of the Sauk nation, refused to retreat, leading his followers back across the Mississippi in an attempt to reclaim their lands in Illinois, which had been taken from them by squatters the year before. The fighting that ensued became known as Black Hawk's War. But in 1832 the old chief was captured and taken east to prison; put on display, he died in captivity in 1838. The governor of the newly created Iowa Territory exhibited Black Hawk's skeleton in his office.[118]

Eventually, the remnants of the five Southern tribes were marched under military "escort" from their ancestral lands all the way to what is now Oklahoma. Cholera broke out along the route, creating an infected corridor through which the unknowing Indians were moved. Many died. The removal was supposed to have been gradual, but in 1838 General Winfield Scott's troops rounded up masses of disconsolate Cherokees and herded them into camps. From there the prisoners were pushed west. On the long winter trek, one of every four Cherokees died of cold, disease, or starvation. An estimated twenty-five thousand Indians perished on this journey, which came to be known as the Trail of Tears.[119]

In the case of the Seminoles, Jackson's policies represented the culmination of more than twenty years of federal conflict with the tribe. In 1818 Jackson had personally led a large expedition against them in the First Seminole War. After Spain had ceded Florida to the United States, and the federal government had begun to pursue its plan of Indian removal, the

Seminoles, under their young chief, Osceola, had refused to emigrate. Federal troops were sent to evict them and a bloody war ensued. After years of fighting, while they were under a sacred flag of truce during a peace conference, Osceola and his supporters were taken prisoner. He died in a military prison three months later. By 1838, it had cost the U.S. government over $20 million to remove nine hundred Seminoles and three hundred blacks (mostly fugitive slaves) from the contested lands. The remaining Seminoles retreated into the swamps and fought a guerrilla war for five more years. When the last of the Seminoles finally surrendered in 1842, the latest war had cost the United States $40 million, and the lives of more than two thousand soldiers and an unknown number of Seminoles and their black allies.[120]

By the mid-1840s, virtually all land east of the Mississippi was safely in white hands. Under the doctrine of Manifest Destiny, white Americans were taught to believe that they were fated to inherit the rest of the continent, from the Atlantic to the Pacific.

REFORM

MEANWHILE, in their first annual report, published in 1826, the managers of the Boston Prison Discipline Society had cited the "degraded character of the colored population" as the foremost cause of crime in the United States. The only support they offered for their conclusion were official prison statistics: the population of New York State was only about 1/35th black, but about 1/4th of its 637 convicts were Negroes; in Massachusetts the proportions were 1/74th and 1/6th; in Connecticut they were 1/34th and 1/3rd; New Jersey's were 1/13th and 1/3rd; and Pennsylvania's were 1/34th and 1/3rd. On this questionable basis, it was asserted that "neglecting to raise the character of the colored population" was responsible for increased crime.[121]

Tocqueville also had noted that race—"the physical and permanent fact of color"—had become "fatally united" with "the abstract and transient fact of slavery," and vice versa, so that the "tradition of slavery dishonors the race, and the peculiarity of the race perpetuates the tradition of slavery."[122]

Slavery in the United States had receded, but the prejudice beneath was proving immovable. Some commentators observed that it actually appeared to be worst in areas where slavery had been abolished. As one Scottish visitor to the North put it, "chains of a stronger kind still manacled their limbs, from which no legislative act could free them; a mental and

moral subordination and inferiority, to which tyrant custom has here subjected all the sons and daughters of Africa."[123] Notions of black inferiority
remained too deeply ingrained to be wiped away.

It was in this context that the British Home Office commissioned William Crawford, forty-three, a London wine merchant and philanthropist
who was secretary of the London Prison Society and a prominent antislavery figure, to investigate prisons in the United States. He was "to ascertain
the practicality and expediency of applying the respective systems of which
they are governed, or any parts thereof, to the prisons of this country."[124] In
his report of 1834 Crawford recounted the usual objections against solitary
confinement, including the argument that such an approach was "unequal
in its effects, operating with greater severity upon active than upon sluggish
minds." Ultimately, however, he favored the Pennsylvania system over the
Auburn plan.

Following the lead of the Boston Prison Discipline Society, Beaumont
and Tocqueville, and others, Crawford presented voluminous statistical
evidence regarding prison systems throughout the United States. His findings showed that at least two-thirds of the states had at least one state
prison, but that most of those without one were in the slaveholding South.
"It is impossible, upon examining the prisons to which these Tables refer,"
he wrote, "not to be struck with the great proportion of crime which the
coloured bears to the white population." Like the earlier investigators,
Crawford concluded that the "causes are too obvious" and was quick to
add: "The force of public opinion has in a remarkable degree contributed
to retard the education and moral improvement of the coloured race.
Hence these oppressed people form . . . the most degraded class of the
community. This prejudice appears to me to be, if possible, stronger in the
free than in the slave States." He went on to say: "From a feeling which
is unknown in Europe, a coloured person, although residing in the most
enlightened of the States, is prevented from attaining that position in society to which his natural intelligence, aided by the benefits of education,
would inevitably raise him. Under such circumstances the only wonder is,
that there should not be more crime among a population so numerous,
and so disadvantageously situated."[125]

E. S. Abdy, another Englishman, who toured the United States from
April 1833 to October 1834, offered still more penetrating insights into the
systems of slavery and prisons.[126] Using terms that were especially popular
with antislavery campaigners, Abdy decried America's "aristocracy of the
skin" as an abomination. Prejudice and discrimination against blacks, he
wrote, "form a barrier to a more liberal and humane intercourse, which
none but the most generous or the most vile among the whites can break

through." One might have expected that the Irish, who had themselves been subjected to persecution, would have shown more sympathy toward blacks and victimized them less, but Abdy found their racism to be more virulent than the norm. Yet racism was not limited to Irish laborers—it pervaded American society. He found it among the trustees of the New-York Manumission Society, who paid higher salaries to white teachers than to black ones, regardless of qualifications or performance. And racism was painfully visible to him in the city's illustrious but racially segregated House of Refuge, which he was shown by Dr. David Hosack, brother-in-law of Thomas Eddy (who had passed away in 1827).[127]

On November 27, 1833, Abdy visited runaway slaves who were being held in the New York City jail. He learned of a recent case in which a runaway Negro with eight or nine children in New York had escaped by boat to that state, only to be reclaimed later and condemned to death in Virginia for stealing the boat. As far as Abdy was concerned, "It was exactly as if a man whose horse had been stolen had gone off with the horse, and had afterwards been executed for stealing the bridle that happened to belong to the thief."

Abdy looked at the so-called greater criminality of blacks in a different light than had most other writers up to that point, noting that some of the racially disproportionate imprisonment in the "free states" may have been due to the difficulty free Negroes had in finding employment there. He pointed out that in Virginia, where work was more easily obtained, there were fewer convictions for crime among that class than in Massachusetts, "where so many departments of honest industry are closed against them." Besides a lack of employment, he added that "ignorance, and the difficulty of finding unprejudiced witnesses and juries, have led too many of this unfortunate race to the prisons and penitentiaries of the country." What kind of society was it, he asked, that exposed blacks to greater temptations and offered fewer rewards for good conduct, then treated honest men like criminals?

He might have also pointed out that, even in the Northern states, blacks were still not allowed as jurors and their standing as witnesses was sharply limited. There were no black governors, legislators, judges, prosecutors, lawyers, police, wardens, principal keepers, chaplains, keepers, or prison contractors. No wonder that Negroes were considered more criminal.[128]

Among those to accompany Abdy when he visited Sing Sing was a famous young Prussian intellectual, Francis Lieber, a veteran of Waterloo, who had twice been imprisoned in Europe for political reasons. He had later emigrated to the United States and become the editor of the *Encyclopedia Americana*.[129] Already well known for his translation of Beaumont and Tocqueville, he had also coined the word "penology," which he defined as "that branch of criminal science which occupies itself . . . with the punishment of the criminal, not with the definition of crime, the subject of accountability and the proving of the crime, which belongs to criminal law and the penal process."[130]

Lieber asserted that human progress had been most retarded in the organization and discipline of prisons. But he thought a good beginning was finally being made, saying that "it is a matter of pride to every American, that the new penitentiary system has been first established and successfully practised in this country," and adding that the "American penitentiary system must be regarded as a new victory of mind over matter—the great and constant task of man." Unlike Abdy, who viewed America's penal institutions with disdain, if not disgust, Lieber found penitentiaries to be "monuments of a charitable disposition of the honest members of society toward their fallen and unfortunate brethren." He acknowledged that several new model institutions, including Sing Sing, stood to produce a profit for the state. He cautioned, though, that "society has a right to punish, but not to brutalize, to deprive of liberty, but not to expose to filth and corruption." He also said, "It ought always to be borne in mind, that a convict is neither a brute nor a saint, and to treat him as either, is equally injurious to himself and to society."[131]

Lieber was particularly critical of sinful and immoral women, whom he considered more depraved than male criminals, perhaps because he saw women as being less amenable to discipline and order. By failing to be virtuous wives and mothers, such women were a major source of criminality in their men as well as in and of themselves.[132]

With input from Lieber and other members, the Boston Prison Discipline Society gathered some of the first comprehensive statistics regarding convicts' family status. In one survey of the Salem jail, the society found that 73 prisoners, 26 of whom were debtors, had 39 wives and 144 children. Three were sons of widows, who had 11 other children; 2 were mothers with husbands and 6 children; 6 had living parents as well as brothers and sisters; 15 had no families; and several were under child-bearing age. The 73 prisoners had a total of 176 near relatives. The probable number of relatives of persons committed to prison in the whole United States that year (1834) was computed as follows: the 113,340 persons who were held in prison had 112,043 children, 30,345 wives, 533,626 brothers and sisters, 9,253 fathers, and 38,042 mothers. At Auburn alone, there were 683 convicts who had left behind a total of 901 children, only 223 of whom had been left with any means of support.[133]

Throughout many of the new American prisons, inmates were forbidden to have any contact whatsoever with their families, because familial influence was considered "corrupting." Eventually, however, some institutions relaxed their rules against correspondence and visitation. By the 1840s, Sing Sing was allowing convicts to send one letter every six months, provided it was penned by the chaplain and censored by the warden. Each prisoner was also permitted to have one visit from his relatives during his sentence, provided it was properly supervised. Still, no reading materials of any kind, except a Bible, were allowed inside.[134]

Following Lieber's example, Samuel Gridley Howe emerged as another important figure in American penology. A graduate of Harvard Medical School, he had travelled extensively throughout Europe, become acquainted with Lafayette and Lord Byron, and, like Lieber, fought in the Greek war of independence. Besides being a leading abolitionist, Howe was keenly interested in prisons; in *An Essay on Separate and Congregate Systems of Prison Discipline* he defended the Pennsylvania system.[135] Howe claimed that the congregate system treated prisoners as masses, whereas the solitary system treated each convict as an individual, which he favored. He also supported the complete separation of convicts, in part because he wanted to keep the races separate. He claimed that a large proportion of the Philadelphia prisoners were mulattoes, "who cannot bear confinement like men of pure Saxon blood," and added that "the colored population whence they are drawn is a very degraded one, and addicted to those sexual excesses which lead particularly to cerebral derangement."[136]

Howe and the Reverend Louis Dwight were part of a growing circle of Massachusetts social reformers interested in prisons. Some others included Dorothea Lynde Dix, Henry David Thoreau, Horace Mann, and Charles Sumner.[137] Dix became one of Howe's closest associates after taking a Sunday school class in the women's department of the house of correction in East Cambridge. Once a shy young theology student, she had become a fearless crusader, embarking on a two-year investigation of the state's jails and almshouses, which she later continued outside Massachusetts. Between 1844 and 1854 she travelled over thirty thousand miles. A convict in the Missouri State Penitentiary, who was serving time for attempting to aid slaves in gaining their liberty, found her to be "bold, affable, and sympathizing." An opponent of operating prisons for profit, Dix sought an end to visitors' fees and advocated allowing convicts to earn wages by working overtime. She also pushed for separating women, juveniles, first offenders, and the insane from regular male convicts. Hardly a total radical, though, she was fond of saying: "It is with convicts as it is with children."[138]

Some other prominent women prison reformers of the day included

Sarah Doremus, Mary Wister, and Elizabeth Farnham. Appointed matron of Mount Pleasant prison in 1844, Farnham allowed the female inmates to decorate their cells with curtains and other domestic touches; she even brought in a piano to accompany their singing. Farnham also instituted a program of prisoner education, which prompted the authorities to dismiss her after only two years.[139]

SOLITARY OR COMMUNAL?

THE early nineteenth century was an age of social experiments and utopian dreams. The rivalry between the prison models of Auburn and Philadelphia was but one example of such thinking. The competition between solitary and communal living arrangements received enormous attention in America, not just in penology but as a major religious, social, and political issue.

When Beaumont and Tocqueville, Crawford, Abdy, Dickens, and other foreign visitors selected American sights to observe, Shaker settlements invariably were among them.[140] Shakerism and imprisonment also had other connections. Like the Pilgrims, the Puritans, the Quakers, and other religious sects, the Shakers had come to America seeking asylum from persecution and imprisonment in England. Accordingly, the history of American Shakerism and American penology intersected and intermingled.

Ann Lee had joined a Shaker sect in Manchester, England, when she was eighteen years old. She had continued to practice her faith despite constant persecution for "profaning the Sabbath" and other alleged crimes. In 1770, while jailed at Manchester, she underwent a deeper conversion, as a result of which she was repeatedly imprisoned and mistreated, sometimes until she was close to death. Finally, in the summer of 1774, Lee and eight of her flock fled to America, eventually settling near Albany, New York. For a decade, Mother Ann made converts throughout the Northeast. After her passing in 1784, she was succeeded by a disciple, James Whitaker, who molded the Shakers into a significant social force. The sect became famous for well-ordered settlements that blended solitary and congregate features into a unique, utilitarian lifestyle, sacralizing every aspect of daily life, down to each distinctive tool and piece of furniture.[141] By the Jacksonian era the Shakers had become one of the largest and most influential religious communistic movements in the United States. Shaker customs— of separation from the world, celibacy, uniform dress, simplicity, silence, industry, and duty—already were being widely (though not always consciously) copied. Many of the sect's virtues became cardinal characteristics of American penitentiaries. Shakers and convicts were under constant watch to ensure the preachings were practiced. Shaker settlements, like prisons, were renowned for their iron discipline. Members of both communities lived a spartan, usually sexually separate existence; they ate in silence and labored incessantly. Even the "lockstep" that became such a hallmark of American prisons may have borne some similarity to the Shakers' "sacred dance," if engravings from the period are any indication. Despite their pursuit of humility, the Shakers were proud of their system, much as American prison reformers glorified their "model" (but terrible) prisons.

Another major nineteenth-century U.S. religious movement—Mormonism—also had prison connections in much of its early history. Unlike most other religious faiths, Mormonism was originally American. Its founder, Joseph Smith, Jr., had been born in 1805 and spent part of his childhood in Palmyra in western New York, not far from the planned site of Auburn prison. The Smiths were poor squatters who dressed in tattered rags and struggled to make ends meet. Some neighbors later described young Joe as "shiftless," "indolent," "prevaricating," and "cunning." But the "burnt-over district" in which they lived was swept by the fire of religious revival and they were part of it. Young Smith said he communed with higher powers, claiming to have discovered golden tablets from God that had been hidden under a rock. He and his father hunted for more treasure with a divining rod. In 1826, after he was caught using a "seer stone" to supposedly help locate some buried treasure, young Smith was arrested and convicted in nearby Bainbridge as a disorderly person and imposter.[142]

Despite these inauspicious beginnings, Joseph Smith quickly rose to become a self-styled prophet. In March 1830, when he was only twenty-five years old, *The Book of Mormon,* revealed by God and "translated" by Joseph Smith, Jr., appeared in New York bookstalls. This extraordinary work became the scripture of the new Mormon Church, and within a few weeks at least forty persons acknowledged the charismatic young Smith as "Seer, a Translator, a Prophet, an Apostle of Jesus Christ, and Elder of the Church through the will of God the Father, and the grace of your Lord Jesus Christ."[143] Intent on founding the New Jerusalem, Smith and his followers moved to Ohio in 1831. By 1835 he had set up an elaborate hierarchy in the church, with himself as president. His flock already numbered in the thousands.

When some of them moved into Missouri, many local residents felt threatened. Mormons had, after all, vowed to gain control of the whole state; moreover, they had showed tolerant attitudes toward Negroes and Indians, which alarmed many whites. Fighting broke out and the Mormons

had to retreat. (The sect also engendered intense conflict in Ohio, particularly for their doctrine and practice of polygamy.) During the fall of 1838,
Smith's forces engaged in guerrilla warfare against the militia; he was
arrested again, and his followers were driven back across the Mississippi.
But he managed to escape from custody and rejoin his flock in Illinois.
There, aged thirty-four, revered as a prophet, he thrived and gathered
more followers.

In 1844 his power seemed so great that he decided to run for president
of the United States. He drew up a platform full of panaceas, saying he
would eliminate unnecessary government, cut congressmen's pay, free the
slaves and pay off their owners, release prisoners from the penitentiaries,
and work other miracles.[144] The controversy surrounding Smith finally
came to a head in southern Illinois when he was jailed on polygamy
charges. A lynch mob attacked the Carthage jail and shot to death Joseph
Smith and his brother Hyrum.[145] The martyred leader of the Mormons,
founder of the Church of Jesus Christ of Latter-Day Saints, was succeeded
by Brigham Young, and in the decades that followed many Mormon men
were imprisoned for polygamy.[146]

Religious zealots and prison reformers were not the only advocates and
practitioners of the solitary life, but they were the most noteworthy exem-
plars, at least until Henry David Thoreau came on the scene.[147] Thoreau
began his famous experiment in solitary living at Walden Pond in 1845.
During his hermitage (which would last for two years) in protest against
the federal government's policies on Mexico and the expansion of slavery,
Thoreau refused to pay his poll tax and was arrested. As a result, in July
1846 he was brought to the Concord jail. It was there that he gained the
inspiration for his classic essay of protest, "On the Duty of Civil Disobedience."[148]

Like many New England intellectuals, Thoreau hated slavery and was
ashamed of his government's support of it. And like Tom Paine, he was a
philosophical anarchist. "[W]hen a sixth of the population of a nation
which has undertaken to be the refuge of liberty are slaves, and a whole
country is unjustly overrun and conquered by a foreign army, and subjected to military law, I think that it is not too soon for honest men to rebel
and revolutionize," he wrote.

In Thoreau's eyes, "Under a government which imprisons any unjustly,
the true place for a just man is also a prison." That was the only place
which Massachusetts had provided for people of conscience. "It is there
that the fugitive slave, and the Mexican prisoner on parole, and the Indian
come to plead the wrongs of his race, should find them; on that separate,

but more free and honorable ground, where the State places those who are not *with* her but *against* her,—the only house in a slave-state in which a free man can abide with honor."[149]

Thoreau spent one night in Concord's jail. What he later described in his essay was not wholly unpleasant. The prisoners seemed reasonably contented and well treated. The jailer pleasantly introduced Thoreau to his roommate and locked their door as if to respect their privacy. The room, freshly whitewashed and simply furnished, was "probably the neatest apartment in the town." His roommate showed him how to get along.

Within a few hours, Thoreau had "read all the tracts that were left there, and examined where former prisoners had broken out, and where a grate had been sawed off, and heard the history of the various occupants of that room; for I found that even here there was a history and a gossip which never circulated beyond the walls of the jail." He later described his experience as "like travelling into a far country, such as I had never expected to behold, to lie there for one night. It seemed to me that I had never heard the town-clock strike before, nor the evening sounds of the village. . . . I had never seen its institutions before. This is one of its peculiar institutions. . . . I began to comprehend what its inhabitants were about."

The next day, to Thoreau's surprise, he was released. It seems that someone had interfered and paid his delinquent tax.

During his brief incarceration, no great changes had taken place on the village common, such as might have happened if he had gone in as a youth and come out an old man. And yet he viewed the town, and state, and country, differently. "I saw yet more distinctly the State in which I lived," he wrote. "This may be to judge my neighbors harshly; for I believe that many of them are not aware that they have such an institution as the jail in their village." By a former custom of the village, a poor debtor coming out of jail might expect to be greeted with a little salute by which his acquaintances would peek at him through their fingers, which they would cross like a barred window. Transformed by his experience, Thoreau felt he was regarded as if he had been on a long journey. History would record that he had.[150]

SLAVOCRACY

AS Thoreau had complained, while Northern states were competing to perfect industrial factories, prisons, and penitentiaries, the whole South remained a massive rural prison farm, holding millions of black slaves who were serving life terms and giving birth to children who inherited and passed on their prisoner status in perpetuity. In fact, more than a generation after the American Revolution, slavery had not only survived— it was growing again.

Since the abolition of the international slave trade in 1808, its domestic counterpart had burgeoned. So had the emphasis upon slave breeding. Slave traders and slave catchers enjoyed a bonanza. Instead of withering away, the "slave power" resurged to become a "slavocracy." Existing prohibitions on the interstate slave trade were lifted, except for criminals, in North Carolina (about 1818), Virginia (1819), Alabama (1832), Louisiana (1834), Mississippi (1846), South Carolina (1848), Maryland (1850), and Georgia (1855–56). Missouri and Arkansas never had barred slaves, except vicious criminals, and the new states of Florida and Texas now permitted interstate slave trading except where it involved criminals. Kentucky prohibited its residents from buying or importing slaves for their own use (1833), but this was widely disregarded. As a result, interstate slave traders did a thriving business.[151]

Coffles of shackled slaves in transit had become a common sight throughout the South. In 1839 James S. Buckingham passed a procession of slaves on the road near Fredericksburg, Virginia, and observed "the men chained together in pairs, and the women carrying the children and bundles [on] their march to the South. The gang was under several white drivers, who rode near them on horseback, with large whips, while the slaves marched on foot beside them; and there was one driver behind, to bring up the rear."[152] On another highway, near Columbia, South Carolina, Charles Ball passed a gang of chained and handcuffed slaves being marched off to market; along the route a local stranger asked, "Are any of your niggers for sale?" After one white man in particular pressed the slave traders to sell him a pair of good "breeding wenches," he was shown two pregnant black women, aged twenty-two and nineteen, who were said to have already delivered seven and four children respectively. The man bought them for $1,000 and shared a liquor toast with the blacksmith who removed their irons. The two women bid a sorrowful farewell to their companions as they were led away.[153]

The hypocrisy of such trafficking within a "free and democractic" nation was glaring to many foreign visitors. In September 1834 an English traveller, G. W. Featherstonhaugh, passed a coffle of three hundred slaves being moved along a southern highway. Farther down the road, at a tavern beyond Knoxville, he came upon none other than President Andrew Jackson sitting at a table, smoking his pipe. Old Hickory was wearing a white hat bound with black crape. A few minutes after Jackson left, another patron appeared, accompanied by his slave. This stranger too was dressed in mourning clothes. Featherstonhaugh described him as a "queer, tall animal about forty years old, with dark black hair, cut round as if he were a Methodist preacher, immense black whiskers, a physiognamy not without one or two tolerable features, but singularly sharp and not a little piratical and repulsive." It was John Armfield, a slave trader from Alexandria, and he proceeded to get drunk at the tavern and boisterously express his admiration for General Jackson, George Washington, and that other beloved champion of liberty, democracy, and equality, the recently deceased Marquis de Lafayette, whose death he was mourning. Featherstonhaugh could barely contain his disgust.[154]

Enlightened Northerners were embarrassed by what they saw down South. While travelling in 1846, Auburn's own William H. Seward, the former New York governor and state senator, witnessed a slave cargo being shipped from Richmond to Norfolk. As seventy-five glum Negroes were trudging aboard the vessel, a Southern gentleman leaned alongside Seward and remarked, "'You see the curse that our forefathers bequeathed to us. . . . Oh, they don't mind it; they are cheerful; they enjoy this transportation and travel as much as you do.'" The ship's captain added, "'Oh, sir, do not be concerned about them; they are the happiest people in the world!'" The words "happiest people in the world!" rang in Seward's ears as he gazed down at the long and miserable human chain as it wound into the ship. Years later, Seward could not help but recall that "[t]he sable procession was followed by a woman, a white woman, dressed in silk and furs and feathers. She seemed the captain's wife. She carried in her hand a Bible!"[155]

Even though it was no longer international, the slave trade remained big business in the South—as big as it had been before the American Revolution. As textile factories in the North consumed more and more Southern cotton, plantation owners scrambled to field a sufficient labor force, and some slaveholders headed west in search of fertile soil. According to one slave trader who fell into conversation with a white business partner on the Potomac in the 1830s, slave prices fluctuated wildly. "Children from one year to 18 months old are now worth about $100," the trader said. Pointing to a black boy of about seven or eight years old, he said, "That little fellow there, I gave $400 for." Noting a lad of about eighteen, he remarked, "That fellow, I gave $750 for last night, after dark." The trader added, "I offered the other day $1,200 for two girls, and their owner got $1,300, a day or two after. A first-rate fieldhand is well worth $900, and would bring it, if the owner did not know it. A good mechanic is worth $1,200. Mine are nearly all fieldhands; but I shall not take a cent under $1,000 [each] for the men, when I get to Carolina."[156] Within a few months, he expected to make 25 to 30 percent on his investment.

Prisons still played a key role in the slave trade, just as they did in upholding slavery. The South was filled with private jails as well as public ones, the primary or exclusive purpose of which was to hold slaves. Most of the extensive slave trading in Washington, D.C., occurred in and around taverns and inns, such as the Lafayette Tavern, at F Street between 13th and 14th NW, and Lloyd's Tavern. Many reputable hotels maintained small jails for their customers' use, just as they offered safes for precious jewels and cash.[157]

On a stifling day in 1833, E. S. Abdy visited Robey's Tavern (on the east side of 7th Street between B Street SW and Maryland Avenue) and spied a wretched slave pen. Inside were several blacks peeking out from between crevices in the palisade trying to breathe some fresh air.[158] Two years later a visitor to John Armfield's slave pen, located between the Capitol and Mount Vernon, described being met in the parlor by "a man of fine personal appearance and of engaging and graceful manners"; he provided his caller with a pungent, frosty julep and summoned a cicerone with the keys. The assistant opened the bolts and padlocks on the grated iron door, and the visitor entered a yard to a high, whitewashed wall surrounding the pen for male slaves. That day there were about sixty men and boys inside, ranging upwards in age from about ten years old. Nearby, the visitor saw a similar pen containing about forty Negro women and girls, some of whom were weeping. Armfield's jail complex included a tailor shop for making slave clothes, a large kitchen, and several tents, wagons, and other equipment used in transporting slaves to and from the market. There was also a small hospital and a long, two-story private jail with grated windows in which the slaves were kept chained at night.[159]

Fredrika Bremer, who visited several private slave pens in 1851, saw in one of them a well-built but forlorn-looking Negro who had reportedly cut off the fingers of his own right hand as a means of hurting his master. Somebody said he was being separated from his wife and children and sold South. At another site Bremer witnessed slaves being tied down and paddled by a keeper. The man explained that his cowhide could "cause as much torture as any other instrument, and even more, because one can give as many blows with this strip of hide without its leaving any outward sign; it does not cut into the flesh." Another jail specialized in "fancy girls," who were sold for sexual purposes.[160]

It was in jails and prisons that many slave sales were conducted, since they enabled dealers to operate with comfort, privacy, security, even secrecy. The squeamish public was spared being exposed to sights that many people plainly preferred not to see. This detachment from the public view enabled traders to more easily engage in practices that were illegal, and it helped to conceal evidence of kidnapping and other crimes that had been committed against free blacks.[161] Solomon Northrup, for example, had been born free in upstate New York and resided in Saratoga with his wife and children, all of whom were also free. But in 1841 two circus managers lured him to the District of Columbia, where he was drugged and kidnapped. The trader James H. Birch imprisoned Northrup in a private jail—Williams' Slave Pen—that was tucked away on a street that was literally within the shadow of the Capitol. From there Northrup was taken to Richmond to be sold into slavery on Theophilius Freeman's Louisiana plantation near the Red River.[162]

Public jails were also made available to slave traders. In most slaveholding cities, a gentleman could send his rebellious slave to jail for whipping or other correction. Between 1824 and 1828, for example, the District of Columbia jail boarded at least 452 slaves.[163]

Moses Roper was a slave of mixed Negro, white, and Indian blood who was sold from his mother in North Carolina when he was six because he bore an embarrassing physical resemblance to his master. As an adolescent he ran away, half-naked, into the woods, was quickly apprehended, and thrown in jail. Roper later explained, "When they put slaves in gaol, they advertise for their masters to own them; but if the master does not claim his slave in 6 months from the time of imprisonment the slave is sold for gaol fees." His master came and claimed him, whipped him severely, and put him to work in the fields with a twenty-five-pound weight attached around his neck. When he misbehaved again, his master responded with another instrument that was several feet high, with cross pieces that were two, four, and six feet in length, strung with iron bells. Roper still refused to capitulate, however, and eventually he escaped to freedom.[164]

Most were not so lucky. At Baltimore in 1837, 149 blacks were jailed as runaways and 148 more were held for not having proper papers. Twenty years later, the combined number had risen to 483.[165]

Public prisons also were used to hold slaves who were accused of insurrection. Of the 79 persons convicted in connection with Denmark Vesey's Charleston slave revolt in 1822, 35 were condemned to death and 44 were ordered transported out of the state via the prisons.[166]

In August 1831 the bloodiest slave uprising in American history occurred in Southampton, Virginia. It was led by Nat Turner, a mystical slave who claimed he had heard voices urging revolt. Turner's followers slaughtered sixty-one whites in an effort to liberate slaves from bondage, but the rebellion was crushed and Turner himself was captured and imprisoned. Chained and helpless, he was awaiting his fate in the Jerusalem jail when an elderly white lawyer, Thomas R. Gray, entered the cell with paper and pens to take down Turner's "confession." Upon conviction, Turner was valued at $375, the amount that the state was required to reimburse the Putnam Moore estate for destroying its "property." A noose was tied around Turner's neck and he was hoisted up. When sufficient time had passed, the corpse was cut down and given to the surgeons for dissection. Later they skinned it and made grease of the flesh. Officially, he was one of seventeen slaves and three free Negroes who were hanged, with twelve others being transported for their part in the rebellion; unofficially, dozens of blacks throughout the region were butchered by mobs.[167]

Ironically, Virginia's system of transportation beyond the limits of the United States was modeled after the British practice that had been one of the abuses cited in the Declaration of Independence and one of the causes of the Revolution. Between 1800 and 1850, Virginia alone transported more than six hundred slave criminals. Slaves were supposed to be held at the penitentiary only until they could be executed or sold out of the country. But administering the law proved difficult. Reimbursement costs posed excessive expense to the state, and it became harder to find foreign buyers. (In 1820 Virginia paid $512.25 apiece for twenty-five Negroes; ten years later the cost was $369.78 per head.)[168] State law allowed the governor to commute a death sentence to imprisonment and then release the slave from the penitentiary on the condition that he or she be deported. In practice there were few legal niceties involved. For example, Governor Henry A. Wise reported in 1857: "I examined the record of the case of Dolly, a slave, the property of B. S. Crouch, who was condemned to be hung by the county court of Henrico, for burning a dwelling house; and because of the insufficiency of the testimony against her, and of the recommendation to mercy by the justices of the peace who composed the court, I commuted the capital punishment, and ordered the prisoner to sale and transportation beyond the limits of the United States."[169]

To carry out this transportation, the state formed business relationships with slave dealers. Once these slave traders took custody of a prisoner, the state washed its hands and looked the other way. A Maryland law of 1818 provided that any slave convicted of a crime, who the court found should not be hanged, might be transported and sold. An 1846 statute provided that any slave who had finished a term in the state penitentiary should be sold at auction and transported. Such laws were particularly aimed at controlling free blacks. In 1848 Governor William Smith of Virginia complained that free blacks were committing ten times more crime in proportion to their numbers as whites, and he said that this adversely affected "the value of our slaves." He lamented that freedom "awakens in the slave new appetites and wants, teaches the road to crime, makes him restless and dissatisfied, and increases the spirit of insubordination."[170]

ABOLITION AND THE UNDERGROUND RAILROAD

THE antislavery crusade began in earnest in the late 1820s and early 1830s, after gradual emancipation had largely been achieved in the North and when other nations, especially Great Britain, were abolishing slavery altogether.

Since the Revolution, the systems of slavery and imprisonment had developed together. At virtually each stage of New York's gradual emancipation process, the state had also gradually created and added to its prison system. Thus, the American anti-slavery movement coincided with the pro-penitentiary movement; efforts to curtail chattel slavery were going on at the same time that reformers were also trying to perfect penal slavery in the North. Both movements were characterized by religious fervor, a sense of moral urgency, and utopianism. Some of each generation's leaders in one movement were also instrumental in the other—men like Thomas Eddy, Benjamin Rush, Caleb Lownes, Francis Lieber, Samuel Gridley Howe, and Franklin B. Sanborn.[171] Sanborn was another leading abolitionist and penal reformer. The anti-slavery and pro-penitentiary movements were partly driven by similar visions of human perfection and human depravity, racial inequality, and class differences. The involvement of Quakers in both movements was strong, and the connections could be complex. Some Friends of conscience even refused to perform jury duty because it might result in someone being imprisoned. Others, like Laura Haviland—a prim Quaker in northern Michigan—took great physical risks in smuggling black fugitive slaves (criminals) to freedom.[172]

Isaac T. Hopper was a prominent Philadelphia Quaker who had started smuggling slaves to freedom in 1787, when he was only sixteen years old. Because he would not renounce the use of violence to combat slavery, however, he was disowned by the Society of Friends. Hopper was also a top penal reformer, who sought to improve imprisonment and help convicts find work and lead honest lives after release. His daughter, Abby Hopper Gibbons, followed in his footsteps by leading the Female Department of the Prison Association of New York as well as a predominantly black antislavery society. She, too, left the Society of Friends due to a dispute over abolitionism.[173] Some other prominent women who were active

in both reforming prisons and opposing slavery included Catherine Sedge-
wick, Caroline Kirkland, Sarah Doremus, Margaret Fuller, Elizabeth Comstock, Elizabeth Buffum Chace, Mary Pierce Poor, and Harriet Beecher
Stowe.

America's leading white abolitionist, William Lloyd Garrison, like many
champions of social change in his era, spent some time behind bars for his
political activities. Wherever he was jailed, he left antislavery graffiti on the
walls; he also published poems and essays about his own imprisonment.
Garrison began putting out a weekly abolitionist newspaper, *The Libera-
tor*, in Boston in 1831, the same time that Beaumont and Tocqueville were
visiting the United States and Nat Turner was leading his bloody insurrection. Garrison insisted that slavery must be overthrown, regardless of the
obstacles, no matter if it took a bloody civil or servants' revolt.[174]

Those working against slavery disagreed among themselves on the extent to which they should assist fugitive slaves in reaching Canada or help
to defend imprisoned abolitionists. Garrison and some of his more radical
colleagues considered such activities too peripheral. They favored direct
action and would settle for nothing less than total and immediate abolition.[175] Reverend Theodore Dwight Weld, an evangelist from New York's
"burned-over district," wrote that enslaving men and reducing them to
things was immoral and against God's commandments.[176] Weld and his
sister-in-law, Sarah Grimké, spent six months scouring Southern newspapers for factual items about slavery, many of them involving jailers and
prisoners; they included them in Weld's documentary exposé, *Slavery as
It Is: The Testimony of a Thousand Witnesses* (New York, 1839). It sold
100,000 copies in its first year alone and set the stage for Harriet Beecher
Stowe's monumental novel, *Uncle Tom's Cabin*.[177]

Even in the free states, reaction against abolitionists sometimes turned
violent. David Walker, the black author of the militant *Appeal to the Coloured Citizens of the World* (Boston, 1829), was found dead in Boston
under mysterious circumstances.[178] In November 1837 Garrison barely
escaped being killed by a mob there. Elijah P. Lovejoy, a Presbyterian minister and newspaper editor who had advocated gradual emancipation, was
murdered by a proslavery mob in Alton, Illinois.[179]

Slaves who tried to escape faced extraordinary obstacles. One choice
was to flee south—to the Dismal Swamp, Florida's Everglades, or Mexico.
For those few who survived the trek, there remained enormous physical
challenges, as well as an uncertain fate at the hands of potential Indian
or Mexican captors. Sometimes the Indians proved sympathetic, just as
Shinnecocks had helped transport runaway slaves from Long Island's
north shore to freedom in Massachusetts, Connecticut, and Rhode Island,

and Ottawas under Chief Kinjeino had sheltered fugitive slaves in western Ohio.[180] After the War of 1812, some slaves fleeing into Florida had ended up living among the Seminoles, whose chief, Osceola, had married a black woman and welcomed fugitives. Although a few of these escapees were enslaved by the Indians, others were accepted, even embraced.[181] Indeed, the First Seminole War had started when U.S. troops had invaded eastern Florida in an effort to eliminate this sanctuary for fugitive slaves. The Second Seminole War extended from 1835 to 1843, beginning after the United States Army tried to drive out Indians and blacks to make way for white settlers. In that conflict, Chief Wild Cat escaped with seventeen others from an army prison at Fort Marion and led the Seminoles and runaway slaves until he was recaptured.[182]

Instead of ending slavery, the Constitution protected it. Article IV, Section 2, stated that any "person held to service or labor in one state" who escaped to another "shall be delivered up on claim of the party to whom such service or labor may be due." But it did not stipulate how this would be accomplished. The federal Fugitive Slave Act of 1793 had provided for enforcement by authorizing slaveowners to cross state lines to recapture their property and bring it before any local magistrate or federal court to prove ownership. The act denied fugitives any protection of habeas corpus, right to a jury trial, or right to testify in their own behalf.[183]

Like England's spirits from two centuries earlier, or press-gangs from the days before the Revolution, American slavecatchers were not finicky about who they grabbed or how. Any black person was fair game. Many saw no need to go to a local magistrate or federal court as the law required. Legal attempts to prevent such abuses were attacked through the courts. Pennsylvania's antikidnapping statute of 1826, for instance, was challenged by slavecatchers all the way to the Supreme Court; in 1842 that tribunal overturned the state law and upheld the right of slaveowners to regain their property as provided by the Fugitive Slave Act of 1793.[184]

By the early 1830s, the volume of black fugitives fleeing the South, and the number of free blacks and white persons of conscience willing to assist them, was so great that an organized smuggling network began to develop. Legend has it that so many slaves seemed to disappear near the home of Levi Coffin, in Richmond, Indiana, that somebody said an "Under Ground Rail Road" must be running to it.[185] Within a few years, journalists were writing about these clandestine activities as if they were part of a full-fledged rail line. The conductors and stationmasters of the Underground Railroad devised passwords, hiding compartments, secret signals, codes, and counterintelligence networks. For security reasons, the stationmaster of an underground depot might know only the names and locations of those colleagues immediately above and below him in the chain. Nobody knew how extensive the whole network really was, or how many runaway slaves it handled. Travel routes and schedules were closely guarded. Those trying to aid escaping slaves faced serious injury to themselves, their friends, and their families if they were detected. The dangers were most acute in the South, but a few courageous whites and blacks actually ventured there to do what they could to help slaves to freedom. Some were killed as a result, white accessories were imprisoned, and blacks were put back in chains.[186]

Leonard A. Grimes of Virginia was caught transporting fugitives and sentenced to two years in the state penitentiary. In 1838 Reverend Charles Torrey left his quiet New England congregation to aid escaping slaves down South. Caught and convicted, he eventually died in prison.[187] Jonathan Walker, a Massachusetts shipwright, was imprisoned at Pensacola in 1844 for trying to carry seven slaves on a sailboat from Florida to the Bahamas; a federal court ordered him branded with "SS"—for "slave stealer"—on his right hand.[188] Lewis W. Paine, a white Northern factory worker caught trying to help slaves escape from Georgia, spent six years behind bars.[189] A free Negro, Sam Green, was sentenced to ten years in the Maryland penitentiary simply for possessing *Uncle Tom's Cabin*.[190]

Having drawn a five-year sentence in Missouri for attempting to aid some slaves in gaining their liberty, the abolitionist George Thompson arrived in prison to find one of the wardens "so drunk, he could scarcely sit up, and he did most of the talking." Thompson and his two accomplices were questioned about their abolitionist doctrines. Who were their contacts on the Underground Railroad? How many slaves had they helped to get away? Their captors made it clear that they considered "slavestealers" to be worse than common murderers or chicken thieves, and they treated them accordingly. After his release, Thompson said his imprisonment had only made him feel more solidarity with the slaves he sought to help free. "We know how the chain feels," he wrote.

> We know what it is to be at the will of another; to do as others
> say; receive what they see fit to give; eat and drink what their
> will supplies, and await their pleasure. . . . We understand what
> it is to be forcibly separated from wife, children, parents and
> friends, and denied the sweetness of their society. . . . To live
> in uncertainty—not knowing what they will do with us tomor-
> row. . . . To be looked upon with scorn, reproach, and con-
> tempt, by men, women, and little children.[191]

Thompson and his associates spread their gospel in the Palmyra jail and the state penitentiary at Jefferson City.

A slave named Henry Brown had himself packed into a 3 × 2½ × 2 foot crate and shipped from Richmond to Philadelphia. Living on a few biscuits and a bladder of water, and with very little oxygen, he was delivered twenty-six hours later and found to be alive. His case generated lots of publicity, much of it humorous. But Samuel A. Smith, the white carpenter who had assisted him, was sentenced to state prison for eight years, and several imitators of "Box" Brown suffocated to death in the mails.[192]

Slaveowners constituted only a small minority, even in the Deep South. By 1850 there may have been fewer than 350,000 slaveowners in a total white population of 6 to 8 million in the slave states. Of these, perhaps 7 percent (about 25,000) of the whites owned nearly three-quarters of the slaves; probably 200,000 or so had only 5 slaves or fewer. Yet, the richest among them continued to wield immense power. In 1850 a new federal Fugitive Slave Law went into effect that favored the slaveholders even more strongly. It provided that alleged runaways in custody were presumed guilty and denied any right to defend themselves. The law created a new federal post of commissioner, before whom any claimant could bring an alleged fugitive to verify that the prisoner was a runaway slave. If the slave-catcher had a supporting affidavit from a state court or testimony from two witnesses, he was supposed to be awarded custody.[193] Critics complained that the law promised a five-dollar fee to a commissioner for ruling against the slavecatcher, but awarded ten dollars if the commissioner ruled in his favor. Federal marshals and deputies were required to assist slaveowners in recapturing their property and were subject to thousand-dollar fines if they refused. The authorities could deputize citizens to assist in slavecatching. Anyone who harbored a fugitive or obstructed the administration of justice was subject to stiff criminal penalties. The act did not carry any statute of limitations, which meant that blacks who had lived in the North for several years could be reenslaved and their free-born children seized as contraband.

Antislavery forces challenged the law in court, but lost. The Supreme Court of the United States upheld the law in 1859.[194] As a result, many blacks throughout the North panicked and sought refuge abroad. During the last three months of 1850 alone, an estimated three thousand of them fled to Canada, many through upstate New York.[195] One legendary fugitive slave, Harriet Tubman, repeatedly risked her life to guide other slaves to freedom north of the border.[196]

Frederick Douglass, the black abolitionist, sometimes had as many as eleven fugitives hiding at his Rochester home. He said he felt obliged to help because he too was an escaped slave and had received assistance from others when he needed it. In his early writings, which were published when slavery still ruled the land, Douglass was reluctant to share many details, primarily because he did not want to incriminate others or close any avenue of escape.[197] But he did tell the story of how, as a youth, he and some companions were suspected as runaways and dragged off to the Easton jail and placed in the sheriff's custody without any rights. He later escaped again and made his way to New York, where he was afraid, homeless, hungry, friendless, and depressed, surviving by his wits on the streets of a foreign city. In time he made a good living for himself and rose to become one of the greatest orators of his era. He never stopped risking his life to help others like himself who had come up the hard way.[198]

Other notable men and women who helped runaway slaves included Allan Pinkerton (who managed a depot of the Underground Railroad beneath his cooper's shop near Chicago, and who was later instrumental in establishing the U.S. Secret Service, as well as being the founder of the noted private-detective agency), Isaac T. Hopper, William Still, Susan B. Anthony, John Greenleaf Whittier, Lucretia Coffin Mott, Horace Mann, Harriet Beecher Stowe, Gerrit Smith, Stephen J. May, John Brown, Parker and Amos Pillsbury, Henry Wadsworth Longfellow, James Russell Lowell, and Louisa May Alcott.[199]

PURGED WITH BLOOD

FRUSTRATED in their efforts to succeed by legal, or at least peaceful, means, abolitionists increasingly condemned the legal system for upholding slavery and appealed to Americans of conscience to follow a higher law. Boston's Anti-Slavery Society declared that the Fugitive Slave Act "is to be denounced, resisted, disobeyed," and many favored civil disobedience or force.[200] When a black waiter in Boston was seized as a runaway slave and hauled off to court, a black mob broke into the courtroom, freed him, and helped him escape to Canada.[201] A few months later, abolitionists tried to free a seventeen-year-old black youth named Thomas Sims who was being held in Boston's courthouse, but military force was used to thwart their efforts and Sims was shipped back to slavery.[202] Other slave rescues occurred throughout the Northeast, much like the attacks on press-gangs of a century before.

In March 1857 the United States Supreme Court handed down its ruling in *Dred Scott v. Sandford*.[203] The case involved a slave named Dred Scott who in 1834 had been taken by his master, Dr. John Emerson, from

St. Louis, Missouri, to Rock Island, Illinois (where slavery had been forbidden by the Northwest Ordinance), and later to Fort Snelling, in the
Wisconsin Territory (where slavery was prohibited by the Missouri Compromise). Scott had remained on free soil for four years or so. Slated to be
taken back to Missouri, he sued for his liberty, claiming that he had become
free by living in a free state and a free territory for a protracted period. The
case remained enmeshed in the legal system for ten years until the question
finally was taken up by the high court.[204] Writing for the seven to two
majority, Chief Justice Roger B. Taney ruled that "people of African
descent are not and cannot be citizens of the United States" and "the black
man has no rights which the white man is bound to respect," and went on
to proclaim that "the enslaved African race were not intended to be
included in the Declaration of Independence." The Court ruled that Dred
Scott had not become free because the Missouri Compromise restriction
under which he claimed his freedom was unconstitutional, since Congress
had no power to prohibit slavery in federal territories.

The ruling enraged many abolitionists and prompted more opponents
of slavery to disdain legalistic approaches in waging their fight. Some abolitionists urged that the North secede from the Union, and a few proslavery
elements proclaimed that the defense of their property depended upon the
preservation of the Union and federal assistance in law enforcement.

Tensions had been mounting throughout the North. At Sing Sing
prison, in November 1855, a keeper was severely beaten by convicts. The
next day, a convict wielding a crowbar charged at a guard in the quarries
and was shot dead. That night a newspaper reported that "the shaking of
eight or nine hundred iron doors, and the unearthly groans of the men
would be somewhat frightful, were it not on the right side of the substantial
stone walls."[205] In early 1858 a convict named Jack Haggerty sprang up in
the saw shop and shouted, "Now boys, liberty or death!" When the smoke
cleared, two convicts lay mortally wounded by gunfire.[206]

John Brown personified the abolitionist who was willing to use violence
to destroy slavery.[207] After fighting many skirmishes against it, he ultimately
decided to wage real war, and drew up detailed invasion plans that were
designed to trigger a massive slave revolt. His scheme was allegedly backed
by the "Secret Six," a group of prominent white abolitionists that included
Howe; Sanborn; Reverend Thomas Wentworth Higginson, a leading
transcendentalist; Reverend Theodore Parker, the Unitarian leader; the
businessman George L. Stearns; and Gerrit Smith, a wealthy New York
philanthropist.

Brown headed a twenty-two-man "Army of Liberation" that included
two of his own sons, assorted white radicals, and several former slaves.

They raided the federal arsenal at Harpers Ferry, Virginia, expecting to seize weapons and free and arm the slaves. Some hostages, but very few slaves, joined their rebellion. After a shootout, Brown was captured by marines under the command of Colonel Robert E. Lee and Lieutenant J. E. B. Stuart, and taken to the Charlestown jail to await trial.

Over eight hundred people visited him there during a two-day period. One step ahead of a lynch mob, Brown was quickly tried and found guilty. On December 2, 1859, he was taken from his cell and put onto a wagon atop his coffin, hands tied behind his back. En route to the gallows he slipped an attendant a handwritten message: "Charlestown, Va, 2d, December, 1859. I John Brown am now quite *certain* that the crimes of this *guilty, land: will* never be purged *away;* but with Blood. I had as I *now think: vainly* flattered myself that without *very much* bloodshed; it might be done."[208]

In the North, Brown's supporters pronounced him a martyr to the cause of freedom. Thoreau called him a "crucified hero." Church bells tolled, songs and poems were composed in his honor. Longfellow wrote in his diary: "The date of a new Revolution,—quite as much needed as the old one."[209]

CHAPTER FIVE

Scandal and Reform

PRISON CAMPS

THE intensified sectional conflict over slavery of the 1850s dominated the presidential campaign of 1860. The platform of the new Republican Party appealed for harmony, emphasizing the importance of the Union and carefully avoiding any condemnation of Negro slavery. Nevertheless, Abraham Lincoln's election prompted the secession of the slaveholding states—South Carolina, Mississippi, Florida, Alabama, Georgia, Louisiana, Texas, Virginia, Arkansas, Tennessee, and North Carolina, plus factional governments in Missouri and Kentucky—which saw him as not serving their interests. The Confederate States of America was declared, with Jefferson Davis as president.

Shortly before dawn on April 12, 1861, Edmund Ruffin of Virginia fired the first cannon shot at Fort Sumter in Charleston harbor, beginning the Civil War. Thirty-four hours later, the garrison surrendered and federal troops were taken prisoner. Full-scale battlefield fighting began a few months later and resulted in significant deaths, woundings, and captures. After only a few months, each side held thousands of prisoners of war.

Many Northerners considered the conflict an illegal rebellion and wanted the Confederates prosecuted for levying war against the United States. (As it would turn out, that did not happen.) Southerners, on the other hand, considered their actions valid, legal, and consistent with their American heritage, regarding the Yankees as foreign invaders and oppressors. Neither side took a kind view of captured enemy troops.

Early on, many prisoners of war were exchanged under a traditional gentlemen's agreement based on rank. Privates were worth less than corporals, a sergeant was equal to so many corporals, and so on up the ranks, so that a single general from one army might be exchanged for hundreds of enlisted men from the other.

Conscription was instituted on both sides. Draftees were allowed to purchase substitutes to serve in their place. When the North finally fielded Negro regiments, the South refused to regard black soldiers as regular personnel, viewing them as rebellious runaway slaves who deserved only to be killed or reenslaved if they were caught. In retaliation, the North charged that many Confederate prisoners who had been exchanged had later returned to duty in violation of their parole. As a result, the new commander of the Union forces, General U. S. Grant, halted the prisoner exchanges. Consequently, captives' lives were devalued by both sides, and prison conditions, which had never been good, deteriorated.

Prisoners of war generally were kept separate from convicts and held in specially built compounds, but these places quickly overflowed. Even at their best, the prison camps of the Civil War were ill equipped for the kind of heavy use they received during massive, protracted campaigns. Additional makeshift prisons were hastily created away from the front, but they too became overcrowded.[1]

Like New York City during the first American Revolution, Richmond became a prison city, holding thousands of Union captives who were collected there before being shipped farther south. The capital's principal Confederate prisons were Libby, an old, rat-infested brick tobacco warehouse, and Belle Isle, a tent city on the James River; the holding pens included Castle Thunder, Crew's, Grant's Factory, Pemberton's, Scott's, and Smith's Factory.[2] Elsewhere in Virginia, captives were held at Danville, Lynchburg, and Petersburg.[3] In North Carolina, they were herded into a stockade at Salisbury, and congregated at Charlotte and Raleigh.[4] At Charleston, a stucco structure housed several hundred men, among them Negro soldiers, deserters from both sides, and military offenders. Also in South Carolina, there were detention sites at Florence and Columbia.[5] Important centers in Georgia included Millen, Camp Oglethorpe in Macon, Atlanta, Savannah, Camp Lawton, Augusta, Marietta, and Blackshear; Alabama had the old Cahaba warehouse called Castle Morgan, as well as Tuscaloosa, Mobile, and Montgomery.[6] Louisiana held prisoners in New Orleans and Shreveport. Texas utilized Camp Groce and Camp Ford.[7]

An inmate who survived to tell about the experience, T. H. Mann of the Army of the Potomac, later recounted being captured during the Wilderness Campaign and moved southward from prison to prison. En route from the front he was taken past General Robert E. Lee, who was sitting upon his horse, smoking a cigar. Mann recalled that Lee "appeared a middle-sized man, with iron-gray hair and full gray beard, not very closely cut; as fine-looking a specimen of a man and soldier as I ever saw." As the Northern captives filed past, Lee remarked, "'Am sorry to see you in this fix, boys, but you must make the best of it.'" According to Mann, "His tone was kind, and spoken as though he really sympathized with us, as I have no doubt he did."

Herded sixty to a boxcar, Mann and his fellow prisoners passed through the desolate North Carolina countryside, past long stretches of noble-looking pine, immense piles of resin, glum-faced Negroes in tattered rags, and shabby-looking poor whites. He came to observe that most soldiers who had seen battle tended to treat their captives well, whereas the dreaded home guard, which often was composed of young boys and old-timers unfit for duty, frequently robbed, abused, and mistreated its prisoners. "A brave man is always humane and generous, while a coward is cruel and vindictive," he wrote. "The brave men of the South were mostly at the front with their armies."

Mann and his companions were brought to Americus, Georgia, deep in the heart of Dixie. The prison nearby was Camp Sumpter, better known as Andersonville. At the time it held thirteen thousand men—"emaciated forms, half human and half spectral, black with filth and smoke, and swarming with vermin."

Inside the log stockade there stretched a slender railing, the "dead line." The sentries were ordered to shoot any person who crossed it. Within this border the stockade enclosed 16½ acres of ground that included two side hills and a small, muddy brook that ran through the little valley in between. The stream, seldom more than a trickle, served as the camp's chief water supply and sewer. According to Mann,

> No provision was made, until near the very close of our incarceration at Andersonville, towards carrying off the refuse and sewerage of our prison, and no sanitary regulations had been put in force. The filth that accumulated through those long summer months can neither be described nor imagined. Most of it collected in and about the three acres of swamp, and I have seen that three acres one animated mass of maggots from one to two feet deep, the whole swamp moving like the waves of the sea.[8]

There were no huts or barracks, and the level of overcrowding was incredible. By March 1864 there were 7,500 prisoners; by May, 15,000 in a space designed to hold only 10,000. As soon as the area was expanded by 10 acres, the population increased to more than 30,000. By August a

Confederate inspector reported that there were only about 6 square feet of ground for each prisoner, and the death toll exceeded 100 a day.[9] During only about four months, 13,000 men perished at Andersonville, and as many more lost their health. Of the 40,000 prisoners of war who entered its walls, fewer than one-third lived as much as 20 years afterward.[10]

Conditions in the North were not much better.[11] After filling all available prisons and penitentiaries, the Union Army improvised its own makeshift camps, such as Camp Douglas near Chicago, a confiscated medical college, and a deserted slave pen in St. Louis.[12]

The prison camp at Elmira was located on New York's prosperous southern tier, where the economy was booming and food and water were plentiful. Yet in the fall of 1864 the hospital surgeon there complained that during the last three months, with 8,347 prisoners in camp, 2,011 had been admitted to the prison hospital, of whom 775 had died. One of eight inmates was seriously sick. He added: "At this rate the entire command will be admitted to hospital in less than a year and 36 per cent, die."[13] It, too, contained a rivulet, which had formed a gummy pond, "green with putrescence, filling the air with its messengers of disease and death." Requests for life-saving medicines, fresh straw for hospital beds, and other supplies were ignored. At last a prisoner exchange was organized, and 1,200 men were pulled out of Elmira and put on trains for Baltimore and shipment south. Five of them died on the train, and 60 more had to be carried off and hospitalized.[14]

At the Union prison at Rock Island, Illinois, more than 1,800 Confederates died, many from smallpox.[15] Point Lookout, which had been set up in Maryland after the Battle of Gettysburg, held as many as 20,000 Confederate soldiers at a time; nearly 3,000 of them died there. Some Rebels were released to fight Indians out west.[16]

Typhoid raged at Fort Delaware, on marshy Sea Patch Island near the mouth of the Delaware River, killing nearly 2,500 Confederates.[17] A Louisianan who spent 16 months imprisoned at Johnson's Island in frigid Lake Erie, three miles north of Sandusky, Ohio, later described the horrors of temperatures of 25 degrees below zero upon coatless prisoners from the Deep South.[18]

Farther west, at the site of a former fairground in Indianapolis, Camp Morton was surrounded by a twenty-foot-high plank wall. The cold and crowding there were so bad that many Confederates dipped their blankets in water before going to bed in a vain effort to retain their body warmth, and slept spoon fashion to avoid freezing to death.[19]

These were not cozy local jails attached to the sheriff's house across the town square from the offender's home, or a fortress-factory state prison located a few counties up the river. Otherwise free white Americans now experienced imprisonment that was hundreds or even thousands of miles from home, in distant places they had never heard of or known existed, in alien climates and cultures.

North and South, the notions of "prison" and "prisoner" assumed new meaning during the war. Suddenly, hideous captivity and even death could await "good" men who had "broken no law" and who had "served their country." One did not have to be black or criminal to be imprisoned. Law-abiding white Southerners found themselves guarded and controlled by armed invaders, including Negroes. Liberty-loving New Englanders might pass their days and nights under the despotic grip of slave-driving Rebs. This was not a penitentiary that sought to separate each inmate from contamination, or a factory-prison that would instill the habits of industry, or a plantation-prison that was founded on chattel slavery. This was a concentration camp, a death trap, founded on total war.

Yankees were not the only victims of atrocities. One former Confederate soldier complained:

> The reputation of the South has suffered not only because the terrible trials of Northern prisoners in Southern prisons have been so fully exploited, but because the truth of the Confederates' prison experience has not been given to the world. My comrades died by the hundreds amid healthful surroundings, almost all of these from the effects of starvation, and this in the midst of plenty. The official records show that at Camp Morton 12,082 prisoners were confined, of which number 1,763, or 14.6 per cent, perished. Excepting the few shot by the guards, the deaths from wounds were rare. The conditions were not malarial, for Indianapolis was not unhealthy. There were no epidemics during my imprisonment of about fifteen months, and little cause for death had humane and reasonable care of the prisoners been exercised.[20]

Near the end of the war, a Rebel officer who had been held at Johnson's Island in Lake Erie crossed paths with returning soldiers who had just been released from Andersonville, Elmira, Point Lookout, Rock Island, Camp Morton, Camp Chase, and Camp Douglas. Victims from both sides stopped and compared notes. The officer later escaped and made his way through Georgia with remnants of the weary Confederate Army. While he was trudging along the ruined Southwestern Railroad, he met a man who asked him if it was true that the Yankees were in Macon. "I at once recognized by his accent that he was a Northerner," the soldier recalled, "and upon my inquiry as to his command he became confused and evidently agitated. As Andersonville was only a few miles off, I was convinced that he was an escaped Union prisoner, and upon so expressing myself he broke down completely, saying, 'For God's sake don't take me back to that place.'" The Confederate concluded, "I had taken my life in my own hands two days before rather than go back to Camp Morton, and I could appreciate this poor fellow's agony."[21]

Prison camps on both sides were incredibly lethal. Indeed, the performance of the military in designing, operating, and supplying prisons during the Civil War proved to be worse than the record of civilian authorities, more horrific even than that of the slave traders and plantation owners, who, after all, had economic incentives to treat their prisoners better. According to War Department figures compiled in July 1866, the North had held a total of 220,000 Confederates and the South had held 126,000 Unionists. Of these, 26,436 Southerners and 22,576 Northerners died in prison camps in less than four years.[22] Revised estimates from the War Records Office placed the numbers at 30,212 dead (of 196,713 held) in Confederate prisons, for a mortality rate of 15.3 percent, and 26,774 dead (of 227,570 held) in Union prisons, for a mortality rate of 11.7 percent. Even those numbers were probably low.[23] To put the matter in perspective, roughly two and a half times as many soldiers were imprisoned as were involved in the great Battle of Gettysburg, yet the prison camps killed nearly ten times as many as did the battle.[24]

THE THIRTEENTH AMENDMENT

EARLY in the war, the journalist Horace Greeley had publicly denounced President Lincoln for catering to the slavery interests and failing to define the war as a struggle to end slavery. He urged him to free the slaves and enlist them to help win the contest. Lincoln wrote back that his goal was to save the Union, not to free the slaves. But a few days later, after the North had finally won a major battle, he sent an ultimatum to the South, stating that as of January 1, 1863, all slaves in areas still in rebellion would be "then, thenceforward, and forever free." Slave states already under federal control, on the other hand, would be exempt from his order. Once the Union was restored, loyal citizens would be compensated for all losses inflicted by the United States, "including the loss of slaves."

When the South failed to capitulate, Lincoln, as promised, issued the

Emancipation Proclamation, freeing all the slaves throughout the states in rebellion. Frederick Douglass called it "a memorable day in the progress of American liberty and civilization," and he noted that the action "was framed with a view to the least harm and the most good possible in the circumstances, and with especial consideration of the latter."[25]

As the war slowly ground to a conclusion, pressure mounted to amend the Constitution of the United States for the first time in over sixty years and abolish slavery once and for all. On January 11, 1864, Senator John B. Henderson of Missouri (a progressive conservative and a former slave-holder himself) proposed a joint resolution, modeled on the Northwest Ordinance, declaring: "Slavery and involuntary servitude, except as a punishment for crime, shall not exist in the United States."[26]

Senator Charles Sumner of Massachusetts, an abolitionist, suggested several alternative versions that would have ended slavery without exception. "Too well I know the vitality of slavery with its infinite capacity of propagation," he said, "and how little slavery it takes to make a slave State with all the cruel pretensions of slavery."[27]

Over Sumner's objections, the Senate passed the following constitutional amendment: "Section 1. Neither slavery nor involuntary servitude, except as a punishment for crime whereof the party shall have been duly convicted, shall exist within the United States, or any place subject to their jurisdiction. Section 2. Congress shall have power to enforce this article by appropriate legislation."

On January 31, 1865, the House finally passed for submission to the states the Thirteenth Amendment. The vote was 119 to 56 with 8 abstaining, a number of Democrats having changed their earlier position.[28] It was not until December 18th—eight months after Lincoln's assassination—that the secretary of state certified that the Thirteenth Amendment had become part of the Constitution of the United States. (Other states eventually ratifying it would include Florida in 1865, Iowa and New Jersey in 1866, Delaware in 1901, and Mississippi never did until 135 years later.)[29]

The Confederacy's defeat ensured that Negroes were no longer doomed to be born and die in bondage. When one young slave girl, Fannie Berry, heard the news she ran to the kitchen and shouted in the window, "Mammy, don't you cook no more. You's free! You's free!"[30] Negroes in Williamsburg danced and sang all night in the cold, and at daybreak walked away with blankets and clothes and pots and pans and chickens on their backs.[31] Another former slave, Annie Mae Weathers, later spoke of "hearing my pa say that when somebody came and bellowed, 'You niggers is free at last,' say he just dropped his hoe and said in a queer voice, 'Thank

God for that.'"[32] And Booker T. Washington later described his emancipation in Franklin County, Virginia. "Finally the war closed, and the day of freedom came," he wrote.

> It was a momentous and eventful day to all upon our plantation. . . . My mother, who was standing by my side, leaned over and kissed her children, while tears of joy ran down her cheeks. She explained to us what this all meant, that this was the day for which she had been so long praying, but fearing that she would never live to see. . . . [Yet] within a few hours the wild rejoicing ceased and a feeling of deep gloom seemed to pervade the slave quarters.[33]

Much of the South was rubble. Roads, railroads, and factories were damaged or destroyed, crops ruined. Hundreds of thousands of Confederate soldiers and civilians killed. The remaining Rebels limping home on parole. Southern society was in shambles, and occupied by the conquering Union Army, complete with armed Negroes in blue uniforms and brass buttons. Official retribution by the North was remarkably mild. Only one Confederate officer was executed, and that was for war crimes, not treason. (Arrested and tried by a military commission on charges of conspiring to weaken and kill Union prisoners and of murder, "in violation of the laws and customs of war," Andersonville's commandant, Henry Wirz, was hanged in the Old Capitol Prison at Washington in November 1865.)[34] Vanquished rebels were not stripped of their remaining property, or disenfranchised, or tried for crimes committed against their former slaves, or forced to pay reparations. Extraordinarily few defeated rebels were imprisoned after the war; even Jefferson Davis, the gaunt former Confederate president, was released without even having been tried or even charged with a crime, after serving only two years' imprisonment in Fortress Monroe. By and large, the survivors were allowed to go home to rebuild their shattered lives.[35]

Meanwhile, in the upheaval, four million Negro men, women, and children throughout the South were suddenly and unceremoniously freed from slavery, ending centuries of bondage. Abruptly on their own for the first time in their lives, without housing or property or means of support, and having received no compensation for what they had endured, they found themselves adrift in a threatening, war-ravaged region that now was under military rule.

Hundreds of thousands of freed slaves quickly fled from their places of captivity, many of them changing their names to evade being traced. Most wanted to escape from the rural plantations they associated with slavery, hoping to find more opportunities and better protection in population centers.[36]

White Southerners and even many Northerners and black leaders urged those who had been freed to avoid the South's devastated cities, which were gutted, depressed, demoralized, disinclined to shelter or support poor black refugees, and swarming with disease and vice. But many former slaves went there anyway, fearing that to remain near the fields might be to risk possible reenslavement if the Union whites reneged on their promise of freedom. Dusty roads were lined with refugees. Massive dislocation ensued. The military authorities struggled to prevent complete chaos and disorder. Many blacks perished from starvation or disease. In Macon, Georgia, during the first December after liberation, five hundred Negroes died, compared to an average loss of forty per month during slavery.[37]

Some blacks who could not find lawful employment were arrested for theft or curfew violations and convicted without counsel or trial. As a result, the first civil right that emancipated blacks sought was not the right to vote but the right to serve on juries.[38] After all, they feared that, according to the Thirteenth Amendment everyone was talking about, anyone convicted of a crime could now be legally enslaved, all over again. And they had good reason to worry. Hadn't the white man's law been used against them for centuries? Wasn't it used against them still? Despite efforts by former slaves and Northerners to help them gain equal-justice protection, blacks continued to be denied the right to serve on juries. In many parts of the South, even the right to testify in court against a white person was withheld.[39]

Lawmakers in several Southern states enacted new legal restrictions that put the Negro's status somewhere between slave and free.[40] These Black Codes provided that freedmen who were found without lawful employment could be arrested as common vagrants; those who failed to pay their fines might be jailed; or if jail space was not available—many slave pens, jails, and penitentiaries having been destroyed in the war—such blacks could be hired out to employers, who paid the fines and deducted the cost from the laborers' wages. Many freedmen found themselves held as prisoners and forced to work for private masters, like indentured servants if not like slaves, rebuilding the white society that had kept them and their families in bondage for generations.

Soon after the fighting stopped, black "vagrants" in Nashville and New Orleans were being fined and sent to the workhouse; in San Antonio and Montgomery they were put to work on the streets to pay for their own jail keep, beginning a sort of penal slavery on the installment plan.[41] A Yankee journalist who entered war-ravaged Selma, Alabama, came upon a chain gang of black prisoners digging the bed for a street under the watchful eyes of Union soldiers. The reporter was told that no white man had ever been sentenced to the chain gang, for any crime, but that blacks were now being condemned to it for such things as "using abusive language towards a white man" or selling farm produce within the town limits.[42] Using this growing labor pool, Alabama's Reconstruction government leased the Wetumpka prison and began developing its state penal machinery.[43] And in North Carolina, the *Raleigh Daily Standard* of September 27, 1865, reported:

> The military on yesterday picked up a large number of gentle-men of color, who were loitering about the street corners, ap-parently much depressed by ennui and general lassitude of the nervous system, and, having armed them with spades and shov-els, set them to play at street cleaning for the benefit of their own health and the health of the town generally. This is certainly a "move in the right direction;" for the indolent, lazy, Sambo, who lies about in the sunshine and neglects to seek employment by which to make a living, is undoubtedly "the right man in the right place" when enrolled in the spade and shovel brigade.[44]

North Carolina's legislature authorized judges to sentence offenders to work on chain gangs on the county roads or on any railroad or other internal improvement in the state for a maximum of one year. Those who escaped would have to serve double the unexpired term.[45] The new state constitution provided for crimes to be punished by death, fine, or impris-onment with or without hard labor. The Reconstruction government decided to build a penitentiary on the Auburn model, but the commission-ers disappeared with $100,000. A second commission paid an Ohio archi-tect to draft a different design. However, it was replaced by yet a third commission, which resorted to leasing convicts to the railroads until a suit-able prison could be constructed.[46] By 1874, 384 of 455 prisoners were Negro, and in 1878 they accounted for 846 of 952.[47]

Mississippi's penitentiary had been devastated during the war, and the state's treasury was empty. In 1867 the military government began leasing convicts to rebuild wrecked railroads and levees. But the convicts and staff remained destitute. Supplies were short, unsanitary conditions bred dis-ease. The penitentiary barely survived for the first several years following the war.[48] By 1872 convicts were being leased to Nathan Bedford Forrest, the Confederate war hero and first head of the Ku Klux Klan, for work on his Selma, Marion and Memphis Railroad. Once again, Forrest was making money from the slave trade.[49]

Georgia's federal governor, General T. H. Ruger, rented Negro convicts to a railroad builder for one year in exchange for $3,500. So did the next ("scalawag") governor, Rufus Bullock.[50]

During the fall of Richmond, 200 of 287 convicts vanished, but Yankees somehow rounded up the rest and—incredibly—returned them to prison, putting some to work repairing the institution.[51] The battered penitentiary remained under military command until March 1866, when General Turner relinquished control to civil authorities. The new superintendent, Burnham Wardwell, had himself been imprisoned during the war, for Yankee sympathies. He remained in charge until early 1870, when he fled to New Jersey to evade arrest for his role in the spreading scandals over corruption and mismanagement at the penitentiary.[52]

Virginia's penal system continued to undergo radical changes. Before the war, most inmates had been white; now they were predominantly black.[53] Overcrowding increased, producing even more unsanitary conditions. Prison authorities increasingly resorted to contracting out the convicts to private companies, who used them to work at reconstruction, toiling on roads, canals, and railroads. In late 1866 Governor Francis H. Pierpont reported the penitentiary was self-sustaining, pointing out that "a favorable opportunity [had] presented itself of employing a number of the colored convicts on the excavation of two short railroad tracts, where they were employed with mutual profit to the institution and the contractors, and doubtless to the welfare of the prisoners; they were not over-worked, and had the benefit of open air."[54] By 1871, 609 of 828 convicts (including all but 4 of 67 women) were black, and the death rate from scurvy, accidents, gunshots, and other causes was running high.[55]

Woody Ruffin was a convict of the Virginia penitentiary who had been hired out with other prisoners to work on the Chesapeake and Ohio Railroad. During an escape attempt, he allegedly killed Louis Swats, an employee of the contractor who had been hired to guard the leased convicts. Ruffin was subsequently captured; tried and convicted in Richmond's circuit court, he was sentenced to be hanged on May 25, 1871.

On appeal the Virginia court found that although Ruffin was not within the walls of the penitentiary, he was still a convict and as bound by its regulations as any other prisoner. Without explicitly citing the Thirteenth Amendment, Judge Christian also declared:

> A convicted felon, whom the law in its humanity punishes by
> confinement in the penitentiary instead of with death, is subject

while undergoing that punishment, to all the laws which the Legislature in its wisdom may enact for the government of that institution and the control of its inmates. For the time being, during
his term of service in the penitentiary, he is in a state of penal servitude to the State. He has, as a consequence of his crime, not
only forfeited his liberty, but all his personal rights except those
which the law in its humanity accords to him. He is for the time
being the slave of the State. He is *civiliter mortuus;* and his
estate, if he has any, is administered like that of a dead man.[56]

After the fall of slavery, Southern prisons increasingly contained black
convicts, whom the states leased to favored contractors in exchange for
fees and graft. After Mississippi enacted measures such as its infamous
"pig law," setting a penalty of five years' imprisonment in the state penitentiary for the theft of any cattle or swine, its prison population swelled from
284 in 1874 to 1,072 at the close of 1877. By the end of radical Reconstruction, Georgia, Tennessee, North Carolina, Florida, Texas, Arkansas, Alabama, Mississippi, South Carolina, Louisiana, and Kentucky were all leasing convicts.[57]

The postwar depression in Texas was particularly acute, and the plum-
meting price of cotton and other woes contributed to increased crime and
a prison population that soared from 146 to 264 persons within the first
few months after the end of the war. Instead of adopting reforms to relieve
overcrowding at the penitentiary, Texas legislators enacted tough new laws
calling for forced labor within prison walls and at other works of public
utility outside the institution. Convicts were leased out to build railroads,
improve navigation and irrigation, and work mines of iron, lead, copper,
and gold. In 1869 the Texas prison population had swelled to 489. In 1871
the institution itself was leased out to the highest bidder—Ward, Dewey
and Company of Galveston—for a period of 15 years. By December 1872
there were 944 convicts. Following a series of prison scandals and political
changes, however, the lease was terminated in 1877 and the institution
passed into the hands of another Texas firm.[58]

Three companies agreed to pay the State of Georgia $500,000 in twenty
annual installments, starting April 1, 1879, to use convict labor. Those
doing the leasing included several prominent onetime Confederates,
among them General Joseph E. Brown, the state's former chief justice, and
his son, Julius; General Joseph M. Brown; and General (and former U.S.
senator) John B. Gordon. A number of other well-connected politicians
also participated.[59]

Tennessee's entire convict population was leased to the Tennessee Coal,

Iron and Railroad Company in order to break a strike by coal miners. However, a thousand enraged white workers seized the mines, freed the five hundred convicts who had been brought in to replace them, and razed the prisoners' cages. A company official later admitted: "One of the chief reasons which first induced the company to take up the [convict lease] system was the great chance it offered for overcoming strikes. For some years after we began the lease system we found that we were right in calculating that the free miners would be loath to enter upon strikes, when they saw the company was amply provided with convicts."[60]

INDIAN PRISONERS

MEANWHILE, farther west, prisons also figured in the fate of the American Indians. After their ill-fated uprising along the Minnesota River in 1862, as many as 303 Santee Sioux were condemned to be hanged and 16 received long prison terms.[61] President Lincoln reduced the number of condemned to 39.[62] The other leaders were taken down the Mississippi by steamer to the prison camp for Confederates at Rock Island, Illinois. One of them, Big Eagle, later said, "If I had known that I would be sent to the penitentiary, I would not have surrendered."[63]

Indians battled Union soldiers throughout the Southwest. Whenever possible, the army tried to capture and imprison their chiefs, and sometimes inflict a worse fate. One of those tortured to death in prison was Chief Mangas Colorado (Red Sleeves).[64] General William Tecumseh Sherman hated Indians even more than Confederates, saying of the former, "The more we can kill this year, the less will have to be killed the next war." Otherwise, they would "all have to be killed or be maintained as a species of paupers."[65] One of those Sherman captured in battle was Set-t-aiint-e (White Bear), a Kiowa chief also known as Satanta. After spending seven years in captivity, he plunged headfirst to his death from a second-story window of the Huntsville Penitentiary hospital, becoming yet another American Indian leader to die in captivity under suspicious circumstances.[66]

Crazy Horse was another. After helping to defeat Custer at the Greasy Grass River (Little Big Horn), he was taken prisoner and murdered by a white soldier, and an Indian policeman named Little Big Man.[67]

The other great Sioux chieftain who had defeated Custer—Sitting Bull—suffered a similar fate. After riding into Fort Buford under a promise that he would be released to the reservation at Standing Rock, he too was taken prisoner. After being interned for over two years, during the summer of 1885 he was allowed to travel throughout the United States and Canada as part of Buffalo Bill's Wild West Show. The military later tried to use Buffalo Bill Cody to lure him to Chicago so he could be arrested again. But that plan failed. On December 15, 1890 (two weeks before the massacre at Wounded Knee), forty-three Indian police under the command of Lt. Bull Head surrounded Sitting Bull's cabin at Fort Yates and shot him to death. They bashed his face, scalped him, and stole his moccasins and other articles as relics, leaving the battered corpse to be taken away to a hospital and dissected.[68]

Indians all across the Plains were chased down until they were killed or imprisoned. The lucky ones were treated as vanquished enemies, regardless of whether they had ever been hostile to white Americans. John Elk had relinquished all ties to his tribe and become a resident of Nebraska, yet he was barred from registering to vote. In 1884 the Supreme Court upheld the finding that Elk, like Dred Scott, was not a United States citizen.[69] A few years later, in *United States v. Kagama,* the Court upheld Congress's power to regulate Native Americans directly and without their consent.[70] Under the Dawes Act of 1887, existing reservations were carved up, and eighty-six million acres of Indian land was given over to white settlement and homesteading.

When Geronimo, the last great Apache war chief, surrendered at Skeleton Canyon, the story was front-page news all over the country. He and his fellow captives were crammed into broiling boxcars and shipped across the desert to San Antonio. Many whites expected him to be hanged. Tourists and souvenir hunters flocked to the fort to see Apaches in cages, though according to one army officer it was "not possible for any human being, other than an Indian" to endure the stench.[71] From there Geronimo was deported with 103 children and 277 other adults to Fort Marion in Florida's humid lowlands, where many contracted tuberculosis.[72] By the time he finally died of pneumonia at Fort Sill, he had been held in captivity for twenty-three years.[73]

For many years to come, prison remained a common fate for Apaches. At Arizona's adobe territorial prison at Fort Yuma, the authorities deployed a Gatling gun to guard their convicts and hired neighboring Quechan Indians to track down any escapees. According to some routine log entries at the prison, on October 30, 1893, a new arrival, an Apache prisoner named Has Ral Te (No. 691), was put into the prison's "Snake Den" for refusing to work. He died of "consumption" the following April. Two others, Say-es and Hos-col-te, began serving life terms for taking part in a stagecoach robbery that had killed a driver. Three and a half years later, Say-es also was found dead in his cell.[74]

ELMIRA REFORMATORY

THE Civil War had profoundly altered America's system of and rationale for imprisonment. Millions of slaves had been let loose, chattel
slavery abolished, and penal servitude expanded. Thousands of inmates
had perished in horrific prison camps kept by their own countrymen.
Many more were badly scarred by what they had experienced.

When the fighting was over, and the traumatized veterans had returned
home, some found themselves in trouble with the law. In 1866 at the Massachusetts State Prison, 171 of 247 entering convicts were war veterans, and
only 6 percent of them had ever been in prison before. "It was a sad sight,"
the warden wrote, "and one to be regretted, that so many noble defenders
of the 'old flag,' some of whom had participated in battles from the first
Bull Run to the surrender of Lee, mutilated and covered with scars (one
had upon his body the scars of eight wounds received in one battle), and
whose record in the war, with few exceptions, was good, should terminate
so glorious a career in the State Prison."[75]

Most state prisons were in sad shape. Even such model institutions as
Auburn and Eastern had deteriorated since their glory days decades earlier—crumbled not just in their physical plant, but overall, as if they had
lost sight of their original goals. The old enthusiasm was gone.

It was in this context that two prominent reformers and members of the
New York Prison Association, Dr. Enoch Cobb Wines and Dr. Theodore
Dwight, reviewed the conditions in New York's aging prisons. Based upon
their study, they suggested some long-needed reforms. In place of a
decades-old preoccupation with profit-making industrial institutions, they
advocated making reformation of the offender the primary object of imprisonment, at least where young offenders were concerned.[76]

The legislature agreed and passed an act creating a new state reformatory. It was to be modeled on Sir Walter Crofton's Irish mark system, the
object of which was to train each prisoner in such a manner that upon his
discharge he would be "able to lead an upright life."[77]

Wines also organized the National Prison Congress, held in Cincinnati
in October of 1870.[78] The meeting's host—General Rutherford B. Hayes,
governor of Ohio and a future president of the United States—embraced
the reformatory concept. "It may seem to be in advance of the present day,"
he said, "but it is, as we believe, but anticipating an event not far distant,
to suggest that sentences for crime, instead of being for a definite period,
especially in cases of repeated convictions, will, under proper restrictions,
be made to depend on the reformation and established good character of
the convict."[79]

The Cincinnati congress adopted a detailed and extraordinarily progressive "Declaration of Principles" which proclaimed that the "supreme aim of prison discipline is the reformation of criminals, not the infliction of vindictive suffering." The delegates called for prison sanitary improvements and an end to political appointments of prison administrators; welcomed the participation of women in prison management; favored the progressive classification of prisoners, based on character, according to a mark system; urged rewards for good conduct, industry, and attention to learning; stressed the importance of prison education; and argued that a prisoner's will must be won over, not destroyed.

Here were reformers who claimed that the prison's regime should strive to cultivate a convict's self-respect, rather than trying to degrade him. Their manifesto favored "moral forces" over physical coercion or brutality, and it condemned the contract system of prison labor as "prejudicial alike to discipline, finance and the reformation of the prisoner, and sometimes injurious to the interest of the free laborer." Although acknowledging that the "proper duration of imprisonment . . . is one of the most perplexing questions in criminal jurisprudence," they advocated long, indeterminate prison sentences for reformatory purposes.[80]

Such views were a sign of the times. The new emphasis upon "reformation," after all, arose during a period of national reconstruction and attempted reconciliation, following the defeat of the Confederacy and the emancipation of blacks from slavery. As part of this movement, some traditional penological beliefs stressing guilt and vengeance now were being replaced by notions of reformation and a medical "disease" approach that was aimed at treatment, improvement, and cure. In both arenas, the reformers showed little understanding of or sensitivity to the condition or needs of free Negroes, in the South or anywhere else. A few years later, as president of the United States, Hayes would employ this same philosophy in ending Reconstruction, when one of his first official acts would be to order the withdrawal of the last federal troops in the South. In effect, as one historian later put it, "The South was 'redeemed.' This favorite euphemism of the white Democrats meant that the Federal government had renounced responsibility for reconstruction, abandoned the Negro, and, in effect, invited Southern white men to formulate their own program of political, social and economic readjustment."[81]

During the Civil War, Elmira had been the site of a large and notorious Union prison camp. Although conditions were not as bad as at Andersonville, thousands of Confederate soldiers had died there without any hindrance from the local citizenry. But now, only five years after the war's end, the legislature selected none other than Elmira as the site of the model new state reformatory. New buildings were constructed and a board of managers appointed. Zebulon R. Brockway, a rising young prison warden who had managed reform-type institutions in Albany, Rochester, and Detroit, became the reformatory's first superintendent. Thirty inmates were received from Auburn on July 24, 1876.[82]

Brockway wrote to his friend, Enoch Wines: "I feel that there are very gross defects in the prison system of the land, and that, as a whole, it does not accomplish its design; and that the time has come for reconstruction."[83] In its place he wanted an institution that would be more like a college or hospital than an ordinary prison. Elmira Reformatory soon proved to be the most ambitious attempt to fulfill the lofty Declaration of Principles that Brockway and others had promulgated a few years earlier at Cincinnati.

The institution held first-time felons, aged sixteen to thirty. Judges sentenced offenders to the reformatory for an indeterminate period; Elmira's managers later decided the actual release date within certain statutory limits. Under this arrangement, convicts had to earn their way out through an elaborate system of grading, after being put through rigorous manual training that was intended to inculcate obedience, discipline, and marketable skills. Brockway's system employed marks, or grades, to rank each inmate's progress, with merits to reward and demerits to punish individual behavior. There were three grades of offenders, each dressed in a different colored uniform. Entering inmates belonged to the second class and were supposed to be advanced or demoted according to their behavior, with privileges being increased or decreased in corresponding fashion. At six months their conduct was examined by the board of managers, who decided whether to release them. If discharged, they remained on parole and were required to write regular letters to the superintendent.[84]

In 1879 Brockway added a "School of Letters." Selected inmates were trained in brush making and hollowware manufacture. He also bought a printing press and used it to produce an endless stream of slick institutional reports, as well as the nation's first inmate newspaper, *The Summary*. Brockway even established an innovative trade school for mentally impaired inmates.

His interest in such slow learners quickly developed into an obsession. By 1884 Brockway was stating that one-half of the prisoners were "incorrigible" due to heredity. A few years later he was reporting that his investigations and efforts had "served to strengthen the opinion that physical degeneracy, however originated, is a common subjective cause of criminal conduct; that the mental powers enfeebled, untrained, uninformed, characterize the mass of criminals on admission." Brockway also contended that modern criminals "are to a considerable extent the product of our civilization and also of emigration to our shore from the degenerated populations of crowded European marts." It was these two sources, he said, that produced the great mass occupying the courts and filling the prisons. "Until the source of supply is staunched, there is no safety for society but in quarantining and curing, in well organized and managed reformatory prisons, the criminally infected individuals brought to our attention by their crimes."[85]

Brockway had managed to advance his reformatory despite mounting pressure by organized labor. The unions wanted to restrict convict labor, claiming that it posed unfair competition to law-abiding workers. He did so in part by packaging Elmira as an "industrial training school" that was free from the usual requirement of fiscal self-support. Nevertheless, in time, all New York prisons, including Elmira, were increasingly affected by a series of restrictive new laws. In 1881 the legislature abandoned convict leasing and all other prison labor arrangements in favor of contract labor; in 1884 contract labor was abolished; in 1888 the "Yates Law" was passed, prohibiting productive labor in prisons. Elmira's labor system was effectively ruled illegal. As a result, Brockway suddenly had to find both another means to occupy his young inmates and another philosophical foundation upon which to build his prison regime.[86] And he had to find it fast.

In the space of only two days, Brockway fixed upon an alternative organizing principle. It happened when a thirty-year-old former newspaper reporter who was serving time for forgery suggested that military training should be made the new core activity. Brockway appointed the inmate as colonel of the regiment and ordered him to select and train the first sixty inmates of the first grade (those closest to parole) for an "officer corps." Soon the group was spending several hours a day marching in formation and learning basic military tactics. The prison yard was renamed the parade ground. Elmira's convict officers were issued snappy uniforms and highly polished brass-hilted steel swords.[87]

By cultivating his relationships in the legislature, Brockway helped to gain the establishment of a state-supply system. It allowed prison industries only for purposes of inmate training, with the further provision that the goods produced were to be sold only to other state institutions or departments. Brockway praised the new state-use law, saying it "makes industrial education of the prisoners the supreme object, directs their classification, gradation and education, permits the conferring of pecuniary rewards, and authorizes the conditional release of such prisoners as properly qualify themselves for safe inhabitancy."[88]

Due in part to Brockway's tireless efforts at public relations, many regarded Elmira as a well-run, model institution. By 1893, however, the reformatory was becoming seriously overcrowded, and some of Brockway's views were becoming controversial. He contended, for example, that "physical degeneracy" was a leading cause of crime, and complained that persons with low intelligence could not learn how to become law-abiding or productive members of society.[89]

Some of his methods also came under fire. In 1894 allegations against him prompted the governor to order a special investigation. It found that he had reserved many of the worst whippings for those he considered most "immoral" and "defective"—boys who suffered from mental or physical disability. His reputation and Elmira's image were tarnished, and he eventually resigned as superintendent in 1900, as bruised as Eddy and Lynds had been before him.[90]

CONVICT LABOR

THE convict lease system that was so prevalent in the post-bellum South had entailed renting out a convict to a private company for a specific term. The state abdicated responsibility for the prisoners' welfare, leaving it to private contractors whose primary or exclusive objective was making a profit. As one Southern convict manager put it, "the State turned over its charges body and soul, and thenceforth washed its hands of them."

Prisoners in the South often were kept in open-air cages and guarded by overseers with bloodhounds; there was no need for major construction and maintenance of the physical plant. Consequently, leasing offered profits to the state of up to three or four times its expense, and the lessee had to pay only a minimal price. Leasing was, however, extremely susceptible to graft and other abuses.[91]

Warden J. H. Bankhead of the Alabama penitentiary observed that "our system is a better training school for criminals than any of the dens of iniquity that exist in our large cities." The state cared nothing for criminals, nor for their well-being. "You may as well expect to instill decent habits into a hog as to reform a criminal whose habits and surroundings are as filthy as a pig's," he remarked. "To say there are any reformatory measures at our prison, or that any regard is had to similar subjects, is to state a falsehood."[92]

One of the few Southerners who spoke out against convict-leasing systems was George Washington Cable of Louisiana, a former Confederate soldier and a novelist.[93] In a major essay on the subject in 1883, Cable exposed the system's sub-rosa nature, and pointed out that Mississippi, Arkansas, and Louisiana did not publish reports or release any statistics about their penal systems in order to conceal rampant abuses. He called convict leasing "a disgrace to civilization."

In response to his charges, a reform committee reported: "The leasing system under any form is wrong in principle and vicious. . . . The system of leasing convicts to individuals or corporations to be worked by them for profit simply restores a state of servitude worse than slavery; worse in that it is without any of the safeguards resulting from the ownership of the slave."[94] As one Louisiana prison official put it: "Before the Civil War we owned the Negroes. If a man had a good Negro, he could afford to take care of him; if he was sick, get him a doctor. He might even get gold plugs in his teeth. But these convicts, we don't own them. So, one dies, we get another."[95]

In fact, the known death rate in Southern prisons was at least three times higher than that in Northern prisons. Many speculated it was actually much greater. Disappearances were extremely common during the early years of the lease system. As late as 1882, a survey found that 1,100 prisoners had successfully "escaped" from Southern prisons during the past two years, compared to an annual rate of only 63 among 18,300 Northern convicts, giving rise to suspicions that some may have met with foul play or perished from wounds.[96]

Accommodations in some prison camps consisted of steel-reinforced railcars—usually about eighteen feet long and seven or eight feet high and wide, one side of which had been covered by iron bars—into which eighteen or so men were put for the night, like circus animals. These cages, which often had tin roofs, were broiling hot and filthy. A Florida prison official from the turpentine camps later described a crude little log house called "Padlock," consisting of open-air platforms on which the convicts slept with shackles binding their legs and waists while an armed guard patrolled in front.[97]

Instead of fortress walls or the silent system, the Southern prison farms and camps used chains, dogs, guns, and brutal punishments to control their convicts. In 1912 Dr. E. Stagg Whitin of the National Committee on Prison Labor observed that the status of the Southern convict was "the last surviving vestige of the slave system."[98]

Writing in the 1920s, more than fifty years after the Civil War, one Northerner described the Southern chain gang as a "peculiar institution." As soon as a new prisoner entered camp, he would be shackled by both ankles with heavy chains that were a foot or two long. "The chain riveted to both ankles tends to drag on the ground and interferes with the working energy of the prisoner," he wrote. "There is therefore another—a longer chain—a kind of cross chain linked at the center of the one that is riveted to the ankles. That chain serves two main purposes. It is used to lift the chain off the ground when the men are working. This is done by sticking the loose end through the belt and raising the riveted chain off the ground. Its other use is to chain the men together at night. A dozen or so men will be chained to each other when they are asleep in their beds."[99]

Mississippi abolished the lease system by constitutional amendment in 1890, and then resorted to segregating the convicts on large state prison farms. And Kentucky assumed full responsibility for managing its penal system in the early 1890s.[100]

Georgia's leasing system was the object of recurring scandals. In 1908 a commission was appointed to obtain a new prison farm where old and sick convicts would be housed; other provisions were made for contractors to pay the state $100 a year for the more "desirable" convicts. After he received a long letter from a former prisoner detailing specific instances of corruption, the muckraker Charles Edward Russell wrote an article for *Everybody's Magazine* exposing hideous conditions in Georgia's lease camps. Stirred by a newspaper crusade and pressure from the federal government, the state finally abolished its leasing system.[101]

Florida's infamous prison conditions—marked by fatal floggings and torture, unsanitary camp conditions, and a lack of basic medical care—ranked among the nation's worst. J. C. Powell, a veteran prison official in the state, wrote a chilling book in which he described an environment ravaged by disease, starvation, and exposure, and keepers who hanged a convict by his thumbs, allowing him to writhe in agony until he died. Powell reported seeing some prisoners' thumbs so stretched and deformed that "they resembled the paws of certain apes" and were extended to the length of their index fingers.[102] And Powell was not alone. After visiting a Florida turpentine camp in 1912, an inspector noted: "Seven convicts died in this camp in a single year from diseases connected with standing or working in water up to their waists at all seasons of the year." Prisoners were forced to work even when sick, upon pain of being beaten or shot to death.[103]

Such conditions in Florida lasted for decades. In 1923, after years of continuous scandals, that state finally ended its notorious convict-leasing system.[104] Alabama followed in 1928.[105]

Meanwhile, under the prison contract labor system that was favored in most of the North, a company contracted with the state for the labor of a specified number of convicts. The state continued to house, guard, feed, and otherwise care for them, but the contractor provided all of the raw

materials, machinery, trainers, and foremen necessary to carry on the contracted business. This system's proponents claimed that contractors were
better businessmen than government employees. They said the arrangement could prove lucrative for the contractors and the state alike, maybe
generating enough revenue to pay for up to two-thirds of the prison's
expenses. They said it could free up prison officials from nagging business chores that distracted them from their real penal mission (whatever
that was).

The workers in a contract prison labor business could not unionize or
strike, and their keepers enjoyed almost complete power over their lives.[106]
Convicts working under the contract system also suffered from treatment
that was often designed to extract their last ounce of labor, regardless of
the physical consequences, and any apparent idlers, malingerers, or
troublemakers faced very harsh consequences. At New Jersey's Trenton
prison in 1878, after Jacob Snook died while being "stretched," an investigating committee determined that the prison authorities had poured alcohol on epileptics and set them afire to detect possible faking. In Ohio's
reformatory that year, unproductive convicts were made to sit naked in
puddles of water and receive electric shocks from an induction coil.[107]

Public investigations of New York's prison contract labor system had
become increasingly frequent (and lurid) during the 1840s, 1860s, and
1870s, but with little effect.[108] Reporting in 1883, the Committee on State
Prisons exposed a catalog of horrors such as the lash, the paddle, the dark
cell, and the cooler, among other instruments of torture. These had
directly resulted in innumerable inmate deaths, and had driven others to
suicide or insanity.

Officials acknowledged that some Sing Sing convicts had actually dived
off the upper galleries and broken their legs in an effort to escape being
paddled. Those less fortunate broke their necks. Eyewitnesses described
how prisoners there had routinely received as many as 315 consecutive
lashes with a three-foot-long heavy leather paddle, for relatively minor
offenses. The blows were administered by the principal keeper and "slug-
gers," after the contractors' instructors or foremen complained that a convict was not working hard enough or not producing his quota of finished
goods. The legislators were told that one rebellious inmate who had
refused to perform, even after severe beatings, was ultimately poisoned to
death for not working. Another uncooperative prisoner, Michael Lawless,
was reported to have been kept chained down on the stone floor for ten
months until he went stark, raving mad and had to be removed to the
lunatic asylum. Inmates were found to have lost limbs or suffered other
permanent injuries due to unsafe working conditions. Convicts assigned

to Sing Sing's infamous stove shop sometimes shrieked when the defective ladles they were using suddenly burst, spilling molten iron onto their shoes and burning their flesh to the bone. Some were later sent back to work with maggots on their wounds. Sing Sing's unusually high death statistics had been published for years, but now human beings with names were being attached to the numbers. Benjamin Myer, twenty-one years old, so dreaded the paddle he had committed suicide. Cornelius Lynch had been making stoves when he became entangled in some machinery and was disemboweled. Another stoveworker, William Anderson, died of overwork, as did James Mackinson, a colored man, and John Moore. Thomas Dolan and William Chambers had complained of work-related ailments shortly before they died; they had received no medical treatment. William McNally had ruptured himself in the stove foundry while putting in extra work to try to earn some extra pay . . .[109]

Sing Sing was not the only New York penal institution experiencing such abuses. Similar reports were delivered about Blackwell's Island, the Albany and Kings County penitentiaries, and Clinton State Prison.

Clinton, located in the Adirondacks near the Canadian border, had been established in 1844 at the site of an iron-ore mine, but mining had been abandoned by 1877 in favor of manufacturing.[110] Arthur Alexander Hessler, who had fought for the Union and who was in ill health from a maritime accident, was sentenced to Clinton for writing a bad check. Shortly after arriving on a frigid January day in 1881, Hessler was forced to wear an eighteen-pound iron yoke, with five sharp spikes garnishing his head, for twenty-four hours. After he collapsed, he was kicked, beaten, and tortured as sport by the guards. Hessler's extraordinarily detailed affidavit provided a rare glimpse into some of the brutality that attended contract prison labor up North.[111]

Similar abuses were publicized in other states. Pat Crowe, a train robber, was sent to the Missouri State Penitentiary at Jefferson City and assigned to work in the prison shoe factory. Under the contract system in effect there, the state was paid forty-five cents per day for each convict's labor. Crowe later claimed it was the most brutal system he had ever witnessed, saying, "I have known men to be whipped to death simply because it was a physical impossibility for them to do the tasks assigned to them under this outrageous contract labor system." First-time offenders were handcuffed to their work posts all night. If, after ten days, a convict failed to achieve his quota, he was taken to "Betsy's sister," a contraption in the punishment hall. He would be handcuffed to it and lifted until his toes barely touched the floor. Then his bare back would be lashed with a rawhide whip and the wounds sponged with salt water. Crowe said he knew several prisoners at the Missouri penitentiary who had died from such treatment. As if to thumb his nose at his former tormentors, Crowe later said that after his release from Jefferson City, he took "a diabolical delight in holding up trains and dynamiting the express safe. I was a real, hard-boiled outlaw and glad of it," he said, "because I felt that anything I did was mild compared with the wrongs that society was inflicting on the men in its prisons."[112]

In the Northeast, organized labor had opposed convict labor since the first workingmen's organizations had been formed and the first prison factories had been established. By the late 1800s, the increased power of labor unions had made them a more formidable force in several states. Labor intensified its long-standing struggle to eliminate "unfair" prison competition, which, its leaders said, threatened all law-abiding wage earners. Led by the Knights of Labor, the Federation of Organized Trades and Labor Unions, and the National Labor Party, union leaders focused their energies in major industrial states like New York and tried to convince key journalists and legislators to support their cause.[113]

New York's pro-union Committee on State Prisons, considering the "serious injury to free labor that is caused by this contract system in prisons," noted that "a number of the leading trades, and more particularly the hatters, stovemakers, hollow ware manufacturers, boot and shoemakers and brushmakers have all been materially damaged throughout the State, and more especially in the larger cities, by the ruinous competition against which they are compelled to struggle." To illustrate what it meant, the committee pointed out that a single penal institution could manufacture a million pairs of boots or shoes per year. It also observed that

> no outside manufacturer can enter the market against the rival whose labor costs him from seventy to eighty per cent below that of the outside manufacturer. Among other advantages, the prison contractor has no rent, repairs, or taxation, to pay for his factory, and he can grind out of his enslaved workman the utmost task which human endurance and man's muscle are capable of performing, even until the victims of this forced exertion often drop down from sheer exhaustion. . . . There was never a more flagrant or unjust monopoly than the one which is enjoyed by the prison contractors.[114]

New York experienced a tremendous growth in its prisoner population during the 1880s. Existing cell space was no longer adequate. Sing Sing had eight or nine hundred inmates double-bunked in its minuscule cells.

Many convicts needed medical treatment for respiratory ailments, chancres, syphilis, and other illnesses; they contracted many of these from each other as a result of overcrowding. It was becoming more difficult to maintain order. Corruption flourished. Medicine money was used to buy whiskey and rum for the prison staff. Huge quantities of food and clothing were stolen. Prisoners bribed staff members to get choice assignments, offering as much as $500 to work in the chaplain's office or land a porter's job.

Convict leasing and the contract labor system were only two of the most common arrangements. "Piece-price" agreements called for the state to receive payment for each piece or article that inmates produced in the prison workshops. The raw materials were furnished by a private contractor, who then received a profit on his investment.[115] Under the public-account or state-account system, a state went into business on its own, using the prisoners to manufacture goods that the state later sold on the open market.[116]

In 1885 a national survey reported that convict labor was being employed in 138 American penal institutions and involved 53,512 persons. New England had 7,451 inmates in 47 prisons, with 1,293 engaged in contract labor, 1,647 on public accounts, 607 on piece-price, and 445 leased out. The Middle Atlantic states showed 15,324 prisoners in 33 institutions, of whom 6,287 were contracted, 3,213 were on public account, 952 were on piece-price, and none were leased. The South listed 14,479 prisoners in only 20 institutions, with 2,110 on contract, 250 on public account, 160 on piece-price, and 9,594 leased out. In the West, 16,258 prisoners were held in 38 institutions, with 6,880 on contract, 2,982 on public account, 638 on piece-price, and 199 leased.[117] An estimated 45,277 American convicts were producing goods valued at about $28.8 million, a relatively small portion of the $5.4 billion that had been produced by the nation's 2.8 million free laborers five years before.[118]

Yet prison labor was big business. In 1885—the same year that the Statue of Liberty arrived in New York in hundreds of wooden crates—convicts accounted for 12.9 percent of America's workers employed in making whips, 21.5 percent of those employed in saddlery hardware, 3.1 percent of the known bootmakers and shoemakers, 3.2 percent of the broommakers and brushmakers, and 7.1 percent of the chairmakers.[119] Besides the tedium, monotony, long hours, and harsh working conditions experienced by other sweatshop workers, prisoners faced severe punishments—ranging from reduced privileges and shortened rations, to flogging, electric shocks, and even torture or death—not to mention their near total loss of civil liberties.

A convict entering Pennsylvania's Western Penitentiary in 1892 told of starting out in Number Seven, the mat shop. It was a dark, low-ceilinged room with small, barred windows, in which the air was heavy with dust and the rattling of the looms was deafening, creating an atmosphere of "noisy gloom." He wrote that it "is beginning to affect my health: the dust has inflamed my throat, and my eyesight is weakening in the constant dusk." Alongside him, a consumptive convict suffered coughing attacks and gushed blood from his mouth. Transferred to the hosiery department, the newcomer spent day after day turning stockings, and observed inmates stealing each other's finished products in order to make their quota. He watched convicts fight to defend their wares.[120]

Writing about his experiences in California's San Quentin prison, Donald Lowrie quoted a former fellow convict named Smoky as questioning the economics of imprisonment. "What I can't get through my nut is why 2,000 able-bodied men cost the State $100 a year apiece," Smoky observed.

> If we had a little town of our own outside we'd have our families
> and children, an' good food an' decent clothes, an' theatres an'
> fire department and everything else, an' we'd all be comfortable,
> an' some of us would have money in th' bank, an' we'd send our
> kids to school, an' all that. By workin' ev'ry day we'd support
> five 'r six thousand people besides ourselves, an' yet in here,
> livin' like dogs in kennels, an' eatin' th' cheapest grub they can
> get, it costs th' State a quarter of a million dollars a year t' keep
> us. There's somethin' rotten somewhere. If they'll get us guys
> work an' pay us f'r it, an' make us pay f'r what we got, y'r'd see
> a big difference. Y'r wouldn't see men comin' back, an y'r'd
> see lots of 'em go out an' take their proper place in th' world.
> They'd have th' work habit then, because they'd know that work
> brings a man all that makes life worth while.[121]

PRISONS AS LABORATORIES

THE period from 1870 to 1920 was an age of great immigration, and the scale and variety of that influx had profound implications for American society and its prisons. Since colonial times, some residents had accused aliens of being more criminal and troublesome than native-born whites. Puritan colonists had ranted about dangerous Quakers and transported convicts, slaveholders had expressed wariness over Negro imports from the West Indies, native Anglo-Saxon-Protestant New Yorkers and

Bostonians had complained about "lawless" Irish immigrants. Following the Civil War, as the volume of foreign immigration increased, nativist feelings also grew, buttressed by pseudoscientific theories about crime-prone races and degenerate nationalities, and pseudoevolutionary notions of biological superiority and inherited inferiority. During the 1870s, as nearly three million foreigners immigrated here, many native-born Americans of old stock were alarmed by the masses of poor, perhaps unassimilable strangers who had flocked to the cities.

In western Europe, Great Britain, and the United States, bastion of capitalism's "survival of the fittest," many social scientists turned their attention to social structures, and particularly to the plight of the "lower class." Charles Loring Brace described the worsened slum environment in graphic detail in *The Dangerous Classes of New York,* which documented the poor's grim struggle for existence. Yet Brace was quick to warn that attempts to cure poverty through charity could backfire, since they might actually lessen the poor's chances of survival by destroying necessary habits of industry, self-reliance, and self-respect. Left uncorrected, he predicted, "a community of paupers, transmitting pauperism to children of like character, would soon become one of the most degraded and miserable on the face of the earth."[122]

In 1874 a civic-minded New York merchant named Robert L. Dugdale toured thirteen county jails as a volunteer inspector for the prestigious Prison Association of New York. While visiting rural Ulster County, Dugdale found in jail six persons—four male, two female—under four family names who appeared to be blood relatives. He set out to trace their family history for clues to explain such an apparently disproportionate involvement in crime. Consulting available official records from prisons, courts, and other sources, he later claimed to have been able to follow the family's roots back to a colonial frontiersman, whom he called "Max," who had been born between 1720 and 1740, descended from early Dutch settlers. In his book *The Jukes* Dugdale supposedly followed the clan over five generations as it produced 1,200 Jukes or persons married to Jukes.[123] Of that number, Dugdale said he had documented 280 pauperized adults, 60 habitual thieves and 140 other criminals, 7 murderers, and 50 common prostitutes. One particular branch of the family had showed distinctly criminal tendencies, according to Dugdale, so he labelled its apparent founder as "Margaret, Mother of Criminals." His genealogy of degeneracy, promiscuity, and crime made titillating reading.[124]

Pseudoscientific arguments like Dugdale's became enormously influential in a nation that increasingly was becoming a mosaic of different races and cultures. In his essay "Crime and Automatism," published in 1875, Dr.

Oliver Wendell Holmes, the Boston physician and intellectual, declared that "in most cases crime can be shown to run in the blood."[125]

In the 1880s, the immigrant influx rose to 5.2 million men, women, and children, many of them refugees from eastern and southern Europe, who had fled political persecution and economic deprivation in Russia, present-day Poland, the lands of the Austro-Hungarian Empire, and Italy; non-Anglo-Saxons who did not speak English and whose appearance, customs, and political beliefs often seemed different, strange. Most of them gravitated to tightly knit enclaves in Chicago, New York, Boston, and other big cities, where they labored in factories and sweatshops, struggling to make ends meet. The zenith in immigration would not occur until the years between 1905 and 1914, when a million or more each year came to start a new life. In 1914 nearly 75 percent of them were from southern and eastern Europe, with only 13.4 percent coming from northern and western Europe.[126]

Crime in the United States was becoming increasingly associated with immigration. Whether or not newcomers were actually any more criminal than native borns was doubtful, but American prisons, reformatories, mental asylums, and other social service institutions clearly were disproportionately populated by immigrants and Negroes. In 1880, 26.4 percent of the United States general population was foreign born or Negro, yet fully 50.4 percent of the nation's prisoners came from those groups (21.8 percent immigrants, 28.6 percent Negro). The rate of imprisonment of foreign born was twice that of native born, and for colored persons it was three times higher. Of the nation's 12,681 prisoners of foreign birth, the most numerous were Irish (5,309), Germans (2,270), English (1,453), British American (1,215), and Chinese (526). In 1892 a third of Sing Sing's convicts and a quarter of Clinton's were foreign born. Germans had begun to replace the Irish as the foreign-born group most prevalent in prison.[127] By 1917 the proportion of immigrants would rise to about one-half in both institutions.[128]

Notions that had been prevalent under slavery continued to remain in vogue through a growing and fashionable eugenics movement, which sought to "improve" the human race through controlled breeding and eliminate "poor" or "inferior" tendencies.[129] Belief in racial superiority imbued government policy during the period of the Indian wars. By the late 1890s, eugenics programs enjoyed a full-blown renaissance in American prisons and other institutions for the insane, feebleminded, and wayward. Some of the leading eugenics adherents and experimenters were prison research directors, physicians, psychologists, and wardens.

The movement had begun rather modestly when a new coterie of physical anthropologists rushed to extend Franz Gall's phrenology—a field of study holding that the functions of the brain are localized in different regions and that their varying development could be observed from conformations, or "bumps," of the skull. Some of these early phrenologists searched for telltale marks of criminality. One of them—Charles Caldwell at Kentucky's Transylvania University—introduced phrenology in the United States during the 1820s. The field had been further popularized by George Combe and other prison visitors, who had followed the fad of using their ever-present instruments to measure the skulls of executed criminals.[130] Thus the cranium of LeBlanc, a murderer in New Jersey, was described as having unusually large organs of "destructiveness," "secretiveness," and "acquisitiveness," whereas the centers of "veneration" and "conscientiousness" in Tardy, a pirate, were found to be small.[131]

One American who was especially fascinated by Combe's phrenological studies of convicts' heads was E. W. Farnham, the matron of Sing Sing prison. In an encyclopedic work, Farnham applied some of the latest phrenological principles to the specialized study and treatment of criminals.[132] Officials at Philadelphia's Eastern Penitentiary also incorporated phrenological data as a regular feature of their prison publications.[133] Paul Broca, the Paris anthropologist, wrote with seeming authority about the peculiar shape and structure of criminals' skulls and brains.[134]

However, it was an Italian physician, Cesare Lombroso, who took this approach to a new level. Lombroso focused the new science of "modern" criminology upon the individual criminal as an animal or physical organism.[135] His book, *L'uomo delinquente* (Criminal Man), inspired by his autopsy of a notorious criminal, posited that there was a criminal type, an atavistic throwback to a more primitive and savage human.[136]

Using the latest methods of physical anthropology (and perhaps some zeal from medieval witch hunting), Lombroso made extensive measurements of thousands of convicts, both living and dead, and compiled a list of positive physical abnormalities, or "stigmata," which he associated with "the criminal type." By 1887 he had cataloged numerous suspicious traits, including an asymmetrical face, prognathism (an excessive jaw), eye defects, peculiarities of the palate, a receding forehead, scant beard, wooly hair, long arms, fleshy or swollen lips, abnormal dentition, a twisted nose, precocious wrinkles, darker skin, inversion of sex organs, a lack of moral sense, vanity, cruelty, a passion for gambling, the use of criminal argot, and cynicism.

In addition to broaching the idea of the born criminal, Lombroso postulated the existence of a "criminaloid," who ranked slightly above the criminal type but below normal man on the evolutionary scale. He had an innate criminal tendency, but could, like a chameleon, be affected by his surroundings. Lombroso ranked noncriminal men highest on the evolutionary scale, followed by criminal men and noncriminal women. Criminal women were said to be the least evolved, with physical traits that resembled those of criminal men. Lombroso classified all "primitive" women as prostitutes.[137] Based on such thinking, he concluded: "We are governed by silent laws which never cease to operate and which rule society with more authority than the laws inscribed on our statute books."[138]

Lombroso's theories were widely accepted in the United States. To some they implied that born criminals were not responsible for their criminality and that perhaps even criminaloids could not be fully blamed for having gone wrong. The impact of Lombroso's views was immediate in the study of the social sciences, especially criminology, which was then being introduced into the sociology curriculum at some American colleges and universities.[139]

The first place that scholars turned to test Lombrosian theories was prison, in part because it was assumed that this was where known criminals or criminaloids could most easily be found. Experiments were quickly conducted at Joliet Penitentiary, the Ohio State Penitentiary, and Blackwell's Island Workhouse and Penitentiary in New York City, to name a few.[140]

Beginning in 1880, the field of physical anthropology began to gain favor in American scientific journals.[141] It focused upon criminals, deviants, and abnormals, viewing the individual criminal offender as both a victim of heredity and a perpetuator of inherited criminality. As the spotlight shifted to one of society's most dangerous groups, the criminal class, much of the evidence that scientists presented had been secretly obtained from meticulously documented experiments, conducted in the controlled social laboratories of prisons, reformatories, jails, and other penal institutions. Prisons, after all, provided a captive population of subjects for study, who were available free of charge; they were also an ideal setting in which to conduct scientific research, to be used at a critical moment in scientific development.

This emerging use of prisons as a social laboratory, complete with inmates as human guinea pigs, confined to tiny cages, would prove to have enormous ramifications for the study of eugenics, psychology, intelligence testing, medicine, drug treatment, genetics, and birth control. Scientists gravitated toward prisons to test their theories of heredity, intelligence, fertility, and physical anthropology. In all of them, efforts at classification assumed greater and greater importance. Criminologists, for example, used their prison-based research studies to classify criminals. August Drähms, a resident chaplain at San Quentin prison in California, published a Lombrosian study in which he used statistics gathered from inmates to support a classification scheme that identified three categories of criminals: "instinctive criminals," whom he said were predisposed to commit crime; "habitual criminals," who resembled the instinctive offenders except that their inspiration was drawn more from their environment than from "parental fountains"; and "single offenders," who committed an isolated violation of the law that was generally out of character and situational in nature. Drähms considered all criminals as being morally, mentally, and physically inferior, but some were just more inferior than others.[142]

Rufus Bernhard von Kleinsmid, a researcher at Indiana Reformatory, reported that his study of fifty-six hundred inmates had convinced him that "these men are physically inferior to the average young man not in prison and presumably normal."[143] A chorus of others produced similar studies.

New methods of positive identification and classification sprang up as a product of this prison-based research. After Darwin's cousin, Francis Galton, photographed the facial features of known criminals, Lombroso quickly adapted photographic composites into his own presentations.[144] Building upon this new technology, France's Alphonse Bertillon developed another, more advanced system of identification that was widely adopted in American prisons during the late 1880s. The Bertillon method consisted of a uniform framework for recording precise measurements of an individual's height, weight, and various body dimensions, as well as other general information, including frontal and profile photographs of each subject.[145] In 1896 New York State required that all persons sentenced to a penal institution for thirty days or more must be measured and photographed according to this system, and the records carefully maintained and cataloged.[146]

Even these criminal identification techniques could not always guarantee that an individual would be positively identified. As Mark Twain disclosed in his popular 1894 novel *Pudd'nhead Wilson*, there was another method available. Called fingermarking or fingerprinting, it supposedly could positively identify every individual based upon the unique patterns on his or her fingertips.[147] Fingerprinting prisoners and criminals was somewhat slow to catch on, but its value was dramatically demonstrated by a number of highly publicized cases of mistaken identity and miscarriage of justice that were exposed with fingerprint evidence. One of them occurred in 1903 when a Negro convict was received at Leavenworth Federal Penitentiary. Prison officials believed they had held him there before under the name of William West. His denials seemed to be refuted by Bertillon measurements and photographs. But it turned out that he was telling the truth, and, to add to official embarrassment, the real William West was found to be still in Leavenworth. A year later, Sergeant John K. Ferrier of Scotland Yard visited the United States and agreed to fingerprint all of Leavenworth's convicts, thus inaugurating a new means of criminal identification.[148] Pretty soon virtually all prisoners could expect to have their fingers inked and rolled over paper.

In the United States, many prison research studies were spearheaded by several key organizations that saw themselves as leading the search for the cause of crime—groups such as the Prison Reform Congress, National Conference of Charities and Corrections, National Prison Congress, Prison Association of New York, and Society for Alleviating the Miseries of Public Prisons.

Zebulon Brockway's Elmira Reformatory carried the latest penological advances as far as possible, working them into the standard prison procedures that had been developed at Auburn and Sing Sing.[149] As described in the institution's *Yearbook* for 1892:

> The morning after arrival, an interview with the General Superintendent takes place. The main object of this private audience is to ascertain the special causes of each individual's crime, for the purpose of determining the treatment to be pursued, experimentally at first, in order to effect a cure. The points gathered in this interview are the names and addresses of parents and relatives, the prisoner's antecedents including the condition of his ancestors, whether criminal, insane, epileptic, intemperate or illiterate, their means and manner of living, and his relation toward them; his own history, comprising an account of previous wrongdoings, the character of his associations, the nature of his home life, his religion, mental attainments, trade relations, and physical type and condition, also the trade he would like to follow and for which he thinks himself more especially adapted. Then other questions are put and answers sought, upon which the General Superintendent usually relies as fair indicators of character, and a certain standard, more or less approximate, is determined upon the quantities of sensitiveness and moral susceptibility. A treatment is then prescribed, subject to any variations that may be found advisable as the treatment progresses.[150]

Each year, Elmira proudly published skillfully prepared reports containing realistic sketches or photographs of actual inmates, identified by face and convict number.

By the 1880s, physicians and social scientists had replaced the chaplains of the 1830s as the most enthusiastic proponents of prison as a vital social laboratory. Elmira's physician, Dr. Hamilton D. Wey, was particularly influential in urging the laboratory study of criminals.[151] Scores of physicians and social scientists answered his call. In 1900 Charles R. Henderson, a sociologist at the University of Chicago, urged in a report endorsed by the National Prison Association that prison laboratories should be substantially expanded and strengthened.[152] Arthur MacDonald, a specialist on the "abnormal classes" for the Bureau of Education, pressed Congress to establish a national laboratory for studying the criminal, pauper, and defective classes.[153] Dr. J. B. Ransom, a physician at Clinton prison, conducted human experiments with convicts which demonstrated that an environment with high altitude and pure air was well suited for the care and treatment of tuberculosis.[154] Just when prison labor was becoming more politically problematic, convicts' bodies were proving to have other uses.

Eugenics researchers found prisons a perfect place to conduct secret studies. Victorian attitudes and criminal anthropology alike encouraged the regulation of sexual conduct and procreation. Mental defectives, inebriates, epileptics, and criminals were thought to be transmitting their tendencies through sexual intercourse. Until the late 1890s, castration (testiotomy) or removal of the ovaries (ovariotomy) remained the only established means of preventing reproduction. Dr. F. Hoyt Pilcher had performed mass castrations in the mid-1890s at the Kansas State Home for the Feeble-Minded.[155] But castration had some distasteful physical and psychological effects.

A more acceptable form of male sterilization was developed near the end of the nineteenth century. Called "vasectomy," it entailed severing the *vas deferens,* the tube connecting the male testes with the urinary canal, thus preventing the sperm from entering the urinary canal into seminal fluid. Dr. Harry C. Sharp, a physician at Indiana Reformatory in Jeffersonville, introduced vasectomy in the case of a nineteen-year-old inmate who had masturbated—excessively, in his expert view. By the end of his first year, Dr. Sharp had sterilized 76 young prisoners. (From 1899 to 1907 he would vasectomize at least 465 men, mostly involuntary patients, all of them by illegal operations.)[156]

Sharp led a campaign in favor of sterilization laws, long after he had already begun secretly performing mass sterilizations of "feebleminded" inmates. "Shall we permit idiots, imbeciles, and degenerate criminals to continue the pollution of the race simply because certain religionists teach that 'marriages are made in heaven' and that the 'function of procreation is divine'?" he asked.[157]

Michigan defeated a proposed sterilization bill in 1897, out of religious fervor, and Pennsylvania's governor vetoed a similar act in 1905. Indiana's statute, enacted in 1907, was the first in the nation authorizing compulsory sterilization, and model sterilization legislation was drafted a few years later by the American Breeders' Association.[158]

Studies involving prisoners were also instrumental in the development of intelligence testing. Henry H. Goddard, a Princeton psychologist who directed the research laboratory at the Vineland Training School for Feeble-minded Girls and Boys, in New Jersey, popularized the use of Alfred Binet's intelligence scale in the United States. Yet, although Binet's IQ tests were age graded, they still had not been adjusted to avoid age-related distortion of intellectual capacity; consequently, unbeknownst to Goddard, the scales tended to grossly exaggerate the extent of mental retardation. Thus, when Goddard examined the results of his IQ testing of juvenile delinquents, he found more feeblemindedness than expected.[159]

Goddard identified feeblemindedness as the major cause of criminality, proclaiming that "25% to 50% of the people in our prisons are mentally defective and incapable of managing their affairs with ordinary prudence." He spent the next several years spreading the alarm through such books as *Feeble-Mindedness* and *The Criminal Imbecile.* Goddard eventually claimed that as many as 89 percent of all delinquents were mentally defective and held that "[e]very feeble-minded person is a potential criminal."[160]

Prison and reformatory officials had long been concerned about the number of mental defectives within their institutions, in part because such inmates were difficult to discipline and often victimized by others. With the availability of new diagnostic methods and intelligence testing, there arose within the prison system a sudden demand for measurement specialists, testing experts, psychologists, and eugenicists. At the same time, intergenerational findings such as Dugdale's "Margaret, Mother of Criminals," and Goddard's "Deborah Kallikak" seemed to validate Victorian beliefs that immoral women were responsible for producing generations of criminals, imbeciles, paupers, and the insane. After all, they drank alcohol in excess, wantonly engaged in fornication and perversion, acquired and spread venereal disease, and gave birth to batches of illegitimate and feeble-minded children who would never amount to anything.

Consequently, eugenic restraints seemed to be society's only hope for averting extinction. Prominent citizens encouraged the state to combat sexual promiscuity, prostitution, vice, and "white slavery." Venereal disease came to be monitored more carefully, and those who spread it faced quarantine and even imprisonment. Women's reformatories and prisons swelled with young prostitutes and became identified with the care and treatment of venereal disease. Incoming prisoners were administered Wassermann and other tests to detect social disease.[161]

Starting with a pilot grant that Superintendent Katherine Bement Davis obtained in 1910, extensive psychological testing was conducted at New York's Bedford Hills State Reformatory for Women. Initial testing by Dr. Eleanor Rowland of Reed College found one-third of the inmates to have subnormal scores, but Davis arranged for further work by Dr. Jean Weidensall, a psychologist who had been trained by Goddard and William Healy of Chicago, who had pioneered the new science of criminal diagnosis.[162]

None other than John D. Rockefeller, Jr., was deeply involved in the project. The Rockefellers were no strangers to social Darwinism, but Junior's particular loathing of the evils of prostitution displayed during the "white slavery" craze in New York City had apparently increased his enthusiastic, behind-the-scenes support for the eugenics movement and criminal reform.

Rockefeller quietly created the Laboratory of Social Hygiene on eighty-one acres of farmland adjoining the Bedford prison in Westchester County. He bought the land for $75,000 and leased it and its buildings to the reformatory managers for a nominal rent. Female inmates were taken there and stripped, measured, examined, and probed. A trained research staff tested their intelligence, recorded and analyzed their family history for eugenic clues, and compiled detailed psychiatric profiles of them all. Each inmate's intelligence, mechanical abilities, eyesight, and other characteristics were compared to those of working women and schoolgirls. Female prisoners generally scored lower in most tests.

Although these activities were conducted by a private corporation upon state prisoners, New York's attorney general issued an opinion that formally authorized the laboratory to utilize women prisoners in its research, provided that the state continued to "bear the mere cost of maintenance of the inmates just as if they remained within the present boundaries of the institution grounds." The testing would help to weed out "defective and criminally inclined persons," who could then be sent to custodial asylums for life rather than being set free after serving a relatively brief time in jail.[163]

This arrangement continued until 1920, when, at Rockefeller's urging, New York purchased the facility for use as a clearinghouse for identifying any woman in the state-supported penal system who was older than sixteen and found to be mentally defective to the extent that she required supervision, control, or care. Weidensall served as director of the laboratory and superintendent of Bedford Hills prison. She eventually joined with other researchers, including Dr. Edith R. Spaulding (Bedford's resident physician) and William Healy, on studies which concluded that low intelligence did not "cause" crime and that criminality was not inherited. Instead, they attributed criminal behavior to a variety of social, physical, and mental causes that are interrelated and interactive.[164]

Mabel Ruth Fernald, another Chicago-trained psychologist who conducted studies at the laboratory, rejected the notion of a female criminal type and concluded that extensive data "fail absolutely to justify the view expressed recently by certain propagandists that delinquency and defective intelligence are practically synonymous."[165]

Using inmates as human subjects, one of Rockefeller's philanthropies, the Bureau of Social Hygiene, also carried out pioneering research into narcotic drugs, helping to formulate the basis for a new federal policy of criminalization and treatment that would loom even larger in the coming decades.[166]

Meanwhile, the eugenics movement continued to spread throughout the country. According to a report to the governor of Kansas in 1919:

> All the feeble-minded lack self-control. . . . Their immoral tendencies and lack of self-control make the birth rate among them unusually high. . . . We know that the social evil is fed from the ranks of feeble-minded women, and that feeble-minded men and women spread venereal disease. . . . Their tendencies to pauperism and crime would seem to be sufficient grounds to justify the claim that the feeble-minded are a menace to society.[167]

Before World War I, no widespread intelligence testing of the American public had been conducted. Hence, it was not until large numbers of army conscripts were tested and the results compared to those for convicts that an empirically based picture began to emerge. One researcher compared the intelligence rating of inmates at the Indiana reformatory with men in the army draft from Indiana and reached the startling conclusion that the prisoners were much more intelligent than the draftees.[168] Research involving 10,413 prisoners in three Illinois penal institutions conducted from 1920 to 1927 resulted in similar findings.[169] Later study of 13,454 men in Illinois penal institutions found prisoners and nonprisoners to be of equal intelligence.[170]

But some of this research also had deleterious consequences for prisoners. Carl Murchinson, for example, concluded that since criminals were not of inferior intelligence they were responsible for their actions. He used this rationale to advocate harsher criminal penalties, including mandatory capital punishment, for anyone convicted of a third felony. Regardless of what the empirically derived data showed, many prison researchers continued to insist that low criminal intelligence was a leading cause of crime.[171]

Frank L. Christian, a psychiatrist specializing in defective delinquents, who served as Elmira's superintendent from 1917 to 1939, blamed the reformatory's high recidivism rates on the inmates themselves, not the institution. He claimed that it was attracting too many defective delinquents.[172]

Not everyone in the prison business subscribed to Lombroso's theories, however. Reverend Frederick H. Wines, the son of Enoch and an indefatigable cataloger of criminal statistics, who was secretary of the Illinois Board of Public Charities and a prominent criminal law reformer, told the National Prison Association in 1898, "I do not believe in inherited crime any more than I believe in the imaginary criminal type."[173] For many years Wines helped to lead the opposition to the connection of criminal anthropology and eugenics with American prisons, writing in one of his books:

> It needs no apparatus for minute and accurate measurements,
> with rules, scales, calipers, and goniometers—no chemical analy-
> sis of blood, tissues, and excretions—no careful experiments to
> test the degree of nervous susceptibility of different sensory
> organs—no specially devised psychical tests—to enable a com-
> mon man, familiar with criminals through his relation to them as
> an officer of the police or of a court or prison, to describe their
> most obvious and striking characteristics.[174]

Wines criticized the reigning positivist notions about "the criminal brain," which were based upon studies by Moriz Benedikt and others.[175] He observed that the list of physiological peculiarities attributed to criminals encompassed an extraordinarily wide and diverse area, including "disordered nervous action, insensibility to pain, quick and easy recovery from wounds, defective taste and smell, strength and restlessness of the eye, mobility of the face and hands, left-handedness, excessive temperature, perverted secretions, abnormal sexual appetites, precocity and so forth." Some medical writers had claimed that criminals possessed defective hearing, others had said it was preternaturally acute. Some reported they were color-blind, others said that was rare. Criminals were labelled as being hypersensitive to climatic and meteorological influences. Some said criminals did not blush.

Wines accused criminal anthropologists of committing serious method-
ological errors, including a common failure to compare their data about
"criminals" with corresponding numbers for an equal population of "non-
criminals" (a controlled study). He was not the only one to question such
methods. Jacob Riis, the muckraker and photographer, had spent years
stalking through the ghettos with camera and notepad, studying "how the
other half lived." He later observed: "We have heard friends here talk about
heredity. The word has run in my ears until I am sick of it."[176]

Some other Americans rejected criminal anthropology on political
grounds. Years before his famous defense in the Scopes Monkey Trial, the
attorney Clarence Darrow told prisoners at the Cook County Penitentiary:
"There is no such thing as crime as the word is generally understood. If
every man, woman and child in the world had a chance to make a decent,
fair, honest living, there would be no jails and no lawyers and no courts."[177]
And after his own incarceration, one prominent labor leader simply said:
"I have heard people refer to the 'criminal countenance.' I never saw one.
Any man or woman looks like a criminal behind bars."[178]

More members of the scientific community ultimately joined the assault
upon criminal anthropology. One of the most important evaluations
involved Dr. Charles Goring, a British prison physician, who had taken
over a massive prisoner study started by another scholar who had been
attempting to test some of Lombroso's theories. Using standard techniques
of physical anthropology, as well as data gathered about age, education,
family background, occupation, intelligence, and other factors, Goring
enlisted the aid of Dr. Karl Pearson, an eminent statistician and eugenicist,
to conduct a rigorous quantitative study of three thousand male convicts
who had been sent to English prisons between 1902 and 1908. All of the
men studied were recidivists, which meant they were precisely the persons
who might most presumably be of the "criminal type."[179] Yet Goring's
book, *The English Convict*, strongly refuted Lombroso's claims, the study
having found no appreciable anatomical differences between the prisoners
and various control groups, including Oxford undergraduates. "The preliminary conclusion reached by our inquiry is that this anthropological
monster has no existence in fact," he declared. "The physical and mental
constitution of both criminal and law-abiding persons, of the same age,
stature, class, and intelligence, are identical."[180]

WEEDING OUT

IN the United States, one of the most astounding examples of scientific experimentation involving prisoners occurred in 1890—the year of the murder of Sitting Bull, and of the Army's massacre of the Sioux at Wounded Knee—when the electric chair was introduced at Auburn prison. At the time, death by electricity was of intense interest to the captains of industry, who were concerned about possible safety problems and resulting civil damages stemming from accidents caused by their new source of power. Scientists were encouraged to discover precisely how electricity killed human beings, in part because punitive awards from the courts might depend on the amount of "pain and suffering" involved in electrocutions. Aided by Thomas Edison, a cadre of state-supported researchers set up electrical appliances in New York's old police headquarters. With still more help from the Society for the Prevention of Cruelty to Animals, they began conducting experiments. Edison's goal was to have the State of New York electrocute its condemned prisoners by alternating current—the type of commercial electricity favored by his rival, George Westinghouse—in order to help define it as lethal in the public mind.

New York became the first state to adopt sweeping new execution provisions. The legislation called for condemned convicts to be transported to the state prison and kept in solitary confinement until it was time to put them to death. The law denied them access to any person except officers of the prison, their counsel, physician, priest or minister (if they should desire one), and members of their family, except by court order. A death warrant would command the prison warden to execute the convict within four to six weeks after the sentence was pronounced and upon some day within a week it appointed. Only specified persons invited by the warden could witness the event. Electrocution was declared the new method of execution. An immediate postmortem examination was to be made by the attending physicians, who would certify the nature of their autopsy. The act was to take effect the following year, in order to give the superintendent of state prisons time to install the necessary electrical apparatus and appliances.[181]

The first convict to be legally electrocuted—William Kemmler—fit neatly into the Victorian criminal profile. Besides having committed desertion, adultery, bigamy, and murder, he was classified as an illiterate of low intelligence (perhaps attributable to a head injury) who also had a chronic drinking problem.

In response to a constitutional challenge to the new method, the United

States Supreme Court found that criminal punishments are cruel only when they involve torture or lingering death, whereas electrocution had been proven to produce "instantaneous and painless death"; although electrical execution might be a new and different way to inflict punishment, it was not constitutionally unusual.[182]

After the sentence was carried out, a physician who had helped to ensure the adoption of electrocution announced to the crowd at the prison gate: "This is the grandest success of the age . . . I tell you this is a grand thing, and is destined to become the system of legal death throughout the world."[183]

Three years later, Henry M. Boies, a penologist for the Pennsylvania Board of Public Charities, the Commission on Lunacy, and the National Prison Association, published a book in which he said that it was "established beyond controversy that criminals and paupers, both, are degenerate; the imperfect, knotty, knurly, worm-eaten, half-rotten fruit of the race." He divided the problem of pauperism and crime into three "elementary phases": prevention, reformation, and extinction. "Preventive measures are like a net which must be dragged through the entire social stream," Boies wrote. "Reformatory treatment is confined to those only who are enveloped in it. The 'unfit,' the abnormals, the sharks, the devil-fish, and other monsters, ought not to be liberated to destroy, and multiply, but must be confined and secluded until they are exterminated."[184]

In 1921 the frontier state of Nevada (population less than eighty thousand) enacted a Humane Death Bill of its own. Not content with shooting or hanging or even electrocuting the lawmakers provided that a condemned man should be approached in his cell when he was asleep and executed by a dose of lethal gas. Nevada's Democratic governor, Emmet Boyle, opposed capital punishment, yet he signed the unusual legislation in the apparent belief that it would be found unconstitutional as "cruel and unusual." But after a convicted tong-war murderer, Gee Jon, was sentenced to death, the Nevada Supreme Court surprised Boyle by upholding the new act. Technicians scrambled to construct a suitable gas chamber.

On February 8, 1924, at the Carson City prison, Jon became the first person to be legally executed by lethal gas. The executioners used cyanide crystals. Within the next two years, Arizona, Colorado, Wyoming, North Carolina, and California also switched to using gas chambers.[185]

Also in 1924, in Landsberg prison near Munich, an Austrian right-wing radical wrote a book entitled *Mein Kampf.* In it, he began to spell out his own notions of "positive" and "negative" eugenics. Within a decade, Adolf Hitler had risen to power and begun putting his ideas into practice.

Assisted by his physician, Karl Brandt, and an old party bureaucrat named Philipp Bouhler, Hitler developed a euthanasia program, starting with "sick" persons. A few years later, Nazi Germany installed its first gas chambers, using Zyklon B, the German trade name for cyanide. The government went on to refine the technique that had been invented in U.S. prisons.[186]

CHAPTER SIX

The Golden Age of Political Prisoners

ANARCHISTS AND SOCIALISTS

FROM the 1880s until World War II, crime and imprisonment were widely considered to be highly politicized, and the United States was recognized as having an assortment of well-known "political prisoners." Some were recent immigrants, others were homegrown; some had been involved in political activities before their arrest and imprisonment, others had not become politicized until they reached prison. Some of the more publicized cases were pointed to as living symbols, either because of what they had done or because of what had been done to them—because of what they were. Viewed collectively, their experiences revealed some important aspects of American society, demonstrating prison's role as a political instrument and raising fundamental questions about the proper role of prison in a free society.

For committing "America's first terrorist act"—attempting to assassinate an antilabor industrialist—the anarchist Alexander Berkman was committed to Pennsylvania's fog-shrouded Western Penitentiary, on the Ohio River, where he was sheared and shaved, assigned a number and a uniform, and ordered to fall in with the other convicts.[1]

Western had been one of the first prisons in the world to be modeled on Jeremy Bentham's panopticon design, which enabled keepers to maintain constant surveillance over their prisoners, amounting to what Aldous Huxley would later call a "totalitarian housing project," devoid of privacy.[2] Berkman found himself living an anarchist's worst nightmare, and he attempted suicide by cutting his wrist with a sharpened spoon. But again the authorities interceded. He later wrote to his lover, Emma Goldman:

"March 4, 1893. . . . Both inmates and officers are at a loss to 'class' me. They have never known political prisoners. That one should sacrifice or risk his life with no apparent personal motives, is beyond their comprehension, almost beyond their belief. It is a desert of sordidness that constantly threatens to engulf one."[3]

Meanwhile, Goldman's own activities as an agitator gained her a one-year sentence at Blackwell's Island penitentiary on New York's East River, where she performed compulsory labor and used her free time to master English in order to be better able to reach the American "natives" through her speeches and pamphlets.[4]

In time, Berkman adjusted to the cellhouse and took on more of the ways of the penitentiary. He came to speak the convicts' language and to practice their code. "I marvel at the inadequacy of my previous notions of 'the criminal,'" he admitted. "I resent the presumption of 'science' that pretends to evolve the intricate convolutions of a living human brain out of the shape of a digit cut from a dead hand, and labels it 'criminal type.' Daily association dispels the myth of the 'species,' and reveals the individual."[5]

Although he had initially been shocked and disgusted by prison homosexuality, Berkman later came to practice expressions of a "very beautiful emotion," on the grounds that it strengthened the bond between imprisoned comrades. He also found the guards to be "of very inferior character," and thought their intelligence was "considerably lower than that of the inmates." Most keepers had worked in the prison for fifteen to twenty-five years, and one had over forty years on the job.

Day after day, Berkman toiled at the same tedious task in the prison shop, then returned to the same desolate cell, beholding all the while how the institution ground and pulverized everyone around him, brutalizing guards, dehumanizing inmates, sapping them of their will to resist.[6]

During the winter of 1893, in Oakland, California, a young high school dropout named Jack London wanted to learn a trade to support himself. London applied to be an electrician's apprentice, believing that electricity was the field of the future. He landed a position at the local power plant, but quit in disgust over working conditions.[7] The following April, at the age of eighteen, he joined Charles T. Kelly's Industrial Army, a West Coast branch of Jacob Coxey's Army of the Unemployed. Its members marched for an end to the class system, hopping freights and panhandling as they went. In late June, while tramping near the Canadian border, London rode into the city of Niagara Falls in a "side-door Pullman," or boxcar, and was arrested for vagrancy.[8] Years later, he described how he had been

denied the right to plead guilty or not guilty, sentenced out of
hand to 30 days' imprisonment for having no fixed abode and
no visible means of support, handcuffed and chained to a bunch
of similarly circumstanced, carted down country to Buffalo, registered at the Erie County Penitentiary, had my head clipped and
my budding moustache shaved, was dressed in convict stripes,
compulsorily vaccinated by a medical student who practised on
such as we, made to march the lock-step, and put to work under
the eyes of guards armed with Winchester rifles—all for adven-
turing in blond-beastly fashion.[9]

London's brief jail experience made a lasting impression, and it provided
material for several later writings.[10]

About the same time London was released from the Erie pen, the Pullman Company lowered its wages by one-third without altering its company
rents or dividends. The leader of the American Railway Union, Eugene V.
Debs, organized the greatest strike yet staged in the United States, for
which he was put into the McHenry County jail in Woodstock, Illinois,
for allegedly violating a court order.[11]

Although the strike was lost and the union broken, Debs became labor's
national hero. Well-wishers flocked to his cell in Woodstock.[12] During his
six-month incarceration, Debs seemed to maintain iron discipline and
"irrepressible optimism." Many who saw him remarked that instead of
breaking his spirit jail seemed to have made him stronger and more determined, as if he suddenly had understood the system and realized how to
change it.[13]

In December 1905 Frank Steunenberg, the former governor of Idaho,
was killed by a bomb attached to the gate at his home in Caldwell. One of
those arrested as an accomplice was Big Bill Haywood, a rising union
official for the Western Federation of Miners. During his confinement
while awaiting trial, he helped to create the International Workers of the
World (IWW), and he continued to follow its development as closely as
he could.[14] Eventually acquitted, he left prison more radicalized, saying:
"I despise the law, and I am not a law-abiding citizen. . . . Those of us who
are in jail—those of us who have been in jail—all of us who are willing to
go to jail—care not what you say or do! We despise your hypocrisy. . . .
We are the Revolution!"[15]

Another union organizer—Mary Harris Jones ("Mother Jones")—was
sentenced in 1913 to twenty years for conspiring to commit murder, but
she was later pardoned by the governor of West Virginia. "To be in prison
is no disgrace," she said.[16]

OSBORNE

WITH all of the political activity leading to and surrounding prisons, the institution itself came under renewed attack. This time, from an unlikely source.

Thomas Mott Osborne had been born to a prominent Auburn family in 1859. As a child he had been taken on a visit to the prison and afterward had recurring nightmares featuring the figure of an escaped convict. Osborne grew up to become a successful industrialist, was twice elected mayor, and served as a trustee of the George Junior Republic, a progressive school for delinquent boys in Freeville, New York. Over the years, he made frequent visits to Auburn prison, where he met many convicts. Some of them became his personal correspondents, and a few were even invited to visit his home upon their release.[17] At the height of the Progressive Era, in the summer of 1913, Governor William Sulzer appointed him to lead a commission on prison reform. Osborne plunged into reading everything about penology he could find. He also concluded that if he was really going to learn anything about prisons he had to find out what it was like to be a prisoner.

That September, Osborne was allowed to address the hushed and rigid rows of fourteen hundred Auburn convicts and officers who were assembled after chapel. To their consternation he announced that he planned to pose as an inmate and be incarcerated, something nobody had ever done before. "I have the feeling that after I have really lived among you," he said, "marched in your lines, shared your food, gone to the same cells at night, and in the morning looked out at the piece of God's sunlight through the same iron bars, that then, and not until then, can I feel the knowledge which will break down the barriers between my soul and the soul of my brothers."[18]

The next day, Osborne presented himself at the prison gate. With the permission of his friend Warden Charles F. Rattigan, he was admitted as "Thomas Brown," with instructions to be treated the same as any newly arrived inmate. No more, no less. As convict No. 33,333x, Osborne was registered and put through all the standard entry rites.[19] Then he was taken through one of the oldest parts of the institution, into a dark and smelly cell that was four feet wide, seven and a half feet long, and seven feet high. It contained a folding iron bed hooked to the wall, mattress and blankets, a stool, a folding shelf, an iron washbasin, a covered iron bucket that served as a toilet, and a tin cup for drinking water. The door shut and he was left alone.

The silent system was still in effect, along with the strict enforcement of endless rules against communication. However, Osborne was introduced to the convict underworld, with its own language, values, and code.

Osborne's willingness to enter the prison world voluntarily gained him the trust of inmates and staff alike. At the same time, he became alert to the prison's state of perpetual tension—the guards constantly watched the prisoners and the prisoners constantly watched the guards and the prisoners watched each other and the warden watched them all. Everyone suspected everyone else. Slight gestures assumed enormous significance. In this fishbowl, he also learned the "first duty and only pleasure of the convict—to deceive a keeper and get away with it."[20]

Some cons complained that having only fifteen minutes for breakfast and eighteen minutes for dinner did not allow a man enough time to chew his food properly. "Why all this hurry to get the meal over with?" one inmate asked.[21]

After a full week as a convict, Osborne bid his fellow prisoners goodbye. "Believe me," he said in a choked voice, "I shall never forget you. In my sleep at night as well as in my waking hour, I shall hear in imagination the tramp of your feet in the yard, and see the lines of gray marching up and down."[22]

After leaving, he remarked to outsiders that the prisoners had been remarkably considerate and showed a willingness to take him into their confidence and treat him like one of themselves. He told the governor: "The first conclusion I have reached, as the result of my stay at Auburn Prison, is the essential *humanity* of the prisoners; the existence among them of a very unexpected amount of manliness, goodness, self-sacrifice, heroic endurance of suffering, and sympathy with the suffering of others. The amount of fine material going to waste in our prisons is shocking to think of; it impugns our intelligence and forms a savage commentary upon our civilization."[23] He also said, "[L]arge numbers of men, broken in health and spirit, white-faced with the 'prison pallor,' husky in voice—hoarse from disuse, with restlessness, shifty eyes and the timidity of beaten dogs . . . are creatures whom we ourselves have fashioned."[24]

Osborne disputed contemporary theories that crime was primarily a result of physical and mental defects, and he roundly rejected the notion that convicts were a distinct and inferior criminal class. "I am no sentimentalist and do not for a moment deny the existence of evil in the natures of the prisoners," he said; "it would be foolish to overlook it. . . . What is not understood and what we need to remember is the other side. Unless we appeal to the good that is in the prisoner, how can we utilize the chance we have to reform them?"[25] As it was, prison only made a good man bad and a bad man worse.

Osborne and his fellow commissioners recommended closing Auburn and Sing Sing and called for sweeping reforms of the whole penal apparatus, including the implementation of a new system of indeterminate sentences. They argued that "[t]he great vice of the present system of prison administration is that it treats all convicts alike making no account of individual differences in character, education or sensitiveness to good influences, and . . . it operates to repress all individuality and to deny all opportunity for the development of self-respect and a sense of responsibility."[26]

After a Westchester County grand jury condemned Sing Sing (eighty-eight years old) and recommended that a new prison be built to take its place, riots and fires rocked the institution. Governor Glynn removed the warden and offered the post to Osborne. He initially turned down the offer, but supporters urged him to reconsider.[27] He received a telegram from Sing Sing that read: "For God's sake, take the wardenship. All the boys are anxious to have you."[28] Osborne finally took the job, went to Sing Sing, and assembled all of the convicts and staff in the mess hall to ask for their support.

He started as warden on November 30, 1914, and promptly began to institute more reforms than Sing Sing had experienced in its entire history. Osborne ended the silent system. He inaugurated a plan of inmate self-government, known as the Mutual Welfare League, which allowed prisoners to establish their own legal disciplinary arm. To show that he meant business, the reform warden granted fifteen of their requests to change the prison rules. Token coins were distributed as a means of starting a legitimate economy. In exchange for receiving $9 a week in wages, each inmate was expected to pay for his own cell, food, and clothing.[29] He said the Mutual Welfare League enabled convicts to "restore their self-respect and belief in their own essential manhood."[30]

Osborne's reforms obtained dramatic results. During the three years before his arrival, Sing Sing's hospital had treated an average of 373 wounds per 1,450 inmates. After he took office, the prison population increased to 1,600, but the number of wounds treated dropped to 155. Escapes decreased. As one prisoner put it, "There we were, all convicts, doing from two years to life, and free to run away, and yet no one did. What is more, I am sure if anybody had tried to do it, the others would have prevented him." Recidivism on the part of Sing Sing ex-convicts plummeted.[31]

Osborne's success was due in part to the reaction he received from veteran convicts. One of them was Canada Blackie. Before the new warden arrived on the scene, Blackie already was legendary as a tough guy, someone who had managed to remain unbroken despite many years of hard confinement. As a result, he enjoyed special status among the long-termers. Blackie was a square-jawed, dark-eyed white man, with jet black hair. After his mother's death, he had left home in Canada and gone on the road, doing stints as a circus performer, cowboy, train bandit, and convict. In 1903 he had been convicted for his part in a bank robbery in Cobleskill, New York, in which a watchman was killed; he drew a life sentence. At Clinton prison, he had maintained a spotless record for seven years until something happened and he began to get into trouble. From that point on, Blackie spent long stretches of solitary in Dannemora's dreaded punishment cell. Somehow he managed to obtain a piece of gas pipe, matches, and other scraps, which he secretly fashioned into a pistol. He pulled the weapon during an escape attempt and ended up shooting a guard through the shoulder before he was captured. For that he received ten additional years, and served the next year and eight months in the "dark cell," without bed or blankets, sleeping on the frigid stone floor. He kept sane by reciting poetry and playing solitary games, such as throwing and retrieving buttons he tore from his clothes. When he was finally brought out, Blackie was blind in one eye and coughing from tuberculosis. For three years after that he remained in solitary confinement in a lighted cell, seemingly cut off from the outside world. Yet somehow he managed to have dynamite smuggled into the prison and hidden for him in the main yard. But he was caught once more and transferred to Auburn, where he was placed in solitary again.[32]

Coincidentally, Donald Lowrie, a writer who was the first ex-convict allowed to visit Auburn, approached Blackie's cell only moments after the inmate had tried a makeshift key in his door and found that it fit. In fact, Blackie had kept his foot pressed firmly against the door during their conversation to ensure that it did not swing open and spoil his escape plan.

And yet, inexplicably, Blackie had a change of heart. After calling Osborne to his cell, he reached into his hiding places and handed the new warden a knife and a key, which he said he had intended to use. Osborne discovered that the key worked. To his astonishment, Blackie told him he was going straight because he had faith in what Osborne was trying to do.

As a reward, the warden allowed Blackie to go for a walk outside the solitary area. As Blackie later recalled:

> After traversing the corridor of the isolation building, we came
> to the double-locked doors—two of them,—which lead directly

into the main prison yard; as we stepped into the pure air, I felt as though I wanted to bite chunks out of it, but the first deep inhale made me so dizzy that I actually believe I would have staggered had I not taken myself into firm control. On rounding the end of the cloth-shop, we came into full view of the most wonderful, as well as beautiful, sight I have ever seen in prison,—or outside, either, for that matter. I hardly know how to describe this sight; but picture to yourself, if you possibly can, fourteen hundred men turned loose in a beautiful park. For years previous to this good work now being promoted by Mr. Osborne and the prison officials, these same men whom I now see running in and out among the beautiful flower-beds and playing like a troop of innocent boys just out of school . . . Instead of the prison pallor and haunted look which once predominated, I now notice smiling eyes, and that clean look which exhilarating exercise in the pure air always brings to the face.

Blackie noticed a ring of boys formed around something in the prison yard; it was a party of Italians, waltzing.[33]

As an idol to the other convicts, Blackie's strong support of Osborne and the Mutual Welfare League proved invaluable. Consequently, as he lay dying of tuberculosis, Blackie was granted executive clemency and moved to a bed in the warden's house. Two convicts were brought over to nurse him till the end. Blackie told the chaplain, "As a friend, you are welcome; but I hope you don't think, after what I've been and after all I've done, that I'm going to try and sneak into Heaven through a back door!"

Canada Blackie died on March 20, 1915. Osborne called him "one of the many thousands of martyrs of the brutal old prison system." His body was given a public funeral at Auburn, with all the convicts attending.[34]

Not long afterward, Osborne's reforms finally ran into serious trouble. He was forced to carry out multiple electrocutions. On December 28, 1915, the conservative local district attorney covering Sing Sing succeeded in getting him indicted for perjury and neglect of duty.[35] Osborne went on leave to prepare his case. The court eventually dismissed the charges, but his power was diminished. Although he returned to duty as warden, he resigned in protest three months later after the superintendent of prisons overturned one of his reforms. Little by little, many of the gains he had made were rescinded or reversed. Contrary to the appeals and promises of grand juries, reform commissions, and governors, old Auburn and Sing Sing were not closed down. They endured.

PROGRESSIVES

MANY on the political left were struggling with women's rights. In 1914 a young feminist named Margaret H. Sanger found herself in trouble for promoting birth control in a women's magazine. After the United States Post Office banned the periodical's distribution through the mails on the grounds that its contraception information was "obscene," she and her husband faced prosecution on smut charges.[36] Although the charges were eventually dropped, she continued to be targeted for her political activities.[37] On October 16, 1916, at 46 Amboy Street in Brooklyn, she and her associates opened the first birth control clinic in America. She was quickly arrested for providing contraceptive information to an undercover vice squad detective. After being held overnight in the Raymond Street jail, she was released on bail and immediately returned to the embattled clinic, where she was arrested again. This time she drew a sentence of thirty days in the Queens County penitentiary.[38]

Although she was an inmate, Sanger stubbornly refused to allow herself to be medically examined or fingerprinted. She discovered that her fellow female prisoners were prostitutes, pickpockets, embezzlers, brothel keepers. Among them were many drug addicts and mothers who were struggling to hide their whereabouts from angry relatives. They resented the fact that their male counterparts received better food and more privileges, such as the right to purchase tobacco and newspapers.[39]

With many radicals organizing against America's involvement in the Great War, San Francisco "hawks" staged a Preparedness Day Parade in support of American military armament and overseas intervention. A massive streetside explosion killed ten innocent bystanders and wounded forty others. Suspecting an anarchist conspiracy, police quickly arrested several known radicals. Four of the defendants were acquitted; one was convicted and sentenced to life imprisonment; and, based upon evidence that would later seem flimsy at best, another—Tom Mooney—was condemned to be hanged.

Mooney's case became an international cause célèbre after anarchists in Russia demonstrated on his behalf. The protests continued after he was moved to death row at nearby San Quentin. A national "Mooney Day" was held in forty cities throughout the United States, but after California's governor commuted his death sentence to life imprisonment, thereby deflating some of the pressure on Mooney's behalf, the case slipped into temporary obscurity.[40]

As President Wilson began his second term, war fever swept the United States. America entered the fighting in Europe, and military conscription was reinstituted. Federal marshals arrested Goldman and Berkman at the office of their paper, *Mother Earth,* for "conspiracy to induce persons not to register" for the draft.[41] After their conviction, the judge sentenced them to the maximum term of two years' imprisonment and imposed $10,000 in fines.[42]

Berkman was shipped to the Atlanta penitentiary and Goldman was taken to the Missouri state prison in Jefferson City. Both were held under close watch and kept at hard labor. A feminist admirer who visited her in prison reported: "Our dear Emma looked as usual, her eyes bright, her lovely complexion rosy. I still felt as if I were dreaming in a topsy turvy world, and that presently I would wake up. . . . One must no longer address her as a 'political prisoner,' because they are not recognized in this country. I asked her to take off her glasses so that I might see her eyes. There are many 'crowsfeet' about them, and they look so sad and tired."[43]

Goldman found companionship with a fellow radical prisoner, Kate Richards O'Hare, a prominent Socialist Party writer who also was being held for antiwar activities, in her case for giving a speech in Bowman, North Dakota. O'Hare was a moderate who did not support the IWW, but despite their ideological and personal differences the two became close friends.[44] Together, they went about trying to reform the predominantly male prison from the inside, by pressuring the warden to provide more-equal treatment to the women convicts.[45] In one account of her experience, O'Hare described the prison's dead, rancid, musty odors; century-old benches and tables that creaked and groaned with use; and rats, roaches, and flies. "One of the most terrible things which I had to endure was that [of] an Indian woman in the last stages of syphilis," she wrote. "Her open sores were never properly dressed, the stench was frightful, and the flies swarmed over her and then awakened us in the morning by crawling over our faces."[46]

Brought to the bathroom to bathe, O'Hare saw a fellow convict named Alice, whose body was covered with open syphilitic sores, leave the bathtub. O'Hare later recalled:

> I asked the matron if it were necessary that I use the same tub
> that Alice had used, and she said it was. I then asked who
> cleaned the tub, and she replied that Alice was too ill and that
> I was to do it. I then asked what disinfectants were used. "Dis-
> infectants!" she snarled: "whatdaya mean?"
>
> "I mean what prophylactic measures do you use to keep the
> clean women from becoming infected with venereal disease?" I
> replied.

She screeched: "Hell, we ain't got none of them high-falutin'
things here. This ain't no swell hotel—this is the pen!"

O'Hare memorialized the discussion in a long letter to her husband,
which she managed to have smuggled out of the prison. It ended up being
published in newspapers and magazines, unleashing a storm of protest all
over the country. In less than three weeks, shower baths were suddenly
installed in the females' wing of the prison.[47]

Nevertheless, O'Hare acknowledged having some sympathy for her
keepers. The matrons, after all, were required to live in the prison and were
seldom allowed outside, prompting her to write, "They were prisoners to
almost the same degree that we were, and they all staggered under a load
of responsibility far too great for their limited intellectual and untrained
powers."[48] O'Hare received a presidential commutation after serving fourteen months, but Goldman remained incarcerated.

Meanwhile, other radicals had also been targeted. The IWW (or Wobblies, as their detractors called them) had long preached antimilitarism and
antipatriotism, but with the onset of wartime hysteria such notions became
extremely unpopular. Furthermore, the Wobblies, like the Reds, pushed
crazy ideas such as the eight-hour workday and decent working conditions
for working stiffs. One of the pamphlets that the postmaster general
banned from the mails was the IWW's *Justice for the Negro*, which pointed
out that colored men were being drafted to fight and die for democracy
abroad while at home they were being lynched and denied basic civil
rights.[49]

During the summer of 1917, the army began rounding up alleged IWW
subversives and putting them in local jails, often without filing any criminal
charges against them, and sometimes claiming it was for their own protection. Federal troops took over copper mines in Arizona and Montana
to guard against the IWW menace. Wobbly organizer Frank Little was
lynched after leading a rally against the Anaconda Copper Company. In
California, Wobblies who were trying to organize farm workers in the San
Joaquin and Sacramento Valleys were tarred and feathered and thrown
into jail.[50]

Agents of the newly created Federal Bureau of Investigation raided
IWW halls and residences throughout the country, confiscating tons of
records and equipment, breaking up union meetings, and arresting virtually the entire Wobbly leadership for allegedly conspiring to violate the
Selective Service Act and the Espionage Act. All without the benefit of
search warrants. Bill Haywood was arrested in Chicago and indicted on
five counts of obstructing the war effort. He and his fellow Wobblies were

put in the Cook County jail, where he was held for six months before finally being released on bail in the spring of 1918.[51] Ninety-seven Wobblies ended up being sentenced to Leavenworth and fined. Haywood drew a term of twenty years and was fined $30,000.[52]

Still, some Americans continued to resist the draft and protest the war. A young attorney named Roger Baldwin deliberately refused to cooperate with his local draft board, for which he was sentenced to one year in the penitentiary. (Baldwin would later found the American Civil Liberties Union.)[53]

Another conscientious objector, Ammon Hennacy, who had vowed he would "fight in a revolution but not in a capitalist war," was sentenced to two years in the Atlanta penitentiary. Once inside, he organized an inmate strike and was put in the dark hole. Immediately upon his release in 1919, he was jailed again for engaging in antidraft activities while he had been in prison. (Converted to the pacifist cause, Hennacy would later become an organizer for the Catholic Worker movement.)[54]

Besides protesting the war, some American women continued to demand the right to vote. Since 1872, when Susan B. Anthony had been arrested and indicted in Rochester, New York, for the crime of attempting to cast her ballot, a growing number of feminists had resorted to civil disobedience in an effort to gain women's suffrage.[55] In 1917 alone, over a hundred suffragists were incarcerated in the Occoquan workhouse in the nation's capital. (The Nineteenth Amendment would not be passed and ratified until 1920.)[56]

REDS

IN October 1918 Congress enacted a sedition law providing for the deportation of aliens holding objectionable views. Mother Jones commented, "Officials of the state and nation squawk about the dangers of bolshevism and they tolerate and promote a system that turns out bolshevists by the thousands."[57]

Following the Bolshevik Revolution and the formation of the American Communist Party, beginning in the fall of 1919 the U.S. Department of Justice under Attorney General A. Mitchell Palmer decided to conduct a massive roundup of radicals. A young federal agent named J. Edgar Hoover planned the dragnet. After one midnight raid in New York alone, seven hundred radicals of all ages were crammed into jails or post offices, and many more throughout the country were held incommunicado under deplorable conditions.[58] "To be a red in the summer of 1919 was worse than being a Hun or a pacifist in the summer of 1917," as John Dos Passos put it.[59]

Meanwhile, Berkman and Goldman had remained under close surveillance, their mail and visitors monitored. Berkman spent some of his time in solitary for protesting the killing of a black convict who had been shot in the back by a guard, but now he and Goldman were nearing the end of their sentences. A month before their scheduled release, however, the attorney general ordered their arrest under the Alien Immigration Act and the Anti-Anarchist Act. Both were interrogated about their political beliefs and activities while federal agents secretly arranged their deportation. Goldman was stripped of her American citizenship and taken under custody to Ellis Island to await exile to the Soviet Union.[60]

In the early morning hours of December 21, 1919, Goldman and Berkman were herded onto an army steamship, the *Buford*, with 247 other Reds. A detachment of 250 heavily armed soldiers stood guard as J. Edgar Hoover spoke to the press. As the vessel prepared to depart, Goldman, who was dressed like a cossack and carrying a typewriter, turned to a newspaper reporter and said: "I consider it an honor to be the first political agitator to be deported from the United States." Then, as the ship pulled away, she thumbed her nose.[61]

Debs had also gotten into trouble for his antiwar views. On June 16, 1918, he was in Canton, Ohio, to address a political convention when he learned that three leftists were being held in the local lockup on charges of obstructing the draft. After visiting the trio in jail, Debs walked to a nearby park and delivered a standard speech in which he denounced the government for suppressing free speech and persecuting citizens who rightfully opposed conscription. In the audience were several federal agents and members of the American Protective League, who were scouring the crowd for men with draft cards in order to build a criminal case under the new law. Soon a federal grand jury in Cleveland indicted Debs for ten violations of the Espionage Act, claiming that he had incited young men to avoid the draft.

At his trial, Debs refused to retract any of his statements and even told the jury that he was committed to helping to bring down the capitalist-competitive system. The jury found him guilty. Later, as Debs stood to deliver a final statement, he told the judge:

> Your honor: years ago, I recognized my kinship with all living
> beings, and I made up my mind that I was not one bit better
> than the meanest of earth. I said then, I say now, that while there
> is a lower class, I am in it; while there is a criminal element, I am

of it; while there is a soul in prison, I am not free. . . . I could
have been in Congress long ago. I have preferred to go to prison.
The choice has been deliberately made. I could not have done
otherwise. I have no regret.[62]

Judge Westenhaver acknowledged Debs's sincerity, but said he had no
choice but to condemn anyone who would impair the nation's ability to
defend itself in wartime. He sentenced him to ten years in prison.

"Tell my comrades that I entered the prison doors a flaming revolution-
ist, my head erect, my spirit untamed and my soul unconquered," Debs
replied.[63]

When he arrived at Moundsville prison in West Virginia, his fellow convicts, who already had heard about what he had said in court, welcomed
him as a hero. Even the warden treated him with unusual respect. So much
so that after two months, worried officials in Washington ordered Debs
transferred to the dreary and more conservative maximum-security Atlanta
Federal Penitentiary, where his privileges were sharply curtailed.[64]

Debs became convict No. 9653. He shared a cell with five other prisoners. A heavy smoker, he quit using tobacco in order to donate his ration to
other inmates. He also always showed respect for other convicts and staff
alike. Visitors and cellmates likened him in manner and spirit to Jesus
Christ and hailed him as a martyr. "The real me, the man within, they can't
touch," he wrote to his brother. "I am simply paying my dues to the
cause."[65]

Even in prison, Debs remained America's leading political radical. In
1920 his name appeared on the Socialist Party ticket for president of the
United States; he received 919,000 votes, or 3 percent of the total. Debs
tallied the results by phone in the warden's office. But prison walls kept
him from participating in society's ongoing struggles, and barred his
unique voice from reaching the American public, at a time when dissenters
on the political scene were undergoing unprecedented repression. Worn
down by fourteen hours a day in a cell, Debs's health and vitality withered
away, and the movement he had helped to build and lead also waned. "I
had a strange dream last night," he confided in an intimate letter from
prison.

> I was walking by the house where I was born—the house was
> gone and nothing left but ashes. All about me were ashes. My
> feet sank in them and my shoes filled with them. A man came
> along and pointed out that my clothes were tattered. I wandered
> on and found a secluded spot. Weary and sad I sat down to read

. . . I awoke. Outside it was thundering and lightning and rain
was falling. I did not go to sleep again—The house was gone—
and only ashes—Ashes![66]

In response to growing petitions for clemency, President Woodrow Wilson told his private secretary that Debs was a traitor to his country and would never be pardoned during his administration. When Debs heard of it, he replied it was Wilson, not himself, who needed to be pardoned.

Debs used some of his time to begin work on a manuscript about prisons. In it he developed the socialist argument that society, not the individual criminal, was responsible for most crime. According to him, "poverty is the crime, penalized by society which is responsible for the crime it penalizes." Take a census of any prison, he said, and you will find that the majority of prisoners are there because they were poor and lacked the means to hire a top lawyer to prevent their imprisonment. "If poverty, of which so many are the helpless victims, could by some magic of power be abolished the prison would cease to exist, for the prison as an institution is cornerstoned in the misery, despair and desperation that poverty entails." Ever the optimist, he predicted that "the time will come when society will be so far advanced that it will be too civilized and too humane to maintain a prison for the punishment of an erring member, and that man will think too well of himself to cage his brother as a brute, place an armed brute over him, feed him as a brute, treat him as a brute, and reduce him to the level of a brute."[67]

During Debs's imprisonment, Haywood jumped bail and fled to the Soviet Union, where he was warmly greeted by Lenin. Back home his departure seemed like desertion, since he had left many of his old IWW comrades behind bars, where they struggled to keep alive a growing prison protest movement. In an effort to defuse mounting unrest over the continued confinement of so many top American labor leaders, President Warren Harding pardoned twenty-four political prisoners, including Debs. (However, he was prevented from running again for elective office.)[68]

As Debs prepared to leave the penitentiary where he had spent the last three years, Warden J. E. Dyche took the unprecedented step of permitting Atlanta's twenty-three hundred convicts out of their cells to bid a final farewell. As Debs walked out the prison gate, a rousing ovation swelled from within the institution. The old man turned, weeping, doffed his hat, raised his cane, and waved goodbye.[69]

Debs was taken to the White House for a brief private meeting with President Harding. Afterward, America's most famous ex-convict rode the train west to Terre Haute, where he was greeted by a huge and cheering crowd. Prison had broken his health, however, and on October 26, 1926, Gene Debs died.[70]

GARVEY

DURING the late teens and early twenties, federal agents also carried on a relentless chase after Marcus Garvey, the Jamaican-born black nationalist who had built a militant movement reaching as many as several million followers. With the Universal Negro Improvement Association as his base, Garvey aimed to lead "Africans" and "Ethiopians" back to Africa, where a new black nation would be established. Following negotiations with Liberia, the Empire of Africa, with Garvey as provisional president, was founded. It adopted a national flag and anthem, ornate uniforms, and the slogan Africa for the Africans, at Home and Abroad. Garveyites staged huge parades and other mass displays. He and his followers formed auxiliary organizations and a steamship company (the Black Star Line), as well as groceries, restaurants, laundries, a hotel, a doll factory, and a printing plant, all affiliated with the UNIA. They urged Negroes to support black-only businesses. Anti-white and anti-American, Garvey and his separatist followers also ridiculed the black bourgeoisie, especially many better-educated, lighter-skinned Negroes who belonged to the National Association for the Advancement of Colored People. Among them was W. E. B. Du Bois, whom Garvey called a "cowardly socialist."[71]

Federal agents arrested Garvey for mail fraud—a deportable offense. He had allegedly misrepresented the assets of the Black Star Line at a time when he supposedly knew the company was near bankruptcy. After a five-year legal battle, he was convicted. When the verdict was announced, Garvey blurted out anti-Semitic remarks. Judge Julian W. Mack sentenced him to five years in prison and imposed a fine of $1,000 plus court costs.[72]

Immediately upon entering Atlanta penitentiary in February 1925, Garvey launched a petition drive for his release, and wrote to his followers: "Look for me in the whirlwind or the storm, look for me all around you, for, with God's grace, I shall come and bring with me countless millions of black slaves who have died in America and the West Indies and the millions in Africa to aid you in the fight for Liberty, Freedom and Life."[73]

On November 28, 1927, President Calvin Coolidge commuted his sentence, and final arrangements were made for his shipment back to Jamaica as an undesirable alien. Garvey was moved to New Orleans and hustled aboard the SS *Saramacca*. Five hundred black supporters, some carrying banners saying GOD SAVE OUR PRESIDENT, were gathered at the dock as the vessel departed into the Gulf.[74]

SACCO AND VANZETTI

UNLIKE Debs or Garvey, who had been major dissident political figures before their imprisonment, two of the most famous political prisoners of the era had been obscure and generally nondescript Italian immigrants until deep-seated questions about their guilt captured worldwide attention. On April 15, 1920, there was a payroll robbery at the Slater & Morrill Shoe Company factory in South Braintree, Massachusetts. A paymaster and a guard were brutally shot dead by two gunmen who sped away with three others in a Buick sedan. The well-planned crime seemed to be the work of professional gangsters. But three weeks later, two local anarchists, Nicola Sacco, a shoemaker, and Bartolomeo Vanzetti, a fishmonger, were arrested by Police Chief Michael Stewart of Bridgewater. He suspected that foreign radicals had attempted an earlier holdup nearby and concluded that they might be implicated in this one as well. Although he had no hard evidence linking Sacco and Vanzetti to either robbery, Stewart arrested them anyway, and the state built a circumstantial case.

The following year, the two were tried and convicted of first-degree murder; Judge Webster Thayer condemned them to death. As lawyers argued their appeals, word of their case spread beyond Massachusetts. The affair came to embody the cause of innocent persons who had been subjected to the judgments of kangaroo courts because of their alien backgrounds and political beliefs.[75]

Personal details about the two men emerged. One of seventeen children, Sacco had come from Torremaggiore, in southern Italy, to seek a better life. He had learned a trade, married, and fathered a son. Life behind bars, awaiting execution, tormented him. By the end of 1921 he had begun to show signs of paranoia, and he refused to eat for four weeks. Agitated, weak, and near death, he was sent to Boston Psychiatric Hospital for examination and later committed to Bridgewater Hospital for the Criminally Insane, where his condition improved enough that he was discharged and returned to the Dedham jail.[76]

Vanzetti, three years his senior, better versed in English, and depicted as being more cerebral, had emigrated from Villafalletto in northern Italy. Besides performing his assigned prison labor, Vanzetti immersed himself in reading and study. Despite his limited English, he became known as a fledgling writer who described Judge Thayer as a "black-gowned cobra" and appealed to a friend, "Try to save us from the flameless fire of the twentieth century." Vanzetti summarized his own plight as follows:

> My conviction is that I have suffered for things that I am not guilty of. I am suffering because I am a radical and indeed I am a radical; I have suffered because I was an Italian, and indeed I am an Italian; I have suffered more for my family and for my beloved than for myself; but I am also convinced to be right that if you could execute me two times, and if I could be reborn two other times, I would live again to what I have done already.[77]

After more than four years in captivity, Vanzetti suffered a nervous breakdown. He too was sent to Bridgewater hospital, where state psychiatrists diagnosed his condition as "hallucinatory and delusional" before discharging him back to jail, five months later.[78]

Hopes for their cause mounted in March 1927, when the *Atlantic Monthly* published an article by a noted law professor, Felix Frankfurter, which passionately argued their innocence and attacked the manner in which they had been tried.[79] But on June 30 Sacco and Vanzetti were abruptly transferred from the Dedham jail to the death house of Charlestown state prison, where they were thrust into two of the three secluded cells on a narrow row that adjoined the execution chamber. Sacco reported they could see nothing but "four sad wall and a lap of sky that disappear under a wing of a bird." Time was running out and they were very close to losing hope.[80]

As death loomed, Vanzetti wrote a final letter to Sacco's fifteen-year-old son. "Remember, Dante," he asked, "Remember always these things; we are not criminals; they convicted us on a frame-up; they denied us a new trial; and if we will be executed after seven years, four months and 17 days of unspeakable tortures and wrongs, it is for what I have already told you; because we were for the poor and against the exploitation and oppression of the man by the man."[81]

The night before their scheduled execution on August 23, 1927, with hopes of a last-minute reprieve virtually exhausted after seven years of fierce struggle, a huge rally was held near the prison, with Sacco's wife, Rosa, and Vanzetti's sister, Luigia, on the speakers' platform. Katherine Anne Porter, the writer, later recalled watching as

> the two timid women faced the raging crowd, mostly Italians, who rose at them in savage sympathy, shouting, tears pouring

down their faces, shaking their fists and calling childish phrases, their promises of revenge for their wrongs. "Never you mind, Rosina! You wait, Luigia! They'll pay, they'll pay! Don't be afraid . . .!" Rosa Sacco spread her hands over her face, but Luigia Vanzetti stared stonily down into their contorted faces with a pure horror of her own. They screamed their violence at her in her own language, trying to hearten her, but she was not consoled. She was led away like a corpse walking. The crowd roared and cursed and wept and threatened.

Fifty years later Porter wrote, "It was the most awesome, the most bitter scene I had ever witnessed."[82]

So powerful was the protest that eight hundred beefy policemen, armed with machine guns and searchlights, were deployed to defend the besieged prison. In the darkness outside the walls, a massive crowd stood vigil till they were informed of the executions.

FREE TOM MOONEY

DURING the years in which Garvey, Debs, Goldman, Berkman, Haywood, Joe Hill, Sacco and Vanzetti, and other political prisoners were removed from the scene, Tom Mooney had remained imprisoned for crimes he insisted he had not committed. His case seemed likely to remain an eternal flame of California labor politics, constantly kept alive by leftist organizations as a symbol of injustice. Since the lifting of his death sentence, Mooney had occupied a tiny stone cell in an old gray-walled section of San Quentin prison. The space measured only four feet wide, eight feet long, and seven feet high, with an arched ceiling that made the space even smaller. Its furnishings consisted of a narrow iron cot with a straw pillow and a thin mattress, a small green wooden table and a stool, two bookshelves over the cell door, and a water pail and a chamber pail. One forty-watt overhead bulb provided all of the light other than what seeped in through a small wicket on the heavy iron cell door. The only ventilation came from a small pipe hole near the ceiling that was connected to a fan on the roof. Sometimes he plugged the vent with newspapers or rags to block the cold or stop the distracting whoosh of rushing air; during the winter, the only way he had to keep warm was to wrap himself in extra clothing or blankets. Mooney maintained his voluminous correspondence using a battered old typewriter that he put on his cot as if it were a desk. Over the years, every available inch of space had become crammed to the ceiling with bulging files, books, yellow newspaper clippings, letters, and legal materials.

Mooney had worked in the prison foundry, the hated jute mill, and the laundry before gaining trusty status that carried choicer assignments, such as operating the donkey engine on the wharf outside the main walls. He also kept a tiny vegetable garden and enjoyed some other privileges.[83]

Despite his public image as a gentle saint, many who knew Mooney well considered him difficult and self-centered; one friend described him as "an aggressive, stubborn fighter; a sensitive, self-willed, touchy individual, not broken but embittered." He was not as universally loved as Debs, and many convicts considered him selfish. Said one: "Hell, Mooney don't know he's a con. He's a martyr!" But such qualities only confirmed his innocence as far as many supporters were concerned. As Roger Baldwin of the ACLU observed, "I think I would speak a good deal stronger if I had done 13 years on a frame-up."[84] Such impressions were underscored when Mooney refused parole on the grounds that he was innocent of the charges and because the conditions of supervision would inhibit his union activities.

Besides his wife and mother, Mooney's visitors had included Debs, Norman Thomas, William Z. Foster, Lincoln Steffens, Upton Sinclair, Theodore Dreiser, Sinclair Lewis, Mayor Jimmy Walker of New York, and his lawyer, Bourke Cockran (who had also handled William Kemmler's unsuccessful appeals to avoid the world's first legally mandated electrocution). Some other prominent supporters were George Bernard Shaw, Stephen Vincent Benét, Edna Ferber, Will Irwin, Carl Sandburg, James Cagney, Edward G. Robinson, Boris Karloff, and William Randolph Hearst. Sherwood Anderson summed up popular sentiment: "He should be turned loose. They should quit it. There should be a limit, even to our inhuman cruelty."[85]

Years of hard confinement and scrutiny under a public microscope had taken its toll on Mooney's health, and he suffered from bleeding ulcers and other nervous problems, which he tried unsuccessfully to remedy by fasting and sunbathing.

Finally, in early January 1939, California's newly elected liberal governor, Culbert L. Olson, announced that he believed Mooney had been convicted based upon perjured testimony. Gallup polls said most Californians and an overwhelming majority of Americans supported a pardon. Mooney was ordered brought to the state assembly's chamber for a highly publicized review of his case. Before a live radio audience, Mooney was officially freed from prison after twenty-two and one-half years. The next day, a crowd of twenty-five thousand turned out to welcome him back to San Francisco with a giant victory procession that wound its way up Market

Street, along the same route followed by the Preparedness Day Parade in 1916. Three years later, Tom Mooney died in obscurity.[86]

THE SCOTTSBORO BOYS

MEANWHILE, like the Mooney case, an episode in the Deep South had drawn international attention for several years. In an era of growing racism abroad, the matter exposed the enduring stain of American racial prejudice, in a part of the country where patterns had remained virtually unchanged since the days of slavery and Jim Crow.

On March 25, 1931, nine black youths were arrested at Paint Rock, Alabama, for allegedly raping two white girls, Victoria Price and Ruby Bates of Huntsville, as they all were hoboing on a freight train that was travelling south from Chattanooga. The nine Negroes were Haywood Patterson, 18; Ozie Powell, 14; Olen Montgomery, who was half-blind; Eugene Williams, who was only 13; Andrew Wright, 19; Roy Wright, 14; Willie Robertson, who was sick with venereal disease; Clarence Norris, 19 years old and the tallest; and Charles Weems, the oldest at age 20. Rape was then a capital crime in Alabama, and an alleged rape of a white woman by a Negro was generally considered suitable grounds for lynching.[87]

According to an account that was later published by Haywood Patterson, "All nine of us were riding the freight for the same reason, to go somewhere and find work. It was 1931. Depression was all over the country." Although the young men in question claimed they had not committed any rape, and that they had not even seen the girls prior to being accused, a mob of armed farmers awaited them upon their return back to Scottsboro, the Jackson County seat, ninety miles northeast of Birmingham, and the terrified Negroes found themselves crammed into a cage in the little two-story Jim Crow jail to imagine their fate. After the worried sheriff warned that he feared a lynching, Governor B. M. Miller called out the National Guard, whose members had to fire warning shots on their way into town to show the mob they meant business. The militia took the youngsters to Gadsden for safekeeping.[88]

On March 31, the nine youths were indicted by an all-white grand jury in Scottsboro. A week later, the capital case went to trial. "Down around that way they'll hoe potatoes kind of slow sometimes but comes to trying Negroes on a rape charge they work fast," Patterson wrote. "We had no lawyers. Saw no lawyers. We had no contact with the outside. Our folks, as far as we knew, didn't know the jam we were in."[89] The fact that they were not represented by counsel was typical of the Deep South at that time.

(Indeed, the Alabama Supreme Court later found nothing wrong with it.) Nor was the conduct of the trial atypical, despite such comments by the prosecutor to the jury as, "'They're not our niggers. Look at their hair, gentlemen. They look like something just broke out of the zoo.'"[90] Although physicians who had examined the young women after the alleged crime testified that no rape had occurred, such evidence carried little weight in the racially charged atmosphere. According to Patterson, "Color is more important than evidence down there. Color is evidence. Black color convicts you. A light Negro stands a better chance in court than a real black one like me. Color sure is important in Southern courts." As he recalled, "The jury kept going in and out of the jury room and coming back with convictions. That was one jury that got exercise."[91]

Judge E. A. Hawkins sentenced eight of the nine to death in the electric chair at Kilby prison on July 10, less than four months after the alleged crime. The ninth, fourteen-year-old Roy Wright, had looked so small and pitiful that one of the jurymen held out for life imprisonment. Patterson recalled the courtroom being "one big smiling white face."[92]

Following the trial, the International Labor Defense took over the appeal. W. E. B. Du Bois complained that the Communists not only asked to take charge of the nine wrongly convicted boys but also "proceeded to build on this case an appeal to the American Negro to join the Communist movement as the only solution of their problem."[93]

As Haywood Patterson awaited execution, he confronted his own illiteracy. "In the death cell I held a pencil in my hand, but I couldn't tap the power that was in it," he remembered. "I couldn't write. I couldn't spell. I was a man without learning." Soon he began to study, and he proved to be a quick learner.[94] As one of the most visible of the so-called Scottsboro Boys, he received donations from admirers through the prison mail. Among his regular contributors were Nancy Cunard of the shipping-line family and Kay Boyle, the writer. (Other supporters included Albert Einstein and Thomas Mann, Madame Sun Yat-sen, and Maxim Gorky.) Patterson used some of these donations to bribe the guards to let him move to another cell for a change of view, to tip the convict porters to get special meals, and to get other favors.

Spared from execution while their case was on appeal, the Scottsboro prisoners learned on November 8, 1932, that they had won a new trial. In *Powell v. Alabama,* the U.S. Supreme Court had reversed their convictions on the grounds that the defendants had been denied their right to adequate counsel.[95]

At the second trial, at Decatur, in Morgan County, Attorney General Tom Knight of Alabama defiantly told the court, "'I never called a nigger

Mister and I never will call a nigger Mister.'" Solicitor Wade Wright bitterly complained that New Yorkers and Jews were trying to tell him what to do.[96]

The jury largely agreed with the state. This time, four of the nine were convicted; one was condemned again to death, and the other three were sentenced to 75 to 99 years. Rape indictments against the remaining five were dropped, although one was convicted and sentenced to 20 years for assaulting an officer during a prison escape attempt.

In some quarters, the case was counted as an improvement; 1933 was a time of growing violence, including lynchings, in Alabama, and the Scottsboro Boys had at least gotten a trial.

Again, the lawyers appealed, and in 1935 in *Norris v. Alabama* the U.S. Supreme Court reversed the convictions again on the grounds that the jury had not been properly selected. Appeals, reversals, retrials, and convictions continued until 1937.[97]

Meanwhile, Patterson and the remaining Scottsboro Boys stayed in prison. He became a hardened convict. He began to lose his faith in the Lord. Both of his parents died.[98] In 1937 Patterson was moved down to Atmore State Prison Farm, near the Florida line. Whereas at Kilby he had been able to purchase sex from women inmates, he now resorted to a "gal-boy."[99]

"Beside what the state did through its prisons and farms, our rackets inside the prison were small," Patterson observed. "Long time ago, old master, he got the take from that. Today the state of Alabama, it gets the take direct, through its prisons and the officials who run them."[100]

After twelve years of confinement, and with little hope of eventual release, Patterson planned his escape. On April 12, 1943, he made his break. Caught and whipped, he got a suit of white and blue stripes that meant he was denied all privileges for sixty days: no exercise or movies, and he would have to earn his way out of the doghouse dark cell. Among his jobs was removing the corpses of victims who had gone to the electric chair. One was an eighteen-year-old Negro boy, Peter Paul, who "wasn't very bright." Patterson added: "He was off. But they killed him. He was terribly burned out. You could see the burns and scorchings all over his face. His mouth was wide open, his eyes open; a bad-looking sight. No hair was on him."[101]

Patterson dug up some human bones while working at the prison farm. He believed the skeletons were those of Negro convicts who had been killed during the 1920s, when the infamous turpentine camps were in full swing. "I saw many a skeleton and corpse in and around Alabama prisons but I never did see a good-looking one," he said.[102]

He also noticed that Negro prisoners outnumbered white ones four to one, six to one. "In Kilby Prison the Negro side was always full up. The white side often had men in only a couple tiers. But Alabama's state population is three whites for every two Negroes." The road camps were the worst. "For a long time the state only sent Negroes to the road camps."[103]

Based on his experience, Patterson cautioned:

> Anybody who thinks that men and women are sent to Alabama prisons to get reformed, they don't know what's going on in the country. I saw men come in with good minds and watched them fade off. I saw men come in sick, then go crazy and murder. I never saw a man come in sick and get well. In nearly eighteen years in Alabama prisons, at the main prisons, in the town and county jails, on the farms, I never saw one man get reformed.[104]

Patterson remained in prison for a crime he insisted he did not commit. Years later, his prosecutor became lieutenant governor; he died and was buried near the spot where he had argued against the Scottsboro Boys. The first judge who had tried the case was identified in his obituary as the "Scottsboro judge." The state official who had stood up in court to say that Alabama justice could not be bought by Jew money from New York was eulogized in Alabama newspapers when he died.

Haywood Patterson identified with his fellow black convicts, complaining that his white captors were always intent on keeping them down. "Whenever Joe Louis fought, the guards, they wouldn't let us talk about it," he later observed.

> They made us shut off our radios and stay in our cells. We couldn't get caught whispering about the fight. There would be bad feeling between us and the white convicts and white guards. The bad feeling always worked up for a few days before each fight. They bet on the white man and whooped for him, we stuck with Joe. The feeling always got deep and rotten inside the prisons because Joe stood for something. That day we were champs, like he was.[105]

THE COLOR LINE

CRIME had emerged as a top political issue in the 1920s and 1930s, as popular attention turned to bootlegging, gangsters, public enemies, and crime waves. Law enforcement became a national craze, glamorized in newspaper extras, comic strips, radio programs, and movies. Negroes were never showcased as mobsters, like Al Capone or John Dillinger or Legs Diamond, but they were increasingly associated with common crimes of the "lower" class—public-order crimes such as larceny, prostitution and vice, and narcotics offenses.

Writing during this period, W. E. B. Du Bois complained it was "to the disgrace of the American Negro, and particularly to his religious and philanthropic organizations," that African Americans "continually and systematically neglect Negroes who have been arrested, or who are accused of crime, or who have been convicted and incarcerated." Tired of being taunted as "criminals," and desperate to disassociate themselves from the lawbreakers, many had been "all too eager to class criminals as outcasts, and to condemn every Negro who has the misfortune to be arrested or accused." He said the black bourgeois had "joined with the bloodhounds in anathematizing every Negro in jail, and has called High Heaven to witness that he has absolutely no sympathy and no known connection with any black man who has committed crime."

Du Bois rejected as "arrant nonsense" all the talk about a black criminal class, saying there was "absolutely no scientific proof, statistical, social or physical, to show that the American Negro is any more criminal than other elements in the American nation."[106]

Gunnar Myrdal, the Swedish researcher who studied American race relations in the 1930s, was astonished to find that, contrary to what he was used to in Scandinavia, most people he interviewed seemed to view crime as if it had nothing to do with social conditions but was simply an inevitable outcome of personal defects or "badness." He also noted that Southern whites tended to exaggerate Negro crime and underestimate white crime to such an extent that many appeared to "consider crime and prison reform part of the Negro problem and therefore not to be discussed."[107]

Ever since slavery days, wherever they had settled, blacks in America had always been disproportionately imprisoned. But as more of them left the South, more black men began to show up as prison statistics in the North. By 1926 a Detroit study reported that twice as many blacks as whites were being sentenced to prison for roughly comparable offenses.[108] About the same time a survey at Pennsylvania's Western Penitentiary found that blacks were being held at a rate nearly fourteen times greater than whites.[109] The United States Bureau of the Census noted that Negroes comprised only 9.3 percent of the adult population, but made up 31.3 percent of the prisoners.[110]

The South continued to have the highest rates of imprisonment in the country, and the highest rates of execution, as well as the highest rates of crime, especially violent crime. Southern convict camps also remained infamous throughout the world, so much so that Myrdal could report that, with very few exceptions, the Southern prison was "a place where prisoners are physically tortured for insubordination of any kind, where the guards are of the lowest stratum of society and receive extremely low pay, where the surroundings are dirty and the food abominable, where there is a tradition of callousness and brutality, where there is not the slightest attempt to reform but only to punish and get work out of the prisoners." He conceded that some Northern prisons were not much better, but added, "there has been a long, hard struggle to improve very bad prisons in the North, but . . . Southern prisons do not approximate Northern penal standards."[111]

Generally speaking, imprisonment in the South appeared to be more closely associated with Negroes than it was up North, both as a result of the experience of slavery and because many Southern prison farms had become predominantly black since Emancipation.

The Great Depression marked a period of despair and pessimism for most Americans. But for African Americans, the situation scraped rock bottom. Blacks' general economic position continued to decline and there seemed to be no significant improvement on other fronts. Not surprisingly, as the economy soured, more people ended up in prison. From 1925 to 1939 the nation's rate of imprisonment climbed from 79 to 137 per 100,000 residents.[112] In large measure, this growth was driven by greater incarceration of Negroes. Indeed, one scholar noticed that during the period between 1930 and 1936 black incarceration rates had risen substantially to a level about three times greater than those for whites, while the white incarceration rate actually had decreased.[113]

As the nation approached World War II, many Negroes had ample reason to feel that America's self-professed democratic aims did not apply to them. As Langston Hughes put it,

> *I swear to the Lord*
> *I still can't see*
> *Why Democracy means*
> *Everybody but me.*[114]

CHAPTER SEVEN

Doing Time

THE CODE

A burglar, brought to the Wisconsin state prison during the early years of the twentieth century, said that when one after another of the iron-barred gates closed behind him, he felt as though he had been eaten and then swallowed into an immense cavern, where he was doomed to remain forever. He thought, "Society had fed another individual into the great iron jaws of the prison hopper."[1] Like being inside the Great Whale.

Even when a novice inmate had not been blindfolded or hooded at the gate, the whirl of terror and excitement often kept him from noticing important landmarks in his new surroundings. As he descended deeper and deeper into the institution, he might overlook what would prove to be the last stretch of green grass he would see in his lifetime, or neglect to memorize the number of locked gates between himself and freedom, until suddenly it was too late and he found himself alone in a bare stone cell, with time standing still and the realization sinking in that he might never get out of prison again. And then he began to wonder, How on earth can I survive here?

The prison authorities put their new arrival through a crunching but meticulously organized admission ritual, which, besides degrading him, was meant to extract every kind of personal information, for entry into the prison record he never was permitted to see. There was the mortification of being stripped naked in front of others, and the mortification of being exposed to naked others. He was probed and tested, and layer by layer his individuality was stripped away, and he was assigned a new identity, and clad in ill-fitting uniformity, of the striped design, striped like the bars of his dreary, desolate cell. Besides the loss of freedom, it was one of the worst pains he would have to endure, what Dostoyevsky called "compulsory life in common."[2] From now on, his life would be under the control of somebody else. All he could do was time.

This official initiation was only part of what lay in store. Every newcomer was also sized up by his fellow convicts, convicts in many instances who had barely seemed to notice him, but who really were master detectives. A veteran prisoner knew what to look for; he didn't miss a detail. He snapped up and stored away the slightest gesture, the smallest clue, the tiniest bit of information. "Convicts know more about prison than anybody else," a Michigan prison official acknowledged.[3] Perhaps fear and long-term sensory deprivation enhanced their sense of smell and hearing and sharpened their powers of observation. Perhaps not. But convicts noticed everything.

Each newcomer (or "fish," in convict parlance) was eyeballed and quickly sorted by race, experience, rap, sentence, and other characteristics. His fellow inmates watched how he handled himself and they communicated his image through the grapevine. The prison's pecking order often ran counter to the state's, so that society's toughest bad guys became leading citizens here. Murderers usually enjoyed high status inside. So did gangsters and professional criminals.

Convicts conducted their own orientation. It started as soon as the coast was clear and they were not being watched by the "hacks" or "screws" (guards). One of them told a fish the institution's "real rules," recounted some recent history of the place, bestowed a nickname, and began showing him how to look, how to act, what to say.

One of the first lessons was how to talk. Language instruction started immediately, as one boyish-looking newcomer to Joliet discovered when he received a smuggled note that said:

L.

Figured there was some of the words and names that is used around the joint here you might not know. So here's a list of some of them:

screw	prison guard	*Holy Joe*	minister
con	prisoner	*kite*	note, letter
punk	bread	*rap*	to talk
buck	Catholic priest	*sticks*	matches

Tear this up after you read it. You ain't supposed to write kites.[4]

Nobody knew for sure how or when American prison argot had originated, but some slang terms dated back to at least the nineteenth century
and a few maybe even to convict-transport days; some expressions were
used in prisons throughout America, whereas others had a regional or
local flavor.[5] "Not only can you usually tell from a man's speech whether
he has ever done time," one particularly savvy convict remarked, "but it is
frequently possible by careful attention to spot the very penitentiary in
which he served his term."[6]

One day during the 1920s, a Chicago street tough named Stanley, who
was only sixteen years old, found himself sharing a cell in the Chicago
House of Correction with Halfpint, a hardened career criminal of about
forty-five. As soon as they were alone, the kid got his first lesson about
doing time. Halfpint recited his prison pedigree. He'd done one to ten in
Sing Sing, five in San Quentin, one to ten in Joliet, three in the Iowa state
pen, four months in the Cook County jail, six months in the Cleveland
workhouse, and lots of other short bids in assorted lockups and jails before
landing in this joint for a con job. "Buddy," he said, "you've got a year to
do, and a year in this joint is like doing ten years in stir. Keep your mouth
shut and mind your own business. And whatever you do, don't be a rat;
they're bumped off when they get out, and it's a dirty trick to rat on a
fellow-prisoner, anyway. Don't antagonize the guards; hate them all you
want to, but work them for your own good."[7]

Another inmate (Broadway Jones) told an interviewer (the criminologist
Edwin Sutherland): "The prisoners get in trouble in two ways: one is to
get high-hat with the guards and try to fight back; the other is to snitch on
other prisoners."[8] The worst label a convict could carry with his peers was
that of rat, snitch, stool pigeon, squealer, informer. The second worst was
sex deviate.

Hans Reimer, a sociologist who conducted an early participant-
observer study of socialization in the prison community that he published
in 1937, found the inmate population to be largely controlled by a small
group. The "politicians," or "shots," held key prison positions that
enabled them to distribute food and exploit other privileges. Their tendency to extort money and services from fellow inmates did not endear
them to others. Another power group was the "right guys," about whom
Reimer wrote: "They are men who can always be trusted, who do not
abuse lesser inmates, who are invariably loyal to their class—the convicts.
They are not wanton trouble-makers but they are expected to stand up for
their rights as convicts, to get what they can from the prison officials, to
never permit an opportunity to pass from which they might secure any-

thing from a better job to freedom."[9] In his view, these were the real inmate leaders.

Sometimes such cons amassed tremendous power, and not just over other prisoners. A convict who had done time in Stateville (Illinois) during the early 1930s, for instance, later described an institution that was run by inmate gangsters. "We were gambling, drinkin', makin' moon, runnin' protection rackets, everything," he said. "Just like on the outside. There were gangs of prisoners runnin' wild over the yard, hijackin' trucks. There were no established shops. The big-shot cons didn't have to make the count in their cells, didn't have to work if they didn't feel like it. They ran the place."[10]

A common pastime in the yard was labelling one's fellow convicts, separating the sheep from the goats, the friends or allies or contacts from enemies. As one old-timer explained:

> X—the heavy-set con leaning against the wall there, with the cap over his eyes, was a queen looking for a new boyfriend, but not a "rat." A rat was an informer, a stool pigeon; anything you told him would reach the warden's office in a matter of minutes. Y and Z—those two standing with their backs to you—were rats: watch out for them. Sometimes a rat would do his work undercover, discreetly: that made him really dangerous; whereas an ordinary rat—like Y or Z—was just a nuisance, easy to handle once you knew what he was up to. Q—the tall, thin con lighting a cigarette—was a "peddler"; anything for money was his motto. Not a man you liked, but a man you might need; not a man to inform on you, but not a man to trust beyond the point where his material interest coincided with your own. He'd get you a comfortable mattress—for a price; get you a quart of whiskey— for a price; get you a law book—contraband—a box of cigars, extra writing paper, a uniform made to your measure. But: handle with care. The two young ones playing catch in the sun were "mickies": newcomers. They'd been shipped in over the weekend, and nobody knew them well enough yet to pin a label on them; but there was a chance they might turn out to be "men," that is to say, members of the elite among the cons. The prisoner who proved himself to be of sound character, who had principles he refused to sacrifice—loyalty to his fellows, disdain for the finks and the rats, the "sharpies" and the "wolves" who exploited fellow prisoners—who would share whatever he had

with his friends, who tried to live up to the "code," that is, refused to act like an animal in spite of the grinding horror of prison life: that prisoner won the respect of his fellows whose respect was worth having, and along with it the title of "man." Among the prisoners there was no higher title to be had. And there was none less flattering than that of "hack lover."[11]

Based upon his stint as staff sociologist at the Menard (Illinois) state penitentiary in the 1930s, Donald Clemmer published the first major sociological study of a prison, *The Prison Community* (1940), detailing life inside a maximum-security institution. In it he analyzed the informal social system, or inmate subculture, that the prisoners had created and maintained. He said that subculture was made up of their

> habits, behavior systems, traditions, history, customs, folkways, codes, the laws and rules which guide the inmates and their ideas, opinions and attitudes toward or against homos, family, education, work, recreations, government, prisons, police, judges, other inmates, wardens, ministers, doctors, guards, ballplayers, clubs, guns, cells, buckets, gravy, beans, walls, lamps, rain, clouds, clothes, machinery, hammers, rocks, caps, bibles, books, radios, monies, stealing, murder, rape, sex, love, honesty, martyrdom, and so on.[12]

Clemmer claimed the system was glued together by unwritten law, the inmate code, which existed beside and in opposition to the institution's official rules. He said its fundamental principle held that "[i]nmates are to refrain from helping prison or government officials in matters of discipline, and should never give them information of any kind, and especially the kind which may work harm of a fellow prisoner." They knew they had to stick together. "Do your own time" and "Be loyal to your class, the cons," were cardinal rules to live by or die.[13]

Convicts needed to conform to the code. They had to be tough to survive in prison. Those who had not grown up tough on the streets and in the alleys and tenements and ports needed to get tough. Fast. A man had to know how to defend himself. Otherwise, he was a sitting duck.

A mother who went to visit her son in the reformatory left shaken and frightened by what she had found. "He'd brushed his hair down to his eyes," she said. "He looked sullen and ugly. At home he wears his hair straight back. Then he has a sweet face." To another she confided, "I says, 'Oh, son, don't wear your hair like that' and he answered gruffly 'I can't help it, mother. It don't do to look good. They get after you. You've got to look hard here to live.'" As one convict explained: "The tougher you are in prison, the more you are held in respect by the average prisoner."[14]

New inmates, like new members of other societies, underwent a process of assimilation.[15] Those who did not know the rules of the game had to learn them fast and conform to the code. Clemmer called this socialization process "prisonization," which he defined as "the taking on in greater or less degree of the folkways, mores, customs and general culture of the penitentiary."[16] The process required inmates to accept an inferior role, to accumulate facts concerning the prison, to develop new habits of eating and sleeping and dressing and acting, to learn a new local language, and to devise ways to survive and prevail in a system by which others in authority sought to control the supply or denial of every human need.

MODERNISM

THE American maximum-security prison was intended as an institution of total control, an island of totalitarianism in a sea of freedom.[17] Originally designed as a detention device to deprive human beings of their liberty, the prison had withstood the mob from within and without to become one of the most formidable weapons in the arsenal of democracy, an apparatus that had changed less and prevented more change than any other institution in American society.

Over the years, the state had refined its design into an art, adding massive walls that might extend thirty feet below ground and just as many in height above a seamless asphalt floor; sally ports at the gate that enabled guards to inspect the undercarriages of passing vehicles; specially reinforced steel bars that could withstand assault by man or time itself; transparent screens to block an anguished kiss between a convict and his spouse; elaborate locking systems that sealed their occupants inside and kept intruders out, like watertight compartments that kept the sea from surging into a battleship's hold; strategically placed canisters of tear gas that could be instantly set off to quell a disturbance; and multitiered cellblocks that allowed a few passing guards to closely inspect hundreds of men in their cages as they slept, read, paced, or defecated. Such were the cumulative contributions of the long line of custodial generations.

By 1933, national surveys reported, there were roughly 4,300 penal institutions in the United States. Of these, 1,500 were municipal jails, workhouses, farms, and stockades for persons convicted of misdemeanors; 2,500 were county jails, workhouses, farms, and chain gangs for convicted misdemeanants; 109 were state prisons, state prison farms, or state chain gangs for convicted felons; 16 were state reformatories for convicted youthful offenders; 3 were federal prisons under military control; and 150 more were juvenile reformatories. Their total inmate population on January 1, 1933, was 233,631, of which the majority, 137,721, were in state penal institutions.[18]

By August 1933, the consecutive numbers that Elam Lynds had begun to assign to Sing Sing's entering convicts in 1825 had surpassed the 88,000 mark.[19] Auburn, Sing Sing, Pennsylvania's Eastern Penitentiary, and several other state prisons were more than a century old and still operating, much as they had for decades, scarcely touched by time. Flogging was still legal in most states and still used in most prisons.[20] The outside world had gone from horse-drawn buggies to automobiles and airplanes, but prisoners in many maximum-security institutions still marched the lockstep. By and large, many old prisons remained essentially unchanged. The fortress prisons had proved remarkably durable: more layers of paint had been added, stone floors had become rounded by shuffling feet, and surrounding villages had become gritty prison towns that turned out third- and fourth-generation guards.

Prisons had been built to last. They were seldom abandoned or torn down, just renovated and enlarged. Auburn, built in 1816, was still in use; so was Clinton (1845) and Sing Sing (1825).

By the early twentieth century, Sing Sing's physical plant had deteriorated so much that many official panels called for its abandonment as a place of confinement.[21] In 1905 a state commission appointed to investigate structural and sanitary conditions there urged that a new prison be built to replace it.[22] In 1912 another state investigation resulted in the indictment of the warden for neglect of duty, and Sing Sing was described as "unfit for the housing of animals . . . a scandal to the State."[23] In 1913 convicts reacted to the practices of a new warden by rioting and burning two prison shops to the ground.[24] In its report to the legislature in 1914, the Governor's Commission on Penal Reform concluded: "Sing Sing Prison, with its archaic equipment, continues as a reproach to the State which maintains it [and] a disgrace [which] should be abandoned."[25] Before a packed house at Carnegie Hall, Governor Martin H. Glynn told concerned members of the Prison Association of New York: "If the number of letters I receive saying 'Sing Sing must go,' and the size of this audience mean anything, I suppose Sing Sing must go."[26] Yet Sing Sing remained. In 1927 the state's new commission of correction concluded that Sing Sing was beyond improvement and should be replaced.[27] During the 1970s the state was forced to close Sing Sing's ancient A and B Blocks because they were deemed by the courts as unfit to house prisoners. Costly renovations were made and Sing Sing resumed its indestructible, relentless existence.[28]

Over the years, prisons gradually relaxed some of their original rules. On July 4, 1864, for example, Warden Gideon Hayes of the Massachusetts State Prison at Charlestown broke a decades-old practice when he suddenly and by surprise permitted convicts to disregard the silence rule for the first time. Initially they did not make a sound. But, as Hayes later recounted, "The shout that then burst forth from those four hundred throats, the delirium of delight into which they were immediately plunged, at once relieved me from all the fear as to the result. They shook hands, embraced one another, laughed, shouted, danced, and cried; one of them caught up my little boy, rushed into the crowd, and I saw no more of him till the bell called them to order." Even then, their reaction was nothing short of remarkable. "At the first stroke of the bell every voice was hushed; silently and quietly they fell into line in their respective divisions, and save for the flush of excitement and the animated expression which flashed from the eyes of all, giving them more the appearance of the men God created in his own image than I had ever seen in that place before, they, in their usual good order, passed into their cells."[29]

At Joliet state prison on the 4th of July in 1875, Warden R. W. McClaughry allowed his convicts the use of the big yard for the first time. The result, he said, was that they "talked, laughed and sang, engaged in athletic sports, and improvised minstrel performances to their hearts' content, while the occasion was enlivened with instrumental music by the Wheaton cornet band."[30]

But many reform efforts struck a stone wall. Reflecting on his thirty-five years of prison life, which had begun in the nineteenth century, an ex-convict named Charles L. Clark recalled how one innovative warden, E. C. Watkins, had single-handedly introduced the grading system and abolished the lockstep, only to be rebuffed in his attempt to end the silent system by the omnipotent contractors, who would not stand for it.[31]

And so, prison customs endured. Rituals that seemed outdated continued. The traditional "bucket brigade," for instance, was still required for entering convicts at Sing Sing, San Quentin, and other prisons well into the 1950s.[32] At Joliet this meant that every morning before breakfast convicts made the daily bucket run from their cells. As one prisoner, Nathan Leopold, described it, "As each man approached he removed the cover of his bucket, dipped it in the trough, sloshed it around several times, and then flung the contents into an enormous cesspool at the right." The air was filled with flying human ordure. A twelve-foot square held the excrement of eighteen hundred men. Leopold thought that, more than anything else, the bucket brigade epitomized prison life as he had known it, and he added: "The very fact that the schedule called for coming directly from the disgusting chore of emptying one's excrement to breakfast, with no chance of washing one's hands, seemed to be deliberately contrived to humiliate the convict and to make his lot as uncomfortable as possible."[33] Well into the 1960s, guards at Sing Sing and Great Meadow rapped on the cell bars with nightsticks to command inmates to move.[34]

Labor was one of the few features of prison life that changed considerably from the nineteenth to the twentieth century. Back in the 1820s, the Boston Prison Discipline Society had urged the use of convict labor because "it is productive, it is healthful, it teaches convicts how to support themselves when they leave prison, it is reformatory, and is consonant with republican principles."[35] For a brief period, prison factories boomed, and some institutions even made a profit. However, over the years, labor organizations in many states had won laws restricting convict labor, so that prisoners would not compete with free workers. Another impediment to the growth of prison industry was the principle of "less eligibility." Essentially, it held that inmates should be subjected to worse conditions than those endured by the lowest classes in free society; otherwise, poor people would commit crimes in order to be sent to prison as a means of improving their lives.

In 1929 Congress passed the Hawes-Cooper Act, which enabled any state to prohibit within its borders the sale of any goods made in the prisons of another state.[36] That same year, only 35 to 45 percent of New York State prisoners were engaged in productive labor, such as making auto license plates. Still, their output continued to be remarkably high: the 1931–32 fiscal year was entered on the record books as Sing Sing's most prosperous ever, with total sales exceeding $860,000; Auburn's annual production of goods consumed by state departments topped the $1 million mark.[37] By the time the Hawes-Cooper Act became effective, in 1934, most states had enacted laws restricting the sale and movement of prison products. In 1935 the Ashurst-Sumners Act strengthened Hawes-Cooper and prohibited the transportation of prison products to any state in violation of the laws of that state.[38]

During the Great Depression, the proportion of inmates in state and federal correctional facilities who were productively employed in prison industries dropped from 52 percent in 1932 to 44 percent in 1940. The value of prison goods actually dropped by 25 percent; the annual value of product per inmate employed dropped by 26 percent, from $916 to $679. In all of the states, 76,775 prisoners out of the total of 173,284 being held were listed as "employed," 60,268 were engaged in prison maintenance, 11,673 were attending school, 14,127 were listed as "sick or otherwise unavailable" to work, and 10,441 were reported as idle.[39] In 1940 Congress enacted legislation to bar, with a few exceptions, the interstate transportation of prison-made goods.[40]

Prisoner wages were not a significant factor contributing to the decline of prison labor: by 1931 only fifty-eight penal institutions in thirty-six states and two of the five federal prisons paid some token money wages to inmates; in 1940 Auburn's average pay for farm workers was still only about five cents a day, and in the shop it was only about twenty cents a day.[41] Nor was the state spending more on employment training in order to better prepare inmates for their release. Rather, prison labor declined as the American economic system fell short in its ability to employ workers who were not in prison. To put still more law-abiding citizens out of work would have been too politically problematic.

Besides, improvement was anathema to all that prison stood for. A prison guarded and enforced the status quo; it didn't try to change it. Some institutions even placed over their entrance Dante's inscription from the Gate of Hell: ONLY THOSE ELEMENTS TIME CANNOT WEAR WERE MADE BEFORE ME, AND BEYOND TIME I STAND. ABANDON ALL HOPE YE WHO ENTER HERE.[42]

Some restraint was physical. As Michel Foucault later noted, prison's raison d'être was containment of motion, confinement of the body, something at which American prisons had proven to be remarkably effective.[43] Among maximum-security institutions, the level of escapes was remarkably low, and a few prisons had never had one successful escape during their entire history.

Such confinement had been achieved only at tremendous physical cost to the inmates. "Visiting the zoo as a child," one long-term prisoner recalled, "I'd been struck by the way a lion—pacing then as I was pacing now—would progressively shorten the distance covered each time, anticipating the presence of the bars before he reached them, anticipating the need to turn and turning a step sooner, then two steps, then three, until finally he was no longer pacing but turning on himself, revolving on his own axis."[44] Now he found himself behaving the same way as the animal in the cage.

But unlike a zoo or a circus, prison remained a drab and lifeless world of granite, steel, and cement, drained of all color and vibrancy. Convicts lived in a barren environment that was reduced to the absolute bare essentials, with less adornment, private property, and services than might be found in the worst city slum. As if that were not bad enough, its designers took this mandate further, continuing to build their penal structures, as one student of prison architecture observed, "in a way which manages by one means or another to brutalize their occupants and to deprive them of their privacy, dignity, and self-esteem, while at the same time strengthening their criminality."[45] A convict who surveyed Auburn's "recreation" yard in the 1920s noted there was "no blade of grass, no tree, no bit of freshness or brilliance. Gray walls, dusty gravel, dirt and asphalt hardness." The whole effect was of being worn down. "We walk about, or during our first few months or years, manage to throw a ball back and forth and in some degree exercise our bodies," he said. "The longer we stay here, the less we do. At last we merely walk at a funeral pace or lean against a wall and talk."[46]

Prison also deprived inmates of heterosexual relationships, subjecting them to involuntary celibacy.[47] Some felt this denied them their very manhood or femininity. Others hungered as much for human touch and caring. Prisoners did the best they could with what they had. In response to those who condemned them for resorting to homosexuality, one former inmate replied that "to talk of 'normal' sexual impulses where prison is concerned is a little foolish unless you can think of sexual starvation as a healthy normal condition."[48]

Regardless of how one came to terms with matters of sexuality, imprisonment threatened a person's feelings of safety and security. Although designed to enforce the law and protect the public, prisons were among the most dangerous places in society, and the people who inhabited them lived in constant tension and fear, wary of prisoners and keepers alike, never able to relax. None could ever put down his guard.

A prison's official regime restricted an individual's movement, not only to the campus of the institution but within it, keeping its occupants confined to a tightly controlled space, which was devoid of privacy. Some men spent years limited to a small sector of an institution, and never got to see what was going on beyond their own cellblocks and walls. Mobility was restricted to a select crew of porters and other privileged types. There was no place to hide, nowhere to retreat to, no sanctuary in which to feel safe. A man could not even talk in his sleep without being heard. His "personal property" was subject to search, his most heartfelt letters could be censored or confiscated or ridiculed. Authorities stood in the way of all news from the outside world, whether it was about riots in the streets or the death of a loved one.

Besides all of their physical constraints, prisons restricted their inmates through an invisible web of rules and timetables. Day after day, week after week, the schedule remained the same. This meant that prisoners were denied the power to govern their lives. They were taught to conform. Days were spent standing for counts, marching to and from work in the prison shop, waiting in line for chow, stepping back for the nightly lockin, just doing time. Monotony was a fact of prison life. A prisoner had to find ways to combat and overcome boredom, or else succumb and become a zombie. For many, that often meant talking with other inmates whenever the chance arose. "We talk at each other," Victor Nelson, who did five years in New York prisons in the 1920s, wrote. "We do not converse; we deliver monologues in which we get rid of the stored up bubblings. We try to live through words and self-dramatization. Our essential need is for actual tangible living, which we cannot have; so we try to live by pretending to live in tall stories based on how we'd like to live, how we long to live."[49]

Sometimes, deliberately or unconsciously, prisoners went into a stupor and lived in a fantasy land of their own making, almost appearing to be in a coma. Victor Nelson described one such pathetic creature, a trusty in striped overalls who was leaning on the handle of his rake on the prison grounds, looking burned-out. "There was an expression of utter indifference in his face and his eyes were glazed with absent-mindedness," he wrote. "He was, although I did not know it then, a living example of the total, final, devastating effect of imprisonment upon the human being."[50]

Jack London wrote a science fiction novel, *The Star Rover,* in which he described a prisoner who developed an ability to counteract some of the deadening effects of solitary confinement by imagining he was travelling through time and space into other lives.[51] London had based his story on the exploits of an actual ex-convict, Ed Morrell, whose use of fantasy had not been wholly unique.[52] But then, what segment of American society could rival prisons as a fantasy world?

LIFERS

ISIDORE Zimmerman was one of five youths who was charged for the fatal shooting of a New York City policeman during a holdup of an all-night gambling joint in 1937. Though he had not even been at the crime scene, he was convicted of murder with the others on the grounds that he had procured the murder weapon. All five were sentenced to death in the electric chair, but his penalty was later commuted to life imprisonment. He was doomed to spend the rest of his life behind bars for a crime he did not commit.

"The years pass; and in the drab gray world I inhabit nothing changes but the dates on the calendar," Zimmerman observed. "I sit in my cell and try one night, after lights out, to establish the chronology of all my wasted years; nine months in the Sing Sing death house; eight years in Auburn; three years in Attica; one year in Greenhaven; eleven years in Dannemora. Nothing changes: only the names."[53]

Over the years, Zimmerman experienced many pains, but none hurt more than the loss of family. He later said a person serving time in prison "imagines his family, his friends outside the walls, will remain somehow as he left them: his wife faithful, his children children. No matter how slowly the clocks tick for him, he thinks, they will have stopped for them."[54] One day he was stunned by the news that his mother was dead. Once again, he'd learned that time was his enemy, the enemy of every prisoner.

When Zimmerman had spent over twenty-four years in prison, evidence that the state had suppressed, which proved his innocence, was magically unearthed. He was cleared. His imprisonment had been a mistake. Not his mistake; the state's. He was free.[55]

In 1909 Robert Stroud, aged nineteen, had killed an older man for assaulting his girlfriend.[56] Young Stroud was sentenced to prison for twelve years. While serving time at McNeil Island penitentiary on Puget Sound, he stabbed another inmate during a fight and was transferred to Leavenworth to do hard time.

One Sunday in 1916 Stroud was sitting at a table in Leavenworth's cavernous dining hall with eleven hundred other convicts when he was confronted by a rookie guard, Andrew F. Turner. Suddenly, as the guard raised his nightstick, Stroud drew a knife and plunged it into Turner's chest, killing him. This time, he was sentenced to death. But after his mother begged for clemency, President Wilson commuted the punishment to life imprisonment, with Stroud to be held in solitary confinement throughout. He spent years in isolation.

One day while walking in his solitary exercise yard, he came upon an injured sparrow, fluttering on the concrete. Stroud managed to smuggle it back to his cell, and over the next several weeks he gently nursed the creature back to health. He became fascinated with it and began studying the sparrow's behavior, teaching it tricks, gaining its trust.

Stroud convinced the warden to let him raise a few canaries in his cell. The birds mated and reproduced. He was able to get birdseed and he constructed an assortment of ingenious contraptions for his winged friends. Although Stroud had only a third-grade education, he began to show some remarkable intellectual abilities and started reading everything about ornithology he could get. Using whatever scraps and bits of materials he could scrounge, Stroud built thirty makeshift cages and acquired a microscope, a microtome, test tubes, and bottles of reagents. Soon he was conducting laboratory experiments on as many as three hundred birds, feeding and caring for the living, recording notes about their health, dissecting the dead. Along the way he compiled two authoritative books about bird diseases; both were published. Some of his readers became supporters of his bid to win release from prison.[57]

In 1942, however, Stroud was abruptly taken out of Leavenworth in leg irons and handcuffs and put onto a train under heavy guard. The journey ended at Alcatraz (meaning, ironically, "the Isle of Pelicans"), where he was put into cell number 41. He was no longer allowed to keep his birds, and all his equipment had been disassembled, packed into crates, and shipped to his brother.[58]

But Stroud would not be broken. He switched to writing a definitive history of the federal prison system, much of it based on his own experience. His health had sharply deteriorated from years of confinement, and he was stooped and in constant pain, yet he continued to labor through the night on his massive manuscript, which he called "Looking Outward." When it had reached several hundred pages, the authorities confiscated it to prevent its publication.[59] Taken to the prison hospital, he remained in isolation for 10 more years. By the time that Thomas E. Gaddis's popular book about him, *The Birdman of Alcatraz,* appeared on bookstands in 1958, Stroud had spent 52 years in prison, 46 of them in solitary confinement. Then, at age 69, he was removed from Alcatraz and sent to a new federal prison hospital at Springfield, Missouri. In 1962 his story became a notable motion picture, starring Burt Lancaster. Stroud died a year later, at the federal penitentiary at Springfield. He was 73 years old.

Stroud had been in prison throughout World War I, and he was still there when the United States entered World War II. Shortly after it began, President Franklin D. Roosevelt issued Executive Order 9066, paving the way for more than 110,000 aliens and Americans of Japanese ancestry to be rounded up along the West Coast and herded into inland internment camps from California to Arkansas.[60] Japanese Americans were held prisoner in these barbed-wire "relocation centers" until mid-1946, almost a year after the fighting had ended.

The news from Pearl Harbor had shocked most prisoners as much as other Americans. Despite their bitterness toward society, many convicts suddenly sensed their country was in danger, and they wanted to do their part to defend her. The new Selective Service Act required all convicts to be registered for conscription, and most of those who could join the armed forces enlisted. The number of inmates dipped for the first time in more than a decade, dropping from 190,000 in 1940 to less than 120,000 in 1943.[61]

Prisons became part of the country's total war effort. Convicts gave gallons of blood to the Red Cross. The institutions became factories once again. Ninety-eight percent of all inmates were productively engaged in war work.[62] They made mattresses for the army, model planes for pilot training, naval assault boats, engines, war ration books, shoes, uniforms, bunks, bomb fins, rubber nets for landing craft, flags. In Illinois alone, some of the prison-made goods delivered to the War Department included: 30,000 Maritime Commission blankets, 10,000 "Lend-Lease" blankets, 99,327 yards of "Lend-Lease" suiting, 1,175 Coast Guard office chairs, 40,482 Army Ordnance Department shell pallets, 22,095 Army Ordnance Department fuse gauges for shells, 439,738 blue chambray shirts for the Navy, 74,979 "Lend-Lease" overalls, 74,979 "Lend-Lease" jackets, 6,000 Army unionalls, 24,248 Army "Bush" shirts, 49,534 Navy "Seabee" shirts, 74,168 "Lend-Lease" wool trousers, 104,190 "Lend-Lease" work shirts, 78,024 "Lend-Lease" dungarees, 6,008 "Lend-Lease" denim jackets, 25,493 Army "Sun Tan" jackets, 26,451 Army "Sun Tan" trousers, 10,270 Army khaki trousers, 819,862 pieces of Army clothing, canvas, and equipage items repaired and returned to Army stocks, 5,113,273 pieces of Army clothing, canvas, and equipage items segregated, classified, and returned to Army stocks, 5,214,100 pounds of "rough dry" Army laundry, and 1,395,423 pounds of "finished work" Army laundry. Convicts also purchased war bonds and rooted for the troops.[63]

Although World War II was strongly supported at home, a few men refused to serve, mostly for religious reasons, and some of them were incarcerated. For example, by 1944 the federal prisons held over 4,000 Jehovah's Witnesses, who were conscientious objectors.[64]

Patriotic feelings ran high. Many prisoners actually felt left out because they could not join the fighting. Knowing that American troops were engaged in deadly jungle warfare across the Pacific islands, Nathan Leopold, the convicted killer, volunteered to participate in a life-endangering experiment on human subjects that was testing the results of various toxic drugs for treating malaria. Leopold was proud when it produced an effective treatment, proud though he remained in prison.[65]

THE BLACK MUSLIMS

NOT everybody wanted to join the United States war machine against the Japanese and Germans. One who didn't was an angry, light-skinned Negro teen-ager named Malcolm Little. When called for his Army induction physical, he convinced the psychiatrist he was a potential security risk and was classified 4-F.[66] Free of his military obligation, he gravitated from Boston to Harlem, started smoking reefer, popping pills, hanging out and playing around as a street hustler and pimp, being cool. Along the way he got hooked on cocaine. Soon he was packing a pistol, pulling stickups.

Arrested for a string of burglaries in Boston, Little was sentenced, in February 1946, to a term of ten years in prison as a first-time felony offender. He was only twenty years old and had not started shaving.

Young Little was sent across the Charles River to the 140-year-old Charlestown state prison, in a town that had been founded by black slaves named Bacchus, Cato, and Jupiter, the same prison where Warden Gideon Hayes had scrapped the silent system 81 years earlier. Not much had changed there since. His ancient cell lacked running water. A covered pail served as his toilet.[67] As No. 22843, he was just another Negro convict. His fellow prisoners called him "Satan" for his antireligious attitude. He worked in the license plate shop. Whenever he could, he got high on nutmeg and reefer sold to him by corrupt guards.

Little might have turned into a career convict, except that a few months into his sentence he came under the influence of a veteran inmate named "Bimbi," who told him stories about Thoreau and encouraged him to use the prison library.

Following his transfer to Concord prison, he received a letter from his brother Philbert, who described his recent conversion to a new religion known as the Nation of Islam, a new movement that was attracting growing attention in the black quarters of some American cities.[68] Another brother, Reginald, urged him to quit cigarettes and pork, saying rather mysteriously that it would help him get out of prison.

Transferred to Norfolk Prison Colony, an experimental, education-oriented institution known for its "intellectuals," Little turned to religion and history, and looked into the thing his brothers had been telling him about.[69]

The Nation of Islam owed some of its black nationalist ideas to Marcus Garvey. Also known as the Black Muslim movement, it had been founded in Detroit in 1930 and later taken over by Elijah Poole, who moved the organization's base to Chicago and began calling himself the Honorable Elijah Muhammad.

Under his authoritarian leadership, the Black Muslims added notions of black supremacy to the traditional beliefs of Sunni Islam. They developed their own ministers, schools, dietary laws, and a cadre of bodyguards known as the Fruit of Islam (FOI). Followers were instructed to refuse alcohol, narcotics, tobacco, and pork. They were forbidden to kill unless ordered to by Allah; as a result, during World War II, some Black Muslims were imprisoned for refusing to serve in the armed forces. (Elijah Muhammad himself spent three and a half years in federal prison for draft evasion.)[70] Many observers would later trace the real growth of the Nation of Islam to 1946 or 1947, after his release from confinement.

It was at this time that Malcolm Little threw himself into the Koran. After lights out, he would feign sleep as the guards passed by his cell and stay up late into the night, reading and studying.[71] He read about the African slave trade and the slavemasters' rape of black women that had produced mixed-race Negroes, light-skinned like his mother, who looked white and was ashamed to speak of her own father. He discovered how the devil had brainwashed blacks to believe that whites were superior, and he learned about how white slavemasters had injected Christian religion into their Negroes.[72]

In his dimly lit cell he scrawled a one-page letter of faith to the Honorable Elijah Muhammad and later dropped it in the mail. To his amazement he received a neatly typed personal reply that welcomed him into the faith and said that the black prisoner "symbolized white society's crime of keeping black men oppressed and deprived and ignorant, and unable to get decent jobs, turning them into criminals." Elijah Muhammad neglected to mention that he had come out of prison just as Malcolm had gone in, but his response offered encouragement. It had a $5 bill attached, too.[73]

By the time Little was paroled in August of 1952, he had served seven years in prison. Shortly after regaining his freedom he dropped his "slave name" and became Brother Malcolm X. In time he became a Muslim minister. When his recruiting had drawn thousands of new believers, Elijah Muhammad appointed him minister of Temple Number Seven in Harlem.[74]

About the same time, a young dark-skinned Puerto Rican convict from New York's Spanish Harlem named Piri Thomas, who was serving a term for robbery, was introduced to the Black Muslims when he stopped to hear several prisoners who were sitting in a circle in a corner of Comstock's big yard.[75] The group's imam, or spiritual leader, was explaining some Muslim beliefs, and Thomas liked the emphasis he had placed upon dignity. He and the imam became friends. Thomas studied Arabic and eventually became a convert, taking the name of Hussein Afmit Ben Hassen. Years later he would write about his prison experiences in a popular novel, *Down These Mean Streets,* and other works.[76]

The Black Muslim movement and the civil rights struggle of which it was part continued to grow throughout the 1950s. Another black man who was in prison during those years, Eldridge Cleaver, had started serving time for possession of marijuana on June 18, 1954, when he was eighteen years old, one month after the United States Supreme Court's historic decision in *Brown v. Board of Education.*[77]

At California's Soledad Correctional Training Facility, Cleaver fell in with a gang of young Negroes like himself who cursed everything American, some of them wondering how white segregationists and Klansmen managed to get away with murder and brazenly flaunt the law while they, ordinary young black men, were put in prison for such crimes as possession of reefer. When Cleaver heard the news from Mississippi about the fate of young Emmet Till, who had been brutally murdered for flirting with a white woman, he had what he later described as a "nervous breakdown," in which he ranted and raved against the white race, especially white women, for several days. Eventually he became aware that he was locked in a padded cell. He had no recollection of how he had gotten there, and all he could recall was having spent "an eternity of pacing back and forth in the cell, preaching to the unhearing walls."[78] In 1958, after being returned to San Quentin for a parole violation, he found that one of his old pals, Butterfly, had converted to the Nation of Islam, and Cleaver too began to study Islam.[79]

By 1961 or so the Nation of Islam had attracted as many as a hundred thousand members, many of them urban males who had been in prison and who now eschewed drugs and other vices and were supposed to give as much as one-third of their legitimate earnings back to Black Muslim temples and schools. Inside the prisons, black convicts kept trying to obtain copies of the Koran and Malcolm X's influential Black Muslim newspaper, *Muhammad Speaks,* while some of their leaders preached a potent message of black nationalism, self-help, and self-discipline. Black Muslim prisoners began demanding pork-free meals and the right to worship in their own temples—actions of separatism and privilege that white prison administrators staunchly opposed. They sued for the right to wear their own religious medals, hair styles, and traditional dress; they also wanted to be able to use their own ministers, enjoy special diets during the month of Ramadan, and receive religious literature.[80]

In response to the first lawsuits brought by Black Muslim prisoners, some courts ruled that the convicts were not exercising religious rights that were protected by the First Amendment. Many prison officials simply viewed them as radical agitators or kooks.[81] When a Black Muslim leader at the Virginia state penitentiary requested permission to hold religious services for his followers, the warden demanded that he identify each one of them by name. When he refused, the warden summarily placed him in the maximum-security unit, where he remained for four years until a court ordered his release.[82]

Black Muslim prisoners were considered so threatening not only because they claimed to hate the "white devil" but also because they were self-disciplined and well-organized, had links to the outside, and knew how to use the courts to get their way. These inmates presented themselves as righteous and incorruptible, making them still more difficult to control, and they advocated rehabilitation and prison reform. In fact, the Black Muslims had taken men who were failures and outcasts, thieves and criminals, men who were in prison, and reformed them, made them proud and upright in their dealings with others. Elijah Muhammad had taught them to renounce narcotics and other vices and stop their criminal ways. He had made some of them into law-abiding, clean-cut, clear-thinking men.[83] One inmate at Indiana state prison, for example, said Islam was "one of the few things that woke me up to recognize and to face reality."[84]

Still, despite having become a Black Muslim in prison, Cleaver later turned into a rapist on the outside. After practicing on black ghetto girls, he assaulted several white women on the pretext that his sexual attacks were an "insurrectionary act." He ended up back in prison, and then was transferred from San Quentin to Folsom as an "agitator."[85]

Malcolm X continued to identify with black convicts, and he frequently used prison metaphors in his political rhetoric. "Don't be shocked when I say that I was in prison," he liked to tell his urban audiences. "You're still in prison. That's what America means: prison."[86] In comments to reporters he characterized President Kennedy as a "warden," former Vice President Nixon as a "deputy warden," and called New York City's mayor, Robert Wagner, a "screw."[87] He also tried to convince Elijah Muhammad to finance litigation that was designed to gain Muslims at Attica state prison the right to worship. But Muhammad was not very responsive to requests that he send ministers into prison. So Malcolm X himself worked in their behalf and helped to continue to build a formidable Muslim prison movement.[88] One of his projects involved preparing to testify in *Cooper v. Pate,* an Illinois prison case that had recently reached the federal court.[89] Thomas X. Cooper was a Stateville convict who claimed the authorities had denied Black Muslim inmates the right to worship as they pleased. He had received eighty-seven tickets for prison infractions from 1953 to 1965, many of them related to his religious activities.[90]

Elijah Muhammad and Malcolm eventually had a falling out that escalated into an open break. Malcolm changed his name to El-Hajj Malik El-Shabazz, made a pilgrimage to Mecca, and started his own program, the Organization of Afro-American Unity. In early February of 1965, he went to Selma, and then gave the biggest speech of his career at Tuskegee Institute, in which he said, "Our objective is complete freedom, complete justice, complete equality, by any means necessary."[91] Afterward he spoke with Coretta King, whose husband, Dr. Martin Luther King, Jr., the recent winner of the Nobel Peace Prize, was then in jail for his efforts to win Negroes the right to vote.[92]

On February 21, prisoners throughout the United States learned that Malcolm X had been assassinated at a rally in Harlem. (The murder was apparently the act of a team of Muslims loyal to Elijah Muhammad.) A onetime inmate named Bobby Seale later remembered, "When Malcolm X was killed . . ., I ran down the street." The future Black Panther leader hurled bicycles at police cars and collapsed into tears until finally telling himself, "Fuck it, I'll make my own self into a motherfucking Malcolm X, and if they want to kill me, they'll have to kill me."[93]

Eldridge Cleaver, who was then serving time in Folsom, attributed Malcolm's death to his rift with Elijah Muhammad, which had become irrevocable after Malcolm had travelled to Mecca and come back renouncing doctrines of hate and racial supremacy. Blaming the elder leader for Malcolm's murder, Cleaver took down Elijah Muhammad's framed picture from his cell wall, destroyed it, and replaced it with a photograph of Malcolm that he had clipped from the *Saturday Evening Post*. Cleaver later recalled:

> Malcolm X had a special meaning for black convicts. A former
> prisoner himself, he had risen from the lowest depths to great
> heights. For this reason he was a symbol of hope, a model for
> thousands of black convicts who found themselves trapped in
> the vicious PPP cycle: prison-parole-prison. . . . One thing that
> the judges, policemen, and administrators of prisons seem never
> to have understood, and for which they certainly do not make
> any allowances, is that Negro convicts, basically, rather than see
> themselves as criminals and perpetrators of misdeeds, look upon
> themselves as prisoners of war, the victims of a vicious, dog-eat-
> dog social system that is so heinous as to cancel out their own
> malefactions: in the jungle there is no right or wrong.[94]

NEGRO PRISONERS

A LTHOUGH the number of inmates had plummeted during World
War II, prisons began to refill when the troops started coming home.
Once again, blacks bore the brunt of increased incarceration. This time
the white share of the inmate population started to shrink significantly.

By 1946, foreign-born immigrants accounted for only 3.2 percent of
American prisoners, which was less than half of the immigrants' proportion among the total U.S. population.[95] Cells were becoming even more
heavily filled by Negroes, Hispanics, and American Indians. In 1950
Negroes comprised only 7 percent of the population of Michigan, but they
accounted for 40 percent of the state's convicts. By 1955 and the end of the
Korean War, America's prison population had reached 185,780, and the
national incarceration rate had climbed back up to 112 per 100,000, nudged
along by the "race problem."[96]

Enforcement of the drug laws played an important role in driving up
the use of imprisonment, especially as it involved minorities. In 1914 Congress had passed the Harrison Narcotic Act, making it illegal to use, sell,
or possess narcotic drugs, and establishing stiff fines and prison terms as
punishment. The immediate effect had been an increase in the prison population, particularly for Negroes.[97] Starting after World War II, in the late
1940s, drug penalties were stiffened once again with the same effect.

One of those jailed on drug charges was Billie Holiday, the young Negro
blues singer. The great-granddaughter of a slave, she had been locked up
at the age of ten for forcibly resisting a sexual assault; her later life led her
to opium and heroin. Arrested on a narcotics charge in May 1947, Holiday
was convicted and sentenced to one year and a day. She served nine and a
half months. After her release she said, "People on drugs are sick people.
So now we end up with the government chasing sick people like they
were criminals, telling doctors they can't help them, prosecuting them
because they had some stuff without paying the tax, and sending them
to jail."[98]

But the criminalization of narcotics, and drug use itself, continued to
escalate, especially in the ghetto. In 1950 the FBI reported that throughout
the United States 3,939 whites and 4,262 Negroes had been arrested for
narcotics offenses.[99]

The 1950s were full of horror stories about the brutal and often racist
way that the drug laws were administered. In one case a Negro military
veteran with no previous criminal record was sentenced to 50 years without
parole for selling marijuana. In 1956 Louisiana enacted laws that provided
mandatory prison sentences ranging from 5 to 99 years for persons who

sold, possessed, or administered relatively small amounts of narcotics. The police there began to arrest suspects. Most of them were not white. Texas punished possession of marijuana with prison terms of 2 years to life.[100] Blacks everywhere were much more likely than whites to be nabbed on drug charges, and they invariably drew longer sentences. Meanwhile, instead of curbing drug abuse, escalating drug-law enforcement had the opposite effect. Drug prices went up, rising profits attracted more pushers, organized crime and official corruption flourished, the incidence of addiction increased, and the stakes of the game went up.

THE PRISONERS' RIGHTS MOVEMENT

TO be a convict in the United States prison system had sweeping legal consequences.[101] Inmates were not entitled to life, liberty, and the pursuit of happiness. A prison did not allow the establishment of religion. A prisoner did not enjoy the free exercise of religion or freedom of speech or of the press, or the right to assemble peaceably or to petition the government for a redress of grievances.

A con could not keep and bear arms, nor could he bar anyone from quartering in his cell. Prisoners did not have the right to be secure in their persons, houses, papers, and effects, against unreasonable searches and seizures, nor were any warrants required, supported by oath or affirmation or particularly describing the place to be searched or the persons or things to be seized.

Inmates could be penalized without due process of law, and just compensation was not required when their private property was taken from them in prison.

They lacked the right to a speedy and public trial for their alleged prison infractions, much less the right to a hearing by an impartial body.

They were not entitled to be informed of the nature and cause of informers' secret accusations against them, nor did they have the right to confront any witnesses against them nor to compel witnesses in their favor nor to have the assistance of counsel for their defense.

Their right to be free of cruel and unusual punishments was blocked by prison walls.

They could not vote, for president or vice president or any other public office. They could not hold public office.

Under the Thirteenth Amendment to the Constitution of the United States, the status of persons duly convicted of crime remained that of slaves.

In short, regardless of their color, Americans' constitutional rights effectively stopped at the prison gate.

For the first 160 years or so of the nation's history, the courts almost without exception had maintained a "hands-off" or "out-of-sight, out-of-mind" posture toward prisoners.[102] The judiciary did not have to worry about responding to convicts' writs or petitions, because convicts generally were not allowed to write (or in later years to mail) letters to outsiders, including the courts, unless they had been specifically approved by the prison warden. Most prisoners had no money to hire a lawyer. Even if convicts somehow had managed to get through to the courts with their complaints, judges and their clerks typically turned a deaf ear.

After 1940, a few changes began to occur. The first group of prison cases in which the courts agreed to accept jurisdiction involved issues concerning the right of access to the courts themselves. In *Ex parte Hull*, in 1941, the Supreme Court of the United States rejected a state regulation that all habeas corpus petitions had to be approved by a "legal investigator" from the parole board as "properly drawn" before they could be transmitted to court. Although the Court seemed to affirm the right of access of state prisoners to federal court, the decision also had the effect of abridging their rights to apply to the federal courts for relief.[103]

Another federal case to suggest important limitations of the courts' traditional "hands-off" doctrine was *Coffin v. Reichard,* decided during World War II, in which the U.S. Court of Appeals for the Sixth Circuit established a new basic standard for judging prison cases, holding that "[a] prisoner retains all the rights of an ordinary citizen except those expressly, or by necessary implication, taken from him by law."[104] In fact, the opposite had been true and still was true, for convicts were not considered to have any rights at all except those that had been spelled out in statutes or granted by prison authorities, and those were precious few.

Judges continued to avoid intervening in prison matters. A typical federal district court decision in 1954 held: "Courts are without power to supervise prison administration or to interfere with the ordinary prison rules and regulations." Eight years later the same court insisted that "supervision of inmates of . . . institutions rests with the proper administrative authorities and . . . courts have no power to supervise the management of disciplinary rules of such institutions."[105]

Moreover, during World War II the U.S. Supreme Court had upheld the internment of Americans of Japanese ancestry in relocation centers.[106]

A 1945 case, *Screws v. United States,* showed how unwilling the federal courts were to take the side of state convicts.[107] The episode involved a drunken jailer in Baker County, Georgia, Sheriff Claude Screws, who had taken into custody a Negro named Robert Hall, hauled him into the court-house yard, and slugged him with a blackjack until Hall was dead. When the state declined to bring any murder charges, federal prosecutors gained his conviction under a civil rights statute from Reconstruction. However, Screws appealed on the curious grounds that he had not intended to deprive Hall of his civil rights, only to kill him. The United States Supreme Court strictly interpreted the word "willfully" in the statute and reversed the conviction. Screws was subsequently acquitted and elected to state office.[108]

During the postwar years it became more evident that an increasingly disproportionate number of inmates were Negro, Hispanic, or Native American, and that virtually all prison administrators and correction offi-cers were white.[109] Inmates were housed and fed in separate sections, and Negroes typically enjoyed fewer privileges in program opportunities, work assignments, and recreational activities. Most American prisons remained racially segregated well after the Supreme Court ordered the integration of the public schools. In fact, apparently the first case to challenge prison segregation, involving a walled-off section of the prison dining hall that was designated for Negroes, was flatly rejected by the Federal District Court in Northern California in 1959 on the simple grounds that "by no parity of reasoning can the rationale of *Brown v. Board of Education* . . . be extended to State penal institutions."[110] Over the coming years, prisoners would have to protest, organize, and litigate in order to obtain minimal racial integration inside American prisons.

A prisoners' rights movement grew out of the civil rights movement of the 1950s and 1960s. Although prison departments remained generally not accountable to the public, either through the process of law or the news media, prisons also assumed increasing political relevance as more individ-uals took part in civil disobedience, protest marches, and desegregation activities, which often carried the risk of imprisonment or worse.

Martin Luther King's *Letter from Birmingham Jail* (1963) expressed no shame at being in prison. On the contrary, King said he was there because Birmingham was the most segregated city in the United States. Although there was both a legal and a moral responsibility to obey just laws, one also had a moral responsibility to disobey unjust laws. Down South, civil rights activists, whether they were black or white, got the same treatment in the criminal justice system as conventional black criminals.

Under Chief Justice Earl Warren, the Supreme Court in the early 1960s issued an unprecedented series of decisions affecting civil rights. Warren, who as the state's attorney general had been the most prominent California official to argue in favor of the internment of Japanese Americans, and who was later appointed to the Court by President Eisenhower, proved to be a surprising champion of prisoners' rights, both in several landmark cases in which inmates challenged actions by the criminal justice system to put them in prison and in a few cases involving the conditions of prison confinement.[111]

The case of *Monroe v. Pape,* in 1961, resulted from a suit by citizens against local police officers. In it the Court resurrected civil rights law from Reconstruction, which delineated the requirements for bringing suit under the Federal Civil Rights Act of 1871, thus enabling attorneys to seek damages and injunctions in federal court against state abuses of an individual's constitutional rights.[112]

In another 1961 case, *Mapp v. Ohio,* involving a repeat petty offender named Dollree Mapp, who was convicted of possessing obscene materials, the Court held that a state's use of evidence that had been secured by unreasonable search and seizure violated due process of law.[113] The decision extended the so-called exclusionary rule to criminal proceedings in state courts, which meant that evidence obtained through an unreasonable search was excluded from state trials. Over the years, many defendants had ended up doing hard time in prison as a result of such practices.

In January 1962 a gaunt and stooped white convict at the racially segregated Florida state prison in Raiford, who had served time for four previous felonies (burglaries), petitioned the U.S. Supreme Court to consider his case. Aged fifty-one, indigent and alone, without anyone on his correspondence list, Clarence Earl Gideon seemed to be an unlikely legal pioneer. However, in *Gideon v. Wainwright,* the Court extended the Sixth Amendment guarantee of right to counsel in state proceedings, and overturned the convictions of defendants who had not been represented by attorneys at trial.[114] As a result, the State of Florida was compelled to release more than a thousand convicts from prison.[115]

In *Cooper v. Pate* (1964), the justices explicitly confirmed that state convicts were protected under the Civil Rights Act of 1964.[116]

That same year, the Supreme Court considered the case brought by Danny Escobedo, who had been denied access to his attorney while he was in police custody. In *Escobedo v. Illinois,* the Court overturned a state conviction and established that a criminal suspect had a constitutional right to consult with an attorney when the "investigation is no longer a general inquiry into an unsolved crime, and has begun to focus on a particular suspect."[117] Two years later, *Miranda v. Arizona* proved even more controversial. The case consolidated for decision the cases of four prisoners who had been incarcerated for kidnapping, rape, robbery, and murder.

They had been convicted on the basis of extended questioning in which they were not informed of their rights to counsel and to remain silent. In his opinion, Chief Justice Warren wrote that upon arrest, a suspect had a constitutional right to "be warned prior to questioning that he has a right to remain silent, that any statement he does make may be used as evidence against him, [and] that he has a right to the presence of an attorney, either retained or appointed."[118] The decision struck a chord with many convicts, most of whom had never received any such warning, and some began to look at the legal process in a different light.

The actions of the Warren Court spawned a growing corps of "jailhouse lawyers," litigious prisoners who churned out reams of crude writs and other legal documents for themselves and their friends.[119] By 1967 the level of judicial intervention in prison matters had become such that a presidential task force warned, "There is some danger that if prisoners are conceded certain legal rights they will devote their energies to fighting legal battles, rather than accepting the correctional regimen and devoting themselves to more productive activities, and that, therefore, rehabilitation will be impeded."[120] Tired of troublesome legal hassles, prison administrators had their antagonists either transferred or removed from the general population and placed in the "hole," without law books and writing materials. But the prisoners persisted. One Stateville inmate resorted to smuggling out a petition to the courts that he had written with his own blood on toilet paper.[121]

For years the lower federal courts had refused to find anything wrong with brutal conditions of solitary confinement. But then, in *Jordan v. Fitzharris* (1966), an inmate at Soledad sued Superintendent Cletus Fitzharris for inflicting "cruel and unusual punishment" by keeping him confined for twelve days in a tiny strip cell (without light, ventilation, clothes, or body covering), where he was forced to sleep on the bare concrete floor, deprived of any means to clean himself, and forced to eat in the stench and filth caused by his own body wastes and vomit, all of this as punishment for a minor disciplinary infraction. Prison officials were astonished when the federal district judge held a full hearing inside their institution to determine if the charges were true, marking "the first occasion that the United States District Court [in that circuit] has undertaken to inquire into the procedures and practices of a State penal institution in a proceeding of this kind." The testimony substantiated Jordan's allegations. The judge was so appalled that he concluded that "when, as it appears in this case at bar, the responsible prison authorities in the use of the strip cells have abandoned elemental concepts of decency by permitting conditions to prevail of a shocking and debased nature, then the court must intervene . . . to restore the primal rules of a civilized community in accord with the mandate of the Constitution of the United States." The court issued a permanent injunction against the imposition of cruel and unusual punishment in connection with solitary confinement and advised the defendants to adopt the disciplinary procedures recommended by the American Correctional Association.[122]

A few months later, the United States Court of Appeals for the Second Circuit, in *Wright v. McMann,* abandoned the "hands-off" doctrine and reversed a district court's dismissal without a hearing of a prisoner's request for an injunction and damages, after Wright claimed that he had been held in a strip cell in Clinton prison under conditions similar to those condemned in *Jordan v. Fitzharris.* The decision represented further change in judicial attitudes toward continual allegations of brutality and administrative abuses in the prisons. The court held that

> civilized standards of humane decency simply do not permit a
> man for a substantial period of time to be denuded and exposed
> to the bitter cold of winter in northern New York State and to be
> deprived of the basic elements of hygiene such as soap and toilet
> paper. [Such] subhuman conditions . . . could only serve to
> destroy completely the spirit and undermine the sanity of the
> prisoner. The Eighth Amendment forbids treatment so foul, so
> inhuman and so violative of basic concepts of decency.[123]

Martin Sostre was a black Hispanic New Yorker, born to Puerto Rican and Haitian parents, who in 1952 was sentenced to 6 to 12 years for possession of narcotics.[124] While in Attica state prison he joined the Black Muslims and became a legendary jailhouse lawyer, winning (with help from Malcolm X) a major suit demanding the rights of Muslim inmates to hold religious services. After he filed another suit protesting the all-white composition of the parole board, he was denied parole and kept in solitary for four years. He served his entire 12-year sentence behind bars. Shortly after his release in 1964, he settled in Buffalo and opened an Afro-Asian bookstore, which came under police surveillance due to his militant activities. In the wake of civil disorders in Buffalo and other cities during the summer of 1967, Sostre was arrested at his store for alleged riot and arson, and for the alleged sale of $15 worth of heroin. The riot and arson charges were dropped, but he was convicted of drug sale and sentenced to 30 to 41 years. Returned to the New York prison system, he was kept in "punitive segregation" in Greenhaven state prison under harsh conditions for 372 days as a punishment for his activities as a jailhouse lawyer. From his cell he filed a handwritten complaint against prison officials and Governor Nelson Rockefeller, suing under the Civil Rights Act of 1871 for deprivations inflicted on him by New York State prison officials. He claimed he had been the target of continual harassment, having been transferred from one institution to another. He said he had been placed in solitary for trying to mail some correspondence to a state court; another time he had been put in "the box" for trying to mail other material to a court. His recreation time was restricted to one hour a day outside his cell, he was isolated from the other inmates, and he was ordered to submit to a regular rectal search (which he refused to do). He was denied use of the prison library, school, and other programs and not permitted to read newspapers or see movies.

Sostre succeeded in gaining a court order restraining his continued punishment in solitary. In May of 1970 U.S. District Court Judge Constance Baker Motley, a black federal judge in Manhattan, handed down her decision. The court outlined the case in detail, recalling that "a federal court once found that in another prison, Martin Sostre had been put in solitary in a cell where a light was kept burning 24 hours a day, making it all but impossible for him to sleep. If he did doze off, it was not for long, as a guard came by every half-hour and ran a 'nigger stick' noisily across the bars." The court concluded that Sostre was being punished "because of his legal and Black Muslim activities during his 1952–1964 incarceration, because of his threat to file a law suit against the Warden to secure his right to unrestricted correspondence with his attorney and to aid his codefendant, and because he is, unquestionably, a black militant who persists in writing and expressing his militant and radical ideas in prison." The court said "punitive segregation . . . is physically harsh, destructive of morale, dehumanizing in the sense that it is needlessly degrading, and dangerous to the maintenance of sanity when continued for more than a short period of time which should certainly not exceed fifteen days." The court upheld Sostre's claim that the punishment procedures used against him violated the United States Constitution. Punitive damages of $13,000 were assessed against the warden.[125]

Judge Motley's order infuriated guards at Attica and elsewhere in New York, particularly as state officials made sweeping changes in the correction department's rules and regulations. In February 1971 the Second Circuit Court modified several findings on appeal, saying in effect that Sostre's punishment was not so bad as to be considered unconstitutional.[126] One of the few Americans to that point to be designated a "political prisoner" by Amnesty International, Sostre won support from foreign dissidents, including Andrei Sakharov. (He finally would receive clemency from Governor Hugh Carey.)[127]

In 1968 Philip J. Hirschkop of the American Civil Liberties Union in Alexandria, Virginia, received a letter that had been kited out of the Virginia state penitentiary, asking him to assist in bringing litigation for better prison conditions. The inmate told of the brutal response to a nonviolent work stoppage by prisoners to protest racial discrimination and other conditions. The inmates were locked into their cells and cut off from visits or mail from anyone, including their families or lawyers. They had remained keeplocked for weeks, even as temperatures reached 120 degrees; those who complained were teargassed in their cells.

Hirschkop went to the prison and became involved in ongoing litigation. He met several committed jailhouse lawyers, including Robert Landman, who had brought two thousand legal cases, and Leroy Mason, a black civil rights advocate who had developed broad-based black and white inmate support for prison desegregation. Both men were being severely punished for their legal activities.[128] Hirschkop and his associates eventually gained an impressive court victory when a U.S. district judge issued a searing opinion. Years later, Fred Cohen, a law professor specializing in prisoners' rights, called the decision—*Landman v. Royster*—"the high water mark in legal safeguards extended to prisoners who are alleged to have violated prison rules."[129]

ARKANSAS THROWBACK

IN the mid–twentieth century, the Arkansas male penal system still consisted of two large prison farms, which remained almost totally cut off from the outside world and continued to operate much as they had during Reconstruction. Because the legislature refused to allocate adequate funds for correctional purposes, in 1966 the ratio of staff to inmates was 1 to 65, compared to the national average of 1 to 7, and authorities were left to rely upon gun-toting inmates, called "trusties" and "riders," to guard the convict longline that trudged to and from the fields. Arkansas prisoners labored ten to fourteen hours a day, six days a week, without any compensation; vocational training, educational programs, or adequate medical services did not exist; corruption was rampant; and violent deaths were commonplace. Arkansas was also the only state where convict whipping was still legal and used on a regular basis.[130]

Then, in August 1966, during a heated gubernatorial race, a Pine Bluff newsman asked Governor Orval Faubus—the ardent segregationist who in 1957 had called out the National Guard to bar Negro children from attending the Little Rock public schools—about documented allegations that had been received regarding systematic brutality and corruption in Arkansas prisons. Faubus launched an investigation and quickly fired three wardens and the Tucker Prison Farm superintendent, each of whom was later indicted on numerous charges. A state police report detailing some of the prison abuses appeared in the press as Faubus was leaving office. Part of the police files reads as follows:

> LL-33 said he was stripped of all clothes. The warden then stuck needles under his fingernails and toenails. His penis and testicles were pulled with wire pliers and he was kicked in the groin. Two other inmates then ground cigarettes into his stomach and legs, and one of them stuck him in the ribs with a knife. The *coup de grace* came from an inmate who squeezed his knuckles with a pair of nutcrackers.
>
> LL-53 came to Tucker in October, 1964, and was told that unless he became the punk of a rider he would be whipped. He refused. Two days later the rider ran his horse over him, knocking him to the ground. The rider then dismounted and beat him with a rubber hose and stomped him until one tooth was knocked out. He received this type of treatment for two or three weeks and was finally sent to the hospital, where the inmate doctor told him he could not stay unless he paid $20. He had only $10 and was allowed to stay one day.[131]

When the chairman of the legislature's prison committee was asked about the allegations, he dismissed them with a smile. "Arkansas has the best prison system in the United States," he said.[132]

After becoming the state's first Republican governor since 1874, Winthrop Rockefeller (Nelson's brother) appointed an outsider to institute some prison reforms. Tom Murton was a thirty-seven-year-old company commander in the Marine Corps Reserve who went to his civilian job in a flat-top wearing blue jeans and flannel shirts. After growing up on a farm in Oklahoma and earning a college degree in animal husbandry, he had gone to Alaska and risen up the ladder from jailer to acting chief of correctional services. He was also a doctoral candidate in criminology at the University of California at Berkeley, and many people didn't know what to make of him.[133]

Murton accepted the post as Tucker prison farm's superintendent on several conditions. Tucker would be autonomous, under his supervision. He would have full authority to hire and fire. He would be a consultant to the governor on correctional matters. He would be a consultant to the prison study commission. If and when a department of correction was established, he would be named commissioner, so that he could guide the development of the correctional system.[134]

Murton inherited a tense, scandal-ridden institution. Several weeks earlier, Tucker's superintendent had been dismissed for menacing the inmates with a loaded submachine gun; the convicts were still in operational control of the 4,500-acre prison; and there were only 34 staff members for 2,000 inmates. According to Paul Keve, an outside consultant who had assessed the situation, "Every modern concept of good prison management was ignored there, and every principle of humane treatment was violated. There was complete dependence on the armed inmate guards, who carried a variety of weapons." Inmates were expected to generate a profit. Any inmate who failed to do his part was liable to be whipped or tortured.[135]

Murton sized up the inmate population as falling into three main groups: "rank men" (the lowest echelon), "do-pops," and "trusties" (the highest). Each group was housed in separate barracks and maintained a distinct lifestyle. Rank men received meager rations of such food as hog's head stew and pig's knuckle soup, and they were issued inferior clothing that did not include any underwear, among other depredations. Do-pops, who popped open doors for their superiors, fared little better. Trusties enjoyed the best food, decent clothing, and numerous other privileges. They not only served as armed guards but were trained and encouraged to shoot; any trusty who killed an escaping prisoner won early parole.[136] Some likened them to kapos in Nazi concentration camps.

Murton's first administrative act was to abolish flogging and torture. He also dismissed the inmate in charge of Tucker's switchboard, radio, and records system, replacing him with a noninmate. Almost immediately, Murton was visited by the superintendent of the other prison farm, Cummins, who complained that his inmates had heard reports that Murton had abandoned corporal punishment at Tucker; now they wanted it ended at Cummins too, but he would not allow it. Despite his appeals, Murton would not reinstate the strap.

When his own trusties heard he planned to remove their weapons, some of them threatened to strike, a move that could force him to close down the institution. In an effort to head it off, he decided to tell the inmates his plans, starting with the trusties, who were, in effect, his staff. He met with them alone and later recalled what had transpired.

"I started off by saying, 'My name's Murton and I'm the superintendent. Normally when I take over an institution I come in and say, This is how it's going to be and this is the way it's going to be and this is the way we're going to run things. But this is ridiculous in a situation like this because you guys have the guns and the keys and you're running things so there's no way I can take over.'

"The men laughed and we were off to a good start."[137]

Murton admitted that he aimed gradually to abolish the trusty system. He also said budget considerations probably would prevent that for at least two more years, which would allow time for a smooth transition. Whenever change occurred, he would not force any trusty to be put into the ranks, he told them, implying he knew that old grudges might result in reprisals, even death.

What Murton did not tell them was that he sought to break the inmate power structure. He realized it would not be easy. "I was only too well aware that the trusties were opposed to me: any reform of the prison operation would affect their power and their relatively easy lives," he later recalled. Such a change would have to be attempted in steps. First he had to gain their confidence.

He wanted to end the wanton exploitation of inmate labor that had existed in Arkansas for more than a century. Although his long-range objective was to achieve productive, modernized farming, the effectiveness and efficiency of the labor program would no longer be measured strictly by the profits turned over to the state; convict labor would have to be productive for the inmates as well, and not carried out through sheer coercion. He expected intense resistance. The state had become accustomed to making fat profits by refusing to spend any money to hire staff or improve living conditions. The labor system depended upon old-fashioned manual labor and mules. Men were pushed beyond their limits in order to ensure maximum profits. Corruption and brutality were not only tolerated; they were an integral part of the regime.[138]

Murton also wanted to make the inmates less dependent on the old system. In order to enable them to avoid exploitation when they got out, he would need to begin equipping them with meaningful skills. He established a school for grades one through nine, and introduced the first women to the institutional staff (as teachers). This also was consistent with a long-term goal, since he wanted men who left the prison to be able to communicate with women on a civilized basis.[139]

He moved the death row prisoners out of isolation and into the regular prison, converting the death house to a hospital. A nonprofit blood bank replaced the one that had earned a local physician from $130,000 to $150,000 a year; inmates got $7 instead of $3 per drawing and the rest of the profits went into the prison's medical fund. From now on, employees would be promoted on merit rather than purchasing jobs. "There will come a time when you will no longer be exploited by other inmates and you will not have to pay for a meal," Murton said. "But in order to get to that time you're going to have to work with me."

The new warden sought to put some of his Berkeley theories into practice. He listened carefully, expressed interest in the convicts as individuals, encouraged them. He had come to believe that corrections departments often made the mistake of judging prisoners solely on their record, rather than by their character. As a result, prisons created a self-fulfilling prophecy, never giving their inmates a chance to change. Instead of denying the existence of inmate power, Murton wanted to recognize it and fuse it with the staff's to form a greater, more positive, combined power that would restructure the prison society for the good of convicts and guards alike.

Within a few months, the reform warden thought he had begun to detect more warmth in his relations with the prisoners. One told him, "You make an inmate feel like a human—which he never felt before." The prisoners also responded to his idea of a camp council comprised of inmate representatives; with his help, they organized and conducted an honest election.[140] He began to assemble a new staff, selecting persons he thought were experienced and trustworthy. He also made a point of hiring five former inmates, who he later said seemed to make good guards.[141]

Many of these changes prompted negative responses. During his first month there were three escapes, in the second there were eight, and in the third there were six. Most runaways were recaptured after a few hours. However, the longstanding reputation of the Arkansas penal system had become so shameful across the country that in one case a judge in Oregon refused to extradite three escapees, saying he did not believe that his state should "encourage Arkansas by aiding and abetting her in the management of her institutes of terror, horror, and despicable evil." The judge also chided the state's legislators and citizens for allowing the prisons of Arkansas to become "a system of barbarity, cruelty, torture, bestiality, corruption, terror, and animal viciousness that reeks of Dachau and Auschwitz."[142]

Murton's announcement that he planned to abolish Tucker's decades-old currency system angered the trusties even more, for it would mean a serious loss of power and status for them. Nevertheless, Murton proceeded to collect the bronzene currency. As a result, twenty-five trusties escaped during the next ten days. Murton saw this as a positive sign, for he took it as an indication that his attack on the inmate power structure was having an effect. It also gave him immediate justification to take drastic measures, such as conducting frisks of the barracks and reclassifying convicts without having to seek the inmates' acceptance. But the escapes alarmed the local residents, the state police, the governor's office, and the legislature, and they gave the newspaper columnists an easy target. To make matters worse, when Murton held a press conference to try to explain away the breakouts, a trusty interrupted him to announce that there had just been another escape.

He had no choice but to slam the lid. "I got the inmates together and told them if they wanted to go back to the old system, they were going about it the right way," he later recalled, "because my opponents were going to use the rash of escapes to organize my downfall." He put them on notice that anyone who ventured outside without permission would be shot.[143]

Although Murton came to feel that he had made gains with the inmates, he had suffered political losses outside. Now he faced friction with the legislature, the governor's staff, and other state officials and consultants; opposition from the three Democrats on the Arkansas Prison and Parole Board; and aroused public opinion, fueled by persons who felt he had cast the state in a poor light. His steps to end corruption and establish controls over the convict labor system had antagonized some prominent businessmen. Legislators were angry that he had increased prison spending, miffed that he refused to provide them with red-carpet treatment, insulted that he had brought them under national criticism. Particularly as he began criticizing other executive departments of the state government, his relations with the governor's office became more strained, and he sensed that Rockefeller himself was straddling the fence, reneging on his promise to appoint him as a consultant and allow him to operate independently of the Cummins superintendent. A gubernatorial aide warned Murton that he could not expect overnight support. Another said his problems stemmed from "poor communication" and urged him to keep disputes "within the family."

When the Cummins superintendent resigned, the penitentiary board refused to endorse Murton for the bigger position. Rockefeller appointed him anyway, and the three Democrats resigned in protest; this enabled Rockefeller to assume control over all appointments.

Upon entering Cummins Prison Farm, Murton immediately fired the executioner and assured the inmates he would not take away their bronzene economy. Then he called the leading troublemaker among the wardens into his office and stunned him by appointing him acting superintendent of Cummins. "Now he was responsible for keeping order through his own men, who were in charge of the prison," Murton wrote. "He had lit the fuse to explode the prison on my arrival; now he would have to put it out or be blown out of the saddle with me." Murton also held a social event for the Cummins inmates, during which some Negro convicts danced with white women visitors. Photos of this mixer infuriated many white Arkansans.[144]

At the same time, one of America's most popular movies was *Cool Hand Luke,* directed by Stuart Rosenberg and starring Paul Newman. Hollywood's story of a convict on a Southern prison farm suddenly had made Murton's drama more meaningful to a national audience.

The climax came when the *New York Times* quoted Murton as saying that he believed that 213 missing Cummins inmates had been murdered and buried in unmarked graves in a mule pasture on the prison grounds. Hordes of national reporters rushed to the scene. Murton ordered an inmate crew to start digging in front of network television cameras. Six feet down, their shovels struck wood. Shutters snapped and newsmen jostled for position as one crude coffin after another was hoisted up. Three human skeletons had been exhumed in unmarked graves. Cummins inmates cheered. State officials panicked.[145]

Arkansas editorial writers fumed that Murton was disgracing the state. Two months later, Governor Rockefeller fired him. Corrections officials throughout the country continued to criticize Murton for his methods, even as many acknowledged that some convicts probably had been murdered at Cummins.[146]

Within two years a federal district judge, J. Smith Henley, condemned the Arkansas prisons as constituting cruel and unusual punishment in violation of the United States Constitution. In the first judicial attack upon an entire penal system, he found conditions in the state's prisons so debased and intolerable that a sentence of imprisonment amounted to banishment from civilized society to a world where human life and the most basic human decencies did not exist. Violent abuses by trusty guards were among the conditions he cited as being in violation of the Eighth Amendment. The judge threatened to close the entire penal system unless state officials presented an acceptable plan to reform it.[147] Arkansas officials narrowly managed to avoid having their prisons shut down.

In 1980, amidst publicity surrounding the making of the movie *Brubaker,* which was based on the Murton episode and also directed by Stuart Rosenberg, another Arkansas governor, Bill Clinton, contested charges that the Arkansas prison system really had not changed since Murton had left. Clinton said it had.[148]

RIOTS AND DISTURBANCES

IN his classic sociological study of a maximum-security prison, *The Society of Captives,* Gresham N. Sykes described prisons as moving "in a cyclical rhythm from order to disorder." He called riots "a logical step in a pattern of repeated social change."[149]

Many of the biggest and best-known prison disturbances occurred in a series, like slave revolts, urban race riots, or revolutions. One such concatenation took place between 1912 and 1915, during the reform-minded Progressive Era. This prompted one prison official at the time to blame "the agitation of so-called social workers."[150] Another, larger wave hit between 1927 and 1931. Folsom prison, known as "California's Siberia," erupted in November of 1927, resulting in eleven deaths. Severe overcrowding was later cited as a leading cause.[151]

In July 1929 at Clinton, the "Siberia of New York," a convict protest against overcrowding escalated into a riot that left three inmates dead at the hands of police and National Guard troops. Once again, overcrowding was blamed.[152] The New York State prison population had risen by 68 percent since 1920, and the political climate had become more punitive toward prisoners: the state had recently built a wall around Great Meadow prison and enacted tough new sentencing laws that called for life imprisonment for four-time losers.[153]

Six days after Clinton blew, another major incident occurred at Auburn. Here, as part of a highly organized escape attempt, a trusty threw acid into a guard's face and grabbed his keys. Within moments, convicts were streaming from their cells and ringleaders were passing out weapons from the prison arsenal. Some inmates went on a rampage, destroying part of the old prison. In the confusion, four of them grabbed guards as shields; they managed to escape over the walls and commandeer getaway cars before they were cornered and nabbed. Although an investigation found that only 80 of the institution's 1,765 convicts had actively participated in the revolt, all privileges were immediately curtailed and all prisoners were locked in their cells. Nevertheless, on December 11, some cons managed to get loose with guns they had obtained the previous summer. After a struggle in which the principal keeper was killed, the rebels took the warden and several guards hostage and threatened to kill them unless the gates were opened. The inmates were told they would be allowed out, but as they proceeded through the guardroom they were ambushed in a fusillade of tear gas and gunfire. The state police rushed in, rescued the hostages, and retook the prison. Eight inmates lay dead and several prisoners and employees had been injured.[154] Following a state police investigation, the

Mutual Welfare League (established by Thomas Osborne) was disbanded as a "hotbed of agitation," and New York became still tougher in its war on crime.[155]

The Auburn riots were followed by one of the bloodiest prison uprisings in American history, at Colorado's rock-hard Canon City penitentiary.[156] Soon after that, on the day after Easter in 1930, 355 of 4,300 convicts who were trapped inside the Ohio state penitentiary (which had been designed to hold 1,500) perished in a raging fire that allegedly had been set by rioting inmates.[157]

Coming after the stock market crash and the onset of the Great Depression, the riots of 1929–30 heightened official concern about prison security. The Federal Bureau of Prisons was created in 1930, and work on what was then the nation's most expensive escape-proof, maximum-security penal institution, New York's Attica state prison, was begun in 1931.[158]

But it was the early 1950s that turned out to be the most riotous period in American prison history to that point. In February 1951, at a time when Americans seemed more concerned about military prisoners of war being held in Korea than fellow countrymen imprisoned within their own borders, thirty-one inmates at the Louisiana state prison at Angola severed their own heel tendons with razor blades in a futile attempt to draw attention to brutal treatment and subhuman living conditions.[159] The next year, a series of prison riots swept the country. At New Jersey's state prison at Trenton, a mass protest followed an incident in which an inmate had been denied permission to see a doctor. Convicts at nearby Rahway prison farm, having heard over their radios about what was going on at Trenton, seized hostages and unfurled banners in solidarity with their fellow inmates. A few days later a full-scale riot broke out at Trenton when convicts in the printshop seized guards and civilians and smashed equipment. They eventually surrendered after four days of negotiations, having won the right to present their grievances to an impartial committee.[160]

Shortly thereafter, a major riot occurred at Michigan's huge Jackson prison. At the time, it held five thousand prisoners (more than were incarcerated in all of Denmark), the largest concentration of inmates in any prison in the United States. The spark seemed to have been a dispute between custodial-oriented guards supported by the warden and treatment-oriented staff supported by a deputy warden and a psychologist. Governor G. Mennen Williams rushed to the scene and agreed to address several of the inmates' demands, prompting their surrender.[161]

Soon a rash of other prison disturbances broke out in Canada, North Carolina, Idaho, Brazil, Argentina, Colombia, Indonesia, Georgia, Kentucky . . . Between 1951 and 1953 it seemed that the whole country and much of the world was rocked by prison revolts. There were at least forty-seven in the United States between 1952 and 1955.[162]

John Bartlow Martin, a political reporter, pointed to the upheavals as proof that "the American prison system has broken down." Acknowledging that some changes might be in order, the American Prison Association changed its name to the American Correctional Association and urged its members to call their prisons "correctional institutions."[163] One leading corrections professional, Austin H. MacCormick, attributed the riots to growing offender pathology, saying "the ringleaders are reckless and unstable men who are not accustomed to weigh the consequences of their actions . . . unstable prisoners . . . 'psychopaths' . . . and 'screwballs.'"[164]

The "rehabilitation" philosophy of the 1950s and 1960s, with its heavy emphasis on "mental hygiene," featured increased education, fresh paint, and improved classification, mixed with some occasional lobotomies, forced sterilizations, shock treatments, and therapy sessions. Yet in reality prison rehabilitation largely remained chimerical. Virtually everyone on the prison scene agreed that prisons, as constructed and operated since the nineteenth century, did not rehabilitate. A common inmate saying developed over the years to the effect that very few individuals are ever rehabilitated *in* prison, and none are truly rehabilitated *by* prison. But some may rehabilitate themselves, *in spite of* prison.

The more characteristic penal response was simple warehousing. Financial considerations had become paramount. Compared to the glory days of the 1830s or the golden era as social laboratory, by the late 1950s prison's lofty ideals had become worn down, faded. The faith of chaplains in dogmatic claims had been replaced by the complex doubts of psychologists; the confident exuberance of prison reformers and criminologists had deteriorated into disappointment and disillusionment over failed experiments. Public pride had given way to shame over prison conditions and other institutional shortcomings. Through it all, one of the most disenchanted groups of all were the inmates. As prison had lost its meaning and mission for society as a whole, their incarceration seemed all the more meaningless, wasteful, and wrong.

Writing in their newspaper in 1954, inmates at San Quentin defined prison as "a metropolis of men without women, a beehive without honey, caged loneliness without privacy, a ranch where all the sheep are black, a cement park with barbed wire shrubbery and an enormous microscope, under which psychiatrists study a smear from civilization's ulcers." Prisons continued as reminders of systemic flaws and social injustice.

This may help to explain why more than 90 percent of all recorded prison riots, strikes, protests, rebellions, and other disturbances in the

United States have occurred since 1960.[165] From 1968 through the first four months of 1971 there were forty-eight reported riots. Sounding like a Southern sheriff or a Chicago political boss, one federal warden pointed to "outside influences" as a major contributor. He told his fellow administrators: "I think you know what I mean . . . there is the problem of well-organized disturbances brought on by the resisters, draft dodgers, professional agitators, Communists, hippies and revolutionaries. . . . Former prisoners, militants, far-out liberals, subversives, and even a few clergymen, educators, and social workers on the outside seem to delight in fomenting unrest in prisons."[166]

In California, prison conflict increasingly involved race. As blacks and Chicanos vied with whites for dominance, frictions among inmates also increased, often fanned by rival street gangs and helped along by worried white staff. In January 1970 an interracial inmate fight in an exercise yard at Soledad resulted in three black prisoners being shot to death by a tower guard. After a local coroner's jury ruled that the killings were justified, a white correction officer was thrown to his death from a third-tier gallery. Three black prisoners were quickly charged with the murder.[167]

One of them, George Jackson, already was becoming a national symbol of the black revolutionary prisoner, due in large measure to his searing political letters. These were published as *Soledad Brother,* to rave reviews from Jean Genet and Jean-Paul Sartre.[168] At the age of eighteen Jackson had been sentenced to one year to life under California's indeterminate-sentencing provisions for robbing a gas station of $70. For being an incorrigible convict, he had spent eleven years in prison, seven of them in solitary confinement. Radicalized along Leninist-Maoist lines, Jackson had relentlessly driven himself into extraordinary physical and intellectual shape through constant exercising and reading. He openly espoused violent revolution and practiced what he preached. He also expressed a growing sentiment when he wrote, on June 10, 1970:

> Blackmen born in the U.S. and fortunate enough to live past the age of eighteen are conditioned to accept the inevitability of prison. For most of us, it simply looms as the next phase in a sequence of humiliations. Being born a slave in a captive society and never experiencing any objective basis for expectation had the effect of preparing me for the progressively traumatic misfortunes that lead so many blackmen to the prison gate. I was prepared for prison. It required only minor psychic adjustments.[169]

His case drew intense international attention. Then, on August 21, 1971, Jackson was shot to death in San Quentin during an apparent escape attempt. He was alleged to have hidden a handgun in his hair. Many black prisoners and their supporters disbelieved the official story.[170]

Police pursued one of Jackson's radical supporters, Professor Angela Y. Davis, on charges that she had participated in a violent courtroom shootout involving Jackson's brother, Jonathan. Arrested, and held in the Marin County jail awaiting trial, she identified herself through writings as a black American political prisoner, and claimed: "Prisoners—especially Blacks, Chicanos, and Puerto Ricans—are increasingly advancing the proposition that they are *political* prisoners. They contend they are largely the victims of an oppressive politico-economic order, swiftly becoming conscious of the causes underlying their victimization." She was ultimately acquitted and freed.[171]

ATTICA

NEW York's penal system tottered on the brink of revolt. Attica inmates organized a two-day work stoppage in July 1970, ostensibly to protest commissary prices and wages. In October, the infamous Tombs jail in Manhattan exploded in a riot.[172] A few weeks later, in November, inmates at Auburn staged a three-hour sitdown strike to demand permission to hold a Black Solidarity Day meeting. Three days after that, four hundred inmates took control of Auburn's yard, kitchen, mess hall, and three cell blocks, seizing thirty-five guards as hostages (who were protected by Muslim inmates). After gaining promises that their grievances would be heard, the prisoners escorted the guards to safety and surrendered. They had made a major statement.[173]

Prison officials throughout the country were more deeply concerned than ever about their ability to maintain control, particularly as the larger society seemed to be getting more embroiled in protest, militancy, and violence over the war in Southeast Asia and other issues. Many black prisoners seemed to be awaiting word that the revolution had begun.

New York's reorganized Department of Correctional Services, as it was now called, had seen the coming of a new reform commissioner, Russell G. Oswald, only nine months earlier, and he was in the process of making sweeping changes at Attica and throughout the system. Oswald already had liberalized visiting and mail privileges, reduced censorship of inmates' correspondence with attorneys and public officials, ordered pork-free meals for Muslim inmates, and increased reporters' access to the prisons. But his actions had angered many staff members and raised inmates' expectations to a level that would be difficult to meet.[174]

During the summer of 1971, cell searches at Attica turned up evidence that some inmates were using their new privileges to circulate messages between prisons, including drafts of petitions from Folsom that were being adapted for New York. Black inmates at Attica had also responded to word of George Jackson's death by wearing black armbands and maintaining a sullen silence.

Trouble had been brewing at the prison for several months. There had been an inmate scuffle in one of Attica's huge recreation yards on September 8. When a corrections lieutenant tried to break it up, he was punched. Word of the incident swept through the prison. As two convicts were taken away to the special-housing unit two hours later, hundreds of inmates jeered their escorts and threw objects from their cells on 5 Company; one of the objects, a full soup can, struck an officer.[175]

On Thursday morning, September 9, 1971, as 5 Company inmates were returning from the mess hall after breakfast, through the A Block tunnel, a passing lieutenant was knocked to the ground. Within seconds, some convicts jumped on their keepers, and pandemonium ensued. Some prisoners grabbed clubs and keys from fallen officers, which they used to release others from their cells. The rioters began destroying everything they could in the hated A Block. Inmates stampeded through the tunnel to the gate at Times Square, the major terminus of the prison, which was designed to permit any of the four cellblocks to be sealed off from the rest of the institution. The mob knocked the gate officer unconscious and burst through into B, C, and D Blocks. Within minutes, thirteen hundred prisoners, over half of Attica's population, were engulfed in chaos, and corrections officials were battling to keep them from taking over the entire institution and flooding into the countryside. As alarms sounded, off-duty correction officers and neighboring police rushed to the scene.

Within hours, Attica's massive concrete walls became surrounded by packs of jabbering news reporters, knots of worried relatives of the hostages, bivouacked National Guard troops, angry correction officers, and state police in riot gear, many of them armed with deer rifles and shotguns. Commissioner Oswald arrived at 2:00 P.M., followed by Professor Herman Schwartz, a Buffalo attorney and prisoners' rights advocate who tried to help gain a peaceful solution through the courts. At the inmates' request over thirty other observers began arriving, to the disdain of correction officers and local residents, many of whom felt that their interests were being ignored. The observers' committee included the columnist Tom

Wicker of the *New York Times;* the radical attorney William Kunstler; Clarence Jones, the publisher of the *Amsterdam News;* Ken Jackson, of the Fortune Society; Assemblyman Arthur Eve of Buffalo; Bobby Seale, the chairman of the Black Panther Party; and two dozen other politicians, ministers, journalists, and activists.

With celebrity also added to the picture, Attica became a major news event, bolstered by the unprecedented access that permitted journalists to get close to the story. Dozens of television cameras and radio microphones penetrated inside the besieged prison, allowing Americans into another world. Lenses zoomed in to focus on the negotiating table, capturing images of an inmate negotiating committee of angry black convicts pointing fingers and spouting off before the microphones, some of them towering over the seated, beleaguered white corrections commissioner. Television picked up the chanting roar of hundreds of inmates, the great majority of them black, some wearing football helmets on their heads or bandanas over their faces, as they gave the power salute. Viewers in their living rooms saw the grim and worried faces of blindfolded hostages, looking like prisoners of war just shot down over enemy territory, but who were being held prisoner in their own jail right here in the United States. A thin young black convict in granny glasses read the prisoners' "immediate demands" to Richard M. Nixon and Nelson Rockefeller:

1. We want Complete Amnesty. Meaning freedom from all physical, mental and legal reprisals.
2. We want now speedy and safe transportation out of confinement, to a Non-Imperialist country.
3. We demand that the Federal government intervene. . . .

Newspapers printed the words of an earlier manifesto of demands by a so-called Attica Liberation Faction:

We the imprisoned men of Attica Prison want an end to the injustice suffered by all prisoners, regardless of race, creed, or color. The preparation and content of this document has been constructed under the united efforts of all races and social segments of the prison. . . .

Some of the inmates seemed intelligent, articulate. Many almost appeared to be normal. Like the televised assassinations and urban riots and war coverage and the Chicago Democratic Convention and the moon landing, Attica was bursting into public consciousness, a real-life human drama, full of powerful images of a secret world. This time Americans and people all over the planet were gaining a glimpse into the epicenter of society's most bitter and terrifying domestic battleground.

Ultimately, on the drizzly Monday morning of September 13, the fourth day of the uprising, after the television cameras had been pulled back from inside the prison, and eight blindfolded hostages had been brought to Attica's wall-top catwalks with inmate "executioners" holding knives to their throats, the rebels announced they had rejected an ultimatum from Oswald to surrender. Tear gas was fired. Gunshots were heard. Helicopters hovered overhead, broadcasting demands for the inmates to surrender. More than 450 shots rang out, hitting 128 men and killing 39, 29 of whom turned out to be inmates and 10 were hostages. In all, 43 persons had died.

"Attica" took its place alongside Chicago, My Lai, Orangeburg, Jackson State, Kent State, a brutal and shocking end to a story that Americans had watched unfold.[176] A New York special commission would later report: "With the exception of the Indians massacred in the late 19th century, the State Police assault which ended the four-day prison uprising was the bloodiest one-day encounter between Americans since the Civil War."[177]

In its wake, state corrections officials claimed that the assault had been ordered to save the hostages, whose throats were being slashed. Several hostages, they said, had been savagely killed by inmates; one guard had been castrated. News syndicates throughout the world immediately condemned the prisoners for their cold-blooded murder of defenseless captives. But the next day, a local medical examiner who had performed the official autopsies announced that all of the hostages had been killed by gunshot wounds and that none had been emasculated. New York officials at first continued to insist that prisoners had killed the hostages, even claiming that maybe the inmates had done the shooting. But ultimately the state conceded that the hostages had been killed by official gunfire. Irate lawyers also began to relate stories of atrocities committed against their clients, both during the assault and afterward, when police were alleged to have carried out mass beatings of naked and defenseless captives.[178]

Governor Nelson Rockefeller brushed aside criticism that he had not gone to the scene. Rocky said the troopers had done a "superb job." He called the shooting of the hostages "justifiable homicide."[179]

The Attica tragedy triggered dozens of criminal trials, countercharges of coverups of official wrongdoing, a sweeping amnesty by the next governor, Hugh Carey, and over twenty years of civil litigation. It also spawned a new generation of prison reformers and galvanized the national prisoners' rights movement to intercede in ways that might prevent future Attica-type tragedies. New York State implemented costly changes in virtually every sphere of its correctional system, building on new mechanisms of security, emergency control, public relations, program services, and inmate discipline.[180]

NEW MEXICO

ONE of the most remarkable aspects of American prison history, even its prison riot history, was the extraordinary restraint that prisoners had shown in their individual and collective outbursts.[181] Attica had demonstrated tremendous discipline and unity among prisoners and conveyed a picture of inmates as victims as far as some observers were concerned.

All of this drastically changed in the 1980s. In the early morning hours of February 2, 1980, the New Mexico State Penitentiary at Santa Fe became the scene of a major disturbance when a mob of prisoners broke into the prison's control center. The explosion unleashed years of pent-up rage, much of it directed against accused informers. Men were burned to death with blowtorches, castrated, hacked apart, and decapitated. Thirty-six hours after the nightmarish orgy of violence had started, the prison was retaken without a shot being fired; all of the hostages were found to be alive. Some New Mexico officials actually congratulated themselves about how well they had handled the situation.[182]

But the scenes of carnage and horror that greeted the rescuers rivalled some of the sights encountered by Allied troops who had liberated Nazi concentration camps at the end of World War II. New Mexico entered the history books as the most savage (on the part of the inmates, at least) prison riot in American history. Thirty-three men had been hideously killed and mutilated, and hundreds of others were raped, beaten, tortured, or terrorized.[183]

Unlike Attica, the Santa Fe penitentiary was not located in a populous state, there were no identifiable radical organizations active there, the news media had not figured prominently in the disturbance, there was no prominent governor involved, the deaths were not attributed to government assault forces, and there were very few inmates promoting legal reform. Compared to Attica, which had been predominantly black, Hispanic-surnamed inmates made up 58 percent of the New Mexico penitentiary's population, blacks only 12 percent, Native Americans 1 percent. Convicts there had shown little ethnic unity.[184] As overcrowding and other effects of fiscal austerity had grown worse, New Mexico authorities had abolished the inmate council and similar programs. They had also instituted a snitch system, which rewarded prisoners for informing on their fellow inmates. The atmosphere thus created led one convict to complain, "Hell, you can't trust your best friend anymore."[185] The administration became so dependent on the confidential informant system that a minister told an inmate, "My son, God wants you to be a snitch."[186] In the process the administrators had totally perverted and then destroyed the prison's social structure, making the climate all the more unstable. "At Attica, the disturbance was tightly controlled by a small group of powerful inmates," a reporting team for *Corrections Magazine* noted. "But in New Mexico, the inmates, leaderless and uncontrolled, went berserk."[187]

Ignored for years, the penitentiary had become what a Justice Department study later described as "one of the harshest, most punitive prison environments in the nation."[188] Officials now acknowledged that the place had long been notorious for its nepotism, totally untrained personnel, corruption, filth, unsanitary and uncomfortable living conditions, fire hazards, sexual abuse, escapes, and violence; a place where mentally disturbed inmates were kept in plaster body casts with holes to allow them to defecate and urinate.[189]

The riot confirmed an image of prisoners that more and more Americans had been conditioned to hold: prisoners were animals. Wild, dangerous, vicious animals.

CHAPTER EIGHT

Full Circle

"SOMETHING HAPPENED"

T HE United States did not begin compiling official national crime statistics until 1930. For many years thereafter, the picture they conveyed was extraordinarily tame by today's standards. During the generally prosperous postwar 1940s and 1950s, the country succeeded in containing most types of crime, and if crime rates increased at all the upward trend was relatively modest, perhaps because the nation was so preoccupied with the Cold War and McCarthyism. Many criminologists were reasonably optimistic about the prospects for reducing serious crime to a minimum. Daniel Bell, the sociologist, wrote in 1960 that "there is probably less crime today in the United States than existed a hundred, or fifty, or even twenty-five years ago, and . . . today the United States is a more lawful and safe country than popular opinion imagines."[1]

But then, something happened. James Q. Wilson, the conservative political scientist, later pinpointed 1963 as the year "the decade began to fall apart," as evidenced by the jump in reported crimes that he later traced to that time.[2] But despite some common assertions that lawlessness was shooting up in response to growing social "permissiveness" (a.k.a. civil rights for Negroes), the crime upsurge then probably was due more to demographics, since the postwar baby boomers were starting to come of an age that was at higher risk for crime, and a greater percentage of them lived in the more crime-prone big cities.

African Americans were especially caught up in such changing demographics. In 1940 half of the black population had been rural, but by 1965 fully 80 percent was urban, and most American inner cities had become predominantly black.[3] Crime rates always had been generally higher in big cities than in suburbs or rural areas, but now economic conditions in those cities seemed to be deteriorating fast. Suddenly there were more impoverished, young urban males—particularly black ones—in the crime-prone age group of 20 to 29. Between 1960 and 1963, the official unemployment rate for persons 16 to 19 years old rose by 23 percent for whites and by 28 percent for nonwhites.[4] Jobless, uneducated, poor, and increasingly addicted to alcohol or other drugs, these young black males were prime candidates for arrest and imprisonment.

Barry Goldwater made crime an issue in his 1964 presidential campaign, but he lost the election. A few months later, after the assassination of Malcolm X and the Watts riot, President Lyndon B. Johnson officially declared "war on poverty" and "war on crime,"[5] at the same time he was escalating the undeclared war in Vietnam.

Special attention was being paid to lawbreaking and abuses of authority. By February 1968, for the first time since the start of scientific public opinion polling in the 1930s, Americans rated crime as the country's top domestic problem.[6] Five months later, after the assassinations of Martin Luther King, Jr., and Robert F. Kennedy, 81 percent of those surveyed said they thought the nation's law enforcement had "broken down."[7] Then came the tumultuous Democratic National Convention in Chicago, which appeared to prove them right. The Republican candidate, Richard Nixon, promised to bring "peace with honor" abroad and "law and order" at home. Two months before election day he told a radio audience: "Under the stewardship of the present Administration, crime and violence . . . have increased ten times faster than population. Now, by way of excuse, the present Administration places the blame on poverty. But poverty is only one contributing factor." Nixon blamed the trend on "liberal" court rulings, which had "handcuffed" the police. "Today it is comparatively safe to break the law," he said. "Today all across the land guilty men walk free from hundreds of courtrooms. Something has gone terribly wrong in America."[8]

In fact, America's rate of violent crime had gone from 190 per 100,000 persons in 1963 to 298 in 1968. This trend continued to 396 per 100,000 in 1971.[9] By 1972, the murder rate had more than doubled from that of the previous decade.[10] (And that did not include what was going on in Southeast Asia.) Exploiting the crime issue helped Nixon gain election in 1968 and reelection in 1972. Yet, as it would turn out, reported crime proved to be his undoing.

In the 1960s, some social reformers focused attention upon the rampant abuses inherent in the discretionary powers of police, judges, and corrections officials. Some of their efforts were directed toward decriminalizing so-called victimless crimes; strengthening due process and other civil rights; and efforts to professionalize the criminal justice system.[11] In response to abuses in California and elsewhere, some critics advocated abolishing the indeterminate sentence and parole release processes that had been conducted without basic due process, saying it was futile to try to improve them. For example, a working group of the American Friends Service Committee (sponsored by the Quakers), several of them ex-convicts or civil rights activists, collaborated to produce *Struggle for Justice* (New York, 1971), a work that attacked the rehabilitative ideal and discretionary justice.

During this period, anti-institutional sentiments ran high, especially among liberals, and many reformers were calling for moving persons institutionalized in mental hospitals, juvenile justice reformatories, and prisons into supervised community care. Based on a series of evaluations of rehabilitation programs through the mid-1960s, Robert Martinson and some of his colleagues at the City University of New York concluded that, "with few and isolated exceptions, the rehabilitative efforts that have been reported so far have had no appreciable impact on recidivism."[12] Such seemingly empirically based findings provided ammunition to prison critics of every stripe, many of whom picked up the chorus of "nothing works." As one criminologist has recalled, "the critique of rehabilitation, in this sweeping and categorical form, was attractive to both ends of the political spectrum." To the Right, it seemed to confirm beliefs that crime reflected fundamental flaws in human nature or individual personalities, and was used to bolster efforts at deterrence, retribution, and incapacitation. To the Left, the apparent failure of rehabilitation exposed the charade that efforts to reform a few inmates could ever succeed in place of needed structural and institutional change.[13] Martinson himself tried to recant and restate his conclusions to appear more in favor of treatment, but he was ignored. Rehabilitative programs of all sorts were ridiculed for being ineffective, counterproductive, needlessly costly, and discriminatory. New York's outgoing governor, Nelson Rockefeller, capitalized on this mood by scrapping a whole system of civil drug treatment in favor of the toughest, most punitively oriented drug laws in the United States.

More conservatives took their cue and began pushing for "sentencing reform." Some of them as well called for abolishing indeterminate sentencing and parole, but for very different reasons than their liberal counterparts, though many on the Left had also adopted the "nothing works" credo. Popular books by conservative commentators, such as James Q. Wilson's *Thinking about Crime* (1975) and Ernest van den Haag's *Punish-*

ing Criminals (1975), added greater academic respectability to retributivist thinking and supported the general concept of determinate sentencing as offering a better chance for swift, certain punishment. Meanwhile, another influential work in policy-making circles at that time was *Doing Justice* (1976), by Andrew von Hirsch, a former staff director of the liberal Committee for the Study of Incarceration. He advocated the rationale of "just deserts" (a more fashionable term for retribution) as an appropriate guiding principle for criminal sentencing. At the time, even Alan Dershowitz noted rather approvingly that dramatically shifting attitudes of reformers toward sentencing marked a growing disdain for indeterminate sentencing among liberals and conservatives alike. He said he foresaw the pendulum swinging toward greater certainty and uniformity in sentencing, which might add to the renewed appeal of determinate sentencing approaches.[14]

In the face of such seeming unanimity, criminal justicians cranked out sentencing guidelines grids, classification schemes, and prison population projections. Such new buzzphrases as the "selective incapacitation of dangerous and chronic offenders" and "mandatory sentences for persistent felony offenders" dominated the criminological conferences and legislative sessions. Within a few years, virtually every state as well as the federal government adopted sweeping penal law changes, often including tougher mandatory prison sentences, determinate sentencing, abolition of parole release, and renewed use of the death penalty.

PRISON EXPANSION

DESPITE the rising crime rates and all the tough talk about fighting crime, during the years from 1962 to 1968 the American prison population had actually declined, by 14.3 percent, underscoring a fact generally understood more by criminologists than the general public: that rates of incarceration are not necessarily related to, or a product of, official crime rates.[15] In 1973 or so, changes began to occur. Amidst the abandonment of the Vietnam War, worsening economic conditions, political turmoil, increased federal funding for law enforcement, and a general shift toward harsher criminal justice policies, the numbers of persons in state and federal correctional institutions started climbing sharply.

This rapid swelling occurred despite some contrary developments: the civil rights movement; a continued trend in favor of deinstitutionalization, particularly for mental patients, the developmentally disabled, and juvenile offenders; some major legal victories of the prisoners' rights movement; and decriminalization of or deemphasis upon some victimless crimes like prostitution, public intoxication, and gambling. It also happened despite the concerted actions of several organizations that had formally begun to seek a halt to expansion of the prison system they said had failed. The National Council on Crime and Delinquency, a nationwide civic body, and the National Commission on Criminal Justice Standards and Goals, a blue-ribbon presidential panel, argued against the construction of any new correctional facilities until alternatives to incarceration were thoroughly explored.[16] In 1974, with support from the Unitarian Universalist Service Committee, S. Brian Willson, a Vietnam veteran, antiwar activist, and attorney, founded the National Moratorium on Prison Construction, a not-for-profit organization dedicated to stopping prison growth.[17] Grassroots efforts to develop community-based alternatives to incarceration also sprang up around the country, but to little avail. A few reformers had even begun to talk about prison abolition.[18]

Some states seemed uncertain about how to respond to increased prison overcrowding. In 1975 U.S. district court judge Frank M. Johnson, Jr., issued a comprehensive order mandating sweeping changes in Alabama's crowded prison system. Noting that 5,100 prisoners were crammed into space designed for only 2,600, he imposed a ban on new admissions until the population was reduced to the system's capacity. Alabama was not unusual. In addition to being populated beyond their designed purpose, many American penal institutions were also old and outmoded: in 1977, 42 percent of all buildings housing state and federal inmates were over 50 years old, 33 percent were over a century old, and some had been built more than 150 years earlier.[19]

State and local governments set aside plans to close old and outmoded correctional facilities and rushed instead to build additional prisons and jails. From December 31, 1971, to December 31, 1978, the U.S. prison population increased by 64 percent. From December 31, 1973, to year's end in 1976, it swelled from 204,000 to nearly 281,000.[20] By December 31, 1983, the count of inmates in custody had reached 420,000.[21]

In large measure, the increased number of prisoners was a natural by-product of the war on crime that had been geared up in the 1960s and running ever since. One key part of the national crime control apparatus—the federal Law Enforcement Assistance Administration (LEAA)—pumped hundreds of millions of dollars into domestic crime fighting from the late 1960s until the late 1970s. Its funding of more police, prosecutors, courts, and prisons ensured that there were more, not less, reported crimes and arrests and convictions and prisoners. In October 1970 there were 701,767 criminal justice employees, 146,273 of them in corrections and 507,877 police.[22] By October 1978 there were 1,123,552 employees, 261,385 in corrections and 622,544 police; in October 1983, 1,270,342 employees, 298,722 in corrections and 723,923 police.[23] Criminal justice agencies were also better equipped and trained to go after criminals than ever before.

Even though bolstered by increased assistance to law enforcement, crime fighting was hampered by the insufficient attention paid to the underlying social and economic problems that led to crime and imprisonment in the first place, and overall the problem got worse. Arrests, indictments, and convictions rose to new levels. Prison sentences were made longer. Commitments of persons to prison increased. Support for probation and parole sagged under the weight of rising caseloads. The use of the death penalty was reinstated after a moratorium of several years. Direct corrections expenditures rose from $2.3 billion in 1971 to $5.5 billion in 1978, then to $9.8 billion in 1983, and $16 billion in 1990.[24] But like Vietnam, the war on crime failed to be won. Instead of deterring crime and selectively incapacitating criminals, the nation's greater use of imprisonment and other get-tough responses was accompanied throughout the 1970s and 1980s by even more murders, rapes, robberies, and other serious crimes. This in turn was followed by redoubled calls to "crack down" on criminals.

Through it all, most of the statistics coming out of Washington masked how prison was really being used. Once again, the upsurge was primarily racial. In 1960 about 39 percent of inmates incarcerated in American state prisons were reported as "nonwhite"; by 1974, the percentage had increased to 47 percent "black" and 2 percent "other" nonwhite races.[25] From 1973 to 1979 the incarceration rate for whites in the fifty states and the District of Columbia rose from 46.3 to 65.1 per 100,000. However, the black incarceration rate skyrocketed from 368 to 544—becoming more than nine times greater than the level for whites.[26] Researchers began to report finding a huge and growing racial gap in the imprisonment rates of every region and state. There was no exception: North, South, East, and West, blacks were many times more likely than whites to be arrested, jailed, convicted, and imprisoned. Some of the jurisdictions with the greatest black incarceration rates tended to be small states with relatively few African Americans in the general population, while those with the highest proportion of black residents tended to have among the lowest rates of African-American imprisonment. Yet, notwithstanding any statistical anomalies, blacks were disproportionately imprisoned in every state, and the disparity was widening fast.[27]

During the span from 1970 to 1990, the overall rate of imprisonment tripled, reaching 455 per 100,000—the highest level in history to that point. Prison populations continued to grow at record levels, fueled by colossal prison construction that was planned to accommodate the projected waves of blacks and other persons of color who were drowning in a sea of urban cases that were flooding the criminal courts.

By 1990, although blacks comprised only 12 percent of the U.S. population, they accounted for more than 44 percent of those incarcerated in local, state, and federal prisons. Meanwhile, the incarceration rate for black males in the United States grew to 3,370 per 100,000. Among Hispanics, 10.4 percent of the males in the prison-prone age group (20 to 29) were under criminal justice control.[28] On June 30, 1994, according to the United States Department of Justice annual survey, nearly 7 percent of all black men nationwide were in prison or jail, compared to less than 1 percent of white men, marking the first time that the number of black inmates surpassed that of whites.[29]

On a given day that year, nearly one out of every four young African-American men in New York State was under the control of the criminal justice system. That was twice the number of full-time black male college enrollees in the state. Eleven percent of New York's black men between 20 and 29 years of age were in prison or jail.[30] From 1955 to 1992, the white share of the New York State prison population had plummeted from about 50.9 percent to less than 16 percent.[31]

One of the implications of these statistics is that a disproportionately large share of African-American men are disenfranchised as a result of their felony conviction and imprisonment, because the laws in thirteen of the most populous states strip convicted felons of the right to vote, and incarcerated persons are also universally prevented from voting.[32]

Nowhere was the prison system more immense than in California, the former Golden State and onetime land of milk and honey. On December 31, 1977, the prison population there had numbered 19,623, the lowest year-end figure since 1959. But in 1978 the state adopted tough new determinate sentencing laws and the prison admission rate began to increase. By the end of 1979 the number of inmates in custody had risen to 22,500. When graphed on a chart, the next several years looked like a missile launched into outer space. During the 1980s, California carried out what one senator called "the largest prison construction program ever attempted by a government entity," a $6.2 billion expansion. By 1991 it had far and away the most prisoners of any state, with more than 97,000 inmates—27,000 more than the population of its capital, Sacramento, and more prisoners than in all of western and central Europe. The number of employees of the department of corrections had grown to more than 32,000. Meanwhile, the operational cost of California's prison system, which had been $826 million in fiscal year 1977-78, had ballooned to $2.3 billion.[33]

Nevertheless, in 1991 there was still no end in sight. Even with a massive

$3.2 billion capital construction effort under way, the prison system was packed to 168 percent of its design capacity, and the state was committed to an additional $5.22 billion expansion program just to avoid rising above 130 percent of capacity over the next three years. A blue-ribbon panel projected a population of 136,640 state prisoners in 1994, rising to 173,000 in 1996, as well as 93,003 jail inmates and more than 19,500 inmates in juvenile facilities, for a total of more than 249,000 inmates expected in 1994, when the maintenance cost was expected to reach $4 billion. (As it turned out, the number of prisoners in custody on January 14, 1996, was 135,249.) Yet despite all of the prison expansion, crime in California did not significantly decrease during this period.

The typical California inmate was not a hardened violent predator, but a young, nonviolent, drug-addicted, semiliterate, unemployed minority male.[34] By 1989, one of every three black men between the ages of 20 and 29 in California was either in jail or on probation or parole; the comparable figure for white men that age was one in every nineteen. Five years later, 40 percent of the state's black men in their twenties were under correctional supervision, in contrast to 5 percent of the whites and 11 percent of the Hispanics.[35]

Even as California struggled to stave off fiscal crisis, and some public figures suggested developing cheaper alternatives to incarceration, the ruling powers would not waver from their lock-em-up course. Passage of the "three strikes" law mandated life prison terms for repeat offenders, even the relatively nonviolent. In one notorious case, a twenty-seven-year-old with two prior robbery convictions was sentenced to twenty-five years to life for stealing a slice of pizza.[36] One study of a thousand criminal cases in Los Angeles found that blacks were charged under the new law at seventeen times the rate of whites.[37]

California was not alone in its enormous prison growth. Texas and Florida were not far behind, and several other states expanded their use of imprisonment even more dramatically during the same period. In fact, in 1990 California still ranked only sixteenth among the states in its rate of imprisonment per 100,000 of the population, and twenty-fifth in its proportion of the population under some form of correctional supervision. The number of inmates in the federal prison system grew from 24,000 in 1980 to 95,000 in 1994.[38]

In the 1990s, most American prison inmates were serving time for drug crimes or were known to have histories of serious drug abuse. Bolstered drug sanctions were a major factor responsible for the ongoing record increase of prisoners. In 1985, 38 percent of federal inmates were sentenced for drug offenses. This was up to 58 percent by mid-1991, and reached 62 percent in 1994, according to the Federal Bureau of Prisons. Among state inmates the comparable numbers were 9 percent in 1986 and 21 percent in mid-1991.[39]

In 1994, 58 percent of the federal prisoners were drug offenders, meaning simply that they were serving sentences for drug-related crimes. Forty-two percent of these were serving time for drug trafficking. In state correctional facilities, 21 percent of the inmates were serving time for drug offenses, 13 percent of them for drug trafficking. (Female prisoners were actually more likely to be serving time for drugs: in federal prisons, it was 66 percent of the women, compared to 57 percent of the men; in state facilities, 33 percent of the women and 21 percent of the men were serving time for drug crimes.) According to the 1994 national survey, 42 percent of the federal prisoners and 62 percent of the state prisoners had reported using drugs regularly at some time during their lives. These numbers were generally recognized as being low, and other indications placed the level much higher. Also according to the prisoners' self-reported data, federal inmates were half as likely as state inmates to have been under the influence of drugs or alcohol at the time of their arrest for the crime for which they were incarcerated. For alcohol specifically, 11 percent of the federal inmates and 32 percent of the state prisoners said they had been drinking at the time of their arrest. But many experts believed these numbers too probably underrepresented the extent of prior use by prison inmates.[40]

By the late 1980s and the 1990s, many prison inmates were longtime drug addicts and/or alcoholics, some of them having returned to prison after only a brief stint on the streets, followed by a very recent and short span of enforced sobriety (possibly including detoxification) in jail. Under the laws in force in many states, they were often sentenced much more severely as repeat offenders, and in some cases their involvement with illegal drugs even had resulted in life without parole. Drugs kept the revolving door moving briskly, filling the prisons.

By 1991 the United States had more than a million persons behind bars and an incarceration rate of 426 persons per 100,000, the highest rate of imprisonment of any nation in the world. South Africa ranked second with 333, and the Soviet Union was third at 268 per 100,000. The European nations generally ranged from 35 to 120 per 100,000, compared to those of 21 to 140 in Asia. One of the starkest indications of the extent to which imprisonment in the United States had become a racial phenomenon was evident in the fact that its incarceration rate for black males was 3,109—more than 4.2 times higher than South Africa's before the fall of apartheid.[41] By 1993, after the dissolution of the Soviet Union, Russia reported

558 prisoners per 100,000, and the United States placed second at 519. Canada, meanwhile, had 116; Mexico, 97; England and Wales, 93; Germany, 80; and Japan, 36.[42]

Still, the number of inmates in federal and state correctional facilities continued to grow, reaching a record high of 1.1 million on June 30, 1995, according to the Bureau of Justice Statistics of the U.S. Department of Justice.[43] The census reflected an increase of 89,404, or about 8.8 percent, during the last twelve months, which was the largest one-year growth ever recorded in the United States, and the equivalent of an additional 1,719 new prison beds every week. Females recorded a greater increase (11.4 percent) than did males (8.7 percent). The rate of total growth exceeded 10 percent in twenty-three states; it was greatest in Texas (nearly 27 percent), followed by North Carolina (18 percent). The states with the greatest numbers of prison inmates were California (131,342), Texas (127,092), and New York (68,526). The federal prison system held 99,466 inmates on June 30. About 6.3 percent of the nation's total in custody, or 69,028, were women. The one-day count of prisoners in custody at the end of 1994 translated to an incarceration rate of about 403 per 100,000 of the U.S. general population. The highest rates were in the District of Columbia (1,722), Texas (859), and Louisiana (573). The lowest rates were reported in North Dakota (90), Minnesota (103), and Maine (112).

From 1990 to 1995 the nation built 168 state and 45 federal prisons, increasing the number of such institutions to 1,500; the number of prison beds rose by 41 percent to 976,000.[44] During the same period, the prison incarceration rate climbed from 293 to 409 per every 100,000 Americans, and by 1996 it was up to 427. Such numbers did not include 3,300 local jails and county or municipal detention centers. By 1991, the jails alone had held 426,479 people, according to the Bureau of Justice Statistics.

Blacks continued to be incarcerated at an increasingly higher rate than whites. In fact, by mid-1995 the incarceration rate for African-American men was almost eight times higher than for white men, and the comparable rate for African-American women was seven times higher. From 1980 through 1994, the total number of persons incarcerated in federal and state prisons and local jails nearly tripled. In other words, four-score and thirty-five years after Lincoln's great Emancipation, and more than two hundred years after the Declaration of Independence, the United States seemed to be heading full circle: it was moving, as a national commission had warned after the Watts riot of 1965, "toward two societies, one black, one white—separate and unequal." This was reflected most graphically in the statistics showing who was in prison and who was not, and who was or was not benefitting from the burgeoning prison system.[45] But that was only part of the alarming picture that was emerging.

THE PRISON BUSINESS

B Y the mid-1990s, the American penal system consisted of more than five thousand correctional institutions scattered in all the states, including more than thirty-three hundred local jails or holding pens. There was a lockup of some sort in virtually every city, and hundreds more state and federal prisons stood guard far outside the cities in hard-nosed prison towns like Dannemora and Stateville and Chino, dotting the countryside like the new red barns of their time.[46] Prisons seemed to be everywhere, but nobody seemed to notice.

It used to be that localities opposed the siting of a correctional facility within their limits, due to strong protests from homeowners—the NIMBY (or not-in-my-back-yard) phenomenon. But by the late 1980s, in harder economic times, some places, particularly sparsely populated locales, switched to lobbying to get a prospective new prison, thereby converting to a sort of PIMBY (please-in-my-back-yard) movement. "We've been trying to get a prison built here for years," a supervisor of one depressed milltown in upstate New York explained. "It would bring a lot of jobs, and that would be pretty nice for the town."[47]

In Texas, the competition during the early 1990s grew so fierce that some communities offered free country club memberships and other perks to prison officials as an incentive to get them to make the right siting decision. Amused journalists referred to the competitions as "prison derbies."[48] In fact, some Texas towns supported their own, independently financed jail-construction projects in the expectation that any excess space they did not use could be leased out to other jurisdictions at a profit, turning imprisonment into a real moneymaker.[49] Some referred to this notion as the "Field-of-Dreams" concept, after the motion picture of that name, meaning build it and they will come, build it and it will be used to capacity. And in time, it appeared they were right. The strategy seemed to be working. For more and more rural communities, prison increasingly had become, by default, both the only show in town and the primary engine of economic development.[50] Prisons were one of the few projects in rural areas that could attract major state investment.

Local representatives of prison towns joined with labor unions and anybody else as staunch opponents of efforts to downsize or close down existing institutions, so much so that it became almost inconceivable for them to think in terms of deinstitutionalization or decarceration. Even the prospect of lowering prison sentences or devising alternative approaches to fighting crime was enough to threaten many prison supporters. On the contrary, they favored getting even "tougher." Instead of gaining expansion of their existing institution, several prison towns in New York State actually lobbied for and obtained additional prisons.

Given their location, prisons often were an area's largest local employer, and consequently the regional economy tended to become inextricably prison based. With little else to turn to, people said they wanted the jobs, the stimulus to the local economy, that prisons offered. Residents were aware that prisons had historically provided jobs of long duration, which seemed to be inflation proof and recession proof, making the institution one of the few enterprises known to humankind that thrived even more in bad times than in good ones. By deciding to build a correctional facility at a particular location, a state committed itself to massive acquisition and initial construction costs, and to very substantial spending over many decades.

In 1994 more than six hundred thousand persons worked for corrections departments alone—a number that did not count many sheriffs' departments and other prison employers—and the total number of others who derived their livelihood from prisons had not been estimated.[51]

Prison employment was the ultimate in job security.[52] There was no danger that the plant would be moved to Mexico, no threat that the industry would become obsolete. Nobody had yet figured out any feasible alternate use or after use for prisons or jails. And there was no incentive to try. In some places, the leading local officials were themselves present or former prison employees or relatives of persons whose livelihood wholly depended on the prison. In such communities, prisoners' families, friends, or supporters were not welcome to linger when they visited or encouraged to take up residence in order to be closer to their loved ones. Programs to help prisoners make the transition from the institution to the community were firmly discouraged. And anything resembling prison reform was considered a dirty word.

Prison expansion has also been aided and abetted by the growth and increasing power of correction officer labor unions. Like their predecessors in criminal justice—the police benevolent associations—these organizations have spearheaded effective campaigns for more jobs and better working conditions, even in the face of budget cuts, layoffs, hiring freezes, and revenue drops in other government programs.[53] Unlike prisoners, whose right to form labor unions has been denied by correction authorities and the Supreme Court,[54] correction officers have generally been allowed to unionize since about the early 1970s. (The first guards' union appears to have been the Correction Officers' Benevolent Association in New York City. In the late 1950s, it became the first correctional employee organization to engage in formal collective bargaining, representing its members in negotiations over a wide range of issues.)[55]

Today, the overwhelming majority of states employ unionized prison guards. Both the number of union correction officers working in U.S. prisons, and their share of the total state and local employee workforces, have been rapidly increasing; with this increase, the uniformed prison staff's political clout has also become extremely formidable. Such public employee unions have typically used this power to bolster their employee rosters, substantially raise their members' salaries, exercise a strong voice regarding working conditions, and affect efforts to control prison discipline. In some instances, they have gained the right to strike, or, lacking such authorization, they have nevertheless undertaken various actions such as lockdowns and wildcat strikes—sometimes violently. Union representatives have also lobbied for prison expansion, tougher sentencing and release policies, and the curtailment of inmate rights and privileges. Many have used incidents of alleged unrest to dramatize their cause, in some cases to such an extent that some critics have charged union officials with intentionally inflaming or exaggerating prison problems in order to serve their own interests.[56]

Starting in the 1980s, prison expansion has proved to be a bonanza for architects, builders, hardware companies, electronics firms, and other vendors who, like defense contractors, managed to pull down astronomical profits under the banner of public security. The state, which usually was under intense pressure to create new space to reduce prison overcrowding, sometimes offered construction contractors handsome bonuses for rapid completion, or its officials threw cost containment measures to the wind in order to get the job done in time to accommodate the lines of backlogged prisoners. Cost-plus arrangements were often in effect.

About $80,000 was needed to build a single maximum-security prison cell, more than it took to build a typical middle-class suburban house.[57] An average-sized maximum-security prison generally ran from $30 to $75 million or so, more than what most medium-sized cities spent on education or transportation or recreation, much less the arts.

The financing of this construction was seldom debated or scrutinized. Under many financing arrangements, the costs were usually spread over twenty or thirty years—a whole generation. By the time the bonds were paid off, a single cell could have cost the taxpayers $1 million to create and maintain. Under one increasingly prevalent financing scheme, the state corrections system "leased" a new prison from a state authority (a quasi-private agency that was not as accountable to the public as a regular government agency), which issued bonds through such private underwriters as Merrill Lynch, Goldman Sachs, or Prudential, offering potential investors a much higher rate of return than would be paid by general-obligation bonds. The financing and siting of new prisons are highly politicized and generally conducted without much public scrutiny, making them especially susceptible to fraud, waste, and abuse. This pattern has not been adequately exposed by the news media, but one scandal came to light in 1995 in Pennsylvania, where a criminal investigation was initiated into questionable practices by the former governor.[58]

Once a prison was finally built, it constantly required huge amounts of funding to keep running. In fact, operating costs usually exceeded building costs. Keeping a person in prison was more expensive than sending him or her to Harvard or Stanford, but not because the accommodations in a correctional facility were so comfortable or the quality of the services so good. In reality, prison food costs were extraordinarily low—generally less per person per day than the price of one Coke and Big Mac at McDonald's; access to hot water was restricted; expenditures for inmate clothing were minuscule compared even to those on public assistance; and the quality of prison medical care was generally rather low, contributing to interminable health problems, complaints, and litigation. (The director of Hawaii's prison medical services was that state's highest paid public official, but she resigned in protest in 1996 because correction officials persisted in allowing correction officers to override a doctor's prescribed course of medical treatment, because they concluded that security considerations should take precedence over medical ones.)[59]

Nor were expensive rehabilitation programs the reason imprisonment cost so much. Prison education programs, vocational assistance programs, recreational programs, job training programs, drug treatment programs, therapy for sex offenders, and programs to address domestic violence and other problems usually accounted for an infinitesimal share of the corrections budget. Moreover, in many prisons, they hardly existed at all. The lack of adequate drug treatment in prison offered a case in point. After all, most persons were in prison for drug crimes.

By the mid-1990s, the presence of so many drug offenders had begun to pose some sticky political problems, not the least of which was that drug policies appeared to be significantly responsible for the growing racial imbalances within a good number of prison systems. Many critics blamed racial disparities in drug-law enforcement and sentencing. For example, the conviction rate for powdered cocaine was higher for whites and lower for minorities, but minorities were much more likely to be convicted for crack-related offenses, which carried penalties that were one hundred times greater than those involving equivalent amounts of powdered cocaine.[60] In October 1995 convict protests over such policies contributed to disturbances at six federal prisons—at Talladega, Alabama; Memphis, Tennessee; Allenwood, Pennsylvania; El Reno, Oklahoma; Greenville, Illinois; and McKean, Pennsylvania. Some of the inmates involved were serving extraordinarily long prison terms because they had handled crystalline cocaine instead of powder.

According to a national survey, on September 30, 1992, there were an estimated 945,000 clients in specialty substance abuse treatment programs throughout the United States. This translated to about 432 clients per 100,000 of the general population aged twelve years or older. Of those receiving treatment, only 3.2 percent were getting it in correctional facilities. Of the rest, 53.6 percent of the clients were being treated in outpatient facilities, 15.6 percent in community mental health centers, 9.7 percent in general hospitals and veterans' hospitals, 6.8 percent in residential facilities, 2.8 percent in specialized hospitals, 2.4 percent in halfway houses, and 5.8 percent in other settings.[61]

Oddly enough, although drug offenders had become much more prevalent as prison inmates since the late 1980s, in 1980 correctional facilities accounted for a higher share—4.8 percent—of the drug and alcohol treatment clients, compared to only 3.2 percent twelve years later, meaning that prison-based drug treatment had fallen behind the expansion of other types of treatment. Moreover, according to other data available from federal surveys, on June 29, 1990, state and federal prisons reportedly had drug treatment programs with an estimated capacity of 132,000 persons, of which 100,200 slots were filled. Only 75 percent of the available treatment capacity in state and federal correctional facilities was being used; the rest was "vacant."[62]

Despite their public image as "country clubs," most prisons remained stripped down to the basic necessities of life, except for the cable television and weight-lifting equipment that right-wingers liked to complain about— programs that correction officials retained because they were such a cheap and effective tool for occupying inmates.

Yet reported cost estimates for correctional departments typically included only the most obvious operating expenditures. Even though these outlays were massive, they tended to grossly underestimate the actual costs of imprisonment because they often left out many other indirect costs, such as fringe benefits and pension contributions, litigation costs and court-imposed fines and judgments, support of government-provided legal services for inmates, parole costs, the operational costs of prison watchdog agencies, the costs of psychiatric and medical services provided by outside hospitals, finance charges, and the burden of increased public welfare to meet the needs of spouses and children left behind, to name a few.[63]

Institutional costs as reported were so astronomical, in part, because today's prison tab included such standard features as modular steel cells, automated collect call telephone systems, inkless fingerprinting, sound activated lighting systems, crash-deterrent gates, drying tumblers that were specially designed for prison use, elaborate property storage systems, inmate identification and classification wristbands, handcuffs, flex-cuffs, telephone monitoring systems, razor wire, abuse-resistant wall and ceiling products, drug testing kits, electronic locking systems, unbreakable glass–clad polycarbonate, and high-security mesh chain-link fabric. Salesmen peddled personal alarms, armor-piercing ammunition, floating jails, X-ray inspection machines, infrared surveillance cameras, canvas footwear, concealed door closers, convex and dome mirrors, and riot-resistant steel toilets. Slick advertisements in the leading corrections magazine pitched such items as reinforced-concrete masonry, intrusion detection alarm systems, impulse radar systems for perimeter security, high-speed computers, stainless foodveyors, "viciously effective" razor ribbon, unbreakable thermal food trays, tamper-proof ceilings, multichannel simultaneous record and playback digital voice loggers, cotton uniforms, and massive quantities of food and tear gas and custom-made prison buses.[64]

PRISONS FOR PROFIT

AFTER decades of relative stagnation, the use of prison labor during the 1980s and 1990s began to experience tremendous growth, reviving many age-old issues in prison reform—and prompting new legal concerns about how to safeguard against inevitable abuses.[65] From 1980 to 1984, as the number of prisoners increased by 221 percent, the number of inmates employed in prison industries increased by 358 percent, and sales of prison-made goods grew from $392 million to $1.31 billion. According to the Correctional Industries Association, by the year 2000 fully 30 percent of state and federal inmates would be working, yielding nearly $9 billion in sales.

Such growth of prison industries and privatization appears to have occurred as a result of several factors: a punitive, "get-tougher" mood among many members of the general public; the need to reduce the skyrocketing costs of imprisonment without causing large-scale releases of inmates; the growth of privatization and anti-government and anti-union sentiments; and the appeal of prison of a source of cheap labor and economic development.

By the mid-1990s, prison management was increasingly being turned over to private companies, which operated to make profits and were not subject to the same scrutiny, standards, or controls as government agencies.[66] Privatization, of course, was hardly new in American corrections, and many recent developments appeared to represent a step back into the nineteenth century, to a time before judicial intervention, legal empowerment of inmates, or laws governing the workplace. Convicts can still be, and many are, compelled to work without pay, and very few receive anything close to the minimum wage.[67] Simultaneous with the recent revival of prison privatization, however, there were strong movements to allow prison authorities to govern prison management without interference from the courts or other government agencies. This important deregulation of prison industry, which might permit prison-made goods to be sold at home and abroad on the open market, for example, was occurring with very little public consideration of its implications.[68]

Privatization was one of the stimuli affecting the changes in prison labor. From 1985 to 1995, there was a 500 percent increase in private prisons; 18 companies had rehabilitated 93 private prisons, creating space for some 51,000 prisoners. By 1996 at least 30 states had legalized the contracting out of prison labor to private companies. From 1995 to 2005, the number of prison beds under private management was expected to increase from 60,000 to more than 350,000.[69] Although in its most extreme form privatization may entail having a private company build and operate a prison or jail on behalf of a government entity, other, lesser variants of privatization—although not as easily identified or quantified—commonly involve government contracts with private companies to furnish medical services, food services, bus transportation, program services, and other parts of the corrections operation.

By the mid-1990s, an estimated 10 percent of Arizona's inmates were working for private companies, earning less than the minimum wage, and performing all sorts of tasks, ranging from manual labor and raising hogs to testing human blood. At California's Folsom prison, inmates worked in recycling and made steel tanks for micro-breweries. Hawaii prisoners packed Spalding golf balls; in Illinois, they sorted inventory for Toys R Us. Nevada convicts converted luxury automobiles into stretch limousines; Oregon's manufactured uniforms for McDonald's. The acting commissioner of New York's Department of Correctional Services announced plans to use inmate labor to help build several new state prisons—a move that until recently would have unleashed an overpowering torrent of opposition from organized labor, but which lately has hardly raised an eyebrow.

Some of the same American politicians who most decry the use of prison labor abroad as a violation of human rights are among the strongest supporters of expanded convict labor and penal servitude at home.[70] Although Americans decried prison labor in China as a major human rights abuse, prison labor at home got less negative publicity, so few consumers were aware they were buying or using prison-made goods. By the mid-1990s, Tennessee inmates were producing $80 custom jeans for the Eddie Bauer company. Women prisoners in Washington State were turning out fashionable clothing under the labels of Eddie Bauer and Union Bay. Oregon, on the other hand, put a different twist on the prison labor scene when it introduced a hip new line of inmate-made casual wear, known as Prison Blues. Sold in five hundred stores nationwide, the line had its own home page on the Internet, where an image of a convict salesman slickly proclaimed, "Prison Blues are as good as you can get in a basic, five-pocket jean." (The program also marketed jackets, bags, and teeshirts.) Oregon Prison Industries, doing business as UniGroup, sold $4.5 million worth of clothes in 1995, thanks to aggressive marketing and a sophisticated appeal to yuppie consumers. The year before, Oregon passed the Inmate Work Act, amending its constitution to provide that if inmates did not "volunteer" to work they could lose good-time credit and other privileges and risk being sent to solitary confinement. Meanwhile, the Beaver State's inmates were paid 28 cents to $8 per hour, but 80 percent of the higher wage was withheld, so that some inmates generated $6,000 a year to defray the cost of their own incarceration. Following Oregon's lead, by 1996 the California corrections system was reportedly considering establishing its own line of casual wear for Japanese markets. It was to be called Gangsta Blues.[71]

Federal Prison Industries, Inc. (UNICOR) produced an assortment of products, ranging from furniture and metal shelving to safety eyewear, which it, too, recently began to sell over its own home page on the Internet. Although UNICOR's primary mission was the productive employment of inmates, it claimed to offer quality products and services at competitive prices, as well as procurement with no bidding necessary.

The Thirteenth Amendment remained the legal cornerstone of prison-labor law, and the provision of the Constitution that set the fundamental parameters for prisoners' rights. For decades following its passage, organized labor gained many important legal restrictions on the use of convict labor, and some states even adopted provisions in their constitutions that limited the ability of prison industry to compete with free labor. The federal Hawes-Cooper Act enabled any state to prohibit within its borders the sale of any goods made in the prisons of another state—a right that most states quickly availed themselves of during the Great Depression. In 1935 the Ashurst-Sumners Act strengthened Hawes-Cooper by prohibiting the transportation of prison products to any state in violation of the laws of that state. Many states adopted laws prohibiting any prison-made goods from being sold on the open market, requiring that they be exclusively sold for state use. Federal law also forbade domestic commerce in prison-made goods unless workers were paid the "prevailing wage." But the law did not apply to exports.

By the early 1990s, however, some of these restrictions were beginning to be changed in ways that favored prison industry. In 1990 California voters approved Proposition 139, allowing the state to use prisoners to make goods that could be sold on the open market. Under the new system, private companies also received various incentives for engaging in prison industry. After 1991, with the state-use system no longer in force, these infant joint ventures with private industry made millions of dollars for private companies and the state's department of corrections.

A San Francisco–based company, DPAS, that opened a data processing operation at San Quentin prison was one such firm that was taking advantage of tax breaks offered under California's Joint Venture Program. Inmates assembled literature for Chevron, Bank of America, and Macy's, for which they received the federal minimum wage of $4.25, minus the 80 percent that was garnished to pay various state deductions. Meanwhile, DPAS received a 10 percent tax credit on the first $2,000 of each inmate's wages.

Prison's unique economic climate enabled companies to earn tremendous profits selling goods and services to a captive market, often under monopolistic arrangements that were provided under lucrative state contracts. At a federal facility in Arizona, for instance, a single prison phone could gross $15,000 a year, five times the take of a regular street pay phone; the RCNA telephone company charged inmates $22 for a fifteen-minute call from Florence, Arizona, to the East Coast, and the federal agency that operated the facility took a 15 percent cut.

History has shown that private prisons, convict leasing, and other profit-oriented arrangements are inherently prone to abuse. Recent events also bear this out. Esmor Correctional Services, Inc., for example, was a publicly traded company based in Melville, New York, with annual earnings exceeding $36 million. It operated private correctional facilities from Brooklyn to Seattle, with a total of about nineteen hundred beds. In June

1995, at a U.S. Immigration and Naturalization Service (INS) processing center at Elizabeth, New Jersey, operated by Esmor, over three hundred detained immigrants rebelled against brutal conditions. The inmates were later transferred and the facility was shut down. Following the disturbance, the company's extensive management troubles were detailed in news reports from coast to coast, and serious questions were raised about the lack of oversight and accountability for private prisons.

Prison labor continued to be subject to charges of unfair labor competition, since companies using inmate workers did not have to pay for health care, welfare, sick pay, vacations, or other common benefits.[72] The United States Supreme Court ruled that inmates lack the right to form unions or engage in collective bargaining. And prisoners received less than minimum wages, if they were compensated at all.

The *AFL-CIO Newsletter* reported that tens of thousands of convicts, who were being paid minimum or sub-minimum wages, generated more than $1 billion in sales in 1995. An inmate at a medium-security prison in Monterey, California, earned 45 cents an hour making shirts, receiving only $60 per month for his nine-hour days. At Oakhill Correctional Facility in Dane County, Wisconsin, seventeen inmates produced $1.5 million per year worth of office chairs, earning for their labor 20¢ to $1.50 per hour, which was applied to their release savings, victim restitution, and court obligations such as child support. In Colorado, AT&T paid fifty inmate telemarketers only $2 per hour for work that ordinarily would have cost three or four times that amount.

Prison labor continued to be linked to union busting. In Ventura, California, inmates started handling telephone reservations for TWA, as part of the company's response to a strike. Workers at Michigan's Brill Manufacturing Company furniture plant lost their $5.65 per hour jobs to prison inmates who were paid 56¢ to 80¢ per hour without benefits.

The use of inmate workers also figured in some of the "downsizing" actions that were being undertaken by American corporations. In Austin, Texas, a plant that assembled computer circuit boards was closed and the work was moved thirty miles away to a prison in Lockhart that was operated by Wackenhut; the convicts, working for IBM, Compaq, and Dell, earned a small fraction of what their predecessors had received. In Ohio, inmates at the Ross County jail assembled auto parts for Honda until the United Auto Workers managed to get the practice stopped. The inmates were later retooled to make toys and rakes and do data entry.

By 1995, the leading company in the field—Corrections Corporation of America—controlled about 50 percent of the private corrections market;

its stock soared 360.5 percent, making it the fourth-best performer on the New York Stock Exchange that year.[73]

American corporations have also been increasingly exporting prison construction, prison management, and prison labor ventures abroad, as part of a globalizing trend that has not been sufficiently noted.[74]

State prisoners are also being transferred long distances—in some cases, to other states, such as from Hawaii, Colorado, or Massachusetts to Texas, or from Colorado to Minnesota—to serve their sentences under the control of private companies. In the process they become subject to the laws of other jurisdictions, regardless of where any crimes of conviction took place.[75] Some jurisdictions have built new jails or prisons on a speculative basis, expecting to rent out space at a profit to private companies.[76]

Still, even by the 1990s the economics of imprisonment was not what it had been a century and a half ago. The international slave trade and convict lease camps had pretty much vanished, although they may have been making a comeback. Instead of being worked to death in quarries or factories, today's inmates were more likely to pass their time in idleness, without work, just as they had been unemployed before going to prison. Instead of hanging out on street corners, they hung out in the yard, and rather than confronting police officers, they confronted correction officers.

In a sense, it was precisely *because* prison was so expensive that made it something of such economic beauty. A cynic might say that the whole apparatus seemed perfectly designed, since imprisonment was one of the few legal ways in postmodern society by which undereducated, unskilled, drug-addicted, antisocial minority males could generate huge amounts of capital for others. A single drug pusher or burglar, sentenced to two or three years, could give rise to a multifaceted, miniature industry worth hundreds of thousands of dollars per whack. The system enabled society to send prisoners from their homes in the slum to out-of-the-way rural areas. Prisoners were overwhelmingly young lower-class urban minorities, but the prisons were predominantly staffed by lower-middle-class white men who came from nonurban areas. In many prisons, there were no black or Hispanic correction officers or supervisors, and the only female employees were secretaries, cooks, and an occasional nurse.

US VERSUS THEM

PRISON benefits one group and one place at the expense of another, somewhat like the convict transportation system in the eighteenth cen-

tury. Under the present arrangement, urban Democratic politicians generally support tougher sentencing laws to remove more criminals from the
cities, while their Republican counterparts cosponsor legislation to build
new prisons in their own rural districts. That way, both interests are
served. In one analysis of corrections policy in New York State, the assemblyman who chaired that house's Committee on Corrections found that
Republican senate districts with relatively low population densities accounted for 89 percent of the prison employees, housed over 89 percent
of the prisoners, and consumed over 89 percent of the state's prison expenditures, while Democratic assembly districts accounted for the overwhelming share of prison inmates. Prison expansion was thus a product of bipar-
tisan collaboration, with the Democrats getting rid of criminals in their
districts and Republicans becoming the beneficiaries of prison pork.[77] "It's
not only lock them up; it's lock them up in my district," New York assemblyman Daniel L. Feldman explained.[78] One result is a greater number
of remote prisons. Whole communities depend for their livelihood upon
correctional institutions. Their long-term fate is tied to the prison.

Society as a whole has become accustomed to this dynamic. For most
Americans, life without prisons is inconceivable, just as the abolition of
slavery was considered out of the question two centuries ago. Ask the average American what should be done about the country's incarceration rate
and he or she will probably shrug and say, incredulously, "Well, my goodness, what would we do without prisons?"

As often as not, the public may expect more, not fewer, prison beds,
just as during the Great Depression when, although there were as many as
three to six million workers unemployed, most Americans still held the
opinion that all who sincerely wanted to work could find it, and the public
reacted to growing crime with anger and demands for more severe punishments.

Leslie T. Wilkins, a distinguished criminologist, observed, "Ask the average layman what ought to be done with thieves, drug addicts, sexual
deviants, and other offenders, and it is almost certain that they will reply
with a considerable degree of assurance." But "ask an expert in the field of
criminology or corrections the same questions," he said, "and he will be
less certain." Pose it to a prison superintendent, and the response might
be, "Send them somewhere, but not to my prison; we've already got too
much to do and there are too many people who don't belong here."[79]

Prison and the criminal justice system as a whole tend to operate on a
war model, not a medical model.[80] Criminals are enemies. Crime control
constitutes domestic defense. Deterrence and other military concepts are
relied upon in the war on crime. The need for more prisons, like the need

for a strong military defense, is portrayed as a matter of public safety. Both the military-industrial complex and the prison-industrial complex are major organizing activities within American society. They go together and are part of the same mind-set. With the end of the Cold War, criminal justice concerns assumed greater importance. During the Reagan-Bush era, prisons were the second fastest-growing item in state budgets, after Medicaid.[81] In fiscal 1991 America spent $20.1 billion on building and operating prisons, and probation and parole costs brought the corrections tab to $26.2 billion. By comparison, that year the United States spent $22.9 billion on the main welfare program, Aid to Families with Dependent Children. Yet there were 13.5 million women and children who were served by welfare, compared to only 1.1 million persons, mostly men, who were imprisoned.[82] By 1995, state governments' proposed Medicaid costs were projected to grow by 4.9 percent, compared to 8 percent for corrections.[83] In 1996, however, "welfare reform" began a series of massive cuts in welfare spending, while prison costs continued to soar.

A large number of politicians portray welfare as a frill and a luxury, even as they approve massive prison spending. Yet many of the same arguments made against welfare can be made just as well against prison. For example, one might allege that prison does the opposite of what was intended, and that in fact it actually makes those who go through it worse off than when they went in; that imprisonment is a revolving door that continues from one generation to the next; and so on. Both institutions are publicly associated with the inner-city poor and linked to minorities; both often involve female-based households. Welfare recipients and prisoners alike get blamed for their own condition and degraded for their own misery. Speaking at the 1992 Democratic National Convention, Reverend Jesse Jackson put it this way: "Once they're jailed, they are no longer homeless. Once they are jailed, they have balanced meals . . . once they are jailed, they will no longer be hit by drive-by shootings."[84]

Meanwhile, the heavy reliance on incarceration has not reduced crime or raised the quality of life in the cities. In fact, it may have done the opposite. A study in the late 1970s argued that massive investment in prisons as a response to crime would bring "a succession of increasingly impossible demands on the budgetary resources of the community," and added: "For every person who goes to prison, two people don't go to college. For every day a person spends in jail, twenty children eat starch instead of protein."[85] Governor James Thompson of Illinois used to say, "A dollar for corrections is a dollar that doesn't go someplace else."[86]

By the mid-1990s, massive prison expansion had affected even some of the smaller states, and the actions seemed to put a lock on the future. In

Washington, for example, tougher sentencing laws were expected to push the annual prison budget to $1 billion in the next decade, regardless of what happens to the crime rate; meanwhile, its voters had approved caps in overall state spending, meaning that other state services will have to be drastically cut in order to pay for the mounting prison burden.[87]

Another important aspect of the cycle of prison expansion to emerge in the 1990s has been that many state governments suddenly have begun to spend more money on corrections than on higher education.[88] In 1995, as a result of recent sentencing changes and for the first time in history, California voters spent more for prisons than for the two state-supported college systems, the University of California and the California state universities. From 1980 to 1995, the prison share of California's budget increased from 2.0 to 9.9 percent, while the higher education share shrank from 12.6 to 9.5 percent. Based on continuing trends, including the full implementation of the "three strikes" law, a Rand Corporation study projected that by 2000 corrections would consume 18 percent of the budget, whereas only 1 percent would be left to the gutted college systems. Similar shifts have been noted in other leading "education-oriented" states, some of them affecting support for the whole system of public education.[89]

The long-range implications of this development are enormous, and they are likely to further retard society's ability to overcome its dependence upon prisons. Tom Hayden, a California state senator from Santa Monica and 1960s radical, characterized the state's prison expansion moves as "another Vietnam moral quagmire in the making, only worse."[90]

Rather than provide more and better housing, medical care, education, welfare, and other services to the population most in need of them, the state spends $100,000 or more to build a prison cell and $30,000 to incarcerate one individual in it per year. The billions of dollars thus spent means that these funds are not available to pay for the services to address the problems that contributed to persons being imprisoned in the first place. Lacking those services, more people are pushed toward prison, and the spiral continues. No wonder that New York's liberal former governor, Mario M. Cuomo, lamented to a group of law enforcement executives: "I am going to go down as having built more prisons than any governor in New York State history, and it disgusts me that they're going to put that on my tombstone."[91]

GET TOUGH

ONE of the central operating notions of both the welfare system and the prison system is the principle of less eligibility, which holds that the standard of living on welfare and within the prisons must be worse than that of the lowest stratum of the working class, so that, given the alternative, people will opt to work under these conditions, and so that punishment will serve as a deterrent. Otherwise, as George Bernard Shaw put it, "If the prison does not underbid the slum in human misery, the slum will empty and the prison will fill."[92]

Over the last twenty years or so, as conditions in the inner city have worsened, the slums have not totally emptied, but they have sent many more of their young persons to the morgue and to the prison. In New York, studies actually showed that fully 75 percent of the state's prisoners came from the seven "worst" (most impoverished) neighborhoods of New York City.[93]

During the same period, conditions in prisons have also deteriorated— in some instances, as a result of conservative movements to cut back on prison "frills," such as education, legal assistance, and rehabilitation programs, even though such efforts were known to have cut the rates of recidivism.[94] The return to a judicial hands-off policy has also ended the brief era of ameliorative court intervention.

Efforts to "toughen" prison programs, along with stricter sentencing policies, returned into vogue during the mid-1980s with the political popularity of military-type "boot camps" and "shock incarceration" programs for youthful drug offenders. By 1995, some states were experimenting with old-style chain gangs, complete with public displays of shackled, shovel-toting convicts in striped uniforms—spectacles that had been abandoned decades ago following a long train of abuses.[95] Alabama became the first to resume using them, and in the ensuing swirl of publicity Florida and Arizona quickly followed suit. Florida's "restricted labor squads" each were made up of thirty prisoners, policed by three armed guards who were empowered to shoot anyone who tried to escape. Arizona even put death-row prisoners on chain gangs. Politicians in several other states announced similar efforts. In California, Republican assemblyman Brett Granlund introduced Bill 2044 to require the department of correction to organize chain gangs by December 1, 1997. "After working 12 hours for 30 to 90 days, shackled to four other prisoners, an inmate is going to think twice about committing another crime," Granlund said.

Shortly afterward, California's lower house passed legislation, authored by Assemblywoman Denise Ducheny, a Democrat from San Diego, designed to force convicts to work forty hours per week and pay for their own prison upkeep. The bill—which also cut prison adult basic education and vocational training by 75 percent—required the department of correction to develop a plan that would put every California prisoner to work by the year 2000. At the federal level, the Texas senator and former presidential candidate Phil Gramm pushed a plan calling for prisoner labor to pay for one-half the cost of the federal prison system. About the same time, New York resumed the practice of double-celling inmates (crowding two prisoners into cells that were designed for one), despite the increased dangers of tuberculosis and HIV transmission, inmate-on-inmate sexual assault, and other problems.[96] New Jersey jails began charging inmates for their medications, and Connecticut passed a bill requiring the state to charge prisoners for medical care.[97] Prison authorities throughout the country cut back on inmate access to weight-lifting equipment, cable television, and other prison recreation.

State governments and the Federal Bureau of Prisons also increasingly resorted to putting "problem inmates" into "supermax" institutions, under harsh solitary confinement. One of the most notorious recent additions has been the huge high-tech control facility at Pelican Bay, in northernmost California—a prison that in January 1995 was condemned by a federal district judge as featuring numerous conditions that were found to constitute unconstitutional cruel and unusual punishment. Another was the Federal Correctional Complex in Florence, Colorado, where inmates are kept locked in their cells for up to twenty-three hours a day and denied most basic privileges.[98] "Many inmates become grossly disorganized and psychotic," according to Dr. Stuart Grassian, a Harvard psychiatrist who studied the effects of a number of supermax institutions. Convicts were reported as "smearing themselves with feces, mumbling and screaming incoherently all day and night, some even descending to the horror of eating parts of their own bodies."[99]

During the 1990s corrections authorities also increasingly resorted to using stun guns, tasers, electric riot shields, and other electronic shocking devices to "control" inmates.[100] Their popularity was linked to the interest in chain gangs, since the devices could keep chained inmates in line in a "more humane" way than by shackling them together.

INTERGENERATIONAL IMPACT

CAPTIVITY leaves deep, sometimes lifelong, impressions. A leading sociologist identified several major "pains of imprisonment," including material deprivation, denial of heterosexual relationships, loss of autonomy, compromised security and feelings of well-being, and suspended liberty.[101] These of course are among the intended consequences of imprisonment.

Others who have tried to measure some of the unintended long-range consequences of imprisonment have suggested that it may actually strengthen ties to criminals, inculcate a criminal code, promote antisocial behavior, and teach criminal skills. Whether or not by design, imprisonment can injure an inmate's physical health and reduce life expectancy. It can damage psychological well-being and impair an individual's ability to function independently, spawning all kinds of post-traumatic stress disorders. Being imprisoned can attach lasting civil disabilities that will plague a person long after he or she has left through the front gate. And it can shatter personal relationships, dissolve friendships, and disconnect and distress fragile families.[102]

By the time offenders are sent away to prison, stress already has torn some families apart. Often as a consequence of their drug addiction and criminal behavior, some inmates have lost their loved ones and alienated their friends. Although prison rules governing correspondence and visiting have been greatly relaxed since the extreme isolation of the early nineteenth century, such contact remains severely hampered by distance, expense, and intrusive security procedures. Just getting to the prison in time for a visit can entail having to help rent a bus to leave before dawn for a ride that is hundreds of miles each way, which is not an easy proposition for poor people.

Links that were often brittle to begin with sometimes snap as the months and years pass by. Prison visiting can also reopen wounds. According to Gresham Sykes, "This may explain in part the fact that an examination of the visiting records of a random sample of the inmate population, covering approximately a one-year period, indicated that 41 percent of the prisoners in the New Jersey State Prison had received no visits from the outside world."[103]

In one case in 1967, a young Connecticut man was sentenced to five years in federal prison for counterfeiting. Shortly after he started serving time, he learned that his wife had decided to end their marriage and retain custody of their two little daughters. His letters to her were returned by the Post Office. The man completed his time and rebuilt his life without ever hearing from his family again until twenty-five years later, when he suddenly received a telephone call from a woman who identified herself as his elder daughter. As best they could, the family reunited. More often, however, there *is* no telephone call. Relationships are simply ended. Inmates often report their anguish is worst around the time of family deaths, holidays, anniversaries, birthdays, funerals, and the dates of romantic breakups.

In a classic example of doublespeak, a 1960s presidential crime commission proclaimed that the "task of corrections . . . includes . . . restoring family ties, obtaining employment and education, securing in the large sense a place for the offender in the routine functioning of society."[104] Nothing could have been further from the truth. For as long as imprisonment has been used, it has done the opposite. Throughout the centuries, prisons have weakened family ties and traumatized relatives, leaving deep emotional scars and inhibiting reintegration into society.

From 1970 to 1990, the share of female inmates doubled. The rate of women's imprisonment grew from 6 per 100,000 in 1925 to 29 per 100,000 in 1989. In every year since 1981, the number of women prisoners increased at a faster rate than did that of men. (Still, only about 6 percent of all American prisoners are girls or women.) The majority of female prisoners are young, drug-abusing persons of color who never completed high school, and who are generally being held for less serious crimes than are men—mostly minor property offenses or drug-related crimes. Most women who are inmates are also mothers—a recent estimate put the number of children left behind while they were incarcerated at 160,000, although many have lost custody by virtue of their legal problems.[105]

Virtually all inmates, men and women alike, have families. Prison not only affects the individual who is locked up; it can also injure others, both immediately and over the long term. The incarceration of one single husband, wife, brother, sister, son, daughter, cousin, niece, or nephew exacts a heavy toll on a large circle of relatives; given its impact on the girls and boys among them, imprisonment is increasingly an intergenerational problem.

Individual family members often react to the incarceration of a relative in different ways, and the family unit itself, the family structure, may be altered because of it. Tocqueville described many scenes of anguished convicts who had been separated from their families, and he wrote that he had detected "a profound and natural antipathy between the institution of marriage and that of slavery."[106] Slave children were said to have felt abandoned by their parents, angry at their own unjust punishment and deprivation, and bitter that they had been robbed of any incentive or reward in their lives. They also resented being forced to see their own parents and friends disgraced before their eyes and being forced to endure the tyranny of other children who happened to be white. To survive, many had to learn to be secretive and duplicitous.[107] Some slaves took solace from the fact that slavery seemed to injure their oppressors as well. "It seems to destroy families as by a powerful blight," one former slave wrote, "large and opulent slaveholding families often vanish like a group of shadows at the third or fourth generation. . . . As far back as I can recollect, indeed, it was a remark among slaves, that every generation of slaveholders are more and more inferior."[108]

Twentieth-century scholars have compiled great volumes about the legacy of slavery and its baneful effects upon the family. E. Franklin Frazier believed that slavery had destroyed the black family.[109] A generation later, Stanley M. Elkins examined how, under slavery, whites had sought to wreck any semblance of the black family.[110] In 1965 Daniel Patrick Moynihan, then an advisor to President Johnson, wrote a report describing the breakdown of black ghetto families, which he largely attributed to slavery, as an urgent national problem.[111] (Since the 1960s, black birth rates have fallen dramatically, and the number of households headed by single mothers has skyrocketed. The percentage of black female-based households rose from 8.3% in 1950 to 20.7% in 1960, 30.6% in 1970, and 46.5% in 1982. The figures for whites were 2.8% in 1950, 6.0% in 1960, 7.8% in 1970, and 15.0% in 1982.)[112]

Some commentators argued for or against Moynihan's controversial thesis that enslavement wrecked the structure of black families and left a "tangle of pathology" that persisted well into the twentieth century. Herbert Gutman and John Blassingame, for instance, countered that black families were remarkably resourceful, resilient, and durable, providing their members one of the few effective buffers from slavery.[113]

Through all the debate, little attention has been devoted to the impact of slavery's kin—criminal imprisonment—on families, black or otherwise. Among urban African Americans, imprisonment is so extensive and deeply ingrained that it may be viewed as the modern equivalent of slavery. Like slavery, prison represents a profound influence upon black culture, black identity, black social and political status, the black family, and race relations. It affects birth rates, the extent of female-based households, and contributes to the forced breakup of families.

In asking where have all the black males gone, somebody ought to look to correctional institutions. Where are the studies examining the effect of prison's forced uprooting upon family structure and relations? What long-term damage does imprisonment (as a slave or otherwise) inflict upon families? Who has determined its contribution to child abuse and neglect, truancy, juvenile delinquency, drug abuse and alcoholism, poverty and crime?

Conservatives and liberals alike agree that the family plays a crucial role in determining whether a person will become delinquent or criminal, regardless of whether the supposed manner is genetic, environmental, moral, or of some other nature. Although it is debatable whether poverty is the cause or the effect of the breakdown of family, it is evident that they go together, and there is general agreement that broken families, poverty, and crime also go together. Yet, there has been little attention given to the extent to which imprisonment may contribute to poverty, delinquency, and criminality on the part of family members in addition to the imprisoned offender. Clearly, the family left behind can become an incubator of social problems.

To the extent that imprisonment actually serves as a source of criminality, blacks' greater exposure to it may have increased the incidence and seriousness of black criminality. Black youths are more likely to suffer from the absence of their father during childhood and to live in poverty, which is more apt to lead them into crime, which increases their chances of being arrested, convicted, and imprisoned. Once in prison, they are more likely to learn criminal ways. Along the way, they leave their own trails of broken families.

Prison life differs from life on the outside, even from life in the ghetto. But prison life and ghetto life have so much in common that some young men who are familiar with both consider them indistinguishable. Going back to the Harlem streets of his youth, thirty years later, Claude Brown observed: "Reformatory and prison bits are still an accepted, often anticipated and virtually inevitable phase of the growing-up process for young black men in this country. They have no fear of jail; most of their friends are there. They are told by the returning, unsung, heroic P.O.W.s of the unending ghetto war of survival that even the state joints are now country clubs."[114] On the South Side of Chicago, a *New York Times* reporter who was present on the day that a young black man named Theodore Russell got out of jail after a long stay observed how a group of neighborhood boys, including Russell's little brother, surrounded him on the stoop of his mother's porch "as if he were a rap star passing out concert tickets." Nearby, a young black girl in the housing project explained, "People always say their brother or cousin is in jail, and you better not mess with them because when they get out they'll have big muscles and beat you up."[115] Lower-class kids are groomed to go to prison. Kids are surrounded with others who are on their way to or from prison, or else headed for an early death.

Imprisonment can affect the family unit economically and socially. Though they were generally poor before the man's incarceration, the family's financial condition invariably deteriorates after his arrest. Finances suffer, and remaining family members often are forced to go on welfare.

Working wives, if they reveal the fact of their husband's incarceration, may find it harder to get a job.

In the late 1920s, the federal government commissioned a sociological study to examine the extent of welfare problems among prisoners' relatives in Kentucky, which was then concerned about the rate of compensation for convict labor and its impact upon prisoners' families. The final report, issued by Ruth S. Bloodgood, a social worker, noted that "[t]o the convicted defendant, sentence to a penal institution means deprivation of liberty and, theoretically at least, opportunity for reformation; to society, protection from the criminal tendencies of the prisoner and possibly a deterrent effect on others with similar tendencies; to the wife and children, deprivation of a father's support and all the economic and social readjustment which such a loss involves."[116] The study reported that Mr. F, serving a life sentence for murder, had been imprisoned for six years when his family was visited. Mrs. F and the three boys, aged thirteen, sixteen, and nineteen, were living in a shack that was described as "little more than a shed, and the agent could scarcely believe that it was occupied by human beings." The mother worked on a small garden plot and did washing and cleaning to earn about $5 or $6 per week. The oldest boy had left school at age thirteen to go to work and he was now earning $3 a day. The second boy had left school at age ten, but he had received a severe injury to his leg that had never healed, making him unable to work. The family were malnourished and in poor health.[117] Outside of a few populous counties, Kentucky was found to be entirely without social services to assist the families of imprisoned heads of households. Bloodgood's study resulted in a slight increase in the amount of compensation for convict labor in Kentucky, but the essential problem remained.[118]

In 1938 a study in the District of Columbia by another social worker (Jerome Sacks) found that most families of incarcerated men were devastated economically and socially by the man's removal.[119] A few other studies since then have concluded that imprisonment punishes the family as well as the prisoner, but there has been little attention paid to the results.[120]

Separation trauma can be especially severe for prisoners' children, who often feel they are to blame for the parent's removal from the home. Family members may also see their pre-prison friendships deteriorate. The family may be stigmatized or ostracized by neighbors, friends, and even members of the larger family because of what their relative has done. Children may be harassed in school. Relatives often feel worried, afraid, and guilty over what has happened to the imprisoned person. Spouses commonly experience heightened emotional and sexual frustration, depression, loneliness, or anger. Managing the children becomes more difficult, resulting in trouble with discipline. Children typically exhibit serious behavioral problems. Mothers are more apt to resort to corporal punishment.[121] Many families complain that they are being treated as criminals, like their imprisoned relative.

This feeling is often acute during visits to prison. As described by John Edgar Wideman, a black college professor and prize-winning novelist:

> The visitor is forced to become an inmate. Subjected to the same sorts of humiliation and depersonalization. Made to feel powerless, intimidated by the might of the State. Visitors are treated like both children and ancient, incorrigible sinners. We experience a crash course that teaches us in a dramatic, unforgettable fashion just how low a prisoner is in the institution's estimation. We also learn how rapidly we can descend to the same depth. Our pretensions to dignity, to difference are quickly dispelled. We are on the keepers' turf. We must play their game, their way. We sit where they tell us to sit. Surrender the personal possessions they order us to surrender. Wait as long as it pleases them to keep us waiting in the dismal anteroom. We come (and are grateful for the summons) whenever we are called. We allow them to pass us through six-inch steel doors and don't protest when the doors slam shut behind us. We let them lock us in without any guarantee the doors will open when we wish to leave. We are in fact their prisoners until they release us.[122]

A transfer from one prison to another can require a major family adjustment. Visitors have to learn new rules, acquire another ride, alter their plans. Usually there is no one to help them negotiate these turns. Loved ones may live in terror over the new life-or-death dangers facing their imprisoned relative.

Increasingly in some families, prison is becoming a second- or third-generation tradition, for keepers and kept alike. Some prisons contain inmates and correction staff who are fathers and sons, brothers, or cousins. Of the five hundred or so correction officers employed at Auburn prison in 1985, there were fourteen sets of fathers and sons, twenty-three sets of brothers, and one husband and wife team.[123] Hundreds of other prison employees throughout the correction system were from the prison town of Auburn. In some instances, prison employees were the second or third or fourth or fifth generation in their family to work in the same institution.

The same is true of the prisoners. One day, a long line of black women and their young children were waiting to enter Auburn to visit their loved ones, just as a group of all-white correction officers emerged at the end of their shift. As the young son of a correction officer ran over to embrace his father, the child turned to the line of somber black people with their toddlers and exclaimed, "Look, Dad—baby inmates!" In his young mind, race and prison went together.

Bobbie Ferguson, a state-raised convict in Iowa who had spent all but sixteen months of his thirty-nine years in state institutions, told the parole board he wanted to remain in prison. "I don't know how to live outside," he said. "My home is inside, and I want to stay there the rest of my life."[124] Ferguson had been born in the Iowa Women's Reformatory, where his mother was being held for a crime long forgotten. "I think her name was Vivian," he later said in an interview, noting that he had become a ward of the state the day he was born and had remained one since, moving from orphanages to a hospital for the mentally retarded, where, he recalled, "We sat at a table all day with our arms folded. If you stood up, without raising your hand for permission, someone hit you." He later graduated to reformatories and eventually landed in prison.[125]

THROUGH THE MIST

PASSING over the rolling hills of remote countryside in autumn twilight, a visitor suddenly comes upon a huge and forbidding form in the mist. Anchored to the land like some medieval fortress, with rolls of gleaming razor wire serving as its moat, and tall watchtowers punctuating the massive stone wall, it sits in a glare of white light and invisible all-seeing electronic sensors, behind warning signs and checkpoints and danger zones—a sight apt to produce in the imagination powerful instinctive feelings of wonder, fear, and abhorrence, if only because it is so awesome, so off-limits, so impenetrable and inscrutable.

Society has gone to extreme lengths to mystify prison, as if to empower the institution by obscuring its inner workings. This mystification serves to absolve society of responsibility, while conferring legitimacy and morality on the prison itself. An aura of secrecy lends mystery and idealization. For, indeed, few human inventions have become so charged with symbolic meaning as the modern prison.

Prison walls protect society and its offenders from each other. They also conceal society's failures and deny its guilt. "We would hide our sins behind its walled towers and barred windows—conceal them from ourselves," Frank Tannenbaum wrote. But its "darkness and isolation only make the sins we would forget fester and grow, and return to stalk in our midst and plague us more painfully than ever."[126]

In reality, few images in today's America are so revealing of society's worst shortcomings. Prisons are museums of society's mistakes, which is one more reason why they are generally kept closed to the public eye. They also serve as cold storage, wherein some of the most infamous offenders are preserved and identified like so many exhibits of state's evidence— prisoners like Richard Speck, Charles Manson, Sirhan Sirhan, James Earl Ray, and Son of Sam, along with others who have outlived their notoriety—although, as everyone knows, most of those incarcerated are simply anonymous, nondescript losers.

We hide them from view, not so much because we are afraid of them, but because we don't want to be exposed to the pain and the harm we're causing; we don't want to have to witness the suffering imposed in our name. Such a reality might prove embarrassing or distasteful. Maybe even confront us with thorny questions or leave us with terrible doubts. Nobody cares to see other human beings defecating, sleeping, masturbating, and weeping in cages. To achieve their intended effect, prison horrors are better left to the imagination.

In the United States, perhaps we avoid looking into prisons very closely because they embody the antithesis of what the nation represents. As Beaumont and Tocqueville observed, "While society in the United States gives the example of the most extended liberty, the prisons of the same country offer the spectacle of the most complete despotism."[127] Actually, prisons were not the only spectacle of despotism in America, since Beaumont and Tocqueville neglected to include chattel slavery as well. Nor have prisons provided the only such spectacle in more recent times. In his sociological classic, *Asylums,* Erving Goffman coined the term "total institution" (short for totalitarian) to describe a variety of diverse closed institutions—mental hospitals, military barracks, leprosaria, cloisters, convents, and monasteries, among others—each of which he defined as "a place of residence and work where a large number of like-situated individuals, cut off from the wider world for an appreciable period of time, together lead an enclosed, formally administered round of life."[128] Prisons, of course, were and still are the most recognizable total institution in America, although many Americans would be reluctant to admit it.

And so, what goes on within prison walls stays hidden from view, to protect the government and to spare the citizens from knowing what is really being done in their name. The same walls, towers, locks, and security procedures that serve to keep the prisoners in also keep intruders out, just as they help to create the terror and mystique central to the prison's success. But they are not the only apparatus of secrecy at work there. The Fourth Estate—journalists representing newspapers, magazines, and broadcast media—have historically avoided covering prisons and jails, except during riots, and legal efforts to gain media access for prisoners (where they have been made at all) have usually been pursued by prisoners rather than the press. In 1978, following a rare challenge by a local television station that was seeking to report on local jail conditions, the United States Supreme Court validated the power of corrections officials to bar any and all journalists and the public from jails and prisons, regardless of institutional conditions.[129] Unfortunately, journalists have largely capitulated to corrections officials' near total control of media access to correctional institutions and the inmates and staff inside them.

Prison is reputed to be one of the least successful institutions in modern society, but the fact it has survived for so long, so intact, suggests otherwise. That it has been reproduced so widely indicates it has performed some important functions. This is not to say that imprisonment's functions have remained the same throughout history, or that they have stayed narrow or limited. On the contrary, as I have demonstrated, imprisonment has served many purposes in American society over the last 500 years, and its multifunctionality has contributed to its ubiquity. Prisons are chameleons that have adapted remarkably well to their changing environment. Unlike other dinosaurs, they appear immune to extinction.

Like its physical components—the rocks and iron and steel—the institution of imprisonment has proven remarkably durable. Over the centuries, some of its forms—most conspicuously, slavery—have largely fallen by the wayside, whereas others, such as the use of penal institutions for holding sentenced criminals, have become more dominant. Indentured servitude persisted for two centuries after its introduction for peopling the colonies. Impressment continued until after the Revolution, was ultimately contested as one of the stated causes of the War of 1812, and lived on until very recently in the modified form of military conscription. The institution of chattel slavery, which had disappeared and reappeared many times in human history before its introduction in the New World, persisted in some states well into the 1860s—a full 250 years after its inception there. Dungeons and other houses of darkness have also endured.

In recent decades, the most common stated goals or rationales of imprisonment have been retribution, incapacitation, deterrence, and reformation, although there has often been disagreement about which should prevail. A few writers have tried to take into account other social functions of prisons.[130] For example, some have pointed out that prisons have been

used to generate capital, furnish slave labor, provide many keepers' positions and ancillary jobs, help to reduce surplus labor, offer an outlet for
reformist needs, help to satisfy authoritarian needs, provide an outlet for
sadistic and masochistic needs, help protect dominant interests and the
status quo, assist in providing important birth control, make available a
social laboratory for purposes of "scientific" research, help to create and
maintain a chronic prisoner class, carry out politicization, and enhance the
self-concepts of some prisoners and others involved in the prison system.
In fact, virtually all of the leading prison historians and theorists have
argued that the modern prison survived and grew because it did more than
respond to crime.

David J. Rothman, a noted social historian, interpreted the rise of the
penitentiary in the Jacksonian era as an attempt to guard against the effects
of increasing social mobility.[131] Michael Ignatieff depicted imprisonment
as the pure form of an industrialist capitalist social order.[132] Michel Foucault, the French philosopher and social theorist, explored prison as in-
stitutionalizing a technology of power and demonstrating the proper
relationship between the individual and the state. In *Discipline and Punish*
he sought to examine prison's birth from the perspective of the body,
arguing that the growing use of imprisonment in place of corporal punishments that occurred following the Enlightenment reflected an important
change by which the direct infliction of pain was replaced by an increased
spiritualization of punishment, so that the soul replaced the body as the
primary target of punishment. Foucault has been one of the most influential writers about imprisonment during the last twenty years or so, and the
impact of his work has been so great that, as one scholar put it, "to write
today about punishment and classification without Foucault is like talking
about the unconscious without Freud."[133] Yet, the usefulness of his work
in explaining the origins and development of imprisonment in America
is rather limited, because he was a philosopher and social theorist, not a
historian, and his work is not historically based; it lacks historical specific-
ity in terms of the American experience of imprisonment.

A more recent study of American imprisonment that was both heavily
influenced by Foucault and based upon serious study of a piece of American history is Michael Meranze's *Laboratories of Virtue*, which links its
development to liberalism.[134] Some other notable works have examined
the rise of the penitentiary in the context of changes in the legal system.[135]
The preeminent cultural analysis of criminal punishment, conducted by
the criminologist David Garland, marshals a synthesis of various interpre-
tive perspectives to offer new insights into penology.[136] To be sure, cultural
considerations affect the ways we think about and respond to criminals.

This is one reason why prisons and imprisonment must be examined in their social context, not as separate, freestanding institutions.

If the economic basis of a society determines its social structure and the psychology of the people within it, then perhaps prison is a creature of economics as much as anything else. Writing on the eve of World War II, Georg Rusche and Otto Kirchheimer contended that fiscal motives shaped the typical punishments developed in modern society, arguing, "Every system of production tends to discover punishments which correspond to its productive relationships." For example, enslavement as a form of punishment arose within a slave economy; prison factories originated during the industrial revolution within an emerging manufacturing system.[137] Rusche and Kirchheimer's was a historically grounded study of western European punishment, focused on the period from the breakdown of feudalism to the rise of laissez-faire capitalism, although their theory is partly based on the development of imprisonment in the United States. They too attempted to show that the use of imprisonment was not a simple consequence of crime; they viewed penal institutions in interrelationship with other social institutions and nonpenal aspects of society. (In another work, Rusche went so far as to claim that "the history of the penal system is . . . the history of relations [between] the rich and the poor.")[138]

Prison still serves the economic system. And it serves it well. When all is said and done, imprisonment has faithfully generated capital, fostered economic development, reduced surplus labor, provided jobs and sometimes slave labor, and protected dominant interests. However, such a strictly economic analysis of imprisonment ignores other factors that have also proved important in its development. For above and beyond its economic utility, corporally and psychologically, imprisonment has also exerted population control, furnished an outlet for reformers, held promise as utopia and dystopia, acted as a potent vehicle of politicization, defined and dramatized evil, and maintained a chronic class of bad guys, a duality of keeper and kept.[139]

The complex psychological dimensions of the public response to crime and punishment have only begun to be explored. Writing in 1918, George Herbert Mead argued that the righteous indignation that society's members feel toward a criminal aggressor is really a cultural sublimation of the self-assertive instincts and destructive hostilities that lie behind human competition and cooperation.[140] According to Mead, hostility toward the criminal helps to promote group solidarity and love among citizens, and the release of aggressive impulses into punitive actions helps to give them their characteristic zeal and energy.

Contrary to some Marxist analysis, popular attitudes toward punish-

ment are by no means simple class-driven responses. In fact, as some writers have pointed out, the lower classes are often among the most vociferous
supporters of punitive policies, even though they themselves constitute
their primary targets or recipients. Writing just before World War II,
the Danish sociologist Svend Ranulf suggested that "the disinterested
tendency to inflict punishment is a distinctive characteristic of the lower
middle class, that is, of a social class living under conditions which force
its members to an extraordinary degree of self-restraint, and subject them
to much frustration of natural desires." He added that "moral indignation
(which is the emotion behind the disinterested tendency to inflict punishment) is a kind of disguised envy."[141]

Legislators, governors, social critics, and criminologists often express
opinions about what prisons should do or what they do or do not accomplish. By the middle of the twentieth century, imprisonment had become
a rather shameful activity, undertaken by professionals and bureaucrats
outside the public gaze. But there is surprisingly little consensus about the
proper aims or even the actual functions of imprisonment.

Today prison is not intended to transform, reform, or rehabilitate
people. If that occurs at all, it is a coincidence, not a primary objective.
There is no longer any pretense that prison makes anyone better; in fact,
most persons tend to assume it will probably make them worse—more
hardened, more embittered, more disabled, and better schooled in the
ways of crime.[142]

Prison is used to get some people out of circulation, off the streets, at
least for a while, for a period of a few years when they otherwise might do
more damage, though the trend is to keep them off the streets for as long
as possible, which increasingly means for the rest of their natural lives. The
number of persons being executed in prisons is also increasing.

Despite what has often been intense debate over the appropriate aims
of imprisonment, the institution we presently think of as prison has gone
relatively unchallenged to the present day. As Norval Morris put it: "Prisons have few friends; dissatisfaction with them is widespread. . . . Nevertheless, prisons have other purposes . . . which assure their continued
survival."[143] In short, as Nathaniel Hawthorne suggested, prison is the
black flower of civilization—a durable weed that refuses to die. Its history
is part of us. Five hundred years later, and it is still growing, spreading out
further into the countryside, fastening its roots deeper into the soil.

For those who subscribe to Dostoyevsky's principle that "the standards
of a nation's civilization can be judged by opening the doors of its prisons,"
or who agree with Winston Churchill's observation that "the mood and
temper of the public in regard to the treatment of crime and criminals is

one of the most unfailing tests of the civilization of any country," the present condition of criminal punishment in the United States would seem to reveal enormously deep-seated, vexing, and troubled conditions within American society.[144] And prison itself is both a source and a response to problems. Even if it were to somehow suddenly end tomorrow, its impact would surely continue to be felt for generations. Until that happens, good people would be wise to fear prisons more while seeking to stem their insidious growth. He who fights monsters should beware that he does not create one or become one.

NOTES

PREFACE

1. Paul L. Montgomery, "Upstate Prison Goes from Crisis to Crisis," *New York Times*, March 4, 1973.

2. See Bruce Jackson, *Wake Up, Dead Man: Afro-American Worksongs from Texas Prisons* (Cambridge, Mass., 1972).

3. For two exceptions, see Thorsten Sellin, *Slavery and the Penal System* (New York, 1976), and Michael Stephen Hindus, *Prison and Plantation: Crime, Justice, and Authority in Massachusetts and South Carolina, 1767–1878* (Chapel Hill, 1980).

4. David Brion Davis, "The Crime of Reform," *New York Review of Books* 27 (June 26, 1980), 14.

5. For an important study of the prison writings of some of these former inmates, see H. Bruce Franklin, *The Victim as Criminal and Artist: Literature from the American Prison* (New York, 1978).

CHAPTER ONE   *The Rise of the Prisoner Trade*

1. The etymology of the term "Indian" can be found in Winthrop D. Jordan, *White over Black: American Attitudes toward the Negro, 1550–1812* (Chapel Hill, 1968), 95.

2. Samuel Eliot Morison, *The European Discovery of America: The Northern Voyages, A.D. 500–1600* (New York, 1971), 66.

3. Eric Williams, *From Columbus to Castro: The History of the Caribbean* (New York, 1984), 33.

4. Morison, *The European Discovery of America*, 66.

5. Williams, *From Columbus to Castro*, 31.

6. Morison, *The European Discovery of America*, 67.

7. Daniel J. Boorstin, *The Discoverers* (New York, 1983), 233–34.

8. Spanish law, including the thirteenth-century code of Las Siete Partidas, already had recognized slavery for centuries before the time of Columbus. Williams, *From Columbus to Castro*, 30.

9. Morison, *The European Discovery of America*, 95–96; Alfred W. Crosby, *The Columbian Exchange: Biological and Cultural Consequences of 1492* (Greenwich, Conn., 1972).

10. Morison, *The European Discovery of America*, 99.

11. Williams, *From Columbus to Castro*, 31.

12. Walter H. Blumenthal, *Brides from the Bridewell: Female Felons Sent to Colonial America* (Rutland, Vt., 1962), 117–18.

13. Williams, *From Columbus to Castro*, 37–38.

14. Ibid., 31-32.

15. Christopher Columbus, narrative of 3rd voyage, in Cecil Jane, ed., *The Four Voyages of Columbus* (New York, 1988), 64; Morison, *The European Discovery of America*, 158-59.

16. Boorstin, *The Discoverers*, 224.

17. Ogden Nash, *The Face Is Familiar* (Boston, 1940), 209.

18. Morison, *The European Discovery of America*, 292.

19. Boorstin, *The Discoverers*, 244.

20. Williams, *From Columbus to Castro*, 33.

21. Boorstin, *The Discoverers*, 631.

22. Williams, *From Columbus to Castro*, 37.

23. Ibid., 42.

24. Ibid., 43.

25. Ibid., 44.

26. Ibid.

27. Blumenthal, *Brides from the Bridewell*, 118.

28. Williams, *From Columbus to Castro*, 97; Richard B. Morris, *Encyclopedia of American History* (New York, 1953), 24.

29. Francis Bacon, "Of Plantations," *Essays* (Everyman Edition), 104.

30. Susan M. Kingsbury, ed., *The Records of the Virginia Company of London* (Washington, 1906); Charles M. Andrews, *The Colonial Period in American History* (New Haven, 1934-38), vol. 1, describes the corporate approach to colonialism. A partial list of the first planters, containing eighty-two names, is found in Captain John Smith, *The Generall Historie of Virginia* (London, 1624), 43-44.

31. The earliest published account of Smith's life is contained in *A True Relation of such occurrences and accidents of noate as hath happened in Virginia since the first planting of that Colony, which is now resident in the South part thereof, till the last returne from thence* (London, 1608). Written by "a Gentleman of the said Collony, to a worshipfull friend of his in England," its authorship was publicly attributed to Smith in 1615. The adventurer's experiences are also recounted in a useful collection of primary source documents — *Travels and Works of Captain John Smith, President of Virginia and Admiral of New England, 1580-1631*, 2 vols., ed. Edward Arber (Edinburgh, 1910) — as well as in numerous biographies, e.g., Philip L. Barbour, *The Three Worlds of Captain John Smith* (Boston, 1964).

32. Alden T. Vaughn, *American Genesis: Captain John Smith and the Founding of Virginia* (Boston, 1975), 30, 32.

33. Smith's accounts are examined in Barbour, *Three Worlds*, 158-70; see also John Seelye, *Prophetic Waters: The River in Early American Life and Literature* (New York, 1977), 281.

34. Her abductor, Captain Samuel Argall, described the snatching in a letter to Nicholas Hawes, dated June 1613, quoted in Conway Whittle Sams, *The Conquest of Virginia: The Third Attempt, 1610-1624* (Spartanburg, S.C., 1973), 195-96. See also Philip L. Barbour, *Pocahontas and Her World* (Boston, 1969).

35. John Curtis Ballagh, *White Servitude in the Colony of Virginia: A Study of the System of Indentured Labor in the American Colonies* (New York, 1969), 23-24.

36. One scholar has compared the colony to a modern-day prison or concentration camp. Karen Ordahl Kupperman, "Apathy and Death in Early Jamestown," *Journal of American History* 66 (June 1979): 24-40.

37. *Minutes of the Council and General Court of Virginia, 1622-1632, 1670-1676, with Notes and Excerpts from Original Council and General Court Records, into 1683, Now Lost*, ed. H. R. McIlwaine (Richmond, 1924), 14.

38. Vaughn, *American Genesis*, 79.

39. Ralph Hamor, quoted ibid., 79-80.

40. Morison, *The European Discovery of America*, 72-73.

41. Edmund Gardiner, *Triall of Tobacco* (London, 1610).

42. Carl Bridenbaugh, *Vexed and Troubled Englishmen, 1590–1642* (New York, 1976), 195.

43. Hugh Jones, *The Present State of Virginia from Whence Is Inferred a Short View of Maryland and North Carolina* [1724], ed. Richard L. Morton (Chapel Hill, 1956), 197, 198.

44. John Pory, quoted in George F. Willison, *Behold Virginia: The Fifth Crown* (New York, 1952), 192.

45. Charles M. Andrews, *The Colonial Period in American History*, vol. 1 (New Haven, 1934), 134. Clifford Dowdey, *The Great Plantation: A Profile of Berkeley Hundred and Plantation Virginia from Jamestown to Appomattox* (New York, 1957), 23, notes that the mortality rate in Jamestown's early years ran as high as 80 percent.

46. Sandys' campaign is described in Bridenbaugh, *Vexed and Troubled Englishmen*, chap. 11.

47. *A True Discourse of the Present Estate of Virginia* (London, 1616), quoted in Philip Alexander Bruce, *Institutional History of Virginia in the Seventeenth Century* (New York, 1910), 4–5.

48. *Virginia Company Records*, vol. 1, 75, 425. As early as 1582 Sir Humphrey Gilbert had provided that every gentleman bringing five or more men to the colony at his own charge would receive a grant of acreage. Abbot Emerson Smith, *Colonists in Bondage: White Servitude and Convict Labor in America, 1607–1776* (Chapel Hill, 1947), 340, n. 18.

49. Andrews, *Colonial Period in American History*, vol. 1, 125–26.

50. *American History Told by Contemporaries*, ed. Albert Bushnell Hart (New York, 1897), vol. 1, 152–57.

51. J. C. Ribton-Turner, *A History of Vagrants and Vagrancy and Beggars and Begging* (London, 1887); Arthur V. Judges, ed., *The Elizabethan Underworld* (New York, 1930); Caleb E. Foote, "Vagrancy-Type Law and Its Administration," *University of Pennsylvania Law Review* 104 (March 1956): 603–50. An early experiment in mandating penal slavery for vagrancy is examined in C. S. L. Davies, "Slavery and the Protector Somerset: The Vagrancy Act of 1547," *Economic History Review*, 2d ser., 19 (1966): 533–49.

52. George Ives, *A History of Penal Methods* (London, 1914), 97–100; John Lewis Gillin, *Criminology and Penology* (New York, 1945), 361.

53. Statement of 1609, quoted in Richard B. Morris, *Government and Labor in Early America* (New York, 1946), 323.

54. Thomas Dale to Lord Salisbury, quoted in *Massachusetts Historical Collections*, vol. 9, 2, 1–4.

55. Quoted in Douglas Campbell, *The Puritan in Holland, England, and America* (New York, 1892), vol. 2, 191n.

56. Smith, *Colonists in Bondage*, 92–93.

57. Andrews, *Colonial Period in American History*, vol. 1, 62n.

58. James Davie Butler, "British Convicts Shipped to American Colonies," *American Historical Review* 2 (1896): 17.

59. Kingsbury, *Records of the Virginia Company*, vol. 1, 256.

60. Ibid., 566.

61. Letter from the Virginia Company in London to the governor and council in Virginia, August 12, 1621, in *Virginia Company Records*, vol. 3, 493–94. H. R. McIlwaine, "The Maids Who Came to Virginia in 1620 and 1621 for Husbands," *The Reviewer* 1 (April 1, 1921): 109–10.

62. Bridenbaugh, *Vexed and Troubled Englishmen*, 419.

63. James I to Sir Thomas Smythe (soon to be governor of the Virginia Company), quoted in Andrews, *Colonial Period in American History*, vol. 1, 135n.

64. Kingsbury, *Records of the Virginia Company*, vol. 1, 270–71.

65. Sandys to Sir Robert Naughton, principal secretary of James I, January 28, 1620, in *Virginia Company Records*, vol. 3, 1933, 259.

66. Great Britain, Privy Council, *Acts of the Privy Council of England, 1619–1621* (London, 1930), 118.

67. Ibid.

68. Smith, *Colonists in Bondage,* 149.

69. John Donne, "Sermon CLVI, Preached to the Virginia Company, 1622," in *Works, 1621–1631,* ed. Henry Alford (London, 1839), vol. 6, 232–33.

70. *The Shorter Oxford English Dictionary on Historical Principles,* s.v. "Kidnapping." See also Smith, *Colonists in Bondage,* 67–68.

71. Jordan, *White over Black,* 73.

72. Wesley Frank Craven, "Twenty Negroes to Jamestown in 1619?" *Virginia Quarterly Review* 47 (Summer 1971): 416–20.

73. Elizabeth Donnan, ed., *Documents Illustrative of the History of the Slave Trade to America* (Washington, 1930–35), vol. 1, 78–79.

74. Adam Smith, *An Inquiry Into the Nature and Causes of the Wealth of Nations,* ed. C. J. Bullock (New York, 1937), chap. 7, "Of Colonies." See also J. Thorsten Sellin, *Slavery and the Penal System* (New York, 1976); William L. Westermann, *The Slave Systems of Greek and Roman Antiquity* (Philadelphia, 1955).

75. Oscar Handlin, *The Uprooted* (New York, 1951), 3: "the immigrants *were* American history."

76. Bridenbaugh, *Vexed and Troubled Englishmen,* 423. One nineteenth-century historian found that a servant might be transported at a cost of from six to eight pounds and sold for between forty and fifty pounds. James Curtis Ballagh, *White Servitude in the Colony of Virginia: A Study of the System of Indentured Labor in the American Colonies* (Baltimore, 1895), 41. Abbot Emerson Smith surmised that the use of professional agents to recruit servants for the colonies probably started before 1620, when the proprietors of Virginia's Berkeley Hundred hired a man for that purpose. Smith also noted that the Providence Company had begun to use an agent by 1633. Abbot Emerson Smith, "Indentured Servants: New Light on Some of America's 'First Families,'" *Journal of Economic History* 2 (1942): 41.

77. William Bullock, *Virginia Impartially Examined* (London, 1649), 14.

78. "Memorial of the Lord Mayor and Court Aldermen, London, to the Privy Council," c. 1638, Public Record Office, State Papers 16/408, no. 117.

79. See Saunders Welch, *Observations on the Office of Constable with Cautions for the more Safe Execution of that Duty, etc.* (London, 1754); C. H. Karraker, *The Seventeenth-Century Sheriff: A Comparative Study of the Sheriff in England and the Chesapeake Colonies, 1607–1689* (Chapel Hill, 1930), xlii, xliv. See also Gamini Salgado, *The Elizabethan Underworld* (Totawa, N.J., 1977), 165.

80. Abbot Emerson Smith contended that "the kidnappers and spirits instead of being deplorable outlaws in the servant trade were the faithful and indispensable adjuncts of its most respected merchants." Smith, *Colonists in Bondage,* 77.

81. Antonia Fraser, *Cromwell: The Lord Protector* (New York, 1973), 327; John W. Blake, "Transportation from Ireland to America, 1653–60," *Irish Historical Studies* 3, no. 11 (1943): 267.

82. Fraser, *Cromwell,* 524.

83. *Calendar of State Papers, Domestic,* 1650, 421, 423, 438; Charles E. Banks, in Massachusetts Historical Society, *Proceedings,* 61 (1928), 4–29; Smith, *Colonists in Bondage,* 154, 157.

84. Blake, "Transportation from Ireland to America," 278.

85. Donnan, *Documents Illustrative,* vol. 1, 276, 331, 415.

86. Blake, "Transportation from Ireland to America," 280; Donnan, *Documents Illustrative,* vol. 1, 121, 180, 392, 393n., 394, 183, 257. His brother, Sir Jeffrey Jeffries, also had extensive interests in the African slave trade.

87. Oglethorpe was a director of the Royal African Company in 1731 and deputy gover-

nor and member of the finance committee in 1732. Donnan, *Documents Illustrative*, vol. 2, 403, 404n., 415, 416, 419, 423–25, 455n., 419n.

88. Basil Sollers, "Transported Convict Laborers in Maryland during the Colonial Period," *Maryland Historical Magazine* 2 (1907): 24; Donnan, *Documents Illustrative*, vol. 2, 23n., vol. 4, 59n., 60, 88.

89. Smith, *Colonists in Bondage*, 74–75.

90. St. Katherine's, the district east of the Tower of London, lay close to the Thames River and was "well supplied with obscure places of detention." Smith, "Indentured Servants," 45.

91. Leo F. Stock, ed., *Proceedings and Debates of the British Parliaments Respecting North America, 1542–1739* (Washington, 1924), vol. 1, 302–4; Ballagh, *White Servitude*, 39; Smith, "Indentured Servants," 51–52; Ives, *A History of Penal Methods*, 117–18.

92. Morgan Godwyn, *The Negro's and Indian's Advocate* (London, 1680), 171. Abbot Emerson Smith held that the figure was "absurdly large," saying it "can only have been given for purposes of propaganda." Smith, *Colonists in Bondage*, 84. However, he does not indicate what number is realistic.

93. The best study of this development is Jordan, *White over Black*.

94. James Pope-Hennessy, *Sins of the Fathers: A Study of the Atlantic Slave Traders, 1441–1807* (New York, 1968), 78. See also Thomas Phillips, *A Journal of a Voyage Made in the Hannibal . . .* [London, 1704], in Donnan, *Documents Illustrative*, vol. 1, 392–413.

95. John Barbor, *A Description of the Coasts of North and Guinea . . .*, translated from the French by the author (Paris, 1732), in Donnan, *Documents Illustrative*, vol. 1, 293–94.

96. These castles were later described, with photographs, in Pope-Hennessy, *Sins of the Fathers*.

97. Phillips, *Journal of a Voyage*, 396.

98. Ralph B. Pugh, *Imprisonment in Medieval England* (London, 1968); Anthony Babington, *The English Bastille: A History of Newgate Gaol and Prison Conditions in Britain, 1188–1902* (New York, 1971).

99. Babington, *The English Bastille*, 71; W. J. Sheehan, "Finding Solace in Eighteenth-Century Newgate," in *Crime in England, 1550–1800*, ed. J. S. Cockburn (Princeton, 1977), 229–45.

100. Christopher Hibbert, *The Roots of Evil: A Social History of Crime and Punishment* (Boston, 1963), 133.

101. Carl Bridenbaugh, *Cities in the Wilderness* (New York, 1938), 75.

102. Ibid.

103. Bullock, *Virginia Impartially Examined*, 47.

104. J. R. Hutchinson, *The Press-Gang, Afloat and Ashore* (New York, 1913), esp. chap. 11. Alleged corruption of these gangs is mentioned in Sir Leon Radzinowicz, *A History of English Criminal Law and Its Administration from 1750* (London, 1968), vol. 4, 82. The operation of the impressment system was also tied to the rest of the prisoner trade, and it involved many of the same individuals, corporations, and vessels. In 1696 the sole power of impressment was given to the governors of the plantations. See *Calendar of State Papers, Colonial: America and West Indies* (Rolls Series, London, 1860), No. 1207, 568 (1697).

105. *The English Rogue: Described in the Life of Meriton Latroon . . .* (London, 1665), pt. 1, 158–60.

106. *The London Spy* (1704 ed.), 54–55, cited in Smith, *Colonists in Bondage*, 60, 351 n. 37.

107. Jonathan Wild (1682?–1725) is the subject of a large body of literature, including Henry Fielding's novel *The History of the Life of the Late Mr. Jonathan Wild and a Journey from this World to the Next, etc.* (London, 1743), Daniel Defoe's *Memoirs of the Life and Times of the Famous Jonathan Wild* (London, 1725), and Christopher Hibbert's *Road to Tyburn: The Story of Jack Sheppard and the Eighteenth-Century London Underworld* (Cleveland, 1957). The best-known early professional criminal, he invented the organized

fencing of stolen goods. Wild was eventually hanged for his crimes. His career apparently began after he was jailed for debt at the Wood Street Prison. Here he came into contact with members of the London underworld, including Mary Milliner, with whom he later opened a brothel. Wild began trafficking in stolen goods and paid his suppliers a commission for their proceeds; he also sold back some of the goods to the victims in return for a fee. He opened offices for the recovery of "lost property" and even set up a business office at the Old Bailey and advertised his wares in the local newspapers. He also "became the leading spirit and head of a large corporation of thieves, whom he organized into gangs, to each of which was allotted a special sphere of work." *Dictionary of National Biography* (Oxford, 1917), vol. 21, 222.

108. Daniel Defoe, *The History and Remarkable Life of the Truly Honourable Col. Jaque, Commonly Called Col. Jack . . .* (Oxford, 1965), 12.

109. This account of Fox's early years and of early Quaker beliefs is based upon *The Journal of George Fox*, rev. ed., ed. John L. Nickalls (Cambridge, U.K., 1952). Other sources consulted include Hugh Barbour, *The Quakers in Puritan England* (New Haven, 1964); John Sykes, *The Quakers: A New Look at Their Place in Society* (Philadelphia, 1959); A. Neave Brayshaw, *The Personality of George Fox* (London, 1933); Samuel M. Janney, *The Life of William Penn* (Philadelphia, 1852); William C. Braithwaite, *The Beginnings of Quakerism* (London, 1923); Henry Van Etten, *George Fox and the Quakers* (New York, 1959); Elbert Russell, *The History of Quakerism* (New York, 1942); and Howard Brinton, *Friends for 300 Years: The History and Beliefs of the Society of Friends since George Fox Started the Quaker Movement* (New York, 1952).

110. Elfrida Vipont, *George Fox and the Valiant Sixty* (London, 1975).

111. Francis Higginson, *A Brief Relation of the Irreligion of the Northern Quakers* (London, 1653), 11–14.

112. Ibid., 175; Sykes, *The Quakers*, 125.

113. Letter dated January 1, 1656, quoted in Sykes, *The Quakers*, 148.

114. Dewsbury, 1689, quoted in D. Elton Trueblood, *The People Called Quakers* (New York, 1966), 13. One of Fox's top preachers, William Dewsbury was of humble origin and had served in Cromwell's army.

115. Isaac Sharpless, *A History of Quaker Government in Pennsylvania*, vol. 1, *A Quaker Experiment in Government* (Philadelphia, 1898), i, n. 18.

116. *The Short Journal of George Fox*, ed. Norman Penney (Cambridge, U.K., 1925), was compiled during his captivity at Lancaster in 1664. *The Journal of George Fox*, 2 vols., ed. Norman Penney (Cambridge, U.K., 1911), covering the period 1650–75, appears to have been started during his confinement at Worcester between 1675 and 1677.

117. E. P. Thompson, *Whigs and Hunters: The Origin of the Black Act* (London, 1975).

118. 9 Geo. 1, c. 22 (1723).

119. The hanging atmosphere is described in Peter Linebaugh, "The Tyburn Riot against the Surgeons," in Douglas Hay et al., *Albion's Fatal Tree: Crime and Society in Eighteenth-Century England* (London, 1975), 66–67, 71, 79; Graeme R. Newman, *The Punishment Response* (Philadelphia, 1978), 128–30; Babington, *The English Bastille*, 32–33.

120. Bernard de Mandeville, *An Enquiry into the Causes of the Frequent Executions at Tyburn* (London, 1725), 20–22.

121. Gerald D. Robin, "The Executioner: His Place in English Society," *British Journal of Sociology* 15 (1964): 234–53.

122. Arthur L. Cross, "The English Criminal Law and Benefit of Clergy during the Eighteenth and Early Nineteenth Centuries," *American Historical Review* 22 (1917): 544–65; Smith, *Colonists in Bondage*, 90.

123. J. M. Beattie, "Crime and Courts in Surrey, 1736–1753," in Cockburn, *Crime in England, 1550–1800*, 158; Babington, *The English Bastille*, 28–29.

124. Smith, *Colonists in Bondage*, 91.

125. Radzinowicz, *History of English Criminal Law*, vol. 4, 151, 157; Newman, *The*

Punishment Response, chap. 7; Douglas Hay, "Property, Authority, and the Criminal Law," in Hay et al., *Albion's Fatal Tree,* 22–23.

126. Hay, *Albion's Fatal Tree,* 22n.

127. Daniel Defoe, *The Fortunes of the Famous Moll Flanders . . .* [London, 1722] (New York, 1949), 318. See Robert Singleton, "Defoe, Moll Flanders, and the Ordinary of Newgate," *Harvard Library Bulletin* 24 (October 1976): 407–13.

128. The convict trade was also profitable for sheriffs, contractors, and others engaged in the trafficking of prisoners. See Richard B. Morris, *Government and Labor in Early America* (New York, 1946), 336. It was not a new idea: as early as the 8th century B.C., an Ethiopian king named Sabbacus had abolished the death penalty in favor of penal slavery in chains on public works. Sellin, *Slavery and the Penal System,* 18. Transportation of troublemakers out of the country also could have political advantages. After the Mar and Derwent uprisings in 1716, for instance, the King ordered two shiploads of Jacobites deported to Maryland and sold. Butler, "British Convicts Shipped," 15.

129. 4 Geo. 1, c. 11 (1717).

130. *Calendar of Treasury Papers, 1557–1728,* ed. H. Redington (London, 1868–89), 1714–19, 389; Smith, *Colonists in Bondage,* 113, 362 n. 6. In 1710 Forward was also listed as a creditor of the Royal African Company. Donnan, *Documents Illustrative,* vol. 2, 126.

131. *Historical Register* (London, 1718), vol. 2, 19; Butler, "British Convicts Shipped," 24.

132. Butler, "British Convicts Shipped." Similar notices in the *Historical Register* indicate that at least 2,138 convicts were transported to America in this manner during the first ten years of the new law, 1718–27. Ibid., 25.

133. Donnan, *Documents Illustrative,* vol. 2, 226, 74.

134. *Calendar of Treasury Books and Papers, 1739–1741,* ed. W. A. Shaw (London, 1857–1903), 18, 20 (regarding Forward's replacement); Smith, *Colonists in Bondage,* 114–15 (Reid and Stewart); Wilfrid Oldham, "The Administration of the System of Transportation of British Convicts, 1763–1793" (Ph.D. thesis, University of London, 1933), 78–80 (Duncan Campbell).

135. A. Roger Ekirch, *Bound for America: The Transportation of British Convicts to the Colonies, 1718–1775* (Oxford, 1987), 86.

136. Blumenthal, *Brides from the Bridewell,* 80–81. Through his many companies, Law also vied with the British for control of the African slave trade. Donnan, *Documents Illustrative,* vol. 2, xxiii, 248n., 249, 334n., 393n.

137. Ekirch, *Bound for America,* 21–22.

138. Amos A. Ettinger, *James Edward Oglethorpe, Imperial Idealist* (New York, 1936); John Pudney, *John Wesley and His World* (New York, 1978), 40–41; Donnan, *Documents Illustrative,* vol. 2, 403, 404n., 415, 416, 419, 423–25, 455n., 419n.; Richard Beale Davis, *Intellectual Life in the Colonial South, 1585–1763* (Knoxville, Tenn., 1978), vol. 1, 61. However, Daniel J. Boorstin has disagreed with the prevailing opinion that Oglethorpe was an imperialist exploiter of prisoners, saying, "It would be hard to find another venture of 18th-century colonizing and empire-building whose leaders were more disinterested or more free of sordid motives." In his estimation, "Very few, perhaps not over a dozen, imprisoned debtors were brought to Georgia," and those were handpicked. Daniel J. Boorstin, *The Americans: The Colonial Experience* (New York, 1958), 75, 79.

139. Smith, *Colonists in Bondage,* 398–99, 117, 118, 119, 134, 364.

140. Ekirch, *Bound for America,* 27.

141. An estimate of 50,000 was offered by John Fiske, *Old Virginia and Her Neighbours,* 2 vols. (Boston, 1897), 183, and Morris, *Government and Labor,* 326. Butler calculated that not less than 10,000 were sent from the Old Bailey alone between 1717 and 1775. Butler, "British Convicts Shipped," 25. Basil Sollers estimated that at least 4,704 were sent from Newgate and the Home Counties between 1729 and 1745, of which 1,236 went to "Maryland," 1,281 to "Virginia," 899 to "Maryland or Virginia," and 1,288 to "America."

Basil Sollers, "Transported Convict Laborers in Maryland during the Colonial Period," *Maryland Historical Magazine* 2 (1907): 43. The accounts of the Old Bailey alone fill 100 volumes in London. Its Session Papers are also available for the period January 1753 through 1831 at the University of Chicago Law Library. These proceedings make fascinating reading, and they have yet to be subjected to systematic analysis by anyone interested in pursuing the shipment of British convicts to America. Professor John H. Langbein of the University of Chicago has used them well for his study "The Criminal Trial before the Lawyers," *University of Chicago Law Review* 45, no. 2 (Winter 1978): 263-316, as well as for an excursion into the link between "Torture and Plea Bargaining," *University of Chicago Law Review* 46, no. 1 (Fall 1978): 3-22. Unfortunately, my own time in the collection was limited to two days. In addition, each Assizes keeps its own records of court indictments and depositions. These are distributed between nine circuits, London records being kept in the Guildhall. In Oxford's circuit, for example, the depositions in criminal cases for the period 1719-1936 are contained in 71 Bundles. These are available in the Public Records Office and require about a week to review. Other useful sources concerning British transportation to America include the first chapter of A. G. L. Shaw's *Convicts and the Colonies* (London, 1966), which is well documented, and Peter Coldham's list of convict names in his edited volume, *English Convicts in Colonial America* (New Orleans, 1974). The *Gentleman's Magazine* started publishing regular notices of the court proceedings on March 9, 1731, and continued them until the eve of the American Revolution. Occasional notices also appeared in the *London Magazine*.

142. Ekirch, *Bound for America*, 77.

143. Cesare Beccaria, *On Crimes and Punishments*, trans. Henry Paolucci [1764] (Indianapolis, 1963).

144. See Marcello T. Maestro, *Cesare Beccaria and the Origins of Penal Reform* (Philadelphia, 1973); Marcello T. Maestro, *Voltaire and Beccaria as Reformers of Criminal Law* (New York, 1942); Elio Monachesi, "Cesare Beccaria," in *Pioneers in Criminology*, 2nd ed., ed. Herman Mannheim (Montclair, N.J., 1972), 36-50.

145. Smith, *Colonists in Bondage*, 124.

146. Bernard Bailyn, *Voyagers to the West: A Passage in the Peopling of America on the Eve of the Revolution* (New York, 1987), 292-93.

147. According to a correspondent of George Selwyn, in Sollers, "Transported Convict Laborers," 41n.

148. Olaudah Equiano, *The Interesting Narrative of the Life of Olaudah Equiano, or Gustavus Vassa, the African* [London, 1789], in Arna Bontemps, ed., *Great Slave Narratives* (Boston, 1969), 27.

149. The use of nets is mentioned by Equiano, *Interesting Narrative*, 31, and in many other accounts of the slave trade. See, e.g., the comments of Dr. Alexander Falconbridge, in John R. Spear, *The American Slave-Trade: An Account of Its Origin, Growth, and Suppression* (New York, 1900), 77.

150. Equiano, *Interesting Narrative*, 38.

151. Most eighteenth-century slave ships had two decks. The space between them was called the upper hold, or " 'tween decks," and it was usually there that the slaves were kept. Spear, *The American Slave-Trade*, 68-69.

152. John Newton, in Pope-Hennessy, *Sins of the Fathers*, 100.

153. Ibid., 101.

154. See, e.g., A. B. Ellis, *The Tshi-speaking Peoples of the Gold Coast of West Africa* (London, 1887), *The Ewe-speaking Peoples of the Slave Coast of West Africa* (London, 1890), and *The Yoruba-speaking Peoples of the Slave Coast of West Africa* (London, 1894); C. K. Meek, *A Sudanese Kingdom: An Ethnographic Study of the Jukun-speaking Peoples of Nigeria* (London, 1931).

155. Pope-Hennessy, *Sins of the Fathers*, 4; Nathan Irvin Huggins, *Black Odyssey: The Afro-American Ordeal in Slavery* (New York, 1977), 39.

156. An estimated one-quarter of the crews engaged in the African slave trade perished from disease, beatings, and other hardships, according to one early study of maritime records. Thomas Clarkson, *An Essay on the Slavery and Commerce of the Human Species, Particularly the African, Translated from a Latin Dissertation, which was Honoured with the first Prize in the University of Cambridge, for the Year 1785, with Additions* (Philadelphia, 1786), 53.

157. Equiano, *Interesting Narrative*, 29.

158. Phillips, *Journal of a Voyage*, in Donnan, *Documents Illustrative*, vol. 1, 406.

159. John Barbot, *A Description of the Coasts of North and South Guinea . . .*, trans. from the French by the author [Paris, 1732], in Donnan, *Documents Illustrative*, vol. 1, 289–90.

160. Phillips, *Journal of a Voyage*, in Pope-Hennessy, *Sins of the Fathers*, 99.

161. Phillips, *Journal of a Voyage*, in Donnan, *Documents Illustrative*, vol. 1, 407–8.

162. Phillips, *Journal of a Voyage*, in Pope-Hennessy, *Sins of the Fathers*, 99. Another standard precaution was meticulous searches of every corner of the ship for hidden weapons—an early shakedown.

163. Ibid., 100.

164. Huggins observed that the absence of race consciousness among Africans also made success improbable. Even if he reached the African shore, a black escapee might face recapture and resale. Huggins, *Black Odyssey*, 44–47. See also Darold D. Wax, "Negro Resistance in the Early American Slave Trade," *Journal of Negro History* 51 (1966): 1–15. For some contemporary accounts of slave mutinies, see the *Boston News-Letter*, September 25, 1729, and *South Carolina Gazette*, January 15, 1732, November 18, 1732, February 10, 1733, June 9, 1733, and July 14, 1733.

165. Philip D. Curtin, *The Atlantic Slave Trade: A Census* (Madison, Wis., 1969), 87.

166. Ibid., 277.

167. Phillips, *Journal of a Voyage*, in Donnan, *Documents Illustrative*, vol. 1, 410.

168. A mortality rate of over 50 percent was not unusual on the so-called White Guineamen. Morris, *Government and Labor*, 321. Daniel P. Mannix and Malcolm Cowley, *Black Cargoes: A History of the Atlantic Slave Trade, 1518–1865* (New York, 1962), 57–58. Abbot Emerson Smith estimated that smallpox and typhus carried off at least 15 percent of the convict passengers. Smith, *Colonists in Bondage*, 116. The vessel that took the Quaker William Penn to America in 1682 lost 30 of 100 passengers to smallpox alone. Francis R. Packard, *A History of Medicine in the United States* (New York, 1931), vol. 1, 62. A ship sailing from Ireland to Philadelphia in 1729 lost 100 of 190 crew and passengers to starvation. *Boston Weekly News-Letter*, October 30–November 6, 1729. In 1741 the sloop *Sea-Flower* left Belfast with 106 passengers; 46 died of starvation. "Records of Board of Selectmen, 1736–1742," *Report of the Record Commissioners of Boston* (Boston, 1876–1909), vol. 15, 317–30. On his voyage, Gottlieb Mittelberger counted no less than 32 dead children who were thrown into the sea. Gottlieb Mittelberger, *Gottlieb Mittelberger's Journey to Pennsylvania in the Year 1750 and Return to Germany in the Year 1754 . . .*, trans. Carl T. Eben (Philadelphia, 1898), 23. See John Duffy, "The Passage to the Colonies," *Mississippi Historical Review* 38 (1951): 21–38.

169. Blumenthal, *Brides from the Bridewell*, 23; Ekirch, *Bound for America*, 108.

170. Ekirch, *Bound for America*, 97, 104.

171. Ibid., 101–2.

172. *Virginia Gazette*, May 22–29, 1746. Smith, *Colonists in Bondage*, 128.

173. Stock, *Proceedings and Debates*, vol. 1, 249.

174. Mittelberger, *Gottlieb Mittelberger's Journey to Pennsylvania*, 19.

175. Durand de Dauphine, *Voyages of a Frenchman exiled for his Religion with a description of Virginia and Maryland in America*, trans. Gilbert Chinard [orig. pub. 1687] (New York, 1934), 95.

176. Mittelberger, *Gottlieb Mittelberger's Journey to Pennsylvania*, 20–21.

177. Quoted in Bailyn, *Voyagers to the West*, 326; [James Revel], *A Sorrowful Account of a Transported Felon, that Suffered Fourteen Years Transportation at Virginia, in America. In Six Parts. Being, a Short History of James Revel, an Unhappy Sufferer* (manuscript in Library of Congress, Ac. 2780). See John Melville Jennings, "Bibliographical Notes: 'The Poor Unhappy Transported Felon's Sorrowful Account of His Fourteen Years Transportation at Virginia in America,'" *Virginia Historical Magazine* 56 (1948): 181–94.

178. Vernon L. Parrington, *Main Currents in American Thought, Vol. I, 1620–1800. The Colonial Mind* (New York, 1927), 136.

179. Bailyn, *Voyagers to the West*, 15.

180. Ekirch, *Bound for America*, 121.

181. *Pennsylvania Gazette*, June 23–30, 1737.

182. The Charleston advertisement appears on the inside cover of A. Leon Higginbotham, Jr., *In the Matter of Color: Race and the American Legal Process: The Colonial Period* (New York, 1978).

183. Henry Laurens (1724–1792) is the subject of numerous biographies, including D. D. Wallace, *Life of Henry Laurens* (New York, 1915). For information on Laurens and the slave trade, see Elizabeth Donnan, "The Slave Trade into South Carolina before the Revolution," *American Historical Review* 33 (1928).

184. Pope-Hennessy, *Sins of the Fathers*, 223–24, 237–28.

185. Karl F. Geiser, *Redemptioners and Indentured Servants in the Colony and Commonwealth of Pennsylvania* (New Haven, 1901), 51 n. 28.

186. Blumenthal, *Brides from the Bridewell*, 42.

187. James Killpatrick, *An Essay on Inoculation Occasioned by the Small-Pox being brought into South Carolina in the Year 1738* (London, 1743), 56. See Joseph I. Waring, "James Killpatrick and Smallpox Inoculation in Charlestown," *Annals of Medical History*, new ser., 10 (1938): 301–8.

188. Philip D. Curtin, "Epidemiology and the Slave Trade," *Political Science Quarterly* 83 (1968): 210; Huggins, *Black Odyssey*, 58–62; Peter H. Wood, *Black Majority: Negroes in Colonial South Carolina from 1679 through the Stono Rebellion* (New York, 1974), chap. 1.

189. The inoculation story is told in Dr. Laurence Farmer, "When Cotton Mather Fought the Smallpox," *American Heritage* 8, no. 5 (August 1957): 40–43, 109. Also, ten years later, a Newgate prisoner named Charles Ray allowed doctors to remove his eardrum in another experiment. Ekirch, *Bound for America*, 62–63. More recent usage of prisoners in medical experiments is described in Jessica Mitford, *Kind and Usual Punishment: The Prison Business* (New York, 1973).

190. Ekirch, *Bound for America*, 107–8.

191. Bailyn, *Voyagers to the West*, 327.

192. Ibid., 326.

193. Ekirch, *Bound for America*, 123.

194. Bailyn, *Voyagers to the West*, 324.

195. Ekirch, *Bound for America*, 123.

196. Cheesman A. Herrick, *White Servitude in Pennsylvania: Indentured and Redemption Labor in Colony and Commonwealth* (Philadelphia, 1926), 201. Stock, *Proceedings and Debates*, vol. 4, 855–56.

197. Bailyn, *Voyagers to the West*, 264.

198. Ekirch, *Bound for America*, 124–25.

199. William Eddis, quoted in Bailyn, *Voyagers to the West*, 325.

200. Alexander Mackraby to his brother, December 2, 1769, in *Pennsylvania Magazine of History and Biography* 11 (1887): 492.

CHAPTER TWO   *A Land of Prisoners and Keepers*

1. Carol F. Lee, "Discretionary Justice in Early Massachusetts," *Essex Institute Historical Collections* 112 (April 1976): 122.

2. Nathaniel B. Shurtleff, ed., *Records of the Governor and Company of the Massachusetts Bay in New England* (Boston, 1853–54), vol. 1, 243, 297, 315, 316; John Winthrop, *Winthrop Papers,* ed. Allyn B. Forbes (New York, 1968), vol. 4, 474–75.

3. Mary Caroline Crawford, *In the Days of the Pilgrim Fathers* (New York, 1920), 193–94.

4. Boston's whipping post stood before the First Church, adjoining the stocks, according to Justin Windsor, *Memorial History of Boston* (Boston, 1881), vol. 1, 506, 539. Examples of whippings of servants included the cases of several runaways. John Noble, ed., *Records of the Court of Assistants of the Colony of Massachusetts Bay* (Boston, 1904), vol. 2, 16, 40, 122, 123, 126. The aversion toward whipping upper-class persons was formally stated in the colony's penal code of 1641, which guaranteed that no "true gentleman, nor any man equal to a gentleman," should be punished by whipping, except in shameful crimes. The Massachusetts Body of Liberties, clause 43, in *A Bibliographic Sketch of the Laws of the Massachusetts Colony from 1630 to 1686* (Boston, 1890), 43.

5. Quoted in Edwin Powers, *Crime and Punishment in Early Massachusetts: 1620–1692* (Boston, 1966), 223.

6. Quoted ibid., 213.

7. Nathaniel Hawthorne, *The Scarlet Letter,* ed. Sculley Bradley, Richmond Croom Beatty, and E. Hudson Long (New York, 1961), 38. Hawthorne's novel was heavily researched and surprisingly factual. See, e.g., Charles Ryskamp, "The New England Sources of the Scarlet Letter," *American Literature* 31 (November 1959): 257–72.

8. For a general topographical description of Boston at that time, see Nathaniel P. Shurtleff, *Topographical and Historical Description of Boston* (Boston, 1871). The account was offered by John Dunton in 1686, cited in Powers, *Crime and Punishment,* 214. See *Letters Written from New England, A.D. 1686 by John Dunton . . .* (Boston, 1687), 118–36.

9. John Winthrop, *Winthrop's Journal History of New England, 1630–1649,* ed. James Kendall Hosmer (New York, 1959), vol. 2, 59.

10. Shurtleff, *Records of the Governor,* vol. 1, 181. See Francis Jennings, *The Invasion of America: Indians, Colonialism, and the Cant of Conquest* (Chapel Hill, 1975), chap. 12. Chausop's internment on Castle Island is noted in Powers, *Crime and Punishment,* 220.

11. Jennings, *The Invasion of America,* 220–25; Winthrop D. Jordan, *White over Black: American Attitudes toward the Negro, 1550–1812* (Chapel Hill, 1968), 69.

12. Jordan, *White over Black,* 68.

13. Max Farrand, ed., *The Laws and Liberties of Massachusetts* (Cambridge, Mass. 1929).

14. Ibid., 4; Leviticus 25.45 and 46: "Of the children of the strangers that do sojourn among you, of them ye shall buy, and of their families . . .; and they shall be your possession. And ye shall take them as an inheritance for your children . . .; they shall be your bondmen forever: but over your brethren with the children of Israel, ye shall not rule over one another with rigor."

15. John Noble and John F. Cronin, eds., *Records of the Court of Assistants of the Colony of Massachusetts Bay* (Boston, 1901–1928), vol. 2, 78–79, 86, 90, 94, 97, 118. Apparently most of the six whites were released within a year, according to Jordan, *White over Black,* 68. See also Bernard Rosenthal, "Puritan Conscience and New England Slavery," *New England Quarterly* 46 (March 1973): 62–71.

16. Emmanuel Downing, quoted in Elizabeth Donnan, ed., *Documents Illustrative of the History of the Slave Trade to America* (Washington, 1934), vol. 3, 8.

17. George F. Dow, *Every Day Life in the Massachusetts Bay Colony* (New York, 1967), 212–13. Deputy Governor Richard Bellingham's own sister-in-law had been executed as a

witch only a few months earlier. Rufus M. Jones, *The Quakers in the American Colonies* (New York, 1911), 31.

18. Jones, *Quakers in American Colonies,* 26–28; Kai T. Erikson, *Wayward Puritans: A Study in the Sociology of Deviance* (New York, 1966), 127.

19. Richard Hallowell, *The Quaker Invasion of Massachusetts,* 3rd ed. (Boston, 1884), 136–37. The act of the General Court of the Colony of New Plymouth, dated June 5, 1655, is reproduced in William Brigham, ed., *The Compact with the Charter and Laws of the Colony of New Plymouth* (Boston, 1836), 99.

20. The Court's order specified that "there shall be a sufficient fence erected about the common prison, in Boston, and house of correction, such as may debar persons from conversing with the prisoners, and the charge thereof to [be] borne half by the county of Suffolk and the other half by the country." Powers, *Crime and Punishment,* 214–15.

21. Samuel Eliot Morison and Henry Steele Commager, *The Growth of the American Republic* (New York, 1962), vol. 1, 88; Harry Elmer Barnes and Negley K. Teeters, *New Horizons in Criminology* (New York, 1951), 377–78.

22. Samuel M. Janney, *The Life of William Penn: With Selections from His Correspondence and Autobiography* (Philadelphia, 1852), chap. 25; Augustus C. Buell, *William Penn as Founder of Two Commonwealths* (New York, 1904), 319; Bonamy Dobree, *William Penn, Quaker and Pioneer* (Boston, 1932), 324–26.

23. See Abbot Emerson Smith, *Colonists in Bondage: White Servitude and Convict Labor in America, 1607–1776* (Chapel Hill, 1947); Jordan, *White over Black;* Richard B. Morris, *Government and Labor in Early America* (New York, 1946); Edmund S. Morgan, *American Slavery, American Freedom: The Ordeal of Colonial Virginia* (New York, 1975); James Curtis Ballagh, *White Servitude in the Colony of Virginia: A Study of the System of Indentured Labor in the American Colonies* (Baltimore, 1895); John Spencer Bassett, *Slavery and Servitude in the Colony of North Carolina* (Baltimore, 1896); Karl F. Geiser, *Redemptioners and Indentured Servants in the Colony and Commonwealth of Pennsylvania* (New Haven, 1901); L. P. Henninghausen, "The Redemptioners and the German Society of Maryland," Society for the History of the Germans in Maryland, *Second Annual Report, 1887–1888,* 33–54; Cheesman A. Herrick, *White Servitude in Pennsylvania: Indentured and Redemption Labor in Colony and Commonwealth* (Philadelphia, 1926); A. Leon Higginbotham, Jr., *In the Matter of Color: Race and the American Legal Process: The Colonial Period* (New York, 1978); John Codman Hurd, *The Law of Freedom and Bondage in the United States,* 2 vols. (Boston, 1858); Marcus W. Jernegan, *Laboring and Dependent Classes in Colonial America, 1607–1783* (Chicago, 1931); Theodore D. Jervey, "The White Indentured Servants of South Carolina," *South Carolina Historical and Genealogical Magazine* 12 (1911): 163–71; E. I. McCormac, *White Servitude in Maryland, 1634–1820* (Baltimore, 1904); Samuel McKee, Jr., *Labor in Colonial New York, 1664–1776* (New York, 1935); Abbot Emerson Smith, "The Indentured Servant and Land Speculation in Seventeenth-Century Maryland," *American Historical Review* 40 (1934–35): 460–72; J. Thomas Scharf, *History of Maryland,* 3 vols. (Baltimore, 1879); Raphael Semmes, *Crime and Punishment in Early Maryland* (Baltimore, 1938); Philip Alexander Bruce, *Economic History of Virginia in the Seventeenth Century,* 2 vols. (New York, 1935); Julia Cherry Spruill, *Women's Life and Work in the Southern Colonies* (Chapel Hill, 1938); Oscar and Mary Handlin, "The Origins of the Southern Labor System," *William & Mary Quarterly,* 3rd ser., vol. 7, no. 2 (1950): 199–221; William Walter Hening, ed., *The Statutes-at-Large, Being a Collection of all the Laws in Virginia, 1619–1792,* 13 vols. (Philadelphia, 1823); E. D. Neill, *Virginia Carolorum (1625–85)* (Albany, 1869); Gary B. Nash, *Red, White, and Black: The Peoples of Early America* (Englewood Cliffs, N.J., 1974); Richard Hofstadter, *America in 1750: A Social Portrait* (New York, 1972); George Alsop, *A Character of the Province of Mary-land* (London, 1666); Rev. Jonathan Boucher, "Letters," *Maryland Historical Magazine* 7–10 (1912–15); William Eddis, *Letters from America, Historical and Descriptive* (London, 1792); Jaspar Dankers and Peter Sloyter, *Journal of a Voyage to New York and a Tour of the American Colonies in 1679–80,*

trans. and ed. Henry C. Murphy (Brooklyn, 1867); John Hammond, *Leah and Rachel, or, the Two Fruitful Sisters, Virginia and Maryland* (London, 1656); John Harrower, "Diary, 1773-1776," *American Historical Review* 6 (1900–1901): 65–107; Hugh Jones, *The Present State of Virginia,* ed. Richard L. Morton [1724] (Chapel Hill, 1956); Gottlieb Mittelberger, *Gottlieb Mittelberger's Journey to Pennsylvania in the Year 1750 and Return to Germany in the Year 1754,* trans. Carl Theodore Eben (Philadelphia, 1898); and Peter Kalm, *Peter Kalm's Travel in North America: The English Version of 1770,* ed. Adolph B. Benson (New York, 1937).

24. Jones, *The Present State of Virginia,* 87. For studies of apprenticeship, see Morris, *Government and Labor,* and R. F. Seybolt, *Apprenticeship and Apprenticeship Education in Colonial New England and New York* (New York, 1917).

25. Morris, *Government and Labor,* 363–71; Seybolt, *Apprenticeship and Apprenticeship Education.*

26. Carl Van Doren, *Benjamin Franklin* (New York, 1938), 13–14.

27. *Acts of the Assembly of the Province of Pennsylvania,* vol. 18 (Philadelphia, 1775).

28. Smith, *Colonists in Bondage,* 271–73; Spruill, *Women's Life and Work,* 314–23; Lois Green Carr and Lorena S. Walsh, "The Planter's Wife: The Experience of White Women in Seventeenth-Century Maryland," *William & Mary Quarterly,* 3rd ser., 34 (October 1977): 547–50. A Virginia law of 1672 admitted that "some dissolute masters have gotten their maids with child, and yet claim the benefit of their service." Hening, *Statutes-at-Large . . . Virginia,* vol. 1, 438, vol. 2, 167 (1672); the latter Virginia statute entitling masters to the service of a maid's illegitimate child may be found in vol. 8, 376 (1769).

29. Lawrence W. Towner, "'A Fondness for Freedom': Servant Protest in Puritan Society," *William & Mary Quarterly,* 3rd ser., 19 (1962): 213. See also Lawrence W. Towner, "A Good Master Well Served: A Social History of Servitude in Massachusetts, 1620–1750" (Ph.D. diss., Northwestern University, 1955); Douglas Greenberg, "Persons of Evil Name and Fame: Crime and Law Enforcement in the Colony of New York, 1691–1776" (Ph.D. diss., Cornell University, 1974); Douglas Greenberg, "Patterns of Criminal Prosecution in Eighteenth-Century New York, 1691–1776," *New York History* 56, no. 2 (April 1975): 133–53.

30. Semmes, *Crime and Punishment in Early Maryland,* 100–110.

31. Smith, *Colonists in Bondage,* 238–41; Jordan, *White over Black,* 48; Morris, *Government and Labor,* 393. For examples of statutes requiring such dues, see Hening, *Statutes-at-Large . . . Virginia,* vol. 1, 257, 435, 439–42, vol. 2, 113–14, 240, 388, and vol. 3, 447–62.

32. Morgan, *American Slavery, American Freedom,* 126.

33. See *William & Mary Quarterly,* 1st ser., 11 (1902–3): 34–37; T. H. Breen, "Changing Labor Force and Race Relations in Virginia, 1660–1710," *Journal of Social History* 7 (Fall 1973): 8.

34. "The Servants' Plot of 1663," *Virginia Magazine of History and Biography* 15 (1907–8): 38–43; Robert Beverley, *The History and Present State of Virginia* [London, 1705], ed. Louis B. Wright (Chapel Hill, 1947), 69; Hening, *Statutes-at-Large . . . Virginia,* vol. 2, 204. Coincidentally, many prison administrators today associate the month of September with prison riots, and September 13, 1971, was the day of the bloody Attica prison assault.

35. Morgan, *American Slavery, American Freedom,* 326–27.

36. Ibid., 246–47.

37. Ibid., 308; Breen, "Changing Labor Force," 12–13. See John Berry and Francis Maryson, "A True Narrative of the Rise, Progresse, and Cessation of the Late Rebellion in Virginia. Most Humbly and Impartially Reported to His Majestyes Commissioners Appointed to Enquire into the Affaires of the Said Colony," reprinted in *Virginia Magazine of History and Biography* 4, no. 2 (October 1896): 117–54; Clarence L. Ver Steeg and Richard Hofstadter, eds., *Great Issues in American History: From Settlement to Revolution, 1584–1776* (New York, 1969), 94–109.

38. Morgan, *American Slavery, American Freedom*, 246–47.

39. Smith, *Colonists in Bondage*, 299–300. See also Nash, *Red, White, and Black*, 220; Hofstadter, *America in 1750*, 61; Thomas J. Wertenbaker, *The Planters of Colonial Virginia* (New York, 1922), 78–80, 96–100; Norman K. Risjord, "Early Virginia: A Prison with Opportunity," *Virginia Cavalcade* 24 (Autumn 1974): 62–69.

40. Smith, *Colonists in Bondage*, 303.

41. Ebenezer Cooke, *Sot-Weed Factor, or, a Voyage to Maryland* (London, 1708).

42. [James Revel], *A Sorrowful Account of a Transported Felon, that Suffered Fourteen Years Transportation at Virginia, in America. In Six Parts. Being, a Short History of James Revel, an Unhappy Sufferer* (manuscript in Library of Congress, Ac. 2780). See John Melville Jennings, "Bibliographical Notes: 'The Poor Unhappy Transported Felon's Sorrowful Account of His Fourteen Years Transportation, at Virginia, in America,'" *Virginia Historical Magazine* 56 (1948): 181–94.

43. Stanley M. Hamilton, ed., *Letters to Washington* (Boston, 1902), vol. 5, 30; Worthington C. Ford, *Washington as Employer and Importer of Labor* (Brooklyn, 1889), 16–17; Walter H. Blumenthal, *Brides from the Bridewell: Female Felons Sent to Colonial America* (Rutland, Vt., 1962), 125; A. Roger Ekirch, *Bound for America: The Transportation of British Convicts to the Colonies, 1718–1775* (Oxford, 1987), 148.

44. Carl Bridenbaugh, *Myths and Realities: Societies of the Colonial South* (New York, 1963), 7; Ekirch, *Bound for America*, 179.

45. Ekirch, *Bound for America*, 148, 144.

46. See William Lee, ed., *Uncollected Works of Daniel Defoe* (Hildesheim, 1968), vol. 1, 72–75; J. R. Moore, *Daniel Defoe, Citizen of the Modern World* (Chicago, 1958); Pat Rogers, "Defoe in the Fleet Prison," *Review of English Studies* 22, no. 88 (1971): 451–55.

47. Moll Flanders appears to have been based on Moll King, an actual criminal of the period. Lee, *Uncollected Works of Daniel Defoe*, vol. 2, 52. See also Robert R. Singleton, "Defoe, Moll Flanders, and the Ordinary of Newgate," *Harvard Library Bulletin* 24 (October 1976): 407–13.

48. Daniel Defoe, *The Fortunes and Misfortunes of the Famous Moll Flanders* [1722] (New York, 1949), 89–90.

49. "Tour through the British Plantations," *London Magazine* (1755), quoted in John Fiske, *Old Virginia and Her Neighbors* (Boston, 1897), 188.

50. Malachy Postlethwayt, *Dictionary of Commerce*, 3rd. ed. (London, 1766), vol. 3, fol. 4M, 2 recto col. 1.

51. Ekirch, *Bound for America*, 178; Blumenthal, *Brides from the Bridewell*, 35.

52. Patrick Colquhoun, *A Treatise on the Police of the Metropolis* . . . [London, 1806] (Montclair, N.J., 1969), 454–55. Colquhoun (1745–1820), the son of a magistrate and registrar of the county records, was born and educated in Dunbarton, Scotland. After he was orphaned, he sailed to Virginia and began a merchant career in the Glasgow to Virginia trade. See Sir Leon Radzinowicz, *A History of the English Criminal Law and Its Administration from 1750* (London, 1956), vol. 3, 211. Colquhoun's involvement in the convict trade is noted in Smith, *Colonists in Bondage*, 116; Massachusetts Historical Society, *Proceedings* (1915–1916): 328–29; *Calendar of Home Office Papers of the Reign of George III, 1760–1775* (London, 1878–1899), vol. 3, 169, 615; *Hertfordshire County Records* (London, 1935), vol. 7, 184, 231, 259, 280, 312.

53. *Colonial Records of Pennsylvania* (1683) (Philadelphia, 1838–53), vol. 1, 72.

54. Gail McKnight Beckman, ed., *The Statutes at Large of Pennsylvania* (New York, 1976), vol. 3, 265–67. See Herrick, *White Servitude in Pennsylvania*, 123.

55. J. Thomas Scharf, *History of Maryland*, vol. 1, 372, 384.

56. Annapolis Mayor's Court Minutes, 1720–1784, fols. 26, 27, 30–32 (1721); Maryland Provincial Court Proceedings, lib. 1719–22, f. 362 (1721).

57. Basil Sollers, "Transported Convict Laborers in Maryland during the Colonial Period," *Maryland Historical Magazine* 2 (1907): 30–31.

58. Ibid., 32–33.

59. Warren B. Smith, *White Servitude in Colonial South Carolina* (Columbia, 1961), 39–40.

60. Ekirch, *Bound for America,* 169.

61. *Pennsylvania Gazette,* May 9, 1751; Morris, *Government and Labor,* 333; Ekirch, *Bound for America,* 169.

62. Radzinowicz, *History of English Criminal Law,* vol. 1, 126n.

63. James Davie Butler, "British Convicts Shipped to American Colonies," *American Historical Review* 2 (1896): 12.

64. Morgan, *American Slavery, American Freedom,* 296–97, 310.

65. Act XII (1662), Hening, *Statutes-at-Large . . . Virginia,* vol. 2, 170.

66. *Archives of Maryland* (Baltimore, 1883), vol. 1, 449, 489, 526, 533–34.

67. Thomas Cooper and David J. McCord, eds., *The Statutes at Large of South Carolina* (Columbia, 1836), vol. 1, 55. Locke's authorship is discussed in Edward McCrady, "Slavery in the Province of South Carolina, 1670–1770," American Historical Association *Report* (1895), 643, and in Higginbotham, *In the Matter of Color,* 429, n. 86.

68. See Jordan, *White over Black,* 235–36, 287, 289, 350–51, 440–41.

69. Ibid., 66–70; George H. Moore, *Notes on the History of Slavery in Massachusetts* (New York, 1866); Philip Foner, *The History of Black Americans: From Africa to the Emergence of the Cotton Kingdom* (Westport, Conn., 1975), 243; Higginbotham, *In the Matter of Color,* chap. 3.

70. Foner, *The History of Black Americans,* 243; Bernard C. Steiner, *A History of Slavery in Connecticut* (Baltimore, 1893); Lorenzo J. Greene, *The Negro in Colonial New England, 1620–1776* (New York, 1942).

71. Foner, *The History of Black Americans,* 244–46; William Johnston, *Slavery in Rhode Island, 1755–1776* (Providence, 1894); Edward Channing, *The Narragansett Planters* (Baltimore, 1886); Jordan, *White over Black,* 70–71. The Rhode Island law of 1652 that forbade enslavement appears in John R. Bartlett, ed., *Records of the Colony of Rhode Island and Providence Plantations, in New England* (Providence, 1856), vol. 1, 243.

72. Foner, *The History of Black Americans,* 244; Charles E. Clark, *The Eastern Frontier — The Settlement of Northern New England, 1610–1763* (New York, 1970).

73. Edgar J. McManus, *A History of Negro Slavery in New York* (Syracuse, 1966); Edwin V. Morgan, *Slavery in New York* (Washington, 1891); Ansel J. Northrup, *Slavery in New York* (Albany, 1900); Foner, *The History of Black Americans,* 235; Higginbotham, *In the Matter of Color,* chap. 4.

74. Foner, *The History of Black Americans,* 238–39; Richard McCormick, *New Jersey from Colony to State, 1609–1789* (Princeton, 1964); and Henry S. Cooley, *A Study of Slavery in New Jersey* (Baltimore, 1869).

75. Foner, *The History of Black Americans,* 231.

76. Edward R. Turner, *The Negro in Pennsylvania: Slavery-Servitude-Freedom, 1639–1861* (Washington, 1911); Darold D. Wax, "The Demand for Slave Labor in Colonial Pennsylvania," *Pennsylvania History* 34 (1967): 331–45; Foner, *The History of Black Americans;* and Higginbotham, *In the Matter of Color,* chap. 7.

77. Higginbotham, *In the Matter of Color,* chap. 6; Richard Reese, *Colonial Georgia: A Study in British Imperial Policy* (Athens, 1963); Foner, *The History of Black Americans,* 616.

78. Greenberg, "Patterns of Criminal Prosecution," 133–53.

79. One of the best-researched studies of these slave codes is found in Higginbotham, *In the Matter of Color.* See also David Brion Davis, *The Problem of Slavery in Western Culture* (Ithaca, 1966); Jordan, *White over Black;* Morgan, *American Slavery, American Freedom;* Carl N. Degler, "Slavery and the Genesis of American Race Prejudice," *Comparative Studies in Society and History* 2 (October 1959): 49–66; Paul C. Palmer, "Servant into Slave: The Evolution of the Legal Status of the Negro Laborer in Colonial Virginia," *South*

Atlantic Quarterly 65 (Summer 1966): 355–70; T. H. Breen, "Changing Labor Force," 3–25.

80. Cooper and McCord, *Statutes at Large of South Carolina*, vol. 7, 396.

81. Ibid., 384.

82. Elkanah Watson, quoted in Bridenbaugh, *Myths and Realities*, 71–72.

83. Ibid., 63.

84. The inventory of Washington's slaves appears in Paul Haworth, *George Washington: Farmer* (Indianapolis, 1915), 193.

85. Ekirch, *Bound for America*, 130.

86. Matthew T. Mellon, *Early American Views on Negro Slavery* (New York, 1969), 35. See also Ford, *Washington as Employer and Importer*.

87. Spruill, *Women's Life and Work*, 77.

88. The 1712 slave rebellion is examined in Kenneth Scott, "The Slave Insurrection in New York in 1712," *New-York Historical Society Quarterly* 45 (January 1961): 43–74; Rosewell R. Hoes, "The Negro Plot of 1712," *New York Genealogical and Bibliographical Record* 21 (1890): 162–63; Joshua Coffin, *An Account of Some of the Principal Slave Insurrections* (New York, 1860), 10–11; Harvey Wish, "American Slave Insurrections before 1861," *Journal of Negro History* 22, no. 3 (July 1937): 299–320, esp. 308; Julius Goebel, Jr., and T. Raymond Naughton, *Law Enforcement in Colonial New York* (New York, 1944), 118–19; Isaac Newton Phelps Stokes, *The Iconography of Manhattan Island* (New York, 1915–28), vol. 4, 474–78; and E. B. O'Callaghan, ed., *Documents Relative to the Colonial History of the State of New York* (Albany, 1856–61), vol. 5, 341–42, 356–57. The 1741 conspiracy is covered in Daniel Horsmanden, Associate Justice of the Supreme Court of Judicature of the Province of New York, *A Journal of the Proceedings in the Detection of the Conspiracy Formed by Some White People in conjunction with Negro and other Slaves, for burning the City of New-York in America, and murdering the Inhabitants* (New York, 1744); Jordan, *White over Black*, 118–19; Leo Hershkowitz, "Tom's Case: An Incident, 1741," *New York History* 52 (January 1971): 63–71; Ferenc M. Szasz, "The New York Slave Revolt of 1741: A Re-Examination," *New York History* 48 (July 1967): 215–30; Thomas Davis, "The New York Slave Conspiracy of 1741 as Black Protest," *Journal of Negro History* 56 (January 1971): 17–30. The Stono Rebellion of September 1739 is examined in Peter H. Wood, *Black Majority: Negroes in Colonial South Carolina from 1670 through the Stono Rebellion* (New York, 1974), chap. 12; Frank J. Klingberg, *An Appraisal of the Negro in Colonial South Carolina: A Study in Americanization* (Washington, 1941), 68; Ulrich B. Phillips, *American Negro Slavery: A Survey of the Supply, Employment, and Control of Negro Labor as Determined by the Plantation Regime* (New York, 1918), 473; and Herbert Aptheker, *Negro Slave Revolts in the United States, 1526–1860* (New York, 1939), 187.

89. Allen D. Candler, ed., *Colonial Records of Georgia* (Atlanta, 1904), vol. 18, 106–7.

90. Ibid., 132–33.

91. Higginbotham, *In the Matter of Color*, 182, 185, 255–58, 262–63, 282; Candler, *Colonial Records of Georgia*, 132–34, 105–6, 137–38, 140.

92. J. Hector St. John de Crèvecoeur, *Letters from an American Farmer* [1782] (New York, 1957), 167.

93. Hening, *Statutes-at-Large . . . Virginia*, vol. 2, 270.

94. See, e.g., Virginia's act of 1705, ibid., vol. 3, sect. 37, 461.

95. *Pennsylvania Journal*, July 19, 1775, in Bernard Bailyn, *Voyagers to the West: A Passage in the Peopling of America on the Eve of the Revolution* (New York, 1987), portfolio.

96. Blumenthal, *Brides from the Bridewell*, 46.

97. For more about runaways, see Gerald W. Mullin, *Flight and Rebellion: Slave Resistance in Eighteenth-Century Virginia* (New York, 1972); "Eighteenth-Century Slaves as Advertised by Their Masters," *Journal of Negro History* 1 (April 1916): 163–216.

98. Ekirch, *Bound for America*, 197.

99. Spruill, *Women's Life and Work,* 134.

100. Daniel E. Meaders, "South Carolina Fugitives as Viewed through Local Colonial Newspapers, with Emphasis on Runaway Notices, 1732–1800," *Journal of Negro History* 60 (April 1975): 288–319.

101. See, e.g., (*South Carolina*) *City Gazette and Daily Advertiser,* August 28, 1766; *South Carolina Gazette,* May 14, 1741, May 11, 1738, July 7, 1737, August 1, 1740, October 25, 1735, April 3, 1736; *Virginia Gazette,* October 17, 1777.

102. E.g., *South Carolina Gazette,* September 3, 1772.

103. Cooper and McCord, *Statutes at Large of South Carolina,* vol. 7, 360.

104. Ibid., Act No. 34 (1686), vol. 2, 53; Act No. 60 (1691), vol. 2, 53; Act No. 383 (1717), vol. 3, 16.

105. Ibid., Act No. 710 (1744), vol. 3, 628; Act No. 314, in Smith, *White Servitude in Colonial South Carolina,* 78.

106. A. S. Salley, ed., *Journals of the Commons House of Assembly of the Province of South Carolina* (Columbia, 1932), vol. 20, 112.

107. *South Carolina Gazette,* June 17, 1745.

108. David William Cole, "The Organization and Administration of the South Carolina Militia System, 1670–1783" (Ph.D. diss., University of South Carolina, 1953), 42n. See also Wood, *Black Majority,* 274–76; H. M. Henry, *The Police Control of the Slave in South Carolina* (Emory, Va., 1914).

109. Wood, *Black Majority,* 275.

110. Candler, *Colonial Records of Georgia,* vol. 18, 25.

111. The earliest apparent reference to imprisonment at Jamestown mentions the jailing of several Indians in 1608 and of a young German in 1609. William Stith, *History of Virginia* (London, 1753), 61, 95. Imprisonment was authorized by James I as necessary for "good order and government" under his articles, orders, and instructions issued on November 20, 1606. Hening, *Statutes-at-Large . . . Virginia,* vol. 1, 69–71. See also Frank W. Hoffer, Delbert M. Mann, and Floyd N. House, *The Jails of Virginia* (New York, 1933), chap. 2; J. M. Moynahan and Earle K. Stewart, "The Origin of the American Jail," *Federal Probation* 32, no. 4 (December 1978): 41–50; Semmes, *Crime and Punishment in Early Maryland;* Carl Bridenbaugh, *Cities in Revolt* (New York, 1965), and *Cities in the Wilderness* (New York, 1955); Harry Elmer Barnes, *A History of the Penal, Reformatory, and Correctional Institutions of the State of New Jersey* (Trenton, 1918); and Powers, *Crime and Punishment.*

112. Hening, *Statutes-at-Large . . . Virginia,* vol. 1, 340.

113. Ibid., vol. 2, 76–77.

114. Paul W. Keve, *The History of Corrections in Virginia* (Charlottesville, 1986), 11.

115. Semmes, *Crime and Punishment in Early Maryland,* 32–33.

116. Ibid., 33.

117. Ibid.

118. Ibid., 32–33.

119. Ibid., 36–37.

120. Norris Galpin Osborn, ed., *History of Connecticut* (New York, 1925), vol. 5, 390. On colonial jails, see Moynahan and Stewart, "Origin of the American Jail," 41–50.

121. Alexander Graydon, *Memoirs of His Own Time, With Reminiscences of the Men and Events of the Revolution,* ed. John Stockton Littell (Philadelphia, 1846), 16–17.

122. Philip A. Bruce, *Institutional History of Virginia* (New York, 1910), vol. 1, 639.

123. Sidney Perley, *History of Salem, Massachusetts* (Salem, 1928), vol. 3, 76, 173–74.

124. For a look at a colonial jailkeeper, see Esther I. Wik, "The Jailkeeper at Salem in 1692," *Essex Institute Historical Collections* 3 (July 1975): 221–27.

125. Reverend Charles Woodmason, quoted in Bridenbaugh, *Cities in Revolt,* 303.

126. Van Doren, *Benjamin Franklin,* 27.

127. Bartlett, *Records of Rhode Island,* vol. 5, 560.

128. Bridenbaugh, *Cities in Revolt,* 118.

129. Bridenbaugh, *Cities in the Wilderness,* 75.

130. Ibid., 385.

131. Ibid., 225.

132. *Colonial Laws of New York* (Albany, 1894), vol. 2, 645.

133. Bridenbaugh, *Cities in Revolt,* 118.

134. *Minutes of the Common Council of the City of Philadelphia* (Philadelphia, 1856), 87.

135. *Newport News Letter,* April 1, 1737.

136. J. T. Scharf and T. Westcott, *History of Philadelphia* (Philadelphia, 1884), vol. 3, 1825; *Mercury,* March 7, 1732; *Pennsylvania Gazette,* October 9, 1729, August 19, 1731, and November 16, 1732. See also Bridenbaugh, *Cities in the Wilderness,* 384, and Carl and Jessica Bridenbaugh, *Rebels and Gentlemen: Philadelphia in the Age of Franklin* (New York, 1942), 250.

137. Bridenbaugh and Bridenbaugh, *Rebels and Gentlemen,* 252.

138. Philadelphia offered regular contributions for the relief of the prisoners and on some occasions held benefit concerts to gain support. Ibid., 250. In 1769 the Newport Fellowship Club sponsored an elaborate dinner at the prison for the debtors' benefit. Bridenbaugh, *Cities in Revolt,* 304.

139. *Colonial Laws of New York,* vol. 2, 753-56. The measure applied only to Dutchess, Kings, Orange, Queens, Richmond, Suffolk, Ulster, and Westchester Counties. See Peter J. Coleman, *Debtors and Creditors in America: Insolvency, Imprisonment for Debt, and Bankruptcy, 1607-1900* (Madison, Wis., 1974), chap. 9.

140. Ekirch, *Bound for America,* 32n.

141. Blumenthal, *Brides from the Bridewell,* 70-71.

142. Ibid., 65.

143. Ibid., 70.

144. Morris, *Government and Labor,* 344; Herrick, *White Servitude in Pennsylvania,* 150-56; Geiser, *Redemptioners and Indentured Servants,* 21.

145. Morris, *Government and Labor,* 343-44; Herrick, *White Servitude in Pennsylvania,* 148-49.

146. Leon Radzinowicz, *A History of English Criminal Law and Its Administration from 1750* (London, 1948-56), vol. 4, 86.

147. Dora Mae Clark, "The Impressment of Seamen in the American Colonies," in *Essays in Colonial History Presented to Charles McLean Andrews by His Students* (Freeport, N. Y., 1966), 200, 216, 222-23.

148. Bridenbaugh, *Cities in Revolt,* 115.

149. Ibid., 115-16.

150. Ibid., 117.

151. Pauline Maier, *From Resistance to Revolution: Colonial Radicals and the Development of American Opposition to Britain, 1765-1776* (New York, 1972), esp. chap. 1.

152. L. Kinvin Wroth and Hiller B. Zobel, eds., *Legal Papers of John Adams* (Cambridge, Mass., 1965), vol. 3, 253.

153. Maier, *From Resistance to Revolution,* and "Popular Uprisings and Civil Authority in Eighteenth-Century America," *William & Mary Quarterly,* 3rd ser., 28 (1970): 3-35. See also Staughton Lynd, "The Tenant Rising at Livingston Manor, May 1777," *New-York Historical Society Quarterly* 48 (April 1964): 163-77; Jesse Lemisch, "Jack Tar in the Streets: Merchant Seamen in the Politics of Revolutionary America," *William & Mary Quarterly,* 3rd ser., 25 (July 1968): 371-407; and James H. Dormon, "Collective Behavior in the American Popular Resistance, 1765-1775: A Theoretical Prospectus," *Historian* 42 (November 1979): 1-17.

154. Jordan, *White over Black,* 195; Thomas E. Drake, *Quakers and Slavery in America* (New Haven, 1950), chaps. 1-3; Davis, *Problem of Slavery,* 317.

155. Jean-Jacques Rousseau, *The Social Contract* [1762], trans. Charles Frankel (New York, 1947), 7.

156. David Hume, *Essays Moral, Political, and Literary* [1752] (Edinburgh, 1817), 377–419; Davis, *Problem of Slavery*, 426–27.

157. Benjamin Franklin, "Observations Concerning the Increase of Mankind," in Leonard W. Larabee et al., eds., *The Papers of Benjamin Franklin* (New Haven, 1959), vol. 4, 229–31.

158. Maier, *From Resistance to Revolution*, 253.

159. John Dickinson, *Letters from a Farmer in Pennsylvania to the Inhabitants of the British Colonies* (Philadelphia, 1768), 38.

160. John Adams, in Bernard Bailyn, *The Ideological Origins of the American Revolution* (Cambridge, Mass., 1967), 233.

161. Ibid., 119–20.

162. George F. Willison, *Patrick Henry and His World* (Garden City, N.Y., 1969), 266–67.

163. Samuel Johnson, *Taxation no Tyranny; an answer to the resolutions and address of the American Congress*, 3rd ed. (London, 1775), 89.

164. Henry Steele Commager and Richard B. Morris, eds., *The Spirit of 'Seventy Six: The Story of the American Revolution As Told by Its Participants* (New York, 1967), 316–17; Mellon, 48–49, 97–98; see generally, Garry Wills, *Inventing America: Jefferson's Declaration of Independence* (Garden City, N.Y., 1978), esp. 377.

CHAPTER THREE   *Prisoners of the Revolution*

1. Danske Dandridge, *American Prisoners of the Revolution* (Charlottesville, 1911), 128. The first known American prisoners of war were twenty-seven persons who had been captured after the Battle of Bunker Hill near Boston in 1775. Larry G. Bowman, *Captive Americans: Prisoners during the American Revolution* (Athens, Ohio, 1977), 28.

2. Richard M. Ketchum, *The Winter Soldiers* (Garden City, N.Y., 1973), 152.

3. Letter from Jonathan Gillet to Elizabeth Gillet, December 2, 1776, New York, reprinted in *The New-York Diary of Lieutenant Jabez Fitch*, ed. W. H. W. Sabine (New York, 1954), 78–80.

4. William Slade, in Dandridge, *American Prisoners of the Revolution*, 494–95. Slade, of New Canaan, Connecticut, kept a diary from November 16, 1776, to January 28, 1777.

5. Alexander Graydon, *Memoirs of His Own Time, With Reminiscences of the Men and Events of the Revolution* (Philadelphia, 1846), 221; see also Mary Ellen Graydon Sharpe, *A Family Retrospect* (Indianapolis, 1909).

6. Peter Force, ed., *American Archives*, 4th series (Washington, 1837–46), vol. 3, 246; William R. Lindsey, "Treatment of American Prisoners of War during the Revolution," *Emporia State Research Studies* 22, no. 1 (September 1973): 8.

7. Force, *Archives*, 4th series, vol. 3, 712.

8. Ibid., 245–46.

9. Ibid., 246, 328; Lindsey, "Treatment of American Prisoners," 6–7.

10. See, e.g., Oscar Theodore Barck, *New York City during the War for Independence* (New York, 1931), 112–13.

11. Mary L. Booth, *History of the City of New York* (New York, 1880), 512–14; Ketchum, *The Winter Soldiers*, 152–53.

12. See Shepherd Knapp, *A History of the Brick Presbyterian Church in the City of New York* (New York, 1909), 69–70.

13. Eugene L. Armbruster, *The Wallabout Prison Ships, 1776–1783* (New York, 1920), 29; Thomas E. V. Smith, *The City of New York in the Year of Washington's Inauguration* (New York, 1889), 142–43; Booth, *History of New York*, 512–14.

14. Bowman, *Captive Americans*, 13.

15. Ibid.; Dandridge, *American Prisoners of the Revolution*, 25-26.

16. Henry Onderdonck, *Revolutionary Incidents of Suffolk and King's Counties: With an Account of the Battle of Long Island and the British Prison-Ships at New York* (New York, 1849), 207-8; Hiram Stone, "The Experiences of a Prisoner in the American Revolution," *Journal of American History* 2 (1908): 527-29; Rev. J. F. Richmond, *New York and Its Institutions, 1609-1872* (New York, 1872), 175.

17. Dandridge, *American Prisoners of the Revolution*, 133. Thomas Stone was a Connecticut soldier who enlisted in April 1777 and was captured at sea in December 1778 off Long Island. Other accounts of the Sugar-House by former prisoners, Oliver Woodruff and Adolph Meyer, appear in William L. Stone, *History of New York City from the Discovery to the Present Day* (New York, 1872), 254-55.

18. William Slade, in Dandridge, *American Prisoners of the Revolution*, 498.

19. Ibid., 108; Booth, *History of New York*, 522-25.

20. Booth, *History of New York*, 527-30. John Fell kept a journal of his confinement in the Provost from April 1777 to November 1778. See Dandridge, *American Prisoners of the Revolution*, chap. 13.

21. Samuel Eliot Morison, *John Paul Jones: A Sailor's Biography* (Boston, 1959), chap. 11.

22. Corey Ford, *A Peculiar Service: A Narrative of Espionage in and around New York during the Revolution* (New York, 1965), 34-40. Cunningham later placed an advertisement in Gaine's paper of August 4, 1781, as follows: "One Guinea Reward, ran away a black man named Richmond, being the common hangman, formerly the property of the rebel Colonel Patterson of Pa."

23. Charles H. Metzger, *The Prisoner in the American Revolution* (Chicago, 1971), 84; John C. Fitzpatrick, ed., *The Writings of George Washington* (Washington, 1931-44), vol. 6, 297 (Washington to Col. Atlee, November 21, 1776).

24. Hiram Stone, "Experiences of a Prisoner," 527.

25. Force, *Archives*, 5th ser., vol. 3, 1429-30; Lindsey, "Treatment of American Prisoners," 11-12.

26. John Fiske, "Charles Lee, the Soldier of Fortune," in *Essays Historical and Literary* (Boston, 1902), vol. 1, 55-98.

27. Thomas Jones, *History of New York during the Revolutionary War* (New York, 1879), vol. 1, 173.

28. Graydon, *Memoirs*, 224-34.

29. Sabine, *New-York Diary*, 84-89, 193-94, 197.

30. Graydon, *Memoirs*, 245-61.

31. Booth, *History of New York*, 529-30; Dandridge, *American Prisoners of the Revolution*, 123.

32. Graydon, *Memoirs*, 242n.; see also Charles A. Huguenin, "Ethan Allen, Parolee on Long Island," *Vermont History* 25 (1907): 103-25; Sabine, *New-York Diary*.

33. Ethan Allen, *A Narrative of Colonel Ethan Allen's Captivity, Written by Himself* (New York, 1930), 171-72.

34. Elias Boudinot, in Dandridge, *American Prisoners of the Revolution*, 38; George Adams Boyd, *Elias Boudinot, Patriot and Statesman, 1740-1821* (Princeton, 1952).

35. Boyd, *Elias Boudinot*, 52.

36. Metzger, *Prisoner in the American Revolution*, 174.

37. Boyd, *Elias Boudinot*, 45.

38. Elias Boudinot to George Washington, March 2, 1778, in Henry Steele Commager and Richard B. Morris, eds., *The Spirit of 'Seventy-Six: The Story of the American Revolution As Told by Its Participants* (New York, 1967), 862.

39. Boyd, *Elias Boudinot*, 54.

40. Robert Hendrickson, *Hamilton I* (New York, 1976), 184-85.

41. *New York Gazette*, May 6, 1777.

42. Jones, *New York during the Revolutionary War,* vol. 1, 174.

43. Commager and Morris, *The Spirit of 'Seventy-Six,* 874. See also Gerald O. Haffner, ed., "A British Prisoner of War in the American Revolution: The Experiences of Jacob Schieffelin from Vincennes to Williamsburg, 1779-1780," *Virginia Magazine of History and Biography* 86, no. 1 (January 1978): 17-25.

44. C. H. Van Tyne, *The Loyalists in the American Revolution* (New York, 1902), 226; Charles W. Dean, "The Story of New-Gate," *Federal Probation* 43, no. 2 (June 1979): 8-14.

45. Richard H. Phelps, *Newgate of Connecticut* (n.p., 1876), 26.

46. Ibid.; Commager and Morris, *The Spirit of 'Seventy-Six,* 875-78.

47. William Evans and Thomas Evans, eds., *The Friends' Library* . . . (Philadelphia, 1842), vol. 6, 288-89.

48. John Pemberton, in Evans and Evans, *The Friends' Library,* vol. 6, 289.

49. Thomas Eddy, in Samuel L. Knapp, *The Life of Thomas Eddy* . . . (New York, 1834), 44.

50. "Charles Willson Peale," in *Dictionary of American Biography,* ed. Dumas Malone (New York, 1934), vol. 14, 344-47.

51. Gen. John Sullivan to John Hancock, August 25, 1777, *Papers of the Continental Congress,* item 160, folio 47, National Archives and Records Service Microfilm publication; Thomas Gilpin, *Exiles in Virginia* (Philadelphia, 1848), 35.

52. Knapp, *The Life of Thomas Eddy,* 45-46.

53. Evans and Evans, *The Friends' Library,* vol. 6, 291-92.

54. Theodore Thayer, *Israel Pemberton, King of the Quakers* (Philadelphia, 1943), 217; Gilpin, *Exiles in Virginia,* 68.

55. Evans and Evans, *The Friends' Library,* vol. 6, 292.

56. Thayer, *Israel Pemberton,* 222-23.

57. Graydon, *Memoirs,* 290; "The Diary of Robert Morton: Kept in Philadelphia While That City was Occupied by the British Army in 1777," *Pennsylvania Magazine of History and Biography* 1 (1877), 5n.

58. Graydon, *Memoirs,* 120; Charles Page Smith, *James Wilson, Founding Father, 1742-1798* (Chapel Hill, 1956), 118.

59. Robert McCluer Calhoon, *The Loyalists in Revolutionary America, 1760-1781* (New York, 1973), 401.

60. Excerpt from "Life of John Pemberton," Evans and Evans, *The Friends' Library* (Philadelphia, 1842), vol. 6, 297.

61. Knapp, *The Life of Thomas Eddy,* 46-47; Isaac Sharpless, *A History of Quaker Government in Pennsylvania,* vol. 2, *The Quakers in the Revolution* (Philadelphia, 1899), 193-95.

62. Sharpless, *The Quakers in the Revolution,* 193-94; Charles R. Barker, "Old Mills of Mill Creek, Lower Merion," *Pennsylvania Magazine of History and Biography* 50, no. 1 (1926): 2-5.

63. Evans and Evans, *The Friends' Library,* 297.

64. In 1775 the annual trade in convicts was conservatively estimated at two thousand souls. Harry Elmer Barnes, Jr., *The Story of Punishment* (New York, 1930), 71.

65. William Bell Clark, *Ben Franklin's Privateers* (Baton Rouge, La., 1956), 10; Francis Abell, *Prisoners of War in Britain, 1756 to 1815* (Oxford, 1915); John K. Alexander, "Forton Prison during the American Revolution: A Case Study of the British Prisoner of War Policy and the American Prisoner Response to That Policy," *Essex Institute Historical Collections* 103 (1967): 365-89, and "American Privateersmen in the Mill Prison during 1777-1782, an Evaluation," *Essex Institute Historical Collections* 102 (1966): 318-40; William Hammond Bowden, ed., "Diary of William Widger of Marblehead, Kept at Mill Prison, England, 1781," *Essex Institute Historical Proceedings* 73 (1937): 311-47, and 74 (1938): 22-48; Rev. R. Livesy, ed., *The Prisoners of 1776: A Relic of the Revolution* (Boston, 1854).

66. John Howard, *The State of the Prisons in England and Wales* . . . [Warrington, 1777] (London, 1929).

67. Derek L. Howard, *John Howard: Prison Reformer* (London, 1958); James Baldwin Brown, *Memoirs of [John] Howard, Compiled from His Diary, His Confidential Letters, and Other Authentic Documents* (Boston, 1831); Charles K. True, *Memoirs of John Howard, the Prisoner's Friend* (Cincinnati, 1878); Hepworth Dixon, *John Howard, and the Prison-World of Europe* . . . (Webster, Mass., 1852).

68. Brown, *Memoirs of [John] Howard;* Christopher Hibbert, *The Roots of Evil: A Social History of Crime and Punishment* (Boston, 1963), chap. 3; Howard, *John Howard,* 42–43; J. Thorsten Sellin, *Slavery and the Penal System* (New York, 1976), 75.

69. W. Brach-Johnson, *The English Prison Hulks* (London, 1957), 3.

70. Ibid., 10–14; Abbot Emerson Smith, *Colonists in Bondage: White Servitude and Convict Labor in America, 1607–1776* (Chapel Hill, 1947), 127.

71. Max Grünhut, *Penal Reform* (Oxford, 1948), 35.

72. Howard, *The State of the Prisons,* 19.

73. Ibid., 13.

74. Ibid., 57–58.

75. Quoted in Torsten Eriksson, *The Reformers: An Historical Survey of Pioneer Experiments in the Treatment of Criminals,* trans. Catherine Djurklou (New York, 1976), 37.

76. Ibid., 37.

77. Howard, *The State of the Prisons,* 41–42.

78. See William James Morgan, ed., *Naval Documents of the American Revolution,* vol. 7, 351, 421, 852. The Americans also used prison ships, such as the schooner *Pease* in New London in 1780. See Robert Owen Decker, *The Whaling City: A History of New London* (Chester, Conn., 1976), 52.

79. *U.S. Naval Institute Proceedings* 101, no. 1 (October 1975): 56. Other accounts include more vessels, among them the *John, Glasgow, Preston, Good Intent, Wales, Lord Dunlace, Judith, Myrtle, Felicity, Chatham, Kitty, Frederick,* and *Scheldt,* as well as prison-hospitals such as the *Hunter, Perseverance,* and *Bristol Packet,* all in New York harbor. Elsewhere, the British appear to have also used the *Torbay, Pack-Horse,* and *Peter.* Bowman, *Captive Americans,* 42.

80. Thomas Andros, *The Old Jersey Captive* . . . (Boston, 1833), in William Dunlap, *History of New Netherlands, Province of New York, and State of New York, to the Adoption of the Federal Constitution* (New York, 1840), 138. See also Armbruster, *The Wallabout Prison Ships,* 26–27; Fox in Dandridge, *American Prisoners of the Revolution,* 255.

81. Letter to the author from Research Assistant, Department of Ships, National Maritime Museum, London, October 26, 1977; letter to the author from the Head of the Naval Library, Ministry of Defence, London, October 24, 1977; *U.S. Naval Institute Proceedings,* 18–65; John Tessier-Yandell, OBE, *HMS Jersey, 1654–1976* (Bagot, Jersey, 1977).

82. Thomas Dring, in *Recollections of the Jersey Prison Ship,* ed. Albert G. Greene [Providence, 1829] (New York, 1961), 11–12. Hereinafter Dring.

83. Andros in Dunlap, *History of New Netherlands,* 139.

84. Ebenezer Fox in Dandridge, *American Prisoners of the Revolution,* 254–55.

85. This inoculation is described in Dring, 19–20.

86. Andros in Dunlap, *History of New Netherlands,* 139.

87. Dring in Dandridge, *American Prisoners of the Revolution,* 258.

88. Ibid.; Dring, 38–39. Apparently, no English physician or any doctor from the city ever came on board the *Jersey.* Andros in Dunlap, *History of New Netherlands,* 140. The commanding officers of the *Jersey* during the Revolutionary War period included William A. Halstead (November 11, 1775–May 16, 1777), Thomas A. Tonken (November 11, 1777–August 1, 1778), David Laird (August 2, 1778–December 12, 1780), and Robert Graeme (February 15, 1781–November 30, 1783), according to the Head of the Naval Library, Ministry of Defence, London, letter to the author, October 24, 1977.

89. These mess groups are described by Fox in Dandridge, *American Prisoners of the Revolution*, 255.

90. Dring, 29-30.

91. Armbruster, *The Wallabout Prison Ships*, 17. Detailed descriptions of the rations and a sample weekly menu appear in Dring, 25-29.

92. Henry Palmer, in Dandridge, *American Prisoners of the Revolution*, 306.

93. Andros in Dunlap, *History of New Netherlands*, 138-39.

94. Dunlap, ibid., 141.

95. Palmer in Dandridge, *American Prisoners of the Revolution*, 307-8.

96. Fox, ibid., 256.

97. Ibid.

98. Van Dyke, ibid., 250.

99. Fox, ibid., 270-71, 277-79.

100. Coffin, ibid., 320.

101. Andros, ibid., 326.

102. Hawkins, ibid., 281.

103. Andros, ibid., 328-31. Hawkins and a boy named Waterman also escaped by swimming to Long Island; see Hawkins, ibid., 280-92.

104. Palmer, ibid., 309-10.

105. Dring, 84.

106. Ibid., 85-86.

107. Ibid., 45-47.

108. Dandridge, *American Prisoners of the Revolution*, 297-98.

109. The burial party is described in detail in Dring, 58-60.

110. Andros in Dunlap, *History of New Netherlands*, 140.

111. Dring, 61, 63.

112. Booth, *History of New York*, 532; Dunlap, *History of New Netherlands*, ccxl.

113. Lewis Leary, *That Rascal Freneau* (Newark, 1941); Philip Merrill Marsh, *Philip Freneau: Poet and Journalist* (Metuchen, N.J., 1967).

114. Mary S. Austin, *Philip Freneau* (New York, 1901), chap. 2.

115. Leary, *That Rascal Freneau*, 83.

116. See "The British Prison-Ship," in *The Poems of Philip Freneau: Written Chiefly During the Late War* (Philadelphia, 1786), 186-206; Robert E. Spiller and Harold Blodgett, eds., *The Roots of National Culture: American Literature to 1830*, rev. ed. (New York, 1949), 951; Nelson Frederick Atkins, *Philip Freneau and the Cosmic Enigma: The Religious and Philosophical Speculations of an American Poet* (New York, 1949); Jacob Axelrad, *Philip Freneau: Champion of Democracy* (Austin, 1967); Philip Merrill Marsh, *The Works of Philip Freneau: A Critical Study* (Metuchen, N.J., 1968); Austin, *Philip Freneau.*

117. Bowman, *Captive Americans*, 27; Henry Laurens, "Narrative of His Capture and his confinement in the Tower of London, etc., 1780, 1781, 1782," *South Carolina Historical Collections* 1 (1857): 18-19.

118. Commager and Morris, *The Spirit of 'Seventy-Six*, 1169-71; Robert V. Remini, *Andrew Jackson* (New York, 1966), 18-19; John Reid and Henry Eaton, *The Life of Andrew Jackson, Major General* (Philadelphia, 1817), 10-15.

119. Boynton Merrill, Jr., *Jefferson's Nephews: A Frontier Tragedy* (New York, 1976), 26.

120. By one study of deaths on the American side, 6,824 were killed in battle, 10,000 died in camps, and 8,500 perished as prisoners of war. Howard Peckham, *The Toll of Independence* (Chicago, 1974). A previously accepted casualty figure had been 4,000 battlefield deaths and 10,000 from all causes. T. Harry Williams, *History of American Wars* (New York, 1981), 45n.

121. Armbruster, *The Wallabout Prison Ships*, 22. Another writer insisted, "It has been ascertained . . ., with as much precision as the nature of the case will admit, that more than

TEN THOUSAND died on board the *Jersey,* and the hospital ships *Scorpion, Strombolo,* and *Hunter.*" Dring, 5.

122. The sinking is described by Henry Palmer, whose father, Capt. Roswell Palmer, had been imprisoned on the *Jersey* in about 1781, as quoted in Dandridge, *American Prisoners of the Revolution,* 305–6.

123. Bowman, *Captive Americans,* 40.

124. Booth, *History of New York,* 531.

125. Alexander C. Flick, ed., *History of the State of New York,* 10 vols. (New York, 1933–37), vol. 4, 274–77; Edith Abbot, *New York in the American Revolution* (New York, 1929), 274–81; Barck, *New York City during the War,* 215, 143; Mary Beth Norton, "The Fate of Some Black Loyalists of the American Revolution," *Journal of Negro History* 58 (October 1973); Herbert G. Gutman, *The Black Family in Slavery and Freedom, 1750–1925* (New York, 1976), 243. Naval inspection records for the ships that evacuated the city in 1783 list most of the émigrés' names and ages, as well as their status as slaves, freeborns, or indentured servants, plus their masters' names and other information. See *Miscellaneous Papers of the Continental Congress, 1775–1785* [1783], Roll 66, microcopy 247, and Roll 7, microcopy 332, National Archives, Washington.

126. Thomas Eddy, in Knapp, *The Life of Thomas Eddy,* 51.

127. D. M. Ellis, "The Rise of the Empire State, 1790–1820," *New York History* 56, no. 1 (January 1975): 5; Booth, *History of New York,* 574–75; Winslow C. Watson, *Men and Times of the Revolution; or, Memoirs of Elkanah Watson . . .* (New York, 1857), 275.

128. Benjamin Rush stated: "The American War is over, but this is far from being the case with the American Revolution. On the contrary, nothing but the first act of the great drama is closed." Rush, *An Address to the People of the United States . . .* (Philadelphia, 1787), in Hezekiel Niles, *Principles and Acts of the Revolution in America,* ed. Alden T. Vaughn (New York, 1965), 334.

129. Booth, *History of New York,* 575; Watson, *Men and Times,* 274–75. The ascension of property rights is examined in Winthrop D. Jordan, *White over Black: American Attitudes toward the Negro, 1550–1812* (Chapel Hill, 1968), 350–52. Regarding the litigation that ensued, see George Richards Minot, *The History of the Insurrections, in the Year MDCCLXXXVI, and the Rebellion Consequent Thereon* (Worcester, Mass., 1788), 29–30.

130. Minot, *The History of the Insurrections,* 201.

131. Stephen Burroughs, *The Memoirs of the Notorious Stephen Burroughs of New Hampshire* [Albany, 1811] (London, 1924); see Alice Felt Tyler, *Freedom's Ferment: Phases of American Social History to 1860* (Minneapolis, 1944), 272–73.

132. Orville J. Victor, *History of American Conspiracies* (New York, 1863), 165; J. R. Pole, "Shays's Rebellion: A Political Interpretation," in Jack R. Greene, ed., *The Reinterpretation of the American Revolution, 1763–1789* (New York, 1968), 416–43.

133. W. E. B. Du Bois, *The Suppression of the African Slave-Trade to the United States of America, 1638–1870* (New York, 1896), 41.

134. See Benjamin Quarles, *The Negro in the American Revolution* (Chapel Hill, 1961); Sidney Kaplan, *The Black Presence in the Era of the American Revolution, 1770–1800* (New York, 1973). But in 1783 the British West Indies received 16,208 slaves from Africa, and in 1787 the number had risen to 21,023. Du Bois, *Suppression,* 41.

135. Betty Fladeland, *Men and Brothers: Anglo-American Antislavery Cooperation* (Urbana, Ill., 1972), 29.

136. Jordan, *White over Black,* 345.

137. Fladeland, *Men and Brothers,* 29–30.

138. David Cooper, *A Serious Address to the Rulers of America, on the Inconsistency of Their Conduct Respecting Slavery . . .* (Trenton, 1783), 12–13.

139. See also Earl Leslie Griggs, *Thomas Clarkson: The Friend of the Slaves* (London, 1936).

140. Thomas Clarkson, *An Essay on the Slavery and Commerce of the Human Species, Particularly the African . . .* (Philadelphia, 1786), vii.

141. Ibid., 24–29, 60.

142. Ibid., 49–50, 53.

143. Ibid., 100.

144. See generally, Fladeland, *Men and Brothers;* Matthew T. Mellon, *Early American Views on Negro Slavery* [1934] (New York, 1969), 65.

145. Jordan, *White over Black,* 354; Benjamin J. Klebaner, "American Manumission Laws and the Responsibility for Supporting Slaves," *Virginia Magazine of History and Biography* 63 (1955): 443–53; Robert William Fogel and Stanley L. Engerman, "Philanthropy at Bargain Prices: Notes on the Economics of Gradual Emancipation," *Journal of Legal Studies* 3, no. 2 (June 1974): 377–401; Arthur Zilversmit, *The First Emancipation: The Abolition of Slavery in the North* (Chicago, 1967).

146. T. R. Moseley, "A History of the New-York Manumission Society, 1785–1849" (Ph.D. diss., New York University, 1963), 9–12; U.S. Bureau of the Census, *Negro Population of the United States, 1790–1915* (Washington, 1915), 51. Slaveholding by the Dutch "boers" of New York, and the effect of slavery's abolition on their way of life, is examined in Alice P. Kenney, *Stubborn for Liberty* (Syracuse, 1975), 77, 214.

147. Philip S. Foner, *History of Black Americans: From Africa to the Emergence of the Cotton Kingdom* (Westport, Conn., 1975), 366–67; Moseley, "New-York Manumission Society," 90.

148. Foner, *History of Black Americans,* 368; Edgar J. McManus, *A Short History of Negro Slavery in New York* (Syracuse, 1966), 163; New-York Manumission Society, *Minutes* for January 25 and February 19, 1785, and November 9, 1786. The minutes of the society from 1785 to 1822 are located in the New-York Historical Society in Manhattan.

149. Thomas Jefferson, *Notes on the State of Virginia* [1785], ed. Paul Leicester Ford (New York, 1894); Jordan, *White over Black,* xii.

150. Mellon, *Early American Views on Negro Slavery,* 115.

151. Job R. Tyson, *Essay on the Penal Law of Pennsylvania* (Philadelphia, 1827), 15–18; W. David Lewis, *From Newgate to Dannemora: The Rise of the Penitentiary in New York, 1796–1848* (Ithaca, 1965), 2–3.

152. Benjamin Rush, *Address to the Inhabitants of the British Settlements in America upon Slave-Keeping* (Philadelphia, 1773), 2–3; David Freeman Hawke, *Benjamin Rush* (New York, 1971), 362–66.

153. Quoted in Harry Elmer Barnes and Negley K. Teeters, *New Horizons in Criminology,* 2nd ed. (New York, 1951), 521.

154. David Brion Davis, *The Problem of Slavery in the Age of Revolution, 1770–1823* (Ithaca, 1975), 252–53.

155. James Edward Gillespie, "The Transportation of English Convicts After 1783," *Journal of Criminal Law and Criminology* 23, no. 3 (1922): 359; Robert Hughes, *The Fatal Shore: The Epic of Australia's Founding* (New York, 1986); L. L. Robson, *The Convict Settlers of Australia* (Melbourne, 1965).

156. "Extracts from the Diary of Ann Warder," *Pennsylvania Magazine of History and Biography* 18 (1894): 61 [entry for 3 mo. 30th (March 30)].

157. Mellon, *Early American Views,* 14–24, quoted at 71. The records of the Pennsylvania Abolition Society are in the Historical Society of Pennsylvania, Philadelphia.

158. N.Y. State Laws, 11 Sess., February 21, 1788, chap. 37, sect. 11.

159. Jordan, *White over Black,* 410–11.

160. *The Federalist Papers: Alexander Hamilton, James Madison, and John Jay* (New York, 1961) [New York, 1788]. For a contemporary view of some of these events, see James Kent to Mrs. Elizabeth Hamilton, December 10, 1832, in William Kent, ed., *Memoirs and Letters of James Kent* (Boston, 1898), 281–331.

161. *The Federalist Papers,* No. 51 (Madison), No. 59 (Hamilton), and No. 27 (Hamilton).

162. Smith, *City of New York.*

163. Booth, *History of New York,* 581; Sidney I. Pomerantz, *New York: An American City, 1783–1803* (New York, 1938), 313.

164. New York City, *Minutes of the Common Council, 1784–1831,* vol. 1, 176.

165. N.Y. State Laws, 8 Sess., March 18, 1785, chap. 40; Pomerantz, *New York,* 313, 315.

166. Booth, *History of New York,* 581.

167. Smith, *City of New York,* 15; Pomerantz, *New York,* 323.

168. Booth, *History of New York,* 581; Smith, *City of New York,* 16.

169. Smith, *City of New York,* 16; Pomerantz, *New York,* 317.

170. Booth, *History of New York,* 583–86.

171. Foner, *History of Black Americans,* 427.

172. Alfred Owen Aldridge, *Man of Reason: The Life of Thomas Paine* (Philadelphia, 1959), 208–19; Audrey Williamson, *Thomas Paine: His Life, Work, and Times* (New York, 1973), chaps. 17–18; W. E. Woodward, *Tom Paine: America's Godfather, 1737–1809* (New York, 1945), 256–76. Adams quote from Massachusetts Historical Society Collections, 5th Ser., vol. 3, 379.

173. Hans Zinsser, *Rats, Lice, and History* (Boston, 1938), 161.

174. Charles Coleman Sellers, *Charles Willson Peale* (Philadelphia, 1947), 111.

175. Benjamin Rush, *An Account of the Bilious Remitting Yellow Fever, as it Appeared in the City of Philadelphia in the Year 1793* (Philadelphia, 1794); Charles-Edward Amory Winslow, *The Conquest of Epidemic Disease* (New York, 1967), chap. 11.

176. Foner, *History of Black Americans,* 422; C. L. R. James, *The Black Jacobins: Toussaint L'Ouverture and the San Domingo Revolution* (New York, 1963).

177. J. P. Martin, "The Rights of Man," in Foner, *History of Black Americans,* 456–57.

178. Belknap Papers, Massachusetts Historical Society Collections, 5th Ser., vol. 3, 402.

179. Jefferson to St. George Tucker, Monticello, August 25, 1797, in Ford, ed., *Works of Jefferson,* vol. 8, 335.

180. Foner, *History of Black Americans,* 452.

181. Ibid., 448–49. In November 1793 several attempts were apparently made to set fire to Albany, and in January 1794 some Negroes were charged with arson.

182. Quoted in Foner, *History of Black Americans,* 451.

183. Governor Charles Pinckney of South Carolina, to Colonial Assembly of St. Dominque, September 1791, quoted ibid., 443.

184. Henrietta Buckmaster, *Let My People Go: The Story of the Underground Railroad and the Growth of the Abolition Movement* (Boston, 1959), 20.

185. *The Public Statutes at Large of the United States of America, 1789–1873,* 17 vols. (Boston, 1850–73), vol. 1, 302–5; Buckmaster, *Let My People Go,* 20.

186. Knapp, *The Life of Thomas Eddy,* 49.

187. Thomas Eddy, ibid., 53.

188. Knapp, *The Life of Thomas Eddy,* 54–55.

189. Ibid., 55; see also Arthur A. Ekirch, "Thomas Eddy and the Beginnings of Prison Reform in New York," *New York History* 24, no. 3 (July 1943): 376–91.

190. Thomas Eddy, *An Account of the State Prison or Penitentiary House in the City of New-York* (New York, 1801), 12–13; Lewis, *From Newgate to Dannemora,* 30; Caleb Lownes to Thomas Eddy, April 19, 1796, and Eddy to Philip Schuyler, July 14, 1796, Schuyler Papers, New York Public Library.

191. Cadwallader D. Colden later wrote that "the laws establishing our State prison, owed their origin more to the part taken by the Society of Friends" than to anything else. Colden to David Hosack, June 23, 1833, in Knapp, *The Life of Thomas Eddy,* 18. Chancel-

lor James Kent said that corporal punishment was definitely abolished for the "first time in the history of American criminal law." Pomerantz, *New York*, 319.

192. Laws of 1796, chap. 30; Knapp, *The Life of Thomas Eddy*, 55–57; Eddy, *Account*, 14.

193. Lewis, *From Newgate to Dannemora*, 29; Thomas Eddy to Philip Schuyler, August 22, 1796, Schuyler Papers, New York Public Library; papers regarding the actions of the Commissioners for the Building of the State Prison in the County of Albany in 1796–97 may be found in Canal Papers, New York State Archives, Albany.

194. Milton W. Brown, *American Art to 1900: Painting, Sculpture, Architecture* (New York, 1977), 150; Knapp, *The Life of Thomas Eddy*, 56–57; Eddy, *Account*, 12–13.

195. Lewis, *From Newgate to Dannemora*, 30.

196. Ibid.; Eddy to Charles Bulfinch, Esq., Boston, March 28, 1800, New York State Archives, Albany. Eddy stated that no keeper should be allowed to strike a prisoner. Eddy, *Account*, 27; Barnes and Teeters, *New Horizons*, 494–95; Negley K. Teeters, *The Cradle of the Penitentiary: The Walnut Street Jail in Philadelphia, 1773–1835* (Philadelphia, 1955), 70, 93, 100, 129–32.

197. Eriksson, *The Reformers*, 41.

198. Knapp, *The Life of Thomas Eddy*, 41; Ekirch, "Thomas Eddy," 376–91; W. David Lewis, "Newgate of New-York: A Case History of New-York," *New-York Historical Society Quarterly* 47, no. 2 (April 1963): 137–71. Eddy acknowledged consulting Howard's work. See Eddy to Philip Schuyler, August 22, 1796, Schuyler Papers; Knapp, *The Life of Thomas Eddy*, 41. He also called Howard "the active and indefatiguable friend of man." Eddy, *Account*, 6. Eddy also acknowledged the influence of Beccaria and Montesquieu.

199. Anonymous, *A View of the New-York State Prison* (New York, 1815), 11.

200. Orlando F. Lewis, *The Development of American Prisons and Prison Customs, 1776–1845* [New York, 1922] (Montclair, N.J., 1967), 44; Eddy, *Account*, 17.

201. Eddy, *New-York State Prison*, 11–13.

202. Eddy, *Account*, 25–26; Eddy to Charles Bulfinch, March 28, 1800, New York State Archives, Albany.

203. Newgate Record Book, 1797–1810, New York State Archives, Albany.

204. Eddy, *Account*, 53; Lewis, *From Newgate to Dannemora*, 32. As a general principle, he believed: "Great changes . . . in matters so deeply interesting to the community, should not too suddenly be made. The work of reformation is slow, and must encounter many and strong prejudices, and the force of long-established opinions." Eddy, *Account*, 15.

205. Lewis, ibid.

206. Eddy, *New-York State Prison*, 32.

207. Knapp, *The Life of Thomas Eddy*, 59. Eddy cited his use of principles of economy of food and the management of fire as contained in Count Rumford's *Essays*. See Eddy, *Account*, 46.

208. William Dunlap, *Diary of William Dunlap (1766–1839); The Memoirs of a Dramatist, Theatrical Manager, Painter, Critic, Novelist, and Historian* (New York, 1930), vol. 1, 251.

209. William Kent, *Memoirs and Letters of James Kent* (Boston, 1898), 122–23.

210. Eddy, *Account*, 34–36.

211. Ibid., 25; Ekirch, "Thomas Eddy," 376–91.

212. Newgate Record Book.

213. Lewis, *Development of American Prisons*, 56.

214. *Prisoner of Hope* (New York), June 7, 1800; Lewis, *From Newgate to Dannemora*, 33–34.

215. David Maydole Matteson, ed., *Minutes of the Common Council of the City of New York, 1784–1831* (New York, 1930), vol. 2, 716; *Daily Advertiser* (New York), November 4, 1801; Anonymous, *New-York State Prison*, 25.

216. William Crawford, *Report on the Penitentiaries of the United States, 1835* (Montclair, N.J., 1969), Appendix, 36.

217. Boston Prison Discipline Society, *Report* (Boston, 1828), 12.

218. Eddy, *Account,* 36.

219. Ibid., 70.

220. Thomas Eddy to Patrick Colquhoun, London, July 15, 1803, in Knapp, *The Life of Thomas Eddy,* 202; *Journal of the Assembly,* 27th Session (Albany, 1804), 87–88.

221. *Journal of the Assembly,* 27th Session (Albany, 1804), 87; Lewis, *From Newgate to Dannemora,* 34.

222. Knapp, *The Life of Thomas Eddy,* 207.

223. Thomas Eddy to Patrick Colquhoun, London, June 20, 1804, and September 27, 1805, ibid., 207–8, 214–15. For the "Rules and Regulations for the Internal Government of the New-York State Prison," dated February 23, 1804, see Lewis, "Newgate of New-York," 149.

224. Paul W. Keve, *The History of Corrections in Virginia* (Charlottesville, 1986), 23.

225. Ibid., 15.

226. Ibid., 21–22.

227. Ibid., 16–17. Latrobe was later commissioned by Jefferson to design the U.S. Capitol.

228. Clayton Mau, *The Development of Central and Western New York, from the Arrival of the White Man to the Eve of the Civil War* (Rochester, 1944); E. Wilder Spaulding, *His Excellency George Clinton, Critic of the Constitution* (New York, 1938), 234–35, 200; and Matthew L. Davis, *Memoirs of Aaron Burr* (New York, 1836), 328–31.

229. Charles Page Smith, *James Wilson, Founding Father, 1742–1798* (Chapel Hill, 1956), 350–51.

230. John Pintard, *Letters from John Pintard to His Daughter, Eliza Noel Pintard Davidson, 1816–1833* (1941), vol. 1, xii–xvi.

231. Robert A. East, *Business Enterprise in the American Revolutionary Era* (New York, 1938); Howard Swiggett, *The Extraordinary Mr. Morris* (Garden City, N.Y., 1952); quote about Morris in Nathan Miller, *The Founding Finaglers* (New York, 1976), 79.

232. Ellis Paxson Oberholtzer, *Robert Morris: Patriot and Financier* (New York, 1903), 345–47.

233. Ibid., 349–52.

234. Knapp, *The Life of Thomas Eddy,* 145–48. In 1793 Thomas Eddy and his childhood friend and fellow Quaker, John Murray, Jr., were appointed to a committee of the New York Yearly Meeting for the Improvement of the Indians, and they went on a Quaker mission to visit the sad vestiges of the Six Nations of the Iroquois Confederation. Ibid., 100–110.

235. John W. Barber and Henry Howe, *Historical Collections of the State of New York* (New York, 1845), 276.

236. P. J. Staudenraus, *The African Colonization Movement, 1816–1865* (New York, 1961), 8; Jordan, *White over Black,* 550–51.

237. Jordan, *White over Black,* 556–59. See St. George Tucker, *A Dissertation on Slavery: With a Proposal for the Gradual Abolition of It, in the state of Virginia* (Philadelphia, 1796).

238. Leo H. Hirsch, Jr., "The Negro in New York, 1783 to 1865," *Journal of Negro History* 16 (October 1931): 390.

239. Laws of 1799, chap. 62; Hirsch, "The Negro in New York," 390–91. The same day, March 29, 1799, chapter 57 was enacted, declaring that a person sentenced to imprisonment for life should be deemed civilly dead. C. Z. Lincoln, *Messages from the Governors* [John Jay, 1798] (Albany, 1909), vol. 2, 399, n. 1. Foner, *History of Black Americans,* 369.

240. See Gresham M. Sykes, *The Society of Captives* (Princeton, 1958).

241. Thomas Robert Malthus, *On Population* [London, 1798] (New York, 1960); see Paul A. Samuelson, *Economics,* 8th ed. (New York, 1970), 28–29.

242. Gertrude Himmelfarb, introduction to Malthus, *On Population,* xxxi.

243. Jordan, *White over Black,* 408–15; Foner, *History of Black Americans,* 508.

244. Foner, *History of Black Americans,* 509–16.

245. See Keve, *History of Corrections in Virginia,* 31; Stephen B. Oates, *The Fires of Jubilee: Nat Turner's Fierce Rebellion* (New York, 1975), 16–18; Herbert Aptheker, *American Negro Slave Revolts* (New York, 1969), 211–19; Joseph C. Carroll, *Slave Insurrections in the United States, 1800–1865* (Boston, 1938), 47–57.

246. James Monroe to Thomas Jefferson, September 5, 1800, in *The Writings of James Monroe,* ed. S. M. Hamilton, 7 vols. (New York, 1898–1903), vol. 3, 201.

247. Oates, *The Fires of Jubilee,* 17.

248. Jordan, *White over Black,* 549–50.

249. Keve, *History of Corrections in Virginia,* 64.

250. Du Bois, *Suppression,* 94–108.

251. Reginald Horsman, *The War of 1812* (New York, 1969).

252. Reginald Horsman, "The Paradox of Dartmoor Prison," *American Heritage,* February 1975, 14.

253. Anonymous, *New-York State Prison,* 36–37, 46–48, 58; Lewis, *From Newgate to Dannemora,* 43.

254. See M. J. Heale, "The New York Society for the Prevention of Pauperism, 1817–1823," *New-York Historical Society Quarterly* 55, no. 2 (April 1971): 153–76; Philip S. Foner, *Organized Labor and the Black Worker, 1619–1973* (New York, 1974), 5.

CHAPTER FOUR   *Little Man in the Big House*

1. See Ralph S. Herre, "The History of Auburn Prison from the Beginning to about 1867" (Ph.D. diss., Pennsylvania State University, 1950); David M. Ellis, "The Yankee Invasion of New York, 1783–1850," *New York History* 22 (January 1951): 9; Whitney R. Cross, *The Burned-Over District: The Social and Intellectual History of Enthusiastic Religion in Western New York, 1800–1850* (Ithaca, 1950).

2. Henry Hall, *History of Auburn* (Auburn, N.Y., 1869), 130; Herre, "History of Auburn Prison," 35–36.

3. E. T. Hiller, "Labor Unionism and Convict Labor," *Journal of the American Institute of Criminal Law and Criminology* 5 (March 1915): 860, n. 21. Herre, "History of Auburn Prison," 34. Records of the Erie Canal may be found in the Canal Papers of the New York State Archives, Albany.

4. For more about the Bank of Auburn, see Hall, *History,* 139–43; Herre, "History of Auburn Prison," 33, n. 7.

5. Hall, *History,* 131–32; Herre, "History of Auburn Prison," 37.

6. Hall, *History,* 131–32; Herre, "History of Auburn Prison," 37.

7. Hall, *History,* 131; Herre, "History of Auburn Prison," 37–38.

8. Hall, *History,* 20–31, 36–45, 62–63; Herre, "History of Auburn Prison," 38.

9. Hall, *History,* 132; Herre, "History of Auburn Prison," 38.

10. Hall, *History,* 134; Herre, "History of Auburn Prison," 39–40.

11. Robert S. Pickett, *House of Refuge: Origins of Juvenile Reform in New York State, 1815–1857* (Syracuse, 1969), 25.

12. Laws of New York, 40th Session, Chap. 137 (passed March 31, 1817). See David M. Ellis, James A. Frost, Harold C. Syrett, and Harry J. Carman, *A Short History of New York State* (Ithaca, 1957).

13. Herre, "History of Auburn Prison," 44.

14. *Military Minutes of the Council of Appointment of the State of New York, 1783–1821*

(Albany, 1901), vol. 2, 993, 1364; *Public Papers of Daniel D. Tompkins, Governor of New York, 1807–1817* (Albany, 1902), vol. 2, 593; Herre, "History of Auburn Prison," 44–45.

15. *Cayuga Patriot*, August 18, 1819; Gershom B. Powers, *Letter of Gershom Powers, Esq., in Answer to a Letter of the Hon. Edward Livingston in Relation to the Auburn State Prison (Read in the Legislature of Pennsylvania, January 23, 1829, and Ordered to Be Printed)* (Albany, 1829), 7; Herre, "History of Auburn Prison," 45.

16. W. David Lewis, *From Newgate to Dannemora: The Rise of the Penitentiary in New York, 1796–1848* (Ithaca, 1965), 45–46; *Journal of the Assembly of New-York,* 42nd Session (1819), 338.

17. *Laws of the State of New-York . . . 1819* (Albany, 1819), 87–89; Lewis, *From Newgate to Dannemora,* 46.

18. Herre, "History of Auburn Prison," 42–43; Lewis, *From Newgate to Dannemora,* 67.

19. Powers, *Letter,* 7; Herre, "History of Auburn Prison," 43.

20. *Cayuga Republican,* October 4, 1820; *Cayuga Patriot,* October 18, 1820; Herre, "History of Auburn Prison," 51–53; Hall, *History,* 134.

21. Hall, *History,* 134.

22. Powers, *Letter,* 8.

23. Ibid., 6; Herre, "History of Auburn Prison," 49; Lewis, *From Newgate to Dannemora,* 67.

24. Hall, *History,* 350.

25. *Cayuga Patriot,* June 20, 1821; Hall, *History,* 133; Herre, "History of Auburn Prison," 54–55.

26. Herre, "History of Auburn Prison," 56; *Journal of the Assembly of New-York,* 44th Session (1820–21), 904.

27. *Journal of the Assembly,* 51st Session (1828), Appendix A, 45; Lewis, *From Newgate to Dannemora,* 68–69.

28. Gershom Powers, *Brief Account of the Construction, Management and Discipline of the New York State Prison at Auburn, together with a Compendium of Criminal Law . . .* (Auburn, 1826), 32–36; Lewis, *From Newgate to Dannemora,* 69.

29. See especially Powers, *Brief Account,* 2, 4–7; *Journal of the Assembly* (1833), 29–30; Sidney Pollard, "Factory Discipline in the Industrial Revolution," *Economic History Review* 16, no. 2 (December 1963): 254–71. Pollard notes that many early-nineteenth-century American factories were modeled on workhouses and prisons.

30. *Journal of the Senate of New-York* (1827), 41.

31. "Report of the Committee Appointed to Visit the State Prisons," in *Journal of the Assembly,* No. 41 (January 15, 1825), 21.

32. *Journal of the Assembly,* No. 199 (1833), 24–25.

33. Powers, *Brief Account,* 3. In 1822 the visitor's fee was raised from 12½ cents to 25 cents. In 1830 the total revenue collected was $1,524. Orlando F. Lewis, *The Development of American Prisons and Prison Customs, 1776–1845* [New York, 1922] (Montclair, N.J., 1967), 91. Lewis was general secretary of the Prison Association of New York, now known as the Correctional Association of New York.

34. Powers, *Brief Account,* 4.

35. John Fowler, a British traveler to New York State in 1830.

36. Boston Prison Discipline Society, *5th Report* (Boston, 1830), 348.

37. Lewis, *From Newgate to Dannemora,* 94–95, 96n., 105, 142, 162–63; *Journal of the Senate,* 60th Session (1827). Appendix A contains the "Report of the Commissioners, directed by the act of the 17th April, 1826, to visit the State-Prison at Auburn, Made to the Senate, January 13, 1827."

38. *Journal of the Senate,* Appendix A, 19–21.

39. Ezra the Scribe [Rev. Silas E. Shepard], *The Chronicles of Auburn* (Auburn, 1838), 3–4.

40. *Journal of the Senate,* Appendix A, 21.

41. *Laws of the State of New-York, 42nd Session* (Albany, 1819), 87.

42. *Journal of the Senate,* Appendix A, 22–24.

43. William Crawford, *Report on the Penitentiaries of the United States* [n.p., 1835] (Montclair, N.J., 1969), 18n.

44. Lewis, *From Newgate to Dannemora,* 95.

45. Estelle B. Freedman, *Their Sisters' Keepers: Women's Prison Reform in America, 1830–1930* (Ann Arbor, 1981), 17.

46. Ibid., 15.

47. Lewis, *From Newgate to Dannemora,* 163.

48. Freedman, *Their Sisters' Keepers,* 34.

49. *Cayuga Patriot,* February 21, 1827, 2.

50. Quoted in [Capt. Frederick] Marryat, *A Diary in America . . . ,* 3 vols. (Paris, 1839), vol. 2, 296–97, citing a book by a convict, *The Rat-Trap, or Cogitations of a Convict in the House of Correction,* in which the author compares the public's visiting prisons with visiting zoos.

51. Alice Felt Tyler, *Freedom's Ferment: Phases of American Social History from the Colonial Period to the Outbreak of the Civil War* (New York, 1944), 279; John M. Duncan, *Travels through Part of the United States and Canada in 1818 and 1819 . . .* (New York, 1823), 63.

52. Negley K. Teeters and John D. Shearer, *The Prison at Philadelphia, Cherry Hill: The Separate System of Prison Discipline* (New York, 1957), 25–26. Regarding conditions in nearby Vermont, see John Reynolds, *Recollections of Windsor Prison; Containing Sketches of Its History and Discipline . . .* (Boston, 1834).

53. Louis Dwight (January 28, 1825), quoted in Gideon Hayes, *Pictures from Prison Life: An Historical Sketch of the Massachusetts State Prison . . . By Gideon Hayes, Warden* (Boston, 1869), 218–19.

54. See William Jenks, *A Memoir of the Reverend Louis Dwight* (Boston, 1856).

55. Quoted in J. P. Mayer, *Alexis de Tocqueville: A Biographical Study in Political Science* (New York, 1960), 13. Alexis de Tocqueville, *Democracy in America,* ed. J. P. Mayer, trans. George Lawrence (New York, 1969); Alexis de Tocqueville, *Journey to America,* ed. J. P. Mayer, trans. George Lawrence (New Haven, 1959); William J. Murphy, "Alexis de Tocqueville in New York: The Formulation of the Egalitarian Thesis," *New-York Historical Society Quarterly* 66, nos. 1 and 2 (January–April 1977): 69–79; Richard Reeves, *American Journey: Traveling with Tocqueville in Search of Democracy in America* (New York, 1982); Jack Lively, *The Social and Political Thought of Alexis de Tocqueville* (New York, 1962).

56. George W. Pierson, *Tocqueville and Beaumont in America* (New York, 1938), 99.

57. Murphy, "Tocqueville in New York," 74–75; Lewis, *From Newgate to Dannemora,* chap. 6. In 1830, for the first time in history, Auburn prison had begun to turn a profit for the state, even if it was only $25.37; by 1831, the sum had grown to $1,803.84. Lewis, *Development of American Prisons,* 279–80.

58. Col. Levi S. Burr, *A Voice from Sing-Sing, giving a General Description of the State Prison . . .* (Albany, 1833), 14.

59. *Assembly Report No. 199* (February 26, 1833), 11–12; *Senate Report No. 37* (1840), 45.

60. *Assembly Report No. 199* (1833), 6; *Senate Report No. 37* (1840), 45.

61. Pierson, *Tocqueville and Beaumont,* 101; E. S. Abdy, *Journal of a Residence and Tour in the United States of North America, from April, 1833, to October, 1834,* 3 vols. (London, 1835), vol. 1, 21. Also see Basil Hall in Thomas Mott Osborne, *Society and Prisons* (New Haven, 1916), 104–5.

62. Hall, quoted in Osborne, *Society and Prisons,* 105–6.

63. Beaumont, quoted in Pierson, *Tocqueville and Beaumont,* 101.

64. Boston Prison Discipline Society, *Third Annual Report of the Managers of the Boston Prison Discipline Society* (Boston, 1828), 61; Lewis, *Development of American Prisons,*

110; James R. Brice, Esq., *Secrets of the Mount-Pleasant State Prison, Revealed and Exposed* . . . (Albany, 1839), 31–32.

65. Lewis, *From Newgate to Dannemora,* 112; Pierson, *Tocqueville and Beaumont,* 104.

66. Quoted in Pierson, *Tocqueville and Beaumont,* 102.

67. Pierson, *Tocqueville and Beaumont,* 103.

68. Burr, *A Voice from Sing-Sing,* 46, 4, 16–17, 21.

69. *Senate Report No. 37* (1840), 70–72; *Senate Report No. 48,* 99, 171.

70. Burr, *A Voice from Sing-Sing,* 23–25.

71. Brice, *Secrets of Mount-Pleasant,* 43, 46.

72. Horace Lane, *Five Years in a State Prison; or, Interesting Truths, Showing the Manner of Discipline in the State Prisons at Sing Sing and Auburn, Exhibiting the Great Contrast Between the Two Institutions, in the Treatment of the Unhappy Inmates* . . . (New York, 1835), 15.

73. Williston H. Lofton, "Abolition and Labor," *Journal of Negro History* 33, no. 3 (July 1948): 263; Nicole Hahn Rafter, *Partial Justice: Women in State Prisons, 1800–1935* (Boston, 1985), 63; Lewis, *Development of American Prisons,* 138–40.

74. Martha J. Lamb, *History of the City of New York* (New York, 1880), vol. 2, 725.

75. Abdy, *Residence and Tour,* vol. 1, 21.

76. Gustave de Beaumont and Alexis de Tocqueville, *On the Penitentiary System in the United States and Its Application in France,* trans. Francis Lieber [1833] (Carbondale, Ill., 1964), 216, appendix n. 1.

77. Pierson, *Tocqueville and Beaumont,* 206.

78. Beaumont and Tocqueville, *Penitentiary System,* 161–65; Pierson, *Tocqueville and Beaumont,* 206.

79. Beaumont and Tocqueville, *Penitentiary System,* 47.

80. Ibid., 93, 264.

81. "Annual Report of the Inspectors of the State Prison at Auburn" (January 15, 1831), in *Senate Report No. 15* (Albany, N.Y.).

82. David J. Rothman, *The Discovery of the Asylum: Social Order and Disorder in the New Republic* (Boston, 1971), 83; see Roberts Vaux, *Letter on the Penitentiary System of Pennsylvania* (Philadelphia, 1827); Franklin Bache, *Observations and Reflections on the Penitentiary System* (Philadelphia, 1829).

83. Quoted from Norman B. Johnston, "John Haviland, 1792–1852," in *Pioneers in Criminology,* 2nd ed. (Montclair, N.J., 1972), 122. Richard Vaux, *Brief Sketch of the Origin and History of the State Penitentiary for the Eastern District of Pennsylvania at Philadelphia* (Philadelphia, 1872).

84. Albert Gardner, "A Philadelphia Masterpiece, Haviland's Prison," *Metropolitan Museum of Art Bulletin,* December 1955, 103. The prison has again become a tourist attraction. See Judith H. Dobrzynski, "For a Summer Getaway, a Model Prison," *New York Times,* July 11, 1997, C1.

85. See Teeters and Shearer, *The Prison at Philadelphia;* Rothman, *The Discovery of the Asylum;* Thomas McElwee, *A Concise History of the Eastern Penitentiary of Pennsylvania* (Philadelphia, 1835).

86. Crawford, *Report on the Penitentiaries,* 10; Beaumont and Tocqueville, *Penitentiary System,* 212 n. 1, 403; Torsten Eriksson, *The Reformers: An Historical Survey of Pioneer Experiments in the Treatment of Criminals,* trans. Catherine Djurklou (New York, 1976), 62–63.

87. George W. Smith, *A Defense of the System of Solitary Confinement of Prisoners* (Philadelphia, 1833), 22–23; Norman Johnston, introduction to Crawford, *Report on the Penitentiaries,* xi.

88. Teeters and Shearer, *The Prison at Philadelphia,* 71–72, 79; Beaumont and Tocqueville, *Penitentiary System,* 403.

89. Demetz and Blouet, quoted in Eriksson, *The Reformers,* 64.

90. Teeters and Shearer, *The Prison at Philadelphia*, 78–79.

91. Ibid., 78–79; Vaux, *Brief Sketch;* Thomas B. McElwee, *A Concise History of Eastern Penitentiary of Philadelphia*, 2 vols. (Philadelphia, 1835); Eriksson, *The Reformers*, 66–67; Charles Dickens, *American Notes, for General Circulation* [London, 1842] (New York, 1972), 148.

92. Dickens, *American Notes*, 149; Teeters and Shearer, *The Prison at Philadelphia*, 70.

93. Beaumont and Tocqueville, *Penitentiary System*, 57.

94. See Negley K. Teeters, "The First Fifteen Years of the Eastern Penitentiary of Pennsylvania," *Pennsylvania History* (October 1949): 261–302.

95. Beaumont and Tocqueville, *Penitentiary System*, 57; see also Reeves, *American Journey*, 253–55.

96. Pierson, *Tocqueville and Beaumont*, 463–68.

97. Crawford, *Report on the Penitentiaries*, 10; quoted in Pierson, *Tocqueville and Beaumont*, 467.

98. Quoted in Teeters and Shearer, *The Prison at Philadelphia*, 84.

99. Boston Prison Discipline Society, *8th Report* (Boston, 1833), 221.

100. Ibid., 222, 224.

101. *Journal of the State of Pennsylvania, 1832-33* (Philadelphia, 1833), vol. 2, 509.

102. Teeters and Shearer, *The Prison at Philadelphia*, 73–75.

103. Ibid., 98–102.

104. Quoted ibid., 102.

105. Ibid., 102–3.

106. Ibid., 101.

107. Ibid., 101–2.

108. See Dickens, *American Notes;* Angus Wilson, *The World of Charles Dickens* (London, 1970); Edgar Johnson, *Charles Dickens: His Tragedy and Triumph*, 2 vols. (London, 1953). For an account of Dickens's visit, see Teeters and Shearer, *The Prison at Philadelphia*, chap. 5.

109. Dickens, *American Notes*, 148.

110. Ibid., 155, 146–47.

111. Winthrop D. Jordan, *White over Black: American Attitudes toward the Negro, 1550–1812* (Chapel Hill, 1968), 480.

112. William Brandon, *The American Heritage Book of Indians* (New York, 1961), 221.

113. Quoted in Nicholas F. Kittrie and Eldon D. Wedlock, eds., *The Tree of Liberty: A Documentary History of Rebellion and Political Crime in America* (Baltimore, 1986), 115. See also Dee Brown, *Bury My Heart at Wounded Knee: An Indian History of the American West* (New York, 1970), 5; George W. Manypenny, *Our Indian Wards* [1880] (New York, 1972), 107–9; Brandon, *American Heritage Book of Indians*, 220; Gary B. Nash and Richard Weiss, eds., *The Great Fear: Race in the Mind of America* (New York, 1970), 79–88.

114. Manypenny, *Our Indian Wards*, 109–10.

115. Quoted in Brandon, *American Heritage Book of Indians*, 226–27.

116. Brandon, *American Heritage Book of Indians*, 229.

117. Nash and Weiss, *The Great Fear*, 79–88; Brandon, *American Heritage Book of Indians*, 229–30.

118. Brown, *Bury My Heart*, 5.

119. Kittrie and Wedlock, *The Tree of Liberty*, 131; Brown, *Bury My Heart*, 7; Brandon, *American Heritage Book of Indians*, 223.

120. Brandon, *American Heritage Book of Indians*, 230–31; Mary F. Berry, *Black Resistance/White Law: A History of Constitutional Racism in America* (New York, 1971), 35–67; see Minnie Moore Willson, *The Seminoles of Florida* (Philadelphia, 1896).

121. Boston Prison Discipline Society, *First Annual Report* (Boston, 1826), 24–25. The authors also concluded that, if public education of free Negroes failed to improve the situa-

tion, "a powerful argument may be derived from these facts, in favor of colonization, and civilized States ought surely to be [as] willing to expend money on any given part of its population, to prevent crime, as to punish it." Ibid., 37.

122. Alexis de Tocqueville, *Democracy in America* (New York, 1948), vol. 1, 358–60.

123. John Duncan, quoted in Leon F. Litwack, *North of Slavery: The Negro in the Free States* (Chicago, 1961), 15–16.

124. Crawford, *Report on the Penitentiaries, 3.*

125. Ibid., 15, 26.

126. Abdy, *Residence and Tour.* See Betty Fladeland, *Men and Brothers: Anglo-American Antislavery Cooperation* (Urbana, Ill., 1972), 239.

127. Abdy, *Residence and Tour,* vol. 1, 44–45, 55, 159, 251, 5, 8, 40.

128. Ibid., 15, 21, 261, 46–47, 95; vol. 3, 151; vol. 1, 92–93, 94–95 (quoting Rev. R. J. Breckenridge of Baltimore), 94–95.

129. Charles Richmond Henderson, ed., *Prison Reform* (New York, 1910), 145.

130. Quoted in Teeters and Shearer, *The Prison at Philadelphia,* 24n.

131. Lieber, in Beaumont and Tocqueville, *Penitentiary System,* viii, xi, xix, 13.

132. Lieber, ibid., translator's preface, 70.

133. Boston Prison Discipline Society, *Ninth Annual Report* (Boston, 1834), 268, 264; "Report of the Chaplain, To the Inspectors of the State Prison, Auburn, B. C. Smith, Jan. 1, 1833," in Boston Prison Discipline Society, *Eighth Annual Report* (Boston, 1833), 161.

134. As one early warden put it: "It is true that while confined here you can have no intelligence concerning relatives or friends. . . . You are to be literally buried from the world." Powers, *Letter,* 14. See Rothman, *The Discovery of the Asylum,* 70–73, 95; "Annual Report of Mt. Pleasant Prison," New York Senate Documents, *No. 39* (Albany, 1842), vol. 2, 25–26; New York Prison Association, *Fifth Annual Report* (Albany, 1850), 186–87; New York Senate Documents, *No. 20* (Albany, 1844), vol. 1, 21–22.

135. Samuel Gridley Howe, *An Essay on Separate and Congregate Systems of Prison Discipline, Being a Report Made to the Boston Prison Discipline Society* (Boston, 1846). See F. B. Sanborn, *Dr. Samuel Gridley Howe, the Philanthropist* (Boston, 1891).

136. Howe, *Separate and Congregate Systems,* 62, 41, 76, 78.

137. See Tyler, *Freedom's Ferment,* 304–7.

138. Ibid., 298, 304; George Thompson, *Prison Life and Reflections . . .* (Hartford, 1853), 369; Dorothea Dix, quoted in John Bartlow Martin, *Break Down the Walls. American Prisons: Present, Past, and Future* (New York, 1954), 49n. See Dorothea Lynde Dix, *Remarks on Prisons and Prison Discipline in the United States* (Philadelphia, 1845).

139. Jocelyn M. Pollock-Byrne, *Women, Prison, and Crime* (Pacific Grove, Calif., 1990), 43; C. Feinman, "An Historical Overview of the Treatment of Incarcerated Women: Myths and Realities of Rehabilitation," *Prison Journal* 63, no. 2 (1984): 17; Freedman, *Their Sisters' Keepers,* 46.

140. Tyler, *Freedom's Ferment,* 140.

141. Ibid., 140–49.

142. Ibid., 86–88. See Cross, *The Burned-Over District.*

143. Sydney E. Ahlstrom, *A Religious History of the American People* (New Haven, 1972), 505.

144. Tyler, *Freedom's Ferment,* 97–105; Thomas F. O'Dea, *The Mormons* (Chicago, 1957); Ahlstrom, *Religious History,* 506.

145. See Dallin H. Oaks and Marvin S. Hill, *Carthage Conspiracy: The Trial of the Accused Assassins of Joseph Smith* (Urbana, Ill., 1975).

146. Douglas F. Tobler and Nelson B. Wadsworth, *The History of the Mormons in Photographs and Text: 1830 to the Present* (New York, 1987), 138–63.

147. See Tyler, *Freedom's Ferment,* part two.

148. See J. Brooks Atkinson, *Henry David Thoreau: The Cosmic Yankee* (New York, 1927); Van Wyck Brooks, *The Flowering of New England, 1815–1865* (New York, 1937).

149. Henry David Thoreau, "An Essay on Civil Disobedience," in *Walden and "Civil Disobedience"* (New York, 1960), 225, 230, 230–31.

150. Ibid., 234–36.

151. Frederic Bancroft, *Slave-Trading in the Old South* (Baltimore, 1931), 272.

152. Ibid., 52–53, 283.

153. Ibid., 282–83.

154. G. W. Featherstonhaugh, *Excursions through the Slave States . . .* (New York, 1844), 46.

155. Bancroft, *Slave-Trading*, 278.

156. Ibid., 55.

157. Ibid., 53n. Another private slave jail was located at Wisconsin Avenue (32nd Street) and M Street (Pennsylvania Avenue), not far from the White House.

158. Ibid., 54.

159. Ibid., 60–62.

160. Ibid., 102, 57.

161. Ibid., 103, 106–9.

162. Solomon Northrup, *Twelve Years a Slave,* ed. Sue Eakin and Joseph Logsdon (Baton Rouge, 1968); see Charles H. Nichols, ed., *Black Men in Chains: Narratives by Escaped Slaves* (New York, 1972), 201, 210; Charles L. Blockson, *The Underground Railroad* (New York, 1989), 132–33; Bancroft, *Slave-Trading*, 57. For a study of slave narratives, also see Charles H. Nichols, *Many Thousand Gone: The Ex-Slaves' Account of Their Bondage and Freedom* (Leiden, 1963).

163. Bancroft, *Slave-Trading*, 53.

164. Nichols, *Black Men in Chains*, 67–73. See Moses Roper, *A Narrative of the Adventures and Escape of Moses Roper from American Slavery* (London, 1839).

165. Richard C. Wade, *Slavery in the Cities: The South, 1820–1860* (New York, 1964), 219; for more about the jail conditions endured by alleged fugitive slaves, see ibid., 184–86.

166. Bancroft, *Slave-Trading*, 270.

167. See Herbert Aptheker, *Nat Turner's Slave Rebellion: Including the Full Text of Nat Turner's 1831 "Confession"* (New York, 1966); Stephen B. Oates, *The Fires of Jubilee: Nat Turner's Fierce Rebellion* (New York, 1975), 120–25.

168. Paul W. Keve, *The History of Corrections in Virginia* (Charlottesville, 1986), 47, 49; Bancroft, *Slave-Trading*, 270.

169. Bancroft, *Slave-Trading*, 274–75; quoted in Keve, *History of Corrections in Virginia,* 47.

170. Bancroft, *Slave-Trading*, 270; Keve, *History of Corrections in Virginia,* 50–51.

171. See Tyler, *Freedom's Ferment;* Fladeland, *Men and Brothers;* M. J. Heale, "The Formative Years of the New York Prison Association, 1844–1862: A Case Study in Antebellum Reform," *New-York Historical Society Quarterly* 59 (October 1975): 320–47.

172. Henrietta Buckmaster, *Let My People Go: The Story of the Underground Railroad and the Growth of the Abolition Movement* (Boston, 1941), 145–46; Blockson, *The Underground Railroad,* 2.

173. Tyler, *Freedom's Ferment,* 480; Buckmaster, *Let My People Go,* 25–28, 107; Freedman, *Their Sisters' Keepers,* 29.

174. See William Lloyd Garrison, *Selections from the Writings and Speeches of William Lloyd Garrison* [1852] (New York, 1969).

175. See John L. Thomas, ed., *Slavery Attacked: The Abolitionist Crusade* (Englewood Cliffs, N.J., 1965); Richard O. Curry, ed., *The Abolitionists: Reformers or Fanatics?* (New York, 1965); Martin Duberman, ed., *The Antislavery Vanguard: New Essays on the Abolitionists* (Princeton, 1965).

176. J. C. Furnas, *Goodbye to Uncle Tom* (New York, 1956), 24; Blockson, *The Underground Railroad,* 237–38.

177. Gilbert Hobbs Barnes, *The Anti-Slavery Impulse, 1830–1844* (New York, 1933),

231. See *Letters of Theodore D. Weld, Angelina Grimké Weld, and Sarah Grimké*, ed. Dwight L. Dumond and Gilbert H. Barnes (New York, 1934); Harriet Beecher Stowe, *Uncle Tom's Cabin* (New York, 1962) and *The Key to Uncle Tom's Cabin* (London, 1853).

178. *David Walker's Appeal, in Four Articles; Together with a Preamble to the Coloured Citizens of the World, But in Particular, and Very Expressly, to Those of the United States of America*, ed. with an introduction by Charles M. Wiltse (New York, 1965); Tyler, *Freedom's Ferment*, 484–85; see Litwack, *North of Slavery*, 232–33.

179. See Edward Beecher, *Narrative of the Riots at Alton* (New York, 1965); Tyler, *Freedom's Ferment*, 503.

180. Furnas, *Goodbye to Uncle Tom*, 200; Charles L. Blockson, "Escape from Slavery: The Underground Railroad," *National Geographic* 166, no. 1 (July 1984): 9.

181. Blockson, *The Underground Railroad*, 10; see Scott Thybony, "Against All Odds, Black Seminole Won Their Freedom," *Smithsonian*, August 1991, 90–101.

182. Thybony, "Against All Odds," 93–95.

183. Blockson, "Escape from Slavery," 9; *The Public Statutes-at-Large of the United States of America, 1789–1873*, 17 vols. (Boston, 1850–73), vol. 1, 302–5; James M. McPherson, *Battle Cry of Freedom: The Civil War Era* (New York, 1988), 78; Tyler, *Freedom's Ferment*, 527.

184. McPherson, *Battle Cry of Freedom*, 79.

185. Tyler, *Freedom's Ferment*, 527; Blockson, *The Underground Railroad*, 2–3; Furnas, *Goodbye to Uncle Tom*, 208.

186. Frederick Douglass, *Life and Times of Frederick Douglass; Written by Himself* [1892] (New York, 1962), 266; Furnas, *Goodbye to Uncle Tom*, 205; McPherson, *Battle Cry of Freedom*, 79; Thomas Brown, *Three Years in Kentucky Prisons* (Indianapolis, 1857).

187. Blockson, *The Underground Railroad*, 131; Tyler, *Freedom's Ferment*, 533.

188. Buckmaster, *Let My People Go*, 130–31; Jonathan Walker, *Branded Hand: Trial and Imprisonment of Jonathan Walker* (New York, 1969); for a facsimile of the 1845 edition, see *Trial and Imprisonment of Jonathan Walker, at Pensacola, Florida, for Aiding Slaves to Escape from Bondage* (Gainesville, 1974).

189. Buckmaster, *Let My People Go*, 192; H. Bruce Franklin, *The Victim as Criminal and Artist: Literature from the American Prison* (New York, 1978), 132.

190. Blockson, *The Underground Railroad*, 94–95.

191. Thompson, *Prison Life and Reflections*, 118, 124, 156, 56–57; see Franklin, *Victim as Criminal and Artist*, 131.

192. Blockson, *The Underground Railroad*, 117–18; Furnas, *Goodbye to Uncle Tom*, 224. See Henry "Box" Brown, *The Narrative of Henry "Box" Brown, Written by Himself* (Manchester, Eng., 1851).

193. McPherson, *Battle Cry of Freedom*, 80.

194. Ibid. *Ableman v. Booth*, 21 Howard 506 (1859).

195. McPherson, *Battle Cry of Freedom*, 81.

196. Blockson, *The Underground Railroad*, 85, 102–4; Buckmaster, *Let My People Go*, 214. See Sarah H. Bradford, *Harriet, the Moses of Her People* (New York, 1886); Earl Conrad, *Harriet Tubman* (New York, 1942).

197. Douglass, *Life and Times of Frederick Douglass*, 265–66.

198. Frederick Douglass, *My Bondage and My Freedom* [1855] (New York, 1969), 298, 301, 340; Carleton Mabee, *Black Freedom* (New York, 1970), 291–95.

199. See Blockson, "Escape from Slavery," 14; Blockson, *The Underground Railroad*.

200. McPherson, *Battle Cry of Freedom*, 82.

201. Ibid., 83.

202. Buckmaster, *Let My People Go*, 204–7.

203. *Dred Scott v. Sandford*, 19 How. 393; 15 L.Ed. 691 (1857).

204. Don E. Fehrbacher, *The Dred Scott Case: Its Significance in American Law and Politics* (New York, 1978).

205. *New York Times,* November 29, 1855; Lewis, *From Newgate to Dannemora,* 273.

206. Lewis, *From Newgate to Dannemora,* 274.

207. Stephen B. Oates, *To Purge This Land with Blood: A Biography of John Brown* (New York, 1972), 19, 53. See also Franklin B. Sanborn, *Life and Letters of John Brown* (Boston, 1885).

208. John Brown Papers, Chicago Historical Society; Oates, *To Purge This Land,* 350–51.

209. Quoted in Oates, *To Purge This Land,* 319; McPherson, *Battle Cry of Freedom,* 209–10.

CHAPTER FIVE   *Scandal and Reform*

1. Editors of American Heritage, *The American Heritage Picture Book of the Civil War* (New York, 1960), 500.

2. Kenneth Radley, *Rebel Watchdog: The Confederate States Army Provost Guard* (Baton Rouge, 1989), 171, n. 19. See William R. Hesseltine, *Civil War Prisons: A Study in War Psychology* (New York, 1964); Earl Antrim, *Civil War Prisons and Their Covers* (New York, 1961); Frank L. Byrne, ed., "A General behind Bars: Neal Dow in Libby Prison," *Civil War History* 8 (June 1962): 164–83; Bruce Catton, "Prison Camps of the Civil War," *American Heritage* 10, no. 5 (August 1959): 4–13, 96–97; William C. Davis, *The Images of War, 1861–1865,* 6 vols. (New York, 1983).

3. Radley, *Rebel Watchdog,* 171–72.

4. Louis A. Brown, *The Salisbury Prison: A Case Study of Confederate Military Prisons, 1861–1865* (Wendell, N.C., 1980).

5. Radley, *Rebel Watchdog,* 172–75. See William Armstrong, "Cahaba to Charleston: The Prison Odyssey of Lt. Edmund E. Ryan," *Civil War History* 8 (June 1962): 218–27.

6. Radley, *Rebel Watchdog,* 171.

7. Ibid., 171–72, n. 19; Hesseltine, *Civil War Prisons,* 163.

8. T. H. Mann, "A Yankee in Andersonville," *Century Magazine* 40, no. 3 (July 1890): 448–55.

9. Catton, "Prison Camps," 5–8; *American Heritage Picture Book,* 504–5.

10. Mann, "A Yankee in Andersonville," 611.

11. Catton, "Prison Camps," 6.

12. *American Heritage Picture Book,* 500.

13. Catton, "Prison Camps," 8.

14. Ibid., 8, 96.

15. Ibid., 8.

16. Ibid., 9–13.

17. Ibid., 96.

18. H. Carpenter, "Plain Living at Johnson's Island," *Century Magazine* 41, no. 5 (March 1891): 710, 715.

19. John A. Wyeth, "Cold Cheer at Camp Morton," *Century Magazine* 41, no. 6 (April 1891): 844–47.

20. Ibid., 852.

21. Ibid.

22. Catton, "Prison Camps," 6.

23. Wyeth, "Cold Cheer at Camp Morton," 852.

24. Catton, "Prison Camps," 6–7.

25. Andrew Delbanco, "To the Gettysburg Station," *New Republic,* November 20, 1989, 31.

26. *Congressional Globe,* 38th Congress, 1st Session, vol. 2, 1313; Herman V. Ames, *Proposed Amendments to the Constitution, 1789 to 1889* (Washington, 1897), 214–15.

27. *Congressional Globe*, 38th Congress, 1st Session, vol. 1, 521, vol. 2, 1482; Lee Wood and Barbara Esposito, *Prison Slavery in the Thirteenth Amendment* (Washington, 1978), 17–20. See Charles Schurz, *Charles Summer* (Chicago, 1951).

28. Wood and Esposito, *Prison Slavery*, 31, 35.

29. Ibid., 35–36.

30. Quoted in Leon F. Litwack, *Been in the Storm So Long: The Aftermath of Slavery* (New York, 1980), 171.

31. Susie Melton, in Federal Writers' Project, *The Negro in Virginia* (New York, 1940), 210–11.

32. Annie Mae Weathers, quoted in Julius Lester, *To Be a Slave* (New York, 1968), 139.

33. Booker T. Washington, *Up from Slavery: An Autobiography* (Boston, 1928), 19–22.

34. Catton, "Prison Camps," 5–8, 96.

35. Kenneth M. Stampp, *The Era of Reconstruction, 1865–1877* (New York, 1967), 10.

36. See Litwack, *Been in the Storm*, 319.

37. *New York Times*, December 31, 1865; C. Mildred Thompson, *Reconstruction in Georgia: Economic, Social, Political, 1865–1872* (Gloucester, Mass., 1964), 46.

38. Litwack, *Been in the Storm*, 287.

39. Ibid., 505, 521–23.

40. Theodore B. Wilson, *The Black Codes of the South* (University Alabama, 1965); Stampp, *The Era of Reconstruction*, 79–80.

41. Litwack, *Been in the Storm*, 319; Edwin C. Woolley, *The Reconstruction of Georgia* (New York, 1901); John S. Reynolds, *Reconstruction in South Carolina, 1865–1877* (Columbia, 1901); William C. Harris, *The Day of the Carpetbagger: Republican Reconstruction in Mississippi* (Baton Rouge, 1979).

42. Quoted in Litwack, *Been in the Storm*, 284–85.

43. Blake McKelvey, *American Prisons: A Study in American Social History prior to 1915* (Chicago, 1936), 176.

44. Quoted in Jesse F. Steiner and Roy M. Brown, *The North Carolina Chain Gang: A Study of County Convict Road Work* (Chapel Hill, 1927), 32–33.

45. Ibid., 21.

46. N.C. Public Laws, 1868–69, chap. 167; Steiner and Brown, *The North Carolina Chain Gang*, 13–14.

47. Steiner and Brown, *The North Carolina Chain Gang*, 15; McKelvey, *American Prisons*, 178.

48. See Harris, *The Day of the Carpetbagger*, 39, 353–56.

49. Ibid., 356–59.

50. McKelvey, 174. See James C. Bonner, "The Georgia Penitentiary at Milledgeville, 1817–1874," *Georgia Historical Society Quarterly* 55 (1971): 321–22; Henry Calvin Mohler, "Convict Labor Policies," *Journal of the American Institute of Criminal Law and Criminology* 15, no. 4 (February 1925): 562–63.

51. Paul W. Keve, *The History of Corrections in Virginia* (Charlottesville, 1986), 65–66; Barnes and Teeters, *New Horizons in Criminology*, 420.

52. Keve, *History of Corrections in Virginia*, 67–68.

53. Ibid., 68.

54. Quoted ibid., 72–73.

55. Ibid., 90.

56. *Ruffin v. Commonwealth*, 62 Va. (21 Gratt), 790, 794–96 (1871).

57. McKelvey, *American Prisons*, chap. 8. See David M. Oshinsky, *"Worse Than Slavery": Parchman Farm and the Ordeal of Jim Crow Justice* (New York, 1996).

58. Donald R. Walker, *Penology for Profit: A History of the Texas Prison System, 1867–1912* (College Station, 1988), 18–20, 26.

59. Walter Wilson, *Forced Labor in the United States* (New York, 1933), 40–41.

60. Ibid., 48–49.

61. Dee Brown, *Bury My Heart at Wounded Knee: An Indian History of the American West* (New York, 1970), 54–60.

62. Abraham Lincoln to Henry H. Sibley, December 6, 1863, ibid., 60.

63. William W. Folwell, *A History of Minnesota* (St. Paul, 1924), vol. 2, 211; quoted in "Big Eagle's Story of the Sioux Outbreak of 1862," Minnesota Historical Society, *Collections* 6 (1894): 399–400; Brown, *Bury My Heart,* 61–62.

64. Brown, *Bury My Heart,* 198–99; William Brandon, *The American Heritage Book of Indians* (New York, 1961), 354.

65. General Sherman, quoted in Benjamin Capps, *The Indians* (1973), 192.

66. Evan S. Connell, *Son of the Morning Star* (San Francisco, 1984), 143–48; Brown, *Bury My Heart,* 253–55, 270–71; Capps, *The Indians,* 6, 192.

67. Brandon, *American Heritage,* 312; Lemly, quoted in Connell, *Son of the Morning Star,* 74–75; Brown, *Bury My Heart,* 313.

68. Capps, *The Indians,* 200, 212–14; Brandon, *American Heritage,* 436–38; Connell, *Son of the Morning Star,* 392–93.

69. *Elk v. Wilkins,* 112 U.S. 94 (1884).

70. *United States v. Kagama,* 118 U.S. 375 (1886).

71. Angie Debo, *Geronimo: The Man, His Time, His Place* (Norman, 1976), 325; quotation, 300.

72. Ibid., 301; quotation, 322.

73. Brandon, *American Heritage,* 411–13; Geronimo, *Geronimo, His Own Story,* ed. S. M. Barrett (New York, 1970), 54, 163–65; Debo, *Geronimo,* chap. 21. See also Walter Reed, "Geronimo and His Warriors in Captivity," *Illustrated American* 3 (August 16, 1890).

74. John Mason Jeffrey, *Adobe and Iron: The Story of the Arizona Territorial Prison* (La Jolla, 1969), 71, 74–75.

75. Gideon Hayes, *Pictures of Prison Life. A Historical Sketch of the Massachusetts State Prison. By Gideon Hayes, Warden* (Boston, 1869), 122.

76. McKelvey, *American Prisons,* 39, 52, 40; quoted in Frederick Howard Wines, *Punishment and Reformation: A Study of the Penitentiary System* (New York, 1895), 203.

77. McKelvey, *American Prisons,* 67–68.

78. American Correctional Association, *The American Prison: A Pictorial History* (n.p., 1983), 70–72; McKelvey, *American Prisons,* 70.

79. American Correctional Association, *The American Prison,* 73, 75; quoted in McKelvey, *American Prisons,* 64.

80. Wines, *Punishment and Reform,* 205.

81. Stampp, *The Era of Reconstruction,* 186–87.

82. Catton, "Prison Camps," 8; McKelvey, *American Prisons,* 67–68.

83. Zebulon Brockway, quoted in McKelvey, *American Prisons,* 52.

84. David J. Rothman, *Conscience and Convenience: The Asylum and Its Alternatives in Progressive America* (Boston, 1980), 33–34; Beverly A. Smith, "Military Training at New York's Elmira Reformatory, 1888–1920," *Federal Probation,* March 1988, 34; McKelvey, *American Prisons,* 108–11.

85. Mark H. Haller, *Eugenics: Hereditarian Attitudes in American Thought* (New Brunswick, 1963), 36; Zebulon Brockway, "The Incorrigible Criminal: What Is He and How Should He Be Treated?" *Proceedings of the National Prison Association* (1884): 105–12; quoted from the *Seventeenth Year Book, New York State Reformatory at Elmira* (Elmira, 1892), B1–B2.

86. Smith, "Military Training," 34.

87. Zebulon R. Brockway, *Fifty Years of Prison Service: An Autobiography* [New York, 1912] (Montclair, N.J., 1969), 355.

88. *DOCS Today* (Albany, New York), October 1988, 14.

89. *Seventeenth Year Book,* B1.

90. Smith, "Military Training," 36; see also *In the Matter of the Charges Preferred against the Managers of the New York State Reformatory at Elmira* (Albany, 1894); Alexander W. Pisciotta, "Scientific Reform: The 'New Penology' at Elmira, 1876–1900," *Crime and Delinquency* 29, no. 4 (1983): 613–30.

91. Mohler, "Convict Labor Policies," 551–52.

92. Quoted in George W. Cable, "The Convict Lease System," in *The Silent South* (New York, 1885), 168.

93. Ibid.; see Arlin Turner, *George W. Cable: A Biography* (Durham, 1956); George W. Cable, *The Negro Question*, ed. Arlin Turner (Garden City, N.Y., 1958); Louis D. Rubin, Jr., *George W. Cable: The Life and Times of a Southern Heretic* (New York, 1969).

94. Cable, *Silent South*, 174; Mohler, "Convict Labor Policies," 564–65.

95. Quoted in Mark T. Carleton, *Politics and Punishment: The History of the Louisiana State Penal System* (Baton Rouge, 1971), 45. See also F. S. Shields, *Prison Reform: Its Principles and Purposes—What It Has Accomplished—Work Yet to Be Done* (New Orleans, 1906).

96. Cable, *Silent South*, 174; McKelvey, *American Prisons*, 182–83.

97. J. C. Powell, *The American Siberia* (Philadelphia, 1891), 17–18.

98. E. Stagg Whittin, *Penal Servitude* (New York, 1912), 1.

99. Frank Tannenbaum, quoted in Harry Elmer Barnes, *The Story of Punishment,* 2nd ed. (New York, 1930), 160.

100. McKelvey, *American Prisons,* 183; Mohler, "Convict Labor Policies," 580.

101. Mohler, "Convict Labor Policies," 566; Charles Edward Russell, "A Burglar in the Making" [June 1908], in Arthur and Lila Weinberg, eds., *The Muckrakers* (New York, 1964), 322–37.

102. Powell, *American Siberia,* 12–13, 15.

103. John Lewis Gillin, *Criminology and Penology,* 3rd ed. (New York, 1945), 405.

104. Barnes, *The Story of Punishment,* 152–54; Rogers in Powell, *American Siberia,* xxii. See N. Gordon Carper, "Martin Talbert, Martyr of an Era," *Florida Historical Quarterly* 52 (October 1973): 115–31.

105. Wilson, *Forced Labor,* 41.

106. E. T. Hiller, "Labor Unionism and Convict Labor," *Journal of the American Institute of Criminal Law and Criminology* 5 (March 1915): 863–64.

107. Barnes, *The Story of Punishment,* 151; Robert Conot, *A Streak of Luck* (New York, 1979), 255.

108. McKelvey, *American Prisons,* 90–97.

109. Committee on State Prisons, *Investigation of New York State Prisons* (Albany, 1883).

110. Ludwig Fink, "Historical Development of Dannemora," paper delivered to Clinton County Historical Association, January 6, 1969, in Clinton County Historical Association, Plattsburgh, New York.

111. Committee on State Prisons, *Investigation,* 132.

112. Quoted in Barnes, *The Story of Punishment,* 2nd ed., 152–54.

113. McKelvey, *American Prisons,* 94–97; Hiller, "Labor Unionism and Convict Labor," 877–78.

114. Committee on State Prisons, *Investigation,* i–iv.

115. Mohler, "Convict Labor Policies," 551; Hiller, "Labor Unionism and Convict Labor," 863.

116. Mohler, "Convict Labor Policies," 548–49.

117. John S. Perry, *Prison Labor, With Tables Showing the Proportion of Convict to Citizen Labor, in the Prisons of the State of New York, and of the United States* (Albany, 1885), 4, 34–36.

118. McKelvey, *American Prisons,* 96.

119. Perry, *Prison Labor,* 10–11.

120. Alexander Berkman, *Memoirs of a Prison Anarchist* [1912] (New York, 1970), 129–33.

121. Donald Lowrie, *My Life in Prison* (New York, 1912), quoted in Gillin, *Criminology and Penology,* 416.

122. Charles Loring Brace, *The Dangerous Classes of New York: and Twenty Years among Them* (New York, 1872).

123. See Haller, *Eugenics,* 21–22, 35–36, 107–8.

124. Robert L. Dugdale, *The Jukes: A Study in Crime, Pauperism, Disease, and Heredity,* 4th ed. [1877] (New York, 1910); Nicole Hahn Rafter, *Partial Justice: Women in State Prisons, 1800–1935* (Boston, 1985), 54.

125. Oliver Wendell Holmes, M.D., "Crime and Automatism," *Atlantic Monthly* 35 (April 1875): 472, quoted in Haller, *Eugenics,* 36.

126. Richard B. Morris, *Encyclopedia of American History* (New York, 1953), 449.

127. E. C. Wines, *The State of the Prisons and Child Saving Institutions in the Civilized World* [1880] (Montclair, N.J., 1986), xxii, xlix; New York State, Prison Department, *Annual Report of the Superintendent of State Prisons of the State of New York, for the Year 1892* (Albany, 1893), 81, 199.

128. State of New York, Prison Department, *Annual Report of the Superintendent of State Prisons for the Fiscal Year Ending June 30, 1918* (Albany, 1918), 90, 289.

129. See Haller, *Eugenics;* Charles B. Davenport, *Heredity in Relation to Eugenics* (New York, 1911).

130. Gillin, *Criminology and Penology,* 77; Fink, "Historical Development of Dannemora," 1–4; Charles Caldwell, *Elements of Phrenology* (Lexington, Ky., 1824).

131. Fink, "Historical Development of Dannemora," 13; "Character of LeBlanc," *American Phrenological Journal and Miscellany* 1 (December 1838): 89–96; "Phrenological Developments and Character of Tardy the Pirate—with Cuts," *American Phrenological Journal and Miscellany* 1 (January 1839): 104–13.

132. Fink, "Historical Development of Dannemora," 15; M. B. Sampson, *Rationale of Crime, and Its Appropriate Treatment, Being a Treatise on Criminal Jurisprudence Considered in Relation to Cerebral Organization,* ed. with notes and illustrations by E. W. Farnham (New York, 1846).

133. Fink, "Historical Development of Dannemora," 15–16.

134. Gillin, *Criminology and Penology,* 77.

135. Marvin E. Wolfgang, "Cesare Lombroso, 1835–1909," in *Pioneers in Criminology,* 2nd ed., ed. Herman Mannheim (Montclair, N.J., 1972), 232–91.

136. Quoted in Stephen Jay Gould, *The Mismeasure of Man* (New York, 1981), 124; see Richard Quinney, *The Problem of Crime* (New York, 1970), 59–60.

137. Stephen Schafer, *Theories in Criminology* (New York, 1969), 126; quoted in Gould, *The Mismeasure of Man,* 124. See C. Lombroso and W. Ferrero, *The Female Offender* [1894] (New York, 1920), 29.

138. Gould, *The Mismeasure of Man,* 124.

139. Haller, *Eugenics,* 40–42.

140. Jocelyn M. Pollock-Byrne, *Women, Prison, and Crime* (Pacific Grove, Calif. 1990), 13.

141. Fink, "Historical Development of Dannemora," 99. See E. P. Fowler, "Are the Brains of Criminals Anatomical Perversions?" *Medico-Chiurgical Quarterly* 1 (October 1880): 1–32.

142. August Drähms, *The Criminal, His Personnel and Environment* (New York, 1900).

143. Quoted from Kenneth Lamott, *Chronicles of San Quentin* (New York, 1961), 128; Wines, *Punishment and Reformation,* 257.

144. Gould, *The Mismeasure of Man,* 128–29.

145. Wines, *Punishment and Reformation,* 249; McKelvey, *American Prisons,* 122.

146. McKelvey, *American Prisons*, 122.

147. Paul W. Keve, *Prisons and the American Conscience: A History of U.S. Federal Corrections* (Carbondale, Ill., 1991), 51–52.

148. Ibid.; Douglas G. Browne and Alan Brock, *Fingerprints: Fifty Years of Scientific Crime Detection* (New York, 1954), 126.

149. See Alexander W. Pisciotta, *Benevolent Repression: Social Control and the American Reformatory-Prison Movement* (New York, 1994).

150. *Seventeenth Year Book*, Q4–Q5.

151. Haller, *Eugenics*, 42–43; Fink, "Historical Development of Dannemora," 92, 115. See Hamilton D. Wey, "A Plea for Physical Training of Youthful Criminals," *Proceedings of the National Prison Association, 1888,* 181–93.

152. Haller, *Eugenics,* 43. See Charles Henderson, *Introduction to the Study of the Dependent, Defective, and Delinquent Classes,* 2nd ed. (Boston, 1901).

153. Haller, *Eugenics,* 43; Fink, "Historical Development of Dannemora," 124; Larry K. Hartsfield, *The American Response to Professional Crime, 1870–1917* (Westport, Conn., 1985), 165–66. See Arthur MacDonald, in *A Plan for the Study of Man, Reference to Bills to Establish a Laboratory for the Study of the Criminal, Pauper, and Defective Classes,* Senate Doc. No. 400, 57th Cong., 1st Sess., serial 4245 (Washington, 1902); Arthur MacDonald, *Juvenile Crime and Reformation, Including Stigmata of Degeneration* (Washington, 1908).

154. McKelvey, *American Prisons*, 123, 156, 165–66.

155. Haller, *Eugenics,* 48; Arthur R. Fink, *Causes of Crime: Biological Theories in the United States, 1800–1915* (Philadelphia, 1938), 189–94.

156. Fink, *Causes of Crime,* 194–97; see Harry C. Sharp, "The Severing of the Vas Deferentia and Its Relation to the Neuropsychopathic Constitution," *New York Medical Journal* 75 (March 8, 1902); Harry C. Sharp, "Vasectomy as a Means of Preventing Procreation in Defectives," *Journal of the American Medical Association* 53 (December 4, 1909): 1897–1902; "Rendering Sterile of Confirmed Criminals and Mental Defectives," *Proceedings of the Annual Congress of the National Prison Association,* 1907, 177–85.

157. Quoted in Haller, *Eugenics,* 49.

158. Ibid., 50; Fink, "Historical Development of Dannemora," 196–97.

159. James Q. Wilson and Richard J. Herrnstein, *Crime and Human Nature* (New York, 1985), 151–52; Gould, *The Mismeasure of Man,* 27.

160. Quoted in Wilson and Herrnstein, *Crime and Human Nature,* 152; Fink, "Historical Development of Dannemora," 220–22. See Henry H. Goddard: "The Responsibility of Children in the Juvenile Court," *Journal of the American Institute of Criminal Law and Criminology* 3 (September 1912), 365–75; "Feeble-Mindedness and Crime," *Proceedings of the American Prison Association* (1912), 353–57; and *Feeble-Mindedness: Its Causes and Consequences* (New York, 1914).

161. Rafter, *Partial Justice,* 67, 54.

162. Ibid., 69–70; Estelle B. Freedman, *Their Sisters' Keepers: Women's Prison Reform in America, 1830–1930* (Ann Arbor, 1981), 116–18; Pollock-Byrne, *Women, Prison, and Crime,* 13–14. Davis had studied under Thorsten Veblen and earned her doctorate in 1900.

163. Rafter, *Partial Justice,* 70–71; Freedman, *Sisters' Keepers,* 118.

164. Rafter, *Partial Justice,* 71; Freedman, *Sisters' Keepers,* 119–20. See J. Weidensall, *The Mentality of the Criminal Woman* (Baltimore, 1916); E. Spaulding, *An Experimental Study of Psychopathic Delinquent Women* (New York, 1923).

165. Quoted in Freedman, *Sisters' Keepers,* 123.

166. Peter Collier and David Horowitz, *The Rockefellers: An American Dynasty* (New York, 1976), 107.

167. Quoted in Nicholas F. Kittrie, *The Right to Be Different: Deviance and Enforced Therapy* (Baltimore, 1971), 311.

168. Gillin, *Criminology and Penology,* 92.

169. Ibid., 92–94.

170. A. W. Brown and A. A. Hartman, "A Survey of the Intelligence of Illinois Prisoners," *Journal of Criminal Law and Criminology* (January–February 1938): 707–19.

171. Gillin, *Criminology and Penology*, 92; Wilson and Herrnstein, *Crime and Human Nature*, 152–53. See Carl Murchinson, "American White Criminal Intelligence," *Journal of Criminal Law and Criminology* (August 1924): 239 and (November 1924): 435. See also Carl Murchinson, *Criminal Intelligence* (Worcester, Mass., 1926).

172. Smith, "Military Training," 38–39.

173. Fink, "Historical Development of Dannemora," 32, n. 33; quoted in Haller, *Eugenics*, 44.

174. Wines, *Punishment and Reformation*, 237.

175. See Moriz Benedikt, *Anatomical Studies upon Brains of Criminals*, trans. E. P. Fowler (New York, 1881).

176. Quoted in Haller, *Eugenics*, 111.

177. Quoted in Richard Quinney, *The Problem of Crime* (New York, 1970), 55–56.

178. Eugene V. Debs, *Walls and Bars* (New York, 1927), 53.

179. Stephen Schafer, *Theories in Criminology* (New York, 1969), 185–86.

180. Charles B. Goring, *The English Convict: A Statistical Study* (London, 1913).

181. "An Act to provide for the proper infliction of the death penalty and to amend the existing provision of law relative thereto," January 17, 1888.

182. Theodore Bernstein, "Theories of the Causes of Death from Electricity in the Late Nineteenth Century," *Medical Instrumentation* 9, no. 6 (November–December 1975): 267; "Electrical Execution," *Scientific American* 62 (January 11, 1890): 26; *In re Kemmler*, 136 U.S. 436 (1890).

183. *New York Times*, August, 7, 1890.

184. Henry M. Boies, *Prisoners and Paupers: A Study of the Abnormal Increase of Criminals, and the Public Burden of Pauperism in the United States; the Causes and Remedies* (New York, 1893), 292–93.

185. Hugo Adam Bedau, ed., *The Death Penalty in America*, 3rd ed. (New York, 1982), 16; George Bishop, *Executions: Legal Ways of Death throughout the World* (Los Angeles, 1965), 160–62; L. C. Berkson, *The Concept of Cruel and Unusual Punishment* (Lexington, Mass., 1975), 21–31.

186. Lucy S. Dawidowicz, *The War against the Jews, 1933–1945* (New York, 1974), 131.

CHAPTER SIX   *The Golden Age of Political Prisoners*

1. Alexander Berkman, *Prison Memoirs of an Anarchist* [1912] (New York, 1970), 99–100.

2. Aldous Huxley, *Prisons, With the "Carceri" Etchings by G. B. Piranesi* (London, n.d.), 13–14.

3. Berkman, *Prison Memoirs*, 148–49, 175.

4. Alix Kates Shulman, ed., *Red Emma Speaks: Selected Writings and Speeches of Emma Goldman* (New York, 1972), 12.

5. Berkman, *Prison Memoirs*, 241.

6. Ibid., 270.

7. Joan D. Hedrick, *Solitary Comrade: Jack London and His Work* (Chapel Hill, 1982), 24.

8. See Sidney L. Harring, "Class Conflict and the Suppression of Tramps in Buffalo, 1892–1894," *Law and Society Review* 11 (Summer 1977): 873–911.

9. Jack London, "How I Became a Socialist," in *The Novels and Social Writings* (New York, 1982), 1119–20.

10. See James Lundquist, *Jack London: Adventures, Ideas, and Fiction* (New York, 1987); Richard O'Connor, *Jack London: A Biography* (Boston, 1964).

11. Barbara W. Tuchman, *The Proud Tower: A Portrait of the World before the War, 1890-1914* (New York, 1966), 495-96.

12. Clarence Darrow, *The Story of My Life* (New York, 1934), 68-70.

13. Nick Salvatore, *Eugene V. Debs: Citizen and Socialist* (Urbana, 1982), 150.

14. William D. Haywood, *Bill Haywood's Book,* (New York, 1929), 205; Leon F. Litwack, *The American Labor Movement* (Englewood Cliffs, N.J., 1962), 187-88.

15. Melvyn Dubofsky, "The Radicalism of the Dispossessed: William Haywood and the IWW," in *Dissent: Explorations in the History of American Radicalism,* ed. Alfred F. Young (DeKalb, 1969), 191.

16. Philip S. Foner, ed., *Mother Jones Speaks: Collected Speeches and Writings* (New York, 1983).

17. Frank Tannenbaum, *Osborne of Sing Sing* (Chapel Hill, 1933), 59-61; Harry Elmer Barnes and Negley K. Teeters, *New Horizons in Criminology,* 2nd ed. (New York, 1954), 692.

18. Tannenbaum, *Osborne of Sing Sing,* 65.

19. "Report of Hon. Thomas M. Osborne on Conditions in Auburn Prison to the New York Commission on Prison Reform," in New York Commission on Prison Reform, *Preliminary Report of the Commission on Prison Reform* (Albany, 1913), 18.

20. Thomas Mott Osborne, *Society and Prisons* (New Haven, 1916), 126-27.

21. Tannenbaum, *Osborne of Sing Sing,* 9.

22. Ibid., 68.

23. New York Commission on Prison Reform, *Preliminary Report,* 18-19.

24. Osborne, *Society and Prisons,* 28.

25. New York Commission on Prison Reform, *Preliminary Report,* 19.

26. Ibid., 11.

27. Tom Murton, *The Dilemma of Prison Reform* (New York, 1976), 200.

28. Tannenbaum, *Osborne of Sing Sing,* 106.

29. Murton, *The Dilemma of Prison Reform,* 204-6.

30. Osborne, *Society and Prisons,* 320.

31. Murton, *The Dilemma of Prison Reform,* 206; Samuel Walker, *Popular Justice: A History of American Criminal Justice* (New York, 1980), 153; Tannenbaum, quoted in Edwin H. Sutherland, *Principles of Criminology,* 3rd ed. (Philadelphia, 1939), 456.

32. Osborne, *Society and Prisons,* 192, 8.

33. Ibid., 199-200.

34. Ibid., 219; Tannenbaum, *Osborne of Sing Sing,* 140.

35. Murton, *The Dilemma of Prison Reform,* 207.

36. Candace Falk, *Love, Anarchy, and Emma Goldman* (New York, 1984), 222, 237.

37. Ibid., 243.

38. Margaret Sanger, *An Autobiography* (New York, 1938), 219-20.

39. Ibid., chap. 19.

40. Ibid.

41. Shulman, *Red Emma,* 15-16.

42. Ibid., 16.

43. Quoted in Falk, *Love, Anarchy, and Emma Goldman,* 284.

44. Quoted ibid., 286. See Kate Richards O'Hare, *In Prison* (New York, 1923); Philip S. Foner and Sally M. Miller, eds., *Kate Richards O'Hare: Selected Writings and Speeches* (Baton Rouge, 1982).

45. Freedman, *Sisters' Keepers,* 152.

46. O'Hare, *In Prison,* quoted in Harry Elmer Barnes, *The Story of Punishment* (Montclair, N.J., 1972), 166.

47. Ibid., 167.

48. Ibid., 185.

49. See William Preston, Jr., *Aliens and Dissenters: Federal Suppression of Radicals, 1903–1933* (New York, 1966), 144–51.

50. Richard H. Frost, *The Mooney Case* (Stanford, 1968), 287; see John P. Roche, "The Red Hunt," in Marshall B. Clinard and Richard Quinney, eds., *Criminal Behavior Systems: A Typology* (New York, 1967), 190–205.

51. See Preston, *Aliens and Dissenters,* chap. 5; Robert K. Murray, *Red Scare* (Minneapolis, 1955).

52. Carl E. Hein, "William Haywood and the Syndicalist Faith," in *American Radicals: Some Problems and Personalities,* ed. Harvey Goldberg (New York, 1957), 194.

53. Paul W. Keve, *Prisons and the American Conscience: A History of U.S. Federal Corrections* (Carbondale, 1991), 147–48.

54. Kittrie and Wedlock, *The Tree of Liberty,* 299; Keve, *Prisons and the American Conscience,* 204.

55. See Godfrey D. Lehman, "Susan B. Anthony Cast Her Ballot for Ulysses S. Grant," *American Heritage* 37, no. 1 (December 1985): 24–31.

56. See Minna Morse, "The Object at Hand," *Smithsonian* 23, no. 12 (March 1993): 28–32; Sherna Gluck, ed., *From Parlor to Prison: Five American Suffragists Talk About Their Lives* (New York, 1976).

57. Foner, *Mother Jones Speaks.*

58. See Max Lowenthal, *The Federal Bureau of Investigation* (New York, 1950). Roche, "The Red Hunt," 190–205.

59. John Dos Passos, *U.S.A.* [1930] (New York, 1960), 399.

60. Shulman, *Red Emma,* 16.

61. Ibid.; Lowenthal, *The Federal Bureau of Investigation,* chap. 21.

62. Eugene V. Debs, "Your Honor," in Isidore Abramowitz, ed., *The Great Prisoners: The First Anthology of Literature Written in Prison. With Analytical Introductions to the Time and Place and Circumstances of Each Prisoner and Imprisonment, a General Preface to the Whole, and a Selected Bibliography* (New York, 1946), 713–14.

63. Salvatore, *Eugene V. Debs,* 308.

64. Ibid., 308–9; Keve, *Prisons and the American Conscience,* 143; Ray Ginger, *The Bending Cross: A Biography of Eugene Victor Debs* (New York, 1949), 390–91.

65. Keve, *Prisons and the American Conscience,* 143; quoted in Salvatore, *Eugene V. Debs,* 314.

66. Keve, *Prisons and the American Conscience,* 143; quoted in Salvatore, *Eugene V. Debs,* 315.

67. Eugene V. Debs, *Walls and Bars* (Chicago, 1927).

68. Salvatore, *Eugene V. Debs,* 326–28; Preston, *Aliens and Dissenters,* 259.

69. Keve, *Prisons and the American Conscience,* 144; Salvatore, *Eugene V. Debs,* 328.

70. Salvatore, *Eugene V. Debs,* 328–30.

71. August Meier and Elliott Rudwick, *From Plantation to Ghetto,* 3rd ed. (New York, 1976), 246–47; George Eaton Simpson and J. Milton Yinger, *Racial and Cultural Minorities,* 3rd ed. (New York, 1965), 319. See E. D. Cronon, *Black Moses* (Madison, Wis., 1955).

72. Judith Stein, *The World of Marcus Garvey: Race and Class in Modern Society* (Baton Rouge, 1986), 186–200.

73. Marcus Garvey, writing from Atlanta penitentiary, February 10, 1925, quoted in *Look for Me in the Whirlwind,* ed. W. Haywood Burns (New York, 1971), v. See *Philosophy and Opinions of Marcus Garvey,* ed. Amy Jaques-Garvey (New York, 1970).

74. Stein, *The World of Marcus Garvey,* 207.

75. See Roberta Strauss Feurlicht, *Justice Crucified: The Story of Sacco and Vanzetti* (New York, 1977); William Young and David E. Kaiser, *Postmortem: New Evidence in the Case of Sacco and Vanzetti* (Amherst, 1985).

76. *The Letters of Sacco and Vanzetti,* ed. Marion Denman Frankfurter and Gardner Jackson (New York, 1930), 6, n. 1; see Feurlicht, *Justice Crucified;* Francis Russell, *Sacco and Vanzetti* (New York, 1986).

77. Quoted in Russell, *Sacco and Vanzetti,* 221; Frankfurter and Jackson, *Letters of Sacco and Vanzetti.*

78. Frankfurter and Jackson, *Letters of Sacco and Vanzetti,* 137–38.

79. See "The Story of the Case," ibid., Appendix I, which summarizes Frankfurter's analysis.

80. Sacco to Auntie Bee, July 3, 1927, ibid., 63.

81. Vanzetti to Dante Sacco, August 21, 1927, ibid., 321–23.

82. Katherine Anne Porter, *The Never-Ending Wrong* (Boston, 1977), 38–39.

83. Frost, *Mooney Case,* chap. 22; Kenneth Lamott, *Chronicles of San Quentin* (New York, 1961), 142–43.

84. Quoted in Frost, *Mooney Case,* 364–65.

85. Ibid., 367, 373.

86. See ibid., chaps. 27–28.

87. Meier and Rudwick, *From Plantation to Ghetto,* 261–62; Theodore Rosengarten, *All God's Dangers: The Life of Nate Shaw* (New York, 1974), 358–59; and Haywood Patterson and Earl Conrad, *Scottsboro Boy* (New York, 1951), 299.

88. Patterson and Conrad, *Scottsboro Boy,* 5–8.

89. Ibid., 299, 8.

90. Ibid., 12.

91. Ibid., 198.

92. Ibid., 299, 12–13.

93. Walter Wilson, ed., *The Selected Writings of W. E. B. Du Bois* (New York, 1970), 166.

94. Patterson and Conrad, *Scottsboro Boy,* 30–31.

95. *Powell v. Alabama,* 287 U.S. 45 (1932).

96. Patterson and Conrad, *Scottsboro Boy,* 36, 43.

97. *Norris v. Alabama,* 294 U.S. 587 (1935).

98. Patterson and Conrad, *Scottsboro Boy,* 60.

99. Ibid., 63, 69–70, 73, 80–83, 115, 96.

100. Ibid., 119.

101. Ibid., 145, 163, 188, 195, 197.

102. Ibid., 94.

103. Ibid., 199, 201, 202.

104. Ibid., 213.

105. Ibid., 215.

106. W. E. B. Du Bois, "Courts and Jails," in *The Crisis,* March 1932, in Wilson, *Selected Writings,* 126–27.

107. Gunnar Myrdal, *An American Dilemma: The Negro Problem and Modern Democracy* (New York, 1962), 557.

108. Thorsten Sellin, "The Negro Criminal: A Statistical Note," *The Annals of Political and Social Science* (1928), 63.

109. William T. Root, Jr., *A Psychological and Educational Survey of 1916 Prisoners in the Western Penitentiary of Pennsylvania* (Pittsburgh, 1927).

110. U.S. Department of Commerce, Bureau of the Census, *Crime Conditions in the United States as Reflected in Census Statistics of Imprisoned Offenders* (Washington, 1926), 59.

111. Myrdal, *American Dilemma,* 554–55.

112. Margaret Cahalan, "Trends in Incarceration in the United States since 1880: A Summary of Reported Rates and the Distribution of Offenses," *Crime & Delinquency* 5 (January 1979): 9–41.

113. Hans von Hentig, "The Criminality of the Negro," *Journal of the American Institute of Criminal Law and Criminology* 30 (March–April 1940): 662–80.

114. Langston Hughes, *The Langston Hughes Reader* (New York, 1958).

CHAPTER SEVEN   *Doing Time*

1. Quoted in Harry Elmer Barnes, *The Story of Punishment* [1930] (Montclair, N.J., 1972), 177.

2. Fyodor Dostoyevsky, *The House of the Dead*, trans. Constance Garnett (New York, 1959), 49.

3. Quoted in John Bartlow Martin, *Break Down the Walls: American Prisons, Present, Past, and Future* (New York, 1954), 21.

4. Nathan F. Leopold, *Life plus 99 Years* (New York, 1957), 95.

5. See generally, Anthony Guenther, "The Language of Prison Life," in Norman Johnston and Leonard Savitz, eds., *Justice and Corrections* (New York, 1978), 528–30; Herbert Yenne, "Prison Lingo," *American Speech* (March 1927); Noel Erskine, *Underworld and Prison Slang* (Upland, Ind., 1933); Donald Clemmer, *The Prison Community* (New York, 1958), 88–100.

6. Leopold, *Life plus 99 Years*, 171–72.

7. Clifford R. Shaw, *The Jack-Roller: A Delinquent Boy's Own Story* [1930] (Chicago, 1966), 151–53.

8. Edwin H. Sutherland, *The Professional Thief: By a Professional Thief* (Chicago, 1937), 135.

9. Hans Reimer, "Socialization in the Prison," *Proceedings of the Sixty-Seventh Annual Congress of the American Prison Association* (Washington, 1937), 151–55.

10. Quoted in Martin, *Break Down the Walls*, 122.

11. Isidore Zimmerman, with Francis Bond, *Punishment without Crime: The True Story of a Man Who Spent Twenty-Four Years in Prison for a Crime He Did Not Commit* (New York, 1964), 150–51.

12. Clemmer, *The Prison Community*, 294–95.

13. See Gresham M. Sykes and Sheldon L. Messinger, "The Inmate Social System," in Richard Cloward et al., *Theoretical Studies in the Social Organization of the Prison* (New York, 1960), 5–19.

14. Madeline Z. Doty, *Society's Misfits* (New York, 1916), 129; Victor Nelson, *Prison Days and Nights* (Boston, 1933), 150.

15. Assimilation generally implies a gradual process of acculturating or socializing a newcomer into a dominant social group. See Donald Clemmer, "The Process of Prisonization," in Robert G. Leger and John R. Stratton, eds., *The Sociology of Corrections: A Book of Readings* (New York, 1977), 175–80.

16. Clemmer, *The Prison Community*, 299.

17. See Erving Goffman, *Asylums: Essays on the Social Situation of Mental Patients and Other Inmates* (Garden City, N.Y., 1961).

18. Edwin H. Sutherland, *Principles of Criminology*, 3rd ed. (Chicago, 1939), 420–21.

19. Lewis E. Lawes, *Sing Sing* (New York, 1933), 10.

20. The gradual replacement of whipping by solitary confinement and other punishments is described in David J. Rothman, *Conscience and Convenience: The Asylum and Its Alternatives in Progressive America* (Boston, 1980), 151–58.

21. Lawrence T. Kurlander, *Report to Governor Mario M. Cuomo: The Disturbance at Ossining Correctional Facility, Jan. 8–11, 1983* (Albany, 1983), 15–17.

22. Elizabeth Benz Croft, "New York State Prisons and Prison Riots from Auburn and Clinton, 1929, to Attica, 1971" (M.A. thesis, School of Criminal Justice, SUNY at Albany, 1972), 22.

23. New York State Commission of Correction, *Third Annual Report for the Year 1929* (Albany, 1930), 24.

24. Croft, "New York State Prisons," 21-22.

25. Commission of Correction, *Third Annual Report,* 25.

26. "Sing Sing Must Go the Way of Carthage," *Survey* 31, no. 25 (March 21, 1914): 763-64.

27. New York State Commission of Correction, *First Annual Report* (Albany, 1928), 19.

28. Croft, "New York State Prisons," 31, 44; Kurlander, *Report to Governor Cuomo,* 16-18.

29. Gideon Hayes, *An Historical Sketch of the Massachusetts State Prison, with Narratives and Incidents, and Suggestions on Discipline* (Boston, 1869), quoted in Harry Elmer Barnes and Negley K. Teeters, *New Horizons in Criminology* (New York, 1951), 678-79.

30. Barnes and Teeters, *New Horizons,* 679.

31. Charles L. Clark and Earle Edward Eubank, *Lockstep and Corridor: Thirty-Five Years of Prison Life* (Cincinnati, 1927), 7.

32. Barnes and Teeters, *New Horizons,* 435.

33. Leopold, *Life plus 99 Years,* 97-98.

34. Paul L. Montgomery, "Upstate Prison Goes from Crisis to Crisis," *New York Times,* March 4, 1973.

35. Boston Prison Discipline Society, *Report* (Boston, 1829), 31.

36. U.S. Code of Laws, Supplement 1925-32, Title 49, Chap. 2 A, s. 65.

37. Walter Wilson, *Forced Labor in the United States* (New York, 1933), 36.

38. Richard F. Jones, Jr., *Prison Labor in the United States, 1940: Bulletin No. 698* (Washington, 1941); Frank Flynn, "The Federal Government and the Prison-Labor Problem in the United States," *Social Service Review* 24, nos. 1-2 (March-June 1950): 1.

39. Barnes and Teeters, *New Horizons,* 730-31.

40. Flynn, "Federal Government and Prison-Labor," 19-40, 213-36.

41. Max Grünhut, *Prison Reform: A Comparative Study* (New York, 1948), 213-14; Barnes and Teeters, *New Horizons,* 741-42.

42. Dante, "Canto III: The Gate of Hell," in *The Inferno,* trans. John Ciardi (New York, 1954).

43. Michel Foucault, *Discipline and Punish: The Birth of the Prison,* trans. Alan Sheridan (New York, 1977).

44. Zimmerman, *Punishment without Crime,* 152.

45. Norman Johnston, *The Human Cage: A Brief History of Prison Architecture* (New York, 1973), 54.

46. Nelson, *Prison Days and Nights,* 16.

47. See Joseph Fulling Fishman, *Sex in Prison* (New York, 1934); Peter C. Buffum, *Homosexuality in Prisons* (Washington, 1972).

48. Nelson, *Prison Days and Nights,* 143-48; quoted in Zimmerman, *Punishment without Crime,* 149.

49. Nelson, *Prison Days and Nights,* 16.

50. Ibid., 14, 219.

51. Jack London, *The Star Rover* (New York, 1915).

52. Kenneth Lamott, *Chronicles of San Quentin: The Biography of a Prison* (New York, 1961), chap. 10; Ed Morrell, *The Twenty-Fifth Man: The Strange Story of Ed Morrell, the Hero of Jack London's "Star Rover"* [1924] (Montclair, N.J., 1955).

53. Zimmerman, *Punishment without Crime,* 174.

54. Ibid., 211.

55. Zimmerman died before he could obtain civil damages from the state of New York.

56. Paul W. Keve, *Prisons and the American Conscience: A History of Federal Corrections* (Carbondale, Ill., 1991), 58; see Thomas E. Gaddis, *Birdman of Alcatraz* (New York, 1955).

57. Robert Stroud, *Diseases of Canaries* (Kansas City, 1933); Robert Stroud, *Stroud's Digest on the Diseases of Birds* (Minneapolis, 1943).

58. See James A. Johnston, *Alcatraz Island Prison and the Men Who Live There* (New York, 1949); Alvin Karpis, *On the Rock: Twenty-Five Years in Alcatraz* (New York, 1980); James P. Delgado, *Alcatraz Island: The Story behind the Scenery* (Las Vegas, 1985).

59. Paul W. Keve, *The McNeil Century: The Life and Times of an Island Prison* (Chicago, 1984).

60. See Peter Irons, *Justice at War: The Story of the Japanese American Internment Cases* (New York, 1983).

61. Grünhut, *Prison Reform*, 228.

62. Harry Elmer Barnes, *Prisons in Wartime* (Washington, 1944).

63. American Correctional Association, *The American Prison: From the Beginning: A Pictorial History* (n.p., 1983), 185.

64. Keve, *Prisons and the American Conscience*, 205.

65. See "Prison Malaria: Convicts Expose Themselves to Disease so Doctors Can Study It," *Life* 18 (June 4, 1945), 43. On other medical experiments involving American convicts, see "Prison Guinea Pigs," *Science Digest* 13 (June 1943); R. Brecher and E. Brecher, "They Volunteered for Cancer: Inmates of Ohio State Penitentiary," *Reader's Digest* 72 (April 1958), 62–66; Jessica Mitford, *Kind and Usual Punishment: The Prison Business* (New York, 1973).

66. See Malcolm X with Alex Haley, *The Autobiography of Malcolm X* (New York, 1965); Peter Goldman, *The Death and Life of Malcolm X* (New York, 1973); Bruce Perry, *Malcolm: The Life of a Man Who Changed Black America* (Barrytown, N.Y., 1991).

67. *Autobiography of Malcolm X*, 152. Malcolm's prison experience is covered in Perry, *Malcolm*, 104–38.

68. *Autobiography of Malcolm X*, 153–55; Jack Rummel, *Malcolm X: Militant Black Leader* (Los Angeles, 1988), 78–79.

69. *Autobiography of Malcolm X*, chap. 10.

70. Ibid.; Comment, "Black Muslims in Prison: Of Muslim Rites and Constitutional Rights," *Columbia Law Review* 62 (1962): 1490–91.

71. *Autobiography of Malcolm X*, 174, 159–60.

72. Ibid., 163.

73. Ibid., 169.

74. Ibid., chap. 11.

75. Piri Thomas, *Seven Long Times* (New York, 1974).

76. Piri Thomas, *Down These Mean Streets* (New York, 1967).

77. Eldridge Cleaver, *Soul on Ice* (New York, 1968), 17.

78. Ibid., 23–24.

79. Ibid., 22–23.

80. James B. Jacobs, *Stateville: The Penitentiary in Mass Society* (Chicago, 1977), 61–62; Ronald L. Goldfarb and Linda R. Singer, *After Conviction: A Review of the American Correctional System* (New York, 1973), 406.

81. See *In re Ferguson*, 55 Cal. 2d 663, 361 P.2d 417, 12 California Reporter 753, *cert. denied*, 368 U.S. 864 (1961); cf. *In re Jones*, 57 Cal. 2d 860, 372 P.2d 310, 22 California Reporter 478 (1962).

82. *Howard v. Smythe*, 365 F.2d 428, 431 (4th Cir.), *cert. denied*, 385 U.S. 988 (1966); *Columbia Law Review*, Comment, "Black Muslims in Prison," 1494, n. 27.

83. *Columbia Law Review*, Comment, "Black Muslims in Prison," 1491.

84. Charles W. Baker, "Interview of Charles W. Baker," in Etheridge Knight, *Black Voices from Prison* (New York, 1970), 37.

85. Cleaver, *Soul on Ice*, 26. See John Irwin, *Prisons in Turmoil* (Boston, 1980), 69–71; Charles E. Silberman, *Criminal Violence, Criminal Justice* (New York, 1978), 158.

86. Malcolm X, quoted in Knight, *Black Voices from Prison*, 5.

87. Perry, *Malcolm*, 239.

88. Ibid., 343-44; Jacobs, *Stateville*, 68.

89. *Cooper v. Pate*, 378 U.S. 546 (1964).

90. Jacobs, *Stateville*, 50, 64-67, 107, 256.

91. Malcolm X, in Jerome Skolnick, *The Politics of Protest* (New York, 1969), 128-29.

92. David J. Garrow, *Bearing the Cross: Martin Luther King, Jr., and the Southern Christian Leadership Conference* (New York, 1986), 392-93.

93. George Breitman, Herman Porter, and Baxter Smith, *The Assassination of Malcolm X* (New York, 1976). Quoted in Bobby Seale, *Seize the Time* (New York, 1970), 3.

94. Cleaver, *Soul on Ice*, 64.

95. Richard R. Korn and Lloyd W. McKorkle, *Criminology and Penology* (New York, 1959), 226.

96. See Scott Christianson, *Disproportionate Imprisonment of Blacks in the United States: Policy, Practice, Impact, and Change* (Silver Spring, Md., 1982).

97. Alfred R. Lindesmith, *The Addict and the Law* (Bloomington, 1965).

98. Billie Holiday in Ross Firestone, ed., *Getting Busted: Personal Experiences of Arrest, Trial, and Prison* (New York, 1970), 130. See also Billie Holiday, *Lady Sings the Blues*, 2nd ed. (New York, 1969).

99. Federal Bureau of Investigation, *Uniform Crime Reports* 21, no. 2 (Washington, 1950).

100. David Courtwright, Herman Joseph, and Don DesJarlais, *Addicts Who Survived: An Oral History of Narcotic Use in America, 1923-1965* (Knoxville, 1989), 19.

101. See Alvin J. Bronstein, "Offender Rights Litigation: Historical and Future Developments," in Era P. Robbins, comp., *Prisoners' Rights Sourcebook: Theory, Litigation, Practice* (New York, 1980), 5-38; Goldfarb and Singer, *After Conviction*.

102. See Note, "Beyond the Ken of the Courts," *Yale Law Journal* 72, no. 3 (January 1963): 506-58; Goldfarb and Singer, *After Conviction*, 364-68.

103. *Ex parte Hull*, 312 U.S. 436 (1941). Also see *White v. Ragen*, 324 U.S. 760 (1945).

104. *Coffin v. Reichard*, 143 F.2d 443, 445 (6th Cir. 1944), *cert. denied*, 325 U.S. 887 (1945).

105. *Banning v. Looney*, 213 F.2d 771 (10th Cir.), *cert. denied*, 348 U.S. 859 (1954).

106. *Hirabayashi v. United States*, 320 U.S. 81 (1943). See Irons, *Justice at War*.

107. *Screws v. United States*, 325 U.S. 91 (1945).

108. Taylor Branch, *Parting the Waters: America in the King Years, 1954-63* (New York, 1988), 408-9, 528, 639, 866.

109. At the time of the 1971 riot at New York's Attica state prison fully 88 percent of the inmates were black or Puerto Rican, and all of the prison guards and administrators were white.

110. *Nichols v. McGee*, 169 F.Supp. 721, 724 (N.D. Cal.), *appeal dismissed*, 361 U.S. 6 (1959).

111. Alexander Bickel, *Politics and the Warren Court* (New York, 1965); Fred Cohen, *The Legal Challenge of Corrections: Implications for Manpower and Training* (Washington, 1969). The Warren Court dealt directly with very few cases involving prison conditions. One of them was *Johnson v. Avery*, 393 U.S. 483 (1969).

112. *Monroe v. Pape*, 365 U.S. 167 (1961).

113. *Mapp v. Ohio*, 367 U.S. 643 (1961).

114. *Gideon v. Wainwright*, 372 U.S. 335 (1963). See Anthony Lewis, *Gideon's Trumpet* (New York, 1964).

115. Goldfarb and Singer, *After Conviction*, 179-80.

116. *Cooper v. Pate*, 378 U.S. 546 (1964).

117. *Escobedo v. Illinois*, 378 U.S. 470 (1964).

118. *Miranda v. Arizona*, 384 U.S. 436 (1966).

119. Goldfarb and Singer, *After Conviction*, 426-28. The U.S. Supreme Court case of

Johnson v. Avery involved a jailhouse lawyer in Tennessee. The number of writs prepared by San Quentin convicts alone rose from about fifty in 1960 to more than five thousand in 1970. Mitford, *Kind and Usual Punishment*, 255.

120. President's Commission on Law Enforcement and Administration of Justice, *Task Force Report: Corrections* (Washington, 1967), 83.

121. Irwin, *Prisons in Turmoil*, 5.

122. *Jordan v. Fitzharris*, 257 F.Supp. 674, 679, 680 (N.D. Cal. 1966).

123. *Wright v. McMann*, 387 F.2d 519 (2d Cir. 1967).

124. See Vincent Copeland, *The Crime of Martin Sostre* (New York, 1970).

125. *Sostre v. Rockefeller*, 312 F.Supp. 863 (S.D.N.Y. 1970), *aff'd in part and rev'd in part sub. nom. Sostre v. McGinnis*, 442 F.2d 178 (2d Cir. 1971).

126. *Sostre v. McGinnis*, 442 F.2d 178 (2d Cir. 1971).

127. David Vidal, "A Freed Activist Sees No Change," *New York Times*, February 15, 1976.

128. Michael Millemann, "VA [Virginia] Prisoners Find Advocates in Early Prison Reformers," *Journal of the National Prison Project* 13 (Fall 1987): 3–4.

129. *Landman v. Royster*, 333 F.Supp. 621, 638 (E.D. Va. 1971); Fred Cohen, "The Discovery of Prison Reform," *Buffalo Law Review* 21, no. 3 (1972): 855–87, at 871.

130. K. Wymand Keith, *Long Line Rider: The Story of Cummins Prison Farm* (New York, 1971); Note, "Arkansas Prison System: An Unconstitutional Outrage," *Missouri Law Review* 36 (Fall 1971): 576.

131. Tom Murton and Joe Hyams, *Accomplices to the Crime* (New York, 1969), 10–13.

132. Quoted ibid., 14.

133. See Richard Korn, "Reflections on Flogging: An Essay Review of the Work of Leslie Wilkins and Tom Murton," *Issues in Criminology* 6, no. 2 (1971): 95–97; Murton and Hyams, *Accomplices to the Crime*.

134. Murton and Hyams, *Accomplices to the Crime*, 21. Murton later said he had believed that he could transform the Arkansas prison system from one of the worst in the nation to one of the best, and in a fairly short time, in part because it would not require the usual investment in concrete and steel. Ibid., 19.

135. Paul W. Keve, review of *Accomplices to the Crime*, by Tom Murton and Joe Hyams, *Crime & Delinquency* 16 (October 1970): 443.

136. Murton and Hyams, *Accomplices to the Crime*, 23.

137. Ibid., 29–31.

138. Ibid., 99. See Tom Murton, "One Year of Prison Reform," *The Nation*, January 12, 1970, 13.

139. Murton and Hyams, *Accomplices to the Crime*, 107. Murton later elaborated on this philosophy in various writings, including Tom Murton, "Inmate Self-Government," *University of San Francisco Law Review* 6, no. 1 (1971): 88–90.

140. Murton and Hyams, *Accomplices to the Crime*, 57–59; Murton, "One Year of Prison Reform," 449–50.

141. Murton and Hyams, *Accomplices to the Crime*, 64–65.

142. Ibid., 71–74; *Pine Bluff (Ark.) Commercial*, June 4, 1967, 12.

143. Murton and Hyams, *Accomplices to the Crime*, 75–76.

144. Ibid., 162–75. See Thomas O. Murton, *The Dilemma of Prison Reform* (New York, 1976).

145. "Hell in Arkansas," *Time*, February 9, 1968, 74; G. Moore, "Buried Secrets in a Prison Farm," *Life*, February 9, 1968, 32–32A; "Telltale Skeletons," *Newsweek*, February 12, 1968, 42–43.

146. Victor Urban, a former member of Murton's staff and his eventual successor as superintendent at Cummins, claimed that Murton had achieved many good reforms, but criticized him for "crucifying Arkansas" and for failing to "compromise." Victor C. Urban,

review of *Accomplices to the Crime,* by Tom Murton and Joe Hyams, *Crime & Delinquency* 16 (October 1970): 444-46. Rockefeller, who was reelected eight months after the firing, tended to downplay the dismissal, stressing that "no man is indispensable" and complaining, "We keep getting bad publicity. I would rather be reading about Arkansas getting a new industry." Quoted in "Politics and Prisons," *New Republic,* April 6, 1968, 7. See also Richard A. McGee, and Paul W. Keve, reviews of *Accomplices to the Crime,* by Tom Murton and Joe Hyams, *Crime & Delinquency* 16 (October 1970): 442 and 442-44; Tom Murton, "Reply to Book Reviews," *Crime & Delinquency* 16 (October 1970): 449-53.

147. *Holt v. Sarver,* 309 F.Supp. 362 (E.D. Ark. 1970), *aff'd* 442 F.2d 304 (8th Cir. 1971).

148. Stephen Gettinger, "Making a Myth Out of a Mortal Man," *Corrections Magazine* 6, no. 5 (October 1980): 42-44, 46; and Bernard Edelman, "In Prison Films, the Institution Is the Star," *Corrections Magazine* 6, no. 5 (October 1980): 45.

149. Gresham M. Sykes, *The Society of Captives: A Study of a Maximum-Security Prison* (Princeton, 1958), 110.

150. Irwin, *Prisons in Turmoil,* 24; quoted in Mitford, *Kind and Usual Punishment,* 251-52.

151. Jim Tully, "Two-Time Losers," *American Mercury* 13 (March 1928): 311-19; *New York Times,* November 25 and November 26, 1927, at 1. For a description of conditions at Folsom several months before the riot, see B. D. Whitlock, "Making Little Ones Out of Big Ones," *Overland* 85 (May 1927): 143-44.

152. New York State Commission of Correction, *Third Annual Report.*

153. Croft, "New York State Prisons," 29.

154. Ibid., 28.

155. Martin, *Break Down the Walls,* 214.

156. Croft, "New York State Prisons," 4.

157. Barnes and Teeters, *New Horizons,* 428.

158. New York State Special Commission on Attica, *Attica* (New York, 1972), 13-15.

159. Martin, *Break Down the Walls,* 210.

160. Croft, "New York State Prisons," 6; Martin, *Break Down the Walls,* 209.

161. Martin, *Break Down the Walls,* 17; Croft, "New York State Prisons," 6.

162. Martin, *Break Down the Walls,* 210-11; Croft, "New York State Prisons," 5-6.

163. Bert Useem and Peter Kimball, *States of Siege: U.S. Prison Riots, 1971-1986* (New York, 1989), 9-10.

164. Quoted ibid., 10.

165. Croft, "New York State Prisons," 7-8.

166. Quoted in Mitford, *Kind and Usual Punishment,* 252.

167. Erik Olin Wright, *The Politics of Punishment* (New York, 1973); Ming S. Yee, *The Melancholy History of Soledad Prison* (New York, 1973).

168. One literary historian referred to Jackson as "the leading theoretician of the prison movement." H. Bruce Franklin, *The Victim as Criminal and Artist: Literature from the American Prison* (New York, 1978), 273.

169. George Jackson, *Soledad Brother: The Prison Letters of George Jackson* (New York, 1970), 9.

170. See Irwin, *Prisons in Turmoil.*

171. Angela Y. Davis, *If They Come in the Morning* (New York, 1971), 37.

172. *New York Times,* August 11, 1970, at 1, August 12, 1970, at 1, and October 3-6, at 1; New York State Special Commission on Attica, *Attica,* 128-29. For a list of the inmates' grievances, see American Friends Service Committee, *Struggle for Justice* (New York, 1971), 2-6.

173. *New York Times,* November 5, 1970, at 57.

174. New York State Special Commission on Attica, *Attica,* 19, 47-48, 55-61. For the

commissioner's own version, see Russell G. Oswald, *Attica—My Story,* ed. Rodney Campbell (Garden City, N.Y., 1972). Oswald is also analyzed in Tom Wicker, *A Time to Die* (New York, 1975).

175. This account of the riot is based on *Attica* (the official New York State report) and on *The Turkey Shoot: Tracking the Attica Cover-Up* (New York, 1985), an account written by Malcolm Bell, a former special state prosecutor.

176. Wicker, *A Time to Die,* 316; *New York Times,* September 19, 1971, 60; "The Bitter Lessons of Attica," *Time,* September 27, 1971, 18–31.

177. New York State Special Commission on Attica, *Attica,* xi.

178. See Bell, *The Turkey Shoot;* Wicker, *A Time to Die,* 301–2; "Looking Back on Attica," *Columbia Journalism Review,* November–December 1971, 2–3. In 1997 the former inmate Frank Smith won $4 million in damages in federal court in Buffalo, in compensation for the abuse he suffered from guards after the uprising.

179. Bell, *The Turkey Shoot,* 1.

180. Costly civil litigation was still going on a generation later. See Andrew Yarrow, "After Seventeen Years, the Attica Trial Lives," *New York Times,* January 11, 1992.

181. Gordon Hawkins, *The Prison: Policy and Practice* (Chicago, 1976), 77.

182. Michael S. Serrill and Peter Katel, "New Mexico: The Anatomy of a Riot," *Corrections Magazine* 6, no. 2 (April 1980): 6–24.

183. The most graphic factual account of the carnage is Roger Morris, *The Devil's Butcher Shop: The New Mexico Prison Uprising* (New York, 1983).

184. Useem and Kimball, *States of Siege,* 89.

185. Quoted ibid., 95.

186. Morris, *The Devil's Butcher Shop,* 86.

187. Steve Gettinger, "Informer," *Corrections Magazine* 6, no. 2 (April 1980): 17–19.

188. Morris, *The Devil's Butcher Shop,* 111.

189. Ibid., 114.

CHAPTER EIGHT *Full Circle*

1. Daniel Bell, *The End of Ideology* (New York, 1960), 151.

2. James Q. Wilson, *Thinking about Crime* (New York, 1975), 5–7.

3. Herbert G. Gutman, *The Black Family in Slavery and Freedom, 1750–1925* (New York, 1976), 466.

4. Wilson, *Thinking about Crime,* 12.

5. See Scott Christianson, "The War Model in Criminal Justice: No Substitute for Victory," *Criminal Justice and Behavior* 9, no. 3 (September 1974): 247–77.

6. Richard Harris, *Justice: The Crisis of Law, Order, and Freedom in America* (New York, 1970).

7. Bert Useem and Peter Kimball, *States of Siege: U.S. Prison Riots, 1971–1986* (New York, 1989), 15.

8. Quoted in Harris, *Justice,* 22–23.

9. See Charles Silberman, *Criminal Violence, Criminal Justice* (New York, 1978).

10. Useem and Kimball, *States of Siege,* 14.

11. See, e.g., President's Commission on Law Enforcement and the Administration of Justice, *The Challenge of Crime in a Free Society* (Washington, 1967); Edwin M. Schur, *Crimes without Victims: Deviant Behavior and Public Policy* (New York, 1965); Ramsey Clark, *Crime in America: Observations on Its Nature, Causes, Prevention, and Control* (New York, 1970).

12. Robert Martinson, "What Works? Questions and Answers about Prison Reform," *Public Interest* 35 (1974); and Douglas Lipton, Robert Martinson, and Judith Wilkes, *The Effectiveness of Correctional Treatment* (New York, 1974).

13. Elliott Currie, *Confronting Crime: An American Challenge* (New York, 1985), 237–38.

14. Alan Dershowitz, "Let the Punishment Fit the Crime," *New York Times Magazine,* December 28, 1975, at 7.

15. Margaret Werner Cahalan and Lee Anne Parsons, *Historical Corrections Statistics in the United States, 1850–1984* (Washington, 1986).

16. National Council on Crime and Delinquency, *Policy Statement* (Hackensack, N.J., 1972); National Commission on Criminal Justice Standards and Goals, *Corrections* (Washington, 1973).

17. The National Moratorium on Prison Construction published a newsletter called *Jericho.*

18. Fay Honey Knopp et al., *Instead of Prisons: A Handbook for Abolitionists* (Syracuse, 1976).

19. Law Enforcement Assistance Administration, U.S. Department of Justice, News Release (September 30, 1977).

20. Useem and Kimball, *States of Siege,* 82.

21. Ibid.

22. *Sourcebook of Criminal Justice Statistics, 1973* (Washington, 1974), 30–31.

23. U.S. Department of Justice, *Expenditure and Employment, 1978* (Washington, 1979), 58–59.

24. *Sourcebook, 1973.*

25. Margaret Cahalan, "Trends in Incarceration in the United States since 1880: A Summary of Reported Rates and the Distribution of Offenses," *Crime & Delinquency* 5 (1979): 9–41.

26. Scott Christianson, "Our Black Prisons," *Crime & Delinquency* 27, no. 3 (July 1981): 364–75.

27. Scott Christianson: "Legal Implications of Racially Disproportionate Incarceration Rates," *Criminal Law Bulletin* 16, no. 1 (January–February 1980): 59–63 and "Racial Discrimination and Prison Confinement—A Follow-Up," *Criminal Law Bulletin* 16, no. 6 (November–December 1980): 616–21.

28. Marc Mauer and Tracy Huling, *Young Black Americans and the Criminal Justice System: Five Years Later* (Washington, 1995).

29. "Nearly 7% of Adult Black Males Were Inmates in '94, Study Says," *New York Times,* December 4, 1995.

30. William Glaberson, "One in Four Young Black Men Are in Custody, Study Says," *New York Times,* October 4, 1990.

31. Statistics from New York State Department of Correctional Services, Albany.

32. Henry Weinstein, "One in Seven Black Men Are Kept from Voting, Study Finds," *Los Angeles Times,* January 30, 1997.

33. *New York Times,* January 18, 1991.

34. Blue Ribbon Commission on Inmate Population Management, *Final Report* (Sacramento, January 1990).

35. Fox Butterfield, "Study Examines Race and Justice in California," *New York Times,* February 13, 1996.

36. Eric Slater, "Pizza Thief Gets Twenty-Five Years to Life," *Los Angeles Times,* March 3, 1995.

37. Butterfield, "Study Examines Race and Justice."

38. Bureau of Justice Statistics, "State and Federal Prison Population Tops One Million," October 27, 1994; William DiMascio, *Seeking Justice: Crime and Punishment in America* (New York, 1995).

39. Caroline Wolf Harlow, "Comparing Federal and State Prison Inmates," NCJ-145864 (Washington, 1995).

40. Ibid.

41. Associated Press, "U.S. Leads World in Imprisonment," *New York Times*, January 7, 1991.

42. Marc Mauer, *Americans behind Bars: The International Use of Incarceration, 1992–93* (Washington, 1994).

43. Results of surveys may be obtained from Bureau of Justice Statistics Clearinghouse, Box 179, Annapolis Junction, MD 20701-0179; http://www.ojp.usdoj.gov/bjs/.

44. "In 90s, Prison Building by States and U.S. Government Surged," *New York Times*, August 8, 1997, A14.

45. National Advisory Commission on Civil Disorders, *Report* (New York, 1968).

46. William G. Nagel, *The New Red Barn: A Critical Look at the Modern American Prison* (New York, 1973).

47. Raymond Hernandez, "Give Them the Maximum: Small Towns Clamor for the Boon a Big Prison Could Bring," *New York Times*, February 26, 1996, B1.

48. Edward Walsh, "Strapped Small Towns Try to Lock Up Prisons," *Washington Post*, December 24, 1994, A3.

49. Robert Bryce, "Texas Posts 'For Rent' Sign on Empty Beds," *Christian Science Monitor*, July 28, 1995, 3.

50. See Shep Montgomery, "Greenwood Chosen as Site of State's Second Private Prison," *Mississippi Business Journal* 17, no. 31 (July 31, 1995): 1; Jane Meade Dean, "What's Next? Westmoreland Tries to Unload Assets," *Business Journal of Upper East Tennessee and Southwest Virginia* 8, no. 9 (September 1995): 18.

51. Bureau of Justice Statistics, *Sourcebook of Criminal Justice Statistics—1994* (Washington, 1995), Table 1.26, 33.

52. See Walsh, "Strapped Small Towns," A3.

53. See Scott Christianson, "Corrections Law Developments—How Unions Affect Prison Administration," *Criminal Law Bulletin* 15, no. 3 (May–June 1979): 238–47.

54. See *Jones v. North Carolina Prisoners' Labor Union*, 433 U.S. 119, 97 S.Ct. 2532 (1977).

55. National Institute of Law Enforcement and Criminal Justice, Law Enforcement Assistance Administration, U.S. Department of Justice, *Prison Employee Unionism: The Impact on Correctional Administration and Programs* (Washington, 1978), 43–45.

56. See Scott Christianson and Richard Korn, "The Other Prison Problem: Regaining Control of Guards," *Washington Post*, August 16, 1981.

57. Criminal Justice Institute, *The Corrections Yearbook: Adult Corrections, 1994* (South Salem, N.Y., 1995).

58. Richard Gazarik and Debra Erdley, "Prison Building Program Probe to Be Continued," (Greensburg, Pa.) *Tribune-Review*, October 28, 1995, A1.

59. "Prison Health Care," *Honolulu Star-Bulletin*, March 12, 1996.

60. Bureau of Justice Statistics, *Sentencing in the Federal Courts: Does Race Matter?* (Washington, 1993).

61. Substance Abuse and Mental Health Administration, *Overview of National Drug and Alcoholism Treatment Unit Survey (NDATUS): 1992 and 1980–1992* (Washington, 1995).

62. Ibid.

63. Rex Smith, "Locking Up Prison Funds: Urban Agency Used to Finance Construction of Jails," *Newsday*, October 9, 1990, 7, 19.

64. For accounts of some of the vendors at annual conventions of the American Correctional Association, see Jessica Mitford, *Kind and Usual Punishment: The Prison Business*, chap. 3 (New York, 1973), and Donatella Lorch, "The Utmost Restraint, and How to Exercise It: The Incarceration-Minded Meet to Buy Mobile Cells, Ballistic Batons, and More," *New York Times*, August 23, 1996, B1.

65. See Christian Parenti: "Making Prison Pay: Business Finds the Cheapest Labor of

All," *The Nation,* January 29, 1996, 11–14, and "Pay Now, Pay Later: States Impose Prison Peonage," *The Progressive,* July 1996, 26–29.

66. Douglas C. McDonald, "Public Imprisonment by Private Means," in *Prisons in Context,* ed. Roy D. King and Mike Maguire (New York, 1994); David Scichor, "The Corporate Context of Private Prisons," *Crime, Law, and Social Change* 20, no. 2 (1993): 113–38.

67. A. B. Wellen, "Prisoners and the FLSA: Can the American Taxpayer Afford Extending Prison Inmates the Federal Minimum Wage?" *Temple Law Review* (Spring 1994): 295–334.

68. See Tim Ferraro, "Crime Bill Is a Boon for Private Prison Industry," *Philadelphia Inquirer,* September 4, 1994; Paulette Thomas, "Making Crime Pay," *Wall Street Journal,* May 12, 1994.

69. Ivan Cintron, "Diversity Helps CCA Expand Lock on Market," *Nashville Business Journal* 12, no. 5 (January 29, 1996): 1, 30.

70. J. M. Cowen, "One Nation's 'Gulag' Is Another Nation's 'Factory Within a Fence': Prison-Labor in the People's Republic of China and the United States of America," *UCLA Pacific Basin Law Journal* (Fall 1993): 190–236.

71. Parenti, "Making Prison Pay," 11–14.

72. Ian Olneirson, "Furniture Dealers Cry 'Foul!'" *Denver Business Journal* 47, no. 24 (February 23, 1996): 1B; L. A. Mitchell, "Prison Break: Inmate Labor Best Deal, Bar None, State Says," *Arizona Business Gazette* 115, no. 46 (November 9, 1995): 1:1.

73. Cintron, "Diversity Helps CCA Expand," 1, 30.

74. See, e.g., Michael Ferrell, "Jail Equipment Company Seeks to Break into Foreign Market," *Capital District Business Review* 22, no. 43 (February 5, 1996): 1; Jim Freer, "Jail Bait: Prisoners' Products Lure International Markets," *South Florida Business Journal,* May 17, 1996, 5A.

75. David Waite, "A Lonely Exile behind Bars," *Honolulu Advertiser,* February 18, 1996, 1; Ian Fisher, "Bartering Inmate Futures," *New York Times,* October 29, 1995.

76. Sam Howe Verhovek, "Texas Caters to a Demand around U.S. for Jail Cells," *New York Times,* February 9, 1996, 1.

77. Daniel L. Feldman, "Twenty Years of Prison Expansion: A Failing National Strategy," *Public Administration Review* 53, no. 6 (1993): 561–66.

78. Assemblyman Daniel L. Feldman, chairman of the Committee on Corrections, as quoted in the *New York Times,* February 26, 1996, B2.

79. Leslie T. Wilkins, *Evaluation of Penal Measures* (New York, 1969), 3.

80. Christianson, "War Model in Criminal Justice," 247–77.

81. *New York Times,* July 29, 1992, 4.

82. Ibid.

83. National Conference of State Legislatures, *State Budget Actions, 1994* (Washington, 1994).

84. *New York Times,* September 13, 1992, 40.

85. Currie, *Confronting Crime,* 90.

86. *Chicago Tribune,* August 24, 1983.

87. Alex P. Fryer, "Fiscal Crisis Looms as Prison Costs Mount," *Puget Sound Business Journal* 16, no. 45 (May 22, 1996): 1.

88. Fox Butterfield, "New Prisons Cast Shadow over Higher Education," *New York Times,* April 12, 1995, A21.

89. See, e.g., P. G. Halpin and L. T. Dickerson, "Schools Make a Better Investment than Prisons," *New York Times,* October 11, 1995, A22; Alton R. Waldon, *Healthy Choice: How New York State Is Sacrificing Education for Incarceration* (St. Albans, N.Y., 1996).

90. Halpin and Dickerson, "Schools Make a Better Investment than Prisons."

91. *New York Times,* February 17, 1992.

92. George Bernard Shaw, quoted in Sidney Webb and Beatrice Webb, *English Prisons under Local Government* (London, 1922), xi.

93. Eddie Ellis, "Developing an Afro-Centric Model for Social Change: A Criminal Justice Discussion Paper," prepared for Black History Month Legislative Caucus, Greenhaven Prison, Stormville, N.Y., February 16, 1990.

94. E.g., Nekesa Mumbi Moody, "State Cuts Prison College Programs: Opponents Say the Move Will Actually Increase Crime," *Albany Times-Union,* June 11, 1995.

95. See Rick Bragg, "Chain Gangs to Return to Roads of Alabama: State Hopes Revival Will Deter Crime," *New York Times,* March 26, 1995, 16. See also David M. Oshinsky, *"Worse than Slavery": Parchman Farm and the Ordeal of Jim Crow Justice* (New York, 1996).

96. New York State Coalition for Criminal Justice, "New York's Double-Celling = Double Trouble," *Coalition Update* (Albany), September 1995, 1, 3-5.

97. Iver Peterson, "Cutting Down on Amenities to Achieve No-Frills Jails: Anger on Crime Drives a Spate of Proposals," *New York Times,* July 10, 1995, B7.

98. See Jonathan Franzen, "Lock It Down," *Details,* December 1995, 65-71, 77-81, 197.

99. Joe Hallinan, "Supermax: Supersecure, Supercostly," *Hartford Courant,* January 7, 1996, C1.

100. Anne-Marie Cusac, "Life in Prison: Stunning Technology," *The Progressive,* July 1996, 18-22.

101. Gresham M. Sykes, *The Society of Captives: A Study of a Maximum-Security Prison* (Princeton, 1958).

102. Anthony Guenther, "The Impact of Confinement," in Norman Johnston and Leonard Savitz, eds., *Justice and Corrections* (New York, 1978), 596-603; Donald Clemmer, *The Prison Community* (New York, 1958); David A. Jones, "The Dangerousness of Imprisonment" (Ph.D. diss., State University of New York at Albany, 1975); Anne Newton, "The Effects of Imprisonment," *Criminal Justice Abstracts* 12, no. 1 (March 1980): 134-51.

103. Sykes, *The Society of Captives,* 65.

104. President's Commission on Law Enforcement and Administration of Justice, *Task Force Report: Corrections* (Washington, 1967).

105. See Jocelyn M. Pollock-Byrne, *Women, Prison, Crime* (Pacific Grove, Calif., 1990).

106. Alexis de Tocqueville, quoted in Gutman, *The Black Family,* xxi.

107. Charles H. Nichols, ed., *Black Men in Chains: Narratives by Escaped Slaves* (Westport, Conn., 1972), 17.

108. "The Fugitive Blacksmith, or Events in the History of James W. C. Pennington, Pastor of a Presbyterian Church, New York, Formerly a Slave in the State of Maryland," [1849] in Arna Bontemps, ed., *Great Slave Narratives* (Boston, 1969), 256.

109. E. Franklin Frazier, *The Negro Family in America* (Chicago, 1932), 40-41.

110. Stanley M. Elkins, *Slavery: A Problem in American Institutional and Intellectual Life* (Chicago, 1959), 53.

111. See Lee Rainwater and William L. Yancey, eds., *The Moynihan Report and the Politics of Controversy* (Cambridge, Mass., 1967).

112. *New York Times,* November 20, 1983. See William Julius Wilson, *The Truly Disadvantaged: The Inner City, the Underclass, and Public Policy* (Chicago, 1988).

113. Gutman, *The Black Family;* John W. Blassingame, *The Slave Community: Plantation Life in the Ante-Bellum South* (New York, 1971); Loren Schweninger, "A Slave Family in the Ante Bellum South," *Journal of Negro History* 60 (January 1975): 29-44.

114. Claude Brown, "Manchild in Harlem," *New York Times Magazine,* September 16, 1984, 44.

115. Don Terry, "More Familiar, Life in a Cell Seems Less Terrible," *New York Times,* September 13, 1992, 1, 40.

116. Ruth S. Bloodgood, *Welfare of Prisoners' Families in Kentucky* (Washington, 1928), 47.

117. Ibid., 25.

118. Donald P. Schneller, "Some Social and Psychological Effects of Incarceration on the Families of Negro Prisoners," *American Journal of Correction* 37, no. 1 (January–February 1975): 29–33.

119. Jerome Sacks, cited ibid.

120. See Schneller, "Social and Psychological Effects"; Stanley L. Brodsky, *Families and Friends of Men in Prison: The Uncertain Relationship* (Lexington, Mass., 1974); L. Alex Swan, *Families of Black Prisoners: Survival and Progress* (Boston, 1981).

121. Velma LaPoint, "Children of Incarcerated Mothers," in *Child Development*, ed. R. Green and T. Yawkey (Lexington, Mass., 1979); W. H. Sack, "Children of Imprisoned Fathers," *Psychiatry* 40, no. 2 (1977): 163–74; Larry L. Hunt and Janet G. Hunt, "Race and the Father-Son Connection: The Conditional Relevance of Father Absence for the Orientations and Identities of Adolescent Boys," *Social Problems* 23, no. 1 (1975): 35–52.

122. John Edgar Wideman, *Brothers and Keepers* (New York, 1984), 52.

123. William LaRue, "Guarding the 'Family Business,'" *Syracuse Post-Standard*, November 21, 1985, 1–2.

124. *New York Times*, December 7, 1973.

125. Andrew H. Malcolm, "For This Convict, 'Freedom' Is Another Word for 'Fear,'" *New York Times*, November 20, 1974, 41.

126. Frank Tannenbaum, *Walls and Shadows* (New York, 1927).

127. Gustave de Beaumont and Alexis de Tocqueville, *On the Penitentiary System in the United States and Its Application in France*, trans. Francis Lieber [1833] (Carbondale, Ill., 1964), 47.

128. Erving Goffman, *Asylums: Essays on the Social Situation of Mental Patients and Other Inmates* (Garden City, N.Y., 1961).

129. *Houchins v. KQED, Inc.*, No. 76-1310 (June 26, 1978), 23 CrL 3164 (June 28, 1978).

130. E.g., see Charles E. Reasons and Russell L. Kaplan, "Tear Down the Walls? Some Functions of Prisons," *Crime & Delinquency* (October 1975): 360–72. They listed prison's manifest functions as reformation, incapacitation, retribution, and deterrence. They suggested as latent functions maintenance of a crime school, politicization, self-enhancement, provision of jobs, satisfaction of authoritarian needs, slave labor, reduction of unemployment rates, scientific research, do-gooderism, safety valve for racial tensions, and birth control.

131. David J. Rothman, *The Discovery of the Asylum: Social Order and Disorder in the New Republic* (Boston, 1971).

132. Michael Ignatieff, *A Just Measure of Pain: The Penitentiary in the Industrial Revolution, 1750–1850* (New York, 1978).

133. Stanley Cohen, *Visions of Social Control: Crime, Punishment, and Classification* (Cambridge, Mass., 1985), 10.

134. Michael Meranze, *Laboratories of Virtue: Punishment, Revolution, and Authority in Philadelphia, 1760–1835* (Chapel Hill, 1996). See also Thomas L. Dumm, *Democracy and Punishment: Disciplinary Origins of the United States* (Madison, Wis., 1987).

135. See, e.g., Adam Jay Hirsch, *The Rise of the Penitentiary: Prisons and Punishment in Early America* (New Haven, 1992).

136. David Garland, *Punishment and Modern Society: A Study in Social Theory* (Chicago, 1990).

137. Georg Rusche and Otto Kirchheimer, *Punishment and Social Structure* (New York, 1939), 5.

138. Tony Platt and Paul Takagi, eds., *Punishment and Penal Discipline* (Berkeley, 1980), 13. See Georg Rusche, "Labor Market and Penal Sanction: Thoughts on the Sociol-

ogy of Criminal Justice," trans. Gerda Dinwiddie, *Crime & Social Justice* (Fall/Winter 1978): 5.

139. Michel Foucault, *Discipline and Punish: The Birth of the Prison,* trans. Alan Sheridan (New York, 1977).

140. George Herbert Mead, "The Psychology of Punitive Justice," *American Journal of Sociology* 23 (1918): 577–602.

141. See, e.g., Svend Ranulf, *Moral Indignation and Middle Class Psychology* [1938] (New York, 1964).

142. See Donald Clemmer, "Observations on Imprisonment as a Source of Criminality," *Journal of Criminal Law and Criminology* 41 (1950–51): 311–19.

143. Norval Morris, *The Future of Imprisonment* (Chicago, 1974), ix.

144. Quoted in Garland, *Punishment and Modern Society,* 215.

SELECTED BIBLIOGRAPHY

Abramowitz, Isidore, ed. *The Great Prisoners: The First Anthology of Literature Written in Prison.* New York: Dutton, 1946.

Bailyn, Bernard. *Voyagers to the West: A Passage in the Peopling of America on the Eve of the Revolution.* New York: Knopf, 1987.

Barnes, Harry Elmer. *The Evolution of Penology in Pennsylvania: A Study in American Social History.* Indianapolis: Bobbs-Merrill, 1927.

Beaumont, Gustave de, and Alexis de Tocqueville. *On the Penitentiary System in the United States and Its Application in France.* Translated by Francis Lieber. Carbondale: Southern Illinois Univ. Press, 1964 (orig. pub. 1833).

Beccaria, Cesare. *On Crimes and Punishments.* Translated by Henry Paolucci. Indianapolis: Bobbs-Merrill, 1963 (orig. pub. 1764).

Bell, Malcolm. *The Turkey Shoot: Tracking the Attica Cover-Up.* New York: Grove Press, 1985.

Blassingame, John W., ed. *Slave Testimony: Two Centuries of Letters, Speeches, Interviews, and Autobiographies.* Baton Rouge: Louisiana State Univ. Press, 1977.

Bontemps, Arna, ed. *Great Slave Narratives.* Boston: Beacon, 1969.

Bowman, Larry G. *Captive Americans: Prisoners during the American Revolution.* Athens: Ohio Univ. Press, 1977.

Brockway, Zebulon R. *Fifty Years of Prison Service: An Autobiography.* Montclair, N.J.: Patterson Smith, 1969 (orig. pub. 1912).

Cahalan, Margaret. "Trends in Incarceration in the United States since 1880: A Summary of Reported Rates and the Distribution of Offenses," *Crime & Delinquency* 5 (Jan. 1979): 9–41.

Clarkson, Thomas. *An Essay on the Slavery and Commerce of the Human Species, Particularly the African* . . . Philadelphia, 1786.

Cohen, Daniel A. *Pillars of Salt, Monuments of Grace: New England Crime Literature and the Origins of American Popular Culture, 1674–1860.* New York: Oxford, 1993.

Coldham, Peter Wilson, ed. *Bonded Passengers to America.* 9 vols. Baltimore: Genealogical, 1983.

Commager, Henry Steele, and Richard B. Morris, eds. *The Spirit of 'Seventy Six: The Story of the American Revolution As Told by Its Participants.* New York: Harper & Row, 1967.

Conley, John A. "Criminal Justice History as a Field of Research: A Review of the Literature, 1960–1975." *Journal of Criminal Justice* 5, no. 1 (Spring 1977): 13–28.

Crawford, William. *Report on the Penitentiaries of the United States, 1835.* Montclair, N.J.: Patterson Smith, 1968 (orig. pub. 1835).

Currie, Elliott. *Confronting Crime: An American Challenge.* New York: Pantheon, 1985.

Davis, David Brion. *The Problem of Slavery in the Age of Revolution, 1770–1823.* Ithaca: Cornell Univ. Press, 1975.

Defoe, Daniel. *The Fortunes and Misfortunes of the Famous Moll Flanders, etc.* . . . New York: Holt, Rinehart & Winston, 1949 (orig. pub. 1722).

Donnan, Elizabeth, ed. *Documents Illustrative of the History of the Slave Trade to America.* 4 vols. Washington, D.C.: Carnegie Institution, 1930–35.

Dostoyevsky, Fyodor. *The House of the Dead.* Translated by Constance Garnett. New York: Dell, 1959.

Durkheim, Émile. "Two Laws of Penal Evolution." Translated by Anthony Jones and Andrew T. Scull. *Economy and Society* 2 (1973): 285.

Ekirch, A. Roger. *Bound for America: The Transportation of British Convicts to the Colonies, 1718–1775.* Oxford: Clarendon Press, 1987.

Erikson, Kai T. *Wayward Puritans: A Study in the Sociology of Deviance.* New York: John Wiley, 1966.

Eriksson, Torsten. *The Reformers: An Historical Survey of Pioneer Experiments in the Treatment of Criminals.* Translated by Catherine Djurklou. New York: Elsevier, 1976.

Feldman, Daniel L. "Twenty Years of Prison Expansion: A Failing National Strategy." *Public Administration Review* 53, no. 6 (1993): 561–66.

Fernald, Guy G. "The Laboratory and the Men's Reformatory." In American Prison Association, *Proceedings,* 1920: 99–102.

Foucault, Michel. *Discipline and Punish: The Birth of the Prison.* Translated by Alan Sheridan. New York: Pantheon, 1977.

Franklin, H. Bruce. *The Victim as Criminal and Artist: Literature from the American Prison.* New York: Oxford, 1978.

Freedman, Estelle B. *Their Sisters' Keepers: Women's Prison Reform in America, 1830–1930.* Ann Arbor: Univ. of Michigan Press, 1981.

Galenson, David W. *White Servitude in Colonial America.* New York: Cambridge Univ. Press, 1981.

Garland, David. *Punishment and Modern Society: A Study in Social Theory.* Chicago: Univ. of Chicago Press, 1990.

———. *Punishment and Welfare: A History of Penal Strategies.* Brookfield, Vt.: Gower, 1985.

Genovese, Eugene D. *Roll, Jordan, Roll: The World the Slaves Made.* New York: Pantheon, 1974.

Gillin, John. *Criminology and Penology.* New York: Century, 1926.

Goffman, Erving. *Asylums: Essays on the Social Situation of Mental Patients and Other Inmates.* Garden City, N.Y.: Doubleday, 1961.

Goldfarb, Ronald L., and Linda R. Singer. *After Conviction: A Review of the American Correction System.* New York: Simon & Schuster, 1973.

Greene, Albert, ed. *Recollections of the Jersey Prison Ship.* New York: Corinth Books, 1961 (orig. pub. 1829).

Greenberg, Douglas. *Crime and Law Enforcement in the Colony of New York, 1691–1736.* Ithaca: Cornell Univ. Press, 1976.

Gutman, Herbert G. *The Black Family in Slavery and Freedom, 1750–1925.* New York: Knopf, 1976.

Hay, Douglas, Peter Linebaugh, John G. Rule, E. P. Thompson, and Cal Winslow. *Albion's Fatal Tree: Crime and Society in Eighteenth-Century England.* New York: Pantheon, 1975.

Healy, William. *The Individual Delinquent: A Text-Book of Diagnosis and Prognosis for All Concerned in Understanding Offenders.* Boston: Little, Brown, 1915.

Herrick, Cheesman A. *White Servitude in Pennsylvania: Indentured and Redemption Labor in Colony and Commonwealth.* Philadelphia: John Joseph McVey, 1926.

Higginbotham, A. Leon, Jr. *In the Matter of Color: Race and the American Legal Process: The Colonial Period.* New York: Oxford, 1978.

Hindus, Michael S. *Prison and Plantation: Crime, Justice, and Authority in Massachusetts and South Carolina, 1767–1878.* Chapel Hill: Univ. of North Carolina Press, 1980.

Hirsch, Adam Jay. *The Rise of the Penitentiary: Prisons and Punishment in Early America.* New Haven: Yale Univ. Press, 1992.

Hood, Roger, and Richard Sparks. *Key Issues in Criminology.* New York: McGraw-Hill, 1970.

Howard, John. *The State of the Prisons in England and Wales. . . .* Warrington: W. Eyres, 1777.

Hughes, Robert. *The Fatal Shore: The Epic of Australia's Founding.* New York: Knopf, 1986.

Ignatieff, Michael. *A Just Measure of Pain: The Penitentiary in the Industrial Revolution, 1750–1850.* New York: Pantheon, 1978.

———. "State, Civil Society, and Total Institutions: A Critique of Recent Social Histories of Punishment." *Crime and Justice: An Annual Review of Research* 3 (1981): 153–92.

Jackson, George. *Soledad Brother: The Prison Letters of George Jackson.* New York: Bantam, 1970.

Jennings, John Melville, ed. "The Poor Unhappy Transported Felon's Sorrowful

Account of His Fourteen Years Transportation at Virginia in America." *Virginia Magazine of History and Biography* 56 (1948): 180–94.

Jordan, Winthrop D. *White over Black: American Attitudes toward the Negro, 1550–1812.* Chapel Hill: Univ. of North Carolina Press, 1968.

Keve, Paul W. *The History of Corrections in Virginia.* Charlottesville: Univ. Press of Virginia, 1986.

Knapp, Samuel L. *The Life of Thomas Eddy.* . . . New York: Conner and Cooke, 1834.

Lewis, Orlando F. *The Development of American Prisons and Prison Customs, 1776–1845.* Montclair, N.J.: Patterson Smith, 1967 (orig. pub. 1922).

Lewis, W. David. *From Newgate to Dannemora: The Rise of the Penitentiary in New York, 1796–1848.* Ithaca: Cornell Univ. Press, 1965.

Litwack, Leon F. *Been in the Storm So Long: The Aftermath of Slavery.* New York: Knopf, 1980.

Malcolm X, with the assistance of Alex Haley. *The Autobiography of Malcolm X.* New York: Grove Press, 1964.

Mather, Increase. *The Wicked Mans Portion.* . . . Boston: John Foster, 1675.

Mead, George Herbert. "The Psychology of Punitive Justice." *American Journal of Sociology* 23 (1918): 577–602.

Meranze, Michael. *Laboratories of Virtue: Punishment, Revolution, and Authority in Philadelphia, 1760–1835.* Chapel Hill: Univ. of North Carolina Press, 1996.

Mitford, Jessica. *Kind and Usual Punishment: The Prison Business.* New York: Knopf, 1973.

Morgan, Edmund S. *American Slavery, American Freedom: The Ordeal of Colonial Virginia.* New York: Norton, 1975.

Morris, Norval. *The Future of Imprisonment.* Chicago: Univ. of Chicago Press, 1974.

Morris, Roger. *The Devil's Butcher Shop: The New Mexico Prison Uprising.* New York: Watts, 1983.

New York State Special Commission on Attica. *Attica: The Official Report of the New York State Special Commission on Attica.* New York: Bantam, 1972.

Oshinsky, David M. *"Worse than Slavery": Parchman Farm and the Ordeal of Jim Crow Justice.* New York: Free Press, 1996.

Paepke, David Ray. *Framing the Criminal: Crime, Cultural Work, and the Loss of Critical Perspective, 1830–1900.* Hamden, Conn.: Archon Books, 1987.

Pisciotta, Alexander W. *Benevolent Repression: Social Control and the American Reformatory-Prison Movement.* New York: New York Univ. Press, 1994.

Rafter, Nicole Hahn. *Partial Justice: Women in State Prisons, 1800–1935.* Boston: Northeastern Univ. Press, 1985.

Rothman, David J. *Conscience and Convenience: The Asylum and Its Alternatives in Progressive America.* Boston: Little, Brown, 1980.

———. *The Discovery of the Asylum: Social Order and Disorder in the New Republic.* Boston: Little, Brown, 1971.

Rusche, Georg, and Otto Kirchheimer. *Punishment and Social Structure.* New York: Columbia Univ. Press, 1939.

Sellin, J. Thorsten. *Slavery and the Penal System.* New York: Elsevier, 1976.

Silberman, Charles. *Criminal Violence, Criminal Justice.* New York: Random House, 1978.

Smith, Abbot Emerson. *Colonists in Bondage: White Servitude and Convict Labor in America, 1607–1776.* Chapel Hill: Univ. of North Carolina Press, 1947.

Sykes, Gresham M. *The Society of Captives: A Study of a Maximum-Security Prison.* Princeton: Princeton Univ. Press, 1958.

Teeters, Negley K. *The Cradle of the Penitentiary: The Walnut Street Jail in Philadelphia, 1773–1835.* Philadelphia: Pennsylvania Prison Society, 1955.

Teeters, Negley K., and John Shearer. *The Prison at Philadelphia, Cherry Hill: The Separate System of Prison Discipline.* New York: Columbia Univ. Press, 1957.

Thompson, E. P. *Whigs and Hunters: The Origin of the Black Act.* New York: Pantheon, 1975.

Walker, Samuel. *Popular Justice: A History of American Criminal Justice.* New York: Oxford, 1980.

Wideman, John Edgar. *Brothers and Keepers.* New York: Holt, Rinehart & Winston, 1984.

Wines, Enoch C. *The State of Prisons and of Child-Saving Institutions in the United States.* Cambridge, Mass.: J. Wilson & Son, 1880.

Wines, Enoch C., and Theodore W. Dwight. *Report on the Prisons and Reformatories of the United States and Canada.* Albany: AMS Press, 1973 (orig. pub. 1867).

Wines, Frederick H. *Punishment and Reformation: A Study of the Penal System.* New York: T. Y. Crowell, 1910.

INDEX

379